THE PAPERS OF ULYSSES S. GRANT

OVERLEAF:

President Ulysses S. Grant, June 2, 1875. *Courtesy James A. Bultema.* "The taking of the photographs in profile was the occasion of my father's shaving for the second time that I ever knew of. My mother had asked him to have a profile taken so that she might send it to Rome to have a cameo cut. Thinking that she wanted a profile of his features, he got shaved and had these pictures taken, very much to the disgust of my mother, who did not accept them for the cameo, but waited until his beard grew out again, and then had another profile taken for the purpose." Frederick Dent Grant in *The Century Magazine*, XXXV, 1 (Nov., 1887), 129.

THE PAPERS OF

ULYSSES S. GRANT

Volume 26: 1875

Edited by John Y. Simon

ASSISTANT EDITORS

William M. Ferraro
Aaron M. Lisec

TEXTUAL EDITOR

Dawn Vogel

—

SOUTHERN ILLINOIS UNIVERSITY PRESS

CARBONDALE AND EDWARDSVILLE

Library of Congress Cataloging in Publication Data (Revised)

Grant, Ulysses Simpson, Pres. U.S., 1822–1885.
　The papers of Ulysses S. Grant.

　Prepared under the auspices of the Ulysses S. Grant Association.
Bibliographical footnotes.
　CONTENTS: v. 1. 1837–1861.—v. 2. April–September 1861.—
v. 3. October 1, 1861–January 7, 1862.—v. 4. January 8–March 31,
1862.—v. 5. April 1–August 31, 1862.—v. 6. September 1–
December 8, 1862.—v. 7. December 9, 1862–March 31, 1863.—
v. 8. April 1–July 6, 1863.—v. 9. July 7–December 31, 1863.—v. 10.
January 1–May 31, 1864.—v. 11. June 1–August 15, 1864.—v. 12.
August 16–November 15, 1864.—v. 13. November 16, 1864–
February 20, 1865.—v. 14. February 21–April 30, 1865.—v. 15.
May 1–December 31, 1865.—v. 16. 1866.—v. 17. January 1–
September 30, 1867.—v. 18. October 1, 1867–June 30, 1868.—
v. 19. July 1, 1868–October 31, 1869.—v. 20. November 1, 1869–
October 31, 1870.—v. 21. November 1, 1870–May 31, 1871.—
v. 22. June 1, 1871–January 31, 1872.—v. 23. February 1–
December 31, 1872.—v. 24. 1873.—v. 25. 1874.—v. 26. 1875.
　1. Grant, Ulysses Simpson, Pres. U.S., 1822–1885. 2. United
States—History—Civil　　War,　　1861–1865—Campaigns　　and
battles—Sources. 3. United States—Politics and government—
1869–1877—Sources. 4. Presidents—United States—Biography.
5. Generals—United States—Biography. I. Simon, John Y., ed.
II. Ulysses S. Grant Association.
E660.G756　1967　　973.8'2'0924　　67–10725
ISBN 0-8093-2499-7 (v. 26)

The paper used in this publication meets the minimum requirements
of American National Standard for Information Sciences—Permanence of Paper for Printed Library Materials, ANSI Z39.48-1992. ∞

Published with the assistance of a grant from the National Historical
Publications and Records Commission.

Contents

Introduction

━━

THE POSSIBILITY THAT Ulysses S. Grant might run for a third term complicated Republican party politics in 1875. Pressed to end speculation, Grant wrote a widely publicized letter in late May. "I am not, nor have I been, a candidate for a renomination. I would not accept a nomination if it were tendered unless it should come under such circumstances as to make it an imperitive duty, circumstances not likely to arise." Grant's answer to the third-term question satisfied some, but others wished that the still popular president had given clearer signs of his intentions.

Despite this distraction, Grant tried to focus on policy goals. In southern states, civil rights for blacks could not be guaranteed. In New Orleans, ominous White Leaguers drilled in the streets, prompting Grant to send Lieutenant General Philip H. Sheridan to stop the cycle of murder and intimidation in Louisiana. Sheridan's characterization of armed Democrats as "banditti" drew criticism from northerners as well as southerners that placed Grant on the defensive. In response, Grant reminded Congress and the nation of a decade's worth of atrocities. "To say that the murder of a negro or a white republican is not considered a crime in Louisiana would probably be unjust to a great part of the people; but it is true that a great number of such murders have been committed, and no one has been punished therefor, and manifestly, as to them, the spirit of hatred and violence is stronger than law." He challenged Congress to take responsibility, adding, "I have repeatedly and earnestly entreated the people of the South to live together in peace, and obey the laws; and nothing would give me greater pleasure than to see reconciliation and tranquillity everywhere prevail, and thereby remove all necessity for the presence of troops among them." When unrest once more threatened Mississippi in September, Grant expressed exasperation. "The whole public are tired out with these annual, autumnal outbreaks in the South, and there is so much unwholsome lying done by the press and people in regard to the cause & extent of these breaches of the peace that the great majority are ready now to condemn any interference on the part of the government."

Spring brought a mounting threat to Grant's Indian policy. A steady stream of prospectors, drawn by rumors of gold, slipped past military patrols into the Black Hills, part of the Sioux reservation. In March, Grant sent an emissary to ask the tribe if they would sell their sacred land. Red Cloud, a Sioux chief, demanded to see the president himself. The Sioux delegation reached the capital in May and found Grant eager to negotiate for the whole reservation. The president alternately threatened and cajoled them to move to the Indian Territory. "There is a territory south of where you now live, where the climate is very much better, and the grass is very much better, and the game is much more abundant, including large game such as buffalo: where you can have good pasturage for animals; and where you can have teachers sent among you to teach you the arts of self-preservation and self support." The Sioux rebuffed Grant's overtures. The talks foundered, and the Sioux went home. In the fall, more government commissioners headed west, but discussion of the Black Hills provoked the Sioux to make an angry demonstration. The commission returned empty-handed. In November, Grant quietly circumvented Indian resistance, ruling that "while the orders heretofore issued forbidding the occupation of the Black Hills country, by miners, should not be rescinded, still no further resistance by the military should be made to the miners going in."

Allegations of wholesale corruption in the procurement of supplies for the Red Cloud Agency further clouded relations with the Sioux. Yale paleontologist Othniel C. Marsh championed the case for the Indians and prodded Grant into ordering Secretary of the Interior Columbus Delano to launch an investigation. "His charges are so specific as to dates and facts that they must either be true or susceptible of undoubted refutation." The resulting revelations and scandal shook the Interior Department and contributed to Delano's resignation. Believing "that public opinion demands a change of the present Commissioner of Indian Affairs," Grant considered numerous candidates and named John Q. Smith to replace Edward P. Smith. All this followed the May resignation of Attorney General George H. Williams after allegations that his wife misused government funds and even attempted blackmail.

Corruption in the management of Indian affairs and cabinet disruption paled before charges of scandal in the Internal Revenue Bureau that came to be known as the "Whiskey Ring." Treasury officials had long suspected fraud in the collection of whiskey taxes, an important revenue source. Directed by new Secretary of the Treasury Benjamin H. Bristow, and solicitor Bluford Wilson, detectives raided revenue offices and distilleries and gathered enough evidence to indict dozens of distillers and revenue agents in Chicago, Milwaukee, Cincinnati, and notably St. Louis, where Grant had taken a personal interest in appointments. Learning that some thought he would shield his friends and that his private secretary, Orville E. Babcock, had been implicated, Grant wrote a memorable endorsement to Bristow. "Let no guilty man escape if it can be avoided—Be specially vigilant—or instruct those engaged in the prosecutions of fraud to be—agains all who insinuate that they have high influence to protect, or to protect them."

Indictments and convictions piled up as the year wore on, and evidence pointed ominously toward Babcock's guilt. In December, as an army officer, Babcock sought a military hearing to avoid criminal trial. Grant, a close observer of the developing situation, reassured Babcock's wife. "I know how much you must be distressed at the publications of the day reflecting upon the integrity of your husband, and write therefore to ask you to be of good cheer and wait for his full vindication. I have the fullest confidence in his integrity, and of his innocence of the charges now made against him. After the intimate and confidential relations that have existed between him and myself for near fourteen years—during the whole of which time he has been one of my most confidential Aides & private Sec.—I do not believe it possible that I can be deceived."

Despite his intention to maintain appropriate distance, Grant found himself drawn deeper into the scandal. A St. Louis prosecutor referred in open court to "presidential interference" early in the Treasury investigation. Grant promptly removed him. When a friend on the grand jury in St. Louis violated his oath and told Grant about the proceedings, the president gave the man's son a consulship. Grant grew suspicious of Bristow and Wilson, and he came to see their pursuit of Babcock as a politically inspired attack on himself. By year's end, the Whiskey Ring had strained the administration, and the crisis appeared to be worsening.

The scandals seemed to affect Grant's work habits. From his summer home at Long Branch, usually a place of retreat, Grant plunged into executive business. A stream of letters and endorsements marked his involvement in otherwise routine removals and appointments. Grant also made himself accessible to the public, traveling extensively in late summer and early fall. From Rhode Island to Utah Territory, Grant met townspeople, schoolchildren, and Mormons (including Brigham Young) as well as veterans, political figures, and businessmen. He drew the line, however, at scandalmongering newspapermen, telling his postmaster general that he would not attend the opening of the new post office in New York City where offending editors would be present. "It never came within my comprehension why a slanderer who promulgated his lies to millions of people should be regarded with so much more favor than the man who only communicates it to the few people with whom he comes in contact."

At a September reunion of army veterans in Des Moines, Grant gave a surprising policy speech that condemned the use of public funds for parochial schools. "In a republic like ours where the citizen is the sovereign and the official the servant, where no power is exercised except by the will of the people, it is important that the sovereign—the people—should possess intelligence. The free school is the promoter of that intelligence which is to preserve us as a free nation." Every child in the nation, he argued, deserved "the opportunity of a good common school education, unmixed with sectarian, pagan or atheistical tenets." At a time of religious and political divisions, sharpened by the onset of mass immigration from largely Catholic countries, Grant's declarations caused an outcry. Grant held firm and two months later, in his annual message, suggested a constitutional amendment "to establish and forever maintain free public schools." In the same message, Grant decried "the accumulation of vast amounts of untaxed church-property" and predicted eventual "sequestration without constitutional authority and through blood" if taxes were not imposed.

Grant's private affairs offered little comfort from political controversy. His farm near St. Louis had never turned a profit, and Grant lost patience with the operation. "I have finally made up my mind that my farming experiment is to wind up with a great loss, increasing as long as the experiment is continued. I will therefore execute the design indicated in my letter from Washington. The best plan probably will be to advertise for sale at private sale until a certain day and then every thing to be sold at auction." The auction, held in September, brought disappointing prices. Grant retained the land, leasing the property for agricultural use while hoping for a lucrative sale to an industrial developer.

As the nation looked ahead to a presidential election, Grant tried to look beyond approaching trials to the end of his term. Apologizing to a friend in Georgetown, Ohio, for his inability to visit, Grant wrote that he would command his time and "be free" when he left office. Still, he remained loyal to his party and took heart in November elections suggesting "that the Republicans will control this Government for at least four years longer."

We are indebted to J. Dane Hartgrove and Howard H. Wehmann for assistance in searching the National Archives; to Harriet F. Simon for proofreading; and to Matthew Olsen and Robyn Rhoads, graduate students at Southern Illinois University, for research assistance.

Financial support for the period during which this volume was prepared came from Southern Illinois University, the National Endowment for the Humanities, and the National Historical Publications and Records Commission.

JOHN Y. SIMON

August 17, 2001

Editorial Procedure

1. Editorial Insertions

A. Words or letters in roman type within brackets represent editorial reconstruction of parts of manuscripts torn, mutilated, or illegible.

B. [. . .] or [— — —] within brackets represent lost material which cannot be reconstructed. The number of dots represents the approximate number of lost letters; dashes represent lost words.

C. Words in *italic* type within brackets represent material such as dates which were not part of the original manuscript.

D. Other material crossed out is indicated by ~~cancelled type~~.

E. Material raised in manuscript, as "4th," has been brought in line, as "4th."

2. Symbols Used to Describe Manuscripts

AD	Autograph Document
ADS	Autograph Document Signed
ADf	Autograph Draft
ADfS	Autograph Draft Signed
AES	Autograph Endorsement Signed
AL	Autograph Letter
ALS	Autograph Letter Signed

ANS	Autograph Note Signed
D	Document
DS	Document Signed
Df	Draft
DfS	Draft Signed
ES	Endorsement Signed
LS	Letter Signed

3. *Military Terms and Abbreviations*

Act.	Acting
Adjt.	Adjutant
AG	Adjutant General
AGO	Adjutant General's Office
Art.	Artillery
Asst.	Assistant
Bvt.	Brevet
Brig.	Brigadier
Capt.	Captain
Cav.	Cavalry
Col.	Colonel
Co.	Company
C.S.A.	Confederate States of America
Dept.	Department
Div.	Division
Gen.	General
Hd. Qrs.	Headquarters
Inf.	Infantry
Lt.	Lieutenant
Maj.	Major
Q. M.	Quartermaster
Regt.	Regiment or regimental
Sgt.	Sergeant
USMA	United States Military Academy, West Point, N.Y.
Vols.	Volunteers

4. Short Titles and Abbreviations

ABPC	*American Book Prices Current* (New York, 1895–)
Badeau	Adam Badeau, *Grant in Peace. From Appomattox to Mount McGregor* (Hartford, Conn., 1887)
CG	*Congressional Globe.* Numbers following represent the Congress, session, and page.
J. G. Cramer	Jesse Grant Cramer, ed., *Letters of Ulysses S. Grant to his Father and his Youngest Sister, 1857–78* (New York and London, 1912)
DAB	*Dictionary of American Biography* (New York, 1928–36)
Foreign Relations	*Papers Relating to the Foreign Relations of the United States* (Washington, 1869–)
Garland	Hamlin Garland, *Ulysses S. Grant: His Life and Character* (New York, 1898)
Julia Grant	John Y. Simon, ed., *The Personal Memoirs of Julia Dent Grant* (New York, 1975)
HED	*House Executive Documents*
HMD	*House Miscellaneous Documents*
HRC	*House Reports of Committees.* Numbers following *HED, HMD,* or *HRC* represent the number of the Congress, the session, and the document.
Ill. AG Report	J. N. Reece, ed., *Report of the Adjutant General of the State of Illinois* (Springfield, 1900)
Johnson, Papers	LeRoy P. Graf and Ralph W. Haskins, eds., *The Papers of Andrew Johnson* (Knoxville, 1967–2000)
Lewis	Lloyd Lewis, *Captain Sam Grant* (Boston, 1950)
Lincoln, Works	Roy P. Basler, Marion Dolores Pratt, and Lloyd A. Dunlap, eds., *The Collected Works of Abraham Lincoln* (New Brunswick, 1953–55)
Memoirs	*Personal Memoirs of U. S. Grant* (New York, 1885–86)
Nevins, Fish	Allan Nevins, *Hamilton Fish: The Inner History of the Grant Administration* (New York, 1936)

O.R.	*The War of the Rebellion: A Compilation of the Official Records of the Union and Confederate Armies* (Washington, 1880–1901)
O.R. (Navy)	*Official Records of the Union and Confederate Navies in the War of the Rebellion* (Washington, 1894–1927). Roman numerals following *O.R.* or *O.R.* (Navy) represent the series and the volume.
PUSG	John Y. Simon, ed., *The Papers of Ulysses S. Grant* (Carbondale and Edwardsville, 1967–)
Richardson	Albert D. Richardson, *A Personal History of Ulysses S. Grant* (Hartford, Conn., 1868)
SED	*Senate Executive Documents*
SMD	*Senate Miscellaneous Documents*
SRC	*Senate Reports of Committees.* Numbers following *SED, SMD,* or *SRC* represent the number of the Congress, the session, and the document.
USGA Newsletter	*Ulysses S. Grant Association Newsletter*
Young	John Russell Young, *Around the World with General Grant* (New York, 1879)

5. Location Symbols

CLU	University of California at Los Angeles, Los Angeles, Calif.
CoHi	Colorado State Historical Society, Denver, Colo.
CSmH	Henry E. Huntington Library, San Marino, Calif.
CSt	Stanford University, Stanford, Calif.
CtY	Yale University, New Haven, Conn.
CU-B	Bancroft Library, University of California, Berkeley, Calif.
DLC	Library of Congress, Washington, D.C. Numbers following DLC-USG represent the series and volume of military records in the USG papers.

DNA	National Archives, Washington, D.C. Additional numbers identify record groups.
IaHA	Iowa State Department of History and Archives, Des Moines, Iowa.
I-ar	Illinois State Archives, Springfield, Ill.
IC	Chicago Public Library, Chicago, Ill.
ICarbS	Southern Illinois University, Carbondale, Ill.
ICHi	Chicago Historical Society, Chicago, Ill.
ICN	Newberry Library, Chicago, Ill.
ICU	University of Chicago, Chicago, Ill.
IHi	Illinois State Historical Library, Springfield, Ill.
In	Indiana State Library, Indianapolis, Ind.
InFtwL	Lincoln National Life Foundation, Fort Wayne, Ind.
InHi	Indiana Historical Society, Indianapolis, Ind.
InNd	University of Notre Dame, Notre Dame, Ind.
InU	Indiana University, Bloomington, Ind.
KHi	Kansas State Historical Society, Topeka, Kan.
MdAN	United States Naval Academy Museum, Annapolis, Md.
MeB	Bowdoin College, Brunswick, Me.
MH	Harvard University, Cambridge, Mass.
MHi	Massachusetts Historical Society, Boston, Mass.
MiD	Detroit Public Library, Detroit, Mich.
MiU-C	William L. Clements Library, University of Michigan, Ann Arbor, Mich.
MoSHi	Missouri Historical Society, St. Louis, Mo.
NHi	New-York Historical Society, New York, N.Y.
NIC	Cornell University, Ithaca, N.Y.
NjP	Princeton University, Princeton, N.J.
NjR	Rutgers University, New Brunswick, N.J.
NN	New York Public Library, New York, N.Y.
NNP	Pierpont Morgan Library, New York, N.Y.
NRU	University of Rochester, Rochester, N.Y.
OClWHi	Western Reserve Historical Society, Cleveland, Ohio.

OFH	Rutherford B. Hayes Library, Fremont, Ohio.
OHi	Ohio Historical Society, Columbus, Ohio.
OrHi	Oregon Historical Society, Portland, Ore.
PCarlA	U.S. Army Military History Institute, Carlisle Barracks, Pa.
PHi	Historical Society of Pennsylvania, Philadelphia, Pa.
PPRF	Rosenbach Foundation, Philadelphia, Pa.
RPB	Brown University, Providence, R.I.
TxHR	Rice University, Houston, Tex.
USG 3	Maj. Gen. Ulysses S. Grant 3rd, Clinton, N.Y.
USMA	United States Military Academy Library, West Point, N.Y.
ViHi	Virginia Historical Society, Richmond, Va.
ViU	University of Virginia, Charlottesville, Va.
WHi	State Historical Society of Wisconsin, Madison, Wis.
Wy-Ar	Wyoming State Archives and Historical Department, Cheyenne, Wyo.
WyU	University of Wyoming, Laramie, Wyo.

Chronology
1875

Jan. 4. U.S. troops evicted Democrats from the state house in New Orleans during a dispute over the composition of the legislature.

Jan. 5. In New Orleans, Lt. Gen. Philip H. Sheridan compared "White League" opponents of Republican Governor William P. Kellogg to "banditti."

Jan. 7. An anonymous Virginian sent USG a death threat, the first of many prompted by events in La.

Jan. 13. In a lengthy message to the Senate, USG defended his policy in La., where, he argued, "the spirit of hatred and violence is stronger than law."

Jan. 14. USG signed a currency bill that committed the U.S. to replace all greenbacks with coin by 1879.

Jan. 27. USG's daughter Ellen Sartoris arrived in New York City from England. School superintendents thanked USG for supporting public education.

Feb. 1. USG sent to the Senate a reciprocity treaty with Hawaii, ratified on March 18.

Feb. 4. USG revoked a Jan. 27 order to transfer revenue supervisors aimed at uncovering collusion between officials and distillers to produce non-taxed whiskey.

Feb. 8. Without consulting the cabinet, USG condemned the new Ark. constitution and asked Congress to act.

Feb. 10. USG approved legislation to aid sufferers from drought and grasshoppers in Kan. and Neb.

FEB. 23.   USG greeted Mexican War veterans.

MAR. 1.   USG signed the Civil Rights Act guaranteeing blacks access to public facilities and the right to serve on juries.

MAR. 3.   Faced with USG's veto, Congress adjourned without passing a controversial bill to equalize bounty payments for veterans.

MAR. 9.   USG signed a bill appropriating $505,000 for executive branch exhibits at the Centennial celebration in Philadelphia.

MAR. 17.   Amid gold rush rumors, USG reported efforts to prevent mining parties from exploring Sioux land in the Black Hills.

MAR. 26.   USG and cabinet rejected Fitz John Porter's appeal for a review of his wartime court-martial.

MAR. 28.   In Neb., Red Cloud resolved to see USG about the Black Hills. "Look at me! I am no Dog. I am a man. This is my ground, and I am sitting on it."

APRIL 15–21.   USG and cabinet traveled to Mass. for the centennial of the revolutionary war battles at Lexington and Concord.

APRIL 22.   Attorney Gen. George H. Williams resigned because of reports of financial irregularities involving his wife.

APRIL 24.   Yale paleontologist Othniel C. Marsh conveyed to USG Red Cloud's allegations of fraud in the distribution of rations.

MAY 10.   Treasury officials raided distilleries in Chicago, Milwaukee, and St. Louis, seizing evidence of whiskey frauds.

MAY 19.   USG greeted Red Cloud, Spotted Tail, and other Sioux leaders delegated to discuss the status of the Black Hills.

MAY 26.   USG warned the Sioux that whites would eventually overrun their land and advised them to resettle in the Indian Territory.

MAY 27.   USG greeted a papal delegation.

MAY 29.   USG ended fervid speculation by announcing that he would not accept a third term unless compelled by "imperitive duty."

JUNE 2.   USG urged the Sioux to relinquish hunting rights in Neb. and to allow mining concessions in the Black Hills.

JUNE 15.   From his summer home at Long Branch, USG ordered the navy to patrol the Rio Grande and to stop raids from Mexico.

JUNE 18.   USG toured the Centennial buildings and grounds in Philadelphia.

JUNE 20.   USG asked Secretary of the Interior Columbus Delano to resign. Delano reportedly threatened blackmail to forestall removal.

JULY 9.   Secretary of State Hamilton Fish visited USG at Long Branch.

JULY 11.   USG's first grandchild, Grant Sartoris, was born at Long Branch.

JULY 21. At the capital, USG and cabinet discussed Cuban unrest and the D.C. district attorneyship.

JULY 24. USG attended the funeral of George Templeton Strong in New York City.

JULY 29. USG met the Board of Indian Commissioners at Long Branch. On a letter detailing whiskey fraud investigations at St. Louis, USG wrote: "Let no guilty man escape," destined to be a watchword for the scandal.

JULY 31. Andrew Johnson died in Tenn.

AUG. 10. In Neb., U.S. commissioners and Sioux chiefs discussed fraud at the Red Cloud Agency.

AUG. 15–19. USG visited Fairpoint and Buffalo, N.Y., then spent three days in R.I. as the guest of U.S. Senator Ambrose E. Burnside.

AUG. 31. USG and family traveled to New York City, where the Sartorises departed for England.

SEPT. 1. Secretary of the Treasury Benjamin H. Bristow submitted his resignation amid press reports of his feud with Delano. Bristow remained in the cabinet.

SEPT. 13. Weighing a Sept. 8 request for troops to quell Miss. unrest, USG acknowledged the public's impatience with such appeals but promised firmness if necessary. Ultimately, no troops were sent.

SEPT. 15–16. USG attended the Army of the Cumberland reunion at Utica, N.Y.

SEPT. 17. USG saw the play "Around the World in Eighty Days" at the Academy of Music in New York City.

SEPT. 20–29. At a Neb. council, U.S. commissioners could not convince the Sioux to renegotiate the 1868 Black Hills treaty.

SEPT. 21. USG and Frederick Dent Grant attended the N.J. state fair.

SEPT. 22. Delano visited USG at Elizabeth, N.J., and successfully pressed for acceptance of his resignation. USG and party left for St. Louis.

SEPT. 24. At USG's behest, Fish and cabinet met after USG had passed Columbus, Ohio, to consider Delano's replacement as secretary of the interior.

SEPT. 26. At St. Louis, USG arranged to liquidate his farm assets and prepared to lease the property.

SEPT. 29. Addressing an Army of the Tennessee reunion in Des Moines, USG championed non-sectarian public education.

SEPT. 30. A livestock auction at USG's farm yielded poor returns.

OCT. 1.   USG spoke to high school students at Omaha.

OCT. 2–4.   USG traveled to Cheyenne and to Salt Lake City, where he met Brigham Young.

OCT. 5–9.   USG visited Denver and other points in Colorado Territory.

OCT. 15.   USG returned to Washington, D.C. The cabinet discussed the pending election in Miss.

OCT. 19.   USG chose Zachariah Chandler as secretary of the interior, ending weeks of awkward uncertainty.

NOV. 1.   USG told local clergymen that he would not abandon his peace policy toward the Indians.

NOV. 2.   Republicans gained ground in state and local elections.

NOV. 3.   USG met key officials on Indian policy and decided to allow miners entry into the Black Hills.

NOV. 8–11.   USG and Julia Grant visited New York City.

NOV. 22.   A St. Louis jury found John McDonald, revenue supervisor, guilty in the whiskey frauds.

NOV. 22.   Vice President Henry Wilson died.

DEC. 3.   USG authorized a military trial for Orville E. Babcock, tied by prosecutors to whiskey frauds in St. Louis.

DEC. 7.   In his annual message, USG proposed a constitutional amendment "to establish and forever maintain free public schools adequate to the education of all the children in the rudimentary branches."

DEC. 8.   USG summoned Solicitor of the Treasury Bluford Wilson for a tense exchange about whiskey fraud investigations.

DEC. 9.   A grand jury in St. Louis formally indicted Babcock for conspiracy in the whiskey frauds. On Dec. 15, Babcock's military court disbanded.

DEC. 17–18.   USG and a large congressional delegation visited the Centennial grounds in Philadelphia.

The Papers of Ulysses S. Grant
1875

To Senate

———

[To the Senate of the United States:

I have the honor to make the following answer to a Senate resolution of the 8th instant, asking for information as to any interference, by any military officer or any part of the Army of the United States, with the organization or proceedings of the general assembly of the State of Louisiana, or either branch thereof; and also inquiring in regard to the existence of armed organizations in that State, hostile to the government thereof, and intent on overturning such government by force.

To say that lawlessness, turbulence, and bloodshed have characterized the political affairs of that State since its re-organization under the reconstruction acts, is only to repeat what has become well known as a part of its unhappy history; but it may be proper here to refer to the election of 1868, by which the republican vote of the State, through fraud and violence, was reduced to a few thousands, and the bloody riots of 1866 and 1868, to show that the disorders there are not due to any recent causes or to any late action of the Federal authorities.

Preparatory to the election of 1872, a shameful and undisguised conspiracy was formed to carry that election against the republicans without regard to law or right, and to that end the most glaring frauds and forgeries were committed in the returns after many colored citizens had been denied registration, and others deterred by fear from casting their ballots.

When the time came for a final canvass of the votes, in view of the foregoing facts, William P. Kellogg, the republican candidate for governor, brought suit upon the equity side of the United States circuit court for Louisiana, and against Warmoth and others, who had obtained possession of the returns of the election, representing that several thousand voters of the State had been deprived of the elective franchise on account of their color, and praying that steps might be taken to have said votes counted, and for general relief. To enable the court to inquire as to the truth of these allegations, a temporary restraining order was issued against the defendants, which was at once wholly disregarded and treated with contempt by those to whom it was directed. These proceedings have been widely denounced as an unwarrantable interference by the Federal judiciary with the election of State officers; but it is to be remembered that by the fifteenth amendment to the Constitution of the United States the political equality of colored citizens is secured, and under the second section of that amendment, providing that Congress shall have power to enforce its provisions by appropriate legislation, an act was passed on the 31st of May, 1870, and amended in 1871, the object of which was to prevent the denial or abridgment of suffrage to citizens, on account of race, color, or previous condition of servitude; and it has been held by all the Federal judges before whom the question has arisen, including Justice Strong, of the Supreme Court, that the protection afforded by this amendment and these acts extends to State as well as other elections. That it is the duty of the Federal courts to enforce the provisions of the Constitution of the United States and the laws passed in pursuance thereof is too clear for controversy.

Section 15 of said act, after numerous provisions therein to prevent an evasion of the fifteenth amendment, provides that the jurisdiction of the circuit court of the United States shall extend to all cases in law or equity arising under the provisions of said act and of the act amendatory thereof. Congress seems to have contemplated equitable as well as legal proceedings to prevent the denial of suffrage to colored citizens; and it may be safely asserted that if Kellogg's bill in the above-named case did not present a case for the equitable interposition of the court, that no such case can arise under the act. That the courts of the United States have the right to interfere in various ways with State elections so as to maintain political equality and rights therein, irrespective of race or color, is comparatively a new, and to some seems to be a startling idea, but it results as clearly from the fifteenth amendment to the Constitution and the acts that have been passed to enforce that amendment, as the abrogation of State laws upholding slavery results from the thirteenth amendment to the Constitution. While the jurisdiction of the court in the case of Kellogg *vs.* Warmoth and others is clear to my mind, it seems that some of the orders made by the judge in that and the kindred case of Antoine were illegal. But while they are so held and considered, it is not to be forgotten that the mandates of his court had been contemptuously defied, and they were made while wild scenes of anarchy were sweeping away all restraint of law and order. Doubtless the judge of this court made grave mistakes; but the law allows the chancellor great latitude not only in punishing those who contemn his orders and injunctions, but in preventing the consummation of the wrong which he has judicially forbidden. Whatever may be said or thought of those matters, it was only made known to me that process of the United States court was resisted; and as said act especially provides for the use of the Army and Navy, when necessary, to enforce judicial process arising thereunder, I considered it my duty to see that such process was executed according to the judgment of the court.

Resulting from these proceedings, through various controversies and complications, a State administration was organized with William P. Kellogg as governor, which, in the discharge of my duty under section 4, art[i]cle 4, of the Constitution, I have recognized as the government of the State.

It has been bitterly and persistently alleged that Kellogg was not elected. Whether he was or not is not altogether certain, nor is it any more certain that his competitor, McEnery, was chosen. The election was a gigantic fraud, and there are no reliable returns of its result. Kellogg obtained possession of the office, and in my opinion has more right to it than his competitor.

On the 20th of February, 1873, the Committee on Privileges and Elections of the Senate, made a report in which they say they were satisfied by testimony that the manipulation of the election machinery by Warmoth and others was equivalent to twenty thousand votes; and they add that to recognize the McEnery government "would be recognizing a government based upon fraud, in defiance of the wishes and intention of the voters of the State." Assuming the correctness of the statements in this report, (and they seem to have been generally accepted by the country,) the great crime in Louisiana, about which so much has been said, is, that one is holding the office of governor who was cheated out of twenty thousand votes, against another whose title to the office is undoubtedly based on fraud and in defiance of the wishes and intentions of the voters of the State.

Misinformed and misjudging as to the nature and extent of this report, the supporters of McEnery proceeded to displace by force in some counties of the State the appointees of Governor Kellogg; and on the 13th of April, in an effort of that kind, a butchery of citizens was committed at Colfax, which in blood-thirstiness and barbarity is hardly surpassed by any acts of savage warfare.

To put this matter beyond controversy I quote from the charge of Judge Woods, of the United States circuit court, to the jury in the case of The United States *vs.* Cruikshank and others, in New Orleans, in March, 1874. He said:

> In the case on trial there are many facts not in controversy. I proceed to state some of them in the presence and hearing of counsel on both sides: and if I state as a conceded fact any matter that is disputed, they can correct me.

After stating the origin of the difficulty, which grew out of an attempt of white persons to drive the parish judge and sheriff, appointees of Kellogg, from office, and their attempted protection by colored persons, which led to some fighting, in which quite a number of negroes were killed, the judge states:

> Most of those who were not killed were taken prisoners. Fifteen or sixteen of the blacks had lifted the boards and taken refuge under the floor of the court-house. They were all captured. About thirty-seven men were taken prisoners. The number is not definitely fixed. They were kept under guard until dark. They were led out, two by two, and shot. Most of the men were shot to death.

A few were wounded, not mortally, and, by pretending to be dead, were afterward, during the night, able to make their escape. Among them was the Levi Nelson named in the indictment.

The dead bodies of the negroes killed in this affair were left unburied until Tuesday, April 15, when they were buried by a deputy marshal and an officer of the militia from New Orleans. These persons found fifty-nine dead bodies. They showed pistol-shot wounds, the great majority in the head, and most of them in the back of the head. In addition to the fifty-nine dead bodies found, some charred remains of dead bodies were discovered near the court-house. Six dead bodies were found under a ware-house, all shot in the head, but one or two which were shot in the breast.

The only white men injured from the beginning of these troubles to their close were Hadnot and Harris. The court-house and its contents were entirely consumed.

There is no evidence that any one in the crowd of whites bore any lawful warrant for the arrest of any of the blacks. There is no evidence that either Nash or Cazabat, after the affair, ever de-manded their offices, to which they had set up claim, but Register continued to act as parish judge, and Shaw as sheriff.

These are facts in this case as I understand them to be admitted.

To hold the people of Louisiana generally responsible for these atrocities would not be just; but it is a lamentable fact that insuper-able obstructions were thrown in the way of punishing these mur-derers, and the so-called conservative papers of the State not only justified the massacre, but denounced as federal tyranny and despo-tism the attempt of the United States officers to bring them to jus-tice. Fierce denunciations ring through the country about office-holding and election matters in Louisiana, while every one of the Colfax miscreants goes unwhipped of justice, and no way can be found in this boasted land of civilization and Christianity to punish the perpetrators of this bloody and monstrous crime.

Not unlike this was the massacre in August last. Several northern young men of capital and enterprise had started the little and flourishing town of Coushatta. Some of them were republicans and office-holders under Kellogg. They were therefore doomed to death. Six of them were seized and carried away from their homes and murdered in cold blood. No one has been punished; and the conservative press of the State dedounced all efforts to that end, and boldly justified the crime.

Many murders of a like character have been committed in individual cases which cannot here be detailed.[1] For example, T. S. Crawford, judge, and P. H. Harris, district attorney of the twelfth judicial district of the State, on their way to court were shot from their horses by men in ambush, on the 8th of October, 1873, and the widow of the former, in a communication to the Department of Justice, tells a piteous tale of the persecutions of her husband because he was a Union man, and of the efforts made to screen those who had committed a crime, which, to use her own language, "left two widows and nine orphans desolate."[2]

To say that the murder of a negro or a white republican is not considered a crime in Louisiana would probably be unjust to a great part of the people; but it is true that a great number of such murders have been committed, and no one has been punished therefor, and manifestly, as to them, the spirit of hatred and violence is stronger than law.

Representations were made to me that the presence of troops in Louisiana was unnecessary and irritating to the people, and that there was no danger of public disturbance if they were taken away. Consequently, early in last summer, the troops were all withdrawn from the State, with the exception of a small garrison at New Orleans Barracks. It was claimed that a comparative state of quiet had supervened. Political excitement as to Louisiana affairs seemed to be dying out. But the November election was approaching, and it was necessary for party purposes that the flame should be rekindled.

Accordingly, on the 14th of September, D. P. Penn, claiming that he was elected lieutenant governor in 1872, issued an inflammatory proclamation calling upon the militia of the State to arm, assemble, and drive from power the usurpers, as he designated the officers of the State. The White Leagues, armed and ready for the conflict, promptly responded.

On the same day the governor made a formal requisition upon me, pursuant to the act of 1795, and section 4, article 4 of the Constitution, to aid in suppressing domestic violence. On the next day I issued my proclamation commanding the insurgents to disperse within five days from the date thereof; but, before the proclamation was published in New Orleans, the organized and armed forces recognizing a usurping governor had taken forcible possession of the State-house, and temporarily subverted the government. Twenty or more people were killed, including a number of the police of the city. The streets of the city were stained with blood. All that was desired in the way of excitement had been accomplished, and, in view of the steps taken to repress it, the revolution is apparently, though it is believed not really, abandoned, and the cry of Federal usurpation and tyranny in Louisiana was renewed with redoubled energy. Troops had been sent to the State under this requisition of the governor, and as other disturbances seemed imminent they were allowed to remain there to render the executive such aid as might become necessary to enforce the laws of the State, and repress the continued violence which seemed inevitable the moment Federal support should be withdrawn.

Prior to, and with a view to the late election in Louisiana, white men associated themselves together in armed bodies called "White Leagues," and at the same time threats were made in the democratic journals of the State, that the election should be carried against the republicans at all hazards, which very naturally greatly alarmed the colored voters. By section 8 of the act of February 28, 1871, it is made the duty of United States marshals and their deputies, at polls where votes are cast for Representatives in Congress, to keep the peace and prevent any violations of the so-called enforcement acts, and other offenses against the laws of the United States; and upon a requisition of the marshal of Louisiana, and in view of said armed organizations and other portentous circumstances, I caused detachments of troops to be stationed in various localities in the State, to aid him in the performance of his official duties. That there was intimidation of republican voters at the election, notwithstanding these precautions, admits of no doubt. The following are specimens of the means used:

On the 14th of October eighty persons signed and published the following at Shreveport:

> We, the undersigned, merchants of the city of Shreveport, in obedience to a request of the Shreveport Campaign Club, agree to use every endeavor to get our employés to vote the people's ticket at the ensuing election: and, in the event of their refusal so to do, or in case they vote the radical ticket, to refuse to employ them at the expiration of their present contracts.

On the same day another large body of persons published in the same place a paper, in which they used the following language:

> We, the undersigned, merchants of the city of Shreveport, alive to the great importance of securing good and honest government to the State, do agree and pledge ourselves not to advance any supplies or money to any planter the coming year who will give employment or rent lands to laborers who vote the radical ticket in the coming election.

I have no information of the proceedings of the returning-board for said election which may not be found in its report, which has been published, but it is a matter of public information that a great part of the time taken to canvass the votes was consumed by the arguments of lawyers, several of whom represented each party before the board. I have no evidence that the proceedings of this board were not in accordance with the law under which they acted. Whether, in excluding from their count certain returns, they were right or wrong, is a question that depends upon the evidence they had before them; but it is very clear that the law gives them the power, if they choose to exercise it, of deciding that way; and *prima-facie* the persons whom they return as elected are entitled to the offices for which they were candidates.

Respecting the alleged interference by the military with the organization of the legislature of Louisiana on the 4th instant, I have no knowledge or information which has not been received by me since that time and published. My first information was from the pa-

pers of the morning of the 5th of January. I did not know that any
such thing was anticipated, and no orders nor suggestions were ever
given to any military officer in that State upon that subject prior to
the occurrence. I am well aware that any military interference by the
officers or troops of the United States with the organization of the
State legislature or any of its proceedings, or with any civil department of the Government, is repugnant to our ideas of government.
I can conceive of no case, not involving rebellion or insurrection,
where such interference by authority of the General Government
ought to be permitted or can be justified. But there are circumstances connected with the late legislative imbroglio in Louisiana
which seem to exempt the military from any intentional wrong in
that matter. Knowing that they had been placed in Louisiana to prevent domestic violence and aid in the enforcement of the State laws,
the officers and troops of the United States may well have supposed
that it was their duty to act when called upon by the governor for
that purpose.

Each branch of a legislative assembly is the judge of the election
and qualifications of its own members. But if a mob, or a body of
unauthorized persons seize and hold the legislative hall in a tumul-
tuous and riotous manner, and so prevent any organization by those
legally returned as elected, it might become the duty of the State executive to interpose, if requested by a majority of the members elect,
to suppress the disturbance and enable the persons elected to organize the house.

Any exercise of this power would only be justifiable under most
extraordinary circumstances, and it would then be the duty of the
governor to call upon the constabulary, or, if necessary, the military
force of the State. But with reference to Louisiana, it is to be borne
in mind that any attempt by the governor to use the police force of
that State at this time would have undoubtedly precipitated a bloody
conflict with the White League, as it did on the 14th of September.

There is no doubt but that the presence of the United States
troops upon that occasion prevented bloodshed and the loss of life.
Both parties appear to have relied upon them as conservators of the
public peace.

The first call was made by the democrats to remove persons obnoxious to them from the legislative hall; and the second was from the republicans to remove persons who had usurped seats in the legislature without legal certificates authorizing them to seats, and in sufficient number to change the majority.

Nobody was disturbed by the military who had a legal right at that time to occupy a seat in the legislature. That the democratic minority of the house undertook to seize its organization by fraud and violence; that in this attempt they trampled under foot law; that they undertook to make persons not returned as elected members, so as to create a majority; that they acted under a preconcerted plan, and under false pretenses introduced into the hall a body of men to support their pretensions by force, if necessary, and that conflict, disorder, and riotous proceedings followed, are facts that seem to be well established, and I am credibly informed that these violent proceedings were a part of a premeditated plan to have the house organized in this way, recognize what has been called the McEnery senate, then to depose Governor Kellogg, and so revolutionize the State government.

Whether it was wrong for the governor, at the request of the majority of the members returned as elected to the house, to use such means as were in his power to defeat these lawless and revolutionary proceedings, is perhaps a debatable question, but it is quite certain that there would have been no trouble if those who now complain of illegal interference had allowed the house to be organized in a lawful and regular manner. When those who inaugurate disorder and anarchy disavow such proceedings, it will be time enough to condemn those who, by such means as they have, prevent the success of their lawless and desperate schemes.

Lieutenant General Sheridan was requested by me to go to Louisiana to observe and report the situation there, and, if in his opinion necessary, to assume the command, which he did on the 4th instant, after the legislative disturbances had occurred, at 9 o'clock p. m., a number of hours after the disturbances. No party motives nor prejudices can reasonably be imputed to him; but honestly convinced by what he has seen and heard there, he has characterized the leaders of

the White Leagues in severe terms, and suggested summary modes
of procedure against them, which, though they cannot be adopted,
would, if legal, soon put an end to the troubles and disorders in that
State.] General Sheridan was looking at facts, and, possibly not
thinking of proceedings ~~that might~~ which would be ~~proper~~ the only
proper ones to pursue in time of peace, ~~but~~ thought more of the utterly lawless condittion of society surrounding him at the time of his
dispatch, and of what would prove a sure remedy. He never ~~intimated
a~~ proposed to do an illegal act nor [Evinced] determination to proceed beyond what the law ~~clearly authorized~~ in the future might authorize for the punishment of the attrocities which have been committed, and the commission of which can not be succesfully denied.
It is a deplorable fact that political crimes and murders have been
committed in La. which have gone unpunished, and which have been
justified or apologized for ~~that~~ which must rest as a disgrace [re-
proach] upon the state and [c]ountry long after the present generation has passed away,

[I have no desire to have United States troops interfere in the domestic concerns of Louisiana or any other State.

On the ninth of December last Governor Kellogg telegraphed to
me his apprehensions that the White League intended to make another attack upon the State-house, to which, on the same day, I made
the following answer, since which no communication has been sent
to him:

"Your dispatch of this date just received. It is exceedingly un-
palatable to use troops in anticipation of danger. Let the State authorities be right, and then proceed with their duties without apprehension of danger. If they are then molested, the question will be
determined whether the United States is able to maintain law and
order within its limits, or not."[3]

I have deplored the necessity which seemed to make it my duty
under the Constitution and laws to direct such interference. I have
always refused except where it seemed to be my imperative duty to
act in such a manner under the Constitution and laws of the United
States.[4] I have repeatedly and earnestly entreated the people of
the South to live together in peace, and obey the laws; and nothing

would give me greater pleasure than to see reconciliation and tranquillity everywhere prevail, and thereby remove all necessity for the
presence of troops among them. I regret, however, to say that this
state of things does not exist, nor does its existence seem to be desired in some localities; and as to those it may be proper for me to say
that, to the extent that Congress has conferred power upon me to
prevent it, neither Ku-Klux-Klans, White Leagues, nor any other
association using arms and violence to execute their unlawful purposes, can be permitted in that way to govern any part of this country; nor can I see with indifference Union men or republicans ostracised, persecuted, and murdered on account of their opinions, as
they now are in some localities.

I have heretofore urged the case of Louisiana upon the attention
of Congress, and I cannot but think that its inaction has produced
great evil.]

To summarise; in September last an armed, organized body of
men, in the support of candidates who had been put in nomination
for the offices of Governor and Lieut Governor, at the Nov. election
in 1872, and who had been declared not elected by the Board of Can-
vassers recognized by all the courts to which the question had been
~~refered~~ submitted, undertook to subvert and overthrow the state
government that had been ~~duly~~ recognized by ~~the Executive~~, me,
and in accordance with previous precedents. The recognized Governor was driven from the ~~soil of the state~~ state house in ~~of over which
he had performed the functions of executive for sixteen months
to the territory of the United States—the New Orleans Custom
House—for protection and probable assassination.~~ was the recognized executive and over which he had presided for the preceeding
sixteen months. But for his finding shelter in the United States Custom House in the Capital of the state of which he was governor it is
scarcely to be doubted that he would have been ~~assasin~~ killed   From
~~that point~~ the state House, before he had been driven to the Custom
House a call was made, in accordance with the the IV section, ~~of the~~
IV Article of the Constitution for the aid of the general government
to suppress domestic violence. Under those circumstances,—and in
accordance with my sworn duties—my proclamation of the [15th]

of September 1874 was issued. ~~commanding the~~   This served to reinstate Gov.r Kellogg to his position nominally; but it cannot be
claimed that the insurgents have, to this day, surrendered to the state
authorities the Arms belonging to the state, or that they have, in
any sence disarmed. On the contrary it is known that the same
armed organizations that existed on the 14th of Sept. 1874, in opposition to the recognized state government, still retain their organization, equipments and commanders, and can be called out at any
hour, to resist the state government. Under these circumstances the
same Military force has been continued in La. as was sent there under the first call, and under the same general instructions. I repeat
that the task assumed by the troops is not a pleasant one to them;
that the Army is not composed of lawyers capable of judging at a moments notice of just how far they ~~could~~ can go in the maintainance
of law and order, and that it was impossible to give specific instructions, providing for all possible contingencies that might arize.[5]
~~They~~ The ~~Army officer~~ troops were bound to act upon the judgement of the commanding officer upon each sudden contingency that
arose or await instructions ~~that~~ which could only reach them after
the threatened wrongs had been committed which they were called
on to prevent. It should be recollected too that upon my recognition of the Kellogg government ~~of La~~ I reported the fact,—with the
grounds of ~~the~~ recognition—to Congress, and asked that body to
take action ~~or else~~ in the matter otherwise I should regard their silence as an acquiescence in my course. No action has been taken by
that body and I have maintained ~~my~~ the position then marked out.
~~To repeat further, it would be singular if a body of men placed in the~~
~~anomolous position which that portion of the Army now in La. has~~
~~been in since last Sept. being called upon constantly to perform du-~~
~~ties belonging more properly to the civil service than the Military,~~
~~should keep constantly within a technical construction of the law.~~ If
~~they have erred~~ errors have been committed it has ~~been~~ always been
on the side of the preservation of good order, the ~~observance~~ maintainance of law, and the ~~preservation~~ protection of life. Their ~~faults~~
bearing reflect credit upon these soldiers, and if wrong has resulted
the ~~fault is with the turbulent elements and in some degree has~~

~~arisen from non action of Congress for its non action when attention was called to the subject in 1873.~~ the blame is with the turbulent elements surrounding them. ~~and to the continued non action of Congress in 1873 when their attention was called to the subject.~~ since its attention was first called to the subject.

I now earnestly ask that such action be taken by Congress as to leave my duties perfectly clear, in dealing with the affairs of La, giving assurance at the same time that what ever may be done by that body in the p[remises] will be executed according to the spirit and letter of [the l]aw "without fear, favor [or] affection."

[I herewith transmit copies of certain documents containing more specific information as to the subject matter of the resolution.

U. S. GRANT.

JANUARY 13, 1875.]

ADf (bracketed material from printed source or in another hand), ICHi. *SED*, 43-2-13. See Endorsement, Sept. 23, 1874.

On Dec. 24, 1874, Secretary of War William W. Belknap wrote to Lt. Gen. Philip H. Sheridan, Chicago. "*Confidential* . . . The President sent for me this morning and desires me to say to you that he wishes you to visit the States of Louisiana and Mississippi and especially New Orleans in Louisiana, and Vicksburg and Jackson in Misissippi and ascertain for yourself and for his information the general condition of matters in those localities. You need not confine your visit to the States of Louisiana and Mississippi and may extend your trip to other States; Alabama, &c., if you see proper; nor need you confine your visit, in the States of Louisiana and Mississippi, to the places named. What the President desires is to ascertain the true condition of affairs and to receive such suggestions from you as you may deem advisable and judicious. . . . The President thinks, and so do I, that a trip South might be agreeable to you and that you might be able to obtain a good deal of information on the subjects about which we desire to learn. You can make your return by Washington, and make a verbal report, and also inform me, from time to time, of your views and conclusions." LS (press), DNA, RG 94, Letters Received, 3579 1874. *SED*, 43-2-13, 19–20; *SD*, 57-2-209, 158–59.

Also on Dec. 24, Merrimon Howard, Fayette, Miss., wrote to USG. "permet me to enclose to a privet Letter from a friend   In Closed find Letter" ALS, DNA, RG 60, Letters from the President. Howard served as sheriff, Jefferson County. On Dec. 17, A. P. Williams, "'Sumner' (Boys) School," New Orleans, had written to Howard. "The weather is wet and cold. Much excitement exists in our city over the admixture of the schools. The streets leading to the different High Schools, are crowded with half grown boys and men who oppose all colored applicants. Several have been severely beaten and numbers driven away. They have organized themselves in to squads of fifty and will to-day visit all of the Grammar and Primary Schools (white) and take therefrom all of the colored pupils and march them to the colored schools. The city superintendent was attacked by a posse of half grown boys and insulted, beaten and even threatened with hanging. The girls of the school interfered and after making an apology to the young ladies for insulting them by allowing negroes to come amongst them, and signing a written document promising to use his influence against the admixture of the schools he was allowed to depart. . . ." ALS, *ibid*.

On Dec. 26, A. J. Carney, "Founder of the United Christian Church," Washington, D. C., wrote to USG. "Please accept a small present from the undersigned. Given as a Momento, For His Excellency's Wisdom & determination in restoring order in Louisiana. And in consequence of being personally acquainted with a brother in Law of His Excellency, (Gen. Frederick. T. Dent.)— " ALS, USG 3.

On Dec. 28, John A. Duble, New Orleans, wrote to USG. "You will remember me, at the first commencement of the late war, when I came to Cairo Ill. with the *first* Gun Boats, fitted up by the U. S. viz—'Tylor' 'Lexington' and 'Conestoga'—I was *directly* connected with you, and your command in all the battles, of 1861 & 1862, untill after the fall of Memphis, and at the fight at St. Charels on White River, on the 16th of June in 1862. Then resigning my commission was ordered to Washington by the Hon. Sec. of the U. S. N. Gideon Wells, was placed in command of the of the Gun Boat off Cincinnati Ohio in the fall of 1862, under the orders of Maj Genl. H G Wright Comdg. the Dept. of the Ohio,— during the invasion of Kirby Smith, of his March through Kentucky,—This whole improvised fleet and expenses attendnt it, was settled up on my vouchers, with the Q M Genl Dept. at Washington—Genl Meigs—from which my record is clear,—afterwards when I fit up the Steamer' 'John H Groesbeck' you saw fit to take her for your Head Quarters Bo[a]t, at Youngs point, Chickasaw Bayou, & Vicksburgh, where she remained untill the fall, after Vicksburgh was taken,   afterwards when you went to the Army of the Potomac, when you made the trip around the Circle, with Prest. Andrew Johnson, my Boat then, the Steamer 'Ruth' was selected by the city of St Louis Mo. to convey the President and his party, from Alton Ill to that city. You will remember as being then my special Guest, during the War on the Tennessee, Cumberland Ohio, & Missi Rivers—I had the confidence— of yourself and all your Staff officers—and you and your Staff, were my guests, after the fall of Fort Donleson up the Cumberland River to Clarksville & Nashville—on the U S Gun-Boat 'Conestoga'   N[o]w Mr President I will state that for over thirty years, I have been directly connected as Captain of Steam Boats, navigating the Western Rivers—to N Orleans La   This city I have made my home for the past five years and perhaps can give you more positive information of the workings here, in the present and past troubles, than any other, who has never been a Politician, never having in my life belonged to a secret society or association—but always voting for those I thought the best fitted for the position & without regard to Politics—Col James F. Casey the Collocter of this Port saw fit some three years ago to have me appointed in the U S Custom House, and I had full charge of all the Bonded goods that went forward from this Port, under the Law of Goods going forward 'without appriesment'—'to whom I refer' as well as Gov Wm Dennison in Washington who is an Uncle of mine by Marriage'—I now write Mr President to you, in regard to the present and past troubles, I know in this state,   I do not disguise the fact that we have very bad men on both sides, which has brought this state to ruin—none of whom in my opinion is worse than than Gov. John McHenry, in his *private* acts, of several of which I know, and from which I make up my mind from mature consideration—I now beg leave to state that I know of agrat deal of Rascality of both sides of those holding office, and those wanting it, and as I have no friends to reward, or Enemies to punish—am willing to give the govt. of the U. S. my firm support, which I have always done—There is brewing here, a big fuss that is bound to ripen shortly, that will require force of Arms to subdue,   Thousands of men are here, demanding employment and starving for want of employment, with the funds of this State, and the Treasury empty, stolen by those in power the past six years or more, and corruption in office, some of whom were filling positions under the U. S. Govt, who were her sworn Enemies a few years since, honest men, suffer, the taxes which bankrupt the property holder—are squandred and stolen away, such is the position of matters here, I shall be glad to give you, or your representatives the full truth of all matters here, I know them all, and can show you those, who now fill positions, who should be confined in a Penetentiary, instead of preying upon the vitals of a starved and bankrupt State—" ALS, DNA, RG 60, Letters from the President.

On Dec. 29, Secretary of State Hamilton Fish recorded in his diary. "Louisiana troubles are referred to and the Attorney General thinks that there are some indications on the part of the Democrats to insist upon installing in office all they think have been elected: but he is of opinion that the action of the returning board has been entirely fair and he inclines to the belief that their returns will be accepted. The President intimates that in case of trouble it may be necessary to place the State under Marshall Guard. Williams thinks that there is some doubt in the law, as to the Presidents authority." DLC-Hamilton Fish.

On Jan. 4, 1875, Louis A. Wiltz, New Orleans, telegraphed to USG. "I have the honor to inform you that the House of Representatives of this state was organized today by the election of myself as speaker, fifty Eight members two more than a quorum voting with a full House present, More than two hours after the organization I was informed by the officer in command of United States troops in this city that he had been requested by Governor Kellogg to remove certain members of the House from the State House and that under his orders he was obliged to comply with the request I protested against any interference of the United states Army with the organization or proceedings of the House but notwithstanding this the officer in command marched a company of soldiers upon the floor of the House and by force removed thirteen member[s] who had been legally and Constutionally seated as such and who at time of such forcible removal were participating in the proceedings of the House, in addition to this the military declared their purpose to further interfere with force in the business and organization of this assembly upon which some fifty two members and the speaker, withdrew declining to participate any longer in the business of the House under the dictation of the military as speaker I respectfully appeal to you to know by what authority and under what law the united states army interrupted and broke up a session of the House of Representatives of the state of Louisiana and to urgently request and demand that they be ordered to restore the House to the position it occupied when they so ~~interrupted~~ interferred and further that they be instructed that it is no part of their duty to interfere in any manner with the internal workings of the General assembly the House is the representation of the sovereignty of the state and I know of no law which warrants Either the Executive of the state or the united states army to interfere with its organization or proceedings," Telegram received (on Jan. 5), DNA, RG 60, Letters from the President. *SED*, 43-2-13, 21; *SD*, 57-2-209, 160−61. See *SMD*, 43-2-45, 43-2-46.

On Jan. 5, John McEnery, New Orleans, telegraphed to USG. "In the name of liberty and of all lovers of liberty throughout the United states I do most solemnly protest against the action of the military forces of the United states on yesterday in the occupation of the state House in the forcible ejectment by troops of members of the legislature and the elected speaker of the House and the subsequent organization of a house by the direct forcible intervention of the military I affirm before the whole american people that the action in part of the military in this City on yesterday is subversive of republican institutions in this free Country," Telegram received, DNA, RG 60, Letters Received, La. On the same day, Sheridan, New Orleans, thrice telegraphed to Belknap. "Please say to the President that he need give himself no uneasiness about the condition of affairs here I will preserve the peace which it is not hard to do with the naval & military forces in & about the city &

if Congress will declare the white leagues & other similar organization white or black banditti I will relieve it from the necessity of any special legislation for the preservation of
peace & equality of rights in the States of Louisiana ~~missippi~~ mississippi arkansas & the
executive from much of the trouble heretofore had in this Section of the country" "I think
that the terrorism now Existing in Louisiana, Miss, and Arkansas, Could be entirely removed and confidence and fair dealing Established by the arrest and trial of the ring leaders of the armed white leagues,　if Congress would pass a bill declaring them Banditti,
they could be tried by a military Commission. The ringleaders of this banditti who murdered men here on the fourteenth of last September and also more recently at Vicksburg
Miss should in justice to law and order and the peace & prosperity of this southern part of
the country be punished. It is possible that if the President would issue a proclamation declaring them banditti no further action need be taken, Except that which would devolve
upon me." "There is some excitement in the rotunda of the St. Charles hotel tonight upon
the publication by the newspapers of my dispatch to you calling the secret armed organization banditti　Give yourself no uneasiness. I see my way clear enough if you will only
have confidence." Telegrams received (the first at 4:47 P.M., the third on Jan. 6), *ibid.*,
RG 94, Letters Received, 3579 1874. *SED*, 43-2-13, 23–24; *SD*, 57-2-209, 161–62. On
Jan. 6, Belknap twice telegraphed to Sheridan. "Your telegrams all received. The President
& all of us have full con-confidence & thoroughly approve your course—" "I telegraphed
you hastily today answering your dispatch. You seem to fear that we had been misled by
biassed or partial statements of your acts. Be assured that the President and Cabinet
confide in your wisdom and rest in the belief that all acts of yours have been and will be judicious. This I intended to say in my brief telegram." ALS (press, telegram sent) and copy,
DNA, RG 94, Letters Received, 3579 1874. *SED*, 43-2-13, 25; *SD*, 57-2-209, 162. On
the same day, Sheridan telegraphed to Belknap. "The city is very quiet to day　Some of the
banditti made idle threats last night that they would assassinate me because I dared to tell
the truth　I am not afraid and will not be stopped from informing the Government that
there are localities in this department where the very air has been impregnated with assassination for several years," Telegram received, DNA, RG 94, Letters Received, 3579
1874. *SED*, 43-2-13, 25; *SD*, 57-2-209, 162.

　　On Jan. 7, "Conservative," Norfolk, Va., wrote to USG. "You had better mend your
corse towards the Sothern States,　if you do not you will not be a living man Two months
from to day,　This is no Idle jest, so take warning, and with Call Phill Sheridan from New
Orleans at once or boath of you will die by the hand of an Assassin in Two month's,—'and
the assasin will be a Virginian, for I owe old Phill and your self '*Hell*,' for burning my home
in the vally of Va,　You may hear from me in a few days through an 'Air Gun" L, USG 3.
On Jan. 15, "Deadshot," New Orleans, wrote to USG. "You are hereby cautioned, against,
allowing the interference of Federal Troops in the politics of this state. Should you not
withdraw the troops and accord, to Louisiana its right, before the expiration of thirty days,
then U. S. Grant will be something of the past. If you cannot well back out of your now
contemptible position, you had better, *PREPARE FOR, THE NEXT, WORLD!!!* If possible, a duel, will be demanded of you, if however, that course should not be deemed advisable, you will be *ASSASSINATED*" L, *ibid.* On Jan. 18, "Charles Howard," Madison, Ind.,
wrote to USG. "I have just arrived from the South and i wish to inform you that there is
an organization just forming for the purpose of raising 2500 men to go to the plains in the
spring to Stir up a war with the indians thinking that they will get the goverment to Concentrate all the troops in the Black hill Country and in the meantime they will have 25000
men ready to Seize all the forts and principal Cities in the South　i have been a member of
the organization for the last 6 weeks　i joined at vicksburgh Missippi . . . there will also
be attempts made to assasinate you and all the leading members of the radical party　they

have Even now got there Spies in Washington City and a letter was read that was recieved
from one of them on the 3d of January   it gave all the news of the day the names of Streets
that the leading members live upon with the number of the houses also a plan of the White
house Showing all of the outlets & inlets to the building and how the foundation was Constructed . . . i Could not rest with out telling you of the danger that is threatening you &
your goverment . . . the above is not my name   i am afraid to tell you as i am going South
Again in 3 weeks . . ." L, *ibid.* On Feb. 2, R. T. [—], New Berne, N. C., wrote to USG "to
inform you of an inpendent Danger in which if not vegillant it may proove fatal to you . . .
I hear from these Southern democratic Conservitive White leagues that they have drawn
A conspiracy to get you out of the way . . ." L (torn), *ibid.* On Feb. 4, Rufus B. Bullock, former Ga. governor, Albion, N. Y., wrote to Orville E. Babcock. "*Confidential* . . . I am not an
alarmist: but the time has arrived when the President is in danger of assassination, and extraordinary caution should be exercised . . . There is, or lately was, a man named Dr J. P.
Hamilton formerly of Atlanta Geo. loafing around Washington. This fellow is a dangerous hot headed zealot. He was implicated in a conspiracy for my assassination, that was
frustrated by Genl Sibley. He then left Georgia & made headquarters in Balto. &
Washn   He is notorious for having named his child 'Jno. Wilkes Booth' after the assassination of Mr Lincoln, & is just the character who would seize an opportunity to win the
applause of the 'Banditti' in that same infamous role. Excuse my intrusion & take such action as you deem best." ALS, *ibid.* On Feb. 8, C. C. Downs, Houston, Mo., wrote to USG
"to inform you that thair is A Conspiracy in the South against you and your Destruction
is well plotted . . . this Conspiracy think that I am A friend to it So I have got 2 Dollars in
the thing to help pay for you assasanation . . ." ALS, *ibid.* Also on Feb. 8, "A *Texan*," Richmond, wrote to USG. "'Ceaser' had his '*Brutus*' 'Charles' the 1st his Cromwell & Abe Lincoln his 'Booth!' You will have your name attatched to History With them just as Sure as
God Made Moses if the Civel rights bill is passed. 'Do not take this as a *banter.* You will
find out in time, or else you will never know [a]nything of it. So old fellow Say your
prayers." L, *ibid.* On Feb. 27, "An American Citizen," identifying himself with the "Ku Klux,
of the North," Philadelphia, wrote to USG. "The '*Booth*' who will give (the '*Drunken*'
'*Blackgaurd,*' '*Ignorant*' '*Imbecile*' '*Dirty,*' '*contemptible,*' Smoking' 'son *of a bitch,*' who now is
Executive Officer of this once great nation) his quietus, does not reside more that a thousand miles from here, and a greatful people will revere his memory by raising a monument
to his patriotism . . ." L, *ibid.*

On Jan. 7, Levi P. Luckey had written to Attorney Gen. George H. Williams. "The
President directs me to send you this note and ask if it will be possible to get in the report
of Southern affairs this afternoon in time to send to Congress to-day, and if it cannot be
sent in to-day, to bring before the Cabinet meeting tomorrow to be sent to Congress afterwards tomorrow afternoon." Copy, DLC-USG, II, 2.

On Jan. 9, Ephraim Hinds, principal, Hempstead Institute, Long Island, N. Y., wrote
to USG. "Just now, amid the abuse heaped upon you, by certain newspapers, calling themselves leaders of public opinion—and the systematic and malicious misrepresentation of
which you are made the subject, I wish to express my most emphatic approval of your
course in Louisiana affairs. Recognizing the unparalleled difficulties of your position, and
appreciating the ease with which a less honest and more crafty President in your place,
might have shirked his duty, and thus have found favor in the eyes of all the ex-rebels and
democrats, as well as a large class of so-called republicans—I cannot but admire your conscientious disregard of what a mere politician would would have thought to be policy—
and your straight-forward performance of the high duty imposed upon you by your oath
of office, . . . Be assured there are multitudes of people, who like myself, have not forgotten
Donaldson, nor Vicksburg, nor Richmond, nor Appomattox,—nor the horrors of Belle-

Isle and Libby-Prison, nor the assassination of Lincoln, nor the massacres of New-Orleans, Vicksburg, Coushatta and other places—and who do not mean that the unrepentant rebels shall subvert ~~the~~ the government or pervert it to their own base uses." ALS, USG 3. On the same day, Wendell Phillips, Boston, wrote to Belknap. "I intrude on your time to thank the Administration for the course taken in Louisa   Sheridan's judgment is entirely correct. You must have, or can easily obtain, abundant evidence to sustain him. I trust the President will support him promptly & vigorously. Be sure the North will rally round Grant in such circumstances. I wish to express to him my gratitude, as a citizen, for this decision & sagacity in dealing with the White League. One firm decisive hour will scatter the whole conspiracy. Left to itself, it will keep the South in turmoil & land her in bankruptcy if not rebellion" ALS, NjP; copy, USG 3. On Jan. 15, William A. Simmons, collector of customs, Boston, telegraphed to Babcock. "Large protest meeting in Faneuil Hall on Louisiana matter Wendell Phillips being a spectator   The audience cheering for Grant and sheridan insisted upon Phillips speaking and he is now upon the platform talking and dealing heavy blows amid great enthusiasm in defence of the President and General Sheridan   Neither Faneuil Hall Boston or the State will sustain the protestants meeting," Telegram received, DLC-USG, IB. On Jan. 18, George W. Calef, Boston, wrote to USG. "Fanuil Hall EXPOSE . . . Not until Louisiana was not 'fugitive from its own hall' could you have done better than you have done. Like a great, but modest soldier, you, with an aching heart and tender solicitude for the bewildered southrons asked light of Congress. Well, sir what have the stupid asses done? For two years they have squat upon their seduced posteriors and *trenchantly smiled*. Refused to instruct you. Every mother's son of them—totidem verbis—thought a cunning quiet was his key to the chair which you occupy. It is a fact not one of those members but thinks one day he will be the President. Poor fellows!!! Walking very fast one day, a big Irishman, with a head like Websters, a face resembling Henan's, and with the (*crude*) intellect of Daniel O Connell—asked me, 'Mr Calef why are the Adams family like a *pota-to*'—'I give it up'   'Well' said he, 'because the best part is under ground.'. . . Wendell Phillips spoke of John Quincy Adams—'not the one who just spoke here' said Mr. Phillips. We all had listened (there Mr. President) in Fanuil Hall to this fellow J. Q A. who is on the anxious seat to his one-sided conundrums,   at last seeing that peerless orator, sitting perched in the gallery, we, in our ignorance called for Phillips—*Damned scene*. Here I must confess that the platform and the chair loudly begged of the excited auditors to hear Mr Phillips. It was a grand scene to see Mr Grey rise like a king alone in his glory, and protect Mr Phillips. Had he not, God only knows the results: When Mr Phillips came, so grand, so fearless, his face so sweetly pale upon that Fanuil Hall platform 'Jack Adams ran like—the—devil—no, he ran like the battle of Bull Run.—home to his 'daddy' in Quincy. Forgive—Mr President—this is not parliamentary talk; but I am not, you know a statesman. *I am a poor man. . . .*" ALS, USG 3. See James Brewer Stewart, *Wendell Phillips: Liberty's Hero* (Baton Rouge, 1986), pp. 308–10.

On Jan. 9, Saturday, Fish had recorded in his diary a lengthy cabinet discussion. "The Louisiana question comes up . . . The President adopts the idea that the Military having been there in pursuance ~~with~~ of a call made in accordance with the Constitution of the United States was to be regarded as a Posse Comitatus . . . I dissent from these ideas—. . . The President in the course of the discussion (and soon after I had suggested disclaimer & denunciation of the action of the military etc) said 'he would ~~not~~ certainly not denounce it' nor would he censure Sheridan—the discussion which lasted until 3 oclock appeared to have some effect upon him, as it advanced he seemed to be somewhat impressed with doubt as to the entire correctness of what had been done   He requested the Secty of War to furnish the Atty Genl with copies of all the correspondence by telegram or otherwise with the officers in command in Louisiana & said that on Monday he would endeavor to send a message to Congress & he desired a Cabinet meeting on Monday at eleven" DLC-Hamilton Fish. See Nevins, *Fish*, pp. 751–54.

On the same day, Sheridan telegraphed to Belknap. "Your telegram of last night received. The object of my despatches has been to break down the White Leaguers whose influence intimidated the citizens and all the State authorities. This even went so far as to openly say that the United States troops here only remained upon their sufferance. There is to day, I will venture to say, more safety for individuals and their opinions than has existed here for the last four years, and the people are now beginning to realize what I have been driving at. The word banditti was taken from the opinion of the Attorney General in the Modoc case." Copy, NjP.

Also on Jan. 9, USG wrote to Belknap. "I wish you would have sent, in cipher, a dispatch to Sheridan asking if he can send ~~me~~ between this and to-morrow evening a synopsis of his intended report upon the number of political murders, &c, in La. since /66." ALS, *ibid.* On Jan. 10, 11:30 P.M., Sheridan telegraphed such a report to Belknap. Copy, USG 3. *SED*, 43-2-13, 29–31.

Also on Jan. 10, M. A. Southworth, New Orleans, telegraphed to USG. "A new Election will Result disasterously to Republican party here & greatly injure Every interest in the state   the proposed full and final settlement by Congressional Committee is preferred by disinterested persons of all parties here and with the guarantees that can be obtained from both parties will doubtless secure real peace and a republican state administration and incidentally settle the present legislative trouble by stopping the purposed revolution fusion claimants have agreed to this plan of settlement   all republican state officials will agree if so advised from Washington   I respectfully suggest that this is the easiest quickest & best solution of the Louisiana question   Have written Casey" Telegram received (at 11:55 P.M.), DNA, RG 60, Letters from the President. On the same day, Edwards Pierrepont, New York City, wrote to USG. "The '*call*' of our enemies concentrates an amount of hostile falsehood not often found in so few words—It is a pure Democratic movement to degrade the Administration, and *enemies*, not known as Democrats heretofore, join in the slander. To call it a *non-partisan* movement is preposterous. There will surely be a re-action when the facts are public—but the signers of this call do not want *facts.* I much regret that we have not a Morning Journal which is not hostile or through which we can be fairly heard—This ought not so to be—it need not be so—If we had had wise management or the least address this would not have been thus. I know Jones and Jennings of The Times well, and I know that they do not desire to be where they *fancy* they have been driven— We cannot afford to lose so much in Newyork as we are losing and we, *need not lose.* We have no NewsPaper of large circulation which is not at present an enemy. The whole object of this meeting is to break down the Administration and build the opposition upon its ruins—this is but one of many measures which will be tried—I am ever truly yours, *in spite of the jealous slanderers who have long tried to undermine me in your esteem.*" ALS, USG 3. William Cullen Bryant and others had called a Jan. 11 meeting in New York City to protest federal interference with the La. legislature. Clipping, *ibid.*

On Jan. 11, the Pa. House of Representatives passed a resolution of protest against the interference, condemning "so heinous an abuse of the power committed to the President." DS, *ibid.* Also on Jan. 11, Isaac B. Gara, Erie, Pa., wrote to USG. "It has occurred to me that at this time of peculiar trial, when your faithfulness and courage are put to the severest tests, a few words of encouragement from a friend you have met, but yet may not remember, may not be unacceptable . . . I feel authorized to assure you that in Erie County, Pennsylvania, long a Republican stronghold, your action, and Genl Sheriden's action, in regard to these difficulties, is cordially approved and commended by a large majority. . . ." ALS, *ibid.* On the same day, Babcock wrote to Adam Badeau, consul gen., London. ". . . The

Presidents head is clear and he is cool and will come out. Sheridans telegram caused the
'old rebel shout all allong the line.' You have heard it so often. Now you hear it here, and
in the Capitol building—I do not believe they can rise up again—. . ." ALS, MH.

Also on Jan. 11, Fish recorded in his diary. "The President and myself are alone for a
few minutes when he spoke of the Louisiana troubles and said that he was determined under no circumstances to apologize for anything that had been done—Finding him in this
mood I referred to the excitement in the minds of some of his best friends on the question
of Military interfearence with a Legislative body, that it involved a fundamental Constitutional principle on which I thought he might place himself properly on record without
severely criticising what had been done and with that view I had just previously placed on
paper for the purpose of seeing if I could frame anything to meet what I thought not only
desierable but very important   I then read him the paper which I had just shown to Bristow   He listened to it attentively but made no comment or reply; at this moment the other
members of the cabinet came in and the meeting was soon organized. . . . The President
stated that he intended in his message to recapitulate the events which he thought would
show the necessity of what had occurred. Robeson followed with the suggestion that the
President might suggest a train of events (in a manner very clearly and forcibly indicated
by him) justifying the presence of the militia in New Orleans under the requisition of the
Governor of September last and relieving the Administration from all responsibility on
that account; for the action of the military on the 4th of Jany had been taken without the
opportunity of consultation of the Government and without its knowledge gradually leading up to the opportunity of disclaiming or at least of not admitting approval—A general
concurrence in the line indicated by him was expressed   Belknap referred with some feeling to the construction which had been put upon his telegrams—by some members of the
Cabinet and disclaimed any approval in them of Sheridans telegrams or of the advice or
suggestions given by him. Bristow and myself insisted that Belknaps telegrams did endorse Sheridan and expressed confidence which we did not feel—the President very
warmly defended the telegrams and said that they did not express more than approval of
Sheridans acts . . . Belknap then read on the hand writing of the President the telegram
addressed to Kellogg on the 9th of December last refusing the use of the military for the
purposes for which Kellogg had requested it and limiting very distinctly the uses to which
the troops could properly be put to   It was suggested from all quarters that this telegram
should be sent with the other papers to Congress; and might be so used as to relieve the
administration of approving or assenting to the use of the military on Jany 4th   It appears
that the Atty General is preparing a draft of the message for congress; the President requests him to let him have it this evening—saying that there are some things which he
wishes to put in it in his own way and wishes to examine carefully the whole of it   He suggests summoning some Senators to meet him tomorrow morning at 10 oclock to whom he
will read the proposed message   The names of Frelinghuysen, Conkling, and Morton are
named; that he had thought of Edmonds, while he had much confidence in him he was
crotchety and apt to dissent   Finally his name was put down as well as those of Sargent
& Logan" DLC-Hamilton Fish.

On Jan. 12, Governor Cyrus C. Carpenter of Iowa wrote to USG. "I have watched
with anxiety the progress and development of the Louisiana imbroglio: And in the recent
climax of an insurrectionary spirit and purpose, shown by a portion of the people of New
Orleans, representing secret organizations hostile to the Government, I have been gratified at the promptness with which their revolutionary schemes were met and defeated. It
is also a source of gratification, and an earnest of the wisdom and moderation with which
the military arm will be used to suppress this incipient rebellion, that the commander of
this Department is a general whose past services to the country, whose brilliant reputa-

tion as a soldier, and whose patriotic devotion to freedom, are recognized and trusted by every man whose heart was with the union during the war of the Rebellion. These people do not believe that he will abuse his power, and they know he will not suffer the rights for which he and his comrades perilled their lives, in the past, to be trampled down by an organized mob. I may safely say, that the masses of Iowa who sympathized with you and your army when you confronted the rebellion at Vicksburg and Richmond sympathize with you in your policy to-day, when confronting its lingering spirit at New Orleans. It is true the people who were with you when civil liberty was imperilled by undisguised and organized warfare will be glad when the spirit of Law and Order shall so far take the place of turbulence and insubordination, and tranquility and peaceful industry shall again so generally prevail, that military interference to preserve peace and prevent bloodshed, will become unnecessary in any of the States. But if the government of any state is to be a government of force, they prefer Federal bayonets, in the hands of men who have proved their fidelity to the country, to shot-guns and bowie-knives in the hands of White Leaguers and Union-haters." ALS, USG 3. On the same day, Edwin H. Nevin, Philadelphia, wrote to USG. "I know you will pardon the liberty I take in addressing you at the present time. I have been your friend and supporter since you were first nominated for the Presidency of the United States. I wish now to say that I admire you more than ever for the position you have taken in regard to our Louisiana troubles. You have the sympathies and prayers of hundreds of Ministers of the gospel of Christ all over our Northern States. Your course will ultimately commend itself to the judgments and consciences of all intelligent loyal citizens. May God be with you and guide and prosper you . . . I write this note from my Son's office, who is the proprietor and Editor of the 'Commercial' This will account for the heading of the letter." ALS, *ibid.*

Also on Jan. 12, Fish recorded in his diary. "The President read his message which was criticised and amended in several particulars, and is much better than I had anticipated from his conversation a day or two ago It is not all that I should wish but contains much stronger expressions of disaproval of the Military interuption than were expected and possibly stronger than the President is himself aware of It will not be sent in until tomorrow" DLC-Hamilton Fish. On Jan. 13, Babcock and Luckey exchanged telegrams concerning delivery of the message to the Senate. Telegrams received and copy, DNA, RG 107, Telegrams Collected (Bound).

Also on Jan. 13, John M. G. Parker, surveyor of customs, New Orleans, telegraphed to USG. "All friends of peace and good order welcome your message with joyful hearts" Telegram received (at 11:11 P.M.), DLC-USG, IB. On the same day, John H. Henry, Selma, Ala., wrote to USG. "Stand firm The true Union men of the South are at your back, You understand the Situation. The South is under the Controle of the White Leages Gen Phil Sheriden has struck the *Key Note* of the situation God help you in your pure motives of protecting the rights of all. We know no party when individual liberty life and hapiness is in the ballance The *Tribune* Herald and Times are bought by the *Democrats* God grant the people of the *North* may stand by their patriotic leaders that saved the nation as true as the the the Suthern people stand by the Reb leaders that would have destroyed the nation Can we comprehend the fact in this nation that Reb that atepted the destruction of the Gov are to be more respected and believed than those that saved the nation Stand firm *Noble* Man with all your traducers and those that will attempt to Seduce you from the path of true liberty—and freedom which you have given to the American people after Washington Your friend and Well Wisher forever" ALS, USG 3. Also on Jan. 13, La. Senator W. Jasper Blackburn wrote to USG. "Your special message to the Senate has been received here and read. The Democrats have but little to say, but I can see that it touches them deeply. It contains too much plain and outspoken truth. From the bottom of my heart I thank you for this most manly and truthful document. If you forsake us, all is lost. You understand the situation here, and I trust Congress does; and I trust that body will act at once." ALS, *ibid.*

On Jan. 14, U.S. Representative Ebenezer R. Hoar of Mass. wrote to USG. "I wish to express to you my extreme gratification in reading your Louisiana message—for which I think the Republican party and the Country owe you a debt of gratitude. It is manly, frank, and vigorous, and I am confident will elicit a response from the People—I do not think it could have been better done, and should not have supposed it could be done so well until I saw it." ALS, *ibid.* On the same day, Speaker of the House James G. Blaine wrote to USG. "I desired to call this morning (but am prevented) to congratulate you on the very admirable Message on Louisiana affairs which you sent to the Senate yesterday—It will exercise an immense influence on the public mind and will bring the People face to face with the real question—dispelling the prejudice which eager misrepresentation has temporarily created in some quarters—You have never been more forcible or felicitous in the presentation of a great public question!" ALS, *ibid.* Also on Jan. 14, Benjamin Aycrigg, Passaic, N. J., wrote to USG. "The Latins had an adage applied to cases like that of Louisiana, where it is dangerous to hold fast or to let go, 'Teneo lupum ab auribus' I have a wolf by the ears." ALS, *ibid.* On the same day, Frederick Dent Grant, Washington, D. C., wrote to [Sheridan]. "You have been the subject of a great deal of talk up here for the last ten day but it has showed who were your strong friends   you never saw any person stand up so strong for an other as the Sectry of War has for you. The Atty Gen the same, and mother carries her endorsement almost to an absurdity   Father is very strong in his feelings but more quiet. Mr Fish was very weak in the knees for several days but is now getting stronger & I hope will soon be all right a-gain. The papers have been talking every which way but all of them are coming into line now.   you have some very strong friends in the Senate, Conkling, O. P. Morton, Logan, Edmunds, Howe, Carpenter Cameron &c. If you wish I will write & let you know all that is going on up here & keep you informed. All would send regards if they knew I was writing to you. I hope you are all well, &c &c" ALS, DLC-Philip H. Sheridan.

Also on Jan. 14, Wiltz telegraphed to USG. "Seeing from your message that the interference by the military on monday the fourth with the organization of the House of Representatives of Louisiana Was unauthorized by you I now as Speaker of Said house ask you to direct the military to restore the statu quo existing at the time Genl DeTrobriand ejected certain members from the house in order that the house of Representatives may proceed in the discharge of its duties without molestation" Telegram received (at 8:00 P.M.), DLC-USG, IB.

On Jan. 15, Ohio Representative Thomas J. McLain, Jr., wrote to USG. "Within a few days there will be sent you, by the Governor of Ohio, a copy of the Resolutions of censure for your course in Louisiana affairs, adopted by the Ohio Legislature. The resolutions were passed through the House, under the demand for the previous question, and carried by a majority of only three, after stifling debate, and an application of the party whip on the part of the Democracy. That your excellency may understand that the Republicans of the House sustain you, I take the liberty of enclosing a copy of a PROTEST which we have had spread upon the Journal of the House. It will explain itself and will show you that the Republicans of Ohio propose to still stand by the government, the President and the Flag." ALS, USG 3. The enclosure is *ibid.* Also on Jan. 15, J. S. Diggs, "Solicitor of Dallas County Alabama," Selma, wrote to USG. "I cannot resist the desire I feel to return you my heartful thanks for the thruthful, eloquent and Manly exposition you have made of the nefarious doings and designs of the White Leaguers of the Southern States and also for the warm sympathy you express for the trials & troubles of the Southern man who has the firmness to maintain that the Union is and ought to be the paramount object with every American

Citizen, in your late message to the Senate of the United States. I as a representative Southern Republican desire to express the hope that you will continue to extend to us the protection we so much need to that extent allowed us by the law and Constitution of the land. No one can imagine the trials and troubles that a native Southern man is subjected until he comes into our midst and stays long enough for the desire of concealment to die out of the minds of the Southern Leaguer and since the last election we have felt that last sheet Anchor of hope that was left to us had passed away and our hearts were sad indeed, but your action and message in relation to the Louisiana matter has again caused day star of hope to arise in hearts and we who but yesterday were despondent to day walk forth with hope beaming from countenances with head and eyes erect, so that all the world can tell that we feel proud of being a Republican and an American citizen. Sir we desire to say that what is true of the Pelican State is also true of our own Magnolia State and we humbly hope that you and Congress may give us that help that is only to be found by placing this Country under a strong military government. To say that we approve your action is but feebly tell the truth for we almost idolize you for your action. Hoping that you will continue to gaurd & protect us to the extent allowed you by law . . ." ALS, *ibid.* On the same day, J. Fillmore, Providence, R. I., wrote to USG. "I am not a politician, but an humble minister of the gospel, yet, I read your message last evening with great satisfaction, it is just right. Sheridan is right, and should be sustained. The politicians are making a great hue and cry over the act of the Soldiers in removing a few men, at the order of the Governor, from the Hall, & seem to think that the whole country should be alarmed at the fact, as the liberty of the nation is in jeapardy, but manifest no concern while hundreds are being murdered in cold-blood. Oh, Shame on such politicians. Had the soldiers shot down the intruders on the spot, and all the leading men that made the disturbance, which made the assistance of troops necessary to quell the same, it would have been a *mild* and justifiable affair, compaired with the bloody murders committed in the state. The present government should be sustained at any cost, until legally displaced. A new election ordered, would not satisfy the rebel spirit, unless those who possess it, were enthroned in power. This Ku Klux, WhiteLeagues, or by whatever name known, business, ought no longer to be handled with gloved hands, but should be put down every where, and whoever does it, will deserve the nation's praise." ALS, *ibid.* Also on Jan. 15, David H. Pannill, Pittsylvania Court House, Va., wrote to USG. "Mr. Davis the late President of the confederacy used to say that he read all letters addressed to him, though he could not reply to them all. Thinking it probable you too might read all addressed to you I venture a few observations on the grave situation of affairs in Louisiana. Though not a member of the Republican party I voted for you in preference to Mr. Greeley, and am, with many others in this portion of Virginia, willing to sustain you for the third time—yea for Life—provided *always*, and provided *only*, that you range yourself on the side of the property holders and intelligence of the country. I believe that the conservatives in Louisiana have by intimidation, force, & blood shed prevented coloured people from voting the Republican ticket. But how are you going to prevent it. The Conservative party in Louisiana represent the intelligence and property of that state;—the Republican party, whatever it may be in other states, in Louisiana represents only agrarianism & ignorance—thieves & plunderers. It is in a very large numerical majority & can control the state and every election if left unawed & unintimidated, and the whole state of Louisiana would be under negro rule. But the white people of Louisiana, representing the intelligence, property, civilization, & refinement of the state cannot and will not submit to be ruled by their former slaves. They would deserve death and worse than death if they did. They cannot leave Louisiana except to starve, for they cannot dispose of their property, and to remain at home & be governed by negroes would be a worse condition than ever imposed by the most cruel conqueror of ancient or modern times upon a subdued people. Therefore say the people of Louisiana we ~~cannot~~ can but die, and die we will before we will submit to such a condition—if it cost 100,000 lives to relieve us from this state of affairs, those lives shall be offered up, and blood shall be shed if necessary in every town, village, or plantation throughout the state. How can it be accounted for that so large a majority can be intimidated by a minority, except that the majority see that the minority are driven to a state of desperation. And, sir, it is right that the tax payers, the property, & intelligence of a country should control it. Politicians recognize this fact, notwithstanding their demagoguical twaddle about universal suffrage. *Non*-property-holders are in a large majority in ~~the state of~~ Virginia, and yet the property holders by management—by hook & by crook—control the state. *Non* property holders are in a still larger majority in the state of New York; yet by bribery and other means the property holders control the state, and so it is more or less in all the states. If this were not the case the whole country would break up into universal anarchy & ruin in less than 12 months. Politicians, who are nearly all demagogues, laugh in their sleeves when they talk to the people about universal suffrage & the majority governing—they use the words in a Pickwickian sense. Europeans wonder how a country can exist governed by a mere numerical majority, and compare such a country to an inverted pyramid;—there is and can be no such country. This country exists because, whatever it may be in theory, it is not in point of fact governed by numerical majorities, but by minorities—by majorities of interest it is true, but not by majorities of mere numbers. The Louisianians are too poor ~~to be~~ to use bribery, and are not in a situation to control by management, they must therefore use the only weapons they have—intimidation or force. If left to themslves the intelligence & wealth of the state would soon control it, establish a good stable government, protecting property as well as persons, and Louisiana would once more be a wealthy & orderly state—a credit to the American Union. The civil rights of negroes are protected in Virginia, so will they be in Louisiana under conservative rule. Your Excellency, notwithstanding the boast of Genl Sheridan, will have to reduce Louisiana to the condition of La Vendée to give the negroes permanent supremacy in that state. Does your Excellency remember how many years it took, & how many lives it cost, ~~to~~ with all the powerful & concentrated energies of the French Republic & Empire to subdue La Vendée—not 150 miles from the city of Paris. Louisiana will be the La Vendée of America before it will submit to be governed by its former slaves." ALS, *ibid.*

On Jan. 16, U.S. Senator John Sherman of Ohio telegraphed to USG from the Senate. "Please send me by messenger for use in debate today a letter of Hon Chas Foster to me about McMillen in New Orleans." Telegram received, DNA, RG 107, Telegrams Collected (Bound). Babcock telegraphed to Sherman. "The President says he remembers conversing with you on that letter but does not remember having ever seen such letter. ~~I~~ We can find no such letter here." ALS (telegram sent, press), *ibid.* Sherman telegraphed to Babcock. "Mr Frelinghuysen says the President took the letter and used it and as I supposed put it away as his authority for some statements of his message. Never mind however I can state the facts contained in the letter" Telegram received, *ibid.* Related telegrams are *ibid.* On Jan. 12, U.S. Representative Charles Foster of Ohio had written to Sherman relaying a conversation with William L. McMillen, elected U.S. Senator by the McEnery legislature, concerning that legislature's intentions. ALS (misdated 1874), USG 3.

On Jan. 16, Sheridan telegraphed to Belknap. "A report has just been received from Major Merrill at Shreveport which is too long for telegraphic transmittal but will be sent by mail. The following is an epitome almost in Merrill's own words. 'The threats made before the election to drive from the community all who voted the radical ticket are being carried out. Combinations among whites are forming and recruiting by every form of pressure by which all negroes who [v]oted the radical ticket are to be refused work or

[l]eases   All whites not forming this combination are [to] be ostracised. Already more than five hundred families including at least two thousand people of all ages and sexes are wanderers without means to go elsewhere, powerless to find other homes where the are and on the verge of starvation in mid winter. Theft and other crimes may result and it is feared that the better feeling naturally resulting from the sense of injustice received may run into one of revenge   these homeless will gradually drift together and the white people are not slow as the past has shown to set afloat inflamat[ory] rumors of intentions of organized violence on the part of the negro and where the revolver and mob law are the common resort in such cases as they usually have been here disorders more or less extensive are sure to result if some preventative is not found for such a state of things." Copy, USG 3.

On Jan. 17, Noah B. Cloud, Montgomery, Ala., wrote to USG at length detailing Southern efforts at disunion since 1832. ". . . *Within the next 2 years they will control the Reconstructed States*—except So. Carolina and possibly Miss.—*with these certain and the middle and Northern & Western Democratic States*—*they will Elect a Democratic President*!   They will then demand *pay for the Slaves lost by the war.*—This denied,—they will RESUSCITATE *The climax of their ambition,* The *'lost cause'*—*call Jefferson Davis to preside*! and who is to prevent it—with the general & State governments in *full sympathy?* Mark well,—Mr President—*this is the Rule!* It is well understood by all,—it will be carried out to the letter—in practice, unless the *government act promptly & efficiently* in the use of *the necessary means,*—to crush it out. I might have been more minute—but the limits & scope of a private letter forbid. . . . P. S. You have doubtless forgotten me—I was introduced to you in the White House, a few days after your first inauguration in 1869,—but I refer you to Senator Spencer or any member of our Republican Delegation.—" ALS, DNA, RG 60, Letters Received. Cloud had served as Ala. representative and superintendent of public instruction. Also on Jan. 17, Henry M. Rawson, Corning, N. Y., wrote to USG. "I venture to write as a friend, who takes an interest in your wellfare and success. In March 1872, I told you a *story of canvassing in New Jersey in 1868 for the Empire,* of wich you may have learned from the New york Herald. I advised in case of your reelection a Broad, generous and open handed Peace, with Nations, as well as our own States.   you have done well, surrounded, as you are by dangerous, Demegogues, whose aim is self. Continue to be the peoples President, and you may openly defy the factions and the Assasins, who howl and threaten you. *I am ready* to shoulder a Musket, to help you Sustain the Laws." ALS, USG 3.

On Jan. 18, W. J. Stevens, Selma, wrote to USG. "As an humble Republican, living amidst the K. K. K. and White Leaguers, yes living in the very community where the people would give any thing they have to distroy you and yours, and as to Gen Sheridan the Newspapers of this Community, openly and avowedly advocate the assassination of him, little as it thought Gen Sheridan had best try and keep his eyes on this rebel element in these turbulents States,   Allow me to congratulate you upon the Message on Louisiana affairs, the tone have time and again cause the loyal hearts South to leap forth for joy, and say in the language of the Christian, 'Amend, Lord give him Strength'   Your Message on Louisiana affairs have done more toward causing the Republicans to hold up their heads then anything that has occurred for some years,   we now believe all of our friends have not deserted us, we now believe that our President is still true to himself and to the people who elected him—we now believe that the Whiteleaguers will not be permitd to slaughter all of the loyal people of the South—I merely write these few lines to say the great Democratic cyclone that is spoken of have not reached us yet—and we are still true to the old ship that so safely waft us over the tempestuous sea of rebellion a few years since—You will ever live in the hearts of the loyal Southren people for your timely Message on the affairs of the State of Louisiana" ALS, *ibid.*

Also on Jan. 18, Governor Adelbert Ames of Miss. telegraphed to USG a resolution of the Miss. legislature supporting Sheridan and the La. policy. Telegram received (at
8:44 P.M.), DLC-USG, IB. On Jan. 20, Belknap wrote to USG. "I have the honor to transmit, herewith, copy of a communication signed by Republican members of the Legislature
of Alabama, expressing confidence in the policy of the Administration in Louisiana affairs."
LS, USG 3. The enclosure is *ibid.* On the same day, Governor John L. Beveridge of Ill.
wrote to USG in support of the La. policy. ALS, *ibid.*

On Jan. 21, John Wills, Baltimore, wrote to USG. "I have watched your course closely
through all the Louisiana difficulties. Your recent special message I read with especial satisfaction. It covered the whole ground truthfully, justly. Governor Wm Pitt Kellogg, is my
nephew. When U. S. Senator I often met him in Washington. My daughter, Helen, spent
portions of several sessions with him and his wife. He always appeared to me honest, upright and the perfect gentleman. I was glad to know you sustained him in his trying difficulties amongst those whom Genl. Sheridan justly designates a bannditti. At no time
would I have been surprised at learning of his assassination by these reckless outlaws. I
think you were right, legally, in sustaining him, though my advice was that he would resign and leave the state. He said his political friends would not consent to his doing so.
I look upon the whole Southern movement, or usurpation, as an effort to disgrace you
because you were victorious over and whipped Secessionism, and Secessionists, thereby
saving to us our glorious Union. Thank God you have had the courage, judgment and
manliness to stand up against so much villification and blackguardism—democratic—
fulminated against you. I suppose you know my Cousin, David Wills (now Judge) of
Gettysburg Adams Co Pa. You may also know me by an interview I had with you two years
ago. I write this gratuitously, asking no favors, to show that one sensible man—and thousands others—approve your course, . . ." ALS, *ibid.*

On Jan. 22, Henry A. M. Bartley, "Near Orange C. H.," Va., wrote to USG. "Feeling
keanly the refusal to grant me employment I had determined to drop from the Republican
party—Nine years of the prime of my life had been spent in its service from consciencious
conviction of right without any reward of any kind. But your action in reference to Louisiana has cemented my admiration and support, I believe, forever. If you will keep Genl.
Sheridan in New Orleans he will brings matters there to a proper focus. My approval, if
publicly known here, might cause me trouble, yet, I believe before God, that Sheridan is
'the right man in the right place.' I am a Southern man—know the Southern people—but
I am a law-abiding man and feel sad to think such a state of affairs disgraces any State of
the Union. I offer you my congratulations for your masterly Message to the Senate on
Louisiana affairs." ALS, *ibid.*

On Jan. 23, John S. Mosby, Warrenton, Va., wrote to USG. "Private . . . I write a line
to say to you that I am not among those who have deserted your flag on account of the
clamor that has been raised over the Louisiana matter. On the contrary I consider your
message a triumphant vindication of your conduct & believe that all the fair minded men
of the country will agree with me in that opinion when they know the facts. I think that
many Republicans who have been frightened by the Democratic victories availed themselves of this opportunity & made use of Louisiana as '*a plank in a ship wreck*' on which to
cross over to the Democrats. Unless you do something worse than you have done in Louisiana I shall continue to stand by you—I mark this *private* simply to indicate that I do not
wish to go in the newspapers." ALS, *ibid.*

On Jan. 23, J. B. Bartlett, Blackberry Station, Ill., wrote to USG. "Your late Message,
on the Louisiana Affairs, has the true ring. I hope you will not hesitate to do your whole
duty. The insane cry of Despot, etc. should not influence you, in the least. I am glad we

have for 'Commander In Chief,' who dares to put down, the insurrectionary spirit, at the South. I hope Congress will do *its* duty, as well as you have done yours. This doctrine of State Rights, is *impractible*, and *false*. We must have a strong Federal Goverment, or our Republic will fall to pieces. Go on noble General. You cut off the head of Secession, now dig up its roots." ALS, *ibid.* On the same day, Thomas J. Reed, Macon, Miss., wrote to USG. "You have no doubt forgotten me as we have not met since the seige of Vicksburg. I was one of Genl A. P. Hovey's Ades, & was at your H.d Qur every day during our stay behind Vicksburg. I like thousands of your old Army was mustered out in the South & have been helping to reconstruct. I have had much harder times arresting K. K. than I ever saw while with you in the field. And I assure you that if you had not of done just what you did do in New Orleans that it would of been imposible for the Union people to of staid in this Country, and we are going to have a hot time the Comeing Election. I blame our own party for part of the feelings of the Southern peoples because we have not put good men in Office as a general thing. we have put too many Colord men in Office that had not the ability to fill them. Our County & State as you know (the State) is largely Colord the white Republicans conceed too much to them. In this County they have recommended a Colord man who is about half way qualified, (for the Post Office. he could run the Office if the Money Order Business was not attached, He will get on about Six Months & will get his Bonds man in for several hundred dollars & then be dismissed as every one has been in this State. I am a Republican from my youth up have ~~I~~ been strictly taught in the faith but I am not going to help any more to put bad or incompetant men into Office. your Course in the past has been the only true one, treat these people who we have been fighting, as Gentlemen, and make I say *mak* them treat you the same, and when they do not take them by the neck & choke them a *few*, as you have done in New Orleans. I will bet all the old Soldiers will sustain you in your action: when the truth goes north as it will, the people will endorce Sharadin, and thank him for acting as promptly as he did. Excuse me for this letter, . . ." ALS, USG 3.

On Jan. 25, Sheridan wrote to Babcock. "Private. . . . I have your letter of Jany 21st & wish to express my obligations for the friendly sentiments contained therein What I have done & said about the people & Condition of affairs down here, is true in evry particular ~~and as~~ The editor of the Times news par of this City said to me last night, that banditti organizations existed politically socialy & commercially in this state, & there could be no peace until they were broken up, but his paper would be ruined if it was known that he held such views, & I may safely say that nearly all the substantial men in this community are of the same opinion, but dare not expres it. I have so often heard expressions that the new rebellion was to be fought under the stars & stripes and in the north as well as the South— that the mistake made in 1861 was to have had their own flag—that I Consider it quite appropriate to mention it & it had better be looked after. When I first reached here the common topic of conversation was about killing people who did not agree politically with these malcontents.—It is not so now but they have only gone back into their holes & will come out again as soon as the sun shines" ALS, ICN; copy, DLC-Philip H. Sheridan.

On Jan. 28, AG Edward D. Townsend telegraphed to Sheridan. "A letter received here which states that a prominent commission Merchant of New Orleans was in Hopkinsville Ky ~~on~~ about the 1st and 2d January—and said he must be at home on 4th as he apprehended terrible work on that day because he had been told by a man distinguished among the Leaguers and prominent in the events of Sept. 14th that they had determined to seat their men if they had to Slay every republican in the house—that they were organized and would make the attack with pistols and bowie knives—that they were determined to make it a private fight in which the Federal troops could not participate as it would take place in the House—It is believed that the New Orleans merchant referred to is R. T. Torian—Have him brought before the Committee and ask him whether he had been ~~So~~ informed as above stated, and ~~what~~ the name of his informant" Df (initialed), DNA, RG 94, Letters Received, 3579 1874. On the same day, Belknap endorsed this telegram. "The President directs that this be sent in cipher to Gen'l. Sheridan at once—" AES, *ibid.*

On Feb. 9, W. P. Grace, Pine Bluff, Ark., wrote to USG. "Your course lately towards the South has been such as to command the approval of the best men in this country. I have always been a citizen of the South, an old whig in politics, and for twenty eight years in Pine Bluff, Ark, and I want to say to you that I think the interest of the whole country demands that you should keep the Republican party in power, and you should be the President for the third term. I am not an office-holder, and do not want an office. . . . P. S. This letter is personal and prvate." ALS, USG 3.

On Feb. 15, Judson Kilpatrick, Deckertown, N. J., wrote to USG. "In view of what I said & what you may have heard that I said in the Presidencial Contest of 72, it would not seeme becoming in me to address you either personally or by letter.—But Gen. I do not think that the events of the hour warrent men who love their Country's welfare to stand on points of etticit—or let past political differences prevent a timely word of sympathy—The whole country is alarmed and justly so at the bold & defiant attitude of those late in Rebellion & their allies at the north,—and it seemes to me as well as to many another soldier that—that line of fire that was drawn in '61 is again flashing into life—That we are rapidly approaching another Contest for the *individual rights* of *man*—(rights paramount to constitutions & States) I have no doubt—we who saved this nation are being driven to the wall by those who upheld the Banner of the Rebellion. The South in the next congress seats from among her soldiers a majority of thos who are to govern & *unless prevented* ruin the Republic—You will be pleased I trust to forget that I raised my feeble arm to strike you down when all the Nation upheld your hands—and accept now when the enemy—victorious—gather—the assurances of my sympathy & support—in your brave effort to save the Republic from the enemy that would destroy it. Pardon me General for intruding upon your time—but I thought it my duty to say to you what I have—and to add that if it becomes necessary I will make reperation for *the past*—deep broad & red—" ALS, *ibid.* Written on stationery of the Union Depot Hotel, Pittsburgh. On Feb. 22, Luckey drafted a reply. "Your letter of — was duly received & laid before the President. He wishes me on his behalf to acknowledge its receipt and in doing so to assure you of his appreciation of the kind feeling which dictated it and to express to you his thanks for it." ADf (initialed), *ibid.* See *PUSG*, 23, 238, 241.

Also on Feb. 15, USG spoke to U.S. Representatives George F. Hoar of Mass. and William P. Frye of Maine, as transcribed by Hoar. "'I believe Gen Sheridan has no superior as a general either living or dead and perhaps not an equal. People think he is only capable of leading an army in a battle or to do a particular thing that he is told to do. But I mean all the qualities of a commander, which enable him to direct over as large territory as any two nations can cover in war   He has judgment, prudence foresight and power to direct all the dispositions needed in a great war. I entertained this opinion of him before he became generally known in the late war'" ADS, MHi. Frye certified this document. AES (undated), *ibid.* George F. Hoar, *Autobiography of Seventy Years* (New York, 1903), I, 209. In Dec., 1874, Hoar had led the first of two committees sent to investigate La. electoral fraud. See *HRC*, 43-2-101, 43-2-261.

On Feb. 16, 1875, J. M. Brian, New Orleans, telegraphed to USG. "Maj E A Burke does not represent the people of La   give us a good Government tis all we ask" Telegram received (at 12:40 A.M., Feb. 17), DLC-USG, IB.

On Feb. 17, James Lewis and eleven others, "ex-soldiers and sailors of the Union army and navy, residing in the State of Louisiana," New Orleans, addressed fellow veterans. ". . . We appeal to all our comrades to listen to the stories of our sufferings which the Grant parish trial, the testimony now before Congress, the truthful statistics of outrage and murder that are familiar to the country, the massacre of Coushatta, and the insurrection of September 14, tell. We appeal to them to aid us by their sympathy and brotherly feeling in our determination, in spite of all, to remain true to our principles, and stand by the party of right, justice and liberty—the great national Republican party." Copy, DNA, RG 60, Letters Received, La.

On Feb. 22, C. E. Girardey, New Orleans, telegraphed to USG. "Compromise recognizing Kellogg as Governor & Penn Lieut Governor giving conservatives control lower house and new organization same would be welcome Relief and give general satisfaction arrangement might include Casey to senate and other minor appointments Kellogg might be provided for say collectorship or otherwise should he desire resign governorship confidential not for publication" Telegram received (at 8:06 P.M.), DLC-USG, IB.

On March 1, Governor Daniel H. Chamberlain of S. C. wrote to USG transmitting resolutions of support passed by the S. C. legislature. LS, DNA, RG 60, Letters Received, S. C.; press, South Carolina Archives, Columbia, S. C. On the same day, Blaine telegraphed to USG from the House of Representatives. "House passed resolution recognizing Kellogg Government by a vote of nearly two to one," Telegram received, DLC-USG, IB. Also on March 1, Oliver M. Wilson, Indianapolis, wrote to USG. "It is a hopeful sign for the future of our country, when we see the Congress of the United States recognizing the duty of the hour, by strengthening the hands of the Chief magistrate, to keep in subjection, without force of arms, the turbulent masses of the South, who, by every unholy pretext have sought to undo the results of the war, by inciting the people to insurrection That our land, would now be the field of another conflict, must appear self evident to the most conservative, had it not been for the strong arm, and resolute will of him, who, but a short time ago, led our armies, and brought victory to our flag, from out of a rebellion It needs no prophetic vision to read what might have been to this hour, had other hands guided the 'Ship of State', nor what may be, if this people, shall, in their passion, and clamour leave the direction of the issues, changed but in name, to other hands, and other heads. The same spirit, that moulded great armies in conflict, and led them on to final victory must dwell with, and watch over this people, until with universal acclaim, the sentiments of our martyred President shall be heard at every threshold, 'with charity for all.' 'with malice toward' none. we are a united and happy people. . . ." ALS, USG 3. Between Jan. and March, USG received nearly thirty additional letters in support of his La. policy, including resolutions from the Kan. and Neb. legislatures. *Ibid.*

On March 3, Belknap telegraphed to Sheridan. "If the Act to retire Genl. Emory as Brig. Genl. does not pass, the President will in a few days retire him as colonel. The President desires Genl. Augur to be in command at New Orleans. Would you recommend Texas to be added to Dept. of the Gulf, Headquarters New Orleans, or what arrangement would you advise? Answer by cipher telegram or by letter to me as you please." Copy, DNA, RG 94, Letters Received, 3579 1874. On March 4, Sheridan telegraphed to Belknap. "I would not advise the merging of Texas into Dept. of Gulf, but would advise that E. O. C. Ord be sent to Texas; he has wanted to go there, and that George Crook be sent to the Department of the Platte, he desires to come in from Arizona. How would it do for me to go to Washington to see you on this, and other matters?" Copy, *ibid.* On March 5, Belknap telegraphed to Sheridan. "I have shown your telegram to the President who thinks it best you should come here when you deem it proper to leave New Orleans." Copy, *ibid.* On

March 27, Brig. Gen. Christopher C. Augur assumed command of the Dept. of the Gulf, replacing Col. William H. Emory. On July 7, Emory, Washington, D. C., wrote to Babcock. "*Personal* . . . I will take it as a favour if you will shew the President the letter from the Hon W. A. Wheeler of which the enclosed is a copy. It is in substance a confirmation, if any is required, of the account I gave him verbally, and in my letter to the Adjt General of March 27th, of the events of 4th January last in New Orleans, referred to by Mr Wheeler. My assignment to command or other duty equal to that from which I was relieved, at this time so near the end of my military service, is only valued as an evidence of the opinion I desire to impress on the President that I was faithful to the high trust he confided to me, and as secondary to my relief from the false position in which I am placed in reference to the event, in the exercise of that trust, referred to by Mr Wheeler. He was on the spot and knows what he writes about. I do not assert there were mistakes made on the occasion referred to, but I do aver, if any mistakes were made, I did not make them. I was only obeying the unmistakeable orders of my superior officer duly empowered to give me orders" ALS, USG 3. On July 1, U.S. Representative William A. Wheeler of N. Y., Malone, had written to Belknap asking that Emory "be promptly assigned to some duty or command, so that it may not appear to the country as I fear it now does, that he was removed from his command at New Orleans, for his conduct on the 4th of January" Copy, *ibid.* Detailed as president of the retiring board in Oct., Emory was retired as brig. gen. as of July 1, 1876.

On March 8, 1875, J. W. Dederick, St. Francisville, La., wrote to USG. "Among the documents accompanying your message on Louisiana affairs I found the following purporting to be a telegram from the mayor of St Francisville. 'Sept 19th.   To the Attorney General: The timely arrival of the Federal troops has saved the lives of unoffending Republicans. We look confidently to the loyal North for the support which they have so generously extended the weak, and hope the protection of the Government will continue until the elections are over. Life is dear to us, and we can't risk an article so precious when surrounded by murderers and White Leaguers.' I know the mayor personally and on inquiry he says he never sent and knew nothing of the telegram until his attention was called to it. The telegraph operator at Bayou Sara says no such telegram was sent from that office. This is the only telegraph station in this Parish. The mayor of St Francisville is a negro drayman was at the time one of the commissioners of the State insane asylum and Parish treasurer. He can neither read or write. His name is Robert Hewlet." ALS, DNA, RG 60, Letters Received, La. See *SED*, 43-2-13, 14–15; Eric Foner, *Freedom's Lawmakers: A Directory of Black Officeholders during Reconstruction* (New York, 1993), p. 102.

On March 12, Mayor James L. Greene of Norwich, Conn., wrote to USG. ". . . I was very much angered during the fortnight preceding your Louisiana message, at the abuse and denunciation which was heaped upon you for your course in the South. I thought you had acted rightly, and in accordance with your sworn duties, and I knew you had done more for the Nation than millions of such men as were hounding you, would do, if they should live on the earth for a thousand years, and when your message gave me the confirmation of my judgement, I felt I must do something to show that there were republicans who knew your course in Louisiana had been right, who knew you deserved gratitude and support, and who had the courage and manhood to say so, even if the air was thick with calumny and abuse. Feeling thus, I issued a brief proclamation giving you my most unqualified and hearty support, and ordering a national salute to be fired in your honor. If a man was ever led by pure and unselfish motives to do any act, I was so led then. I had no other thought in my mind, except to say, Grant has done right, I know it and nothing shall prevent my saying it. I never thought or cared how my action might affect me; but it proved however that I struck the key note in republican hearts, and when our State Convention met in New Haven, on the 20th day of January, for the purpose of naming a State ticket, the delegates were determined to run me for Governor. . . ." ALS, USG 3. Greene, who urged USG to write a letter declining a third term, lost in Nov.

On March 30, Luckey wrote to Williams. "The President directs me to say that, if you are legally authorized to do so, he desires that you will direct additional Counsel to assist the District Attorney of Louisiana in defending Generals Sheridan, Emory and De Trobriand for damages in ejecting members of the La. legislature." ALS, DNA, RG 60, Letters from the President.

On May 1, Roland T. Bull and more than 200 others, "col. Citizens of the State of Louisiana," Caddo Parish, petitioned USG at length. ". . . Mr President congress have don[e] met and congress have done adjourned all the State Legislation have done met, and all have Adjourned and we dont See no chance for Justice yet. never Seen no change made yet for us to be colonized Mr President?   for Gods Sake and for heavens Sake let us know if Such things is possible   it Seems to us that it is not impossble for us to be colonized. no more than it was for England and France. and Spain. and Prussia. and Russia, and Mexicans, and all other nations are colonized to them Selves . . . President Grant. the actions from the White Lague towards the carpet Bagger And our Selves directly Shows what their Sentiments is ~~but the~~ towards us. We cant make a crop of cotton and Recieve the Benefit of it   We cant enter a pece of Goverment Land and live quietly upon it. We cannot get upon a mans Stemboat and make a round trip but what Some of us are whipped or Beat or Killed or Driven ashore.   if we Stand up as men for the protection of our Wives and our Daughters or any of our relations, these white men men of these Southern States Says that we must die and We do die, and we have resolved to not Stand that any longer. . . . We are determined to apply to faren Nations to help us out of this terrible Struggle. We intend to Send men there with our Credintials.   if it kills us we will die, if it Saves us We will live, and if it brings war let it come. Sink or Swim, live or die, our feets and our hearts are upon the rock.   this is the Voice of the whole African race of the Southern States The Injustice of England drove the americans to arms, and we believe that the Americans whites in the Southern States will drive us to the Same. . . . Mr President please have that Freedman's Bank, established so we colored people can get our money.   if we had our money we could help our people who are Starvig   The ~~people~~ white League of our Southern States ~~and~~ have taken away the ~~money~~crops from our people. who caused us to be nearly Starved to death and clothless And it Seems to us like the whole United States is down on the whole colored race. . . ." D, *ibid.*, Letters Received, La. For related petitions, see Proclamation, Sept. 15, 1874; Endorsement, Sept. 23, 1874.

On May 5, Gen. William T. Sherman, St. Louis, telegraphed to Belknap. "Genl Sheridan reports that the seven companies of twenty second Infty can be spared from Louisiana.   do you object to their returning to their posts on the Lakes." Telegram received, DNA, RG 94, Letters Received, 2359 1875. On the same day, Belknap telegraphed to Sherman. "The President desires me to defer a reply to your telegram concerning the seven companies of Twenty Second Infantry until Friday" ALS (telegram sent), *ibid.* On May 7, Friday, Townsend telegraphed to Sherman. "Referring to your telegram of the fifth (5th) the President assents to return of companies of twenty second (22d) regiment to north." ADfS, *ibid.* See Joseph G. Dawson III, *Army Generals and Reconstruction: Louisiana, 1862–1877* (Baton Rouge, 1982), pp. 197–215; Paul Andrew Hutton, *Phil Sheridan and His Army* (Lincoln, Neb., 1985), pp. 263–73.

1. "I hope in a few days to [be able to] give an approximate [estimate of the] number of ~~the~~ political murders committed in L[ouisiana] within the last few years, and where no

punishment has been administered for the crime" ADf (fragment, bracketed material not
in USG's hand), ICHi.

2. See *PUSG*, 24, 124.

3. See telegram to William P. Kellogg, Dec. 9, 1874.

4. "The question here arises whether the Constitutional Amendments added after
the great conflict through which the country has passed to maintain its integrity and perpetuity mean any thing or not." ADf (fragment in USG's hand), ICHi.

5. USG drafted an alternate version. "but it must be remembered here that the army
is not composed of lawyers fully competent to judge just how far they can technically
legally go in executing general orders to maintain peace, [good] order, [&] good government and ~~but~~ that in the duties assigned ~~them~~ the troops in L[ouisiana] if they have tran-
scended any technical legal authority it has been on the side of protecting life and in the
maintainance of law and order. Their task has been one repugnant to their feelings, deplorable to the whole law abiding citizens of the republic that it should ever [have] been
necessary and not of their seeking. They have performed a painful duty according to their
best understanding of their obligations at a time when non-~~actions~~ might have caused an
amount of blood-shed and anarchy not now possible to conceive of, and which, if it had
been allowed, ~~would have~~ might have cast upon them the reprobation cast upon civil conservators of the peace when they fail in their duties." ADf (fragment, bracketed material
not in USG's hand), *ibid.*

To Senate

————

[*Jan. 14, 1875*]

TO THE SENATE OF THE UNITED STATES:

Senate Finance Bill No. 1044, [To provide for the resumption of
specie payments] is before me and this day receives my signature of
approval. I venture upon this ~~metho~~ unusual method of conveying
[the notice of my approval] to the House in which the measure originated ~~my approval~~ because of ~~the~~ its great importance to the country at large ~~of~~ and [in order] to suggest further legislation which
looks [seems] to me ~~as~~ essential to make this law effective. It is a subject of congratulation that a measure has become ~~a~~ law which fixes a
~~period~~ [date] when specie resumption shall commence, and implies
an obligation on the part of Congress—if in its power—to give such
legislation as may prove necessary to redeem this promise.

To this end I respectfully call your attention to a few suggestions. First; the necessity of an increased revenue to carry out the
promise [obligation] of adding to the Sinking Fund annually, one per

cent of the public debt—amounting now to about 34 Millions of dollars pr. annum—and to carrying out the promises of this measure,
to redeem, under certain contingencies, 80 Millions of the present
Legal Tenders, and, without contingency, the fractional currency
now in circulation.

How to increase the surplus revenue is for Congress to devise,
but I will venture to suggest that the duty on tea and coffee might
be restored without [permanently] enhancing the cost at last to the
Consumers; and by repealing [that] the ten pr. cent horizontal reduction of the tariff on articles specified in the law of [June 6, 1872
be repealed.] The [The supply of] Tea and Coffee already on hand in
the United States would in all probability be advanced in price by
adopting this measure. But it is know that the adoption of free entry
to these articles of necessity did not cheapen them, but merely added
to the proffits of the countries producing them, or of middle men
who have the exclusive trade in them.

Second: The first section of the bill now under consideration
provides that the fractional currency now in circulation shall be re-
deemed in silver coin as rapidly as practicable. There is no provision
preventing the fluctuation in the value of the paper currency. With
gold at a premium of any thing over ten per cent above the currency
in use it is probable—almost certain—that that silver would be
bought up [for exportation] as fast as it was put out, for exportation
[or] until change would become so scarce as to make the premium on
it equal to the premium on gold, or sufficiently high to make it no
longer proffitable to buy for export, thereby causing a direct loss to
the community at large, and great embarrassment to trade.

As the present law commands final resumption on the first day
of January 1879, and as the gold receipts by the Treasury are larger
than the gold payments; and the Currency receipts are smaller than
the currency payments, thereby making monthly sales of gold necessary to meet current currency expences, it occurs to me that these
difficulties might be remedied by authorizing the sec. of the Treas to
redeem legal tender notes whenever presented in sums of not less
than $100 00 and multiples thereof, at a premium for gold of ten per
cent, less interest at the rate of 2½ per cent pr annum from the 1st

day of January 1875, to the date of putting this law into ~~execution~~ opperation, and diminishing this [the premium gradually] premium at the same rate until final resumption, changing the rate of premium ~~claimed~~ demanded from time to time as the interest amounts to one quarter of one per cent. I suggest this rate of interest because it would bring currency at par with gold at the date fixed by law for final resumption. I suggest ten per cent ~~at~~ as the demand premium at the begining because I believe this rate would insure the retention of silver in the country for change. ~~To prevent combinations being formed to exhaust the Treasury of Coin the provision in the second~~ third ~~section of the Act under consideration authorizing the Sec. of the Treas. to use surplus revenues, sell bonds &c where should go into effect at once with the new law~~

The provisions of the third section of the Act will prevent combinations being made to exhaust the Treasury of coin   With such a law it is presumable that no gold would be called for not required for legitimate business purposes. When large amounts ~~are required a~~ of coin ~~may~~ [should] be drawn from the treasury corresponding[ly] large amounts of currency would be withdrawn from circulation [thus] causing a [sufficient] stringency in currency ~~would be produced that would tend to prevent further drain and sufficient~~ to stop the outward flow of coin   †The advantages of a currency of fixed, known, value would also be reached. In my opinion [by the enactment of such a law] business and industries would revive, and the begining of prosperity, on a firm basis, would be reached[.] ~~by the enactment of such a law~~

Other means of increasing revenue than those suggested should probably be devised, and also other legislation than that suggested. In fact to carry out the first section of the Act another mint becomes a necessity. With the present facilities for coinage it would take a period probably beyond that fixed by law for final specie resumption to coin the silver necessary to transact the business of the Country.

There are now smelting furnaces for extracting the silver & gold from the ores ~~of~~ brought from the Mountain territories, in Chicago, St. Louis and Omaha,—three in the former city,—and as much of the change required will be [wanted] in the Miss. Valley states; and as the metals to be coined comes[e] from West of those states, and, ~~as~~ as I understand—the ~~expen~~ charges for transportation ~~for~~ of bullion from either of the cities named to the Mint in Philadelphia, or to New York City, amounts to four dollars for each one thousand dollars worth, with an equal expense for transportation back, it would seem a fair argument in favor of adopting one or more of these cities as the place, or places, ~~for establishing new mints~~ [for the establishment of new coining facilities]. ~~I would~~

I would also recommend extending the provisions of Sec. two of the present law ~~to any new law passing enacted on the same subject~~ [providing] for the [free] ~~coinage of gold free as well as silver to the coinage of silver   There is less tendency to export coin than bullion, and, particularly so with that [coin] of a less denomination than twenty dollars, and so long as it is coined free in Europe and there are coinage charges here there is just that much premium on bullion for exportation over the same metal for coinage at home.~~[1]

I have ventured upon this subject with great diffidence because it is so unusual to approve a measure—as I most heartily do this, even if no further legislation is attainable at this ~~sesstime~~—and to announce the fact by message. But I do so because I feel that it is a subject of such vital importance to the whole Country that it should receive the attention of, and be discussed by, ~~Congr~~ Congress and the people, through the press and in every way, to the end that the best and most satisfactory course may be reached of executing what I deem most beneficial legislation, on a most vital question to the interests and prosperity of the Nation.

ADf (bracketed material in another hand), ICHi; copy, DNA, RG 130, Messages to Congress. *SED*, 43-2-14. On Jan. 7, 1875, Speaker of the House James G. Blaine telegraphed to USG. "Senate Bill for Resumption of Specie Payment has passed the House by 136 to 99" ALS (telegram sent), CSmH; telegram received, DNA, RG 107, Telegrams Collected (Bound). On Jan. 11, Secretary of State Hamilton Fish recorded in his diary. "The President then read the rough draft of a message which he proposed to send to Congress announcing his approval of the finance bill and suggesting some further legislation—Bristow pointed out some points in which it would need alteration." DLC-Hamilton Fish. See *U.S. Statutes at Large*, XVIII, part 3, p. 296; *John Sherman's Recollections of Forty Years . . .* (Chicago, 1895), I, 507–18; Irwin Unger, *The Greenback Era: A Social and Political History of American Finance, 1865–1879* (Princeton, 1964), pp. 249–65.

On Jan. 13, "Confidence Man," New York City, wrote to USG. "Permit me to inform you that I would not give two cents for your life if you vetoe the Specie bill. and if there is not a change for the beter in financies. as the power lies within you. to make the change.

you will, will, therefore beyond a doubt meet the fate of your friend—Abraham Lincoln, for we have had Enough of your government thieves, and now the end is close at hand when honorable men will protect their rights. the People of these U. S. has Stood it to their Ruin. we give you until the 4 day of March, to make amends. or resign and let and honest true Patriot. Occupy the Presidential chair. you had better look the mater Square in the face for your Ilgotten gains will not Save. you. for the Confidence men throughout in there meetings resolved to force matters to a close. this removing and appointing men to Suit your thieving Convenience is prepostrous. to Save yourself of an Ignominious death look after things and commence to build up the government you have torn down, before it is too late" L, USG 3.

On July 15, Secretary of the Treasury Benjamin H. Bristow wrote to USG. ". . . The market is now in good condition, and I have no doubt we shall close up the entire five per cent loan before the meeting of Congress. I have further agreed with the contracting parties that they shall have the privilege of selling whatever bonds may be put on the market between now and the 15th of November next under the specie resumption act of January 14th last I hand you also a memorandum statement of the revenues and expenditures for the first fifteen days of this month, by which it will be seen that the revenues are greater and the expenditures less than for the corresponding period of last year. The recent decline in gold has stimulated our customs receipts considerably. Internal revenue receipts under the increased taxation of last winter should have been larger than they are, but our receipts from this source are affected by the large quantity of illicit whisky on the market, and also by the fact that spirits which had paid a tax at seventy cents were forced into the market." LS (press), DLC-Benjamin H. Bristow.

1. The final message omits this paragraph.

To Congress

To The Senate and House of Representatives:

In my annual message of December 1. 1873 while inviting general attention to all the recommendations made by the Secretary of War, your special consideration was invited "the importance of preparing for war in time of peace by providing proper armament for our sea coast defenses. Proper armament is of vastly more importance than fortifications. The latter can be supplied very speedily for temporary purposes when needed. The former cannot."

These views gain increased strength and pertinence as the years roll by, and I have now again the honor to call special attention to the condition of the "armament of our fortifications" and the absolute necessity for immediate provision by Congress for the procurement of heavy cannon. The large expenditures required to supply the number of guns for our forts, is the strongest argument that can be adduced for a liberal annual appropriation for their gradual accumulation. In time of war such preparations cannot be made, cannon cannot be purchased in open market, nor manufactured at short notice, they must be the product of years of experience and labor.

I herewith enclose copies of a Report of the Chief of Ordnance and of a Board of Ordnance officers on the trial of an 8 inch rifle converted from a 10 inch smooth bore which shows very conclusively an economical means of utilizing these useless smooth bores, and making them into 8 inch rifles capable of piercing 7 inches of iron. The 1294 10 inch Rodman guns should in my opinion be so utilized, and the appropriation requested by the Chief of Ordnance of $250.000 to commence these conversions is urgently recommended.

While convinced of the economy and necessity of these conversions, the determination of the best and most economical method of providing guns of still larger calibre should no longer be delayed. The experience of other nations based on the new conditions of defense brought prominently forward by the introduction of iron clads into every navy afloat, demands heavier metal and rifle guns of not less than 12 inches in calibre. These enormous masses hurling a shot of 700 pounds, can alone meet many of the requirements of the national defenses. They must be provided, and experiments on a large scale can alone give the data necessary for the determination of the question. A suitable proving ground with all the facilities and conveniences referred to by the Chief of Ordnance, with a liberal annual appropriation, is an undoubted necessity. The guns now ready for trial cannot be experimented with without funds, and the estimate of $250.000 for the purpose is deemed reasonable and is strongly recommended.

The constant appeals for legislation on the "Armament of Fortifications" ought no longer to be disregarded, if Congress desires in peace to prepare the important material, without which future wars must inevitably lead to disaster. This subject is submitted with the hope that the consideration it deserves may be given it at the present session.

U. S. GRANT

EXECUTIVE MANSION
JANUARY 20TH 1875.

Copy, DNA, RG 130, Messages to Congress. *HED*, 43-2-126, 44-1-1, part 2, III, 93–94. On Dec. 14, 1874, Brig. Gen. Stephen V. Benét, chief of ordnance, wrote to Secretary of War William W. Belknap concerning heavy guns. *HED*, 43-2-126, 3–5. Related papers are *ibid*. On June 23, USG had nominated Benét, USMA 1849, for promotion to brig. gen. and chief of ordnance.

To House of Representatives

TO THE HOUSE OF REPRESENTATIVES:

I have the honor to transmit herewith a report from a Board composed of one person named by the head of each Executive Department and of the Agricultural Department and Smithsonian Institution, appointed March 25th 1874 for the purpose of securing a complete and harmonious arrangement of the articles and materials designed to be exhibited from the Executive Departments of the government at the International Exhibition to be held in the city of Philadelphia in the year 1876 for the purpose of celebrating the one hundredth anniversary of the Independence of the United States.

The report gives a statement of what is proposed to be exhibited by each department, together with an estimate of the expense which will have to be incurred.

Submitting to Congress the estimate made by the Board, I recommend that Congress make a suitable appropriation to enable the different departments to make a complete and creditable showing of the articles and materials designed to be exhibited by the Government and which will undoubtedly form one of the most interesting features of the Exhibition

U. S. GRANT

EXECUTIVE MANSION
JANUARY 20TH 1875.

Copy, DNA, RG 130, Messages to Congress. *HED*, 43-2-125. On Jan. 8, 1875, Maj. Stephen C. Lyford, chairman, transmitted to USG the indicated report. LS (press), DNA, RG 56, Records Relating to Expositions. *HED*, 43-2-125, 1–3. Related papers are *ibid*. On Oct. 18, Lyford wrote to USG submitting additional estimates for exhibit appropriations. *Ibid*., 44-1-1, part 9. See Order, March 9, 1875.

Proclamation

———

To all to whom these presents shall come, Greeting:

Know Ye, that reposing special trust and confidence in the integrity, prudence and abilities of Hamilton Fish, Secretary of State of the United States, I have invested him with full and all manner of power and authority, for and in the name of the United States, to meet and confer with any person or persons duly authorized by the government of the Hawaiian Islands, being furnished with like power and authority, and with him or them to agree, treat, consult and negotiate of and concerning commercial reciprocity, and of all matters and subjects connected therewith, and to conclude and sign a Convention or Conventions touching the premises, for the final ratification of the President of the United States, by and with the advice and consent of the Senate thereof, if such advice and consent be given.

In witness whereof I have caused the seal of the United States to be hereunto affixed.

Given under my hand at the City of Washington the twenty-second day of January, in the year of our Lord one thousand eight hundred and seventy-five, and of the Independence of the United States the ninety-ninth.

U. S. Grant

DS, DLC-Hamilton Fish. On Oct. 13, 1874, King Kalakaua, Honolulu, wrote to USG. "Although Our Predecessors have on several occasions endeavoured to conclude a Special Treaty of Commercial Reciprocity with the United States to the end that the mutually free and unrestricted exchange of the products and manufactures of each country might add to the wealth, commerce and general prosperity of both people, and although these endeavours have not been ultimately successful, notwithstanding that two Treaties have been negotiated, still impressed as Our Predecessors were with the advantages of such unrestricted interchange of products with our nearest neighbour, the country with which the greater part of our foreign commerce is even now carried on, We have determined to follow their good example, and with much hope of better success. With these views We have accredited to Your Excellency, as Our Envoy Extraordinary and Minister Plenipotentiary, the Honorable Elisha H. Allen, Chancellor of Our Kingdom, Chief Justice of Our Supreme Court, Member of Our Privy Council of State and of Our Cabinet, to whom we have given Full Powers for the purposes aforesaid to negotiate a new Special Reciprocity Convention similar to those which have been hitherto negotiated, and for all other acts and measures tending to the interests of My people and Government and to the honor and stability of

Our Crown. And I have also appointed the Honorable Henry A. P. Carter, Member of My Privy Council of State, a Special Commissioner to co-operate with the Honorable Elisha H. Allen in the negotiation of the proposed Reciprocity Treaty. Therefore, We desire Your Excellency to give full faith and entire credit to the things that Our before named Plenipotentiary may say to you in Our name, and more especially when he assures Your Excellency, as he is commanded to do, of Our earnest desire to improve and perpetuate all Our existing relations between Our Kingdom and the United States of America, so as that while Providence has made them near neighbours, they may be, for ever good friends" LS, DNA, RG 59, Notes from Foreign Legations, Hawaii. On Nov. 16, Elisha H. Allen and Henry A. P. Carter, Washington, D. C., wrote to Secretary of State Hamilton Fish requesting an audience with USG to transmit this letter from King Kalakaua. LS, *ibid.* On Feb. 1, 1875, USG transmitted to the Senate a reciprocity treaty concluded between Fish and the Hawaiian officials on Jan. 30. Copies, *ibid.*; *ibid.*, Reports to the President and Congress; *ibid.*, RG 130, Messages to Congress. On March 5, USG again transmitted this treaty because the Senate failed to ratify before the close of the prior session. Copy, *ibid.*, RG 59, Reports to the President and Congress. On March 18, the Senate amended and ratified this treaty. On May 31, USG authorized Fish to exchange ratifications. DS, DLC-Hamilton Fish. On June 3, Fish exchanged ratifications with Allen. Hamilton Fish diary, *ibid.* Concerns over U.S. relations with Hawaii, retaliatory actions by foreign powers, reduced federal government income from duties, and outcry from domestic producers of hemp and refined sugars complicated negotiations and delayed legislative implementation until Sept. 1876. USG consistently supported a reciprocity treaty. See letter to Hamilton Fish, Dec. 11, 1874; Fish diary, Jan. 4, 7, 15, 19, 20, 22, Feb. 11–12, 18, 27, 1875, DLC-Hamilton Fish; *Senate Executive Journal*, XX, 41–43; *Foreign Relations, 1876*, pp. 318–20; Sylvester K. Stevens, *American Expansion in Hawaii 1842–1898* (Harrisburg, Pa., 1945), pp. 46–59, 76–140; Gavan Daws, *Shoal of Time: A History of the Hawaiian Islands* (New York, 1968), pp. 203–5; Merze Tate, *Hawaii: Reciprocity or Annexation* (East Lansing, Mich., 1968), pp. 108–17.

To Congress

To The Senate and House of Representatives:

I have the honor to transmit herewith for the information of Congress, a report of the progress made to this date by the United States Centennial Commission appointed in accordance with the requirements of the Act approved June 1. 1872

U. S. Grant

Executive Mansion
January 26. 1875

Copy, DNA, RG 130, Messages to Congress. *HED*, 43-2-129. On Jan. 20, 1875, Joseph R. Hawley, president, Centennial Commission, Philadelphia, reported to USG and requested government funding. *Ibid.*, pp. 1–4. Related papers are *ibid.* See Order, March 9, 1875.

On July 4, William S. Lewis, Minden, La., wrote to USG. "... I am a native born American, am proud of my Country, and I am honorably descended through Father and Mother from ancestry distinguished in the Councils as well as in the Wars of this Nation. I refer with pride to the Clevelands, Marions, Morgans and Langdons; and to Francis Lewis one of the Signers of the Declaration of Independence who was grandfather to my own distinguished father the late Col John Langdon Lewis *your only champion*, in this Section of Louisiana, at your election as President in 1868—since which time my father died. As for myself I am only—as my political enemies say—'the head and front of the Republican Party in *Webster Parish*.' Having told you something of who I am, I make bold to tell you *what I want*: and it is an *honorable place* in the Celebration of our *great* nation's birthday next year at Philadelphia. If the Commissioners have not already been chosen I would be proud to represent Louisiana in that capacity . . ." ALS, DNA, RG 59, Miscellaneous Letters. Lewis and his father had served in the C.S. Army. No appointment followed.

On Aug. 26, James H. Bell, New York City, wrote to USG. "... I learn from the newspapers of Texas that you will be asked by the Governor of that State to remove from their positions as United States Centennial Commissioners Hon W. H. Parsons and Hon J. C. Chew, on the ground that they have ceased to be citizens of Texas. I suppose the law in reference to the Centennial Exhibition did not intend that your Excellency should be made the instrument of injustice or of political prejudice upon the *ex parte* statement of the Governor of a state; and I venture to request, in the interest of truth and justice, that your Excellency will not act in the matter of the removal of the above named gentlemen without full information as to the facts of the case. These facts I will undertake to state to your Excellency, if I can have the honor of a personal interview at Long Branch during the ensuing week, which for other reasons I very much desire." ALS, USG 3. On Sept. 17, Gideon Strother, New York City, wrote to USG. "Having a great desire to see the centenial the greatest Sucees ever innaugerated in America and that my State should be fully represented (Texas) I have taken the liberty of laying before you a few facts which have come to my knowledge since I have been in this city and also in Phila   the present commissioner, a resident of N. Y. is obnoxious to the people of our State and our legislature will never appropriate one dollar while he remains in that position, as he is a non resident, and has not been in the State for the last three years yet he draws his mileage from the centenial fund every time the commission meets, as coming from Texas   I understand that should your Excellency commission an other our legislature will make an appropiation from thirty to forty thousand dollars. I do not know the feeling of northern part of the State but the Southern part is very anxious to see 'Texas' take a prominent place in this great national exhibition and as a representative of the collered race of that state I have taken this liverty, with a hope and a firm belief that your Excellency will give us another commissionr . . ." ALS, DNA, RG 59, Miscellaneous Letters. On March 4, 1876, Secretary of State Hamilton Fish recorded in his diary a conversation with USG. "I call his attention of the case of the nomination, by the Governor of Texas, of a Commissioner & alternate for the Centennial, which had been signed by him last September at Long Branch, and that the parties had now left the state and that now there was a bill before Congress which provided for the keeping of them and that Genl Hancock had told me this morning that Parsons one of them—had been a confederate who at the close of the war went to Brazil and was subsequently brought home in one of our public vessels; that he was a member of a disloyal and disreputable organization which he and some loyal Democrats were instrumental in breaking up; that Parsons then professed to become a member of the Loyal League was elected to the State Senate; made considerable amount of money in some very questionable operations, and left the state, and had not resided there for several years, that Chew the alternate had become a newspaper man never having an established residence in the state   The President thereupon signed the nomination of A. M. Hobby for Commissioner and J. W. Jennings for Alternate" DLC-Hamilton Fish. On March 27, William H. Parsons and John C. Chew, New York City, wrote to USG defending their relocation "as a matter of convenience." ". . . Gov Coke recognized us as U. S. Centennial Commissioners *from* Texas up to within *five days* of the date of our supersedure. We state the question fairly when we say that the allegations of our removal from our State was only a pretext made to subserve the purposes of partisans who wished to accomplish our removal because we were the nominees of a Republican Governor." LS, DNA, RG 59, Miscellaneous Letters. Parsons and Chew continued as commissioners from Tex.

In [*Sept.*], 1875, Governor Daniel H. Chamberlain of S. C. had written to USG. "*Confidential* . . . I am induced to write you a confidential note on account of the great desire on the part of many citizens here to have a change made in the Centennial Commissioner for this State. The present Commissioner is William Gurney of Charleston, appointed by you on the recommendation of my predecessor, Gov. Moses. As a matter of fact he is personally so obnoxious to the white people of the state that we are unable to do anything towards having our state represented at Phila. under his auspices. It is perhaps not necessary to indicate the *grounds* of objection to him. They are not *political*, at least not wholly or principally. Whether well-founded or not, the objections are so serious as to make it impossible to accomplish any thing while he holds this office. I am urged by the officers of the Centennial Commission to do all in my power to have S. C. represented at the Centennial. I have done all in my power and but for this one hindrance we could succeed—Mr. Gurney will not withdraw in any recommendations yet addressed to him; and I am reluctantly driven to think we shall have to leave our place in the Centennial vacant. I deemed it proper to make this statement to you *confidentially*, because you might possibly see some solution of the difficulty. I see none which I can apply—I should be glad of any suggestion or advice which you may give in this matter, but I do not wish you to take the trouble to answer this note unless you see something which may be done to forward the object for which it is written." ALS, USG 3. USG endorsed this letter. "Refer to Gov. Fish Confidentially for answer, this letter not to go on file." AES, *ibid*. On Sept. 11, Saturday, Fish, Garrison, N. Y., wrote to Levi P. Luckey. "I have your note of 8th covring a confidential letter from Govr Chamberlain to the President. My *impression* is that the Commissioner can be removed *only* with his own consent—As I expect to return to Washington on Tuesday I shall delay an answer until then—I think the question has already been decided in a similar case" ALS, USG 3; press, DLC-Hamilton Fish. On Oct. 9, Fish wrote to Chamberlain. ". . . The question involved in your inquiry was presented to this Department in a case from another state some two years ago, and after a careful consideration of the acts of Congress relating to the Centennial Exhibition it was conceived that the President was not invested by law with authority to remove Commissioners appointed under the acts in question. Upon a re-examination of the matter, I am unable to discover any ground for changing that view." Copy, USG 3. William Gurney, former col., 127th N. Y. vols., and bvt. brig. gen., continued as Centennial commissioner.

To John F. Long

Washington, Jany. 29th 1875

DEAR JUDGE:

Enclosed I send you my check for $2500%/₁₀₀ with which to pay off the last call on my Carondelet property. I do not know whether a portion of this is to be returned to me by the Court or not, after settlement. If it is please retain it and pass to my credit. The entire expenses of the farm for the next four months must be all outlay unless Carlin can sell the mares you speak so highly of. I would not have him sell them however except for a good price if they are as promising as he thinks them. I would prefer keeping them a year more on the farm and then dispose of those I have here and keep the others for my own driving.

Mrs. Grant's and my kindest regards to yourself and family.

Yours truly

U. S. GRANT

JUDGE J. F. LONG SURVEYOR &c.

Copy, DLC-USG, II, 2. See *PUSG*, 24, 16–20, 49–50; letter to John F. Long, Dec. 1, 1874.

On March 27, 1875, John F. Long, St. Louis, wrote to Nathaniel Carlin, "Whitehaven." "Personal . . . Learning from a neighbor on the Fenton Road, that, old Linton Sappington has been notified, to vacate the shanty he now occupies,—I regret this, because *he himself*, is old, poor and as honest as the world goes, and it would be a pity, *in the absence of absolute necessity*, to turn him out. Again Mr. Carlin, refering back to Genl. grant's Letter of 1873, he intimates, if not inimical to the interests of the farm, he would like old Linton to have a house—soowhere on the farm—if not the Orr. house. Hence I would ask as a favor, if not detrimental to your interest or that of the President, to let L. S. remain in the cabin, untill the President comes on. This is only a wish or suggestion, ~~not a wish~~ on behalf of *him individually*. However your own sense of justice will dictate the propper course." ALS, OClWHi.

To Congress

TO THE SENATE AND HOUSE OF REPRESENTATIVES:

I have the honor to lay before Congress a communication of the Secretary of War relative to the action taken in issuing certain supplies to the suffering people in Kansas and Nebraska in consequence of the drouth and the grasshopper plague, and to respectfully request that such action be approved.

U. S. GRANT

EXECUTIVE MANSION
FEBRUARY 3D 1875.

Copy, DNA, RG 130, Messages to Congress. *HED*, 43-2-143. On Jan. 29, 1875, Secretary of War William W. Belknap wrote to USG. "I have the honor to state that with your approval, and in view of the emergency existing, there has been issued by the Quartermasters Department, to the suffering people of Kansas and Nebraska Woolen Blankets, Great Coats, Sack Coats, Trousers, and Pegged Bootees. These issues were made as an Act of charity to the people in the States mentioned, who were rendered destitute by reason of the drouth, and the grasshopper plague. Although made by your authority, in response to a very general demand, the issues were without authority of law, and I have the honor to request that this matter be represented to Congress in order that the action taken may be legalized. As precedents for such action I would refer to the Acts of April 23rd, May 13th, June 23d, 1874 (Sec. 6:) and the Joint Resolution of May 28th, 1874, for the relief of the suffering and destitute people on the lower Mississippi; the Tombigbee, Warrior, and Alabama Rivers." Copy, DNA, RG 107, Letters Sent, Military Affairs. *HED*, 43-2-143, 1–2.

On Sept. 26, 1874, William T. Barnard, War Dept. clerk, had written to Joseph Wildt, Covington, Ky. "The President having referred to this office your communication of the 21st instant, transmitting petition, from settlers on the Kansas Pacific Rail Road, for assistance on account of ravages to their products by the late grasshopper plague, I am directed by the Secretary of War to inform you, that while the utmost sympathy is felt for those who have suffered, with such severity, by this unlooked for calamity, it is with regret that he announces to you the inability of the Department to render the desired assistance, as there is no appropriation available for the purpose. I return the petition as requested." Copy, DNA, RG 107, Letters Sent, Military Affairs.

On Oct. 29, William H. Nelson, postmaster, Cora, Kan., wrote to USG. "I address these few lines to you in behalf of the citizens of Smith County Kans. who are, as you perhaps well know, suffering from the visitations of the *drouth* and *grasshoppers*—and some of them are at present in destitute circumstances. Cold weather is now coming on, and many are without sufficient clothing to keep them warm even were we favored with an exceedingly warm winter, and although they can by some means procure food, it will be utterly impossible to supply all with clothing. Cannot the General Government do something to alleviate this at least in a measure? Is there not Government clothing so damaged as to be rendered unfit for farther use in the service? This could be used for *patches*, and could be made into clothes for children. if it is possible, let something be done to do away with some of the suffering in this County. Hoping this may meet with favor with you . . ." ALS, *ibid.*, RG 94, Letters Received, 4391 1874.

On Nov. 11, Belknap wrote to USG. "I have the honor to inform you that this Department is in receipt of letters from the Postmaster at Cora, Smith County, Kansas, the Cincinnati Chamber of Commerce, and General Ord, setting forth the suffering of the people of Kansas and Nebraska, by reason of the drouth and the grasshopper plague, and requesting that sufficient condemned army clothing, to relieve immediate wants, be issued to them. The Quartermaster's Department has on hand at Jeffersonville Depot a few thousand unservicable forage caps, lined and unlined sack coats, jackets, boots and bootees, and about one thousand unserviceable great coats, which could be issued without much loss to the United States. . . ." Copy, *ibid.*, RG 107, Letters Sent, Military Affairs. On Nov. 12,

Orville E. Babcock wrote to Belknap that USG had authorized "the issue of clothing to the sufferers." Copy, DLC-USG, II, 2. On Feb. 10, 1875, USG signed a bill appropriating $150,000 for this purpose. *U.S. Statutes at Large*, XVIII, part 3, pp. 314–15.

On July 16, U.S. Senators Algernon S. Paddock and Phineas W. Hitchcock of Neb., Omaha, telegraphed to USG, Long Branch. "Secretary Delano hesitates about compliance terms your letter   we again appeal to you for protection for our Grasshopper state" Telegram received (at 7:00 P.M.), DLC-USG, IB.

On Aug. 2, James S. Snoddy, La Cygne, Kan., wrote to USG enclosing an undated petition from John Calvin *et al.* to USG. ALS, DNA, RG 75, Letters Received, Central Superintendency. "We the Undersigned citizens of the State of Kansas most respectfully represent that the Settlers upon the Miami Reserve in the State of Kansas are in a destitute condition caused by drought, the Grass hoppers and the extraordinary stringency of the money market. That by reason of such destitution among the settlers they will be unable to meet the payment which falls due on the 30th day of October 1875, which failure will under their contract work a forfeiture of their rights to their homes. That under ordinary circumstances these people would have been able to meet their payments promptly as they fall due and their inability to pay is the result of circumstances beyond their control. That the prices which these Settlers have contracted to pay for their lands are fully as much as the lands are worth and are greater than the lands could now be sold for. That unless these Settlers get relief in some way from such punctual payments as are required of them by their contracts they must forfeit their homes and thus be subjected to great want and loss of property land and homes. We therefore ask that the period at which a failure to pay upon the contract shall work a forfeiture, *be extended* and be to the 30th day of October 1876, upon such equitable terms as to interest and the payment thereof as the Department may prescribe. For this your petitioners earnestly pray:—" DS (more than 100 signatures), *ibid.* In Sept., 1874, the Kan. legislature had passed a resolution requesting USG and Congress to extend to Oct. 30, 1876, the deadline for settlers to pay for land on the former Miami reservation. Copy, *ibid.* On May 23, 1876, USG signed legislation granting a two-year extension.

To Edward M. McCook

———

February 5th 1875.

DEAR GOVENOR.

As you expressed to me some months since a desire to retire from the Governorship of Colorado—I am able now to offer you a transfer to the position of Second Assistant Postmaster General, to take effect at once.

Very truly yours
U. S. GRANT.

GOV. EDWD. M. McCOOK
WILLARDS HOTEL.

Copy, DLC-USG, II, 2. On Feb. 5, 1875, Governor Edward M. McCook of Colorado Territory, Washington, D. C., wrote to USG. "I have the honor to acknowledge the receipt of your communication of to day tendering me the position of 'Second Assistant Postmaster General'. I thank you most sincerely for this kind offer and regret that I cannot in justice to my personal and business affairs, accept the position. Referring to our conversation of December last, I renew the request I then made 'to be relieved from duty as Governor of Colorado.' As Congress will adjourn soon, I think my successor should be confirmed before the adjournment takes place. I shall therefore be glad to have you consider this a resignation of my position as Governor. Please accept my thanks for this additional evidence of your friendship and for the many favors, personal and political, shown me in Civil and Military life—You can always command me for any service that I can render to your administration or to yourself." ALS, USG 3. On Feb. 8, USG wrote to McCook. "I have before me your letter of the 5th instant announcing your inability to accept the position of Second Assistant Postmaster General. I suggested this transfer knowing your desire to be relieved from the Governorship of Colorado Territory, your resignation of which I reluctantly accept. Thanking you for your kind expressions of personal friendship, . . ." Copy, DLC-USG, II, 2. On the same day, USG nominated John L. Routt, 2nd asst. postmaster gen., to replace McCook. On Jan. 22, 1876, Levi P. Luckey wrote to Routt. "The President has read your letter of the 13th inst. and directs me to say that he has never doubted your loyalty to the Republican party nor your personal friendship for him; nor has he suspected that you are other than the 'right man in the right place.'" Copy, *ibid.*, II, 3. See *PUSG,* 24, 467.

On Feb. 4, 1875, Julius White, Evanston, Ill., had telegraphed to USG. "I am urged by many prominent republicans of Colorado to apply for the governorship of that territory & am informed that a delegation is now on the way to Washington to represent their wishes   while I do not make such application I respectfully request a suspension of any action in the matter till they arrive If not incompatible with the public interests or in conflict with any views you may have already formed." Telegram received, DLC-USG, IB. On Feb. 5, White, Chicago, wrote to Orville E. Babcock on the same subject. ALS, ICN.

On Jan. 5, Tuesday, and Jan. 22, Secretary of State Hamilton Fish had recorded in his diary. "Bristow called at my house tonight . . . He says that Babcock is engaged with Delano in the efforts against him   He refers to a Conversation in Cabinet on Tuesday about the 'Colorado Land Thieves' and asks if I remember Delano's proposition to change all the Territorial Officers including McCook. He says that McCook and John Delano were engaged in the land frauds and have quarreled about the division—that Cowen tells him that Delano (the Secretary) was also interested deeply with them in their fraudulent practices." "*Cabinet* . . . A long discussion took place on the subject of the Territorial Appointments in Colorado; and with reference to what are called the Land Thefts—Delano was anxious for a general change; Bristow, notwithstanding what he had said to me on a former occasion, on this subject was silent." DLC-Hamilton Fish. See Ross A. Webb, *Benjamin Helm Bristow: Border State Politician* (Lexington, Ky., 1969), pp. 171–73; letter to Jerome B. Chaffee, March 13, 1875.

On Sept. 27, 1874, fifty-three "practising members of the Bar," Denver, had petitioned USG to retain Ebenezer T. Wells as associate justice, Colorado Territory. DS, DNA, RG 60, Letters from the President. On Jan. 22, 1875, John W. Roberts, *Oskaloosa Independent*, Oskaloosa, Kan., wrote to USG concerning Colorado Territory. ". . . I see a report that you are about to remove the judges of the court of that territory, and appoint others at the solicitation of Gov. McCook. I hope this is not true. I do not personally know either Judge Wells or Belford, and have no interest in them. But I mingled with the people in all the populous portions of the territory last year, and I know how they feel. We must save Colorado to the Republican party. *This cannot be done by sustaining McCook.* I know of what I speak. I would not advise sustaining either faction of the party there. I have friends on both sides. Judge Wells time will soon expire. Let him serve out his term. Then appoint some new man if you deem best, not obnoxious to either side. Dismiss Gov. McCook, and appoint some one who is not on the war path with the party. Let Belford alone. I was in Colorado during the political campaign last year. I do not know that I shall ever be there again. I have no 'friends to reward or foes to punish there,' but I do wish to see harmony restored, which cannot be done by *perpetuating the strife between the factions.* After the election there, the editor of the Denver *News* wished to go east, and being acquainted in all the newspaper offices, Mr. Byers requested me to edit the *News* during the absence of Mr. Thomas. I did so, avoiding territorial politics. . . ." ALS, *ibid.* On Feb. 1, Henry K. Steele, Denver, wrote to U.S. Representative Lewis B. Gunckel of Ohio. "For some time rumors have been rife, that the President does not intend reappointing as Judge in this district, Hon E. T. Wells the present incumbent. I write to you hoping, that by some means, you may be able to induce the President, to change his determination in this matter. This territory has been kept in a continued state of agitation for the last year by reason of the new appointments to office; some of them are good, some are not. . . . If the Republicans think it important to carry this territory, or as a state, they should not allow our present judiciary to be meddled with, neither of the Judges Wells—Belford—Hallett. If they are removed I have no hesitancy in saying that we cannot elect Senators or Congressman who will support the present administration. The Republican party here has been disturbed and agitated beyond measure, and it needs but a straw or two more to accomplish its ruin. As for the question of admission as a state I have no care either way. I hope you will excuse my troubling you with this long letter." ALS, *ibid.*, Letters Received, House of Representatives. On Feb. 6, Gunckel endorsed this letter to USG. AES, *ibid.* See *PUSG*, 19, 500.

On Dec. 15, 1873, Judge William B. Woods, 5th U.S. Circuit, Savannah, had written to USG. "I have the honor to state that I am well acquainted with the private and professional character and abilities of Amherst W. Stone Esq, formerly a member of the Bar of this City, but now and for about two years past a citizen of Denver Colorado Territory. Mr Stone's professional learning is varied and extensive. He has keen, quick and discriminating legal mind, broad common sense, and great forensic power. While practicing law in this city he stood in the front rank of the profession. His private character is above reproach. He is and always has been a devoted friend of the Union and ever since the war a consistent and leading member of the Republican party. He would worthily fill and adorn any judicial position to which your Excellency might see fit to call him." LS, PHi. USG endorsed an envelope written in the same hand as this letter. "File—Intended as recommendation ϵfor the office of Dist Judge in case Colorado is admitted as a state." AE (undated), IHi. On March 9, 1869, Amherst W. Stone had written to USG requesting appointment as U.S. attorney, Ga. ALS, DNA, RG 59, Letters of Application and Recommendation. Related papers are *ibid.* See Woods and John Erskine to USG, Nov. 15, 1876, NIC; Thomas G. Dyer, *Secret Yankees: The Union Circle in Confederate Atlanta* (Baltimore, 1999), pp. 11–23, 115–32, 216–30, 264.

On Jan. 22, 1875, Judge Lewis B. Woodruff, 2nd U.S. Circuit, Albany, N. Y., wrote to USG. "I am informed that Genl. Andrew W. Brazee of Lockport, New York, has been proposed to you for the Office of Judge of the Territory of Dakota. Genl Brazee has appeared before me, as Assistant U. S. District Attorney for the Northern District of New York, in the discharge of the duties of that office for more than three years. I take pleasure in Testifying to the high Estimate I have formed of Genl Brazee while witnessing the manner in which his professional duties have been performed & also during the Social intercourse which grew out of his relations to the Court.—His uprightness, fairness courtesy and fidelity to duty as well as his professional Experience and capacity commend him to your consideration, and as I think give assurance of the just and Efficient performance of the duties of the Judgeship.—I hope that you will find it agreeable to your sense of duty to confer upon him the appointment." LS, NHi. On Jan. 26, George D. Lamont, N. Y. Supreme Court, Lockport, wrote to USG. "I recommend Genl. Andrew W. Brazee of Lockport N. Y. as a suitable person to be appointed Judge of the Supreme or Territorial Court of Dacotah, or any of the territories. I can speak from long acquaintance and intimate knowledge of his qualifications—He is an excellent lawyer—of long standing—industrious, well-read in his profession—Served his country in the late War of the Rebellion—and would discharge the duties of such an office properly—" ALS, NIC. On Feb. 5, USG nominated Stone and Andrew W. Brazee as justices, Colorado Territory, in place of James B. Belford and Wells.

On June 15, 1874, W. W. Lander, Denver, had telegraphed to USG. "The Speedy appointment of Genl Fisk as Marshall is regarded as vital to prosecution of Indictments found against Chaffees partner Moffatt Cook and others" Telegram received (at 5:49 P.M.), DLC-USG, IB. On July 6, McCook, New York City, wrote to USG. "I have the honor to Enclose herewith the copy of a letter, the original of which was ~~placed~~ filed with the Attorney General of the United States for his information. A C. Fisk the writer served in our army during the war, won the rank I believe of Colonel, and is at present a reputable citizen of the Territory of Colorado. Should his statement be true, then all the good you have anticipated from changes in Colorado officials, will be counteracted by the action of the Judicial Officer he refers to. The 'D H. Moffat Esq.,' referred to is the present *Territorial Treasurer*, was appointed by Ex Gov., Elbert, and is historically familiar to yo[u] in connection with chaffee and Elberts administrati[on] of the Las Animas portion of Colorado affairs. I will not Embarrass the Administration by endeavoring to remove Territorial officers, and making an appeal to the President afterwards. I am satisfied that the majority of these places should be filled by new men.—Without this, the change in the Executive would be barren of results; but I wish to fortify myself with the opinion of the law advisers of the Government, so that no ignorant or corrupt Territorial officer will be able to nullify your action as President or mine as your subordinate. Consequently, I have the honor to request that you will advise me at an early day whether under the Organic Act, and laws of Colorado, and in compliance with the laws of the United States, the Territorial Governor posesses the power to *remove* or *suspend*, the Auditor, Treasurer or other Territorial Officers *for cause* or otherwise?. . . If not, and the whole local Territorial machinery, can be forcibly retained by men for whose Official conduct I will be held responsible, and yet who are my most bitter personal and political Enemies, and the open, and avowed enemies of Your Administration, then neither I nor any other man can hope to make headway against the abuses which exist, or relieve the people of the Territory from oppression and misrule" ALS, DNA, RG 60, Letters from the President. On June 23, Archie C. Fisk, Denver, had written to McCook concerning indictments against David H. Moffat, Jr., and others. Copy, *ibid.* On July 24, Samuel F. Phillips, act. attorney gen., wrote to McCook. ". . . The Auditor and the Treasurer, mentioned by you, are officers created by a territorial statute, and appointed by the Governor with consent of the Council, to hold for two years . . . They are therefore not removable by the Governor. . . ." Copy, *ibid.*, Opinions. *Official Opinions of the Attorneys-General*, XIV, 422–24. On July 30, John W. Jenkins, secretary, Colorado Territory, wrote to Attorney Gen. George H. Williams disputing Phillips's ruling. LS, DNA, RG 60, Letters from the President. On the same day, McCook endorsed this letter. "I hope the letter of Secretary Jenkins may receive Early attention from His Excellency the President   I have the honor to thoroughly concur in the views Mr Jenkins has expressed, and believe that the decision of the President is of great importance, so far as the political and financial future of this Territory is concernd" AES, *ibid.* On Aug. 14, McCook telegraphed to Babcock. "I have recd no answer yet from Atty Genl in relation to question submitted by me to Prest   what is the decision" Telegram received (at 5:42 P.M.), *ibid.*

On Aug. 6, J. F. McKenna, Denver, had telegraphed to USG. "The territorial convention has sustained your Colorado policy by nominating for Congress a grant & mcCook man   The convention was composed of the most intelligent & honest men that have ever assembled in Colorado   the main plank in the platform endorses the national republican party" Telegram received (at 5:55 P.M.), DLC-USG, IB. On Aug. 18, McCook telegraphed to USG. "Please do not make any Changes in Colorado appointments until you hear from me by mail" Telegram received (at 3:45 P.M.), *ibid.* On Oct. 26, McCook telegraphed to Babcock. "Please request the President to make no appointment of Colorado Marshall until I write" Telegram received, *ibid.* On Feb. 5, 1875, USG nominated Charles C. Tompkins as U.S. marshal, Colorado Territory.

To Senate

————

To the Senate of the United States.

Herewith I have the honor to send, in accordance [with the resolution of the Senate of the 3d instant,] [1] ~~with Senate resolution~~ all the information ~~in my possession~~ [in my possession] not heretofore furnished ~~the~~ relating to affairs in the State of Ark.

I will venture to express the opinion that all the testimony shows that in the election of 1872 Joseph Brooks was lawfully elected Governor of that state; that he has been unlawfully deprived [of the] possession of his office since that time: that in 1874 the Constitution of the State was, by violence, intimidation and ~~fraud~~ revolutionary proceedings, overthrown and a new Constitution adopted, and a new State government established. ~~The precedent I believe is one which should not be tolerated.~~ The[se] ~~precedent~~ proceedings, if permitted to stand, practically ignores all rights of Minorities in all the States. ~~and if not in the United States~~   ~~a~~Also What is there to prevent ~~every one~~ each of the states, recently re-admitted to federal relations on certain conditions, changing their constitutions and violating their pledges if this ~~precedent~~ action in Ark is ~~allowed to stand?~~ acquiesced in. ~~Why may not a national convention be called, under this precedent, to inaugurate a new Constitution and government of the United States?~~

~~With the light before me I earnestly recommend that the recent proceedings by which the new Constitution and new Government have been set up in Arksas be declared nugatory and void, and that the Constitution of 1868 be declared the only legally existing Constitution of the state; and that Joseph Brooks — who it is now known received the Majority of the legal votes cast at the last gubernitorial election held thereunder — be declared the lawful governor.~~

I respectfully submit whether a precedent so dangerous to the stability of state government, if not of the National Government also, should be recognized by Congress.

I earnestly ask that Congress will take definite action in this matter to relieve the Executive ~~branch of the Govt.~~ from acting upon questions which should be decided by the Legislative branch of the Govt.

[EXECUTIVE MANSION
FEBRUARY 8TH 1875]

ADf (bracketed material in another hand), DLC-USG, III. *SED*, 43-2-25. On Feb. 9, 1875, and subsequently, Secretary of State Hamilton Fish recorded in his diary. "The papers of this morning gave a copy of a message sent by the President yesterday to the Senate, on Arkansas affairs (it is a message on which there has been no discussion or consultation in Cabinet and to which, had I been consulted, I should never have advised; it is dangerous in its tendencies, and inconclusive in its argument. Too many of the states have changed their constitutions by proceedings similar to those under which the new constitution of Arkansas has been adopted, to question the rightfulness of the proceedings by which the present constitution of that state has been adopted. No allusion was made directly or indirectly to the message, during the Cabinet session. I did not wish to introduce the subject but was prepared to express a dissent had an opportunity of so doing been offered to me." "Feby 11th . . . The message bears evidence of having been written by the President. So far as I can learn no member of the Cabinet was consulted with respect to it. I first saw it in the public prints and had not heard that a message on the subject was contemplated. Bristow tells me that the same was the fact with him; as also does Jewell who says he saw the President on Sunday (the day previous to its being sent to the Senate) and that no allusion was made to the subject. Bristow understands that Shepard and Dorsey induced the President to send the message   It is said that Dorsey & Clayton and their friends 'Counted out Brooks' who was undoubtedly elected governor in 1872 and 'Counted' Baxter in   That subsequently Baxter refused to sign a large amount of Rail Road bonds (two millions it is said) which were to be issued in fraud and then the party who had counted him in turned around and said that Brooks had been elected. The President's proclamation of May 15th 1874 declared Baxter to be Governor and denounced Brooks and his adherents   his message of the 8th instant declared Brooks to have been elected   Dorsey (Senator from Arkansas) is a tenant and neighbor of Shepard and intimate with him   Whether there are any other relations between them I know not but I believe that there is a large steal in the Arkansas matter and fear that the President had been led into a grevious error." "Feby 21st

. . . Sen Boutwell, Judge Hoar and Secty Bristow come in during the evening—Bristow remains after the others leave; says he saw the President yesterday who introduced the subject of the Arkansas question and said that he had no other object in his message than to urge Congress to make some expression of opinion—that he (Bristow) had remarked that he had understood the concluding part of the message as intimating a determination Prest disclaimed—Bristow expressed gratification: during the inteview Babcock came in as (Bristow says) 'he always does he never allows me to be with the President without coming into the room.' that Babcock took part in the conversation that Bristow after expressing satisfaction at the Presidents disclaiming any other object than to induce Congress to relieve him of the entire responsibility of deciding and of any intent of definite action; had inquired whether he was at liberty to communicate the purport of the Presidents declaration, saying that to his knowledge many of his friends, including some of his most pronounced and ostentatious friends were very much distressed by what they feared was the significance of the message and that the knowledge of his views and purposes as now declared would greatly relieve them and as he believed the country The President said he saw no objection but Babcock interposed and said that he thought that nothing should be said, that it was necessary to be bold and take decided ground and not enter upon explanation or disclaimer (or something to that effect I may not have Babcocks language as stated by Bristow but this is the general purport, thereupon the President withdrew his assent and said that he did not wish anything said about it" "March 9th . . . The President directed that I should issue commission to the party nominated by Gov Garland of Arkansas as commissioner to the Centennial Exposition He also directed the Sectretary of War to issue the arms for which recognition had been made by Gov Garland Robeson remarked that this would be a recognition of the Government The President replied that that was what he wished" DLC-Hamilton Fish. In 1874, a congressional committee had found clear evidence of voting fraud detrimental to Joseph Brooks in his race for Ark. governor with Elisha Baxter in 1872. Later in 1874, Augustus H. Garland was elected governor of Ark. under a controversial new state constitution. In its majority report, the congressional committee concluded that Garland properly held the office. USG's message sparked a Senate argument over the propriety of federal intervention to designate a governor and resulted in a vote accepting the majority report on March 2, 1875. See Proclamation, May 15, 1874; *HRC*, 43-2-2; *CR*, 43–2, 1055–56, 1078, 2085–118; *New York Times*, Feb. 8–11, 1875; George H. Thompson, *Arkansas and Reconstruction: The Influence of Geography, Economics, and Personality* (Port Washington, N. Y., 1976), pp. 159–69.

On Nov. 13, 1874, Volney V. Smith, Little Rock, had telegraphed to USG concerning his role as lt. governor during the constitutional crisis. ". . . on my return to the state after a brief absence I find that Elisha Baxter the Recognized Govr of the state has abdicated & abandoned the office of Governor & turned the same over to one A. H Garland who pretends to Execute the office of Governor under & by the authority of a pretended Constitution which he claims was ratified by the people of said state on the thirteenth day of October last the manner & mode of amending or Changing the Constitution of the state is distinctly stated in article thirteen the Change of Constitution attempted to be made was not & is not in accordance with said article but under the provisions of an act to provide for a Convention to frame a new Constitution 'approved May sixteenth Eighteen hundred & seventy four a Copy of which is hereto attached Marked "A" the state of Arkansas was admitted to Representation in Congress upon Certain fundamental Conditions named in the act of June twenty second Eighteen hundred & sixty Eight which I claim are violated by the pretended new Constitution I also claim that the Constitution of the state of Arkansas can not be altered or amended in any other manner than that provided by the Constitution itself & that the pointing out of how this Constitution should be altered or amended is an *inhibition* on the General assembly & the people of the state to pursue another or a different mode   the abdication of the office of Governor and the abandonment thereof by Elisha Baxter in Law amounts to a Constructive or *parol* Resignation   in such case under the provisions of section ten article six of said Constitution the duties of the office of Govr. devolve upon me as Lieutenant Governor   by and through the treachery & Connivance of Elisha Baxter I find A. H. Garland in the Executive office discharging the duties thereof   not only this I find a body of men in the legislative Halls who pretend to be the Members of the General Assembly of the state of Arkansas & who are attempting to Legislate for the people who were not Elected at the time nor in the manner provided by the Constitution & laws of said state   I also find a new set of pretended Judicial officers acting as supreme & Circuit Judges who were not chosen at the time nor in the manner provided by the Constitution & laws of said state   in short I find a new Government set up during my absence that is not the legitimate offspring of that of Eighteen hundred & sixty Eight & that the officers of the pretended Govmt have in some instances by violence & force displaced officers holding similar positions under the Constitution alluded to   by Reason of this state of affairs and other Causes all Contributing to the same end domestic violence Exists in this state which too powerful to be suppressed by ordinary process of the law or the Militia at my Command   Now therefore I,—V. V. Smith Lieutenant Governor of the state of Arkansas Elisha Baxter the Recognized Governor of said state having abdicated & abandoned said office do hereby and by these presents make application to the president of the United states and the Laws passed in pursuance thereof to guaranty to said state of Arkansas a Republican form of Government & protect the same against domestic Violence   The Legislature of said state is not now in session & Can not be Convened at this time without great detriment to the public interests   any attempt to do so would Result in augmenting Confusion & anarchy and would probably lead to strife & unnecessary bloodshed . . ." Telegram received (on Nov. 14, at 2:20 A.M.), DNA, RG 60, Letters from the President. *SED*, 43-2-25, 24–25. On the same day, Smith wrote to USG a letter with text similar to the telegram. LS, DNA, RG 60, Letters from the President. On Nov. 14, via St. Louis, Smith telegraphed to USG a message dated Nov. 13 "To the People of Arkansas" asserting his claim to be governor. Telegram received (on Nov. 14, at 11:35 P.M.), *ibid*. Related papers are *ibid*. See also *SED*, 43-2-25, 26–28.

On Nov. 14 and 16, Smith again telegraphed to USG. "On account of delay in publication my Proclamation was not made public until three oclock this afternoon,   immediately a large crowd gathered in the streets & the proprietor of republican was arrested for treason,   Garlands' sheriff has just visited my house With warrants for the arrest of myself & Edward Wheeler secy of state   I have no militia force organized & desire to avoid hostilities if possible   Without Presidential interference no alternative is left but organizing militia or submitting quietly to overthrow of the state Gov't   early Action on your Part is earnestly solicited" "The State Government is as Completely overthrown by the Connivance of Elisha Baxter as that of Louisiana was by Penns militia   it is true that the revolution by which it was accomplished was bloodless but it is just as effectively done as though it had Cost a thousand lives   Baxter himself used the office of Governor to organize the present revolutionary *Govt*   it was perfected in all its Departments Civil & military before he abdicated the office & turned the Same over to the Garland   So long as Baxter occupied the office I could not assume to discharge its duties   when he ceased to act as Governor he yielded the office to a person who was the head of new Government which is backed by a well armed & *the thoroughly* organized militia   in the face of such overwhelming advantages on the part of the Garland government it would be worse than madness for me to undertake to reestablish the overthrown Government by force of Arms   had I been able to do this I should not have Called on You for aid   it is because I am powerless that I appeal to You any attempt on my part to reestablish the Government under the Constitution of eighteen hundred & Sixty eight without Your recognition or during the pendency of the application now before you would result in embroiling the Citizens of the State in a Sanguinary Conflict before the life of any citizen of the State is Sacrificed I desire to know from You who are the arbiter between Garland & myself whether I will be regarded as the executive of a lawful Government or as being as guilty of treason against if you have no authority under the Constitution & laws to restore a Government to its lawful officers from whom it has been wrested by revolution & treachery instead of by actual Conflict of arms & bloodshed it is a sad Commentary on the legislation of the Country" Telegrams received (at 8:55 P.M. and 4:30 P.M.), DNA, RG 60, Letters from the President. *SED*, 43-2-25, 76–77.

On Nov. 17, Fish recorded in his diary. "The Arkansas difficulty is discussed—Williams says that so many of the States are now governed under Constitutions adopted in the mode of that recently adopted in Arkansas that it will not be safe to deny the validity of a Constitution thus adopted, viz: by a legislative authorization of a Convention to revise an existing Constitution, notwithstanding the fact that such existing Constitution provides the means of amendments to itself—This opinion seems generally concurred in. Williams states that he is importuned & his office continually filled by parties from either side urging action, & wishes to know what answer he shall give—President refers to the fact of a Congressional Committee now being in Arkansas, investigating state of affairs & suggests a reply that no action will be taken until the report of that Committee is known—I object that possibly some action may become necessary in the interval & that such answer wd commit him too strongly to the conclusions of the Committee—Bristow warmly endorses this view—It is finally determined simply to say that with the information now before the Government no action will be taken—" DLC-Hamilton Fish. See *New York Times*, Nov. 15–18, 1874.

On Nov. 18, Thomas Allen, president, St. Louis, Iron Mountain & Southern Railway, St. Louis, telegraphed to USG. "There is no more crime and disorder in Arkansas than in any other Equal quantity of humanity on earth our trains running daily through the state three hundred miles bring us into immediate contact with the people, the corruptions of a few selfish politicians haply are about ceasing and with in improved and advanced constitution the state is entering a bright career of material prosperity. people exposed to fire frost and grasshoppers in the north west are seeking safty in the timber of Arkansas," Telegram received, DNA, RG 60, Letters from the President.

On Nov. 19, Stephen Wheeler and four others, Little Rock, telegraphed to USG. "We the undersigned who were elected to the state office indicated opposite our names on the same ticket with Lieut Govr, fully indorse his application to you to re-establish reinstate the lawful Government of the state of Arkansas," Telegram received (on Nov. 20, at 9:45 A.M.), *ibid. SED*, 43-2-25, 77–78. On the same day, U.S. Senator Powell Clayton and U.S. Representative Oliver P. Snyder of Ark., Little Rock, telegraphed to USG. "The republicans of the state regard the Government of eighteen hundred and sixty Eight as the lawful one and Garland as revolutionary they Consider the recognition of Gov Smith as being not only demanded by law but necessary for their protection they Confidently rely upon you, You to afford the aid necessary to re-establish the legitimate Govt which when done they are amply able to maintain without further assistance, Messrs Hines and Hodges are absent from the state but concur with us in these views—" Telegram received (on Nov. 20), DNA, RG 60, Letters from the President. *SED*, 43-2-25, 77. On Nov. 20, A. D. Thomas, pension agent, and seven others, Little Rock, telegraphed to USG. "We take this occasion to say that the entire republican party of the state almost without exception sustain Lieut Gov Smith & we join therein," Telegram received, DNA, RG 60, Letters from the President. *SED*, 43-2-25, 78.

On Dec. 11, Robert E. Doran, Napoleon, Ark., wrote to USG on a printed petition meant to protest the removal of county officers under the new constitution, but altered to favor the new constitution. "I was beaten for the County Clerk Ship of my county by a Republican & a negro to boot. And it was fair I I gave him up my office & the people both black and white dont want the Goverment the voted in changed—I say I would rather give my claims up than to have it changed   one of your Supporters . . . a Democrat & Late clerk of Desha County Ark" ALS, DNA, RG 60, Letters from the President. *SED*, 43-2-25, 97–98.

On Jan. 13, 1875, Garland telegraphed to USG. "If there is a white league or any kindred association in this state I do not know it & I have asked for those who assert it to be brought before the Grand Jury of this country now in session to show the fact pledging all the Power of this Government to break them up & to punish those that belong to them & I call upon the Legislature now sitting to pass the most stringent laws to this end." Telegram received (at 6:36 P.M.), DLC-USG, IB.

On Jan. 23, Louis L. Hyman *et al.*, Waldron, Ark., petitioned USG and "People of the United States." "We the undersigned union Soldiers in the late war of the Rebellion do hereby heartily indorse and approve the course of Leiut Gen Sheridan in Louisiana   We are Residents of Arkansas and know the Statements Made by him concerning the condition of Union Men and the terrorism existing in this State to be true in every Particular . . ." Copy, DNA, RG 60, Letters Received, Senate. Levi Hill and others, "Soldiers of the Confederate States Army Residents of the State of Arkansas," favorably endorsed this petition. Copy, *ibid.* See message to Senate, Jan. 13, 1875.

On Jan. 24, H. S. Dodd, Doddsville, Ark., wrote to USG. "The Republican party and war Democrats of north arkansas are Solid in favor of your action regarding Southern affairs   Stand firm to the right as you have done in the past and we will help you fight it out no matter how long it takes: the northen people cannot understand this matter as we do living as we do in the south   they Say we are all rascals & thieves: perhaps I am a thief but I did not Steal it from the rebels but have built up a $30000 lumber manufacturey business which is acknowledged to be a great benefit to the County: I am no politician never asked for an office in my life, and never held one only *During the Rebellion*   Stand Firm General and may God help you to See the right: . . ." ALS, USG 3.

On Jan. 24, Miss E. M. Bartlett, Little Rock, wrote to USG. "By telegram from Washington, I have noticed that you are not in favor of our present State administration—Although but a woman, I cannot refrain from thanking you for the stand taken, and humbly pray, that you may be sustained in your position, not on my account, but for the sake of all good republican people here. Northern people (and I include both Democrats and Republicans) who have never been South of Mason's and Dixon's Line, cannot understand the situation here—I am constrained to write you this morning, hearing as I have, that Judge Wilshire and others have sent here saying, they must have $150,000 and they can gain their cause. Can it be, that we live in an age, when right and wrong have nothing to do, with guiding those in authority, in matters pertaining to our great National welfare! God forbid—We have lived in this State since 1859. Are from Mass. I could write at length of persecutions, insults, &c, to northern people—but it has nothing to do with the question to be decided, neither have you the time to read it. We learn that your good wife is with us in this matter, may the Lord bless her. Trusting this question may be speedily settled, and in such a way as may prevent greater evils in our country, . . ." ALS, DNA, RG 60, Letters from the President.

On March 16 and 19, Clayton and U.S. Senator Stephen W. Dorsey of Ark. wrote to

USG. "We respectfully recommend that James Torrans be appointed U. S. Marshal for the Eastern District of Arkansas—" LS, PHi. "We have the honor to request the appointment of Hon Volney V Smith late Lieutenant Governor of Arkansas, as United States Consul at Prescott Canada in place of Clifford S Sims who has served about six years. . . ." LS, DNA, RG 59, Letters of Application and Recommendation. Related papers are *ibid.* On March 17, USG nominated James Torrens as marshal, Eastern District, Ark.; on Dec. 9, USG nominated Smith as consul, St. Thomas.

On June 8, M. E. Hedges, East Pittsburgh, Pa., wrote to USG. "For the first and I trust only time—Allow me to intrude upon your most valuable time, to beg at your hands a favor—justly due! I refer to *Ex Chief-Justice McClure*, of Ark,—who has togather with his family Suffered great privations—and persecutions because of the 'lost Cause'—for which he Struggled So bravely. I have known him as a man of honor & firmness of character and a Superior Judge—having thus Suffered—and fallen with the 'Cause' I therefore think him deserving of notice and help at your hands. An appointment as Judge in a Territory, or anything in Short to enable him to Start life again and get from that hated place, where he can never rise even as a Lawyer—because of his malignant foes. Hoping you will kindly remember him in the many gifts you have for your people—believe me you will have the Prayers of his worthy family for your welfare—and many more thanks than I am able to express . . ." ALS, *ibid.*, RG 60, Records Relating to Appointments. No appointment followed for John E. McClure, Ark. chief justice, 1871–74.

1. See *CR*, 43–2, 922.

To George F. Edmunds

———

February 19th 1875.

Dear Sir.

In sending papers relating to Louisiana District Judgeship, I did not desire to ask if any particular nomination if made, would be confirmed, but to say to the Judiciary Committee that although I had said that I would not appoint Billings under any circumstances. I now withdraw that determination so far as to submit the question to the Committee to suggest between the candidates which one of them should receive the nomination. If the Committee will make the examination and suggestion, I will follow it.

> Very truly,
> Yours
> U. S. Grant.

Hon. George F. Edmunds U. S. Senate.

Copy, DLC-USG, II, 2. On Feb. 16, 1875, Attorney Gen. George H. Williams wrote to U.S. Senator George F. Edmunds of Vt., chairman, Committee on the Judiciary. "I am requested by the President to forward you the enclosed papers recommending E. C. Billings, Esq. for Judge of the District Court in Louisiana. He has heretofore been disinclined to appoint Mr. Billings; but is now willing to do so in case he is satisfied that the nomination if made will be confirmed by the Senate. He does not wish to submit any more nominations for the office until he is satisfied that they will be acceptable to the Senate. Your attention is respectfully directed to the enclosed recommendations, and I will ask that after you have used you will cause them to be returned to this Department. My own judgement is that Mr. Billings is well qualified for the place, as I have had some opportunities to know what his legal attainments are." Copy, DNA, RG 60, Letters Sent to Executive Officers. On Dec. 24, 1874, George L. Smith, New Orleans, had written to USG. "I take great pleasure in joining in suggesting the name of Edward. C. Billings of New Orleans, as a fit person to be appointed as United States District Judge for the District of Louisiana, to fill the vacancy now existing there. Mr Billings was a graduate of Yale College, studied law at the Cambridge Law School, and in an eleven years practice at the bar of New Orleans in which he has dealt with the heaviest and most complicated cases,—has shown his great ability and learning in the law. He represented the Government in the wine cases and by his fearless advocacy of the enforcement of the law in the face of the powerful and angry combination of the wine trade, secured the fair invoicing of the red wines; . . ." LS, *ibid.*, Records Relating to Appointments. Letters to USG from U.S. Senators William M. Stewart of Nev. (Feb. 14, 1875), Oliver P. Morton of Ind. (Feb. 14), and Hannibal Hamlin of Maine (Feb. 15) recommending Edward C. Billings are *ibid.* On Feb. 19, U.S. Representative Jeremiah M. Wilson of Ind. wrote to USG. "Having been informed that it has been asserted that the evidence taken by the Committee on the Judiciary of the House relative to the impeachment of Judge E. H. Durell ~~contained~~ disclosed fact unfavorable to the Hon E. C. Billings it gives me pleasure to say that any such assertion is wholly unwarranted. I am familiar with that testimony having been present at the examination of all the witnesses and I am quite sure that a careful scrutiny of it will fail to disclose anything derogatory to his honor or integrity. And lest any inference might be drawn of an unfavorable character because of this statement being limited to the disclosures of that evidence I will add that all the knowledge or information I have of him is that he is a gentleman of high character, and acknowledged ability—" ALS, *ibid.*, Letters Received, House of Representatives. On Dec. 17, Wilson, Washington, D. C., again wrote to USG defending Billings. ALS, *ibid.*, Records Relating to Appointments. Related papers are *ibid.* On Jan. 10, 1876, USG nominated Billings as judge, La. See *New York Times*, Dec. 2, 1893.

On May 28, 1874, Elizabeth S. Durell and M. A. Durell, Dover, N. H., had written to USG. "We, sisters of E H. Durell of New Orleans, beseech that you will not permit the great injustice which threatens to crush our brother. Those who have known him from early youth to old age, *know* that he is not guilty of the crimes of which he is accused, The accusation causes us unspeakable anguish." LS, DNA, RG 60, Letters from the President. Appointed in 1864 by President Abraham Lincoln, Judge Edward H. Durell, U.S. District Court, La., was threatened with impeachment by the House of Representatives for drunkenness and abuse of his authority. On Dec. 1, 1874, Durell, New York City, wrote to USG resigning his office. ALS, *ibid.* See *PUSG*, 19, 434–35; *HRC*, 42-3-96, 43-1-732; *CR*, 43-2, 319–24.

On Dec. 4, U.S. Representative Lionel A. Sheldon of La., New Orleans, telegraphed to Orville E. Babcock. "Please ask the President to delay appointment of Judge for this District for a few days, will leave for Washington tomorrow" Telegram received, DLC-USG, IB.

Also on Dec. 4, Governor William P. Kellogg of La. telegraphed to USG. "I take the liberty of suggesting to you the name of Judge P. Morgan of this City for appointment as

U. S. District Judge of Louisiana. Judge Morgan as you was formerly U. S. District Attorney. He is an old resident, a warm friend of yours and your Administration and possesses the respect and confidence of the Bar and the community here. Ex Attorney Genl. Hoar, Genl Butler & W. M. Evarts, are well acquainted with him" Telegram received, *ibid.* On Dec. 7, Joseph P. Bradley, U.S. Supreme Court, wrote to USG. "It is so difficult to find the proper man fas successor to Judge Durrell,—that I gladly enclose to you the within letters recommending Judge *Philip H Morgan*, formerly District Attorney. The person wanted is, one acquainted with the people, the institutions, the laws of Louisiana; well affected to the U. S. Government; capable, trustworthy and of legal qualifications. From what I have heard of Judge Morgan (I do not know him personally) I think he is the man. I have been trying to think of some one qualified in all respects—whom I could recommend in case I should be questioned—and I am relieved to hear that he is urged for the place. The Louisiana bar has men of much ability and high character; but their connection with the cause of the Confederacy or their views on public questions, would probably render them objectionable. Against Mr. Morgan I do not know of a single objection." ALS, DNA, RG 60, Records Relating to Appointments. Similar letters of the same day from Charles A. Peabody and Thomas J. Durant to USG are *ibid.* On Nov. 1, 1869, Philip H. Morgan, New Orleans, had written to USG resigning as U.S. attorney, La. ALS, *ibid.*

On Dec. 8, 1874, A. K. Johnson, New Orleans, wrote to USG. "as the appointment of U. S. Dist Judge for this dist is of great importance Excuse me if I Sugest the name of the Hon Judge. John. B. Cotton. a practicing attorney Since 1848—for four (4) years Judge of —dist court of this city—a *man able just & fearless*—whos personal character is above reproch. an original *democrat* but a conservative—consistant and fearless advocate—of the reconstruction acts and your administration Since 1868 ripe in years—and Experience —now about 50 years old his appointment would I believe give more general Satisfaction than that of any other. man. in *La* the Judge does not know—that his name will be mentioned in connection with the position but, I am Sure he would accept and honorably fill. the *high* office if tendered to him. for his character and abillity—I refer you to the Hon T. J. Durant and his Partner Mr Horner of your city, also A. P. Field attorney Genl—of this State now in your city Satisfactory Endorsements can be furnished if required . . . Confidential Don. A. Pardees. appointment would in my opinion be a *great mistake* for reasons that I could explain if called upon" ALS, *ibid.* Related papers are *ibid.* On Jan. 27, 1875, Johnson telegraphed to USG on the same subject. Telegram received (at 10:50 P.M.), DLC-USG, IB.

On Dec. 4, 1874, E. Howard McCaleb *et al.* had petitioned USG. "The undersigned members of the New Orleans Bar would most respectfully recommend the Honl Don A. Pardee for appointment to the vacant Office of Judge of the United States District Court for the District of Louisiana. Judge Pardee was elected Judge of the Second Judicial District of Louisiana in 1868 and re-elected in 1872. During the time he has occupied the bench he has gained the confidence respect and esteem of the members of the bar by his courtesy, dignity, impartiality and thorough knowledge of law." DS (16 signatures), DNA, RG 60, Records Relating to Appointments. Related papers are *ibid.* On March 9, 1869, Sheldon had written to USG recommending Don A. Pardee as U.S. attorney, La. ". . . Judge Pardee entered the military service from Ohio and throughout the entire war served with great merit and gallantry. He has resided and practiced the legal profession in the city of New Orleans since the close of the war. . . ." ALS, *ibid.* Among several undated favorable endorsements is one from James F. Casey. AES, *ibid.* On Dec. 14, 1874, USG nominated Pardee as judge, La. See letter to George F. Edmunds, Feb. 27, 1875.

On Dec. 10, 1874, George Norton, New Orleans, had telegraphed to USG. "Will you do me the kindness to extend my recommendation for clerkship to the successor of Judge Durell" Telegram received (on Dec. 11), DNA, RG 60, Records Relating to Appointments.

On Jan. 8, 1875, Thomas J. Durant and Joseph P. Horner, Washington, D. C., wrote to USG. "We enclose herewith, as requested by Mr Kearney, a petition to you for his appointment as U. S. District Judge for Louisiana. As the appointment has been made already, it seems somewhat supererogatory to send you this petition: but it will do no harm and may do good to our Friend R. M. Kearney." L, *ibid.* Two undated petitions recommending Robert M. Kearney, one signed by "citizens of Kentucky," including James, Joshua F., and John J. Speed, are *ibid.*

On Jan. 12, Simeon Theodore, St. Louis, wrote to USG. "I learn from the dispatches published in the St. Louis Democrat of this date, that it is proposed to Substitute the name of Gen. Butler, for that of Mr. Pardee, as the nominee to fill the seat in the U. S. District Court, made vacant by the resignation of Judge Durell. I hope this is but an idle rumor. I am unwilling to believe that the Chief Executive of this great nation can be so insensible to the common instincts of justice, as to contemplate an act so monstrous and outrageous. Such an expression of malignant hate might well be expected of from that class of whom Wendell Phillips, is a befiting representative, whose moral sensibilities are so distorted, that they believe it to be a religious duty, to anoy and humiliate the Southern people, for no other reason than because they were once a prosperous and arogant people. God forbid that the President of the U. S. should ever be influenced by sentiments so brutal" ALS, *ibid.*

On Jan. 13, J. Madison Wells, New Orleans, wrote to USG "in behalf, of the Republican party of Louisiana and more particularly those of State nativity," recommending George S. Lacey as judge, La. LS, *ibid.* On Feb. 23, Wells again wrote to USG. "Some weeks since I intruded upon you the wishes of the Native Republicans of our State, Members of the Bar, and my own, as to the successor of Judge Durell. From this general desire for the appointment of Mr Geo. S. Lacey, I am constrained to say, or give it as my opinion, it will remove the complaint of the rule of the Carpet bagger, and may molify the feelings of the better class of our people. Judge Pardee is so strongly advocated by the White league organ (the Bulletin) although he is a Republican it is true, but the support from that quarter throws a suspicion over his fidelity to the party. Hoping for your continued good health, and your future political success, . . ." ALS, *ibid.* On July 2, Wells wrote to USG introducing Lacey. ALS, *ibid.* Related papers are *ibid.* On March 2, 1877, USG nominated George S. Lacey as U.S. attorney, La., to replace James R. Beckwith. On March 24, 1875, Wells, Washington, D. C., wrote to USG. "I take the liberty of asking the appointment of Naval Officer for the Port of New Orleans Louisiana—Fully adequate to its duties, and assure you of their faithful execution   A Louisianian by birth a life long resident an unflinching unionist before and during the rebellion—Extensively related to and Connected with many prominent and influential families in west and north west Louisiana,   This federal position would I am satisfied strengthen me with these and many others of my people and enable me to render much good Service to the Republican party in 1876 and advance materially your political interest for a third term if your friends desire it   The present incumbent is a citizen of Wisconsin unable to control but his own vote but reaping the political fruits labored for and achieved by such partizans as your Applicant—The general rule President in all political organizations in the distribution of the political gains—is I believe to award those who were most proficient in accomplishing the Success—Claiming to be of that number and knowing that through me the Republican party was sustained in their political control of the State of Louisiana thereby sustaining your action there in, I shall President expect your favorable consideration of my claims to this asked for position—" ALS, *ibid.*, RG 56, Naval Officer Applications. On Dec. 8, USG nominated Wells as surveyor of customs, New Orleans.

On Jan. 21, La. Speaker of the House Michael Hahn had written to USG. "This will introduce to your acquaintance Hon. O. J. Flagg, Judge of the Fourth Judicial District

Court of this State. Judge Flagg thinks that in case there should be any difficulty in getting a suitable successor for Judge Durell's position, he might prove such. He resides in my Parish (St. Charles) where, and throughout his District, he enjoys the esteem and confidence of all parties. As a Judge he is faithful, competent and impartial; and as a republican he is earnest and bold. He will explain his case, and I bespeak for him your kind attention." ALS, *ibid.*, RG 60, Records Relating to Appointments.

On Feb. 1, Secretary of State Hamilton Fish recorded in his diary. "The President stated that Mr West of Louisiana had called in relation to the appointment of a District Judge, and was opposed to Mr Pardee. He thought West would be opposed to anyone unless he named them himself; and that he had sent a message to Messrs Frye and Hoar in cipher through Genl Sheridan requesting them to obtain information in regard to the appointment" DLC-Hamilton Fish. USG wrote two undated notes. "Telegraph to Sheridan in cyipher to ask Mr. Hoar or Frye if they will ascertain whether in their judgement to confirmation of Pardee is desirable and conducive to the best interests of the public good." "Add to dispatch to New Orleans. Please ~~recommend~~ suggest name or names of persons that would make satisfactory District Judge." AN, DNA, RG 94, Letters Received, 3579 1874. On Feb. 2, Babcock endorsed the second note. "The Secty will please send this also—" AES, *ibid.* On the same day, Lt. Gen. Philip H. Sheridan, New Orleans, telegraphed to AG Edward D. Townsend. "Mr. Hoar has made no investigation and has no opinion but wishes to say that he has great confidence in Mr. Frye's opinion who has investigated and who says that Pardee is the best appointment for District Judge all things considered and that Mr. Beckwith is the next. Mr. Frye has no confidence in Morgan for this position." Telegram received (in cipher), *ibid.*

On July 6, Richard Crowley, U.S. attorney, New York City, wrote to USG recommending Robert H. Shannon, "formerly of the City and State of New York. but at present a Commissioner of the United States Circuit Court, for the District of Louisiana," as judge, La. Printed copy, *ibid.*, RG 60, Records Relating to Appointments. Horace Porter, Chester A. Arthur, and others endorsed this letter. *Ibid.* On Nov. 17, Peter J. Kramer *et al.*, New Orleans, petitioned USG recommending Shannon. DS (23 signatures), *ibid.*

On Aug. 7, Kellogg wrote to USG. "Permit me to introduce Mr. C. S. Kellogg of New York who visits Washington on private business. Mr. Kellogg has been a resident of the South since 1851. and for a number of years a resident of this City, is a lawyer of high standing in the community, and was formerly Ass't U. S. Dist Atty for District of Louisiana and since 1867 has held the position of Register in Bankruptcy for First Congressional District of Louisiana." Copy, *ibid.* On Aug. 16, Louis C. Roudanez, New Orleans, wrote to USG. "In view of the importance both of an early installment of a Judge upon our vacant U. S. District Court Bench and of a cautious selection to that end, I venture to commend for consideration Mr C. S. Kellogg, a lawyer of this city. Mr Kellogg is not a relative of the Governor nor conspicuous in politics, but a sterling Unionist and of liberal culture in the law. A native of New York, he settled in Woodville, Mississippi, in 1851, and there practised his profession, with increasing success until 1863, when he entered New-Orleans, a Union refugee, . . ." LS, *ibid.* Related papers recommending Chauncey S. Kellogg are *ibid.*

On Nov. 5, James W. Flanagan, Flanagans Mills, Tex., wrote to USG. "I have been Strongly importuned to write you in behalf of Judge Loony of Shreveport *La*, in reference to the vacant Judgeship in that State. I have been Hesitating in doing so, as I am a Texan, not wishing to interfere in The Politicks of Louisiana, but when Strongly urged by old personal & Political Friends, I must act, and Simply Say, That Judge Loony is an excellent *man*, a good District Judge, a fine Lawyer, fully competent to Discharge the duties of the office he aspires to, a good Republican, and Remote from the City of New Orleans where the Political Cauldron boils So Strong; his appointment, I think would be well Reced by the Masses,   I am taking but little *trouble* as to the Political movements in my State,   The Democrats, have all in their own *hands*, and cannot agree, but if they had to *yield* they would be Ready to fall in the last Ditch, *Rather* than do, so,   They Detest the United States Laws, and all those that Sympathise with them,   I trust Judge Loonys application may Recive kind and favorable notice   I have known him long & favorably" ALS, *ibid*. Related papers recommending Robert J. Looney are *ibid*.

On Nov. 27, J. Hale Sypher, Franklin, La., wrote to USG. "I appreciate your difficulty in finding a suitable person to fill the vacant U. S. Judgeship in Louisiana,   Last winter I supported Judge Pardee who you nominated to the Senate and I regret that he was not confirmed,   assuming that he is no longer a candidate I now desire to call your attention to a gentleman who is in *every respect* well qualified to fill such a position—It is Wm. Grant Esq of New Orleans—who during the war was a gallant officer in the Union Army and since the War he has devoted himself to the practice of law in New Orleans in which profession he has achieved a reputation second to no practitioner at the bar. Beside his high attainments in the law, his social standing in the Community is of the *first order*. His appointment I know would give universal satisfaction—I hope you may see proper to confer upon him the nomination" ALS, *ibid*. Related papers recommending William Grant are *ibid*., as are papers recommending Jacob Hawkins, George Williamson, and Emmet D. Craig. A draft letter recommending John S. Whitaker is in DLC-Caleb Cushing.

To Columbus Delano

Washington, D. C.
Feby. 27th 1875

SIR:

I have read, and considered carefully, your report, and the report of the Commissioner of the Land Office, against compliance with the Resolution of the House of Representatives of the 26th of Jany. 1875, and fully concur with you. You may if you please report to the Speaker of the House that you find it wholly impracticable and illegal to comply with such Resolution, and that you have so reported— with your reasons in detail—to the Executive, and that you are sustained in them by him. You may also communicate copies of the Commissioner's and your report.

Very truly yours
U. S. GRANT

HON. COLUMBUS DELANO
SECTY. OF THE DEPT. OF THE INTERIOR.

Copy, DLC-USG, II, 2. *HED*, 43-2-180, 5. On Jan. 26, 1875, the House of Representatives adopted a resolution offered by U.S. Representative Benjamin F. Butler of Mass. "for the purpose of directing the proper officer of the Government, having charge of the public lands, to determine the title of the United States in the valuable quicksilver mines known as the New Idria Company mines, or sometimes as the McGarrahan claim." *CR*, 43–2, 763. See Fish diary, Feb. 12, 19, 1875, DLC-Hamilton Fish; *PUSG*, 20, 240–45, 292–302.

USG wrote an undated note on this subject. "I do not.   I have read the papers in the New Idria case and while I think there is sufficient evidence on which to issue patents yet I think, in view of the subject having become a matter of Congressional enquiry, before the incoming of my first administration it is better to defer final action until the meeting of Congress and then refer the whole matter to that body for instructions." AN, DLC-USG, IB. On June 1, Levi P. Luckey wrote a letter to Secretary of the Interior Columbus Delano incorporating USG's note. Copy, *ibid.*, II, 2. On the same day, Delano wrote to USG. "The name of Mrs McKinney is not on the list for discharge from the Pension Office. She need therefore give her self no uneasiness. Will you be good enough to send by the bearer, all the papers in the New Idria case. . . . I send Henry's appointment" ALS, *ibid.* Frances A. McKinney worked as a Pension Office messenger. For John J. Henry, see *PUSG*, 24, 139–40.

To George F. Edmunds

February 27th 1875.

Sir.

Your note of yesterday enquiring if I wish the name of Pardee, nominated for District Judge of La, withhold any longer is received. In answer I would state, that I made the nomination believing it to be the best I could make from the candidates named for the office. I have seen or heard nothing since to change that view, except the two statements made by the Chairman of the Judiciary Committee, at our last interview. If they cannot be satisfactorily explained I would say that the nomination was an unfit one to be confirmed. In that case I would be glad of a suggestion from the Republican members of the Judiciary Committee, as to who they would think the best of, my judgement leaning rather towards Beckwith,[1]   I would be glad however if there should be no action before Monday next, before which time I will see the Chairman of the Committee.

Very truly yours.

U. S. Grant.

Hon. Geo. F. Edmunds.
Chairman Judiciary Committee U. S. S.

Copy, DLC-USG, II, 2. On March 24, 1875, U.S. Senator George F. Edmunds of Vt. telegraphed to USG. "It seems to me impossible in view of the third section of the Tenure of Office Act to fill the vacancy in the Office of District Judge for Louisiana during the vacation as the place became vacant before the commencement of this session of the Senate   If therefore any different action is to be taken it would seem necessary to take it before we adjourn" Telegram received, DLC-USG, IB. Also on March 24, Orville E. Babcock telegraphed to Edmunds. "The President says in reply to your telegram that he is not prepared to take any other action now—and that the place will remain open if it cannot be filled after adjournment." ALS (press, telegram sent), DNA, RG 107, Telegrams Collected (Bound). On the same day, the Senate adjourned, after tabling the nomination of Don A. Pardee as judge, La. See letter to George F. Edmunds, Feb. 19, 1875.

1. James R. Beckwith continued as U.S. attorney, La. See *PUSG*, 21, 384–85.

To James A. Garfield

February 27th 1875.

SIR.

I respectfully suggest to you, and to the Conference Committee on the Indian Appropriation Bill—that $300.000. be added to the appropriation as at present reported to find and clothe something over 3000 Indian prisoners captured and surrendered to the Army during the past winter. These Indians are now under guard and really without law and appropriations for their support. They embace about all that are inclined, or can give us trouble south of the Union Pacific Railroad.

This appropriation, if made, should be available at once, and is estimated to answer for the remainder of this fiscal year, and all of next. These Indians would then be brought to Fort Leavenworth and would be under Military controll until it might be deemed safe to place them on reservations.

Very truly yours.
U. S. GRANT.

HON. JAS. A. GARFIELD
CHR. APPROPRIATION COM.
HOUSE OF REPS.

Copy, DLC-USG, II, 2. On Feb. 27, 1875, AG Edward D. Townsend telegraphed to Gen. William T. Sherman, St. Louis. "Your dispatch of the twenty-sixth (26th) to the Secretary of war has been considered by the President, Secretaries of war and Interior and Commissioner of Indian Affairs. The President approves General Popes proposition to bring the Indians referred to by him to Fort Leavenworth, and also those under General Augur at Fort Sill   The Secretary Interior has gone to committee on appropriations with letter from the President asking for three hundred thousand dollars to *support these Indians* remainder of this and during next fiscal year, with authority to turn it over to the Secretary of war. The President desires the Indians to remain where they are at present until result of endeavor to get ~~to get~~ money is known when you will be immediately informed by telegraph." Copy, DNA, RG 94, Letters Sent. Congress appropriated $300,000 "for the support, education and civilization of three thousand, or more, captive Cheyenne, Arapahoe, Kiowa, and Camanche Indians," provided that "as soon as he may deem it expedient, the President shall cause said Indians to be placed on a permanent reservation." *U.S. Statutes at Large*, XVIII, part 3, p. 448.

In June, 1874, U.S. troops had begun a sustained campaign against Cheyenne, Kiowa, Comanche, and Arapaho forces. On Oct. 6, Secretary of War William W. Belknap telegraphed to USG, St. Louis. "Following telegram received yesterday from General Sheridan: 'Chicago, October 5th 1874. GENERAL W. W. BELKNAP, Washington, D. C. Some few of the hostile Cheyenne Indians, and a few of the Kiowas, probably Satanta among the number, have surrendered themselves as prisoners of war, delivering up their arms to Colonel Neill at the Arapahoe Agency, and it is more than probable that before long we will have to determine what shall be done with four or five hundred. I think myself that all who have committed murder or stolen cattle within the last two years, should be tried by a military commission, that the horses of all who have been hostile, and which will be captured property, should be sold at auction and the proceeds invested in cattle for the tribe. I have also thought that the ringleaders who may be exempt from a military commission could be confined at Fort Snelling. Can you give me an answer before the eighth, as I go to the Indian Territory on that date. P. H. SHERIDAN. Lieut. General.' I have replied to General Sheridan as follows: 'GENERAL P. H. SHERIDAN, Chicago, Illinois. Telegram of fifth received. I have consulted with Acting Secretary Cowan, and the Commissioner of Indian Affairs. The conclusion is that if Satanta is among the number he should be delivered to the Governor of Texas; that the others who have committed murder or stolen cattle within the last two years, should be tried by a military commission; that the horses of all who have been hostile and which may be captured should be sold at auction and the proceeds invested in cattle for the friendly portion of the tribe. Of course all should be deprived of their arms. The decision as to the ringleaders who may be exempt from military commission, will be made hereafter. I have informed the President of this by telegraph. Acknowledge receipt.'" Copies, DNA, RG 94, Letters Received, 2815 1874; *ibid.*, RG 107, Telegrams Collected (Bound); *ibid.*, Letters Sent, Military Affairs. Also on Oct. 6, Orville E. Babcock, St. Louis, telegraphed to Belknap. "The President says your action as to Indians is correct." Telegram received, *ibid.*, RG 94, Letters Received, 2815 1874. On Oct. 7, Belknap telegraphed to USG. "Gen'l. Sheridan request that the contents of yesterdays telegram as to disposition of captured Indians be *not* given to the public" ALS (telegram sent), *ibid.*, RG 107, Telegrams Collected (Bound).

On Nov. 13, Belknap wrote to Townsend. "Please communicate the following to General Sheridan through the General of the Army:—To-day the President instructed the Secretary of the Interior to telegraph to the Governor of Texas requesting him to take no immediate action relative to the Indian Chiefs lately turned over to the State authority until further consideration and advices. In the meantime General Sheridan is desired to give the Secretary of War for the information of the President his opinion as to the guilt of these Indians and generally the history of their alleged violations of their promises; and of the

laws and treaties." LS, *ibid.*, RG 94, Letters Received, 2815 1874. Paroled by Tex. authorities in 1873, Kiowa chiefs Satanta and Big Tree fought in the 1874 campaign before surrendering to U.S. troops in Sept. See James L. Haley, *The Buffalo War: The History of the Red
River Indian Uprising of 1874* (Garden City, N. Y., 1976), pp. 188–90; *PUSG*, 22, 388–90;
ibid., 24, 439–40.

On March 12, 1875, Edward Earle, Washington, D. C., wrote to USG. "I learn that a
portion of the Indian prisoners of war are to be sent to Dry Tortugas with their families
as a punishment for their past marauding and wickedness—I do entreat that their families may not be sent because 1st the women and children are not responsible for the acts of
the men And 2nd The peril of the women in such a situation is very great and there can be
no chance for the improvement of t in civilization of the women or children. It must be far
better for the children to remain at Fort Sill where they can attend a good school all ready
established and for the Women to go with the greater number of the prisoners of war—
whom friends connected with the central superintendency, I beleive, would desire should
be placed in the North Eastern portion of the Indian Territory adjacent to or in the Quapaw Agency where the Modocks are. I crave for these suggestions thy serious consideration" ALS, DNA, RG 75, Letters Received, Central Superintendency.

On March 13, Belknap wrote a "Memorandum for a telegram and letter to General
Sherman, and for letter to the Secretary of the Interior." "The President decides that of the
captured Indians the ringleaders & such as have been guilty of crimes are to be selected to
be sent to such military posts as may hereafter be designated. They are *not* to be accompanied by their families. The remaining captured Indians, with the exception of the two
Chief's who were guilty of outraging the German girls, to be turned over to the Indian
Department, at their respective Agencies. The two Chief's, before referred to, are to be
retained as prisoners of war, and held in confinement, hereafter, in such place as the
Commander of the Military Division may direct." DfS, *ibid.*, RG 94, Letters Received,
2815 1874. Cheyennes had abducted four daughters of John and Lydia German, killed in a
Sept., 1874, raid near Fort Wallace, Kan. See Grace E. Meredith, ed., *Girl Captives of the
Cheyennes* (Los Angeles, 1927).

In May, 1875, seventy-two captured chiefs, primarily Cheyenne and Kiowa, were
transported from Fort Leavenworth, Kan., to Fort Marion, St. Augustine, Fla. On June 11,
1st Lt. Richard H. Pratt, Fort Marion, wrote to Townsend. "I have the honor to report that
the Indian prisoners confined here under my charge have made very urgent appeals to have
something done in their cases. They are particularly distressed about being separated from
their women and children. On the 9th. instant the Kiowas and Comanches gave me a talk
through the Kiowa Chief, Male-Mante, which they desired me to send to 'Washington,'
and to ask 'Washington' to do something for them. The Cheyennes have talked in the same
manner. Male-Mante said—'We are termed by all the white people a very lazy class of
men, not willing to do anything for our own support. This is not so. We have been taken
away from our wives and children, relatives and friends, shackled and sent down to this
place to remain, we do not know how long. We are willing to show that we are not too lazy
to support ourselves, if there is anything 'Washington' wishes us to do, tell us what it is,
and 'Washington' will see how willingly we do it. We don't care what kind of work it is.
We want to show 'Washington' that we are willing to do anything he wants us to do. We
want to learn the ways of the white man. First we want our wives and children, and then
we will go any place and settle down and learn to support ourselves as the white men
do. . . . There are a great many Indians at Fort Sill and in that country who have done more
bad work than we have, and why should they be allowed to go free, and be happy with
their families, and we sent down here as prisoners, to live in these dark cells. That is not
right. . . ." Copy, DNA, RG 94, Letters Received, 2815 1874. Richard Henry Pratt,

Battlefield and Classroom: Four Decades with the American Indian, 1867–1904, ed., Robert M. Utley (New Haven, 1964), pp. 122–23. On June 26, Lt. Gen. Philip H. Sheridan, Chicago, telegraphed to Belknap. "I have the Indian Talk made to Lieut Pratt   it is more indian twaddle   I have heard the Same in almost the Same Language at Least one hundred times all the Indians at St Augustine are unmittigated murderers of men women and children without a single particle of provocation   Knowing the Present appeal would arise not only from these Indian but from the families left behind I recommended when it was first proposed to send them to St Augustine that their families Should accompany them but my recommendation was rejected by the Indian Department   I now again renew it not on account of the Sympathy which their Simple but diplomatic talk creates but as a matter of good policy to Save ourselves from numerous Similar appeals which will follow from these Indians and their families now at Fort Sill   if the wives and families are sent care Should be taken to allow none to go but the immediate family circles" Telegram received (at 8:00 P.M.), DNA, RG 94, Letters Received, 2815 1874. Babcock endorsed these papers. "The President says he thinks it ~~would~~ will be well to carry out the recommendation of Gen Sheridan—" AE (initialed, undated), *ibid.* On July 22, Secretary of the Interior Columbus Delano wrote to Belknap. "Referring to War Department letter of the 13th instant, relative to the removal of the wives and families of the prisoners at Fort Marion, Florida, requesting information as to the number of persons for which accommodation will be required, I inform the Honorable, the Secretary of War, that the Commissioner of Indian Affairs, who was directed to carry the recommendation of General Sheridan into effect, being in doubt, as to the scope of the order of the President in the premises, asked whether, in cases where an Indian had a plurality of wives, they should all be sent with all their children to Fort Marion. The subject was submitted, on the 16th instant, for the further direction of the President. The papers have been returned to the Department, with the Executive endorsement, as follows; 'Send the actual *wives* not exceeding one wife to one Indian, and send the children under twelve years of age. The women and children need not be confined within the Fort if there is not ample room.' The Commissioner of Indian Affairs has been this day directed to take appropriate action in accordance with the President's order." LS, *ibid.* On Aug. 5, Benjamin R. Cowen, act. secretary of the interior, wrote to USG. "I have the honor to submit, herewith, a copy of a telegram, referred to this Department, by the Commissioner of Indian Affairs, reporting that the Kiowa and Comanche women are unwilling to go to Florida. As there removal to Florida was ordered upon the recommendation of General Sheridan, and by your direction, in view of the discontent among the Indian prisoners, who had asked for their wives and children, I deem it proper to request your further instructions in the premises." Copy, *ibid.* On Aug. 9, Babcock endorsed this letter. "The President directs that the order sending the women and children be for the present revoked." Copy, *ibid.* Related papers are *ibid.*

On July 19, Delano had written to USG. "I have the honor to present, herewith, a communication addressed to this Department, on the 3d ultimo, by the Honorable the Secretary of War, with accompanying report of Lieut: F. W. Mansfield, A. A. Q M., of the disposition made of the mules and ponies captured from hostile Indians; and requesting information 'as to the disposition the Interior Department desires to have made of the proceeds of the sale.['] I also present a report dated the 16th instant of the Commissioner of Indian Affairs, to whom the subject was, on the 4th ultimo, referred. The Commissioner intimates that if it be deemed advisable to commit the Qua-ha-da band of Comanches or any number of the captured Indians to the charge of the Military as recommended by Col. McKenzie, the use of the funds as proposed would be proper; but if, the control of the Indians is to remain, as at present, with the Civil authorities, the proceeds of the sale of the stock should be used for the benefit of the Indians who are to be placed on the Quapaw reservation, and should be turned over to the Agent of the captured Indians at said reservation. I respectfully invite your attention to the subject, and solicit your advice and direction in the premises. A return of the papers is requested." Copy, *ibid.* On July 24, Levi P. Luckey endorsed these papers to Delano. "The recommendations of the Secretary of the Interior are approved—viz—If the Indians or a portion of them are transferred to the military force—the money may be used by the military Commander. If they are turned over to an Indian Agent, the money may be transferred to him for support of the Indians." Copy, *ibid.* See Henry T. Crosby, chief clerk, War Dept., to Delano, Aug. 6, 1875, copy, *ibid.*, RG 107, Letters Sent, Military Affairs.

On March 14, 1876, Bishop Henry B. Whipple, St. Augustine, wrote to USG. "Personal . . . I have been at this place for my health and have been much interested in the Indian prisoners at Fort Marion   You are aware that they are Chiefs & Soldiers of the Comanches, Kiowas, Cheyennes & Arapahoes. I cannot speak too highly of the wisdom and kindness of the officers who have them in charge—Capt Pratt who is their immediate officer, is perfectly acquainted with Indian character, very firm and decided, & yet with a heart keenly alive to those obligations which demand that we shall give to these poor heathen christian civilization   General Dent who is in command of the post seconds every good work with all the weight of his authority—They have done much to solve the question 'what shall we do with hostile Indians'? The Indians came here sullen & defiant—One committed suicide on his way here—all were brought in irons—as soon as they arrived the Indians had their hair cut—they were uniformed & drilled as soldiers. They were taught lifes' great lesson 'to obey.'   a school was opened—some noble Christian Women volunteered as teachers. The Indians have made good progress in learning to read & write. They have been taught the Lords prayer & sing some christian hyms very sweetly—They have non commissioned officers of their own people, act as sentinels in charge of the fort, go into town to attend church, and I doubt if there is a garison in the land where the Soldiers are more obedient & circumspect—When you remember that a few months ago these men were engaged in war, and in their blind hatred for real or fancied wrongs murdering women & children, it touches the heart to see them sitting at the feet of women as docile children—I am sure that when they go back to their people they will be leaders in the work of Civilization—A portion of these chiefs & and headmen are old men & since they came have done all they could to advise & council the young men right—They are pining for their homes & I fear another summer here might prove fatal—They show in every way that a human being can show that they have learned the lesson—& I am confidant that it would be wise to exercise executive clemency towards them—It will be better to select out some of the older men of each tribe and send them home first, with the understanding that if their people cease war, all will be released—If you should authorize General Dent and Capt Pratt to select such persons, they would act wisely and such clemency would offer a still greater incentive to those who remain—I fear that if this is not done, some like Nemmick will pine & die during this summer and the effect of it prove very disastrous— I have been in constant intercourse with these Indians during my stay here, have preached to them regularly and often conversed with them—I have not the slightest doubt of the propriety and the wisdom of this act of mercy to these old men—I believe it will do great good—Genl Dent can readily find a proper person to go with them—Mr Fox the interpreter ought to remain here—He is an excellent interpreter speaks also the sign language perfectly—He deserves great credit for his faithful cooperation with the officers—He is one of those men who ought to be retained in the service—Pardon this long letter—I have never before asked the pardon of an Indian, but my convictions are so strong as to the propriety & wisdom of this, I do respectfully ask the priviledge of presenting these facts to you—Assuring you of my high regard . . ." ALS, *ibid.*, RG 94, Letters Received, 1618 1876.

On March 15, Lt. Col. Frederick T. Dent, St. Augustine, wrote to USG. "I transmitt herewith a letter from Bishop Whipple sudgesting that the time has come when it would be good policy to exercise clemency toward some few of each tribe of the Indian prisoners now here—All of these Indians have behaved well they are tractable obedient docile shewing great eagerness to learn and in many cases an aptitude simply surprisin[g] they are no longer prisoners save to themselves the guard at the Fort is composed entirely of Indians and in no case have they failed in alertness or reliability—I do think to pursue the course indicated above [is] a simple act of mercy toward some of the old men and in the event of a war with the Sioux the presence of such men as Minimic and Howling Wolf with the Cheyennes. Black Horse with the Comanches and others from the different tribes represented by the prisoners now here being sent home to their people would have a restraing influence on those tri[bes] and prevent their joining the Sioux. may I request speedy action one way or the other in this matter as time is important" ALS, *ibid.* On March 30, Sherman endorsed these letters to Secretary of War Alphonso Taft "with an expression of regret that I do not agree with Bishop Whipple & Genl Dent as to the policy of pardoning *now* a few of the Indians now confined at Fort Marion Fla. They have made good progress in the right direction and if kept in a Body, can safely be returned to their people at Fort Sill *in a body*, to form the nucleus for the organization and Subjugation of these tribes" AES, *ibid.* On April 5, Taft wrote to Whipple concurring in Sherman's views. LS (press), *ibid.* See *New York Tribune*, April 1, 1876.

On June 23, Stumbling Bear and twenty-three others, Kiowa and Comanche Agency, Indian Territory, petitioned USG. "As children look up to their real father, and feel a freedom to bring their matters of grievance and objects of desire before his notice, so we feel towards you, believing your ears will not be shut against us, or our petitions, unnoticed or unheeded cast aside as unworthy of consideration. Some of us have had the privilege of looking into your face, and holding you by the hand, and all believe you to have a heart warm and generous towards all your children, of whatever color they may be. We know too, that you are the Chief of a great people, a powerful people who cannot afford to be ungenerous or unjust towards the unfortunate and uneducated remnant of those who once held undisputed sway of all the lands, over which you now hold control. For generations it has been our custom to live upon the plains; each generation has educated the succeeding one, in the ways peculiar to our race, ignorant of White man's laws and governed only by our own, we have regarded as worthy of commendation many acts which white man's laws visit with punishment According to our laws in former years, those only who were regarded as brave and daring, were elevated to position and power among us. The minds of the children were educated by listening to the tales of daring adventure, as told around our Camp fires, to desire similar distinction for themselves. Is it any wonder that they should be led out to commit deeds which are in violation of white men's laws? But with us these things are passing away—Changes have taken place; we have given our children to go to school, many of them are now reading in the white mans books, and will soon obtain a knowledge of his laws and ways. We, too, have cast aside our swords and spears, have taken the plow's instead, and with it by our own labor, have plowed and planted many acres of corn. Last year and this year we have worked hard, believing that by so doing, we would not only be rewarded with crops, but would please our Great Father by doing what he desired us to. For a long time now we have been encamped near our Agent and have tried very hard to do as he has asked us to, and we believe he will bear us out in the assertion, that we have not in any way violated good faith and loyalty to the requirements which have been made of us. We have listened eagerly with our ears open towards Washington and at all times have been ready to do quietly, what he might require of us. Two years ago misfortunes overtook us. Some of our people voluntarily and others forced by circumstances beyond their control, were placed in hostile position to the laws of the Government; besides those unwillingly in the hostile class, there were many of us who remained near the Agency loyal and true to good order, during all the troubles. Of the eleven hundred Kiowas, the enrolment of our names showed only about two hundred and seventy men, women and children as classed among the disloyal. In compliance with your requirements, the loyal of us, who could came in and encamped near the Agency, and gave many of our young men to act as scouts for the military. While we were so encamped, hundreds of our ponies were stolen by some of our Fathers white children, who were as disloyal to good laws and order as any of our people, but notwithstanding our losses in property were very great, in some instances all we had, reducing us to poverty, our hearts have not grown weary or tired in well doing neither have we regretted that we did not cast aside, but listened to the talks of our great Father, as they come down to us through his Agents, believing that in good time he would see that our wrongs were righted, and our loyalty to his requirements appreciated. At the close of the troubles to which we have referred, a large number of our people were taken as prisoners to a different part of the country, and are now held in confinement there. They were taken without any trial and, as we believe in some instances, with very partial investigations and without cause. One of them 'White Horse' Kiowa, was regularly enrolled among the loyal, and while encamped near the Agency, without having taken any part in the disloyal acts of his people, and under the assurance of the enrolling officers that he would not be disturbed for the past, or acts previous to 1874, but would be protected, was arrested and sent away as a prisoner. Our people are anxiously waiting and watching for the return of our kindred, towards whom our feelings of attachment are as strong as those of the white man for his kindred, and we now humbly and respectfully ask of our Great Father that he will cause them to be returned to us, promising him, that we will in every way maintain our loyalty and in all things in which we are able, do just as he asks us to; that we will use all our power and influence to keep every member of our tribe from doing wrong or violating the law, and should any disregard it and violate our promises, we will not object, but render assistance for his arrest and punishment. Trusting our humble petition will be heard in a favorable light . . ." Copy, DNA, RG 94, Letters Received, 2815 1874. See Arrell Morgan Gibson, "The St. Augustine Prisoners," *Red River Valley Historical Review*, III, 2 (Spring, 1978), 259–70.

To Fitz John Porter

[*Feb., 1875*]

Your appeal, ~~Dated~~ dated Oct. 28th 1875[4,] reached me on the 10th inst. I have not had [time]   I had before been made aware of the *possible* existence of such an appeal through an unfriendly press—or an unfriendly portion of the press—

Your letter makes a demand on me upon grounds which I cannot admit. First; you had about three years of the administration under which your trial occured to appeal to if any injustice had been done you: you had four years of another Administration preceeding ~~mine~~, my first inauguration, as president, in which to make your appeal: and if a rehearing is as imperitive a right as you claim I do not see why you did not get it then.

Second; you sight insubordination and conduct on the part of your former military commander towards the then president of the United States as justification for your course. You do not do this directly but by implication. I do not hesitate to say that had any subordinate of mine, in the trials the country was going through at the date the dispatches from which you quote were sent, had been sent to me, occupying the position Mr. Lincoln did, the command of that Gen.l would not have continued one moment beyond the time necessary to communicate his dismissal. That dismissal would have been accompanied by an order of arrest, for trial. Possibly this might have been accompanied by a resistince on the part of some *officers* to a carrying out of the decree. In fact I think your letter demonstrates the fact that it would. But the rank and file were patriotic, brave, true and fighting for a principle which now I am convinced you had forgotten. I sincerely hope that there were but few who were only serving men. I will consult with my Cabinet, and gentlemen in whos sence of justice I have confidence as to whether a re-hearing can be granted, and as to whether the developed facts would justify such a rehearing. I must say however that your letter of the 28th of October 1874—which only reached me Feb.y 10th 1875, though commented on largely by the public press before—does not impress me favorably, and I do not believe that it was the work of your hand, nor that your uninfluenced judgement would have dictated it. But you are responsible and must take the consequences of it.

There is much in your letter to take exception to, but I will limit myself to what is here stated; adding only that if you have been wronged I will take all legal methods of ascertaing the facts, and will correct the wrongs so far as lay in my power.

GEN. FITZ JOHN PORTER.

ADf (bracketed material not in USG's hand), Mrs. Paul E. Ruestow, Jacksonville, Fla. On Oct. 28, 1874, Fitz John Porter, Morristown, N. J., wrote at length to USG. "Respectfully, but very urgently, I renew my appeal to you to order a review of my case. . . . The campaign of 1862, on the peninsula, resulted in one of the common controversies between minister at war, and general in the field. After the battles before Richmond, General McClellan charged his failure to capture Richmond, and all its momentous consequences, to the interference and mismanagement of the War Department. He wrote to Secretary Stanton 'if I save this army no thanks to you, or any one at Washington.' When soon after, Pope lost the great battle at Manassas, Mr. Stanton, in turn, charged the fatal result on Mc-Clellan; in not getting the necessary supplies and reinforcements to Pope. . . . Mr. Lincoln thought it necessary, instead of dismissing McClellan, to remove Pope, and restore Mc-Clellan to the command of the army. . . . Stanton's charge and remedy against McClellan had been disposed of by the necessity for him at the time, and his subsequent victorious campaign. But Pope looked for his defence, and the defence of the administration, in the same direction Mr. Stanton had looked. He said the troops sent him from McClellan's army of the Potomac 'wouldn't fight.' I commanded a corps of that army in his battle. The severest fighting and heaviest loss of the battle fell upon these troops and especially upon my corps; they led in the attack; after the battle they held the post of honor and danger; to cover the retreat: which was successfully accomplished until his army was brought within the defences of Washington. Pope did not see a case against me, until the War Department exhibited to him my telegrams warning the government of his fatal incapacity. 'Then'— he said 'his eyes were opened.' The general accusations against 'McClellan's troops,' were converted into specific charges against me, who had commanded the principal corps of his army in Pope's campaign. . . ." *SED*, 46-1-37, part 1, pp. 527, 529. See letter to John Pope, May 9, 1874. On Aug. 14 and Sept. 2, 1874, on behalf of their state legislatures, Governors James A. Weston of N. J. and John F. Hartranft of Pa. forwarded resolutions to USG urging that the charges against Porter be reexamined. Copies, DLC-Fitz John Porter. *SED*, 46-1-37, part 1, pp. 546–47. On Aug. 26, Fisher A. Baker and Charles H. Drew, formerly 18th Mass., addressed a similar request to USG. *Ibid.*, p. 549.

On March 26, Secretary of State Hamilton Fish wrote in his diary after a cabinet meeting. "Genl Belknap read a letter from Genl John Pope suggesting that the President ought to make an answer to Fitz John Porters application for a rehearing in his case and settle it. This led to considerable discussion   The President said that he intended to examine into the matter and dispose of it now that congress had adgd; he said that he had suggested to the Secretary of War the adviseability of taking the advice of the Atty General 1st Whether an investigation could now be made   2d Whether good grounds existed. The Atty Genl suggested that Judge Holt should do it—and report   The President said that he thought he ought not to write a letter with his conclusions himself as he might be applied to in all cases. He said that some time since Genl McClellan and Gov (now Senator) Randolph came to him with a pamphlet and asked his personal examination. He said he promised to examine it; that before that time he had no idea that the officers in the Army of the Potomac were hostile to Pope and preferred to be beaten than to be commanded by him and that Porter had been caught impressing them and on reading the pamphlet he could not see why he had not been shot. He read some conclusions to which he said he had hastily arrived in reading this last pamphlet   Bristow suggested that the President had better say what he now said   Jewell thought it might not be wise to say anything, but in hearing the Presidents strong opinions changed his mind   The general opinion was against Porter" DLC-Hamilton Fish. On March 28, Secretary of War William W. Belknap wrote a memorandum. "The foregoing statement telegraphed to the 'Tribune' is not true. The subject of F. J. Porter's application for a rehearing was discussed in Cabinet, Friday March 26th—but with no final decision save a direction from the President to myself to furnish him with a statement of the case, including a synopsis of the so-called new testimony, in order that he might come to a conclusion as to Gen'l. Porter's application, and he suggested, ~~that~~ the applications & statements of Gen'l. Porter & his friends as well as all the papers in the case be referred to the Judge Advocate General for report, which course will be pursued & the papers returned to the President for his examination & action. The President did say that an examination of Gen'l. Porter's pamphlet gave him a very strong inclination to regard him as properly convicted. I did not make the remark above attributed to me in the 'Tribune's' special. What I did say was this—Gen'l. Porter 'seems to take it for granted that upon a re-investigation of his case he would be acquitted. Although he cannot properly or legally be tried again, it is not probable, that, (while he desires to be reinstated, if upon examination he should be deemed innocent) he would consent to be shot, should he be deemed guilty.' I stated also that I came to Washington in 1869, with an impression upon my mind that Gen'l. Porter had been badly treated, that the first official paper which was placed in my hands for examination was Porter's appeal to the President, dated June 10, 1869, & that a perusal of this paper went far toward convincing me that he was properly convicted: that a few weeks afterwards Gov. Randolph and Admiral Porter called to see me concerning the case and that I had informed them that after reading General Porter's pamphlet, I could not, on account of the impression it gave me of his guilt, recommend his restoration. . . . P. S. On March 30th I alluded, in Cabinet meeting to the publication in the 'Tribune' referred to above. Mr. Jewell stated that he gave the information to a gentleman, but he could not remember to whom, although Sec'y. Bristow, after Cabinet meeting informed me that Gov. Jewell had informed him, before, that he had informed Mr. Ramsdell, the correspondent of the 'Tribune.'" ADS, DNA, RG 94, Letters Received, R574 1867. Clippings and related papers are *ibid.*

On May 28, Fish recorded in his diary. "The Secty of War reads a long report on the subject of Fitz John Porter's application for a board to review the decission of the Court Martial by which he was tried: Porter appeals for this on the ground of subsequent discovered evidence obtained from the official reports of the confederates; his application and accompanying papers had been referred by the President to the Secretary of War for examination and for the looking into the newly discovered evidence. It was referred to Judge Advocate General Holt who represented to the Secretary of War that he had been so much criticised for his conduct in connection with the trial that he would prefer not to be called on to report, therefore the case had been referred to Genl Dunn the Assist Judge Advocate General who had made a very elaborate investigation and report from which it appears that the new testimony adduced does not conflict with that before the court but is supposed on the contrary to strengthen the grounds on which Porter was charged with having failed of duty; from the report there would seem to be no ground for criticism of the verdict of the court, or for any action by the President   It is evident that a new trial cannot be had & the question is raised whether any answer should be made to Porters printed appeal to the President. The general opinion is that no reply should be made, but to await till his friends bring the matter before congress" DLC-Hamilton Fish. See letter to Fitz John Porter, Sept. 27, 1881.

To House of Representatives

———

To The House of Representatives:

House Bill No 3341, is herewith returned without my approval for the reasons; first, that it appropriates from the treasury a large sum of money at a time when the revenue is insufficient for current wants and this proposed further drain on the treasury. The issue of bonds authorized by this bill to a very large and indefinite amount would seriously embarrass the refunding operations now progressing whereby the interest of the bonded debt of the United States is being largely reduced. Second, I do not believe that any considerable portion of the ex-soldiers who it is supposed will be the beneficiaries of this appropriation are applicants for it, but, rather it would result more in a measure for the relief of claim agents and middlemen who would intervene to collect or discount the bounties granted by it. The passage of this bill at this time is inconsistent with the measures of economy now demanded by the necessities of the country.

U. S. GRANT

WASHINGTON, MARCH 3D 1875

DS, Herman Blum, Philadelphia, Pa. On March 4 and 5, 1875, Secretary of State Hamilton Fish recorded in his diary. "Bristow tells me that the President had prepared a veto of the Bounty Bill which he has brought in his pocket for the purpose of use in case the bill passes   This morning again we are all present at the Capitol again at nine oclock; at about half after eleven oclock the Bounty Bill was brought to the President   He calls the members of the Cabinet together (the room being full of other persons) and reads the draft which he had prepared. No objection is expressed by any member to the bill failing to become a law   The President asks whether it be better to let the bill fail without his signature or to send in a veto, and if so whether the paper he had read met our approval   Appealing to me first I say I think decidedly an expression of opinion is better than a silent defeat of the Bill suggesting however that an additional objection to the bill may be presented on account of the provision authorizing the raising of additional money by the Government to meet the requirements of the Bill   Bristow cordiall endorsed this suggestion and no dissent is made either to the veto or to the argument proposed   The President hands his draft to Bristow for alteration he Bristow called me in consultation and on his knee wrote the additional lines   The message was then copied, there being but 12 minutes from the time they began it   The President signed it and called to Babcock to take it to the House; Babcock remonstrated saying you are making a terrible mistake—the President replied quietly I have signed this and wish it to go to the House   Babcock left taking with him only the last sheet of the message and returning it was found that he had delivered it to the Senate instead of to the House in which place the Bill originated   Bristow tells me that on his return Babcock claimed that he had left the first sheet with him, whereas he had handed both together to Babcock   The lateness of the hour and the hurry were evidently the causes of this mistake. P. S—Since writing this sentence I have reason to reconsider that opinion expressed & to think that the lateness of the hour &c only was availed of, as a plausible excuse for a deliberate design to suppress the veto—" "The misrepresentation which appeared in the papers of this morning (copy from the Chronicle hereunto annexed) with regard to the Bounty Bill were discussed and met with universal condemnation. Bristow said that Logan had seen him this morning and was quite indignant at the idea that the Bill had been defeated by such means as the Chronicle alledged but was quite content when told that the President entertained views that the condition of the Treasury did not allow such large expendatures and hence had used his veto   The President wished it understood that he had vetoed it although the veto had not reached the House before its adjournment; and intimates that he will give the text to the press. Bristow further states that Logan told him that he knew it was vetoed as he had seen the President seign the veto message" DLC-Hamilton Fish. The attached clipping chronicled "the failure of the bill to equalize the bounty of soldiers" and pointed to U.S. Senator John A. Logan of Ill. as misrepresenting the action of the House and Senate conference committee. *Ibid.* On March 3, the Senate had tabled the conference report for a bill providing bounty money to eligible soldiers or their survivors, a step that should have prevented the bill from coming before USG. See *CR*, 43–2, 1256–65, 2037–50, 2205–6, 2264–65; *HRC*, 44-1-239, 45-2-1000; Mary R. Dearing, *Veterans in Politics: The Story of the G. A. R.* (Baton Rouge, 1952), pp. 219–20.

On March 4, Levi P. Morton, New York City, telegraphed to USG. "Your veto of the bounty bill gives very great satisfaction in this neighborhood," Telegram received, DLC-USG, IB. On the same day, U.S. Senator George F. Edmunds of Vt. wrote to USG. "I cannot let the day go by without taking the liberty to thank and congratulate you for your brave and noble message on the 'Bounty Bill.' That Ruler will receive the gratitude of the people, who preserves them from the schemes of demagogues." ALS, USG 3.

On March 16, Samuel Bard, postmaster, Atlanta, wrote to USG. "A practical Sug-[g]eston or two as to matters in [t]his Section of the County may not [b]e out of Place. I call your attention [t]o the fact, that we have may of your appointees, who are not in Sympathy with your 'Southern Policy.' I am advised that Col. P. W. Perry 'Supervisor of Int. Rev,' for this 'District,' is in full accord with Mr Blaine. I have never *knowingly* mislead you, and give this as one instance out of *many*. [T]he frinds of Wilson and Blaine [ar]e at work in evy Southern State. [I] tell you this as a duty, so that [y]ou may govern youself accord[i]ngly. He that is not for you, [(]*now*) is against you. It is due your 'Adminstration' that all places of trust shuld be filled by open outspoken frinds—Not men who will Smile to your face and Stab you in the back. *Systematic determined action* is necessary here. 'Weak-Kneed' miscreants should not be continued on guard—" ALS, *ibid.* A note from Bard dated March 17 disparaging Vice President Henry Wilson and a clipping describing Wilson's opposition to USG's veto message on the bounty bill are *ibid.*

Order

March 9th 1875.

In order to carry out the provisions of the 5th section of the act of Congress entitled "an act making appropriations for sundry civil expenses of the Government for the fiscal year ending June 30th 1876, and for other purposes," approved March 3d 1875, the Board heretofore appointed to take charge of the articles and materials to be exhibited by the several Executive Departments, the Smithsonian

Institution and the Agricultural Department at the International Exhibition of 1876, is hereby continued under the following regulations and distribution of duties, viz:—

The funds appropriated by the above named section will be drawn from the Treasury upon the requisition of the Chairman of the Board, and to be disbursed as are other public moneys, under the existing laws relating to disbursing officers.

An officer of the Army will be detailed by the Secretary of War as disbursing officer of the Board.

Each representative of an Executive Department, and the representative of the Smithsonian Institution, of the Agricultural Department and the U. S. Commissioner of Food-Fishes, will have charge of the matters pertaining to his respective Department, subject to the general advisement of the Board; and all bills will be paid by the disbursing officer upon vouchers certified by such representative and countersigned by the Chairman of the Board.

The disbursing officer will render monthly accounts current of all advances to and disbursements by him to the First Auditor of the Treasury, for audit and settlement in the same manner as are other accounts of disbursing officers of the Government.

Each representative will be held responsible to the head of his respective Department for all public property of the United States furnished by the head of such Department or otherwise coming to his hands for the purposes of the Exhibition, and will render proper accounts of the same to such head of Department until the property is returned.

U. S. GRANT
President U. S.

DS, DNA, RG 56, Records Relating to Expositions. On March 3, 1875, USG signed a bill appropriating $505,000 for executive dept. exhibits at the Centennial Exhibition. *U.S. Statutes at Large*, XVIII, part 3, p. 400. USG had recommended this appropriation. See messages to House of Representatives, Jan. 20, 1875, March 27, 1876.

On March 11, Maj. Stephen C. Lyford, chairman, wrote to USG recommending William A. De Caindry, War Dept. clerk, as secretary to the Board on U.S. Executive Depts. at the Centennial Exhibition. LS (press), DNA, RG 56, Records Relating to Expositions.

To Jerome B. Chaffee

March 13th 1875.

DEAR SIR.

Your favor of yesterday is received by me with much pleasure, and I accept it in the same spirit in which it is written. From the date of my first visit to Colorado to the present I have believed that the Territory had the Mineral and Agricultural resources to make it a populous and prosperous state, and an intelligent and energetic population calculated to develop these resources and to maintain republican government. I sincerely hope that all strife in the embrio state may cease, and confidently believe it will.

Yours truly
U. S. GRANT.

HON. J. B. CHAFFEE

Copy, DLC-USG, II, 2. Born in 1825 in N. Y., Jerome B. Chaffee engaged in banking and real estate and moved to Colorado Territory in 1860. Active in mining and a founder of Denver, Chaffee served in the territorial legislature and as U.S. Delegate (1871–75). In 1875, Chaffee wrote to USG defending himself against charges of intemperate and improper expressions. William Evarts Benjamin, Catalogue No. 42, March, 1892, p. 6.

On March 29, 1875, Henry C. Alleman, U.S. attorney, Colorado Territory, wrote to USG. "I have the honor to address Your Excellency and beg pardon for this apparent presumption, which I think, the necessity of the occasion fully justifies. Hon. J. B. Chaffee is using his utmost exertion to have me removed, and for this purpose, is operating through Senator Harvey of Kansas. The object of Mr. Chaffee in trying to get rid of me, is purely selfish. I am prosecuting his partner—D. H. Moffat Jr.—for defrauding the government of some five thousand acres of land in the Las Animas District, and I filed a statement in Court of what I expect to prove by Mr. Chaffee, as a witness, at the June term of Court. Mr. Chaffee is in a very unpleasant dilemma. He will either be compelled to commit Perjury, or his testimony will convict his partner. He wishes to avoid being a witness in order to save his chances for U. S. Senator; but as the prosecuting officer of the government, with my knowledge of the importance of the evidence which he can give, I cannot agree to let him off. Criminal Informations and Bills in Equity are pending against Mr. Moffat and others, as the result of my instructions from the Attorney General, to prosecute the Land grabs, and bring the guilty parties to justice. These cases will be tried in June next. If Mr. Chaffee succeeds in having me removed, it will be heralded as a repudiation by the government of my official acts in the premises, and an endorsement of the rascalities of the land thieves in this Territory. Mr. Chaffee pursues me because I did my duty in carrying out the instructions of the government, and refused to be bribed by the corrupt ring of which Mr. Chaffee is the reputed and recognized head and leader. If I failed to honestly discharge my whole official duty, I should be promptly removed. If I have continued to discharge my official duties honestly and faithfully; but for the sake of harmony, criminal proceedings should be dropped for political effect, then I should be transferred to some other place. If the Administration sustains my official course, then I should be retained. Or if I did my full duty, and nothing but my duty; but the interests of the government would be better served by sending a stranger to fill my place, then, as a reward for duty well and faithfully performed, I should be promoted. I am entirely willing to accommodate myself to Your Excellency's own good judgment. If my resignation is wanted, it shall be promptly forwarded; which will necessitate my speedy return to Philadelphia, be a great loss to me professionally, and an expense, for travel, of some five hundred dollars, which I cannot very well afford. If Your Excellency concludes that the appointment of another in my stead would aid the Administration in making Colorado a Republican State, by uniting the Chaffee element with the Republican party,—although I have given entire satisfaction to the government,—then, I will not object to be transferred to an equally important position in Washington or Philadelphia, or a Judgeship in Utah, where coming changes are reported." ALS, DNA, RG 60, Letters Received, Colorado Territory. Alleman enclosed a court document describing Chaffee's expected testimony in the upcoming trial. Copy, *ibid.* See letter to Edward M. McCook, Feb. 5, 1875. For the Las Animas land claim, see Orville E. Babcock to Attorney Gen. Edwards Pierrepont, May 25, 1875, ES, DNA, RG 60, Letters from the President; Pierrepont to USG, May 15, 1876, copy, *ibid.*, Opinions. *Official Opinions of the Attorneys-General*, XV, 94–104.

On May 14, 1875, Attorney Gen. George H. Williams wrote to Secretary of the Interior Columbus Delano. "I have the honor to enclose a copy of a letter addressed to the President by Mr. J. B. Chaffee and a copy of a resolution adopted by the Republican Central Committee of Colorado, asking the removal of the District Attorney now Secretary of that Territory. As the Secretary is an officer under the jurisdiction of your Department, I submit these copies for your information and such action as you may deem advisable." Copy, DNA, RG 60, Letters Sent to Executive Officers. Alleman did not serve as secretary, Colorado Territory.

On May 15, Governor John L. Routt of Colorado Territory wrote to USG. "During my recent illness, Mr Chaffee read to me a letter which he had written to you, relative to a change in the U. S. District Attorney's Office for this Territory; in which I fully concur. I have been—since my arrival here—importuned almost daily, to ask for a change in that Office—Complaints come from all parts of the Territory against Mr Alleman's management of the Office. In some localities—the feeling is so intensely bitter—that it is difficult to secure a conviction before a jury, for the most flagrant violations of law. I have listened patiently to these complaints, and declined to make any recommendation in the case, until I had taken ample time to fully acquaint myself as to whether there was a just cause for this universal opposition—After carefully considering the case in the light of the facts, I am convinced, that it is absolutely necessary for the interests of the public service, that a change should be made at an early day—This is one of the most important positions in the Territory,—and should be filled by a thoroughly competent *Lawyer*—who would discharge the duties of the Office, in a manner calculated to reflect credit to the Government, and your administration, and who would command the confidence and respect of the people. Should you, upon this statement of facts, agree with me—that a change aught to be made, I would respectfully recommend to your favorable consideration Mr E. O. Wolcott—of Georgetown, as a suitable person for the position. Mr Wolcott is a young lawyer—of much promise,—a good *Republican*, and his appointment would give general satisfaction, he being a citizen of the Territory—Although the people will be satisfied with any one you may be pleased to appoint, as they are with the U. S. Judge's and Marshal, which you recently sent us—Hoping that this recommendation will meet with your approval—. . ." LS, *ibid.*, Letters Received, Colorado Territory.

On May 20, Charles C. Tompkins, U.S. marshal, Colorado Territory, wrote to USG.

"From letters rec'd from Washington City, I am credibly informed that there is a movement on foot, looking to the removal of H C Alleman, U S Dis't Att'y, and that Jerome B Chaffe, & one J C Wilson, Chairman Rep' Com'te, charge him with incapacity & dishonesty. They also charge him with being distasteful to the Rep Party, in this Terr'. My official relations with the U S Dis't Att'y, are neccessarily of an intimate character,—we meet daily—I have seen much of him, & *know* his official actions, & am free to state that all charges of inefficiency & dishonesty, are *wholly*, & *entirely without foundation*. I also assert that the opposition to the U S Dis't Att'y has been confined almost entirely to the 'Ring', which he has been, & is now, bravely fighting for glaring & well known frauds upon the Government, (& consequently whose interests can best be subserved by his removal). Col Alleman is industrious & untireing in his efforts to protect the interests of the Gov't, & his name is a terror to evil-doers. His removal would be of great pecuniary loss to the Gov't, no advantage, (upon the contrary really a serious disadvantage), to the success of the *true* Republican Party in this Terr'; & at same time would give strength to an element here, claiming to be Republican, but *openly, avowedly, & notoriously; bitter* and *implacable enemies*, of your Administration. In writing this letter I am actuated by my allegiance to the Republican Party, as well as a duty, I consider I owe your Administration. I expect to go East for my family in July, (after the spring term of the Courts are over), & will then go to see you. With sentiments of the most profound respect . . ." ALS, *ibid.*

On June 14, Alleman, Pueblo, wrote to USG. "I have the honor to state, that during the past week, I tried the case of the United States against David H. Moffat Jr., Irving W. Stanton and Charles A. Cook, for Conspiracy. This is the celebrated Las Animas land grab case. Mr. Stanton was Register, and Mr. Cook Receiver of the U. S. Land Office at Pueblo, and for corruption and irregularities in their offices, as shown by Mr. Robinson's report, they were removed upwards of a year ago. Mr. Moffat—the partner of Mr. Chaffee—as capitalist, furnished the money, obtained through fraud possession of U. S. patents, and now claims title to, and has possession of some five thousand acres of land in the Las Animas land grant, obtained through fraudulent proofs of right of pre-emption. About fifteen months ago, you instructed me, and the Attorney General ordered me, to prosecute the offenders of the law in defrauding the government of those lands in the Las Animas grant. In obedience to said instructions and orders, I prosecuted the matter before the U. S. Grand Jury and had bills of indictment found at the June Court 1874. These cases were continued at the last December Court for the good and manifest reason that Judge Belford, who then temporarily held the Court, did so for the corrupt purpose of forcing the acquital of those defendants. Chief Justice Hallett presides at this term of Court, and retried the case. The defendants were ably represented by three of the best lawyers in Colorado, who actively engaged in the trial, while other Attorneys assisted as advisory counsel. I, alone, represented the government, and had no assistance whatever. The defense fought with unprecedented personality and acrimony. The vilest and most malignant abuse was heaped upon me by counsel, in order to distract the attention of the jury from enormities of the offenses, and prejudice them against me as the malicious representative of a persecuting government. They even went so far as to assure the jury that I would certainly be removed for prosecuting those defendants, and this case. With all their threats, abuse and contumely, they failed to swerve me from my path of duty, or decrease my energy or vigilance in this prosecution. Hon. J. B. Chaffee was called as a witness for the government, and after remaining here three days, suddenly left the Court House, on learning that he was about to be called upon the witness-stand, and took the cars for Denver. When his time as a witness arrived, I called him, and learning of his *escape*, I took out an attachment for him, and he was brought back. But he appeared singularly deficient in memory and facts, and evidently committed wilful and deliberate perjury to save his friend Moffat, and his own

reputation. With all the efforts and appliances of the 'ring,' the jury cannot be forced to acquit the defendants. The jury have already been out upwards of forty-eight hours, and just
informed the Court that it will be impossible for them to agree. They will likely be discharged to-day for disagreement, and the case will be for trial again next December. Moffat and his friends have too much money to warrant a conviction of these defendants in this
Country, and the consequence is, a failure of the jury to agree. Every effort, honorable and
infamous, has been made to secure an acquital by this jury; but the integrity and vigilance
of Col. Tompkins, U. S. Marshal, who has the jury in charge, has been put to its severest
test, and he has been equal to the occasion, and proved himself an incorruptible and
efficient officer. Even the disagreement of the jury is a grand triumph. It proves that there
was probable cause for the prosecution, and evidence of guilt. The defendants are mortified
and their associates dispirited. The corruptions and infamies of these scoundrels have been
exposed, the 'ring' is now completely broken, and the honest peoples 'rejoice and are exceeding glad.' This prosecution will have a salutary effect in this Territory. It has virtually
ended the power of a once formidable 'ring.' I have an abiding conviction of having performed my duty, my whole duty and nothing but my duty in this vexatious matter, and yet
for prosecuting these 'ringsters,' Mr. Chaffee has demanded my removal. Since I have accomplished the glorious triumph of overpowering, and breaking up this gigantic and corrupt 'ring,' I am ready to retire, feeling that I have done a grand work, and in doing it,
withstood the temptations of money and influential power. I received a letter from the Attorney General one week ago, stating that you would accept my resignation, and that I
could forward the same at an early day. I immediately wrote him the status of my official
business, requesting him to name the day when my resignation should take effect, and not
jeopardize the interests of the government, as I did not want to embarrass my successor,
or injure government interests by hasty action. As soon as I receive his suggestion, I will
forward you my resignation, to take effect on the day designated by the Attorney General.
I did expect support, and think I am justly entitled to it, in carrying out the instructions
of yourself and the Attorney General; but as Mr. Chaffee has sworn that he would have me
removed,—bitter as he expresses himself against you and your administration,—I will not
complain here and now. I was in hopes, that if you would conclude to gratify Mr. Chaffee
by relieving me, you would transfer me to some other place, without being requested to
resign, to satisfy the revenge of an unrelenting and most unscrupulous foe. I take this occasion to earnestly renew my thanks to you for your kindness towards me. I will continue
to support most heartily your Administration, and will never cease to be your personal and
political friend, admirer and advocate." ALS, *ibid.*, Letters from the President. On June 16,
Wednesday, Alleman, Denver, wrote to USG. "I have the honor to report, in the case of the
United States against Irving W. Stanton, Charles A. Cook and David H. Moffat Jr.—indicted for Conspiracy to defraud the United States of patents to lands in the Las Animas
land grant, which was tried before the District Court at Pueblo last week;—that the jury
failed to agree, and were discharged by the Court, and the defendants were bound over for
their appearance at the next term of Court, when the case will again be tried. The defendants have made application for a change of venue, feeling that their chances for escape are
not altogether safe in the hands of Chief Justice Hallett. I will go to Pueblo on Friday and
argue this motion on Saturday. If the defendants can secure a change of venue (which really means a change of Judges), *and get rid of me*, they feel that they will have a better
chance for success at the next trial. I took the liberty of writing you on Monday from
Pueblo in this matter, and write you again to-day, believing that you feel a decided interest in this case, and will be glad to know the result of the trial. The disagreement of the
jury is a glorious victory for the government, and I feel in it a personal and official triumph.
It is a complete vindication of my course in pursuing and prosecuting those offenders of

the law. On the opposite page, please find two printed slips, which I cut from the 'Pueblo Chieftan,' a daily paper, of the issue of Monday and Tuesday last. This newspaper is in the interest of the land-grab-outfit, and a word of kindness or praise of me has only been extorted from them by the force of decided public opinion. The paper is hostile to me. The defendants and their friends are exceedingly despondent." ALS, *ibid.*, Letters Received, Colorado Territory. The clippings are *ibid.* On June 21, Alleman wrote to Babcock that the change of venue motion had been rejected. ALS, *ibid.*

On July 3, Alleman wrote to USG resigning his office, effective July 20. ALS, *ibid.* On July 2, Pierrepont had written to USG, Long Branch. "Hon. Wm A. Phillips wishes me to advise you that he has filed an application in favor of J. G. Nohlen of Kansas, recommended by several for district attorney at Denver." Copy, *ibid.*, Letters Sent to Executive Officers. On Dec. 15, USG nominated Charles D. Bradley to replace Alleman. On Aug. 9, 1876, U.S. Senator Frederick T. Frelinghuysen of N. J. wrote to USG. "Charles D. Bradley was the District Attorney of the Territory of Colorado and has been suspended by the nomination of another person for that office since Colorado became a State. Mr. Bradley is the brother of Mr. Justice Bradley. He is a good lawyer, a man of superior intellect and of good character. He may not understand politics so as to have a fair chance in a new country, but should you appoint him District Judge I do not think you would regret it; and I feel confident that he would fill the office with credit to himself, and to the satisfaction of the bar and litigants in the Court." LS, *ibid.*, Records Relating to Appointments. On Nov. 28, Bradley, Denver, wrote to USG seeking reappointment as U.S. attorney, Colo. ALS, *ibid.* Chaffee and two others favorably endorsed this letter. AES (undated), *ibid.* On Jan. 9, 1877, USG nominated Westbrook S. Decker as U.S. attorney, Colo.

On Oct. 13, 1875, Tompkins had written to USG. "Since you left Denver, I have seen Col John W Jenkins & incidentally asked him, how he would like to assist in the prosecution of the U S cases in this Terr; his reply was that he would prefer that to any appointment that the President could give him at this time. This letter is suggested by a question, asked by yourself at the last interview I had with you. As I stated at the time, Col Jenkins is eminently qualified, & I have the most perfect confidence in his honesty, & I believe he would perform his duty well, & acceptably to the Gov't. As the time for the trial of the West Las Animas land cases, is set for December, it will require much preperation upon the part of the law officers of the Gov't, to be ready by that time as the defendants have employed the finest array of legal talent in the Terr, & they will have the advantage over the prosecution of familiarity with the case, gained by previous trials. I know it to be an exceedingly difficult case to manage, one that will require much study, & preperation; & in view of these facts, I respectfully suggest that in the event the Gov't considers this case of sufficently grave importance to justify employing competent counsel, to conduct the prosecution, that it be done at an early day, & that it be some gentleman, not *easily intimidated nor averse nor afraid to do his duty*, though the heavens should fall. Hope your trip to Washington was in every respect pleasant. With sentiments of the most profound respect, . . ." ALS, *ibid.*, Letters from the President. On Oct. 22, USG approved this suggestion. E (on docket), *ibid.* On Dec. 9, USG nominated John Taffe as secretary, Colorado Territory, in place of John W. Jenkins.

On June 7, 1876, Jenkins, Denver, wrote to USG. "I learned a few days ago that charges had been made at the Department of Justice against me as to my conduct in the Shaffenburg cases   The charges were for drunkenness and general misconduct in the cases. Under ordinary circumstances I would not take notice of such charges, but in as much as I was given this employment on your Excellencies recommendation I have taken the trouble to refute the slanders on your account and that of my wife and children and not on my own. Judge Brazee sat in this court until the 25th of May when he changed with

Judge Hallett he taking Halletts place at Pueblo and Judg Hallett taking his place here so that I have all the time been under the eye of either one or the other of these two Judges— I enclose you the letter of Judge Brazee endorsed by Judge Hallett also by U S Atty Bradley. I also send you the letter of Gov Routt. who hering of these charges sent me this letter without my asking for it. If necessary I can get every member of the bar (except those engaged in the Shaffenburg cases) to endorse me both for ability and rectitude of purpose The truth is Mr President I have been offered the most enormous bribes only to let up in the Shaffenburg cases to the extent of allowing the cases to be continued for this term After a hard fight I have succeeded in getting one of the cases to trial   The Special agent of the Department of Justice, (Mr Forney) is no very good friend of mine but I believe he will tell the truth and I am willing to stand or fall by his report on my conduct in these cases   This letter is not written with much thought Mr President for the reason that my mind is entirely taken up with the case now on trial   I would be pleased if your Excellency would refer these letters to the Honorable Atty General" ALS, *ibid.* The enclosures are *ibid.* On Aug. 3, Tompkins wrote to USG. "Please accept my most grateful acknowledgements, for the very high compliment conferred upon me by my re-appointment, & rest assured that in the future, as in the past I shall endeavour to so conduct the office as to merit your favourable consideration. Please pardon a suggestion which I shall make; viz, that Mr P W Forney, who is in the First Auditors Office, & who was detailed as special Agent by the Dep't of Justice in the Shaffenberg cases, at both of the last terms of the Dis't Court, be again detailed for the same purpose, & that it be done *without delay*, that the case may be fully ready for trial, at the next term of Court, thus obviating a continuance, which would add very materially to the cost. In few words, this would result in a great saving to the Gov't. As a matter of economy it must be apparent. There is great anxiety manifested here as to whom you will appoint as Dis't Judge, many aspirants, all with friends, but to my *personal knowledge no one* more eminently qualified to fill the place with credit to the appointing power, & himself; and no one who has proven himself a more consistent, & true friend of your Administration, & yrself personally than Judge Andrew W Brazee at this time Judge of the First Dis't Court of Colo. I am most glad to know that Congress will so soon adjourn, then the opportunity will be afforded you to enjoy that rest which you so much need." ALS, *ibid.* On Jan. 15, [*1877*], Mrs. John W. Jenkins wrote to USG. "I hope you will forgive me for again intruding upon you. You have been very kind to me, and I feel very grateful; but I must now beg of you to continue your kind favor in my behalf and request that my Husband be retained in those cases. The Atty. Genl. said if you made a request he would have him retained   Indeed Mr. President I am forced to beg you to do this for me, for if Col. Jenkins is discharged the children and myself *must perish this winter*. It is all I have depended upon   Col. Jenkins has no other business but those cases, if they are taken from him he has nothing—. . . If you will not see me, will you Mr. President kindly send me word if you will do this favor for me—I will await—" ALS (stamped Jan. 17, 1877), *ibid.* On Sept. 15 and Oct. 16, [*1876*], Mrs. Jenkins, London, had written similar letters to USG. ALS (docketed 1876), *ibid.* For M. A. Shaffenburg, former U.S. marshal, see *New York Times,* July 28, 1877; *PUSG,* 18, 504–5.

On Jan. 5, 1876, Tompkins twice had telegraphed to USG. "A petition has been gotten up to have H. P. Bennett appointed Surveyor Genl   Bennett is one of the most violent of the ring here & his appointment would be fearful in its consequences,   For God sake do not make the appointment" "The immediate appointment of a recever of land office at Pueblo Col is much needed   the appointment of Mark G Bradford turned out by Chaffee to make room for one of the defendants in the las animas land Grab would be a master stroke" Telegrams received (at noon and 9:40 P.M.), DLC-USG, IB. On Feb. 11, Philip King *et al.,* Denver, petitioned USG. "The undersigned citizens of Colorado, learning that an assault has been made upon Surveyor General Searight, beg leave respectfully to bear testimony to the ability, fidelity and industry with which he has discharged his office, and to express the belief that his removal would be detrimental to the public interests and prejudicial to the harmony of the friends of your administration." DS (26 signatures), DNA, RG 233, 44A-D1. Related papers are *ibid.* On Jan. 5, 1877, USG nominated Ferdinand Barndollar as land office register, Pueblo, to replace Keyes Danforth; on Jan. 10, USG nominated William L. Campbell as surveyor gen., Colo., to replace Thomas B. Searight.

To Senate

To The Senate of the United States.

I have the honor to transmit herewith communications from the Secretaries of War and the Interior in answer to the Resolution of the Senate of the 15th instant requesting "any information in my possession in regard to the proposed emigration to the Black Hills Country in the Sioux Indian Reservation; whether such emigration is with the consent of the Indian tribes holding said country under the Treaty of February 24. 1869, and if not what measures will be taken in relation to the same."

U. S. Grant.

Executive Mansion,
March 17th 1875.

Copy, DNA, RG 130, Messages to Congress. *SED*, 44-Special Session-2. On March 17, 1875, Secretary of War William W. Belknap wrote to USG. "I have the honor to enclose copies of correspondence from the files of the Department, relating to the proposed emigration to the Black Hills Country, and the measures taken by the military authorities in the matter prepared in compliance with Senate Resolution of the 15th instant." LS (press), DNA, RG 94, Letters Received, 1356 1875. *SED*, 44-Special Session-2. On the same day, Secretary of the Interior Columbus Delano wrote to USG. ". . . Statements published in the newspapers indicate a determination on the part of many persons throughout the country to explore the Black Hills in search of minerals. Measures have been adopted by the Secretary of War, with the concurrence of this Department, to prevent further intrusion upon the reservation in question, and looking to the removal of the persons now unlawfully there. . . . This Department has taken steps to bring to this city a delegation of the Sioux (parties to the treaty) for the purpose of negotiating for the extinguishment of their right to the reservation embracing the Black Hills country, with a view to opening up the same to settlement, and until such an arrangement has been effected it is the intention of this Department, with the co-operation of the War Department, to protect the rights of the Indians as guaranteed to them by the treaty of 1868, and to prevent any further infraction of those rights. It is also the intention of this Department to use every effort possible to extinguish the Indian title to the Black Hills country, and open the same to settlement and explorations for mineral wealth at the earliest day practicable." *Ibid.*, p. 15. On

March 16, AG Edward D. Townsend had telegraphed to Gen. William T. Sherman, St. Louis. "The President requests you to make public the following 'all expeditions into that portion of the Indian Territory known as the Black Hills Country must be prevented as long as the present treaty exists efforts are now being made to arrange for the extinguishment of the Indian title & all proper means will be used to accomplish that end If however the steps which are to be taken towards the opening of the Country to settlement fail these persons at present within that territory without authority must be Expelled—please acknowledge receipt." Telegram received (at 3:10 P.M.), DNA, RG 108, Letters Received. *SED*, 44-Special Session-2, 14.

On March 15, Oliver W. Barnes, Union League Club, New York City, had written to USG. "Permit me to suggest a solution of the pending difficulty relative to the desire of our enterprising miners to enter the Black Hills. I would recommend as follows *First.* That the Government make a new treaty with the Indians, buying out their title to the Black Hills Reservation for $100 000—& pay them an annuity besides, so that there may be no charge of unfair dealing. *Second.* Give the Indians a new Reservation at some distance from the Black Hills where they would not molest our Miners—*Third*—Permit miners to enter the country of the Black Hills only by Licence from the Government granted through the Department of the Interior—Let the Licence stipulate, that one third of the miner's product shall be paid over to the Government as a Royalty—*Fourth*—The Government should place sufficient Military Force near the Mining Region to maintain good order, protecting the Miners during their labors, giving safe conduct to the transportation of supplies in and the product of the mines out of from Black Hills. *Fifth.* If machinery is necessary to reduce the ores let the Government furnish it at a fair toll, and also furnish assay offices at or near the mines—*Sixth*—Let the Royalty derived from the mines be applied to the reimbursement of the amount paid to the Indians & their annuity and the balance to the reduction of the National Debt—" ALS, DNA, RG 75, Letters Received, Dakota Superintendency.

On March 17, Ely Adams *et al.*, Plum Creek, Neb., petitioned USG. "The undersigned citizens of the State of Nebraska having watched with deep interest the accounts relative to what is known as the Black Hills of Dakota and being thoroughly of the opinion that the opening of the same to occupancy by all who may desire is but Simple justice and would promote the general welfare of the country, we would therefore Humbly pray your Excellency to inaugurate such steps as will at the earliest possible moment render the said Black Hills occupiable by the white people with safety, . . ." DS (138 signatures), *ibid.*

On March 22, Delano telegraphed to Orville E. Babcock. "When can I see the President, and the Commissioner Indian Affairs and Bishop Hare? Bishop Hare leaves at 1. O'clock" Telegram received, DLC-USG, IB; DNA, RG 107, Telegrams Collected (Bound). Babcock endorsed this telegram. "He will see you at any time" ADfS, *ibid.* Also on March 22, Delano wrote to Belknap. "The importance of determining with accuracy whether the 'Black Hills' country does, or does not, contain valuable mineral deposits cannot be over-estimated. To settle this question satisfactorily the Department has decided, under the advice of the President, to send a competent Geologist to explore that region.—Should it be found to contain the precious metals in large quantities it will be very desirable to extinguish the Indian title guaranteed to the Sioux by the treaty of 1868. Negotiations for this purpose have been instituted, and will be pursued with unremitting efforts until it is ascertained whether the Indians will, or will not, consent to such relinquishment. The Department has recently obtained information leading to the belief that the trespassers now in that country, in violation of law and treaty stipulations, will endanger the success of these negotiations. I have the, honor, therefore, to request that all persons now unlawfully in that territory be be notified by your Department to leave immediately; and that they be informed that a refusal to leave will lead to their expulsion by military force. Should it become necessary to employ such military force, the Geologist about to be appointed can accompany the expedition, and, if such force proves unnecessary, I may hereafter call for a suitable escort for the geological party." LS, *ibid.*, RG 94, Letters Received, 1356 1875. Walter P. Jenney led a small geological team that explored the Black Hills from May to Oct. See *HED*, 44-1-1, part 5, I, 683–85; *SED*, 44-1-51. On May 28, Asahel W. Hubbard and four others, Sioux City, Iowa, telegraphed to USG. "Capt Walker first Infantry attacked Evans train of twenty wagons and one hundred men in Camp on Niobrara river near Antelope Creek Nebraska burning wagons arms and Provisions starting men in Destitute condition for Ft Randall   men didn't contemplate Encroachment upon Sioux reservation   is action to be sustained" Telegram received (at 11:40 P.M.), DNA, RG 94, Letters Received, 1356 1875. Related papers are *ibid.* See Speech to Sioux Delegation, May 26, 1875.

On June 9, 1874, Delano had written to USG. "Owing to the absence of Secretary Belknap, I deem it my duty to send you a copy of a letter which I have this day sent to him, accompanied by a copy of a letter from Bishop Hare to me, relating to the dangers which Bishop Hare apprehends will result from a military expedition into the Black Hills in consequence of our relations with the Sioux Indians. You will concur with me in the opinion, that under any circumstances a general war with the Sioux would be deplorable. It would undo the good already accomplished by our eforts for peaceable relations, and, at this particular time, just upon the heel of the resignation of the members of the Board of Indian Commissioners, I feel an increased anxiety that every precaution, which prudence and wisdom dictate, shall be taken to prevent an Indian war. You will pardon the freedom of this letter when you recur to the circumstances surrounding the department at this moment, and when you remember that Gen. Belknap is absent and I leave here tonight for Ohio to remain a few days and that I omitted to say this during Cabinet meeting this morning." Copy, Delano Letterbooks, OHi. On the same day, Bishop William H. Hare, Yankton Agency, Dakota Territory, telegraphed to Delano. ". . . Agent Bingham reports that his Indians have gone to fight the Rees   they ought to be struck without mercy   so should all marauders.   the Black Hill expedition is a different matter,   we are the marauders in this case   I write at length to-day" Copy, DNA, RG 94, Letters Received, 1741 1874. Also on June 9, Hare wrote to USG. "In the month of February a commission of which I had the honor to be chairman, was appointed by the Hon. Secretary of the Interior to visit the Red Cloud and Whetstone agencies and to make such recommendations as upon examination should seem to them judicious as to the line of policy to be pursued towards the Indians connected with those agencies and towards the Indians from the North, large bodies of which Indians had made the above named Agencies their resort during the past Winter. That commission unanimously recommended that a special effort should be made this summer for the conciliation of the Northern Sioux, and that, in order to deter them from pushing South as Winter approaches to draw rations at the Red Cloud and Whetstone Agencies and thus increasing the dangerous element on the northern border of Nebraska, an Agency should be established for these Indians near the Black Hills, or elsewhere, in their own part of the Sioux Reserve. I had the privilege of bringing this recommendation of the commission before your mind in the personal interview with your Excellency with which I was favored in April last. It was approved and adopted by the Hon. Secretary of the Interior, and I have now in my possession a letter from the Department of the Interior continuing the commission and instructing it to put into effect the recommendation rehearsed above. On returning from Washington to this part of the country, I found, to my surprise, that the newspapers were teeming with news of a *military expedition fitting out for the heart of the Sioux country, the Black Hills*, and with proposals that Sioux City and other

towns should not fail to be represented in the large party of adventurers who were prepared to follow in the wake of the military. Having learned from the Secretary of the Interior that such a military expedition is preparing, I gladly avail myself of an invitation given
by him to address you on the subject, and beg to present the following points:—1st That
the appointment of a commission to invite a delegation of Northern Sioux to make a
friendly visit to Washington and accept the bounty of the Government and the invasion of
their country by a Military expedition are incompatibles. Either course may be pursued,
but not both. 2d That such an expedition would, almost beyond a doubt, provoke an Indian war. The Yellowstone Expedition of last Summer, though it did not invade the territory assigned the Sioux, so greatly alarmed and excited them that warriors hastened to resist it from most of the Sioux tribes, and confronted it, it has been reported, several
thousand strong. What may be expected then as the result of an Expedition which not only
invades the Sioux country but penetrates it through & through, and cuts into that particular part of it, which by common consent, is the hive of the hostile Sioux, their place of
council when war parties are sent out, their retreat in times of danger, and the pride of the
nation! Acting under the peace policy the Commissioners recently sent out by the Secretary of the Interior recommended that a feeding agency protected by a friendly garrison
should be planted near this part of the Sioux country. They argued an Agency and a garrison planted somewhere near these hills would put the whole Sioux country and people
under the control of the Government as they have never been before, and open up this at
present impenetrable heart of the nation to the rays of civilizing influences; and if the bottom lands of the forks of the Cheyenne and of the streams which flow into them from the
Black Hills should prove upon examination good for agricultural purposes, as many represent that they are the commission believe that the planting of an Agency in the Black
Hills country worth all the expense which its establishment would involve. This plan followed out would, I believe, get the Northern Sioux under control and yet preserve the
peace,   An invasion of the Black Hills means, I fear, or at least will surely result in, *War*,
and war to the knife. 3d That this invasion of the Indian territory will almost beyond a
question be made the occasion of the inroad of large numbers of rapacious and unprincipled civilians. Indeed, as the extracts taken from the 'Sioux City Journal' which I enclose
clearly indicate, a party is already organizing with that intent. Such intrusion, as the Report of the Indian Peace Commissioners of 1867, (comprising Genls Sherman, Augur, Harney, and others) emphatically represents, have been the most frequent causes of our past
Indian troubles. 4th That the exasperation which would ensue from such an expedition
would seriously imperil the existence of the struggling but numerous missions, which encouraged by your policy, the Episcopal Church is nourishing among the Sioux, and endanger the lives of her Missionaries. Of the dimensions of this Missionary work the following recapitulation will give you some idea—. . . 5th That in 1872, as recorded by Genl.
Walker, late Commissioner of Indian Affairs, an expedition was projected and partially organized in Dakota for the purpose of penetrating the Black Hills for mining, and lumber-
ing and an invasion of the Territory was imminent, which would beyond a peradventure,
General Walker remarks, have resulted in a *general Sioux War*. In this case the Executive
acted with great promptness. A proclamation was issued warning evil-disposed persons of
the determination of the Government to prevent the outrage and troops were put in position to deal effectively with the marauders. No one can read the papers hereabouts without coming to the conclusion that the Military expedition now projected will be used by
bad men for the accomplishment of that wrong, which your own action, to the joy of good
men, discountenanced and thwarted in 1872. 6th That the proposed Military Expedition
would be a violation of the National honor, which in the treaty of 1868, pledged the Sioux
the safety of their Territory both from invasion and intrusion. It cannot, indeed, be affirmed,

that all the Sioux have observed the obligations laid upon them by this treaty, but neither can it be maintained that they have as a people so violated it as to effect, *ipse facto*, its annihilation, nor has the U. S. declared it annulled. It may be well to declare the abrogation of the treaty of 1868, but until that is done what but some emergency can justify a Military invasion of their land? I have written Mr. President, in no spirit of opposition to the discreet employment of the Military in controlling Indians. The recommendations contained in Pages 7, & 8, & 13, of the Report on the condition of the Sioux, lately presented by me as Chairman, is clear proof that I hold a contrary opinion; nor in the spirit which would discourage thorough castigation of all marauding bands, who in my judgment ought to be punished more severely and persistently than they generally have been, and if war ensues, from this administration of justice, let it come and be so rigorously prosecuted that it shall be plain to all, the U. S. means that every soul within its domains shall obey its will. I have written in the fear that the expedition at present under discussion, which I believe to be dangerous, may be at the same time gratuitous, and bring the nation no honor. Thankful that in appealing to you, Mr. President, I appeal to the ear of moral courage and justice, and cordially acknowledging how much the Indians, and those who would do them good, owe to your administration, . . ." Copy, *ibid.* On [*June*] 17, Delano wrote to USG. "The Rt. Rev'd. W. H. Hare, Missionary Bishop of Niobrara, is the Chairman of a Commission, appointed by this Department, to investigate Indian Affairs at the Red Cloud and Whetstone Agencies. He performed the service devolved upon him with great ability and good judgement. The Commission has been continued and instructed to visit the Northern and hostile Sioux in the interests of peace. Bishop Hare has, from time to time given me information in personal communications, touching the rumors that had reached him in relation to a contemplated expedition to the Black Hills Country, and I suggested the propriety of his presenting his views upon the subject, to the President. The letter I now have the honor to enclose, is the result of my suggestion. I will remark that Bishop Hare is a discreet cautious and just man, whose views and judgement in all matters are given after mature reflection, and are not the prejudiced statements of an enthusiast." Copy (misdated), *ibid.* Related papers are *ibid.* See *PUSG*, 23, 369–70; M. A. DeWolfe Howe, *The Life and Labors of Bishop Hare: Apostle to the Sioux* (New York, 1914).

On June 22, Belknap wrote to Delano concerning Hare's letter to USG. ". . . While this Department has issued no orders for an expedition to proceed to that country, it is understood that, for the purpose of ascertaining the best location, if in the future it should become necessary to establish there a military post, General Sheridan has directed that a reconnoissance be made well out on the Belle Fourche, and among the Black Hills. This Expedition is understood to be merely a scout or reconnoissance, and no civilians are to be taken, and its purpose, is to seek information, in a peaceable manner, in regard to the character of the country entered. It is well known to the Department, that at various times the settlers in the adjacent country have contemplated explorations to the Black Hills, and the Department has uniformly discountenanced such movements; but it has now almost become a military necessity that accurate knowledge should be possessed by the Army as to this portion of our territory, and for that purpose only is the present expedition undertaken. The military authorities do not share in the apprehension of Bishop Hare, that any grave result, in the nature of an Indian outbreak, will result from this reconnoissance. The same apprehensions were entertained by many civilians in regard to the Yellowstone Expedition, of last year, but events proved that the fears aroused were groundless. In conclusion, I may say that the policy of this Department has been to make, and keep, peace with the Indians, and to th[is] end will always be glad to co-op[er]ate with the Department of the Interior." LS (press), DNA, RG 94, Letters Received, 1741 1874.

On May 1, Friday, Lt. Gen. Philip H. Sheridan, Chicago, had written to Sherman. "I returned from Fort Abraham Lincoln on Monday. It is the most complete army post I have ever seen, and was a model of economy in its construction. I would like to start Colonel Custer with a column of cavalry out, about the 15th of June, to examine the Black Hills country and the north fork of the Sheyenne, known on the map as the Belle Fourche. This country is entirely unknown, and a knowledge of it might be of great value in case of Indian troubles. It will take Col. Custer about six weeks to make the examination . . ." LS, *ibid.* On May 25, Sheridan wrote to Col. William D. Whipple, asst. AG. ". . . The expedition will examine a country heretofore unknown, and for the ultimate object of establishing a military post in the Black Hills, on or about the western line of the Sioux Reservation, which seemed to meet the approval of the Secretary of the Interior at a consultation last fall in Washington, when the President, Gen. Sherman and the Secretary of War were present." LS, *ibid.* On July 25, Sheridan telegraphed to USG, Long Branch. "Custer has been heard from at Longitude one hundred & three 103 forty six west & latitude forty five 45 twenty nine 29 north all well command excellent plenty of good grazing & water on line of march" Telegram received, DLC-USG, IB; copy, DLC-Philip H. Sheridan. On Aug. 12, Sheridan again telegraphed to USG. "Gen. Custer's command was at Harney's Peak August 3rd It will start home August 11th. Col. Grant is well." Telegram copies, *ibid.*; DNA, RG 393, Military Div. of the Mo., Letters Sent. See telegram from Sheridan to Sherman, copy, Sept. 1, 1874, *ibid.*, RG 94, Letters Received, 1741 1874; *ibid.*, 4028 1873; Belknap to Sherman, Nov. 28, 1873, ALS, DLC-William T. Sherman; *HMD*, 42-3-65; *SED*, 43-2-32; *HED*, 43-2-1, part 5, I, 548; Donald Jackson, *Custer's Gold: The United States Cavalry Expedition of 1874* (New Haven, 1966).

On July 13, Mary A. Calkins, Onondaga, Mich., had written to USG. "The interest which I feel in the cause of humanity; and the welfare of our country, prompts me to petition thee on behalf of the Sioux Indians. I know it seems presumptious for a lone, undistinguished woman to thus address the President of the United States; it is but as a drop of water to the boundless ocean. But the humane policy which thee adopted towards the Indians in the commencement of thy Administration, and has thus far maintained throughout, leads me to hope that this Administration will not be marred by the foul blot which designing men would fain bring upon it. I allude to Gen. Custar's proposed expedition to the Black Hills, which is declared to be in direct violation of the treaty made with the Sioux nation in 1868, is disapproved by all friends of the Indian, and actuated by unworthy motives. May it be thy pleasure to countermand the orders, which if carried out will no doubt plunge our beloved country into the horrors of a bloody and expensive war. Praying that God may imbue thee with wisdom to fill with honor the high trust imposed in thee, . . ." ALS, DNA, RG 75, Letters Received, Dakota Superintendency.

To Horace Porter

March 24th 1875.

DEAR SIR.

I am in receipt of your letter of the 22nd inst, and take an early opportunity to reply. I do not recollect that the subject of the proposition submitted by the U. P. R. R. Co. was ever alluded to in a conversation between you and me, except during a purely social visit you paid my family on the evening of the 22d Feby. last. The subject was then mentioned in a very casual manner in the presence of half a dozen ladies and gentlemen who were calling at the same time, and you remarked that you had heard the Secretary of the Treasury say in a conversation that day that the proposition did not meet his approval and had not met the approval of myself or the cabinet, and that although he had drawn up the proposition in the shape of a letter to be forwarded to Congress without approval, he did not think that it would be forwarded even in that shape on account of the end of the session being then so near at hand, that you had believed and you thought the general belief was that the proposition would be recommended and sent in at the present session,   I remarked that there were features of the proposition which had struck me very favorably, although it would be impossible for me to approve it in its present shape, that if there were more time an equitable adjustment could no doubt be arrived at and submitted to Congress, but that I would be entirely unjustifiable in in sending a proposition to Congress even without my recommendation at so late a period of the session, and that the matter would have to go over till the next session. I remember your speaking in my presence in a very complimentary manner of the of the road and its present management instancing the relations of your Co. to it as a means of knowing of its steady improvement, and you certainly manifested an interest in its success.

I have no hesitation in saying that the rumors you mention are so far as my knowledge extends entirely false, and without the least foundation in fact.

Yours truly.
U. S. GRANT.

GEN. HORACE PORTER
V. P. P. P. C. Co. NEW YORK.

Copy, DLC-USG, II, 2. On Feb. 12 and 16, 1875, Secretary of State Hamilton Fish recorded in his diary cabinet discussions concerning enforcement of a law calling for payments of five percent on net earnings from the Union Pacific and other railroads to the federal government. DLC-Hamilton Fish; *HED*, 43-2-2, XLII–XLIII, 44-1-127, 6–15. Disputing both the definition of net earnings and the business prudence of such payments, railroad managers sought alternatives. On Feb. 19 and 23, Fish again wrote in his diary.

"The proposition of the Central Pacific Rail Road was brought up by the Secretary of the Treasury—. . . Bristow says that this will not meet the Amount of the bonds and interest until about nine years after the last bond falls due   The proposition from the Union Pac he reads and states that the Companies do not wish their proposals sent to Congress except with a recommendation from the Administration. The President does not authorize an approval but a statement to Congress that a settlement of the difficulties with the Companies is very desirable." "The President speaks to Bristow about the proposition of the Union and the Central Pacific Rail Road's; and states that he understands that there is a stock jobbing project in the submission of the proposal; that Jay Gould and others having purchased large quantities are intending to sell out on the advance of prise which it is supposed will take place on the recommendation to Congress of the proposal that Horace Porter had told him last night that such were the facts and that the price had already advanced in consequence; that the Administration had agreed to recommend this proposal and that Gould and his friends were already unloading . . . The proposals of the Central and Union Pacific Rail Roads were considered and Bristow read draft of a paper prepared for submission to Congress presenting the terms of their proposals but not recommending acceptance, concluding with a statement of the advisability of some adjustment of the differences with these Companies   Considerable discussion ensues the President inclining against any presentation of the subject to Congress   Bristow refers to the fact that the determination of the Cabinet at a former meeting to submit the proposals had been made public through the press and that the with drawing it at present might subject the Administration to the charge of yielding to a stock Jobbing operation or influence   After much discussion it is concluded that the submission of the question will give an opportunity to attach some proposition in connection with these words to some of the appropriation Bills and thus jeopard their passage and make necessary an extra session of Congress therefore that the subject must be deferred to the next session of Congress in December 1875." DLC-Hamilton Fish. Grenville M. Dodge, acting for Jay Gould, principal Union Pacific stockholder, proposed compromises considered in cabinet and never revived. See Ross A. Webb, *Benjamin Helm Bristow: Border State Politician* (Lexington, Ky., 1969), pp. 169–71; Maury Klein, *The Life and Legend of Jay Gould* (Baltimore, 1986), pp. 167–68.

On March 22, 1875, Horace Porter, Pullman Palace Car Co., wrote to Secretary of the Treasury Benjamin H. Bristow. "I wish you would telegraph me care Babcock authorizing me to see the letter you took to Cabinet meeting with you in reference to the Union Pacific settlement, and the endorsement put upon it after Cabinet meeting, and make a copy of them, to show to an individual to whom you have been lied about terribly   I shall treat it confidentially, and explain when I see you. I want it for your good and shall make no improper use of it, nor let it go out of my hands if you say so. I know it is not confidential entirely as you showed it to Dodge. Please do this and oblige . . ." ALS, DLC-Benjamin H. Bristow.

Order

———

March 25th *1875*,

In pursuance of the 4th section of the act entitled, "an act making appropriations for sundry civil expenses of the Government, for

the fiscal year ending, June 30th 1876, and for other purposes," approved, March 3rd 1875,[1] a Board is hereby appointed to consist of:
Lt. Col. T. T. S. Laidly, Ordnance Department, U. S. Army
     President of the Board,
Commander L. A. Beardslee, U. S. Navy,
Lt. Col. Q. A. Gillmore, Engineer Dep't., U. S. Army,
David Smith, Chief Engineer, U. S. Navy,
W. Sooy Smith, Civil Engineer,
A. S Holly, Civil Engineer,
R. H. Thurston, Civil Engineer,
who will convene at the Watertown Arsenal, Massachusetts, on April 15th 1875, or as soon thereafter as practicable, for the purpose of determining, by actual tests, the strength and value of all kinds of iron, steel, and other metals, which may be submitted to them, or by them procured, and to prepare tables which will exhibit the strength and value of said materials, for constructive and mechanical purposes, and to provide for the building of a suitable machine for establishing such tests, the machine to be set up and maintained at the Watertown Arsenal.

The funds appropriated for the purposes of these tests, will be disbursed under the Ordnance Department, of the Army, and the Board will receive instructions from, and make its report to, the Chief of Ordnance.[2]

Mr. R. H. Thurston, Civil Engineer, is designated as Secretary of the Board, at an annual compensation of Twelve hundred dollars.

Actual travelling expenses, as provided by law, will be allowed the members of the Board.

U. S. GRANT

DS, DNA, RG 94, Letters Received, 1605 1875. On March 15, 1875, Orville E. Babcock wrote to Secretary of War William W. Belknap. "The President will be pleased to have you address a communication to the Society of Civil Engineers, requesting them to suggest some names from which ~~to~~ he could select the members of the Commission for testing iron and steel—as provided by an Act of the last Congress." Copy, DLC-USG, II, 2. See *HED*, 45-2-98; Jeanne McHugh, *Alexander Holley and the Makers of Steel* (Baltimore, 1980), pp. 336–38.

On March 24, 1875, Belknap telegraphed to Alfred B. Mullett, New York City. "The President offers to you position as one of the Civil Engineers and Secretary on Board for tests of American Iron & steel. Answer" ALS (telegram sent), DNA, RG 107, Telegrams

Collected (Bound). On the same day, Belknap wrote to Mullett, Washington, D. C., on the same subject. Copy, *ibid.*, Letters Sent, Military Affairs. On March 25, William B. Franklin, Colt's Patent Fire Arms Manufacturing Co., Hartford, wrote to USG. "Having noticed that a law was passed by the last Congress authorizing the appointment of a joint Board of Army & Navy officers and civilians to investigate the subject of testing metals, I recommend for appointment on such Board, Prof W. P. Trowbridge of the Yale Scientific School, and Mr C B. Richards of this place. Prof Trowbridge is a graduate of the Military Academy of 1848, has been in charge of the Novelty Iron Works of New York, and is now in charge of the Department of Dynamic Engineering in Yale College & the subject of tests of metals necessarily comes in his Department. His reputation as an Engineer is the best possible. Mr Richards is the Engineer of the Colt's Arms Co & has devised & used a testing machine of very great efficiency, and has had more & better experience in testing the strength of metals than any person I know. He would be of the greatest assistance to the Board in its investigations, and he would be second to none of them in practical & theoretical knowledge of the subject. My particular object in asking these appointments is to have the Board use our machine, which is the best in the United States. I cannot doubt that the results obtained from this ma- machine will exceed in accuracy & general utility any that could be obtained anywhere else, or on any other machine, so that at the risk of being suspected of trying only to get grist for my mill, I make the recommendation for these apptmts. Prof Trowbridge & Mr Richards are not politicians, but the first may be considered a Democrat & the second a Republican. Gov. Jewell can give you information as to both men if you require it." ALS, *ibid.*, RG 156, Letters Received.

On June 7, 1876, USG wrote to Congress transmitting a report from the testing board and recommending additional appropriations. Copy, *ibid.*, RG 130, Messages to Congress. *SED*, 44-1-71. On April 17, Col. Theodore T. S. Laidley, Watertown Arsenal, Mass., had written to USG requesting $50,000 for the coming year. *Ibid.*, pp. 3–4. On May 19, William Sooy Smith, Washington, D. C., wrote to USG praising the testing board's contributions to science and industry. *Ibid.*, pp. 1–2. On July 31, USG signed a sundry civil appropriation bill committing $19,396.98 but discontinuing the board after this expenditure. See *U.S. Statutes at Large (Public Laws)*, XIX, 119; message to Congress, Jan. 30, 1877.

1. See *U.S. Statutes at Large*, XVIII, part 3, pp. 399–400.
2. On June 15, 1875, Brig. Gen. Stephen V. Benét, chief of ordnance, wrote to Belknap concerning a proposal to remove the board from Ordnance Dept. oversight. ALS, DNA, RG 94, Letters Received, 1605 1875. On June 19, Belknap wrote to Laidley, Watertown Arsenal, "that in compliance with the request of the Board for testing Iron, Steel, &c., and with the concurrence of the Chief of Ordnance, the words, 'the Chief of Ordnance', in the Executive Order of March 25, 1875, appointing the said Board have been stricken out, and the words 'the President of the United States' substituted therefor." LS (press), *ibid.* Related papers are *ibid.*

To Francis E. Spinner

—————

March 30th /75

My Dear General:

Your letter of resignation of the office of Treas. of the United States, of yesterday—and your very kind private note of the same date—are received, and in return I wish to say how much I, in common with the great mass of people of this country, appreciate your zeal and devotion to the arduous duties you have been called upon to perform in the last fourteen years. In retiring from these duties I hope you will find the rest and restoration to vigorous health so long denied to you.

You take with you my best wishes for your welfare and happiness, and my confidence in your patriotism, zeal and ability. But few men have performed more labor for the public than you. None have retired from their labors retaining a stronger confidence in the public mind for constancy, integrity and unselfishness.

> With great respect
> Your obt. svt.
> U. S. Grant

Hon. F. E. Spinner, U. S. Treas.

ALS, NIC. A merchant in N. Y. and frequent Democratic office holder, Francis E. Spinner switched to the Republicans while in Congress (1855–61) and began his tenure as U.S. Treasurer on March 16, 1861. On March 29, 1875, Spinner twice wrote to USG. "More than fourteen years ago, I entered upon the duties pertaining to the office of the Treasurer of the United States, with a solemn promise, made to myself, faithfully to do my whole duty. I feel conscious that the promise, then so made, has been honestly kept.—I now feel that I need that rest, that the arduo[u]s duties of the office have so long denied me.—If agreeable with the views of the President, I would most respectfully beg to have my resignation accepted, and be relieved from further service in the office, after the close of the current fiscal year, ending with the thirtieth of June next." "In the formal letter, of to-day's date, in which I tendered to you my resignation of the office of Treasurer of the United States, it would hardly have been proper that I should express my heartfelt feelings towards you: and in our recent interviews, your kind treatment so filled my heart, that I could not give utterance to my grateful thoughts. Now, that it is all over with, and that I stand on the threshold of Emancipation, I desire to express to you my deep gratitude for your great confidence, for your marked friendship, and for the many kindnesses and favors that you have bestowed upon me.—It was your kind countenance and steady support, that more than all else, sustained and held me up, during my long years of vexatious and arduous official labor.—I shall always look back upon these marks of esteem and favor, commencing with the time when you took the command of the Army of the Potomac, and growing through the time that you were in Command of all the Armies of the republic, and since you became president of the United States, as the events of my long life of which I shall ever feel most proud.—For all these kind manifestations towards me, from one who stands so high in the esteem of the World for his great achievements, please permit me, now that our official relations are about to end, to tender to you the sincere thanks of a truly grateful heart.—" ALS (press), *ibid.* On April 12, Spinner again wrote to USG. "Your very kind and highly complimentary letter, of the 30th Ultimo, was this day received. It will be filed with the commission, that it supersedes, that I received from the lamented Lincoln, more than fourteen years ago; and will go to my children as a proof of the confidence that the two great men of the time placed in their father. It is the best legacy that I will be able to leave to them.—In their behalf I thank you—As for myself, I am bankrupt in words to express to you my deep gratitude.—" ALS (press), *ibid.*

On March 29, a correspondent had reported from Washington, D. C., on Spinner's replacement, "John C. New, Cashier of the First National Bank of Indianapolis, . . . Mr. New is about forty years old, and a wealthy banker. He was recommended for the appointment by Senator Morton, . . ." *New York Times,* March 30, 1875. On March 1, 1885, John C. New, Indianapolis, wrote to Frederick Dent Grant, New York City. "Words cannot express the sorrow I feel at the reports of your fathers failing health. It always seemed to me that General Grant was too true, too good and too great, to suffer the ordinary ills of mankind, and that he would be spared to his friends and the world for long life and and a happy and peaceful old age. His name and fame will be eternal, would, that his life could be as enduring. Mrs New joins me in tenderest love to him, and sincerest sympathy to your Mother, and the family. I should be glad to hear from you anything that you may have time to telegraph or write me as to his condition. My love for him is only less than your own in the kinship that makes it." ALS, USG 3.

On March 24, 1876, U.S. Senators Phineas W. Hitchcock of Neb., Timothy O. Howe and Angus Cameron of Wis., and one other, telegraphed to USG. "We earnestly recommend the appointment of Albert U. Wyman U. S. Treasurer in event of resignation of Treasurer New,   He is better fitted for the position than any one who can be named on account of thorough knowledge of the Bureau & is as honest & faithful as any man in the world" Telegram received, DNA, RG 107, Telegrams Collected (Bound). On June 20, New tendered his resignation to USG to pursue private business activities. See *New York Times,* Feb. 7, June 21, 1876. On March 17, 1875, USG had nominated Albert U. Wyman as asst. treasurer; on June 28, 1876, he nominated Wyman as U.S. Treasurer.

Probably on June 23, Gus Bither, Saginaw, Mich., had telegraphed to USG. "Cant take the Treasurership before July fifteenth" Telegram received, DLC-USG, IB.

To John F. Long

———

Apl. 4th /75

DEAR JUDGE;

In my last letter to you I intended to state that my plans in relation to my proposed visit to St. Louis this Spring have been changed. It occurs to me now that I closed my letter without saying any thing on the subject, and that possibly my young friend, Gen. Harney,[1] may be placing himself at some inconvenience in consequence. I find now that Nellie will will not be able to go West and consequently Mrs. Grant will not go. My stay will therefore be short, and later in the season than I proposed. I have accepted an invitation to be in Boston on the 17th & 19th of this month and can not go before I have paid this visit.

I am very anxious to see you for a day, in St. Louis, to see if some plan can not be hit upon to make my farm less expensive. It has cost so much now that I must keep the land until it is worth something.

My kindest regards to your self and family.

Yours Truly
U. S. Grant

Judge John F. Long

ALS, CSmH. USG did not visit St. Louis until Sept., 1875.

On April 17, Henry T. Crosby, chief clerk, War Dept., had written to John F. Long, St. Louis. "Your letter to the President, of the 7th. instant, asking for the discharge of Nathaniel Able, Co. F, 3d. Infantry, has been received, and you are respectfully informed that the man was discharged April 9th., on an application presented by Hon. D. D. Pratt." Copy, DNA, RG 107, Letters Sent, Military Affairs.

On May 18, U.S. Senator Oliver P. Morton of Ind., Indianapolis, wrote to USG. "Seeing in the papers that you are coming West in a few days, for ourselves, and at the desire of many friends, we invite you to stop at Indianapolis and make us a visit. The people here will be glad to see you and pay their respects. We shall be glad to entertain you, and trust that Mrs Grant will be with you. Mrs Morton and the ladies of Indianapolis would be happy to receive her. Please let me hear from you" ALS, ICHi.

1. On Dec. 8, William S. Harney, St. Louis, wrote to USG. "You know how much I dislike to trouble about official Matters, but this in favor of a son of one my oldest & most intimate Friends & I hope you will Excuse me for doing so now—Col. Schaumburg is one of the most elegant & highly respected young Gentleman of this City—you, no doubt, remember all his connections here—The Col is anxious to get a Commission in the Army, & I will say here that, no man could do more credit to the Army than himself—He wishes to get the appointment of Pay-Master, & I must tell you frankly that, having no turn for a *Civil* Appointment, his object is to Exchange from the Pay Dept. into the *Cavalry* which he can effect without any difficulty with the approval of yourself I hope My Dear General, you will gratify this young Gentleman & add another Obligation to the many you have done . . ." ALS, DNA, RG 94, Applications for Positions in War Dept. A related paper is *ibid.* No appointment followed.

To William W. Smith

Apl. 6th 1875,

Dear Smith:

Can't you & Emsy, with Gertrude, come and pay us a visit during this month, or the first part of next? I go to Boston on the 15th to be absent until the 20th,[1] so I would like your visit after the latter date, but as early after as convenient. I want to run out to my farm for a few days before going to Long Branch—early in June—and would like to have you visit us before I go. Nellie[2] is with us and will remain until next fall, but with the exception of her our house is empty, and will be—not counting us two old fogies—for the balance of the season. At Long Branch we will be rather fuller. Buck will then be coming down every evening from the City; Jesse will be at home; Fred's wife will be with us, and Mr. Sartoris will have returned from England. He goes—sails—on Saturday next[3] to be absent about seven weeks. Fred goes to the Yellow Stone and probably will not get back until the latter part of August.

Give our love to Emsy and the children, and kindest regards to the Judge[4] and family. As to yourself you were an old bachilor so long that you have no rights to be respected by those more fortunate than you.

Yours Truly
U. S. Grant

ALS, Washington County Historical Society, Washington, Pa. On May 2, 1875, Julia Dent Grant wrote to Ida Honoré Grant. ". . . We are all well & just now we have the house full of company   Willie Smith & Emsy & Genl Dent & wife are with us—We have a large dinner on Tuesday next for Genl Badaux & wife   Nell & I had a lovely visit to N Y.   Nellie expects Algee back in about two weeks   I hope you are having a very nice time you & Freddie   I hope he will not be gone long from you little girlie? We are all getting dreadfully tired of your absense & will not submit any longer to such desertion   So hurry home. Cant Freddie bring you? . . ." ALS, Ulysses Grant Dietz, Maplewood, N. J.

1. On April 2, a correspondent reported from New York City. "Among the visitors to the President at the Fifth Avenue Hotel this morning were Collector Arthur, General Sharpe, Hon. Thos. Murphy, General Babcock, and a number of gentlemen representing the Massachusetts Legislature, who tendered him the hospitalities of the State on the occasion of the Centennial commemoration of the battles of Concord and Lexington, on the

19th inst. The invitation was accepted." *Philadelphia Public Ledger*, April 3, 1875. See letter to Joseph A. Harwood, April 27, 1875.

2. On Jan. 27, USG had telegraphed to Frederick Dent Grant. "Steamer Baltic now at Sandy Hook coming up. Be sure and meet your sister at landing about two thirty." N. Y. Book & Art Auction Co., No. 74 (1938). On April [22], Julia Grant wrote to Frederick Grant. ". . . When it came so near the time for Nellies departure (Algee engaged passage for the 24th) I just could not consent that she should be any place else than with me in her approaching trial & insisted upon her remaining with us this summer   Algee at length consented that she should remain But said that he *must* go home for a few weeks. So he sailed on the 9th & will be with us again by the 1st of June, & they will be with us the ballance of the summer. . . ." ALS (misdated April 2), USG 3. Grant Sartoris was born July 11 at Long Branch.

3. April 10.

4. William W. Smith's father-in-law, Judge William McKennan, 3rd U.S. Circuit, also lived in Washington, Pa.

To George H. Williams

———

Washington. D. C.
April 8th 1875.

To the Hon. George H. Williams,
Attorney General of the United States.
Sir:

Your attention is requested to the enclosed Petitions of George Chorpenning: One addressed to me as the President, and the other to the Hon. Marshall Jewell, Postmaster General of the United States.

From these papers you will observe, that under and by virtue of a joint Resolution of Congress approved July 15th 1870, Postmaster General Creswell, acting in a judicial or quasi-judicial character, on the 23rd of December 1870, awarded and determined, that there was due and owing to George Chorpenning from the United States, the sum of Four hundred and forty three thousand and ten dollars and sixty cents.

A copy of the late Postmaster General's Report, detailing his manner of making up this award, and his reasons therefor, is also enclosed for your consideration.

In January 1871, before a Warrant issued for the payment of the amount allowed the Claimant, further proceedings under the award were suspended by a resolution passed in the House of Representatives, instructing the Committee on Appropriations to inquire into the allowance and manner of the allowance of the claim of George Chorpenning under the Act approved July 15th 1870, and the Sixth Auditor was requested to delay the payment of any Warrant for the money until the Committee should report.

By joint Resolution of Congress approved Feb. 9th 1871, the Joint Resolution of July 15. 1870, was repealed.

The Petitioner contends, that his rights under the aforesaid Award became vested when the award was filed, and could not be abrogated by a subsequent repeal of the joint Resolution under which the award had been rendered: that the repealing Act is unconstitutional and void: that Congress had no more power to set aside his award, than it had to set aside a judgment of the Supreme Court of the United States: that Congress did not even attempt to set aside the award, but merely repealed the law under which the award had been made: that jurisdiction over the Award, and over his rights vested under it, belongs to the judicial, and not to the Legislative branch of the Government; and that even a judicial tribunal of competent jurisdiction could not impair those rights, except for good and sufficient legal cause:—that no such cause having been shown he is entitled to his award, and all the benefits arising therefrom; and he has called upon the Executive branch of the Government to enforce his rights under the Constitution and laws of his Country.

In the papers herewith enclosed, you will find reference to all the Laws of Congress, commencing with the Act of March 3rd 1857, which bear upon his case; and your attention is invited to their careful consideration.

I wish your opinion, as the law-officer of the Government, on the following points:

1. What is the legal effect of the repealing resolution of February 9th 1871? Does it set aside the award? Or, does it invalidate the vested rights of the claimant under that award, in whole or in part? If in part only, to what extent, and in what particular?

2. If the award stands in full force and virtue in law, can the amount

be paid, in whole, or in part, '*out of the Treasury,*' under the Act of Congress approved March 3rd 1857: or, under the joint resolution of Congress approved July 15th 1870: or, out of the general appropriations for the transportation of the mails under any other act or resolution of Congress?

3. The Petitioner, you will observe, claims interest on his award from the time it was filed: Can this claim be sustained in law, and have I the power to order its payment?

Your opinion on the points suggested is respectfully solicited. at an early day.

[*U. S. GRANT*]

L, DNA, RG 60, Letters from the President. The enclosure from George Chorpenning to Postmaster Gen. Marshall Jewell is *ibid.* On March 27, 1875, Chorpenning, Washington, D. C., wrote to USG. "As the chief executive officer of the nation whose duty it is to see the laws faithfully executed, permit me to present for your consideration the following statement of facts. . . . The truth is, when stripped of all irrelevant matter, and the newspaper prejudice created against the case, the action of Congress in the premises, was an absolute indorsement of the justice and validity of the award, and left me, at that time, a clear right to demand the money from the Post Office Department. Owing, however, to the deep-seated prejudice created by false and unfounded statements of the press, being utterly destitute of means to procure the publication of a single article in my defense, having been denied a hearing either by myself or counsel before the appropriation committee while the matter was pending in their hands, and with a determination to have a fair and thorough investigation into the question of fraud or irregularity; whereby the guilty parties, if any were found, might be made to suffer, or my rights be so far vindicated that there need no longer remain a timidity on the part of an executive officer to take such steps and assume such responsibility as would bring about a due execution of the laws, and thus render the justice so long withheld and so manifestly due me. To these ends, indorsed and encouraged by all the leading minds of my native county in the State of Pennsylvania, I brought the matter before the Judiciary Committee of the House of Representatives in the 43d, Congress. After months of investigation, the Committee, through their chairman, Hon. B. F. Butler, made a report sustaining the claim, accompanied with a Bill providing for my relief, which was, by the House, sent to the Private Calendar, where, as with hundreds of other bills, it was not reached for action, because of the great pressure of important public legislation with which that body was overwhelmed during the last session. Driven to absolute poverty and want, as I have been, during the past seventeen years of weary effort to obtain my rights from the Government, the contemplation now of my utter inability to support myself and family during another prolonged controversy, either through the Courts or before Congress, compels me to appeal directly to you, into whose hands the people have intrusted the administration of that right and justice to which all men are entitled, and beg such early and favorable action as your sense of justice commensurate with the dignity and power of your official position will warrant." LS, *ibid.* On April 24, Levi P. Luckey wrote to Jewell. "Have you any papers which you desire to have accompany the reference of Mr Chorpennings letter to the President to the Attorney General other than the

printed document signed by Mr. Creswell. 'The President has made a reference of the letter for decision first—as to whether acts of Congress referred to, make settlement in this
case obligatory by the P. O. Dept.' Second whether if not obligatory, settlement is authorized, under the acts referred to; whether the case can be given a status in the Court of
Claims." Copy, DLC-USG, II, 2.

On July 23, Attorney Gen. Edwards Pierrepont reported to USG. "The questions referred by the President to the Attorney General in the Chorpenning case are these:
First. Whether the Postmaster General is obliged to make settlement and payment under
the law as it now stands:—and *Second*; Whether the case has any status in the Court of
Claims. . . . My conclusion is that in the present state of the law the amount found due by
the late Postmaster General can not be paid, out of any existing appropriation and that the
Court of Claims has jurisdiction in the case and that the claim now made against the Post
Office Department may be transmitted to said Court under Sec. 1063 of the Revised
Statutes. But I am clearly of opinion that the amount found due on the reference to the late
Postmaster General cannot be sued upon as a binding award; and unless Congress shall in-
terpose I think the Statute of Limitations will bar the claim." DS, DNA, RG 60, Letters
Received, Ky. *Official Opinions of the Attorneys-General*, XV, 19–26. On July 29, USG en-
dorsed this opinion. "Returned to the Atty. Genl   The parties interested may let this opin-
ion stand, or they may withdraw the application for reference of the Case to the Atty Gen.
if they see fit, and the Atty Gen. deems it proper that such course should be authorized."
AES, DNA, RG 60, Letters Received, Ky. On July 24, Pierrepont had telegraphed to USG,
Long Branch. "Please let your Secretary return opinion in Chorpenning; a leaf left out."
Copy, *ibid.*, Letters Sent to Executive Officers. Chorpenning never received satisfaction
from the government on his controversial claim. See *CG*, 41–3, 833–37, 1011–13, 1028–
31; *HMD*, 41-3-66; *SRC*, 41-3-346; *HRC*, 43-1-622; William T. Otto, *Cases Argued and Ad-
judged in the Supreme Court of the United States* (Boston, 1877), IV, 397–400; *New York Times*,
Dec. 30, 1892; *DAB*, IV, 91–92.

To Adam Badeau

—————

Apl. 23d 1875.

DEAR GENERAL:

I write to express my regrets that I shall not be able to be present at your wedding as I had expected, and so much desired. Invitations that I had given—not for particular date—for company to
spend a week with us has been accepted, and the company will arrive
during the early part of next week. Allow me therefore to heartily
congratulate you, in behalf of Mrs. Grant and myself, and wish you
a happy journey through life.

Please to say to Miss Niles that I very much regret that I shall not have the pleasure of confering her upon my old—not in years, but in date of service—Staff Officer.

Ever your friend,
U. S. Grant

Gen.l A. Badeau

Consul Gen.l London Eng.

P. S. I hope you will take Washington in your tour and give Mrs. Grant and me an opportunity of having you and Mrs. Badeau meet some of our friends—and your old ones—socially.

U. S. G.

ALS, Munson-Williams-Proctor Institute, Utica, N. Y. On [*April 29, 1875*], USG tele-graphed to Adam Badeau, New York City. "Please accept my hearty congratulations upon the auspicious event of to-day, and my regrets that public business prevents my being pre-sent to present the bride and congratulate you in person, as I had expected to do." *New York Times*, April 30, 1875. Marie E. Niles was escorted by her brother, Nathaniel Niles, Jr.

On April 9, Orville E. Babcock had written to Badeau. ". . . The President has agreed to be in N. Y. on the 28th to attend Miss Nellie Murphy's wedding   Now if your day is not fixed why not make it the 27th the Presidents birth day or the 29th. The Cardinal is to marry Miss Murphy also. I take the liberty of suggesting these days to insure the presence of the President. for he wants to be present. . . ." ALS, MH. See Babcock to Badeau, April 25, 1875, *ibid.*

To Nathaniel Carlin

Washington, Apl. 24th, 1875.

Dear Sir:

Your letter of the 12th only reached me on the 22d, probably ow-ing to my absence during the greater part of the time between these dates. In regard to asking Mr. Sprague[1] to send the horse Rhode Is-land to my farm I cannot do it. If he does not send at the request of Mr. Akers he need not go. I regret to learn the missing of so many foals. I had hoped to get a few more colts from Jennie. She is only eighteen years old. Do you think the smallest black mare is in foal?

In regard to the cows on the place I wish you would turn over one of them to Mr. Jackson.[2] The remainder you can take on the

terms contained in your letter. Let me know how many colts we are
likely to have this year.

Yours &c.

U. S. GRANT.

N. CARLIN, ESQ.

Walter B. Stevens, *Grant in Saint Louis* (St. Louis, 1916), p. 170.
    On April 5, 1875, B. F. Akers, "Kansas Stock Farm . . . Sprague & Akers," Lawrence,
wrote to Nathaniel Carlin. "Yours, of a few days ago recd & have being waiting to hear from
Sprague before answering, think certain must hear tomorrow, am so buisy I cannot spare
time to go myself & requested him to send the horse—why he dont, I cannot say, but expect the horse men of Providence are trying to keep him there—will telegraph you soon
as I hear from him—" ALS, OCIWHi. On April 29, John F. Long, St. Louis, wrote to Carlin. "Beverly-Porter, tells me your were in on the 27th—our office being closed, I did not
see you,   I have no news of Rhode Island at all, nor have I had a line from the Prest. since
I saw you. B. H. Sale produced a bill of $22 95/100 for corn.—I could not pay without your
certificate, also Wm Barr & Co. a bill, in same condition,   Next week, Genl. Sherman, Col.
Easton, Maj. Wright & self, will run out to see your horses. All well,—regards to Madam."
ALS, *ibid.* On May 1 and 4, Akers wrote to Carlin. ". . . I have written Col Sprague—repeatedly, but to none of my letters have I received any reply further than that he would
write me about Rhode Island in a few days—never in all my connection with him in buisness matters—has he ever wanted to know anything further than that it was my wish—
and I dont understand this, but buisy as I am, shall start east in a day or two & find out—
I know he is no friend of the Generals—but this is my matter and if you dont get the horse
forthwith, the Col & myself are friends no longer—. . ." "I finally got the reason of Col.
Spragues silence.   so I shall not go on. I have several fine horses here—come up & see them
—I think Bay Star will suit you—both for a stallion. trotter & Show horse   you can have
any except Ethan—as I want to make all amends I can for—the dissapointment which no
one regrets as much as myself—. . ." ALS, *ibid.* On May 10, Akers again wrote to Carlin
concerning horses for USG's farm. ALS, *ibid.* See letter to Nathaniel Carlin, Dec. 26, 1874.

    1. Born in 1828, Amasa Sprague, Jr., was a partner with his brother, former U.S. Sen-
ator William Sprague of R. I., in the family's textile and manufacturing business. A trotting horse enthusiast, he owned "Ethan Allen."
    2. USG had hired Jackson to work on his farm. See letter to Nathaniel Carlin, Aug.
24, 1875.

To Joseph A. Harwood

———

Apl. 27th 1875.

DEAR COL.

    Permit me through you—the Chairman of the Committee of the
Mass. Legislature, appointed to meet the Cabinet and myself, on the

occasion of the late Centennial Celebration of the battles of Concord-Lexington, and convey to us the invitation of the State to be its guests for the time—to tender my thanks, and the thanks of the accompanying Cabinet Ministers for the courtesies received from his Excellency the Govenor of the State—and staff, your Committee and citizens generally. Nothing was left undone to make our short stay in the State most pleasant.

With great respect,
Your obt. svt.
U. S. GRANT.

HON. J. H. HARMOND
CHM. LEGISLATIVE COM.

Copy, DLC-USG, II, 2. Recently-elected Mass. Senator Joseph A. Harwood, a prosperous leatherboard manufacturer, had served as postmaster, Littleton, and on the staff of Governor William B. Washburn of Mass. On April 16, 1875, Harwood welcomed USG and party to Mass. See *Boston Evening Transcript*, April 17, 19–20, 1875; Hamilton Fish diary, April 13, 21, 1875, DLC-Hamilton Fish; *New York Times*, April 20, 1875; *Proceedings at the Centennial Celebration of the Battle of Lexington, April 19, 1875* (Lexington, 1875); David B. Little, *America's First Centennial Celebration: The Nineteenth of April 1875 at Lexington and Concord, Massachusetts*, 2nd ed. (Boston, 1974).

On Dec. 29, 1874, USG had replied to an invitation. "I am in receipt of your very cordial invitation to be present on the interesting ceremony of celebrating the Centennial Anniversity of the battle of Lexington. Though the numbers were small, the principals they fought for were of the greatest possible value to struggling, advancing mankind. The battle of Lexington though but the commencement of the strife, yet it decided that on which all rested viz—that the people of the Colonies knew their rights, and as brave people dared to maintain them. It would afford me great pleasure to be present and witness the ceromonies, but at this time I am unable to say that I can be, and am of the opinion that I shall not be able to accept." Copy, DLC-USG, II, 2.

On May 15, 1875, USG wrote to Mass. Senator George B. Loring. "I have the honor to acknowledge the receipt of the kind invitation of your committee on behalf of the Legislature of Massachusetts to accept the hospitalities of the Commonwealth upon the occasion of the Centennial Celebration of the Battle of Bunker Hill on the 17th of June, and beg to tender my sincere thanks therefor. I regret extremely that I shall not be able to attend the Celebration." Copy, *ibid.* On the same day, USG wrote a similar letter to G. Washington Warren, William W. Wheildon, *et al.* Copy, *ibid.*

To George H. Williams

Apl. 28, 1875.

DEAR SIR:

In accepting your resignation of the office of Attorney General of the United States, to take effect on the 15th of May 1875, as tendered by your letter of the 22d inst., allow me to express my appreciation of the ability, zeal, and efficiency with which the trust confided to your charge has been performed.

My sincere friendship accompanies you in the new field of life you have chosen and best wishes for your success.

Very respectfully yours
U. S. GRANT

HON. GEO. H. WILLIAMS
ATTY. GEN. OF U. S.

Copy, DLC-USG, II, 2.

On March 12, 1875, Secretary of State Hamilton Fish described in his diary a conversation related by Postmaster Gen. Marshall Jewell. ". . . he had told the President that several members of Congress, and he named Carpenter, Edmunds, and Sherman, (and adding that he might have named many more) who had told him that the investigations of the Judiciary Committee had developed facts which if Judge Williams remained in the Cabinet would lead to investigations and exposures which could not fail to be extreemly damaging to the Administration" DLC-Hamilton Fish.

On March 14, Horace Porter wrote to Secretary of the Treasury Benjamin H. Bristow. "When will you have a half hour for a little chin-music? Are you going to attend the Sanctuary this morning or worship nature at home? I shall call whenever most convenient today" ALS (on White House stationery), DLC-Benjamin H. Bristow. On March 16 (Tuesday) and 28 (Sunday), Bluford Wilson, solicitor of the treasury, wrote to James H. Wilson. "I have your favor of yesterday and have also seen the very excellent letter to Bristow. As he handed it to me just as he was going to Cabinet, I had no time to discuss it with him or ascertain his views as to the way you have put things. I may not see him to talk with him for two or three days but that is less important for the reason that I spent Sunday evening with him and went over the subject with him and Mrs Bristow in all its aspects. I was highly gratified with the result and left with the distinct understanding that he would 'stick,' and without any avowed purpose to put himself in the hands of his friends would nevertheless accept all the responsibilities that may fairly follow his continuance in public life. He was very positive however in his views as to the reorganization of the Cabinet, and agrees with you that Delano & Williams must go. In this Porter is also in accord, and I am satisfied that Porter carried out in good faith the assurance to you & Mr. Pullman. HeI have from Porter & Bristow confirmation that the former was frank and outspoken and produced an extremely favorable impression on the mind of the Secretary, and opened up the whole field of '76 not however in a very direct way. Since writing the above Bristow sent for me to go to the Senate with him. He gave me a full account of an important interview with Mr Conkling. the result of it all is that they have joined hands against Williams & Delano and they today made a direct appeal to the President against Williams telling him substantially that Williams ought to go. They were not encouraged very much but made some impression and proposed to renew the fight.—The most gratifying result of Porter's visit is that it brought Conkling & Bristow together. I was very sorry to find however that Bristow thinks he has evidence today of Porters bad faith and he bases it on the ground that he and Babcock are not helping him make you Commissioner. He says they are afraid you will smash the 'whiskey ring' and believes they have been talking up Cowan with the President. It is enough to say that I was not convinced by what Bristow said of Porter's bad faith and told him so—that I would suspend my judgment until I had more evidence. At the outset Babcock doubtless influenced the President against you but now sees his error and will doubtless fall in with Porter's views. Bristow will be in New York on Friday and will explain evrything to you. Meanwhile I am sure you had better go in for Commissioner and I urge you to go to Porter and make a straight issue with him at once and if necessary have him write to the President—You should be Commissioner and succeed Delano in the Summer, letting Cowan have the place vacated by you if it is thought best." ". . . A week ago last Saturday I struck the writer of certain anonymous letters to Belknap, Robeson & Bristow. The letter to Bristow comparatively trifling, but those to Belknap (three) and to Mrs Robeson (two) of the most infamous character. The writer was Mrs. George H. Williams, upon the most conclusive evidence both from the extrinsic circumstances, and on a comparison of writings. I at once laid the facts before Belknap and had a long discussion with him as to his course, advising prudence in the interests both of his family and the administration. He recognized the necessity for caution, and especially for the reason that he wanted to complete his case against Mrs Williams without reference to Bristow's letter by which I had been enabled to touch bottom in my inquiries. He refused however to consult with Bristow, claiming that on a matter affecting his honor and that of his wife he must reserve to himself the sole right to judge as to the proper course, or as to the measure of reparation or reprisal. As he seemed very deeply affected by the outrage, and expressed his purpose to bring the affair home to Williams and give him opportunity to force the issue, I felt called upon at once to write Bristow which I did, notifying him of the letter by telegraph. I felt then and feel now that I had uncovered material for a national scandal that would make that of the Eatons respectable in comparison and which if made public would cover the administration with a cloud of infamy. The President has sinned against light in keeping the Williams' in his Cabinet and society and the public would not spare him in the face of the infamous exposure. For these reasons I wanted Belknap to have the advice of Bristow's cooler head and Porter's also. The result of my letter was to bring Bristow & Porter together. A plan was agreed upon based on Williams' prompt removal and such prudent measures to suppress the scandal as might be devised from time to time. Porter sent Babcock a cipher telegram stating he had a plan and promising to come down Wednesday. On Monday by request I met Belknap Robeson & Babcock—The case was again carefully gone over—further discussion was had as to the course without reaching any definite conclusion. We met again on Wednesday Porter taking Robeson's place, the latter having gone to New York. After full consultation it was determined that Babcock should open the attack on Williams at once, giving the President the Falls story as the ground of action. This however was against my judgment as I held and meant that the President should know the *whole* truth. Especially as Babcock had produced at the Monday meeting as a new and startling contribution to the pile of filth already before us a letter to *Mrs Grant* from the very same source—the meanest of the series—and only received Saturday night previous.—Another proposition was advanced from which I dissented at the time and still do: Whitley was to be seduced from his allegiance to Mrs Williams, and turning traitor to her was to become her keeper compelling silence on her part through intimidation, or threats of the Penitentiary for her share in the Falls peculation. I am willing enough in the interests of common decency, the administration and the party to see the scandal suppressed. I am not willing however to invoke the aid of an infernal damned scoundrel like Whitley who himself upon the strongest proof has seduced Mrs. W. into her new field of infamy. Nor am I willing to see the President placed unwittingly in the power of such a man. If knowing the facts he still wants Whitleys help I have nothing to say. It is his matter—He should deal with it and not his aide de camp who I am sorry to say is sadly in fear of Whitley for the past, and must therefore trust him with the future.—On Bristow's return Thursday night we went over the whole ground. I am glad to say we agreed fully that the President should know all and that Whitley should be kept out—During the day of Thursday Babcock was in to see me, told me he was going to New York that night and expected to have the change made in a very few days. I again urged him to deal frankly with the President but obtained no assurance except that he would manage the affair. In the evening however Bristow told me that Babcock who had stopped in enroute to the depot claimed to have told the President all. I also learned that Pierrepont was to be Williams' successer, as part of a scheme I imagine to drive Fish out. Bristow accepts Pierrepont as perhaps the best under all the circumstances that can be done. Precisely the true significance of Pierrepont and the leaning towards Sharpe on the part of Babcock & Porter I am unable to say. I interpret it thus however. The ghost of a third term still haunts their brains. They want those in, who if the signs are right, will need no spur. If not, they will exact better terms from Bristow. Sharpe as Commissioner in their interests will hold the Secretary in check and through him they will retain their grip on power. This I have explained to the Secretary as my view. He is inclined to concur and will accept Sharpe only on the positive refusal of the President to appoint you. I do not think he will refuse as the only point he has ever made was so obviously suggested by Babcock that I have hopes it will be overcome by the Secretary in good time. I havent time to write more but you will see from all this how important to the Secretary & the President it is that you do not permit the good natured but wily policy of Porter and Babcock to prevail against you and the Secretary. Your presence here as Commissioner would be of incalculable value to the country and to your friends. *I do not over-estimate*. Possibly it might be well for you to capture Sharpe. Do it if possible, and set him on the President when the latter goes to New York. He will do you good as against Babcock and in a legitimate way. It won't do in skirmishing with your *two* friends to take too high ground. They have read Machiavelli and follow some of his precepts. Bristow insists that they have set the cards up on you with the President. As to this letter I presume you had better burn it though if I thought Babcock had not dealt fairly with the President I would be perfectly willing to have you use the facts herein to enlighten on the President, the first opportunity you have. . . ." ALS, WyU.

On March 27, Secretary of War William W. Belknap telegraphed to Horace Porter, New York City. "Letter mailed Babcock last night in your care. If he leaves before receiving it read & destroy it" ALS (telegram sent), DNA, RG 107, Telegrams Collected (Bound).

On April 12 and 26, Fish recorded in his diary. ". . . The President asked me what I thought of the appointment of Pierrepont   I replied that personally it would be to me a very agreeable selection, whereupon he remarked there can be no objection to having two members from the same State in the Cabinet, that New York was a large State. I replyed that there would be criticism on that point, that local Jealousies were very strong and that I doubted whether the selection would be agreeable to Conkling   He said that he wanted a person whose character and ability would give assurance of no occasion for the Democratic Party in the next house of challenging the administration of the Department. That from what he had heard he should be glad ~~be glad~~ to avoid an investigation of the past That the Secretary of the Treasury had told him some things with regard to transactions in NewYork which were very alarming which Bristow said he had mentioned to Belknap who however had no mention of it to him   I asked whether he had heard of anything in connection with the firm of Pratt & Boyd   he had not; I told him that while in NewYork I had heard some very startling things with regard to it. That it is a suit for the recovery of a large amount for false Custom House entries that I was told that a large sum had been paid to certain parties to obtain a discontinuance of the suit and that a certain lady exacted $30.000 in consideration of which she promised to have the suit discontinued   I told him Bristow might give him some information   He spoke of the anonymous letters which have been addressed to several parties and says that they are undoubtedly written by this lady that they have peculiarity of expression as well as undoubted peculiarty of hand writing which place their authorship beyond doubt" "Received a note from Genl Babcock stating that the President wished to see me at 11 o'clock this morning. Messrs Belknap Robeson & Jewell had likewise been summoned and were in attendance   The President stated that he desired to confer upon the appointment of a new Attorney General   That Williams had resigned to take effect on 15 May, he read his note of resignation and said that in the filling of Cabinet appointments he did not feel bound to observe State limits   That while he might desire to select his Cabinet from different parts of the country there were difficulties in so doing, that as to political advantage which might result it was uncertain as in some of the states the Republican Party was divided into two factions to such an extent that the selection of a person from one of the factions would disturb and distract the party by giving offense to the other more than the equivalent ~~more than the~~ good which would result from giving a Cabinet appointment to the State. He instanced Pennsylvania from which no man could be appointed as he thought who would not be objectionable to either the Cameron or the Anti Cameron party referred to his own selection of Mr Borie from that state as having been about the only man not identified with either and then made a humorous allusion to the appointment of Robeson to succeed Mr Borie as being a Pennsylvanian in matters of business relations and New Jersey in voting. He stated that he had received several letters warmly urging the appointment of Judge Pierrepont and among the number one from A. B. Cornell of NewYork which he read, also one from Bristow which he likewise read   He then mentioned the name of Judge Pierrepont for the vacancy saying that he would not however make an appointment which would be objected to by any of the Cabinet   Belknap Robeson & Jewell each expressed themselves cordially in approval Robeson adding that the Secretary of State being from New York and knowing Pierrepont more intimately should have more to say on the subject. I replied that the President ~~had~~ had spoken to me of Pierrepont who was a warm friend of mine some two or three weeks ago and I had expressed to him my personal approval of the selection but had then suggested a doubt owing to an apprehended opposition which was however removed by the letter just read from Cornell   The President then remarked ~~yets~~ that the Secretary of State had told him he feared the appointment would not be acceptable to Sen Conkling; Robeson & Jewell stated that they entertained the same apprehension but it was agreed that Cornell's letter might be taken as Conklings approval. Belknap read a letter addressed to him by Bristow, from NewYork, dated yesterday, *approving* of Pierrepont, for Atty Gen   The question was then raised whether Pierrepont should be asked whether he would accept the appointment or a Commission at once be sent to him   The President decided to send the commission immediatly and requested me to write to Pierrepont asking him to telegraph his decission and to give no publicity to the affair until an appointment should be officially announced from Washington" DLC-Hamilton Fish. On April 27, Fish wrote to USG. "Since returning to my Office, I have a telegram from Judge Pierrepont, in acknowledgment of my letter, and signifying his acceptance of the position offered" ALS (press), *ibid.* On May 17, Fish recorded in his diary. "Bristow called on me in the afternoon and referred to the letter from him read at the Cabinet Meeting on April 26 respecting Pierrepont's appointment; said he had been induced to write it from an application made to him by Judge Cartter urging the appointment of General Butler as Attorney General that Cartter after pressing the fitness of the appointment had said that if Butler be made Attorney General he would favor Bristows election to the Presidency and that on the Sunday evening before the meeting at the Presidents Horace Porter had told him in NewYork that a special meeting of the cabinet or a part thereof was to be held on the following day for the purpose of considering certain changes in the Cabinet   ~~Belknaps~~ Babcock's letter convening the Meeting of the Cabinet was directed and dated on Monday morning but it seems that Horace Porter was advised in NewYork on Sunday evening of the meeting" *Ibid.* See Nevins, *Fish*, pp. 769–73; *HMD*, 44-1-186, 406–7, 464–66.

To Michael John Cramer

————

May 11th 1875.

DEAR SIR.

This will introduce the Hon. John M. Francis proprietor and editor of the Troy Times, an able and tried advocate of the Union Cause in the most trying days of the republic, and for some time U. S. Minister to Greece, who visits Europe again with Mrs Francis on a tour recreation and pleasure. As personal as well as political, friend, I take great pleasure in introducing Mr. Francis & Lady to you and bespeak your good offices in his behalf.

Yours truly,

U. S. GRANT.

HON. M. J. CRAMER, U. S. MINISTER, COPENHAGEN DENMARK.

Copy, DLC-USG, II, 2. On May 11, 1875, USG wrote a similar letter to ministers and consuls. Copy, *ibid.* In 1846, John M. Francis had married Harriet Tucker, daughter of a newspaper editor. See *PUSG*, 21, 181–82.

On Oct. 19 and Nov. 2, 1872, Francis, U.S. minister, Athens, had written to USG. "I send you greeting from the Levant upon your reëlection to the Chief Magistracy of the United States. The act of the People will have been consummated ere this meets your eye. An active participant in every Presidential election except the present one during the past thirty years, I can say this with all sincerity: The results of none of these has given me more joy than your merited and sublime triumph, which is in fact a triumph of the People—a victory of integrity over stupendous fraud and vindictive calumny. I am proud of my country. The Republic is *not* ungrateful. If your enemies had taxed their ingenuity to invent methods by which to *help* you most effectually, they could not have adopted agencies more potent for that purpose than those they have employed to injure you. Their very malice has served to magnify the object of their unreasoning and insane hate. With a heart full of joy and gratitude I congratulate you. And Mrs. Francis unites with me also in congratulations for Mrs. Grant." ALS, USG 3. "As a souvenir from this far-off classic land, I enclose herewith a copy of an Athens Greek newspaper containing an editorial on the recent elections in America and complimentary expressions concerning yourself. The article is marked on last page of the paper, and I transmit a translation of the same." ALS, Babcock Papers, ICN. The translation is *ibid.*

On Jan. 30, 1875, Francis, Troy, N. Y., wrote to USG. *"Private . . .* You honored me with a diplomatic appointment in 1871. I discharged the duties of the place to the best of my ability. I held the office for a period of about two years. Then my personal affairs at home impelled me to resign. I did this reluctantly, for I felt that I had only just educated myself to a position for usefulness in the service. Now I would deem it a very high honor to receive another similar appointment. There is the vacant place at Constantinople. My knowledge of affairs at the East might possibly render my services there useful. The record of my work at Athens I may refer to in this connection. If reappointed now I shall have less than four years of official service altogether under your administration. I think I understand something of the perplexity of geographical quotas in respect to a distribution of these offices. And yet it might be possibly assumed in my case that experience is worthy of consideration, and that I held my first place but for a limited time. An office of this character coming without importunity, and as evidence of Executive confidence, the choice being made substantially upon the principle you have sought to apply in our civil service, would certainly be deemed by me a very great honor, and for which I should be ever grateful." ALS, USG 3. No appointment followed. See *New York Times,* Nov. 10, 1873.

On June 1, Francis, Fire Island, N. Y., wrote to Edward M. Smith. "I enclose you the letters to President Grant and Secretary Fish. The General, with some other influential friends & yourself should have earnest interviews with both the President and Mr. Fish, and the *urgency* of the proposed appointment should be put in the strongest possible way. . . . Do you know Gen. Porter, Grant's former secretary, now Sup't of Pullman's cars? If you can get him to back you, a point would be gained. Or, if you can get Tom Murphy to take hold in your behalf earnestly it would be well. Try by all means to have Conkling back you vigorously. Move with real strength if at all. . . ." ALS, DNA, RG 59, Letters of Application and Recommendation. On June 3, Francis, Troy, wrote to USG. "The Hon. E. M. Smith, formerly Mayor of Rochester, N. Y., and recently Postmaster in that city, is an applicant for a United States consulship at some suitable European post. I do earnestly hope it may be in your power to gratify his wish. . . . Under the peculiar circumstances which may be explained to you, I am convinced that the effect of such appointment would be most happy, while the honor conferred would be altogether deserving. I have never, Mr. President, made to you a plea in behalf of an appointment wherein I have felt the earnest convictions and very clear perceptions of what it seems to me is both just and due and most desirable, as in this case." ALS, *ibid.* On July 21, USG endorsed this letter. "If Mr. Smith could be given a Consulate in place of some New Yorker who wants to—or who should—retire I would be pleased to see him get it." AES, *ibid.* USG also wrote an undated note. "Ed. M. Smith (Rochester, N. Y.) desires Consulate" AN, Columbia University, New York, N. Y. On Dec. 21, 1870, USG had nominated Smith as postmaster, Rochester, N. Y.; on Jan. 10, 1876, USG nominated Smith as consul, Mannheim.

To Ministers and Consuls

May 11th 1875.

SIR:

I take pleasure in presenting to you Rev. Dr. S. S. Mitchell of this city, who visits Europe for health and pleasure. Dr. Mitchell is accompanied by his wife, and Mrs. J. M. Thompson and family.

I beg to bespeak for them your kind attention while they may remain near you.

Very truly yours
U. S. GRANT

To U. S. MINISTERS & CONSULS IN EUROPE

LS, State University of New York at Buffalo. Samuel S. Mitchell was minister of the New York Avenue Presbyterian Church in Washington, D. C.

On Feb. 18, 1875, USG wrote to ministers and consuls in Europe. "This will present to you Mr. A. D. Jessup of Philadelphia who proposes traveling in Europe for pleasure. Mr Jessup is a gentleman worthy of such courtesies as you may be able to extend to him, and I take pleasure in commending him to your good offices while he may remain in your vicinity." Copy, DLC-USG, II, 2. USG wrote similar letters introducing Dickinson Woodruff, retired lt. col. (Feb. 27), John V. Farwell of Ill. (March 2), U.S. Representative Lyman K. Bass of N. Y. (March 5), Mrs. M. N. Babcock of Saratoga Springs, N. Y. (April 8), and R. Suydam Grant of New York City (Oct. 15). Copies, *ibid.*, and *ibid.*, II, 3.

On March 1, USG had written to ministers and consuls. "I take great pleasure introducing to you Col. John J. McCook, now of New York but formerly of Ohio, who proposes calling upon you in his travels. He, together with his father and brothers, served through the war with distinction, and his services entitle him to the respect and esteem of his countrymen. I beg to commend him to your good offices while he may remain in your vicinity." Copy, *ibid.*, II, 2.

On March 13, USG wrote to U.S. diplomats in Mexico. "I take pleasure in presenting to you Judge W. L. Helfenstien of Pa.—a gentleman much eteemed by the people of his state. Judge H— is about to visit Mexico, and I beg to commend him to you as worthy of such courtesies as you may be able to bestow while he remains near you." Copy, *ibid.*

On March 16, USG wrote to ministers and consuls in Europe. "This will present to you Gen. S. W. Crawford, who visits Europe for the purpose of study and pleasure. Gen. Crawford has been placed on the retired list of the army on account of wounds received in battle. You will please extend to him such courtesies as are customary while he sojourns in your vicinity." LS (facsimile), Joseph Rubinfine List 145, [*2001*], no. 21. On March 3, USG had signed an act raising the rank and retirement pay of Samuel W. Crawford, previously retired as col., to that of brig. gen., the rank he held when he was wounded. The act applied the same principle to all officers retired because of wounds received in action. See *U.S. Statutes at Large*, XVIII, part 3, p. 512.

On April 29, USG wrote to ministers and consuls. "I take pleasure in introducing to you Mr Chales S. Baylis, of New York City, who proposes making a tour around the world, and will visit your post of duty. I commend him to your good offices, while he may remain in your vicinity." Copy, DLC-USG, II, 2.

On May 11, USG wrote to ministers and consuls introducing "Wm A. Richardson, Judge of the Court of Claims formerly Secty. of the Tres." Copy, *ibid.*

On May 28, USG wrote to ministers and consuls. "I take particular pleasure in introducing to you Major Genl. S. P. Heintzelman of the U. S. A. who with his wife and daughter propose spending some time in Europe. Genl. H—whose entire life has been given to his country; his active service commencing in 1826—continuing through the Mexican War and the late rebellion—until 1869. when by special act of Congress he was retired with full rank of Maj. General   He is entitled to the grateful thanks of his countrymen & the best offices of our foreign officials & I beg to commend him to you while he may remain in your vicinity." Copy, *ibid.*

To Chester A. Arthur

May 12th /75

Gen.l;

This will introduce Co[l.] Geo. G. Pride, who served on my Staff with the Western Armies, who desires to call on you.

The Col. I know to be an able and efficient man in any capacity he undertakes, as I found him while with me. After the return—or falling back—of the Army from Oxford, Miss, in Dec. /62, the roads —R. R from Holly Springs to Memphis were entirely rebuilt under his supervision and Engineering with only such aid as could be got from the ranks and freedmen of the country in an incredibly short time.

Yours Truly
U. S. Grant

Gen.   Arthur Col. Port of New York.

ALS, IHi. On May 11, 1875, USG wrote to Secretary of the Treasury Benjamin H. Bristow. "Will the Sec. of the Treas. please see Col. Geo. G. Pride? Col. Pride served on my Staff at Pittsburg Landing, and after for a considerable time." ANS, DNA, RG 56, Letters Received from the President.

To Oscar H. La Grange

———

May 12th 1875.

DEAR SIR.

This will introduce to you Mr. Frank C. Berdan who goes to San Francisco with his bride to make that City their home—I have known Mrs. Berdan for some years before her marriage and she is the daughter of an officer who served for thirty years in his country's service. Mr. Berdan is very desirous of securing employment in the Mint under you, and if you can aid him either in that direction or in securing him some other suitable position, if a place in the Mint should be impracticable. I shall esteem it in the light of personal favor to myself.

Very truly yours
U. S. GRANT.

GENL. O. H. LA GRANGE
SUPT. MINT SAN FRANCISCO, CAL.

Copy, DLC-USG, II, 2. As of Sept. 30, 1875, Frank C. Berdan served as workman at the U.S. mint, San Francisco. See Kate I. Berdan to Hamilton Fish, March 8, 1875, DNA, RG 59, Letters of Application and Recommendation.

On Dec. 7, 1869, USG had nominated Oscar H. La Grange, former col., 1st Wis. Cav., and bvt. brig. gen., as superintendent, U.S. mint, San Francisco. On Sept. 23, 1875, La Grange wrote to Orville E. Babcock seeking appointment as assay commissioner. ALS, ICN.

To Ministers and Consuls

May 22d 1875.

SIR,

This will present to you Mr. A. B. Mullett of this City, who visits Europe in pursuit of information in the line of his profession—An Architect and Civil Engineer—Mr. Mullett held the position of Supervising Architect of the Treasury Dept. for fourteen years, during which time he planned and built many of our finest public buildings—Notably among them the New York Post Office—San Francisco Mint, New State War & Navy Depts. building in this City.— Any assistance you may be able to give him, will be extended to a worthy gentleman.

Truly yours
U. S. GRANT.

To U. S. MINISTERS & CONSULS IN EUROPE.

Copy, DLC-USG, II, 2. On Nov. 21, 1874, Alfred B. Mullett, Washington, D. C., wrote to Secretary of the Treasury Benjamin H. Bristow resigning as supervising architect of the U.S. Treasury. Suzanne Mullett Smith and Daisy M. Smith, eds., *A. B. Mullett Diaries &c. . . .* (Washington, 1985), p. 107. See *New York Times*, Nov. 24, 1874.

On Dec. 16, Chester A. Arthur, collector of customs, New York City, wrote to USG. "Understanding that Mr Wm Appleton Potter has been spoken of in connection with the appointment of Supervising Architect of the Treasury, it affords me pleasure to say in regard to him, that I know him personally to be a gentleman of the highest character and of very high attainments in his profession as an Architect." ALS, DNA, RG 56, Appointment Div., Letters Received. On the same day, James McCosh, president, Princeton College, *et al.*, wrote to USG. "Mr William A. Potter of New York has been employed by the Trustees of the College of New Jersey as the Architect of the two finest buildings that have been erected for the College, to-wit, the Chancellor Green Library and the John C. Green School of Science, and we cheerfully certify not only to the great beauty and excellence of these buildings as to their Architectural effect and the adaptation of the plans to the purposes of their building, but to the practical skill exhibited by Mr Potter in the mechanical structure of the parts and details." LS (16 signatures), *ibid.* Related papers are *ibid.* Willam A. Potter was appointed supervising architect. See *New York Times*, Dec. 30, 1874; Sarah Bradford Landau, *Edward T. and William A. Potter: American Victorian Architects* (New York, 1979).

On Dec. 27, 1875, USG wrote to George Williamson, U.S. minister, Central American States. "I take pleasure in introducing to you Mr. A. B. Mullett, late Supervising Architect of the Treasury, who informs me he expects to visit the country to which you are accredited. I beg to commend to you Mr. M. as a gentleman who will appreciate any kindness you may be able to extend to him while he remains in your vicinity." Copy, DLC-USG, II, 3.

Endorsement

———

Will the Sec. of the Treas. please read and forward to the Atty. Gen. so that he may see this before Cabinet meeting to-day.

U. S. Grant

May 25th /75

AES, DNA, RG 60, Letters Received, Mo. Written on a telegram dated May 24, 1875, from Chester H. Krum, St. Louis, to USG. "Since the earliest rumers concerning the U S attorneyship here I have made careful inquiry into all insinuations and reflections against Mr Patrick   I respectfully represent and am prepared to show that he has had no intimacy with suspected persons and that the reflections ~~against~~ upon his private character which have bee[n] made as I understand in Washington are based upon malice and untruth   I hope that I shall not be deemed officious in suggesting that the mode of proceedure against Mr Patrick by interested parties from this city has been so unusual as to have been of itself suspicious   I beg leave to call attention to the fact that a change in the U S attorneyship would lead to confusion and might hazard substantial interests of the United States as you honored me with your confidence so far that upon my resignation Mr Patrick was appointed upon my own recommedation I have sifted matters here to the bottom so as to learn if I could what there was to be urged against Mr Patrick as a public officer   I beg to assure you that I am not mistaken or deceived when I say that Mr Patrick stands before our people with an unblemished reputation as a capable and honest officer   I have heard regrets expressed on all sides in regard to his probable suspension   If I have shown unusual interest in this matter I respectfully submit that knowing as I do how free from blame Mr Patrick has been it is but natural that I have not been able to refrain from remonstrating against what I am told here is a probable suspension based upon charges which have been made without his knowledge and which are simply untrue and malicious It does seem to me that such favorable assurances as to Mr Patricks honorable and upright conduct have already been received that unwarrantable aspersions against him might with safety be ignored" Telegram received (at 1:30 A.M.), *ibid.* On May 7, Krum had written to USG on the same subject. ALS, *ibid.* See *PUSG,* 23, 281–82.

Also on May 7, Thomas C. Fletcher, St. Louis, wrote to USG. "It has been suggested to me by some of our friends here, that there would probably be a change in the District Attorneyship for the Eastern District of Missouri. If it should be so, I believe I could do the U. S. some good service in that position and will, if necessary have our friends here, upon whose judgment and integrity you can rely, to write or telegraph you to that effect." ALS, DNA, RG 60, Records Relating to Appointments.

On May 8, John F. Long, surveyor of customs, St. Louis, wrote to USG. "A rumer is prevalent in the City to the effect, that Capt. William Patrick, United States Dist. Attorney is to be releived. I regret exceedingly to hear this.—I hope it may prove erronious, because of Mr. P's legal ability, his stern integrity as an officer, And of his irreproachable Character and high sense of honor as a gentleman. I know the President may be imposed upon, in such matters, by friends, who from immaginary wrongs or unfounded evils, jump at conclusions, which imply error or wrongdoing in a faithful officer. But of this you will be sole judge" ALS, *ibid.,* Letters Received, Mo.

On May 20, Levi P. Luckey wrote to Attorney Gen. Edwards Pierrepont. "The President directs me to write and say that, such information is received as seems to make it advisable to change the District Attorney, both at St. Louis and Milwaukee." ALS, *ibid.* On the same day, USG suspended William Patrick as U.S. attorney, Eastern District, Mo. See William Patrick to Edwards Pierrepont, May, 1875, *ibid.*, RG 118, Letters Sent, U.S. Attorneys, Eastern District, Mo. On May 20, Luckey wrote to Alexander J. Falls, chief clerk, Justice Dept. "The President says he has not decided upon the successors to the suspended Dist. Attorneys, but for the Atty. General to consult with the Secty. of the Treasury, who has been investigating these matters." Copy, DLC-USG, II, 2. On the same day, Pierrepont wrote to Secretary of State Hamilton Fish requesting a commission for David P. Dyer to replace Patrick. Copy, DNA, RG 60, Letters Sent to Executive Officers.

On May 22, Chauncey I. Filley, postmaster, St. Louis, wrote to USG. *"Personal & confidential* . . . The news of the nomination of D. Pat Dyer yesterday, for the U S Dist Atty of this district was as great a suprise, as was the subsequent report of its withdrawal a relief, to the Republicans generally and especially your friends who are familiar with his past record—While I would not continue the differences of the past—yet there are some persons, who by reason of their positions—should not have been traitors to the party and to you—and Pat Dyer is one of them. He openly & bitterly denounced you in 1870, was allied to the Bolters, and at the Philadelphia Convention of 1871—would with Orrick, Stanard, and some others have opposed your renomination and *so stated* before leaving here, if there had been any show to unite upon any one else. Henderson came to me the other day to join in reccommending Dyer. I did not, & would not do it, for I dont beleive in rewarding traitors, and men whom I have no confidence in sticking by the party—if a personal insterest arose to the contrary. The Republicans of his own the 13th District would not unite upon him & this recognition of him will prove a discouragement to them & other true Republicans in [t]he State. I do not know whom [He]nderson induced to sign his reccommendations but it seems easy for people to forget that Dyers past & present affiliations are more with the Liberals than with the Regulars. The whole state recognizes the ability and reliability of Jeff Chandler. He was the Candidate in '72 for Attorney General, and canvassed the State. He has been always true and will so remain. He is the brother in law of Hon Isaac C. Parker, and is one of, if not the most rising young lawyer, & so looked upon and acknowledged by Henderson and the legal fraternity—in the State. He is above suspicion, and the recognition of such a man, and such a Republican, would be benefi[c]ial now and hereafter, and meet with general approbation   Henderson undertook to prove to me that Dyer had always been your friend,   I knew, & know better,   An opportunity in '71 or any other time would show the contrary." ALS, *ibid.*, Records Relating to Appointments. Related papers recommending Jefferson Chandler to replace Patrick are *ibid.*

On May 25, Jesse B. Woodward, St. Louis, wrote to USG. "I beg leave herewith to make application for appointment to the office of United States District Attorney for the Eastern District of Missouri   I have been actively engaged in the practice of law in the States of Tennessee and Missouri for eleven years, having been County Attorney in the Memphis District in Tennessee for two successive terms during the republican administration there—I have practiced in this City the four years last past—My age is thirty five years—I would also call attention to the indorsement and recommendation forwarded to you in regard to my qualification for the office, and I would also refer you to the government officials cognizant of the facts as to recent services rendered by me in investigating and exposing the frauds against the internal revenue laws in this and other cities" ALS, *ibid.* Related papers are *ibid.* On April 25, 1876, Charles S. Bell, former special agent, Post Office Dept., testified before a select committee of the House of Representatives that he had been ordered to remove evidence against government officials during the investigation of the St. Louis Whiskey Ring. ". . . I had taken three or four letters that were written by a lawyer in Saint Louis named Jesse D. Woodward, dated in 1873 and 1874, in which he gave information to Mr. Douglass of the frauds committed at Saint Louis; and I noticed that the names mentioned in his reports in 1873 and 1874 were the names of the same parties, some of them, who have since plead guilty or been convicted. In fact, his report of 1873 was complete, and the line of investigation laid down by him is that which has been followed by the Government. Those reports were published in the Saint Louis Republican of the 9th of November, and I know that Mr. Woodward came out in a card and accused Mr. Bristow of a gross breach of confidence in publishing his name signed to the reports. He was very bitter against the Secretary for making the thing public, because it made him a great deal of trouble there. He had spent a good deal of his own money in working against the 'ring;' and I understood that he expected to be made district attorney for the services he had rendered, but he was not. Mr. Dyer was made district attorney." *HMD*, 44-1-186, 111–12. See *ibid.*, pp. 143–44.

On May 26, 1875, John A. Scudder and eight others, St. Louis, had telegraphed to USG. "The undersigned citizens of St Louis learning with Surprise their U, S Atty Wm Patrick may probably be Suspended by direction of Your excellency & from a long personal acquaintance with him being very loth to believe that any just reason can exist for his Suspension or removal Respectfully Submit that his removal at this time would cast a blemish on a gentleman whose reputation in this Community is beyond reproach & would be a serious detriment to the local interests of the U, S" Telegram received (at 4:40 P.M.), DNA, RG 60, Letters Received, Mo.

On May 27, Matthew H. Carpenter, Milwaukee, telegraphed to USG. "Levi Hubbell district atty here is a faithful & able officer   Geo Q. Erskine is as honest a man as lives, Has done his duty always,   the removal of these men at this time is wrong, & will do great harm,   I beg of you not to act until I see you and Bristow which will be between the fifth & tenth June,   The recommendation of mr Bean for Erskine place is an unfortunate one He was a bolter last winter,   Is very unpopular & not the man at all," Telegram received, *ibid.*, Letters Received, Wis. On June 1, USG suspended George Q. Erskine as collector of Internal Revenue, 1st District, Wis.; on Dec. 8, USG nominated Irving M. Bean to replace Erskine.

On May 31, Secretary of the Treasury Benjamin H. Bristow, Louisville, had written to USG. "A letter from Senator Howe has been forwarded to me at this place, which he intimates a desire for you to see, and I, therefore, take the liberty to enclose it. I am sure he is entirely right in what he suggests touching the whiskey ring in Wisconsin. I find by personal contact with people in the West, that there is a very general and earnest desire that these revenue frauds shall be cleaned out, and a very strong wish among the good men of all parties to support your Administration in the effort we are making to suppress the frauds and collect the revenue. What is to me one of the most gratifying political signs of the times is the tendency among Liberal Republicans throughout the West to return to their party allegiance. The treatment they have received at the hands of Democrats shows them what they may expect in the future, and has disgusted them with their present party affiliations   Of course the contest with the Whiskey ring is going to be a very hot one, and they are supported by some hitherto strong political influence and backed by enormous sums of money, and we are going to have great trouble in some places in securing the services of lawyers competent to cope with the counsel that will represent the ring. This will be particularly the case in St. Louis. I hope you are comfortably located in your summer quarters." LS, USG 3.

On June 12, Jefferson C. McKenney, asst. U.S. attorney, Milwaukee, wrote to Bristow. "I took the great liberty of telegraphing to you to-day on the subject of the appointment of a District Attorney for this District—It may have been great presumption in me to do so, and my only excuse is that I am too deeply interested in the success of the Government in the whisky war here to remain silent when I think that success is endangered—I thoroughly believe in the honesty of the great mass of the people, but here in Milwaukee we have a peculiar state of affairs—A large portion of the city is composed of Germans; nearly all of the liquor men are Germans; their workmen and employes are Germans, and in most instances the bondsmen of the distillers are wholesale business men, also Germans—The constant inquiry of the German part of the population is, whether this raid is made in the interest of honest reform in the collection of the revenue, or whether it is a grand political Scheme—So far, the German press has been with us, but timid and fearful—Our greatest opposition comes from the former federal officers, their attorneys and newspapers—We are daily maligned, lied about and traduced by both the 'Sentinel' and the 'News', the former owned by Carpenter and Murphy, the attorneys of the whisky men, and the latter in their pay—In these cases we have the law and the evidence on our side, we want also to retain the active sympathy of the honest portion of the community—This can only be done, in my opinion, by carefully avoiding every appearance of using the appointing power to reward past political service—The appointment of Mr. Hazleton, *from another District*, I fear would raise a storm of indignation here that would well nigh break us down, while the appointment of a good lawyer and unexceptionable man here would add a tower of strength to our side—I deem it not only desireable to win, but also to have the verdict of the jury applauded by the people—I have presumed to write this much, as an an Attorney writing to a client, with no political aspirations to gratify, no enemies to pull down, and no friends to promote—I believe Senators Howe and Cameron would not have approved the appointment had they fully known the feeling here and thought a good man could be found in this District, as certainly can be done—" ALS, DNA, RG 60, Records Relating to Appointments. On June 16, Bristow endorsed this letter. "The Attorney General being away I take the liberty ~~of~~ to forward this letter to the President" AES, *ibid.* On June 14, Bristow had written to USG. "I hand you herewith a message from Mr McKinney relating to the appointment of a District Atty at Milwaukee. The Atty General is out of the city and no one in his office knows anything about the Matter   It may be that papers favoring Hazletons appointment have been sent to you hence I send you McKinney's message. You will no doubt recollect that Mr McKinney was employed as special counsel at the instance of Senator Howe. I do not know him personally but have a good opinion of him   I hand you also a message from Dist Atty Dyer of St Louis for your information. I fear the whiskey frauds in St Louis reach much further than we have supposed. I have replied to Mr Dyer that while it is important to go to the bottom of the frauds, it is desirable to institute no proceeding which is not fully sustained by proofs in his possession." ALS (press) and typescript, DLC-Benjamin H. Bristow. On the same day, 8:15 A.M., Dyer had telegraphed to Bristow. "The Grand Jury has returned bills against McDonald, Joyce and others and will hive the whole gang before they adjourn. The extent and magnitude of the frauds is perfectly appalling." ALS (press, telegram sent), DNA, RG 118, Letters Sent, U.S. Attorneys, Eastern District, Mo.; telegram received (at 9:30 A.M.), USG 3. On July 7, Pierrepont wrote to Fish requesting a commission for Gerry W. Hazelton to replace Levi Hubbell as U.S. attorney, Eastern District, Wis. Copy, DNA, RG 60, Letters Sent to Executive Officers. See *PUSG*, 19, 366–67; Endorsement, July 29, 1875.

Speech to Sioux Delegation

————

Executive Mansion, May 26th, 1875.

I want to say something about the object for which you have been brought here. I want to say a few words for you to think about; and I do not wish you to say anything now, until you have had time to think about it.

I have always been a friend to the Indians, and I am very anxious to do what I think is best for them.

The country where you now live, as you must be aware, is entirely incapable of supporting you, if the government should cease to support you. By the treaty of 1868, clothing was granted to you for thirty years, and provisions for only five years. The food and provisions which have been given you for the l[a]st two years, have been a gratuitys on the part of Congress. They may be taken from you at any time without any violation of the treaty. My interest now is, to make some arrangement with you, by which you and your children will be secure for the future.

I said in the beginning it must be evident to you that if food were witheld by the white people, it would be entirely impossible for you to live where you are. Another thing that I would call your attention to, is this: you must see that the Indians (whites) outnumber the Indians now, about 200 to one, taking all the Indians within the United States. This number is increasing so very rapidly that before many years it will be impossible to fix any limits to your territory[1] where you can prevent their going.

It will become necessary for the white people to be able to go from one place to another, whether occupied by Indians or not just as they now go from one state to another; th[a]t while you have a friend here to look after your interests, you shall be situated where you will be able to get a support beyond any contingency.

I do not propose to ask you to leave the homes where you were born and raised, without your consent. I want to point out to you the advantage to you and your children, if you will make such arrangements as will be proposed to you.

There is a territory south of where you now live, where the climate is very much better, and the grass is very much better, and the game is much more abundant, including large game such as buffalo: where you can have good pasturage for animals; and where you can have teachers sent among you to teach you the arts of self-preservation and self support.

Now this year we have had great difficulty in keeping white people from going to the Black Hills in search of gold; but we have so far prevented their going, or prevented their remaining there.

Every year this same difficulty will be increased, unless the right of the white people to go to that country, is granted by you; and it may in the end lead to hostilities between the Indians and the white people without any special fault on either side. If such troubles should occur and become general, it would necessarily withold for the time at least, the supplies which the government would be sending to you. All this trouble I want to avoid. I want to see you well provided for, and I want to see the provision made in such a way that it will have to be respected by my successor, and by other administrations in future. I want the Indians to think of what I have said. I do not want to say anything more to-day; but think among yourselves, and be prepa[r]ed to hear the Commissioner of Indian Affairs, and the Secretary of the Interior, who will always speak for me, and will never speak without advising with me either before or after they have spoken.

That is all I want to say to-day. What I have said has been written down and will be repeated to you.

Typescript, DNA, RG 75, Letters Received, Dakota Superintendency.
    On May 19, 1875, USG greeted a Sioux delegation from the Red Cloud, Spotted Tail, and Cheyenne River agencies. "I have sent for you to come simply to see you, and to congratulate you upon your safe arrival, but not to talk to you on any business. I shall see you again from time to time, while you are here. In the meantime I want you to talk with the Commissioner of Indian Affairs on all matters of business, and whenever there is a misunderstanding, the matter will be referred to me, and I will see you on such business; but to-day I don't want to see you on business. While you are here, take the word of the Commissioner of Indian Affairs and the Secretary of the Interior, and do not rely on any word except as it comes from them. If Spotted Tail and Red Cloud want to say a word in response, I will hear them." *Ibid.* Lone Horn spoke. "My Great Father I am glad to see you. I see my people here. They are relatives of mine. There is a great countty that belongs to me, and I think this country here, belongs to me; but it is not mine to-day; and part of the

countty which I own now, the white people wish to take from me. My father was a great
chief, something as yourself. We called him Great Father. He was my great grand-father:
also my father was a chief, and I am a chief myself. I am the Indian chief. I have never
claimed that I owned all the country around, but to-day I claim that I own it. These people
that visited you before, and shook hands with you, [a]nd councilled, those were soldiers;
but these are chiefs, and I and that man are chiefs." USG replied. "We don't want to discus[s] that question to-day. You will be s[p]oken to by the Secretary of the Interior, and by
the Commissioner of Indian Affai[r]s. We have the interests of the Indians at heart, and in
view of the great growth of the population among the white people, we know better what
is for your ~~good~~ interests than you can know yourselves; and it is your interests we are
looking after." Spotted Tail spoke. "Great Fathe[r] I am very glad to [see] you, and shake
hands with you. We are very glad to see each other. We wish to have a council here, and
sometime we will do much business. I used to have councils with this man, and we want to
have councils together. And we will say the truth to you, and you will to me." Red Cloud
concluded. "My Great Father, I have come to see you and shake hands with you. I hope you
will appoint a day for us to come and talk with you again." *Ibid.* On May 21, the Sioux delegation met with Interior Dept. officials to discuss grievances. Typescript, clippings, *ibid.*
See Council with Sioux Delegation, June 2, 1875.

On March 28, John S. Collins, Red Cloud Agency, Neb., twice wrote to USG. "I have
the honor to inform you, that in accordance with your request that I procure what Information I could from the Indians concerning the Black Hills, I came to this Agency, called
upon U. S. Indian Agent J. J. Saville and informed him that I desired to procure information, and meet in council such cheifs and leading Indians as could be assembled for the purpose above named; that my object is to procure a truthfull expression without in any way
conflicting with his wishes, and to get such expression would with his permission meet the
Indians in a Lodge, to prevent any influence that might govern them if the council was
called by him. I accordingly employed a Half Breed Louis Richards to call the Indians in
council, having accomplished this, I invited to be present The Agent Saville, Capt. Jordan and two or three officers that he might select. All being assembled at Eleven O'clock
today I read to the Indians the enclosed copy of questions and conversation. Before proceeding Agent Saville, asked by what authority do you council with these Indians, my reply was, 'At the Verbal request of President Grant. have you any objections to offer,' he
answered 'no.' I here enclose you the speaches made in council, also a list of Indians and
others present. It is my impression that the presence in council of the Agent and others, in
a measure influenced the Indians and prevented an extended and candid expression and
further that it would be impossible in council to get the candid expression of the Indians.
it is my beleif that were commissioners sent here to treat with them no desirable result
could be attained. Should a delegation from their number be selected to go to Washington,
I beleive they would be perfectly willing to sell the Black Hills, unless influenced by the
persons selected to conduct them there. I go to Spotted Tail Agency tomorrow, on my return will see the Indians again, and report to you as soon thereafter as possible. That the
Indians are willing to sell the Black Hills I have not a doubt, and if a Delegation be sent
on, no trouble would be experienced in accomplishing the desired result" "In the event of
a delegation of Indians being called to Washington I have the honor to submit the following: for your consideration. As many as 30 or 40 white men and halfBreeds who are
married to squaws and living on Government rations, are working among their Indian relations, and want to accompany them to Washington. a majority of them are indolent,
worthless, and unprincipaled, but have some influence over Indians, as 'Red Clouds and
'Red Dog's speaches indicate. A disinterested citizen not connected with the Indian Bu-

reau, by selecting his own interpreters, and one or two intelligent persons familliar with the wants and character of the Indian, could conduct them without difficulty. The Black Hills question seems to be with the Indians as exciting a topic as with the whites, and the impression with them is that they will be allowed to go on to Washington in unlimited numbers. 'Red Dog' stated since the council that the Indians 'would sell the Black Hills, if the great Father would give them blankets and provisions for 50 years. He no doubt had previously been told to say nothing in council about selling the Black Hills. upon such facts I base the beleif that nothing could be accomplished here, while if 30 to 40 prominent ones, representing the various tribes are taken to Washington, a desirable treaty could be made." ALS, DNA, RG 75, Dakota Superintendency. Collins had read a statement to the assembled Sioux. "I am your friend. I came here to talk with you, from the Great Father in Washington. I did not come to make promises, but to hear what you have to say about white men going to the Black Hills to hunt for Gold. Last fall, white men came from the Missouri River, across your country, and into the hills that lays between the two Cheyenne Rivers. Some of them are there now. In a little while a great many people will come from the Missouri River, and from the Rail Road, across your country, and into the Black Hills to hunt for gold. The Great Father tells them they must not go there, for it is the Indians country. If they do go, he will send his soldiers to bring them back, and he will employ some of your young men to help them. There are many roads where the white men can travel, where the soldiers cannot go, and it will be hard to find them. Before the winter comes, the white men will be many there, like the people in your villages. The Great Father will send many more soldiers, but if there is Gold there he has not got soldiers enough to keep the white men out of your country. The Great Father told General Bradley at Ft. Laramie to send his soldiers to the Black Hills, and bring the people out that are hunting Gold. Six days ago Genl. Bradley sent 40 or 50 soldiers to bring the white men out, and when they come to Fort Laramie you can know how many. Do you want to make a treaty with the Great Father for the Black Hills? if you do not, he will have to send a great many more soldiers out to protect your country. Is it not better to sell the country between the two Cheyenne Rivers, then the Great Father would not have any trouble trying to keep the white men from stealing it from you. The Great Father has only one word, that is the truth. If any promises are made to you, that are not kept, it is not the word of the Great Father. I want you to tell me what you want the Great Father to do for you. Do you want the Commissioners to come and see you, or, do you want some of your Cheifs and head soldiers, to go to the Great Father, and hold council with him. I am going to Spotted Tail Agency, to talk about this with the Indians there. The words you give me will go to the Great Father. I have nothing more to say." AD, *ibid.* Red Cloud responded. "Yesterday, I made up my mind and told the agent about it. I think the White men are beginning to know that this is my land. Look at me! I am no Dog. I am a man. This is my ground, and I am sitting on it. You tell me about the Great Fathers Troops. He has troops all over the world, and I do not beleive that the gGreat Father has not Troops enough to keep white men away from the Black Hills. The Great Father sends Commissioners out here to tell the truth, and they pray to God to help them, but they all lie to me and want to steal every thing I have. When I go to my Great Father, and see a peice of land fenced in, I do not pass through or take any thing from it. I want you to tell my great Father, not to let the Commissioners come out here. I want to go myself and see the great Father and settle the matter with him. I forgot one thing: there is a man sitting here that I want to take along with me, and that is the Agent, Dr. Saville. My Friend when you go to Spotted Tail, tell them the same news you told me. When you get back, I will tell you some more about taking some of the old Traders and halfBreeds with me to Washington" D, *ibid.* Responses from Blue Horse and Red Dog, and the list of attendees, are *ibid.* On March 29, Collins again wrote to USG. "I have the honor to inform you that since the council referred to in my communication of yesterday I have learned that The Indians do not want their agent to go to Washington *in charge of them* but to have him present in telling you of his administration here of their affairs. I am convinced that the Indian Soldiers are rising in influence and if a delegation is selected to go to Washington they and not the cheifs will choose. There are 8 Bands who may ask for 5 from each band, but a leading cheif and two soldiers from each would represent them as well as a larger number. 'Red Skin' a friend to the whites, and who killed his nephew for stealing Horses from whites is deserving of praise. My Interpreter informs me that the Indians have decided who they will ask for to escort them, also the whites and HalfBreeds, and on my return from Spotted Tail Agency will give me their names. Three facts I am convinced of, Viz: 1st. The Indians are willing to sell the Black Hills. 2nd. To this end they desire to go to Washington   3rd. That if commissioners are sent out to Treat with them nothing satisfactory can be accomplished. Owing to a snow storm I could not leave for spotted Tail today. I expect within 8 days to return to Ft. Laramie and report to you such further information as I can obtain, unless stormy weather prevents." ALS, *ibid.* On April 4, Collins, Fort Laramie, Wyoming Territory, telegraphed to USG. "I returned from Indian Agencies this Evening   will forward my report tomorrow by Courier to Cheyene thence by mail" Telegram received (at 10:48 P.M.), *ibid.*, Letters Received, Miscellaneous.

On May 7, Collins, Fort Laramie, telegraphed to USG. "Agents with nineteen Indians here   Indians asked for council with me   are very much dissatisfied with only two Interpreters   Say their people not Satisfied   want four   Insist on my telegraphing Great Father they may go on   Liable to turn back and ask for Commissioners   are not in good temper   liable to complicate Black Hills matter   Please answer—" Telegram received (at 8:10 P.M.), *ibid.*, Letters Received, Dakota Superintendency. USG endorsed this telegram. "Refered to the Sec. of the Int. who will please answer this dispatch. If the Indians can be accomodated by permitting Mr. [Co]llins to come on with them I have no objection, nor to their having ~~an~~ additional Interpreters. On this subject decide as deemed best." AES (docketed May 8), *ibid.* See James C. Olson, *Red Cloud and the Sioux Problem* (Lincoln, Neb., 1965), pp. 175–89.

1. On Jan. 11, USG had issued an executive order expanding the Sioux reservation along the Missouri River in Dakota Territory. DS, *ibid.*, Orders. *HRC,* 44-1-799, 550; *HED,* 45-2-1, part 5, I, 636, 45-3-1, part 5, I, 743, 47-2-1, part 5, II, 323, 49-2-1, part 5, I, 539; *SED,* 49-1-1, 10, 19, 72, 91; *SD,* 57-1-452, 924. USG issued related orders on March 16 and May 20. DS, DNA, RG 75, Orders. Printed in the sources listed above. On Feb. 9, Henry F. Livingston, agent, Crow Creek Agency, Dakota Territory, had endorsed a copy of the Jan. 11 order. "In accordance with the above Executive order of the President, no person will be permitted to reside, or trade within the said described country, except those duly authorized" ES, DNA, RG 75, Letters Received, Crow Creek Agency. On May 8, Edward P. Smith, commissioner of Indian Affairs, wrote to Livingston. "I send you, herewith enclosed, copy of a letter from Governor Pennington of Dakota, dated the 27th ultimo, and copy of petition enclosed by him from citizens of Buffalo County, Dakota, presenting claims for damages sustained by said citizens, by reason as alleged of Executive Order of January, 11th 1875 extending the Sioux reservation   I also enclose copy of Department letter to [th]is Office dated the 4th instant; and in accordance with the instructions therein you are directed to restrain the Indians and forbid their molesting the settlers, and inform the petitioners that the views of Governor Pennington are correct, and that the Executive Order was not intended to interfere in any manner with their peaceful occupancy of the country, but to prevent the introduction of whiskey into the reservation,

and that there must be no further interference with the settlers." ALS, *ibid.*, Letters Received, Dakota Superintendency. On May 19, Peter Nelson, Yankton, Dakota Territory, wrote to Governor John L. Pennington of Dakota Territory. "Enclosed I send you copy of Presidents Order, with reference to the Reservation on the Missouri: also order of Indian Agent H. F. Livingston which explains itself. I desire that you should assist us in obtaining some relief from the Government in order that we may extricate ourselves from absolute want occasioned almost wholly by the action of the Government and its Agents in prohibiting us from residing or trading in and upon land taken in good faith under the laws and inducements held out by said Goverment. Two of the settlers upon said newly made reservation arrived here yesterday, and I am informed by them that those who remain are in a pitiable condition.—that they have no work, nothing to eat and cannot get away. Something ought to be done for them immediately" Copy, *ibid.*, Letters Received, Crow Creek Agency. On May 26, Smith wrote to Pennington. ". . . I would respectfully state that the object of the order in question is to aid in the suppression of the liquor traffic with the Indians on the Missouri river. The order does not affect existing rights of any persons, residents within the limits of the territory withdrawn, nor is it supposed that the withdrawal will be made permanent, or that any purchases will be made by the Government of property owned by individuals in the tract of country withdrawn. There will be no interference with the legitimate business pursuits of any person lawfully residing within said limits." ALS, *ibid.*, Letters Received, Dakota Superintendency.

On May 13, Secretary of War William W. Belknap had written to Secretary of the Interior Columbus Delano. "I have the honor to transmit, for your information, copy of a communication from Lieut. Colonel Lugenbeel, dated, Fort Randall, Dakota Territory, April 23rd relative to portions of the river front, near the Sioux reservation, being the resort of whisky dealers, horse thieves, &c., Also that whisky is sold on a similar piece of land near the Yankton reservation &c" LS (press), *ibid.*, RG 94, Letters Received, 2392 1875. Related papers are *ibid.*, including a copy of the May 20 order, which set aside the land in question.

Endorsement

I know Gen. W. S. Smith but do not know Clark.   Smith would be entirely competant and satisfactory but might not be able to act, he being one of the Eng. Board selected to test iron & steel.[1] Either of the parties named would be satisfactory to me.

U. S. GRANT

MAY 26TH /75

AES, DLC-Benjamin H. Bristow. Written on a letter of May 26, 1875, from Secretary of the Treasury Benjamin H. Bristow to Orville E. Babcock. "Please say to the President that Genl Webster declines to act on commission to examine Chicago Custom House, and suggests Genl Wm Smith, or L. H. Clark Chf Engineer Ill Central RR. Potter suggests Chesbrough City Engineer of Chicago. I know none of them & have no preference but would like to have the Presidents direction, or at least his opinion if he knows any of the men named. Potter is in N. Y. waiting directions by telegraph & I would like to advise him at once." ALS, *ibid*. William A. Potter was supervising architect, U.S. Treasury. On June 15, William Sooy Smith, George B. Post, and Orlando W. Norcross, Washington, D. C., "commissioners appointed 'to examine and report upon the condition of the United States custom-house in course of construction at Chicago, Ill.,' and to report 'if, in their opinion, it is practicable to continue said construction,'" wrote to Bristow, concluding "that it will be impracticable, unadvisable, and a waste of time and money to proceed further with the construction of the building." *HED*, 44-1-2, 651–55.

On June 16, Benjamin H. Campbell, U.S. marshal, and others, Chicago, telegraphed to USG. "In case custom House building Shall be condemned we hope you will do all in your power to have the taking down begun at once & not await the tedious action of congress as the delay will be very damaging to our city" Telegram received, DLC-USG, IB. On June 17, Alfred B. Mullett, former supervising architect, U.S. Treasury, Chicago, wrote to Babcock. "I arrived here this morning and after calling on some of our friends, I visited the building in company with Mayor Colvin and Ex. Supt J. C. Rankin and to my utter astonishment I found that there is absolutely so little the matter with the building that the whole damage can be repaired at a cost not to exceed five thousand dollars and I do not believe that it will cost over one. There is not the slightest evidence of settlement, and there is *not a crack in the outer walls*. The inner partition walls have been lifted by the frost a little more than the outer walls and as a consequence four cracks opened but as the frost went out the cracks have closed and a couple of hundred dollars will make the work as good as new. As regards the stone it is an excellent job of work and the stone is good. The whole outcry is the most infamous piece of vilany I ever met. Potter is either an unscrupulous knave, or a first class fool, for my part I think he is sometimes one and sometimes the other. And I feel sure he is in this case acting under the special inspiration of Mr. Bristow who is straining every effort to destroy my reputation and that of every other friend of the President. I know you will smile at this but if the President could hear what I have heard the past three weeks, I know he would remove Mr. Bristow before night. The 'Globe Democrat' will open on him as soon as they can complete some evidence in their position, and every friend of the President in St. Louis looks on aghast at the stabs he is delivering at the hearts of the supporters of the Administration. The Inter Ocean is as you are aware in open war with him but what is published is a mere nothing to the opinions expressed in conversation. So it is in Cincinnati and wherever I go, or have been. Holman the Superintendent who Potter has sent here is a scoundrell as you will see by the enclosed slip. I am informed that he is with the representatives of the Democratic papers the whole time, he does nothing but get up such rumors every day, and unless the President desires to see every friend of his here maligned he should direct Mr. Bristow to remove him at once Mr. Van Oesdell the oldest Architec here and the best constructor agrees with me in regard to the building, and can be induced to accept the Superintendency if Offered. it would restore confidence here, and do more to please his friends than any thing he can do. At any rate Holman should be removed at once. Please say to the President that I pledge my reputation as an architect and my honor as a man that the building is all right and that I have made no mistake. Rankin has been foully slandered and has done well. He is an earnest friend of the President, and was a brave soldier, and has been stricken down by a malicious fool, who knows no more of his duties than a boy knows of a mans. I write earnestly in this matter because I know that the interests of the President, the Republican party and of the Public are at stake. A boy like Mr. Potter cannot tear down one and a quarter millions dollars of property without a searching investigation and an investigation cannot but sustain me. Please see Gen Porter in regard to this and get the President to look into this at once . . ." ALS, USG 3. The enclosure concerning cracks and leaks in the Chicago Customhouse building is *ibid*.

On June 29, Mullett, Brooklyn, wrote to USG. "I am in receipt of the enclosed letter from Major James R. Willett U. S V. formerly an Engineer Officer under Genl Geo. H. Thomas U. S. A. from whom he receved very high testimonials of approval as a brave Soldier and competent Officer. Major Willett is an experienced and accomplished architect, and now holds an appointment as superintendent of the proposed Custom House at Nashville Tenn. He was also employed for many years under me as Supt of Repairs and I can unhesitatingly vouch for his integrity and ability, and would very respectfully recommend him as Superintendent of the Custom House at Chicago where he has practiced his profession since the fire with great success. in the place of the present Superintendent Genl J. H. Holman, who I know from actual observation to be doing all in his power to damage the building, And injure it by persistently refusing to protect it in any manner. The so called commission of experts cut away without cause or excuse large masses of the concrete foundations, and these cavaties were when I inspected the building a few days since filled with water which of course was seeping under the foundations to the serious injury and peril of the work. I do not believe that any competent and honorable Architects would have perfected such an act of vandalism, or left the work in such condition. Neither do I believe that any superintendent who desired to protect the property and interests of the Government would have neglected to repair the damage a single moment. And I do not hesitate to express the opinion that the present Superintendent is doing all in his power to make good the outrageous statements in regard to the condition of the work now being so industriously circulated in the 'Independent and Democratic papers, and in the report of the commission. Which report so far as relates to the present condition of the work I am reluctantly compelled to pronounce untrue, and grossly exaggerated. And to deny that there is or has been any good reason for suspending work a single day. I therefore respectfully submit that so much valuable property should not be left in the charge of a person who denies that it is of any value. Who is interested in a rival stone quarry, and is therefore an interested party, And who is notorously permitting the destruction of the property he is sworn to protect. And that it should be placed in the in the hands of some honorable man who will not only protect it, but who is an expert in Chicago soil. Trusting you will pardon the length of this letter and the liberty I have taken in recommending Major Willett . . ." ALS, *ibid*. The enclosure is a letter of June 22 from James R. Willett, Chicago, to Mullett, Washington, D. C. "In answer to your inquiries I will state that about a month ago I visited the Custom House here & spent about an hour examining the building. I perceived a number of defects but none whatever that would justify the taking down of the structure, none that could not be comparatively easily remidied. I see no reason to doubt that the building could be completed on its present foundations by a competent Architect who was familliar with the Chicago foundations" ALS, *ibid*. On June 29, Mullett, Brooklyn, wrote to Babcock. "I was greatly disappointed at not meeting you on either of my trips to Long Branch. I had however the pleasure of meeting the President who receved me with great kindness and heard me with equal patience. I will not trouble you with my views at full but I assure you that there is nothing whatever the matter with the foundations of the Chicago building, or any thing the matter with the building itself that cannot be repaired at a cost not to exceed a few hundred dollars   Five thousand dollars would be an extravagant estimate of the amount necessary. And I feel no hesitation in saying that more money has been squandered in the so-called investigations. . . . I am willing to day to contract for the completion of the work guaranteeing it to be a permanent and substantial structure, and the stone to be durable and equal to any of the Same Kind. And will find friends who will give bonds to any amount that the President may decide necessary. What more can I do? You must remember that the same clique pronounced the foundations of the New York Post Office insecure and that this is the sixth Commission (some unofficial) that has pronounced me incompetent yet in all other cases I have proved by the actual results I was correct. . . ." ALS, *ibid.*

On June 30, Mullett, New York City, wrote at length to USG. "The recent extraordinary action of the Secretary of the Treasury and his subordinates in regard to the Custom House at Chicago, and the systematic and persistent efforts that have been made to destroy my reputation, and the confidence of the public in the public works designed and commenced by me; Seem to make it my duty to place you in possession of certain facts that appear to me to have an important bearing on the case. . . . I have in another commission expressed the opinion that there is not the slightest excuse for suspending work on the Custom House at Chicago, and made positive denial that any material damage has been done to the building by the frost, or that there is any evidence of Settlement. And expressed the opinion that the opinions of the commission are entitled no no consideration being on their face either absurd or malicious, but I desire in addition to call your attention to the fact that in organizing the commission every man of recognized capacity and integrity was excluded. . . . I respectfully submit that after 22 years experience: 15 of them in the Govt Service, and about 10 in the capacity of Supervising Architect, during which time I have never met with a failure that my opinion is entitled to greater consideration than theirs. I am willing to show my faith by my works and am willing should you desire to enter into a contract to complete the building according to the original plan and guarantee its stability by ample bonds. I do not see how I can do more, and with many thanks for your great courtesy and kindness to me, and with apologies for the great length of this communication . . ." ALS, *ibid.* On the same day, Mullett wrote to Babcock. "I enclose herewith in accordance with the request of the President a letter in regard to the treatment I have receved from the Treasury. I regret it is so long but I could do no better. And I must also apologise for the delay in preparing it which was unavoidable with the pressure of business on me. I have taken no copy and therefore trust that the President will not suffer the original to go out of his hands without keeping a copy,   I sail on Saturday on business for our Company   I would see you before I go but it appears to be impossible. I hope to be home in ten weeks . . ." ALS, *ibid.* See letter to Benjamin H. Bristow, Aug. 7, 1875.

1. See Order, March 25, 1875.

To Lt. Gen. Philip H. Sheridan

———

Washington, D. C. May 26th *1875*

MY DEAR GENERAL;

I have yours of the 24th of May asking Mrs. Grant & myself the pleasure of attending your wedding on the 3d of June. I have been intending for some time to send you my congratulations for the event which is so soon to take place, but have defered to see whether Mrs. Grant and I might not arrange to attend the wedding and deliver our congratulations in persons. It seems now that it will be impossible for us to go, and I take this method therefore of saying how glad I am of your proposed union to one who I know is so well calculated to make you happy.

Again repeating my congratulations, and my earnest wish for health, long life and prosperity for you and your bride, I am,

Faithfully & truly
your friend
U. S. GRANT

LT. GEN.L P. H. SHERIDAN,

ALS, DLC-Philip H. Sheridan. On June 3, 1875, in Chicago, Lt. Gen. Philip H. Sheridan married Irene Rucker, daughter of Col. Daniel H. Rucker.

To Edwin Cowles

―――――

Washington, D. C. [May 29] 187[5]

SIR:

I have your note of   in which you ask

The whole question has been forced upon the republican party by its enemies, ~~and~~ I think needlesly—and heretofore I therefore have thought it beneath the dignity of the office which I have been twice called on to fill to answer it.[1] But the great state of Pensylvania, represented in Convention to nominate a state ticket having thought it wise to adopt a resolution in [op]position to a third term, and in view of the fact that other state conventions are to follow which may feel it incumbent on them to adopt some resolution on the subject, I deem it now not improper to respond to your ~~inqu~~ letter.

I have never been a candidate for re-nomination. It is not probable that the subject of a third term for any president would have ever been thought of again, unless in time of great commotion when it might not be deemed prudent to make a change but for this ruse of the enemy of the republican party, and of this Administration, to force upon it an issue intended only to cause dissention and division. If the number of terms of a president is to be limited to one, two, or any other number, then the question should be one as to the propriety of amending the Constitution to effect this. This would be a question in which both political parties could engage.

I left a life position of which I was very proud, to accept a first term, very much against ~~against~~ my inclination. Twice I have been nominated to the office with great unanimity ~~of the~~ by Conventions convened to make the nomination. It is not in my nature to struggle for position and I assure you that a nomination grudgeling give in the past would not have been accepted, and in the future I shall stand in this respect as I have in the past.

ADf, ICN. Edwin Cowles edited the *Cleveland Leader*. On Tuesday, May 26, 1875, Cowles, Cleveland, telegraphed to USG. "Can I have an interview with you on Political matters friday or Saturday if I should go to washington   Answer—" Telegram received (at 7:28 P.M.), DLC-USG, IB. On May 30, Secretary of State Hamilton Fish recorded in his diary. "Robeson called in the morning saying he had seen the President on the evening before who had requested him to ask me with himself to be at the White House at 3 oclock; at which hour we were there and Belknap & Pierrepont appeared. The President said that after the meeting of the cabinet on Friday he had been thinking of the proceedings of the Philadelphia convention which had been referred to in some of our conversation on that day & had 'scratched off something' in the form of a letter to the President of the convention on the subject of the 'Third Term' but had not determined whether he should send it or not, or write anything on the subject. He said that Mr Cowles the editor of the Republican paper in Cleveland Ohio whom he knew personally and who was a good friend of his personally as well as a good republican had telegraphed to him enquiring whether in case he came to Washington he could have a conversation with him on political subjects and he had replied in the affirmative and had seen him Saturday; that he had referred to the resolution of the Pennsylvania Convention on the subject of 3d term also to the approaching state convention to be held in Ohio on Tuesday and to the probability of resolutions on the same subject being introduced at the convention that he had prepared & read to him a letter inviting an expression of opinion on the subject but said he would not leave it with him unless he (the President) desired him to do so & felt inclined to reply, that he had also 'scratched off' an answer to such letter   he then proceeded to read both of these drafts. When the reading was through after a slight pause Robeson expressed the opinion that some statement by the President was very desirous; in general terms he approved the tone of the letter intimating that there might be some changes of expression . . . Robeson & Pierrepont seemed to think that the letter might be more appropriatly addressed to the late President of the Penna Convention, but my object was attained in the main by the suggesting that there might be something in the draft to Mr Cowles which might be inserted in the letter to be sent to Penna   The draft was then taken up and read through by paragraphs—many expressions were changed & many passages omitted   Some new ideas were thrown in and some were left which the President seemed tenacious to retain in which however some modification of language were made. The President seemed anxious to retain his argument on constitutional reëligibility for an indefinite number of terms & the right of the people to select an incumbent as often as they please. He consented quite readily to state that he was not nor ever had been candidate for renomination and accepted quite graciously the suggestion of several expressions both of language & of sentiment. Finally the letter was agreed upon substantially in the form in which it was to be sent. We left him copying it out. . . ." DLC-Hamilton Fish. See following letter. On May 18, Allen T. Wikoff, Columbus, Ohio, had written to USG. "*Private & Confidentiail* . . . This personal letter is addressed to you at the request of the Republican State Executive Committee of Ohio. The approaching political canvass in the State bears promise of being a thoroughly contested one, and the importance of its result can scarcely be ever estimated. The republicans are desirous of presenting *the* national issues involved squarely to the people, relieved of extraneous or feigned questions. Let this be done, and the result is not doubtful; for the people of Ohio are true to the Union and the principles settled by the war. One of the matters out of which our adversaries seek to make an issue, and which is likely to prove a stumbling block to quite a numerous class of citizens who would otherwise heartily cooperate with us, is the third term agitation. The committeee entertain no doubt that your convictions on this subject are in entire harmony with those of the party generally, and belive that an expression from you of them anterior to the Republican State Convention, June 2d, would remove the dificulty alluded to and be of great service to the cause of the party, which is also the cause of the country. We fully appreciate, as I think, the embarrassment of your situation, in answering this communication, but hoping that it may not prove insurmountable, . . ." ALS, USG 3.

1. On Jan. 22, Thomas C. MacDowell, Harrisburg, Pa., had written to USG. "I know not whither you will Consider me Officious or not, but at the risk of being Considered so, I shall take the liberty of writing to congratulate you upon the course pursued in the Louisiana affair, and your complete vindication in your special Message. The course adopted was the only one dictated by sound policy and good judgment, and 'the sober second thought of the American people' will fully sustain you in the end. Hon Henry Wilson's recent letter on the State of the party, and Mr Blaine's hobnobbing with Whitelaw Read, of the NewYork Tribune, and the general hubbub, created by your special Message are but parts of the plan adopted to create a diversion of public opinion in a direction adverse to your Administration with the White House in view, for some of the men who think, that if they Can break down your administration now, and Keep the Republican party in tact, their ends will be accomplished; but they will fail, signally fail. These men do not seem to take into their account, the fact, that the people are determined to rule the question of the next Presidency in their own way in 1876; and in that event, you will distance all Competitors. Circumstances as they have transpired since September last, when I wrote my letter to the Grant National Club of Atlanta Georgia, have only tended to confirm the Convictions I then entertained on the next Presidency. If you will take the trouble to look over that letter, you will find, that I have predicted just such a state of things as do now exist in this Country as regards the position of parties; from which I argue, that no man in the nation possesses half the strength with the masses, that you do, and my word for it, your strength will increase with every revolving month till 1876. The hypocritical Carpings of the crew of Republicans who seeck to circumvent you, and the insane howlings of the Burbon Democrats, who take hold of every circumstance, no matter how trivial, to make partasan capital, will not win in this Contest. The Republican party must support you, or go under, 'horse, foot and dragoon,' and the people will do the rest. All that you have to do is, to hold fast to the position already assumed, and triumph will follow as sure as light succeeds to darkness in the natural world. Hoping and trusting, that the God of battles, will sustain you in the discharge of every duty, and that you may be successful in the assertion of principle and right, . . ." ALS, *ibid.* On Sept. 7, 1874, MacDowell had written to USG. "I take the liberty of enclosing to you a copy of a letter, which I addressed to 'The Grant National Club,' of Atlanta, Georgia, 2500, copies of which, have been printed by our mutual friend Sam Bard Esqr. P. M. at Atlanta, for distribution. In the brief interview I had the pleasure of having with you on Wednesday last, at Long Branch, I fore bore to allude to the enclosed Argument, from sheer modesty on my part, preferring, (as I knew it was in the hands of the printers,) that you should first see it in print, when you could read it

for yourself and form your own judgment of its merits, as well as, the motives of the author, in writing it. . . ." ALS, *ibid.* The enclosure, "An Argument for a Third Presidential Term," is *ibid.* On Nov. 8, 1875, MacDowell again wrote to USG in support of a third term. ALS, *ibid.*

In a letter docketed March 10, Thomas G. Webster, Jr., had written to USG. "You have some Office holders in this State who, doubtless, will be applicants to you for reappointment. Now what claims have some of them on you? When the last Repn State Convention met at Harrisburg a resolution was gotten up by Genl. H. H. Bingham opposing any Presidential 3d term. Did Collector Comly, Naval officer Heistand, Surveyor Goodrich Marshal Kerns or Appraisers Blodget and Moore interest themselves in preventing the passage of this resolution striking at and insulting to you? Ex-Congressman Dickey, the townsman & bosom friend of Naval Officer John A. Heistand, urged the passage of that resolution in a speech. These Officers, holding positions under you, were *all* at Harrisburg and never tried to stop this matter. How much time do Goodrich & Heistand devote to their Offices—not three days in any one month. Consult your Secy. of the Treasury and Commissioner of Customs & you will find out the truth of this statement; & yet they wish to be re-appointed. They first help to insult you & weaken you, and then demand thanks for so doing, & endorsement from you. Consider this matter over before you act. In confidence. . . . I want no Office of any kind, please remember." ALS (undated), DNA, RG 56, Letters Received from the President. USG either renominated or retained Seth J. Comly, collector of customs, John A. Hiestand, naval officer, E. O'Meara Goodrich, surveyor of customs, Lorin Blodget, gen. appraiser, and Edward B. Moore, appraiser, Philadelphia, and James N. Kerns, marshal, Eastern District, Pa.

On March 27, L. Montgomery Bond, Philadelphia, wrote to USG. ". . . I have thought that you might agree with me, and with a large majority of the people, no doubt, in the propriety of giving expression to your dissent to the question of 'a third term.' I am satisfied that you have never entertained the proposition, or harbored a thought of a re nomination, because I have looked in vain for anything pointing to such a conclusion in either your utterances or actions. But you have been so often represented as desiring, if not favoring a departure from the settled policy of the nation, that it would seem that the time had come when a public expression of denial through a private medium would be not only re assuring to the national sentiment, but would strengthen the hands of the party of the country. An influential journal now before me says 'how easy would it be for the President by a single word of denial to settle this vexed question, and strengthen the hands of his friends.' I would close with an earnest request that you will allow me to give publicity, in any way you may direct, to a few words from your own hand, authorizing a denial of the now serious assertion, which, if not given, will be used by the Democracy to the hurt of the national party in the coming campagnes, which is being a thousand times repeated by the venal Press of the country." ALS, USG 3.

On March 31, L. J. Messervy, Charleston, S. C., wrote to USG. "I have been extremely interested within the Period of the last twelve months about the matter of a third term. I have taken bets freely against odds that you will be Elected, I have not the slightest doubt of it; your popularity is legion. The Press is no indication of the Public mind   it is swayed by present passing events as vacillating as the prices of the Market. . . ." ALS, *ibid.*

On April 30, Robert T. Kent, Atlanta, wrote to USG. "We the Colored Men and Women Boys & Girles yes Even the Litle Children Thank you dear Sir   we thank you for your Faithfullness to us in the Field and in the office you So Worthly Fill   May God Almighty Bless you & your Family Long to Live in this World and that What Ever you do Prosper and Finley in the Heven of the Blessed & faithfull may Each and all find and Everlasting Home is our daily Prayer   you have bin a Good President to both White & Colord and Men all over this County Privately Expess themselve that you was the Man for the office—and if you would Cosent its the Best thing For the whol County to be reelected the third 3rd terme and dear Mr President we shall Ever Feel our obligations to you & the Rest of our True Friends for all the Pass Blessing under the assisting Hand of a Good and Mercifull God   Again we thank you all for the Cival Right Bill that Will Be a Lasting Blessing to all the People White & Colord shall Pray & Act so as to Prove that the Kindness is not in Vain Bestowed on us   I am Sir Presiding Elder in 19 County Midell Georgia" ALS, *ibid*. On March 1, after extensive congressional debate, USG had signed "An act to protect all citizens in their civil and legal rights." *U.S. Statutes at Large*, XVIII, part 3, pp. 335–37.

On June 15, 1874, Jacob Manthe, Marshall, Tex., had telegraphed to USG. "If possible for Gods sake and the welfare of Our County please veto the Civil rights bill and Oblige a Man fought with Genl Siegel and Genl Dodge a friend of Carl Schurz a friend of yours" Telegram received (at 4:07 P.M.), DLC-USG, IB. After the Aug., 1874, elections, USG received an essay entitled "The proper solution of the 'Civil Rights' question," which argued against passage of the pending civil rights bill and recommended annexing Santo Domingo as a colony for blacks. D (undated), USG 3. Also in 1874, Governor James L. Kemper of Va. wrote to USG transmitting resolutions from the Va. assembly opposing civil rights legislation. William Evarts Benjamin, Catalogue No. 34, Jan., 1891, p. 21. On March 1, 1875, Anonymous, Baltimore, wrote to USG. "This is to notify you that if you sign the 'Civil Rights Bill' you shall not live long to enjoy with the negroe the privilege you give him. We will bear much for peace, but we will not bear all that you and your contemptable set choose to inflict. A word to the wise is sufficient. Believe me, many like the noble J. W. Booth still live and we like him will gladly yield our lives to rid our country of its despot and several others shall share your fate. Our last word is 'Beware.'" L, USG 3. On March 2, another anonymous letter was sent to USG. "if you Signe that Civil rights bill you will not live one month longer   By order of K K K   you old beet" L, *ibid*. USG also received a communication marked *"Mollie Maguires"* and "James Wallace" headed Pottsville, Pa. "Assassination of Prest. Grant. Tremendous excitement all over the country. His Assassin escapes. Supposed to be a member of his Cabinet—$100,000 for his body, dead or alive. His wife and Mrs. Sartoris carried away insensible. &c., &c., &c. The Civil Rights bill has passed the House." D (undated), *ibid*.

To Harry White

———

Washington, D. C. May 29th *1875*.

DEAR SIR:

A short time subsequent to the Presidential election of 1872, the press—a portion of it—hostile to the republican party, and particularly so to the administration, started the cry of Cæsarism and the "third term" calling lustily for me to define my position on the latter subject. I believed it to be benath the dignity of the office which I have been twice called upon to fill, to answer such a question before the subject should be presented by competant authority to make a nomination, or by a body of such dignity and authority as not to make a reply a fair subject of ridicule

In fact I have been surprised that so many sensible persons in the republican party should permit their enemy to force upon them, and the party, an issue which cannot add strength to the party no matter how met. But a body of the dignity and party authority of a convention to make nominations for the state officers of the second state in the Union having considered this question I deem it *not improper* that I should now speak.

In the first place I never sought the office for a second, nor even for a first, nomination. To the first I was called from a life position, one created by Congress expressly for me for supposed services rendered to the Republic. The position vacated I liked. It would have been most agreeable to me to have retained it until such time as Congress might have consented to my retirement, with the rank, and a portion of the emoluments—which I so much needed—to a home where the balance of my days might be spent in peace, and the enjoyment of domestic quiet, relieved from the cares which have oppressed me so constantly now for fourteen years. But I was made to believe that the public good called me to make the sacrifice.

Without seeking the office for the "second term" the nomination was tendered to me by a unanimous vote of the deligates of all the states and territories, selected by the republicans of each to represent their whole numbers, for the purpose of making this nomination. I cannot say that I was not pleased at this, and at the overwhelming endorsement which their action received at the election following.

But it must be remembered that all the sacrifice—except that of comfort—had been made in accepting the "first term." Then too, such a fire of personal abuse, and slander had been kept up for four years, notwithstanding my conscientious performance of my duties, to the best of my understanding—though I admit, in the light of subsequent events, many times subject to fair criticism—that an endorsement from the people, who alone govern republics, was a gratification that it is only human to have appreciated and enjoyed.

Now for the "third term:" I do not want it any more than I did the first. I would not write or utter a word to change the will of the people in expressing, and having, their choice. The question of the number of terms allowed to any one Executive can only come up fairly in the shape of a proposition to amend the Constitution— a shape in which all political parties can participate—fixing the length of time, or the number of terms for which any one person shall be elegible for the office of President. Until such an amendment is adopted the people cannot be restricted in their choise by resolutions further than they are now restricted—as to age, nativity, &c.

It may happen in the future history of the country that to change an Executive because he has been eight years in office will prove unfortunate if not disastrous.

The idea that any man could elect himself pPresident,—or even re-nominate himself—is preposterous. It is a reflection upon the intelligence and patriotism of the people to suppose such a thing possible. Any man can destroy his chances for the office, but no one can force an election or even nomination.

To recapitulate: I am not, nor have I been, a candidate for a renomination. I would not accept a nomination if it were tendered unless it should come under such circumstances as to make it an imperitive duty, circumstances not likely to arise.

I congratulate the convention over which you presided for the harmony which prevailed, and for the excellent ticket put in the field, and which I hope may be triumphantly elected.

With great respect,
Your obt. svt.
U. S. GRANT

GEN. HARRY WHITE,
PRES. PA REP. STATE CONVENTION

ALS, DLC-USG, IB; copy, USG 3. Harry White, unsuccessful Republican candidate for Pa. governor in 1872, had served as maj., 67th Pa., and was breveted brig. gen. On [*May*] 30, 1875, Orville E. Babcock telegraphed to White, Indiana, Pa. "Have mailed you a letter from the President of the twenty ninth   Copy given to the Press" Telegram sent, DLC-USG, IB. On June 1, White wrote to USG. "Your letter of the 29th ulto in relation to your candidacy for 'the third term, addressed to me, as President of Pennsylvania Republican State Convention, has just been recd, although I had already read it, through the Press, to which, I was informed by telegraph, you had directed a copy to be given. Your frank & pru-

dent expressions as to your present attitude before the Country should be entirely satisfactory to all who have an *honest* desire to be informed on the subject matter of your letter.
As a private citizen, desiring nothing from your administration but good government, I
feel assured, I only utter popular Sentiment in saying, thus far you have recd, from your
fellow citizens nothing but what your eminent & patriotic Services have justly entitled you
to. It is no bad taste, I fancy, for me further to say—no special power of prophesy is required to predict, the impartial pen of future history will record, your administration of
our affairs was animated by a constant purpose to advance the strength, wealth & integrity
of the nation that the happiness & comfort of the individual citizen in all his conditions
might be permanently secured. Be good enough to accept my earnest hope, your administration may continue to its close to merit & receive, as I believe it now does, the confidence
of the American people—Accept thanks for your kind congratulations to the convention
on the result of its labors & your hope for the Election of the ticket nominated—With best
wishes for you personally" ALS, USG 3.

On May 31, Henry O. Wagoner, Sr., Denver, had written to USG. "I have read, with
profound interest, your letter to Genl Harry White, President of the recent Pennsylvania
Republican State Convention. In that letter you Say Some things which I have so often said
to croakers about 'third term,' that I am irresistibly impelled to take the liberty of inditing
this humble *private* letter. I have often said that it is a well known fact, to the Nation, that
you never even Sought the *first* or *Second* term; that the people took you up of their own
free will and accord, and elected you, both terms; and, therefore, why should you presume
to refuse a 'third term' before it were offered to you, or indicated from such a Source as
arose to the dignity of some sort of authoritative capacity. This, I have all a long imagined
was your own View of the subject. Now, if the ~~Administration~~ Clamorers, Liberal Republicans and Democrats are really sincere in their pretentions about abolishing 'Third term,'
why dont they Unite in Some sort of authoritative Capacity and declare their purpose
boldly to the people for their decisive action?—in the shape of a National Convention to
Amend the National Constitution, prohibiting the *Choice* of 'third term' *by the People*, and
submitting such proposition to the Vote of the people. The fact is, and all right thinking
men know it, that if all the aspirants for office Could have gotten office, and been retained,
whether they did their duty or not, no word of Complaint would have went up. Oh how
unwise in the Republicans to lose their prestige by Cowardly falling back to the defensive.
How well you, as a successful military man, know the force and charm of taking the initiative in war. But whoever be the next Republican Candidate for the Presidency, I trust he
may be a true man, and that the Colored men of the Country may act wisely and well, as
citizens worthy of their new Condition. May Heaven bless you is my prayer" ALS, *ibid.* On
the same day, Frederick Douglass, Washington, D. C., wrote to Babcock. "Again the President has spoken the right word at the right time: Again he has given convincing evidence
of wisdom and patriotism and of his ability to lead in times of trouble. I am not quite sure
however, that circumstances will release him from a third term. There are many great and
good men in the land; but to whom among them all, has the order of events given greater
powerer to serve the country than to President Grant? His name stands for national peace,
Liberty prosperity and stability. He has been the shelter and savior of my people in the
hour of supreme danger and naturally enough we feel great concern as to who is to come
in his stead—" ALS, *ibid.*

On June 1, John F. Long, surveyor of customs, St. Louis, wrote to USG. "Confidential. . . . The papers of our city contained, on yesterday morning, your Letter 'to Genl.
Harry White,—Prest. of Penn. Convention, of Rep. party; And it is just such a high toned
and lofty paper, as the circumstances calling for it.—demanded. And I am rejoyced at its
tone, for it leaves *the matter* of a 'third Term' in the hands of *the people*, in *that* people who

are not to be dictated to, nor to be ruled or influenced by weeklies Newspapers or disappointed aspirants.' I was called upon this morning by. McKee of the Globe-Democrat. Genl. Harny. Genl. McDonald & many others and all are now satisfied, that your Letter was a wise, gentle & master-stroke of policy. I keep my own counsels, and hear a great deal. And When I see you, I will have something to say to one whom I know, & whom the people of the greatest Govnt, in the world know, to their advantage." ALS, *ibid*. On the same day, Samuel R. MacLean, New York City, wrote to USG. "Allow me to congratulate you upon your so called 'Third Term Letter.' It is dignified in tone—full of good and wise counsel and will undoutedly make '*the people*' feel more reliant & confident in your administration. Shall be pleased to have you call when in this city. With my best regards to your brother Orville and namesake Jas McLean when you see them . . . I'm sorry that the Sec'y has had to resort to selling Gold again—thereby aiding abetting—Exciting 'Speculation'—and correspondingly it demoralizes the legitimate and active business intrests of the country. . . ." ALS, *ibid*. On June 9, 1873, MacLean, Pittsburgh, had written to USG. ". . . Financial affairs are such and the business of Banking so cut up I have about concluded to quit—and as I have a sick wife and am myself desirous of recuperating my bilious nature from long & close confinement to business cares & duties I would thank you for a Mission to Europe worthy of my position and capabilities? I would ask for a commission to London Liverpool France or Germany . . ." ALS, DNA, RG 59, Letters of Application and Recommendation. No appointment followed.

On June 2, 1875, Charles H. T. Collis, Philadelphia, wrote to USG. "*Private* . . . A year ago the Republican party of this State permitted itself to be imposed upon by the 'Third term' scare, and disgraced itself by the passage of a Resolution for which there was no earthly necessity. I was at Harrisburg at that time, and although for years past I had been afforded an opportunity of reading the platform in advance, yet upon that occasion I was not permitted to see it—when the Third term Resolution was read, I understood *why*— . . . There is no disguising the fact that the Resolution of last year was conceived and 'set up' by a few men in the State who have failed in their efforts to *control you*—The Resolution of this year however was simply a political blunder, nothing more. . . ." ALS, USG 3.

On June 15, John Scott, Pittsburgh, wrote to USG. "When in Philada a few days ago, I met Mr Childs and he stated to me the complimentary terms you were pleased to use when my name was the subject of your consultations. I cannot forbear expressing to you the pleasure it affords me to know that my discharge of public duty has secured your good opinion and your confidence to the extent manifested by those expressions. My duties to others require me while I have health for labor, to be engaged in remunerative employment and to forego the thought of holding public office, but that I should have been deemed by you worthy of a place in your Administration, will ever be to me a source of gratification, and to my children just cause of pride. I trust it is not too late to congratulate you upon your letter disposing so justly of the third term phantasm which was so frighting the souls of your fearful adversaries. If it is, it certainly is not too late to congratulate you upon the fact that for every President who has lived since Washington, *except yourself*, a third term has been considered impossible. The war made upon you by your political enemies as well as the declarations made by conventions of your party friends will unite in leaving the historical record that your third election was considered not only possible but probable, while your letter gives you the advantage of saying for yourself that such a desire had not its origin with you. With my warmest wishes for the continued success of your Administration and for the personal welfare and happiness of yourself and family . . ." ALS, *ibid*. USG had considered Scott for secretary of the interior. See Hamilton Fish diary, May 17, 1875, DLC-Hamilton Fish.

On June 27, William H. Macomber, Brough, Iowa, wrote to USG. ". . . I rather think that the opposition to a third term comes mainly from presidential aspirants who fear they will not be able to reealize the consumation of their hopes if one man is allowed to monopolize more than two terms. With the masses of the people I believe it makes no difference how long a President serves provided he gives general satisfaction. When I get a good hand on my farm I keep him just as long as I can if he continues good, & I do not know why we should make it any reason for discharging our faithful public servants, because they ha[ve] served us a certain number of years; I hope you will excuse my presumption in addressing this to you, & consider it as the sentiments of a friend & well wisher, also from one who served in the great struggle for freedom under your command and if circumstances required, would again do the same. With the kindest of wishes for the future welfare of yourself & family . . ." ALS, USG 3. Other commendatory letters are *ibid.* See *Julia Grant,* p. 187.

On Aug. 3, Henry A. M. Bartley, "near Orange C. H.," Va., wrote to USG. "I inclose a communication for Harper's Weekly. If you approve it please forward to them or to any other medium that you may think proper. It contains the popular sentimen[t] of many people of the South, and I believe you are stronger in Va now than you were four years ago. Although you have persistently refused to give me any encouragement or employment I nevertheless must take my position for you in the approaching campaign. I nearly lost my life before   I may come out better this time" ALS, USG 3. The enclosure, "President Grant and the 'Third Term,'" is *ibid.*

On Aug. 26, John Phelan, Charlotte, N. C., wrote to USG. "I write you, (hoping you will not consider this presumptive in me).   in a free Republic like ours, the master is not greater in the sight of the law than his Servant! all are equal. My object is to tell you that if you will come out for the 3rd term on the *'hard money basis'* you will be elected. . . ." ALS, *ibid.*

On Sept. 1, L. Falkenburg, Memphis, wrote to USG. "In order to save time, pardon me to avoid ceremonies. If you desire a third Term, I feel confident that my plans would prove beneficial to that purpose. This is all for the present. I referre you, as to my character, to Mr. Deloach, P. M. of this City" ALS, *ibid.*

On Sept. 3, Rudolph Wieczorek, New York City, wrote to USG. "I am informed, that you decline to accept the nomination for presidency for the next term. I am proud to say, that in both the campaigns for presidency I stood on your side and I will stand there so often you will be the candidate for said office and I am aware that there are hundred thousands who will do the same.—Your last victory was the third, by which you humiliated the traitors of the United-States. Is there any one else in the whole Republican party, who, if nominated, would have the chance to succeed?—I dont know of any. And you will surrender the presidential chair to the Democratic party?—Since Democracy became identical with treason, rebellion & secession under their states rights theory—no good & true citizen should cast his vote for a candidate of this party; but democracy here is manufactured of the ignorant and uncultivated masses—just like the roman catholic church. Thanks god, that the philosophers of Green-Erin are not the majority of the people of the Union!—The leaders of the last Rebellion here are the leaders of this party, just as the jesuits are the rulers of the roman catholic church—and with those leaders of the democracy here the jesuits are united in their principles like husband and wife. Shall we surrender?—. . . For my person I will stand by you and fight for you in the private and in the public—from the pulpit and from the lecture chair, in the news-papers and in pamphlets as I have done before. . . ." ALS, *ibid.* Wieczorek enclosed clippings and a pamphlet. *Ibid.*

On Oct. 21, E. B. DuRoy, Jacksonville, Fla., wrote to USG. "Although I am not a Native of America, having arived in this Country during the Rebelion, & takeing a deep interest in the welfare of the nation, I have made its laws a constant study. I beleave with thousands of others, that the Country will sucseed better under your administration, than by makeing a change. I sincearly hope that you will allow your Honored Name, to be nominated for the third term, for the Presidency, as your many Friends wish. . . ." ALS, *ibid.*

On [*Dec. 15*], Ward H. Lamon wrote to USG. "I cannot refrain from giving expression to what I feel in relation to the most singular and unheard of action in the House of Representatives to day in the introduction and action on the Resolution protesting against *the third Term* Bug-Bear. This was brought about through the instrumentality of the Democrats, but it is my judgement, that it had its emanation, its birth and its incentive in the minds of Ambitious Republicans, not perhaps so much through ill-will to you, as from a desire, by supplanting you, to afford them a chance of being your Successor. Such strategy will be looked upon by every independent thinking man in the country as unprecedented and as futile as it is disgraceful. Your course in relation to the Henderson matter at St Louis will be commended by every independent man in the Government. Let the opposition wage its war against you—let it come from the subdued Democracy of the North—their more intrepid confreres of the South or the ambitious devotees of our own party   The *people*—the great masters of Office holders, have made up their minds that Genl U. S. Grant *shall* serve another term as President of these United States. I have nothing to ask. I can therefore speak my sentiments freely and fearlessly—" ALS (undated), *ibid.* On Dec. 15, U.S. Representative William M. Springer of Ill., a Democrat, offered a resolution. "That, in the opinion of this House, the precedent established by Washington and other Presidents of the United States, in retiring from the presidential office after their second term, has become, by universal concurrence, a part of our republican system of government, and that any departure from this time-honored custom would be unwise, unpatriotic, and fraught with peril to our free institutions." *CR*, 44–1, 228. The resolution passed 233 to 18.

Council with Sioux Delegation

———

[*June 2, 1875*]

The President.—If they accept the conditions, I will appoint good commissioners to make these purchases for them and to distribute them among them. If they have any choice of persons who shall act as such commissioners, I will be glad to hear who they are, and if I think them suitable persons, I will consult their pleasure. ~~and~~ But I make the appointments myself; but if they will suggest the name of any person that I think is good to put on the commission, I will consider it. Now I want to speak to them again about what I have said before. Let them understand distinctly that this $25,000, cannot without a violation of law be paid to them in money: it must be paid in presents bought with the money. I want to impress upon them what I said to them when they called on me before. The necessity of their making provision for themselves and their children in the future, in view of the great increase of white population in the country. I don't ask them to give any answer now, or to agree to leave their homes and go to a new country, but it is something for them to think of, and talk to their tribes about when they go back among them

In regard to the Black Hills, I look upon it as very important to them to make some treaty by which if gold is discovered in large quantities, the white people will be allowed to go there, and they receive a full equivalent for all that is rendered.

If gold is not found there in large quantities, of course the white people won't for the present, want to go there, and their country will be left as it is now.

The Secretary of the Interior, and the Commissioner of Indian Affairs, will explain to them hereafter, about what would be probably a fair equivalent to the white people and to them which should be given in case they should surrender the Black Hills, or th[a]t portion in which gold may be found. As I pointed out to you before, there will be trouble in keeping white people from going there for gold, if it should be dis[covered, and under another administration,] it is possible that strong efforts might not be made to keep them out.

My interest is in seeing you protected, while I have the power to make treaties with you which shall protect you. After you go back to your homes and have been there a sufficient time to talk pretty generally with your people if I get such a word from you as to make it seem desirable, I will appoint commissioners to go out to confer with you. But it is important to you that while you are here, you settle the question of the limits of your hunting grounds, and make preliminary arrangements to allow white persons to go into the Black Hills. If it should come to the purchase of the Black Hills or a portion of that country from you I would try to see you get a full equivalent in value, and that that money be paid out in U. S. bonds and deposited here, so that the interest would be drawn twice a year for your benefit, and be expended for your benefit each year as might be agreed upon, and I look upon it as very important to you, and your children the Indians who come after you, that you encourage all you can, the children attending schools, in speaking English and preparing yourselves for the life of white men

Secretary [*of the Interior Columbus Delano*]. The agreement for the relinquishment of the hunting privilege in Nebraska, has been drawn up ready for you to sign.

The President.—That agreement has been shown to me and I approve of it and would be glad to have you sign it. I will say again whenever the Secretary of the Interior, and the Commissioner of Indian Affairs talk to you, they talk for me, and if there is any point they cannot quite agree upon they will submit the views of the Indians and their own views to me to decide between them

One word more that has nothing to do with this   I have always felt ever since I was a young officer of the army, a great interest in the welfare of the Indians   I know that formerly they been abused and their rights not properly respected. Since it has be[e]n in my power to have any control over Indian affairs I have endeavored to adopt a policy which should be for your future good, and calculated to preserve peace between the whites and Indians for the present; and it is my great desire now while I can—retain some control over the matter, that the initiatory steps should be taken to secure you [a]nd your children hereafter. If you will co-operate with me I shall look always to what I believe is for your best interests. Many of the Indians who accepted an early day, what we propose to you to-day, are n[o]w living in houses, have fences around their farms; have school houses, and their children are reading and writing as we do here.

Spotted Tail. My Great Father, yesterday the Secretary of the Interior told me some things, and some of them did not please me. I ask that I might see my Great Father on the next day face to face. I thought it would be best that we should settle this matter openly and all of us hear it. I want to know if the money is collected by Congress.

The President. The money is appropriated by Congress.

Spotted Tail. If it already collected, I would like to have it counted and given to me.

The President. It is all collected and is now in the treasury, and ready to be spent for presents and if you have any choice as to what shall be bought, you may express it.

Spotted Tail. I am speaking about the money that was collected for the purpose of buying the right to hunt buffalo.

The President. Yes, that is the money.

Spotted Tail. I was afraid that the money was taken from the money for feeding the Indians.

The President. N[o], this was additional. There were $1,200,000, appropriated for feeding the Indians. They commence getting that from the 1st of July. This $25,000, is appropr[i]ated now in addition, to be given you for the right of hunting in that particular locality; and you cannot get that money without surrendering that right, and you must surrender that right before the first of July, for then the money goes back on the to the United States.

Spotted Tail. My Great Father, you have men under you to assist you. The Secretary of the Interior, the Commissioner of Indian Affairs, and Indian agents. You also have missionaries. Last year you sent out a commission; Bishop Hare and Mr. Hinman were members.

They told me that I was only to give up the right to hunt on the Smoky Hill Fork of the Republican—not all of the Nebraska.

The President. The law says all of Nebraska. Spotted Tail was right in what the commissioners said, but when Congress made the appropriation they took in the whole.

Secretary. We could not get the appropriation on any other terms.

Interpreter. He asks when that part of Nebraska that is included in the neutral lands has been purchased and why, if purchased, they ask them to give it up.

Secretary. They have not anything in Nebraska that belongs to them They have simply the right to hunt.

Interpreter. They understand that the Niobrara line which runs to the North Platte, belongs to; them, and th[e]y think it is unceded land.

Secretary. It is unseded land; but that is only for the time being and Congress now assumes the right to it; it was not ceded to them

Spotted Tail. You are helping the Omaha people.

Secretary. We have to fight both sides: the whites and the Indians.
President. You can tell them I am very anxious to see them become like Omaha people, so that they can build farms, towns and houses for themselves; so that they can have farms and houses and own them, and buy and sell, and go where they please, and if they cannot, I want to see their children prepared for it anyhow.

Interpreter. They called me into council this morning; there is another misapprehension about that neutral land: they claim that until it is purchased it belongs to them. Now this right they give up for $25,000 is merely the right of hunting. I told them the question of the right to the lands might be left until next summer.

Secretary Delano. What they relinquish now is merely their right to hunt.

The President. That is all. Nothing else.

Secretary Delano. And then we distinctly agree that they shall not be disturbed along the Divide, north of the Niobrara. If Congress gives anything more, we will be glad to pay it, but we can't promise it.

Interpreter. When the Black Hills question comes up cou[ld] not that be put in with it?

The President. Yes, it might be put in together with that.

Spotted Tail. Yesterday, when this matter was mentioned, I understood that I was only giving up the right to hunt on the Republican and in Kansas, and afterward it was explained that this was for all my hunting on the North Platte and in the country which I considered as my own, and when I went home I felt very badly about it and desired to see you.

The President. Down the North Patte, according to my observations, there is n[o]thing to hunt at all, until they get down among the buffaloes in Kansas.

Interpreter. But they are afraid this will include the use of territory which they claim.

The President. This has nothing to do with any territory, only with the right to hunt. In the territory where I proposed they should go, in our first interview the other day, they would have a good portion of the year, right within the territory to be given them, the main herd of buffaloes on the plains; for it is right in the country where they cross to go north and south where they winter and stay.

[Se]cretary.—I would like to explain to them that this agreement is drawn up in such a way that if they relinquish their right to; the unceded territory north of the North Platte, it secures to them all that lies north of the Niobrara, and that would be a consideration for giving up the unceded territory.

Interpreter.—That is the point they make. He says that while they sign this, it does not secure it to them.

Secretary.—Yes it does; because Congress will have to ratify this. It will secure it to them.

Spotted Tail.—Mr. President: that country you have spoken to me about at the south, where there are so many buffalo, does not concern me

This is what conserns me; [i]n the country [w]here t[h]e buffalo roam, the white people are killing many of them; and will soon destroy the whole herd. These people are the ones you ought to send to the Indian Territory.

The President.—When the buffalo are all gone, from that territory just as many cattle can live there, as buffalo now live there; and if they owned the territory, the[y] would own the cattle; and no person could come in and kill them.

Spotted Tail.—I do not like it that the children of the Great Fat[h]er a[r]e offering money to me for something that belongs to me; and are making themselves well off from the buffalo that are mine.

I would like to consider the m[a]tter a little more: that is a right that belongs to me; and I don't want to answer without considering.

Secretary.—How much longer time does he want?

Interpreter.—He will give an answer to the President directly.

Spotted Tail.—My Great Father; I wish to say again that it does not please me that your white children have collected money to pay for something that belongs to me. It also does not please me that your soldiers have settled down in my country; and that they cut my wood and my grass, without paying for them. I have told them to pay for them, and they say the Great Father says they can have them without paying for them.

The President.—We cannot go into a discussion of this question to-day.

Where there is a population of industrious people, who understand how to work, they cannot let their population be pent up and be destroyed while there is territory where they can go, and get a subsistence. And what I want to do, is to prepare the Indian for a contingency that will be sure ~~to arrive~~ to arise; so that he will be able to live upon the ground and get a support from it. the same as white people. This question that he is discussing, is one of sentiment, b[u]t it will have to give way before the growth of numbers who are not going to starve, merely out of a sentimental consideration of a title that others may have.

In all this matter, and in all my dealings with the Indians, as I have explained frequently, and once or twice to-day, I am looking more to their interests than to ours; and I am very anxious that the government of the United States should pay them in a way that will be of most benefit to them, a full equivalent for all that they have given up.

And this is the only way that I see a chance of their having in the future, a fair equivalent for what they surrender.

You may say to Red Cloud, in answer to what he stated a little while ago, that he did not like to have money collected for what is his, that what we are doing, is paying money which is not his, for buffalo which he claims, but which he has not the right to.

Spotted Tail.—My Great Father, I wish to settle this matter in some way that is possible to settle it; and I think the way I have considered, is the only possible way. I said yesterday, that I would take this money in cash; take it myself; and my two friends there said it was impossible.

The President.—You may say what you would like to bu[y] with it; and the commissioners could buy it better than you could.

Spotted Tail.—I would like to h[a]ve the money taken out of the treasury, a[n]d put in the hands of some good person, that you or I could name and I will go home and consider what to buy.

The President.—I have to select the man. You may name the person and if it pleases me, I will take him.

Spotted Tail.—I would like to have the money taken and put in the hands of some person and go home and have a council with my people and consider what ought to be bought with it. And I would like to go home and sign the treaty there after the goods are bought. The President.—That could not be done. The money must be expended, if at all, within four weeks. The receipts taken, and used as vouchers, before the auditor of the treasury. If you name any person whom you want as commissioner, if there is no objection, I will appoint him

Spotted Tail.—I have thought over the matter, and I think I can get home and have the whole matter settled before the end of the month. The President.—I will leave you to settle that with the secretary. B[u]t I think it would be too late: it will be impossible. This has to be settled now or not at all. If you settle it now, the agent can be appointed, and go to Philadelphia and New York, and make the purchases at once for you. and I could appoint them at once.

Spotted Tail.—I am afraid of my people: that if I make purchases here, they will not please my people. If I can go home and sign and council there, and buy the things, it will please my people and make their hearts glad.

The President.—If you will mention whom you would like to have for an agent to purchase the articles, we will wait as long as we can. after you go home, to hear what you want; and if we do not hear from you in time, we will purchase ourselves. Of course you will have to sign first. I will leave you now to talk with the others.[1]

Typescript, DNA, RG 75, Letters Received, Dakota Superintendency. USG attended a council with Sioux representing the Spotted Tail, Red Cloud, and Cheyenne River agencies. "The President began by explaining to them that Congress had appropriated $25,000, to pay to them for the relinquishment of their right to hunt in Nebraska, and that this money was in the treasury, and that in order to get it out of the [t]reasury, it was necessary to sign an agreement that has been drawn up, in which they agreed to relinquish all rights of hunting in Nebraska, and on Smoky Hill Fork, of the Republican, and to reserve right of occupation of the country of Nebraska north of the divide, south of and near the Niobrara and west of the 100th meridian. This agree[me]nt he had read and approved, and was ready to appoint a special commissioner to take the money and buy therewith, such things as they desired." *Ibid.* USG wrote a memorandum for this meeting. "It may be understood definitely that the present treaty, if signed, and ratified by Congress is not to touch the future title to the lands in Nebraska, claimed as unceeded lands, or it may be understood to settle for ever, or until otherwise disposed of, the ~~claim~~ title of the indians to the lands north of the divide spoken of in the Treaty, and their entire relinquishment of all south of it." AN (dated June 2 in another hand), Gilder Lehrman Collection, NNP. See Speech to Sioux Delegation, May 26, 1875; letter to Columbus Delano, June 16, 1875.

On June 5, Benjamin Tatham, New York City, wrote to USG, Long Branch. "I have observed with great interest the negociations & interviews with the representatives of the Sioux and especially the proposition for them to emigrate to the Indian Territory—It seems to me that there can be no difference of opinion when the honor of the nation and the consistency of professing Christians is concerned—both of which are inseparable from the even handed administration of Justice and right.—I should be glad of an opportunity for a little conversation upon this broad subject—In the mean time I have to day telegraphed to Secty Delano as follows: 'Why not send Red Cloud and party to visit the Cherokees and other civilized Indians that they may see their prosperity and report to their people' A single piece of tangible evidence—occular demonstration, is worth *a flood* of *talk*; and would do more to convince the Indians of the advantages, as well as of the necessity of civilization, than any other process. If they should be stung by a sense of injustice from the rapacious greed of the whiteman and driven to desperation, the honor of the nation will be compromised;—Your own bright chapter of history will be tarnished; and the industry of the people will be taxed for at least one hundred millions of money to be extracted from an already overburdend people:—to say nothing of the loss of life which will inevitably accompany it—I forbear to add more from an overburdened heart, whilst in the language of Jefferson 'I tremble for my country when I remember that God is Just—' With earnest desires that you may so act in this matter as to yield a peaceful retrospect . . ." ALS, DNA, RG 75, Letters Received, Dakota Superintendency.

1. Secretary of the Interior Columbus Delano spoke after USG. "I want to make an explanation to Spotted Tail. If you sign the agreement now, and the agent is appointed, the money will be retained until you have time to get home; and if you can get home and consult with your people, and send us word what you wan[t] to buy, we will wait till the last hour; but if you do not send us word a little before the time expires, then we will have to buy the goods before the time expires. I think there will be time, because you can, after consulting with your people, come back to Laramie, and telegraph to us from there. I think there will be time. We will give you the very last hour we can wait." Red Cloud responded. "My friend, do you think that all the people you see about here, have no brains, no eyes, no ears, no heart? I think you tell the truth too. I told you a long ti[m]e ago, that I did not come to dispute any matter with the President. You have the President here in the midst of you, and a good many have gathered about you, and discuss matters day and night. And when you have determined anything, you tell him, and it is put on paper. I am 54 years old; I understand the ways of the whites. When we sign papers, something is put before us for us to take and that is divided among us after we have signed the paper. I have told you that I wish to live like the whites. I have come to Washington to ask for those things that we want to live like white people. I have been to Washington twice before, and then our treaty when it was made, was to last for thirty-five years. I have not forgotten anything; and I have nothing to lay aside. The President gave me the land that we have: it is not a very large country for m[y]self and my children to live upon. I have none to spare. You have asked us to give up the right to hunt buffalo. We are willing to agree to that, but we cannot sign any papers, until we see the goods. [Th]is is the way we do business; we cannot do it any other way. I came here to see the President, and to ask him for those things which I want. I have been here fourteen days; . . . I have the same opinion about the matter under discussion, as Spotted Tail—that it is not best for me to sign the papers till I see the

goods   What shall I say to my people when I come home and say I have signed papers and have no goods?" Delano replied. "When friends meet together to make agreements for their common interests, they ought always to try to respect each others rights and feelings. I know the [P]resident is the best friend that the Indian has had in the presidential chair for a great many years; and I know the President wants every thing done for the present and future good of the Indians. The President told me after we went out of this room, that that was his feeling. And I and the commissioner, always speak the President's wishes. Now the President's term of office will expire in a little less than two years. Then there will be ano[the]r Great Father. It is not certain that the next Great Father will be as good a friend to the Indians, as the present one is; but what treaties and agreements the present Great Father makes, he will be bound by. . . ." *Ibid.* See *New York Times*, June 4, 1875; *HED*, 44-1-1, part 5, I, 681–82.

To Hamilton Fish

Long Branch, N. J.
June 3d /75

Hon. Hamilton Fish,
Sec. of State,
Dear Sir:

W. Cornell Jewett has been here requesting a letter from me to our mMinister to France authorizing or directing him to exert his good offices in facilitating his—Jewett's—obtaining from the govt. of France a concession for landing an American Cable. I declined giving any letter but said I would obtain from the State Dept. for him what had been the uniform answer to such requests.

I enclose you a printed programme of the company which Jewett professes to represent.

You may if you please answer Mr. Jewett. His address in New York City I do not remember; but if you will send the letter to me I will find the it and forward the letter

Very Truly
Your obt. svt.
U. S. Grant

ALS, DLC-Hamilton Fish. On June 10, 1875, Secretary of State Hamilton Fish, New York City, wrote to USG, Long Branch. "I recd your letter in reference to Mr Jewett on my way to the Station, in Washington this morning   Mr Washburn is at present endeavouring to negotiate a treaty with France for the regulation of Submarine Cables between the two

Countries, & I fear that any special intervention of his in behalf of Mr Cornell Jewetts or any other of the several projects just now being agitated, might embarass his negotiation of a general treaty—There are several *projected* schemes for Cables between the U. S. and France, now on foot—but none, so far as I am aware, has yet been able to secure the Capital necessary—Mr Jewetts association has been a long time before the public   I enclose a letter to Mr Jewett saying it has not been usual either for the U. S. or other Governmts to solicit concessions from other Powers in favour of their Citizens—& that the pending negotiations between the two Governmts preclude any present efforts on the part of Mr Washburn in favour of any particular interest   Mrs Fish came on this morning & although much fatigued has borne the journey well . . . PS. I leave the letter for Mr Jewett open, for subject to your approval" ADf, *ibid*. W. Cornell Jewett had earned a notorious reputation as a diplomatic and financial schemer. See *PUSG*, 24, 400–401.

On July 16, USG wrote to Fish. "I know you will feel bad when you read the enclosed." ALS, DLC-Hamilton Fish. The enclosure is a clipping with a letter of July 15 from Jewett, Long Branch. *"To the Editor of the N. Y. Express:* The impression from my late published national appeal is that I oppose Democratic principles and advocate a third-term for Gen. Grant. It is not so. . . . As to General Grant, I intimated his late letter created him a self-constituted candidate, and should have added, committees in each State should be raised to secure funds for the erection of a mammoth asylum, in which to place, as lunatics, all office-holders and others favoring his third election for President. Gen. Grant's rising star set with his allowing the execution of the Modoc Indians and in his desertion of the Southern people by yielding to an unconstitutional and unjust reconstruction power of Congress. . . . Who envies Gen. Grant's past glory, in connection with his selfish, unstatesmanlike, forbidding kingly character. Seward's selfish policy ruled Lincoln. Fish's unstatesmanlike policy rules Grant, and Grant, a despot, rules the people blindfolded. . . ." *Ibid*. On July 17, Fish wrote to USG. "I do feel bad—very bad—It was cruel in Jewett not to give me the chance which the Coon had to come down before Col. Scott fired—or at least the notice that Tilton gave Beecher to 'step down and out'—He is right—there is need of another Lunatic Asylum—his whole life has demonstrated this—We are moving, & on Monday will transact business in the new Building—" ALS (press), *ibid*.

To Edwards Pierrepont

———

Long Branch, N. J.
June 10th /75

HON. EDWARDS PIERREPONT,
ATTY. GEN.L;
DEAR SIR:

I am in receipt of your letter of the 8th inst. at the hands of Judge Carey, W. T. I am not possessed of such information as to warrant the removal of either of the Judges of Wyoming Territory—except as you have heard the statements made against them as well as myself—and approve the suggestion of an entire suspension of action until a full investigation can be had. Such an investigation may show other parties as those unworthy, or unfit to retain their positions

Very Respectfully Yours

U. S. GRANT

ALS, DNA, RG 60, Letters from the President. On May 31, 1875, Attorney Gen. Edwards Pierrepont wrote to Joseph M. Carey and to Edward A. Thomas, associate justices, Wyoming Territory, requesting their resignations. Copies, *ibid.*, Letters Sent. Thomas retained his position.

On June 7, E. S. Whittier and many others, Evanston, Wyoming Territory, petitioned USG. "Having learned that your Excellency is about to cause to be removed from office the Honorable Joseph M Carey, Judge of the 3rd Judicial District of Wyoming Territory, we the undersigned residents of said District beg leave to remonstrate against such removal, for the reasons that Judge Carey is an upright, honest and able officer and that his removal would be detrimental to the interests of the people of this district, he understanding their wants and being interested in their welfare. We therefore respectfully petition Your Excellency to retain Judge Carey in his present office, as he has in every way fulfilled his duties and no better man could be appointed to fill his place." DS, *ibid.*, Records Relating to Appointments. On June 25, Carey wrote to Pierrepont. "The Attorneys of this Territory, have I understand prepared a paper in reference to my standing, as one of the judges of the Territory,—which will be forwarded to you as soon, as it can be submitted to the lawyers in the Western Counties—I have been closely occupied every day in Court, since my return here. Just as soon as I can get a spare day, I will see that evidence is furnished you in reference to my proposed resignation—" ALS, *ibid.*

On Feb. 2, 1876, following the expiration of Carey's term, USG nominated Jacob B. Blair as associate justice, Wyoming Territory. On July 20, 1875, Thomas B. Swann, Charleston, West Va., had written to USG. "The Honorable Jacob B. Blair of this State, formerly a Member of Congress from the Parkersburg District, & afterwards our Minister at one of the Central American States, before the consolidation act of Congress, forming these States into one Ministerial District, has urged me in person & by letter to ask your Excellency to Send him as Minister to Ecuador. There is no Friend whom I would more cheerfully serve (if it is in my power to serve) & no Gentleman in West Va who would fill the position with more credit. An Ardent Republican & admirer of your Administration, he has many fine qualities which adorn private life, & the address of a gentleman of Culture. Your Excellency must know I do not presume I have any influence with the administration. Events beyond my controul have suggested to others to make me the Medium of communication with Your Excellency & I cannot be indifferent to the wishes of my fellow-man, if he is worthy & I can aid him." ALS, *ibid.*, RG 59, Letters of Application and Recommendation. See Lewis L. Gould, *Wyoming: A Political History, 1868–1896* (New Haven, 1968), pp. 47–53.

On Aug. 21, Governor John M. Thayer of Wyoming Territory wrote to USG concerning a report that he had been replaced by John A. Campbell. "*Private*. . . . The enclosed appeared in a Laramie paper two days ago.   of course I know not whether it is true or not. My removal will ruin me ~~polically~~ politically and financially. I appeal to you, whom I have supported and defended for fourteen years, not to permit this injustice to be done to me. My losses and misfortunes for the last four years have left me without a dollar. If I could hold the office till next Spring when the Black Hills are opened for settlement, I can then start anew, and try to ~~rev~~ recover myself. I have been travelling through the Territory and have been received every where with the utmost cordiality and good feeling. I know the people are with me. If you have removed me, or are inclined to, I know you have been deceived by erroneous information. I do not complain, for I have the fullest confidence in your intention to do what seems to you to be right. I should like to know my fate. I know not what I am to do if I go out. I will ask that you destroy this on reading it. . . . If you are in doubt on account of conflicting information, I respectfully suggest that you send some competent man, a stranger, here to investigate." ALS, USG 3. A clipping is *ibid.* Orville E. Babcock endorsed this letter. "Gov Thayer—Ansd Aug 27th Never contemplated change—" AE (initialed), *ibid.* On Feb. 10, USG had nominated Thayer as governor, Wyoming Territory, after former governor Campbell had been nominated as 3rd asst. secretary of state. Probably at an earlier date, USG wrote. "Gen. Thayer desires a mission which will send him abroad as bearer of dispatches; or a place in his state." AN (undated), Columbia University, New York, N. Y.

To George M. Robeson

———

LONG BRANCH N.J. JUNE XVTH. [*1875*] SEC. OF THE NAVY WASHN. DC. IF VESSEL WITH PROPER LAUNCH FOR PATROLLING THE RIO GRANDE HAS NOT ALREADY BEEN SENT TO THAT RIVER PLEASE SEND ONE FROM THE MOST CONVENIENT POINT AND WITHOUT DELAY. U.S. GRANT.

Telegram received, DNA, RG 45, Letters Received from the President. On June 9, 1875, Orville E. Babcock, Long Branch, wrote to Secretary of the Navy George M. Robeson. "The President will be pleased to have you station one or two naval vessels. at or near the mouth of the Rio Grande Texas,—and to instruct the commanding officer to use his transports in assisting the US troops and the state troops to prevent marauding bands from crossing Mexico—and then recrossing to Mexico. Steam launches will be of good service." ALS, *ibid.* On June 15, Secretary of War William W. Belknap, West Point, telegraphed to Babcock. "Please inform the President that telegram received from Army Hd Qrs. says company of Texas troops had an engagement June 12 near Palo Alto, in Europe with Mexican cattle thieves, killing twelve, Part of killed recognized as belonging to Matamoras Report says 40 crossed to rescue Mexicans party. A company of U. S. troops sent from Fort Brown to cut it off. Gen'l Ord says Infantry may be needed from New Orleans if Cortina crosses & Genl Sheridan thinks it advisable that a vessel of war be sent to Mouth of Rio Grande, & a good surf tug to patrol the river, and thinks there is one at Savannah or New Orleans. Please give order for tug to Sec'y of Navy in addition to launches & gunboats heretofore ordered." Copy, *ibid.*, RG 94, Letters Received, 1653 1875. On June 16, Lt. Gen. Philip H. Sheridan, Chicago, telegraphed to AG Edward D. Townsend. "There is a well founded fear that Cortina may retaliate for the just punishment administered a few days ago on. A Band of mexican robbers and although the garrison at Fort Brown has been increased by three Companies of Cavalry and one of Infantry Still I would recommend that the President make his conditional Order about navy Vessels and a tug to the rio Grande a positive one—" Telegram received (at 8:55 P.M.), *ibid. HRC*, 44-1-343, 81. On June 17, Belknap telegraphed to Henry T. Crosby, chief clerk, War Dept. "Sheridan's telegram receivd, I have repeated it to the President and suggested that it be complied with, . . ." Telegram received, DNA, RG 94, Letters Received, 1653 1875. See Belknap to Babcock of the same date, telegram received, DLC-USG, IB. On June 17, USG, Long Branch, telegraphed to Belknap. "Positive orders were sent the Secretary of the Navy to send vessel & launch to the Rio Grande on receipt of dispatch announcing the engagement between cattle thieves & Texans" Telegram received, DNA, RG 94, Letters Received, 1653 1875. Related papers are *ibid.* On June 18, Robeson telegraphed to USG. "Ship of war, with two steam launches has been ordered to the Rio Grande, in accordance with Genl. Babcocks letter. I have also seen and consulted with Genl. Ord, and propose to send another ship with more launches very shortly. First ship will reach the Rio Grande, in about a week from this time." Copy, *ibid.*, RG 45, Letters Sent to the President. See *Foreign Relations, 1875,* II, 899–918, 946–47; *HRC,* 44-1-343; *HMD,* 44-1-170, part 5, pp. 682–83; *PUSG,* 23, 123–30; message to Congress, May 26, 1874.

On March 30, Governor Richard Coke of Tex. had telegraphed to USG. "The depredations of organized bands of robbers from the republic of Mexico have of late increased in frequency and atrocity to an extent which threatens the depopulation of the lower Rio Grande Country the alarm in the country between the Nueces and Rio Grande consequent upon ~~the~~ these raids in which our people are ruthlessly murdered and their property forcibly taken by these foreign desperadoes is wide spread and unless relieved by some assurances of protection must result in a general break up of the settlements. On the twenty sixth of this month a large party of these robbers penetrated the interior as far as within eighteen miles of Corpus Christi robbing stores and ranches, and murdering and capturing citizens and capturing and destroying United States mails. I appeal to your Excellency for protection for the people of that country against these invasions of outlaws from Mexico since they have been of almost weekly occurrence for several months past and are increasing in force and boldness. The citizens of that country have been compelled for the most part to move to the towns for protection and no security exists outside of these corporations for life or property and the people in the towns even hold themselves in constant readiness for defence. I trust that Your Excellency will deem it proper to give security to the people on the Rio Grande border in view of the assurance I now give you that an extreme necessity exists for it." Copy, DNA, RG 94, Letters Received, 1653 1875. *Foreign Relations, 1875,* II, 891–92; *HRC,* 44-1-343, 71. On March 31, Belknap telegraphed to Coke. "The President being absent your telegram has been sent to me. Orders will be given to the military authorities to take immediate steps towards the protection of the people of Texas on the Mexican frontier ~~and to pursue the invader~~." LS (telegram sent, press), DNA, RG 94, Letters Received, 1653 1875. *HRC,* 44-1-343, 71.

On April 6 and 23, Secretary of State Hamilton Fish recorded cabinet deliberations in his diary. "The only subject discussed was the troubles on the Mexican frontier Belknap read a communication from the officer in command at Fort Brown also a telegram from Genl Sherman The officers on the frontier admit that parties on both sides of the River are engaged in the raids; they speak of those on the Texas side as Mexicans alluding to the original nationality or their descent and state that when parties are captured and brought before Mexican Judges and Juries they are sure to escape. The President directs me to suggest to Mr Mariscal (Mexican Minist[e]r) that an arrangement might be entered into between the two Governments for a more efficient suppression of outrages by allowing the troops of either Governments in persuit of actual merauders to cross the frontier and continue the chase in the territory of the other—to my inquiry whether he would allow the Mexicans to enter our territory—he answers that he would I remind him that Cortina who was in Military command of the territory embracing Matamoras, he thought that he had been superceeded I corrected his impression on this point but he does not change his instructions as to the communications to be made to Mariscal" ". . . During the conversation the general subject of the raids made on either side across the Rio Grande were discussed and Belknap asked whether Mexico would consent that the Government troops on either side should be authorized to follow in actual pursuit into the territory of the other Government and to punish actual merauders. I replied that I had not been authorized to make any such proposal but that the Mexican minister professed a strong desire on the part of his Government to put an end to the lawlessness which exists on the frontier The President authorized me to make suggestion to Mr Mariscal and ascertain whether his Government would assent to such arrangement." DLC-Hamilton Fish. See also Fish diary, April 22, 27, 30, 1875, *ibid.*

On May 18, Belknap wrote to Coke. "I have the honor to invite your attention to the enclosed copy of telegram from General Sheridan, dated the 15th instant, relative to affairs in Texas, in the country bordering the Rio Grande, and reporting the arrest of United States soldiers. The President desires me to call your attention to this subject, and to say that if soldiers of the United States forces placed in that state for the protection of the citizens, are to be treated in the manner indicated in this dispatch when they have simply done their duty, it may become necessary for him to withdraw the United States troops from that locality." LS (press), DNA, RG 94, Letters Received, 1653 1875. A copy of the enclosure is *ibid.* Soldiers ambushed while on patrol had been arrested for allegedly killing a Mexican assailant. See numerous related papers, *ibid.*; *HRC*, 44-1-343, 143—44.

On May 21, Fish recorded a cabinet discussion in his diary. "The President suggested that I send for Mr Mariscal & represent to him that the condition of affairs on the frontier necessitate some immediate action on the part of Mexico in default of which he apprehends that it will be impossible to allay the public excitement on the borders of Texas and prevent some outbreak or possible invasion of Mexico. I read to him the draft of an instruction to Mr Foster dated 19 May suggesting that the Mexican Government might not be indisposed to allow the U. S. troops to cross the frontier and temporally occupy the territory from whence the raiders are in the habit of coming and directing him to sound the Minister of Foreign Affairs on this point; he approves the dispatch and authorizes its being sent. . . . I raise the question however whether the Executive is authorized to consent without the action of Congress to the occupation of any part of our territory by foreign troops. He replies that he had authorized me to propose to the Mexican Minister that the troops of either Government might in actual pursuit follow lawless bands into the territory of the other. In answer to this I am of opinion that the Executive may waive objection to such momentary pursuit and regard it in the light of friendly exercise of police authority & that it appears to me different from a formal consent to the occupation which carries the idea of more or less disorder duration; this view is accepted & I am directed to transmit the note as read." DLC-Hamilton Fish. See *Foreign Relations, 1875*, II, 924—25, 943—46.

On May 29, Coke wrote to USG. "It again becomes my duty to call your attention to the extraordinary condition of affairs in that portion of the territory of this State bordering the Rio Grand[e] river, and extending back for the most part to the river Nueces. The invasion of that country by predatory bands from the Republic of Mexico, to which your attention was called by my communication of March 30th, continues unabated, and is of a character to be no longer borne. Citizens are being murdered, thousands of cattle being driven across the Rio Grande, the roads are infested with bands of robbers, Ranches and plantations are abandoned, the owners seeking safety in flight to the towns, and on account of the terror reigning in the country and the absence of any security for life or property, revenue officers of the State are unable to assess or collect taxes. The country must be defended, or our people and jurisdiction be left to the mercy of foreign robbers. The forays which have devastated, and are daily desolating that country, have been for a year past, and are now growing bolder in execution, and more extensive in their proportions, and give abundant evidence that they are the manifestation of an organized and settled purpose to overrun that Country. Gen. Cortina, a notorious Mexican bandit, who on a former occasion invaded that country with a large force, is believed to be one of the principal instigators of the present war on that border. I have two Companies of State troops on duty in that country, but they, as well as the forces of the United States, are powerless as long as the Rio Grande river is an inviolable line beyond which the invaders can not be pursued. There is in my judgment no efficient mode of defending the Texas border, other than through retaliatory measures on the territory and people west of the Rio Grande. The information I give you as to the deplorable condition of that country and the imminence of a sanguinary border war, is corroborated fully by Gen. Ord, in his correspondence with me. Necessity for prompt action exists, and must be taken by the State authorities unless the arm of the General Government, is interposed in our defence. I respectfully but earnestly ask that relief be given, and the State authorities relieved of the responsibility of dealing with this Subject, which pertains properly to the national administration. I invite the attention of your Excellency to the Enclosed extract from a letter written by myself on this subject to Gen. Ord, Commanding in this Department, which gives my views more in detail." LS, DNA, RG 94, Letters Received, 1653 1875. The enclosure is *ibid.* See *HRC*, 44-1-343, 76–78.

On the same day, Halbert E. Paine, Washington, D. C., wrote to USG. "I have the honor to lay before you the enclosed letter, received from Theodore W. Gillette, respecting the murder of D. D. Lovell and George Hill, committed, as is alleged, in the State of Texas, by armed Mexicans, who invaded that State and, having perpetrated these crimes, returned for protection to Mexican territory. During the late war I was well acquainted with the writer of this letter, as also with Dr Lovell. They were soldiers of the 4th Wis. Regt., of which I was the first colonel, and were both upright & intelligent men. The regiment, when discharged from the service of the United States, in the summer of 1866, was stationed on the Rio Grande, and many of its members, including Dr Lovell, remained in the western part of Texas, and became citizens of that State. Inasmuch as the 6th article of the treaty of 1861, now in force, admits of no demand upon Mexico for the extradition of these murderers for trial & punishment in the State of Texas, and the Governor of Texas is not authorized to make reprizals within mMexican territory, I respectfully ask that you will take such steps as shall seem proper to secure the punishment of the murderers and the adequate compensation of the families of the murdered men—" LS, DNA, RG 59, Miscellaneous Letters. The enclosure is *ibid.* See *HRC*, 44-1-343, 53–54.

On June 6, Coke telegraphed to USG. "I am informed by W Steele adjutant Genl of the state now at Brownsville that Cortina the mexican bandit is now shipping cattle from the mouth of the Rio-Grande to Havana & that an investigation if one can be had at Havana will show complicity of Mexican authorities in the depredations in Texas I am further informed by Genl Steele that the Commanding officer at Brownsville refuses to send troops to defend the people & their property against mexican raiders now in the County saying that he acts under recent instructions I request to be informed if it be true that the forces of the U. S are instructed not to defend that Country" Telegram received (at 11:43 P.M.), DNA, RG 94, Letters Received, 1653 1875. On June 8, Belknap telegraphed to Coke. "No instructions of the character named in your telegram of June 6 to the President have been given to the officer commanding the U. S. forces in Texas. Gen'l Ord is here & has given the Comd'g Officer at Brownsville proper orders in the matter." Telegram sent, *ibid.*

On June 20, John Embleton, Cincinnati, wrote to USG. "Having resided most of my life time in Mexico, and mostly on, or near the U. S. boundary line, I respectfully ask the privilege of submitting my knowledge of facts connected with the late difficulties on and near the Rio Grande. I am not partial to the Mexican government, having descended from English parentage, but being somewhat familiar with the causes—as I understand them—of the several conflicts, resulting in the death of most of the Mexicans engaged. I shall—without desiring notoriety—state all the facts fairly. There are in Texas, at most of the prominent rail way stations, and at their Hotels, a set of fellows, whose ostensible business is to search out, and purchase homes; but whose business is, though not Texans, to induce such as go in with money to buy lands or cattle, to unite with them 'as they are in the same business' in procuring horses and buggies &co to look at the country. In those schemes they generally succeed, and such as are enticed out ~~and~~ are left lifeless in some obscure spot, divested of all their money, watches &co. and if suspecion falls on this disperate companion, which it some times does, he is the first to propose to hang some Mexican; for there still reside some Mexicans in every county in Texas, and thus escape himself. The true state of such cases on reaching Mexico creates sympathy for the Mexican, and a spirit of revenge toward his murderers. This class in Texas is composed of those adventurers, united in many instances with railway employees, who have the same *daring*, and are like themselves, nonresidents. Allow me to state—which I do with ~~with~~ the greatest sincerity—that no negro nor Mexican belongs to this party; and beside they—the negroes and Mexicans—are too friendless and defenceless to go among a people as desperate and brave as are the Texans, on a thieving raid. Here too allow me to contradict a statement going the rounds of your papers, charging General Cortena with being at the head of party of 'cattle thieves,' and the late dozen or more, who were murdered in Texas, were murdered by the class heretofore described, for their money and effects. There are none in Mexico insane enough to provoke a war with the U. S. willingly, and but few, if any, who would give their sanction to the annexation of any part, or all of Mexico to this or any other country. I regret much to see, in my late travels from Matamoras, Mexico, and leisurely through Texas to this place, an entire people so unjustly incensed against the (Greasers) Mexicans; and especially as I see in it—unequal as it may be—a great and bloody strife impending. My father, Robert Embleton resided in the State of veracruz during the war between the U. S & Mexico, and became a scout for Genl Scott, and his son, the undersigned is neutral.... While on my way to visit my relatives in Canada, I have seen proper to address you the following facts, which have come within my own knowledge Please excuse the liberty I have taken in doing so." ALS, *ibid.*

On July 7, Gen. William T. Sherman, St. Louis, telegraphed to Belknap conveying a dispatch from Sheridan questioning an order from Brig. Gen. Edward O. C. Ord to "arrest any men who may Come from Mexico with arms in their hands & Confine them in the guard house notifying Civil authorities at once of Such arrests & in Case parties attempt to resist Shoot them if necessary to make the arrest . . ." Telegram received (at 4:26 P.M.), *ibid.* On the same day, Crosby telegraphed to Sherman. "Your telegram about Texas affairs recd & sent to president   Genl Belknap is in Keokuk . . ." Telegram received, *ibid.*, RG 108, Letters Received, 928 1875. On July 8, Belknap, Keokuk, telegraphed to Sherman. "Your telegram recd—on account of its importance I have directed that it be repeated from washington to the presedent for such instructions as he may give—. . ." Telegram received (at 2:46 P.M.), *ibid.*

On July 9, Fish conversed with USG at Long Branch. "I spoke to him of the disturbances on the Mexican frontier with regard to which he thinks no immediate measures need be taken." Fish diary (retrospective entry dated July 7), DLC-Hamilton Fish.

On Aug. 30, Monday, Daniel Ammen, Washington, D. C., wrote to Babcock. "I enclose a graphic description of the situation along the Rio B[r]avo, rec'd late on Saturday from Gen'l Ord. The saying that the worst use a man can be put to is to shoot or hang him has done a great deal of harm. I suppose the world would be far better off if nine out of ten of the vagrants described by Gen'l Ord were '*despatched.*' The comparison the Gen'l makes of corsairs is very just and it seems that they should be rooted out wherever they are sheltered. If it is supposed advantageous we can have two steamers on the river, but crossing the cattle as they do would seem to afford little chance for incepting them. I trust you are all well and that we will soon have the pleasure of seeing you." ALS, USG 3. The enclosure is a letter of Aug. 19 from Ord, San Antonio, to Ammen. "I am just back from an examination of the lower Rio Grande, and finding that matters there still look serious, write you that if you can do so conveniently, you may present the subject to the President, or Cabinet—. . . Quite a large population, mexican and indian, live in mud huts and dirt, their little patches lining the road and river bank, all the way from Brownsville to Ringold Barracks. Cultivation is scant, and the ranchmen, with few exceptions, seem to have no visible means of support—At nearly every ranch I noticed a number of men lounging around, and generally one or two horses saddled; we received as we rode by none of the customary salutations, but generally a sullen hostile look—I was told by every U. S. official, and by the Army officers, that they were either in league with the cattle thieves, and murderers, of Americans those who might be peaceably disposed, are afraid to give information against them—. . . Now, how can the civil, military, or naval, authorities, be expected to put a stop to this raiding? There is but one prompt, proper, and effectual way of doing it; notify the Mexican Government, that if a single case of raiding occurs on the river, after a certain time, that reprisals will be at once made on the towns of Matamoros, Reynosa, ~~and~~ Camargo, Mier and Guerero; to cover the damage already done; *notice* of such intended action, with a good force of sailors and soldiers to back it, would be all that would be necessary; Cortinas would'nt come back, and some of the other leaders of raiders would follow him, or be shot, and the nests of robbers at Las Cuevas, La Balsa, Guerero, and other points along the river, well know to the mexicans, would be broken up—. . . As Col. Potter, said to me when I spoke about his pushing things with the black cavalry 'If you can get any thing out of these d——d negroes it is more than I can' so if the President, does threaten reprisals,—and the threat alone will do,—he should send white troops to back it—The mexicans have a contempt for the negroes soldiers, and it is not surprising that they do— what few officers of snap there are in the colored regiments, are longing for a change to white troops; and, indeed, I must have a white regiment very soon vice the 24th for its soldiers will soon be nearly all discharged, and there are next to none enlisting—. . ." ALS, *ibid.*

On Sept. 17, Belknap wrote to Edmund J. Davis, Austin. "Among the many letters that have accumulated on my table during my absence, I find your very interesting communication of June 29th. I do not reply to it fully at this time for the reason that I desire to give it further consideration, and to present it to the President, in order that his views on the subject may be obtained." LS (press), DNA, RG 94, Letters Received, 1653 1875. On June 29, Davis had written to Belknap concerning unrest along the Tex. border with Mexico. LS, *ibid.*

On March 9, 1876, Fish wrote to Robeson, act. secretary of war. "In view of the information through the Department of War and from other sources as to an attempt at revolution in Mexico, and especially in that part of it contiguous to the Texan frontier, I am directed by the President to request that an order be issued by telegraph as well as in writing to the proper military officer in that quarter, to tolerate no armed expeditions from this side the Rio Grande, or any organizations for such purpose, that the aid of troops be granted if necessary to cause the neutrality of the United States to be respected, and for the arrest of offenders for prosecution according to law, and, if any armed men cross from

Mexico to the American side of the boundary, that they be at once arrested, disarmed and sent under arrest to a point in the interior of the country." LS, *ibid*. On March 21, Sheridan endorsed this letter. ". . . Prisoners, if captured, would only be a rascally lot of chaparral scalawags, who, it seems to me, should be simply dis-armed and let go. I tried this matter of taking prisoners to the interior—as far as San Antonio—on a previous occasion, and felt afterwards a little ashamed of myself for giving such an amount of consideration to such a set. . . ." ES, *ibid*.

On July 7, John L. Cadwalader, act. secretary of state, wrote to Secretary of War James D. Cameron. "I have the honor to enclose a copy of a telegram this day received from Thos. F. Wilson, the Consul of the United States at Matamoras. The President gave directions that the Consul be informed that the Government could not authorize an interference in the difficulties at Matamoras, by troops of the United States, but that the authorities would be instructed to lend aid for the protection of the lives and property of American citizens. . . ." LS, *ibid*.

On July 18, Fish wrote to Cameron enclosing a telegram "in regard to the alleged crossing the Rio Grande of an armed band of Mexicans, and the seizure by them of three Mexican citizens who had taken refuge in Brownsville." LS, *ibid*. The enclosure is a telegram of July 17 from Wilson to Fish, reporting that the prisoners might be summarily shot. ". . . It is understood that Mexicans claim that they were captured on Mexican soil, though on Texas side of Rio Grande, and that they have understanding with Gen. Ord through Lieut. Colonel Devine, commanding Fort Brown, to pass armed parties of Mexicans into Texas to pursue criminals. There is considerable excitement in Brownsville, and, if the alleged understanding exists with Genl. Ord to allow armed Mexicans to cross into Texas, State authorities will not submit, and armed conflicts will doubtless occur." Copy, *ibid*. On July 18, Fish recorded in his diary that USG directed Wilson's telegram to Cameron "to enquire whether there be any such understanding as is alleged between Genl Ord & the Mexican Authorities." DLC-Hamilton Fish.

Endorsement

WAR DEPT.

This apt. and that of Wells[1]—formerly Capt, 4th Inf.y—may be made early; the latter in the Artillery.

                                        U. S. GRANT

JUNE 15TH /75

AES, DNA, RG 94, ACP, 2779 1875. Written on a letter of June 12, 1875, from Ann Mary Coleman, Louisville, to USG. "I have received a letter from my sister Mrs Thomas Crittenden, begging me to remind you of your promise as to her son John J. Crittendens appointment and to ask as a great additional kindness that his commission might bear the same date as that of his graduating class   I have written to my sister that you told me you would give John J his commission when his class graduated, and that you did not forget your promises, but as she requested I venture to write. I will only say in conclusion General Grant, that I love you and thank you for all your kindness. I have more reason for love and gratitude to you than any one I know. Would it be out of order for my nephews commission to be sent to me to forward to him, this would give me pleasure" ALS, *ibid*. On Dec. 6, USG nominated John J. Crittenden as 2nd lt., 20th Inf. On June 25, 1876, he was killed in action at the Little Big Horn. For Coleman, see *PUSG*, 16, 551–52.

On April 10, 1870, Col. Thomas L. Crittenden, Camp Grant, Richmond, had written to USG. "I have the honor most respectfully to solicit an appointment to a Cadetship at West Point, for my son John J Crittenden who is now at school in Kentucky and is sixteen years old. My son was promised an appointment from Arizona, but as he is not now a resident of that Territory he could not be appointed by the Delegate from there. There is no prospect of obtaining for him an appointment by any representative in Congress from Kentucky . . ." ALS, DNA, RG 94, Correspondence, USMA. On May 4, John P. Kennedy, Baltimore, wrote to USG. "In a recent interview which I have had with General Thomas Crittenden, who passed through this City on his way to the Indian frontier, I found him very earnestly interested in the success of an application he had made to get his son into the Academy at West Point under one of the appointments at large.—Since he left the City his sister, Mrs Coleman, has called on me, at his instance, to ask me to recall this subject to your notice . . . We of the Border States have a keen perception of the merit of those who could preserve their faith in the midst of the many influences, persuasions and threats which were used to draw off our best men from the support of the Government. No family, perhaps, felt this trial more painfully than that of Genl Crittenden—. . . He is, I am told, in straitened circumstances, having lost his small inherited property by the accidents of the war. . . ." ALS, *ibid*. On April 20, Lt. Gen. Philip H. Sheridan, Chicago, had favorably endorsed Crittenden's application. AES, *ibid*. On July 13, 1874, U.S. Senator John W. Stevenson of Ky., Covington, wrote to USG. "I hope I shall be pardoned for an appeal to your generous & manly impulses for an exercise of Executive power, if the same be not deemed by you, detrimental to the public service   John Jordan Crittenden, a son of Genl T. L. Crittenden & a grandson of the illustrious Kentuckian, whose name he bears, has been found deficient in Natural Philosophy at the late examination at West Point, where he has been as a cadet for three years past, & is recommended for dismissal—for his failure in the study named. His friends are aware that he cannot remain without the recommendation of the Academic Board, & no such recommendation has been made   But is it asking too much of you in respectfully soliciting you to order that Board to reassemble, in order that this noble boy—*well known to me*, & beloved by all who know him may be reexamined—& put back a year in his studies. . . ." ALS, *ibid*. On the same day, Stevenson wrote to Secretary of the Treasury Benjamin H. Bristow. "I enclose you an open letter to the President, which I ask you to read—If you deem it indelicate or improper in me to address him in the premises destroy it—If you do not please see it delivered promptly to the President . . ." ALS, DLC-Benjamin H. Bristow. On July 14, Thomas L. Crittenden, New York City, wrote to USG. "I have traveled a long distance in order to hold a few minutes conversation with you about my son who has just been discharged from West Point. When I called yesterday at the Fifth Avenue Hotel I learned from General Babcock that you were in the act of starting for Saratoga. He also informed me that you had been talking over my son's case, and although very kindly disposed towards him, you could do nothing, because the law of Congress forbid his reinstatement or reappointment. I was aware of this law, and of course should not have solicited any such action from you. What I hoped and still hope General is, that you might reconvene the Academic Board of Examiners or direct the Superintendant to do so, and see if the Board would not so modify their report as to put the boy back a year instead of discharging him from the Academy. . . ." LS, DNA, RG 94, Correspondence, USMA.

On July 2, Coleman, Baltimore, had written to USG. "The 'Ides of March' are upon us, that is to say *July* and I ask permission to remind you of Burnley Crittenden and the vacancy in the 4th Infantry, Captain Powell. I was in Washington a few days since & saw Gen Bristow, who first recommended Burnley Crittenden for one of these appointments. The General told me that you were absent, but that if I would write to you on the subject, he would see that you got the letter. He is an intimate friend of my Brother Robert, & can answer any questions you may ask with regard to him. Our Paymasters bill did not become a law   Mr President, I watched for it as, 'They that watch for the morning.' But there are Pay masters & pay masters." ALS, *ibid.*, ACP, 4153 1873. On Dec. 7, USG nominated A. Burnley Crittenden as 2nd lt., 4th Inf.

In [*June*], U.S. Senator Thomas C. McCreery of Ky. and eight others had petitioned USG. "We—the representatives from the state of Kentucky—respectfully ask the appointment of John J Crittenden Jr. to West Point   He is the son of Maj Eugene W Crittenden—now of the regular army—and the Grand son of John J Crittenden—deceased" DS (docketed June 23), *ibid.*, Correspondence, USMA. On Sept. 1, 1876, Coleman, Ocean Beach, N. J., wrote to USG. "I write to ask that you will give an appointment in the army to John Jordan Crittenden, the son of Major E. W. Crittenden deceased. This young man is twenty years of age, well grown, has a fine constitution, and good abilities. He lives at Frankfort. Kentucky." ALS, *ibid.*, ACP, 532 1877. On Sept. 11, USG endorsed this letter. "The Sec. of War. Some time during my term of office I would like to confer this apt." AES, *ibid.* Related papers are *ibid.* On Dec. 6, USG nominated J. Jordan Crittenden as 2nd lt., 22nd Inf.

1. On Jan. 5, 1875, Eugene Wells, Washington, D. C., had written to USG. "I respectfully request the appointment of Consul in Class "1st". I would state in making this application that I have served ten (10) years in the Regular Army, commencing in May 1861, and for my services therein, would respectfully refer to enclosed recommendations. During the past year I have been engaged in business in Alabama—said business was however ruined because of the murder of my brother in law and business partner Mr W. P. Billings, who was murdered because of his political opinions." LS, *ibid.*, RG 59, Letters of Application and Recommendation. Related papers are *ibid.* On [*Aug.*] 2, 1874, Wells, Livingston, Ala., had written to Lewis Dent, who had died on March 22. "I have just this moment received information, from a gentleman who saw the body, that my brother in law Mr. W. P. Billings of Missouri after making a Republican speech within five miles of this place, was basely murdered while on his way to his plantation. Five shots were fired and both he and horse were killd. Now Genl Dent the charge can not be brought against Mr. Billings or myself of being carpetbaggers, simply out spoken Republicans   And if Genl Grant the representative of our party is to see us slaughtered, with impunity then we wish to know it. I served ten years in the Regular Army, and both you and the President knew my father R. W. Wells U. S. Dist Judge of Missouri. I refer you for character to Montgomery &. F. P. Blair of Mo—and to Senator Louis V. Bogy and Chas D Drake of U. s Court of Claims. I am laboring under such emotion that I can scarcely express my thoughts coherently. Please write me by return mail" ALS (misdated July 2), *ibid.*, RG 60, Letters from the President. *HRC*, 43-2-262, 1224. See *ibid.*, pp. 1122, 1129, 1255; *New York Times*, Aug. 14, 1874.

In May, 1875, John F. Long, surveyor of customs, St. Louis, wrote to USG recommending Wells for a military appointment. ALS, DNA, RG 94, ACP, W225 CB 1870. About this time, Wells wrote to USG applying for appointment as 2nd lt., art. ALS (undated), *ibid.* On June 27, USG endorsed this letter. "Refered to the Sec. of War. I approve the apt. of this applicant." AES, *ibid.* On Dec. 6, USG nominated Wells as 2nd lt., 1st Art., to date from July 6. Allegations of drunkenness followed Wells through his military career. See *HED*, 53-2-259; *HRC*, 55-3-2210.

On Sept. 21, Wells wrote to Long. "On my arrival in the East, I was unable to see President Grant, as he had left for the West, and was not at Long Branch. I therefore take the liberty of enclosing to you the application of the President of the 'University State of Missouri' of and of Major Rollins 'President Board of Curators' of the same; and most earnestly hope you will present it to President Grant on his arrival in St Louis; and use your influence to have it granted. . . ." ALS, DNA, RG 94, ACP, 4131 1875. On Sept. 15, Daniel Read and James S. Rollins, University of Missouri, Columbia, had written to USG to request that Wells be assigned as military professor. LS, *ibid.* Related papers are *ibid.* No appointment followed.

To Columbus Delano

Long Branch, N. J.
June 16th 1875.

DEAR SIR,

I see announced in to days papers the names of the Commissioners to negotiate with Soux for possession of the Black Hill Country. Among the names announced is that of Col O'Beirne[1] of the New York Herald. I immediately telegraphed to have Gen Lawrence[2] substituted for O'Beirne and J S. Collins[3] for Dywyer[4] as Secty—I had previously caused a despatch to be sent to the Int Dept asking to have Collins appt as Secty. In regard to the former I am decidedly and unalterably opposed to the New York Herald being recognized on this or any other Commission, appointed by me or with my sanction, and desired therefore, notwithstanding the publication of the names of the Commissioner that this change should be made.

Very respectfully yr ob Svt
U S GRANT.

HON C DELANO
SECTY OF THE INTERIOR

Copies, ICarbS; DLC-USG, II, 2; Df, USG 3. On June 16, 1875, USG, Long Branch, telegraphed to Secretary of the Interior Columbus Delano. "Please substitute the names of Gen. Lawrence and J. S. Collins for Obeirne & Dwyer on the Commission to negociate with the sioux Indians. You are authorized to add Mr. Ashby to the Commission." ALS (telegram sent), USG 3. On June 8, Delano had telegraphed to Orville E. Babcock, Long Branch. "Please say to the Prest that among the names suggested for commissioners which seen to meritorious are bishops Ames & Haven and Dr Newman" Telegram received, DLC-USG, IB. On the same day, Babcock wrote to Delano. "The President directs me to say in reply that he would suggest Gen. Frank Palmer of Chicago and Genl. Alf. Terry of the Army. The Commission will then consist of Bishop Hare Bishop Whipple Rev. Mr. Hinman Gen. Palmer Gen. Terry. The President says he has no suggestions to make in the matter of their instruction." Copy, *ibid.*, II, 2. On June 14, Babcock wrote to Benjamin R. Cowen, act. secretary of the interior. "The President directs me to forward you the enclosed letter and to say that he has no objection to adding to the names already appointed on the Commission to the Black Hills Country, that of Mr. Collins, and also General Gallatin Lawrence. The latter full name and address you can procure from the Secretary of the Navy. Will you please notify Mr. Collins of your action in the matter." Copy, *ibid.* On June 15, Cowen wrote to USG. "The Secretary has appointed the following named persons to constitute the Commission to negotiate with the Sioux Indians: Senator Allison, chairman; Hon. F. W. Palmer of Chicago; Hon. Abram Comingo of Missouri; Rev. S. D. Hinman of Dakota; General A. H. Terry of the Army; Mr. Beauvais of Missouri, recommended by Senator Bogy; Colonel O'Beirne of the New York Herald; Bishop Ames of the Methodist Church; with J. W. Dwyer of Ohio as secretary. Since the Secretary's dispatch was received, making the above appointments, the Senators from Nebraska telegraphed him asking the appointment of William H. Ashby, of that State, as a member of the Commission. He telegraphs me to communicate the wishes of the Nebraska Senators to you, and take your suggestions in the matter, which I do. Bishop Ames has not yet accepted the appointment, but telegraphs that he will be here next week and will then give his reply. The appointments, as named above, will be announced to-day. If you have any suggestions to make in regard to Mr. Ashby, he can be added to the Commission, if desired, or if Bishop Ames should finally conclude to decline the appointment, Mr. Ashby could be named in his place." LS, USG 3. On Aug. 2, Delano wrote to USG. "Bp. Ames has been compelled to decline his place on the Sioux Commission Will you name a Successor. I have no one in my mind to suggest I will re examine the Case of Peters, and Communicate my Conclusion in a day or two The weather and a pressure of business begins to tell on my health and I must as soon as I can take a few days rest some where I prefer my home in Ohio—but I will advise you when I leave ... P. S Letters marked personal will be sent me & official business will be attended to by the Asst Secty" ALS, *ibid.* The commission, chaired by U.S. Senator William B. Allison of Iowa, included Brig. Gen. Alfred H. Terry, former U.S. Representative Abram Comingo of Mo., Samuel D. Hinman, Geminien P. Beauvais, William H. Ashby, Albert G. Lawrence, and John S. Collins as secretary.

On March 23, James L. Crane, postmaster, Springfield, Ill., had written to USG. "I see from despatches that you design appointing Commissioners to treat with the Indians for opening up the Black Hills so that citizens of the states may go there. In such an event allow me to ask that my neighbor & friend *Rheuna D. Lawrence* of Springfield Ill. be appointed as one of said Commissioners. Mr. L. I have known long & well. He is an honorable upright, & efficient business man. He is not a politician in the general meaning of the term, but a thorough business man. Could you know him fully I think you would be inclined to appoint him. I would be exceedingly gratified if you would select him." ALS, DNA, RG 75, Dakota Superintendency.

On June 15, the Kansas City, Mo., board of trade adopted a memorial to USG protesting the possible relocation of the Sioux to Indian Territory as "a policy that would lead to the concentration in that territory of the wild Indians of other regions also, and a dedication of this fair and fertile section, lying in the heart of the country and amidst populous states, to savagery and barbarism forever." Printed copy, *ibid.* On June 28, Governor Charles H. Hardin of Mo. wrote to USG endorsing this memorial. ALS, *ibid.* On July 6, Governor Thomas A. Osborn of Kan. wrote to USG. "I have the honor to signify my concurrence with the remonstrances which, I am informed, have been forwarded to you, against the policy of locating the Sioux tribes of Indians in the Indian Territory. I do so in the name of the people of this State, of whose views upon the subject I am thoroughly cognizant, and who would ratify a respectful protest against the policy in question with a marked approach to unanimity. While the people of Kansas are far from believing that the wild Indian tribes upon our frontiers have no claims upon the justice and humanity of the white race, they do believe that there are no interests of such transcendent importance associated with the future of those tribes as to justify the arrest of civilization by locating them permanently in its pathway. Such is the ardor of American enterprise, and so rapidly is the theater of its exercise extended, that to the people—those of the West, especially— the proposition to set apart that magnificent domain known as the Indian Territory to the exclusive occupancy of the savages forever, savors almost of sacrilege. It is idle to discuss an abstraction. The practical question is: Are the interests which demand that, within a reasonable period, the Territory shall be opened to settlement, upon terms just and equitable to the tribes already located there, superior to those of the roving and troublesome barbarians whom it is proposed to concentrate there? To this question, I think, there can be but one answer. Indeed, the generosity of the Government will scarcely be appreciated by those in whose behalf it is exercised. To them the arid wastes and mountain fastnesses, with the facilities which they offer for the chase and for the primitive occupations of nomadic life, are superior in attractiveness to the unexcelled fertility of the region to which it is proposed to transport them. It is useless to anticipate profitable intercourse with the gulf ports, through the Indian Territory, while the resources of that Territory remain undeveloped. If it were not so, I very much doubt whether, upon grounds of natural right and justice, the Government would be justified in dooming that land to perpetual barrenness. The interests of the Indians are clearly subordinate to those of the White race, indeed, are of but trifling consequence in the comparison; and in determining questions respecting the future welfare of both, this vast disparity should not be lost sight of. I think I know the sentiment of the West on this subject, and I hazard the prediction that the day is not distant when the States west of the Mississippi will demand that this obstacle to the progress of industry, of development and of civilization be removed. But for the fact that, heretofore, by solemn treaty, lands were patented to some of the Indian tribes, the barrier would have been broken down ere this. But it is of the first importance that the difficulties in the way of such a consummation shall not be increased by the action of the Government itself, as would be the case were the Sioux or other uncivilized tribes located there. I cannot forbear to add that the policy of dealing with the scattered and roving tribes through the medium of treaties is one that, in my judgment, ought to be discontinued. With all its sanctions of history and precedent, it can scarcely be claimed, at this day, to comport with the dignity of the nation or the spirit of the people. The Government ought to exercise complete authority over the Indians within its territorial jurisdiction, and—the relative interests of the races being considered—should so exercise it as to insure the largest measure of usefulness. Conventions with the Indians are now a very general subject of derision throughout the country. A scarcely less important objection to the location of any more wild tribes in the Indian Territory is, the danger which it will occasion to the neighboring States. Upon this subject Kansas feels deeply, and I would be derelict in my duty to this people were I to withhold my protest against such a project. Their mere removal to the Indian Territory will not change the nature of the savage and treacherous tribes whose barbarities have disfigured almost every page of our history. More than one hundred and fifty thousand of our people have, within the past few years, made their homes upon territory subject to the encroachments of those tribes, and which has been the scene of their frequent depredations. Since the organization of Kansas hundreds of citizens have been ruthlessly murdered and their property destroyed. During the very last year twenty-seven citizens of this State were butchered, within the State, by savages who had no shadow of right

to be upon our soil, but who had roamed from their reservations in defiance of the authority of the Government. Since Kansas became a State considerably more than three hundred thousand dollars has been expended in defending the people against Indian hostilities, an indebtedness of about forty thousand dollars having been incurred during the last
year, and paid by authority of the Legislature at its late session. Claims to the amount of
more than three hundred and fifty thousand dollars, for property stolen and destroyed by
hostile Indians, have been properly investigated and verified by authority of the State. This
amount, it is believed, represents but a small part of the total loss and damage to which
our people have been subjected from this source. In Texas the loss of life and property has
been vastly greater than in Kansas. Is it a matter of wonder that people who have been thus
harassed and afflicted should betray apprehension at the idea of massing upon their very
border all, or at least the worst, of their savage enemies? Is it proposed to increase the dangers of settlement on the frontier to such an extent as to compel these States, in self-
defense, to enter upon a line of policy which can only result in the complete annihilation
of the wild tribes? At this time crime is alarmingly prevalent in the Territory. That region
has become a convenient skulking place for the thieves and outlaws of the surrounding
States, and it is difficult, if not impossible, to compel their surrender for trial and punishment. Congress should, in its wisdom, erect there some sort of a political government, in
order that crime may be adequately punished, and the Territory prevented from becoming
a secure asylum for fugitives from the justice of the several States. In conclusion, Mr. President, I beg to assure you of my profound conviction that your course with reference to the
Indian policy of the country has been inspired by a sincere desire to do the best that could
be done, under the circumstances, for the welfare both of the Indians and of the country at
large. Many features of that policy I believe to have been mistaken; and I am impressed
with the belief that the massing of the Indian tribes in the Territory south of Kansas would
be a greater mistake than any that have preceded it. Therefore, for reasons hastily and imperfectly set forth in the foregoing, I most respectfully, but earnestly, remonstrate against
the prosecution of such an enterprise." LS, *ibid.*

On July 2, John Watson, Boston, had written to USG. "A thought comes to me that I
will suggest to you. By the newspapers, it is reported that efforts to treat with the Indians
for the purchase of territory have been frustrated. And that efforts are being made to obtain minerals in their territory. For the preservation of peace and good-will with a weak
portion of the human race—Cannot a tax be levied on the substance taken so as to offer
to the owners of the soil a fair compensation for the privelege usurped. And a communication made to them that the United States Government will superintend the operations
so prosecuted so as to compensate them and make them wealthier for the intrusion and so
far as possible maintain order and good-will and every alleviation of anger or bitterness
that may be engendered by self-will. I have a feeling that the whole race of *man* need an
abiding education to subject self or self-will to good. If the suggestion can be made available by those in authority my object is gained. The preservation of good-will." ALS, *ibid.*

On July 3, Henry T. Crosby, chief clerk, War Dept., telegraphed to Babcock. "The following telegram has just been received. Will you please communicate it to the President?—It is from General Sheridan to General Sherman. There should be no longer any
doubt of the existence of gold in paying quantities in the South eastern corner of the Black
Hills of the Cheyenne. No odds what Professor Janney may report, and if the government
expects me to keep the miners out of that locality & other points further west of it Professor Janney should be ordered home. To Expect me to keep miners out of the Black Hills
while the Indian Bureau by the examination is afforded an opportunity with skillful and
practical miners to ascertain the valuable minerals in it and newspaper correspondents to
publish it to the world is putting on me a duty which my best skill & most conscientious

desire to perform it with the means I have at hand will make a failure for the Black Hills have not only gold but there is good soil good grass good water & magnificent timber. Signed P. H. SHERIDAN." LS (telegram sent), *ibid.*, RG 107, Telegrams Collected (Bound).

On July 12, Maj. Thomas M. Vincent, asst. AG, telegraphed to Gen. William T. Sherman. "Referring to your despatches of the third 3 inst the Prest. directs that you issue the necessary Orders to continue to keep people from going to the Black Hills Country at least until the result of the labors of the commission to treat with the Indians is known   please acknowledge receipt" Telegram received (at 3:10 P.M.), *ibid.*, RG 108, Letters Received.

On July 29, Babcock wrote to Delano. "In reply to yours of the 27th transmitting copy of telegram from Prof Janney relative to the discovery of gold in the Black Hills Country &c. the President directs me to say that he thinks it will be well to furnish the Commission to treat with the Indians a copy, and to say to them that this information increases the desirability of obtaining a treaty with the Indians—as he believes a treaty will be advantageous to the white people as well as the Indians—" ALS, *ibid.*, RG 75, Letters Received, Dakota Superintendency.

On Sept. 14, Delano wrote to USG. "I have the honor to return, with this, the papers referred by you to this Department on the 4th instant, being a communication from General George Crook, and its accompaniments, having relation to a request from miners— in regard to their property now in the Black Hills country—that six of their number be allowed to remain where they now are, to guard their property after the others shall have evacuated the country in accordance with proclamation issued by General Crook. The subject having been referred to the Commissioner of Indian Affairs, I transmit herewith, a copy of his report, dated the 13th instant, containing reference to certain articles of the treaty of April 29. 1868, bearing upon the subject, and his views thereon, to the effect that the request of the miners cannot be complied with without violating the provisions of said existing treaty, and also suggesting the impropriety of such occupancy by whites during the pendency of negotiations for the purchase of that country. The views of the Commissioner are concurred in by the Department." LS, *ibid.*, RG 94, Letters Received, 1356 1875. Related papers are *ibid.* During tense negotiations in Sept., the commission failed to secure any change in the treaty status of the Black Hills. See *HED*, 44-1-1, part 5, I, 686–702; James C. Olson, *Red Cloud and the Sioux Problem* (Lincoln, Neb., 1965), 199–213.

On Nov. 9, Lt. Gen. Philip H. Sheridan wrote to Terry. "Confidential. . . . At a meeting which occurred in Washington on the 3rd of November, at which were present, the President of the United States, the Secretary of the Interior, the Secretary of War and myself, the President decided that while the orders heretofore issued forbidding the occupation of the Black Hills country, by miners, should not be rescinded, still no further resistance by the military should be made to the miners going in; it being his belief that such resistance only increased their desire and complicated the troubles. Will you therefore quietly cause the troops in your Department to assume such attitude as will meet the views of the President in this respect?" LS (press), DLC-Philip H. Sheridan. See Edward Lazarus, *Black Hills White Justice: The Sioux Nation Versus the United States, 1775 to the Present* (New York, 1991), p. 343.

On March 16, 1876, Culver C. Sniffen wrote to Augustine S. Gaylord, asst. attorney gen. "The President directs me to say, in returning, to you Senator Allisons telegraphic inquiry of yesterday that he does not know under what authority Prof. Janney's exploration of the Black Hills, was made last year, nor does the Secretary of War, to whom the inquiry was referred to-day. It is now suggested that the information on this subject, if anywhere, must be at the Department of the Interior" Copy, DLC-USG, II, 3. On March 21, A. E. Barns, Bushnell, Ill., wrote to USG. "I see by the Inter-Ocean of 20th inst' that Senator Allison has the Bill in Charge Authorizing the President to appoint a Commision of five to make the necessary negotiations with the Indians for the Black Hills Country—having been a Republican ever since the organization of the party and spent nearly four years in the Army—much of the time an officer under your Command—I thought to ask your Excellency for an appointment as a member of that Commission—. . ." ALS, DNA, RG 75, Letters Received, Dakota Superintendency. In June, U.S. Delegate Jefferson P. Kidder of Dakota Territory, and two others, wrote to USG. "We take pleasure in recommending to your favorable consideration for the appointment of one of the Commissioners to make a treaty with the Sioux Indians, pursuant to what is called Senator Allison's bill as amended for that purpose, Ex Gov. Newton Edmunds of Dakota Territory, considering him eminently qualified, in all respects, to fill such position. . . . Governor Edmunds whilst Gov. of Dakota was *ex-officio* Supt of Indian Affairs." LS, *ibid.* For Allison's bill, ultimately unsuccessful, see *CR*, 44–1, 1796–1801, 1829–30, 3530–39.

1. Born in 1844 in Ireland and brought to the U.S. as an infant, James R. O'Beirne served as capt., 37th N. Y., and won promotion to bvt. brig. gen. After the war he served as secretary to President Andrew Johnson before joining the *New York Herald.* On July 9, 1875, O'Beirne, Washington, D. C., wrote to USG. "It has been represented to Officials at present holding office under your administration that you were personally opposed to my receiving office or other recognition by them on ac/c of my past connection with the 'N. Y. Herald,' as one of its special correspondents. As your friend no less in the past than in the present, which I have attested unwaveringly & to your own knowledge I believe—may I not take the liberty of asking you in a manly straightforward way thro' this medium if there be any foundation for such a belief or statement as above referred to" Copy, USG 3. On July 28, O'Beirne wrote to Babcock enclosing the above copy and asking for a reply. ". . . I write as one who has spoken and worked as President Grant's friend unwaveringly, from the start, & I respectfully but firmly submit, I have a right to be regarded accordingly." ALS, *ibid.* On Aug. 2, Babcock wrote to O'Beirne. "I am in receipt of your favor of July 28th. In reply I have to say the President did receive your letter. He did not answer it, as he never answers letters requesting him to deny a rumor. You give no authority but say, 'it has been reported by officials'—but give no officials name. I can tell you though that no such statement has been made by the President, or any such statement applying to you personally— I know the President has no unkind feeling towards you, and has therefore no reason to make such remarks—I am sure you have no reason to suppose the President feels unkindly towards you—" ADf (initialed), *ibid.* On Oct. 6, O'Beirne wrote to Babcock on the same subject. ALS, *ibid.*

2. Born in 1834 in New York City, Albert G. Lawrence graduated from Harvard, where he also received a law degree, and served as a diplomat before joining the 54th N. Y. On March 10, 1869, U.S. Senator Henry B. Anthony of R. I. wrote to USG. "Gen Albert Gallatin Lawrence served with great credit and gallantry in the war. He particularly distinguished himself at Fort Fisher, and left an arm on that bloody field. For his conduct on that occasion, he recd. a brevet. No military record could be clearer than his   I learn that Gen Lawrence desires some position in the public employment, suited to his service & talents. I should be pleased to see him gratified. . . ." ALS, DNA, RG 59, Letters of Application and Recommendation. On Jan. 25, 1876, Anthony renewed the request. ALS, *ibid.* Related papers are *ibid.* No appointment followed.

3. See *PUSG*, 23, 332–33; John S. Collins, *Across the Plains in '64* (Omaha, 1904), pp. 76–96.

4. See *PUSG*, 21, 487–88. On June 2, 1876, Joseph W. Dwyer, chairman, Coshocton County Republican Central Committee, Coshocton, Ohio, wrote to Babcock. "I here en-

close an Editorial clipped from the Cin. Gazette, which is but a repetition of the articles published by the papers friendly to Bristow. They have repeatedly charged that the President desired to be rid of B. but dared not ask for his resignation, for fear of B. making trouble for Fred, and Orville Grant, and now that the prince of sneaks, Yarahan has received his deserts—they are repeating these things. You and other friends of the President ought send to the world, through the friendly press, such facts as will place Bristow and his lackeys in their true light. That he, through his subordinates did, at Chicago, attempt to subornate witnesses to indict persons against whom they directed their malice, carrying their devilish designs into the Presidents own family, for the purpose of ~~getting~~ finding indictments against Fred and Orville, and thus raize higher his reputation for reform. Bristow owes evry thing he is to the President, and in return attempts his assasignation in this way. The liberal element at the back of B. are trying hard to gain the good graces of Gov. Hayes, and are gushing over him very much, claiming that they nominated him &c and that he must vindicate B. by re instating him in the Treasury. I presume you hear enough of all this an are sick of it, but I could not desist from writing you." ALS, ICN.

To Nathaniel Carlin

Long Branch, N. J.
June 16th /75

DEAR SIR;

I find that the horses I got in Mo. last fall are of no account whatever. Whether they have been injured since I got them or not I can not tell. They seemed all right this Spring but suddenly, and without hard or fast driving, the brown horse gave down all at once, in wind and spirit, and while he seems well in every other way he can not be forced beyond about a six mile gate. The bay is a blower. I shall have to dispose of them for waggon or farm horses. Now what I want to ask is will the two filleys you have been driving make me a good team for this summer? I hope you will answer me without delay, and answer at the same time questions asked in my two or three last letters.

Yours Truly
U. S. GRANT

NAT. CARLIN, ESQ.

ALS, OClWHi.

To Columbus Delano

Long Branch N. J.
June 20th 1875

MY DEAR MR DELANO

In our last conversation on the subject of your resignation I advised against it at that time, and stated that I would speak freely to you if I should have anything to say on that subject. I think now would be a good time to carry out the intention which you expressed a desire of as early as last December and again spoke of in April, but which I advised against at that time. With assurances of my high regard and esteem, and appreciation for your public service I remain

yr obt svt
U S GRANT

Copy, USG 3. On July 26, 1875, a correspondent reported from Washington, D. C. "The only tangible source to which can be traced the origin of the report that President Grant in June last requested Secretary Delano's resignation seems to be this: That Generals Porter and Babcock both knew of the action of the President, and each sharing the opinion that Mr. Delano would comply with the request, made the fact public to several confidential friends. It came from a reliable source that Babcock, about the 21st of June, visited this city and communicated to several the event which was expected to transpire. Meanwhile Mr. Delano was in Mount Vernon, Ohio, and did not receive the President's letter until his return here, two or three days after it had been received at the Interior Department. It is known that upon his return he went at once to Long Branch and had a conference with the President. There was given from the Interior Department to members of the press after his return the information that the Secretary's relation with the President remained unchanged. Now it is asserted here on the other hand, and from sources usually deemed eminently reliable, that the meeting between the President and Mr. Delano was anything but a pleasant one, and that Mr. Delano actually made threats of exposure concerning privileges granted Orville Grant, a brother of the President, if his resignation was enforced, but gave assurances that if not molested until after the Indian frauds investigations had been concluded, he would quietly step down and out. It can be stated most positively that in June President Grant did ask Mr. Delano to resign. Why he saw fit to further indulge him is known only to himself. Again, it may be equally positively stated that Mr. Delano's official Cabinet relations will soon be dissolved, and that, in all probability, he will be succeeded by ex-Governor Dennison, of Ohio, now one of the District of Columbia Commission. Secretary Delano is now absent from the city in Virginia, and General Cowan, the Assistant Secretary, declines to commit himself one way or the other on the subject." *Baltimore American and Commercial Advertiser*, July 27, 1875. See letter to Benjamin H. Bristow, June 28, 1875; letters to Columbus Delano, Aug. 26, Sept. 22, 1875.

To Edwards Pierrepont

————

Long Branch, N. J.
June 23d /75

Hon. Edwards Pierrepont,
Atty. Gen.l;
Dear Sir:

I think the public service would be benefited in the state of Delaware by a change of Marshal.

The present incumbent, Mr. Dunn, I have been advised for some time, is not a suitable person for the place. Henry W. Cannon has been suggested for the place, and knowing the father I am ready to approve the apt. of the son.[1]

Very Respectfully
Your obt. svt.
U. S. Grant

ALS, DNA, RG 60, Letters from the President. On Aug. 25, 1875, Attorney Gen. Edwards Pierrepont wrote to USG, Long Branch. "A commission has this day been received for Henry W. Cannon, to take effect on the 20th of July last. I do not know whether this is sent by mistake or not. If there is to be a new Marshal, his commission ought to be so made as to take effect in the future, as the acts of the present Marshal have continued, and will create confusion. It is possible that this commission has been sent by mistake, and that the Commission of Hazelton, which has not arrived may have been intended to have been sent in its stead. I call your attention to the case; and suggest that a new commission must be made out, if that is the intention. I rather suspect that this has been sent by mistake in place of Hazelton's; but, of course, I do not know. I hold it until I hear from you." Copy, DNA, RG 60, Letters Sent to Executive Officers. See letter to Edwards Pierrepont, July 7, 1875.

1. Wilson L. Cannon's son Henry W., an ardent Republican, edited the *State Sentinel* in Dover, Del.

To Benjamin H. Bristow

———

Long Branch, N. J.
June 28th /75

Hon. B. H. Bristow;
Dear Sir:

I return herewith Stevens' letter to you. The papers refered to are in the front part of the drawer at my seat at Cabinet table. Mr. Luckay has the key and will get them out for you.

Very Truly Yours
U. S. Grant

ALS, DLC-Benjamin H. Bristow. On June 24, 1875, Secretary of the Treasury Benjamin H. Bristow wrote to USG. "I had hoped that it would not be necessary for me to mention the matter of the Stevens papers to you again and I am reluctant now to give you further annoyance about them; but I am to day in receipt of the third letter from Mr Stevens urging me to return the papers to him, and do not see how I can refuse to make some kind of reply to his request. I do not know Stevens; never heard of him before I received his letter with enclosures which were handed to you, nor have I written him a word in answer to any of his communications. But he writes like a man of sense & character, and I feel that it is due him that the papers should be returned to him, or a reason given for not doing so. If no notice is taken of his request, can he not justly charge me, & possibly yourself with having suppressed evidence of official wrong? I desire to do nothing in the matter against your wishes, but I submit for your consideration whether I can afford to refuse compliance with his request. . . . P. S. I take the liberty to hand you Stevens last letter to me. Please return it" ALS (press), *ibid.* Leverett C. Stevens, former chief clerk under Silas Reed, surveyor gen., Wyoming Territory, had charged Reed and John Delano, son of Secretary of the Interior Columbus Delano, with corruption and blackmail, increasing pressure on Delano to resign from the cabinet. See *HRC*, 44-1-794, 1–4, 22–37; Harry James Brown and Frederick D. Williams, eds., *The Diary of James A. Garfield* (East Lansing, Mich., 1967–81), III, 65–68; Nevins, *Fish*, pp. 773–75.

On July 30, Bristow wrote to USG. "Of the many despatches ~~that~~ of the same purport that have been sent from this city since your recent visit here I have clipped & hand you two; one from the N. Y. Herald of Saturday the 24th, the other from the N. Y. Evening Post of Wednesday the 28th inst. These are but specimens of the general tenor of despatches sent from here by the Associated Press and several special correspondents. It has not been my habit to ~~take n~~ give the slightest heed to newspaper despatches affecting my personal or official conduct, but in this case the false statements have been repeated so often & adhered to so persistently that there can be no doubt as to their ~~origin~~ authorship or the purpose for which they are sent out. Besides I have heard from trustworthy sources that statements of like purport have been repeatedly made by the Secty of the Interior & certain associates & friends of his to newspaper correspondents & others. It is obvious that there is a fixed & deliberate purpose to involve me in a personal quarrel with a view to create a diversion from charges ~~with~~ that have been publicly made & with which I have had nothing whatever to do. ~~I do~~ I neither desire to engage in such a quarrel nor do I shrink from it, but a proper regard for the interest of your administration, as well as a decent respect for the office I hold have hitherto restrained me from taking notice of these wilfully false reports; but it seems to me that I cannot afford longer to be silent ~~on this~~ in the face of their repeated announcement in the newspapers, and by personal statements   I ask no protection against these authors of these insidious falsehoods, but am unwilling to enter upon my own defence at the expense of the harmony which you have a right to expect in your Cabinet & without which the public business cannot be satisfactorily, or successfully conducted, and for this reason I now write you to say that I shall be pleased to have you accept my resignation of the office of Secretary of the Treasury, & thus relieve me from all embarrassment in making that defence & exposing the motives ~~th~~ which have induced ~~these~~ the false statements in question. ~~I might~~ Other reasons might be given for tendering my resignation at this time but I ~~do not~~ cannot doubt that you will consider this sufficient and therefore forbear to mention others. I propose to leave here tonight for Louisville but will return here at least as early as Thursday of next week when I hope to receive your acceptance of my resignation. Thanking you, Mr President for the personal & official kindness which I have received at your hands & with assurances of my high regard for you. . . ." ADf, DLC-Benjamin H. Bristow. On July 23, Friday, a correspondent had reported from Washington, D. C. "At the meeting of the Cabinet on Wednesday last, after Secretary Delano had retired, the other members formally gave expression to their opinion whether Mr. Delano ought to remain in the Cabinet or yield to the pressure made upon him through the press and tender his resignation. The conversation continued for some time, and although no vote was taken the opinion of the members, as derived from an authoritative source, is as follows:—Secretary Bristow thought Mr. Delano should retire immediately, . . . Mr. Delano, it is understood, is personally aware of Mr. Bristow's hostility, and is not disposed, after so many years spent in public life, to be driven into retirement by one who, it is said, he has befriended on former occasions." *New York Herald*, July 24, 1875. On July 25, Secretary of State Hamilton Fish recorded in his diary next to a clipping of this article. "Bristow refers to the letter of the Herald and says he knew that it was written in the Interior Department, that he also has evidence that an article which went the rounds of the newspapers some time since to the effect that the charges against Delano were gotten up by persons who were disappointed in control had been set up in the Interior Department and distributed to the press from thence. He says he will not submit to the insinuations put out by Delano" DLC-Hamilton Fish. On the same day, a correspondent reported from Washington, D. C. "A statement originating at the Interior Department is in circulation, to the effect that at the Cabinet meeting last week the case of Secretary Delano was discussed, and only two members were in favor of his retiring from the Cabinet, namely Secretary Bristow and Postmaster-General Jewell, and that all the others favored his remaining. So far from this being true, the case of Mr. Delano was not even mentioned at that Cabinet meeting. Furthermore, every member of the Cabinet has, within a few weeks past, privately expressed the opinion that the time has come when the interests of the Administration and of the Republican party require that he should go out. Further than this, the President, about June 20, addressed Mr. Delano in writing, asking for his resignation. When Mr. Delano received this letter on his return to the Department, a few days later, he left at once for Long Branch. He had a most remarkable interview with the President, in which he insisted that he should not be removed under fire, and that he should be allowed to remain till the pending investigations into Indian affairs were finished. He finally ended with what was virtually a threat, that if he was forced out of the Cabinet, the Administration would regret it. . . ." *New York Tribune*, July 26, 1875. On

July 26, Fish recorded in his diary, next to a clipping, that this article "bears the mark of Bristow containing much the same language as was used by him yesterday at dinner." DLC-Hamilton Fish. On Sept. 1, Bristow wrote to USG. "Referring to our conversation last winter I beg to say that considerations of private interest forbid me to continue longer in office. I, therefore, have the honor to submit my resignation of the office of Secretary of the Treasury, and to ask that you will designate as early a day for my retirement as may suit your pleasure and convenience, not later than the first day of October proximo. Be pleased, Mr President to accept assurances of my high regard, and earnest wish for the complete success of your Administration, . . ." ALS, DLC-Benjamin H. Bristow. Bristow remained in the cabinet. See letter to Columbus Delano, June 20, 1875; letter to Benjamin H. Bristow, June 19, 1876; Ross A. Webb, *Benjamin Helm Bristow: Border State Politician* (Lexington, Ky., 1969), pp. 171–75, 186.

To Matthew H. Carpenter

Long Branch, N. J.
June 28th /75

DEAR SIR:

I am just in receipt of your letter of the 23d inst. enclosing a paper containing your speach before the Citizens of Madison. I made no such remark about your speach as is attributed to me. I am sure I have not seen the speach, in full, in print until now, and your position on the La. question I have know from the time it come up in Congress. I have no fault to find with your speach.

Very Truly Yours
U. S. GRANT

HON. MATT CARPENTER

ALS, Mr. and Mrs. Philip D. Sang, River Forest, Ill. On Feb. 3, 1875, following his defeat for reelection, U.S. Senator Matthew H. Carpenter of Wis. delivered a speech in Madison defending his proposal for a new election to determine the legitimate state government in La., upholding his positions on other policy questions, and calling for Republican unity. See *New York Times*, Feb. 9, 1875; E. Bruce Thompson, *Matthew Hale Carpenter: Webster of the West* (Madison, Wis., 1954), pp. 228–30.

To Edwards Pierrepont

LONG BRANCH N. J. JULY IST. [*1875*]
ATTY. GENL. WASHN. DC.
WOULD SUGGEST THAT MARSHAL PURNELL BE GIVEN
AN OPPORTUNITY TO ANSWER CHARGES AGAINST HIM
BEFORE MAKING REMOVAL. FOR A NUMBER OF YEARS
PERSISTENT ATTEMPTS HAVE BEEN MADE FOR HIS DE-
CAPITATION AND SO FAR HE HAS BEEN ABLE TO MEET
EVERY CHARGE.

U. S. GRANT.

Telegram received, DNA, RG 60, Records Relating to Appointments. On July 1, 1875, Attorney Gen. Edwards Pierrepont telegraphed to USG, Long Branch. "Marshal Purnell of Texas whose deputy allowed the celebrated counterfeiter to escape must resign or be removed. Evidence has accumulated of such a nature and of such authority that there can be no doubt of the necessity of this course. Shall I direct him to send his resignation" Copy, *ibid.*, Letters Sent to Executive Officers. On July 27, Pierrepont wrote to USG. ". . . Mrs Purnell is now here and I have permitted her to see the charges made by Gov. Davis and others against the Marshal. The matter has assumed such importance from political as well as other causes that I have deemed it my duty to make a thorough investigation and from a trusted agent now in Texas I shall soon have a report from a thorough investigation made upon the spot. I shall then submit the whole matter for your consideration." Copy, *ibid.*

On June 18, J. W. Johnson, Jefferson, Tex., had written to USG. "being an old Union man of this State and a republican I for the first time ask of you an appointment.   Learning that Marshal Purnell would be removed I respectfully ask of you to be appointed in his stead as Marshal of the Western district of Texas. If required can furnish you any recommendation as to my ability honesty & integrity and my republicanism." ALS, *ibid.*, Records Relating to Appointments. No appointment followed.

On Oct. 19, Thomas F. Purnell, U.S. marshal, Austin, telegraphed to Pierrepont. "It has come to my knowledge today that Davis & Britton prepared and had signed affidavits by a number of hangers on of the courts representing that the marshal would not pay their fees as jurors & witnesses concealing the fact they were not entitled to such pay & that I had no authority to pay them   they hold no certificates from the court to justify such payment   I only ask the opportunity of answering these & all other charges made by Davis & Britton against me & I will show them to be false" Telegram received (at 2:25 P.M.), *ibid.* On Oct. 26, Purnell telegraphed to USG. "The charges made by Davis & Britton were abandoned as soon as I was permitted to answer them   They have now sent by mr Payton to the Dpt of Justice others which I have not been permitted to see, or know, but they are false and I am fully prepared to vindicate myself when permitted to do so,   A combination of corrupt officeseek[ers] here have been trying to remove me without cause, and without a hearing." Telegram received, *ibid.* On Dec. 3, former Governor Elisha M. Pease of Tex. *et al.*, Austin, telegraphed to USG. "The republican meeting held here last Evening was called by those opposed to Maj Thos F. Purnell to make an Expression against this gentleman, & does not represent the feelings of the republican party of the City of Austin   His republicanism cannot be successfully impeached   His guilt or innocence of the criminal charges preferred are questions of fact for the Govt to determine, not Questions of politics,   statement with signatures will be forwarded by mail," Telegram received, *ibid.* On the same day, Webster Flanagan, Henderson, Tex., wrote to USG. "I have been informed, that Marshal Purnell thinks of vacating his office *soon*, and in the event a change is made, I ask that you take my claims into consideration. I have appealed to no one *else* nor shall I do so—. . . I do not ask the removal of Maj Purnell   on the contrary he is a good officer and my *friend.*" ALS, *ibid.* On Dec. 10, USG nominated Purnell to continue as marshal, Western District, Tex. See *PUSG,* 19, 426; Endorsement, May 18, 1876.

On June 10, 1872, James P. Newcomb, Tex. secretary of state, New York City, had written to USG. "After my arrival at Philadelphia, I received a telegram from Governor Davis urging the presentation of the name of Gen. A JG. Maloy for the position of U. S. Marshall for the Western Dist. of Texas.—I reserved this telegram in consequence of the lack of unanimity on the part of the delegation, and also in consequence of the endorement of Col. Ochiltree. Should Col. Ochiltree's chances not be good I cheerfully endorse Gen. Maloy and know him to be the choice of the Governor and all others in prefference to any one else. We believe it is very important that this position be filled by a thoroughly competent and reliable man." ALS, DNA, RG 60, Records Relating to Appointments. A related letter is *ibid.*

On Nov. 13, James G. Tracy, chairman, Republican state committee, Houston, wrote to USG. "I would most heartily recommed Capt. Frank L. Britton as a suitable person to fill the office of US. Marshal for the Western Texas District. Capt. Britton has for three years acted in the capacity of Private Secretary to Gov. Davis, and has ever proven himself an active, zealous and devoted Republican. The present incumbent Mr. Purnell is no party man, but in fact a positive obstacle to the success of our party in this State. Capt. Britton's appointment will be hailed with satisfaction by every true friend of your Administration in Texas." ALS, *ibid.* On Nov. 12, Frank L. Britton, Austin, had written to USG. "I have the honor to herewith make application to your Excellency for the appointment of U. S. Marshal for the Western District of Texas vice J. A. Purnell who now fills that position. Mr. Purnell does not aid in sustaining the principles of the party which your Excellency has again led to victory, Viz—protection of the weak and obedience to the laws. . . ." LS, *ibid.* Related papers are *ibid.*

On Feb. 28, 1873, Joseph Glenn, *Cincinnati Gazette,* wrote to USG. "Another effort, I learn, is being made to remove *Maj. Thos. F. Purnell, U. S. Marshall for the N. E. Dist. of Texas*; and a man named Ochiltree has been sent on, in the belief that he has personal influence with you to strengthen his recommendations. The principal party at the bottom of this movement is a notorious Rebel named Mayberry—a man whom I personally know to be destitute of honor or principle, and who is solely actuated by personal ends; but the movement is of course, I presume, under cover of certain so-called Republicans. From 25 years acquaintance, I can testify to Maj. Purnell's character, ~~and~~ integrity, and faithfulness in the performance of his duties—to say nothing of his services during the war; and he has been too consistent a Union man during his residence in Texas since the war, and at times when it was dangerous ~~and~~ as well as in conflict with his interests to be so, and is too staunch in his principles now, to suit ~~a portion of the~~ certain Rebel and Hybrid elements there as U. S. Marshall. I trust you will not allow any flank movements of this character to succeed. I have had some experience with the people in that quarter, and would not give a continental for the real Unionism of nineteen twentieths of the ~~s~~ so-called Republicans thereabouts, outside of the colored population. They will scruple at no means of accomplishing their object." ALS, *ibid*. On March 10, Glenn telegraphed to USG on the same subject. Telegram received, *ibid*., Letters from the President. On March 6, USG had nominated Adam G. Malloy to replace Purnell. On March 10, Levi P. Luckey wrote to Attorney Gen. George H. Williams. "The President directs me to ask if there is any objection to the retention of Purnell as Marshal of Texas until the end of his term. If there is no objection, he desires a withdrawal sent to the Senate of the nomination of his successor." Copy, DLC-USG, II, 2.

On March 12, Governor Edmund J. Davis of Tex. *et al*. petitioned USG. "The undersigned Republican State Officers and Members of the Legislature earnestly recommend that Thomas F. Purnell be not continued in the office of U. S. Marshal of the Western District of Texas and that some other man recommended by the Republicans of Texas be appointed." DS, DNA, RG 60, Records Relating to Appointments. On March 13, Davis wrote to USG. "I today forwarded you a telegram as follows—'Petition forwarded you today by mail signed by officers State Government, chairman Republican central committee, and Republican State Senators, as follows ... I now enclose you the Petition itself, and ask your favourable consideration of the Same. I am sure it expresses the opinion of the mass of the Republicans of this State. It has been a matter of the greatest wonder here, how, in the face of the many complaints from Texas, Mr. Purnell can persuade you to retain him in office, and we have come to the conclusion that misstatements in his favour, are made to you from some source having more influence with you, than your true friends in this State. The U. S. courts in Texas have been used to oppress the Republicans, and for this we do not without good ground attribute largely the blame to Mr. Purnell, who by hook and crook always manages to *pack juries* for the occasion, but at the same time takes care to avoid any direct responsibility therefor by putting it off, when found out, on some Scape Goat of a Deputy. It may be, Mr. President, that you have too little confidence in our representations to permit them to weigh in the scale against, that unknown influence, which has hitherto closed your ear to our complaints against this official. In that event, we must wait for such relief as time, which rights all wrongs, may bring us. In addition to the above telegram, I sent you on the 11th Inst. the following—'Nelson Plato is not a proper person to be entrusted with the collectorship at corpus christi. The moneys of the Government will be in unsafe hands, you have been misinformed as to his character, and for the credit of the Government I beg you to withdraw his nomination.' To speak plain English about this man Plato will require me to term him a mere 'Shyster'. You, Mr. President, if you knew him as we do here, would as soon entrust him with five dollars (unless you wanted to give it to him) as you would to the individual known about Washington as Beau Hickman. It is stated here that he *partly* owes his nomination to the influence of Generals Dent and Chipman. If those gentlemen have recommended Plato, I can only suppose that their slight army acquaintance with him has left them a very incorrect estimate of his fitness to handle government money. You will soon have proof of that, after he is installed in office. But I do not think that those gentlemen could have been instrumental in doing us this damage. There is some malign influence at work that we have not yet been able to divine. I have written a longer letter than I can usually devote to such matters, but the interest we naturally take in the good name and success of the party, which has placed you in your high position for a Second Term, may serve as my excuse for writing, & you for reading it, as long as it is." ALS, *ibid*.

On Nov. 4, 1874, Nelson Plato, Corpus Christi, wrote to Orville E. Babcock. "I take this liberty as a former comrade. Tonight, I received notice of *Suspension*, as Collector of this Port. There is an act of gross injustice in this. I know not upon what '*ex-parte*' reports the Presidents action is based, but I do know, that so far as *facts* are concerned, there are *none existing* which will justify a final substantiation of *cause* for suspension. No Collectoral District in Texas can exceed this in integrity of administration, efficiency, or political accomplishments. . . ." ALS, *ibid.*, RG 56, Letters Received from the President. On Nov. 16 and 30, Plato wrote to USG transmitting petitions for his retention as collector of customs, Corpus Christi. ALS, *ibid.* The enclosures and related papers are *ibid.* On Dec. 7, USG nominated Ridge Paschal as Plato's replacement. On Dec. 10, Plato again wrote to Babcock concerning his case. ALS, ICN. On Dec. 15, Plato wrote to USG. "*Personal.* . . . I trust your sanction to the liberty I take in addressing you personally, will be agreeably accorded. Having been recently suspended from Office, without knowing who my accusers are, or of what accused, I am left to mere conjecture as to any possible cause which led to such action, and deem it my duty, to assert most positively, that I am totally unaware of anything having transpired in my administration of the affairs of this Collectoral District, which could be construed discreditably towards me as an Officer, or warrant the action taken. Any evidence to the contrary received by the Department, must, therefore, be only '*ex-parte*'; and I hope you may become convinced of the great injustice done me in the matter, and at least, furnish me an opportunity to vindicate myself. If Mr. A. J. Bennett, through his reports and statements, was instrumental in bringing about my suspension, I invite your attention to *his record*, furnished by the Collector of Port of Brownsville, and enclosed herewith. Special Treasury Agent A. J. Bennett was the only Officer who visited this District just previous to my suspension, and from his known personal hostility to, and threats against me, I have reason to believe he basely used his Official position, to vilify and injure me with the Department. In another instance for conjecture; should it transpire, that Ex Govr *E. J. Davis*, has again sought to injure me, by reopening a political difference which existed between he & I in *1869*, when I endorsed and supported the Hamilton wing of the Republican Party, at the election in this State, I have the following statement to offer for your consideration; 'Viz':—that I was led to believe all our differences were honorably healed and settled at the Dallas Convention, in 1873, where I attended as a delegate, representing several counties, and aided and supported the nomination of E. J. Davis for Governor, afterwards giving my best efforts towards his election, also contributed liberally in funds to the State Executive Committee for necessary expenses of the Canvass, and moreover, carried this District by a good majority for Davis as Governor. I should therefore be greatly surprised to find that he had been active in procuring my suspension. With regard to my political services as a Republican, I can truthfully say, that no man in this section of the State, has exceeded me in zeal, organization and successful work, and as a leading Republican Exe Officer, of Western Texas, I shall continue my efforts diligently & faithfully to maintain & increase the Party." ALS, DNA, RG 56, Letters Received from the President. The enclosure is *ibid.* On Feb. 10, 1875, Luckey wrote to Secretary of the Treasury Benjamin H. Bristow. "The President directed prepared and sent to the Senate on the 5th inst. the withdrawal of the nomination of Ridge Paschall to be Collr of Customs at Corpus Christi, Texas. This was done as an act of justice to Mr Plato who is thus restored." ALS, *ibid.* On March 31, Plato, Laredo, wrote to Babcock. "Just arrived here yesterday on my quarterly Inspection & collection trip & tonight news reaches me that I am again suspended, & Paschal reinstated. A telegram from Paschal is the authority for the report. If true, there is deep villiany & conspiracy invented by my enemies to bring about such a result. It was intimated that Ridge Paschal & his father were engaged in preparing charges against me for alleged irregularities while I was Chief Quartermaster at Brownsville, Texas. If such is the case, every act of my administration there, is susceptible of the clearest explanation, . . ." ALS, *ibid.* On May 22, Plato, Corpus Christi, wrote to USG. "Per-

SONAL. . . . On several occasions since my second suspension, I have had in view this pleasure. From impressions received through your assurances at our interview in the Executive Mansion early in February last, when you announced that Mr. Paschal's appointment had been withdrawn from the Senate by message, and consequently my reinstatement followed; I returned to duty in full confidence; armed with requisite authority. Soon after, without any warning or thought of danger, Official notice of my suspension was received. Whatever the alleged cause, I am confident Your Excellency was misled into taking such action; and I now appeal to you, to know why this action was taken in my case. In conclusion, General; I desire to assure you of my unalterable friendship in any event; and as some evidence of same, I enclose certain Proceedings; by which, you will observe that, notwithstanding my grievances; I have waived personal power & prerogatives, to assist in extending the political influence of my successor, in behalf of the Republican Party, by virtue of his Federal position." ALS, *ibid.* The enclosure is *ibid.* On the same day, Plato wrote to Babcock concerning his removal as collector of customs and recent election as mayor of Corpus Christi. ALS, *ibid.* On Dec. 8, USG nominated Paschal as collector of customs, Corpus Christi.

To Edwards Pierrepont

———

Long Branch, N. J.
July 1st 1875

DEAR JUDGE:

Your letter of the 28th of June was duly rec'd. If the Commissions for Brdley & Cannon have come to me, the first for Dist. Atty. Colorado, the second for Marshal of Delaware, I have signed them. If not I will sign them when forwarded. I am clearly of the opinion that both changes should be made.

Statements that I see in the papers make it my duty at least to enquire whether good reasons do not exist for a change of Dist. Atty. in the district of Columbia?[1]

In regard to the Marshal in Texas I think it would be well to be sure of the grounds before making a removal. The politicians of that state has been anxious for his removal for several years—for some time before his re-appointment. It is difficult both to get accurate information from that state, and to get reliable men to fill the offices. Purnell is the Son-in-law of Bishop Ames of Baltimore. He served as a disbursing officer during the war, and since as Marshal, without, so far as I have ever heard, the slightest difficulty with his accounts.

Gen.l Fagan[2] I know but little about. We have always had difficulty with Marshals in that district of Ark. The other changes you speak of I will be glad to get your suggestions about as soon as you get the further information you are after.

Very Truly

Your obt. svt.

U. S. GRANT

HON. EDWARDS PIERREPONT, ATTY. GEN.L

ALS, ICarbS. On June 28, 1875, Attorney Gen. Edwards Pierrepont wrote to Secretary of State Hamilton Fish. "I am directed by the President to request you to issue the follow-commissions   Charles D. Bradley to be Attorney of the United States for Colorado Territory in place of H C Alleman resigned, this commission to take effect on the 20th proximo. Henry W. Cannen to be Marshal of the United States for the District of Delaware in the place of John M. Dunn resigned this commission to take effect on the 20th proximo" Copy, DNA, RG 60, Letters Sent to Executive Officers. See letter to Jerome B. Chaffee, March 13, 1875; letters to Edwards Pierrepont, June 23, July 7, 1875.

1. See letters to Edwards Pierrepont, July 8, 17, 1875.

2. Born in 1828 in Ky., James F. Fagan, maj. gen. in the C.S. Army, later supported Joseph Brooks in Ark. politics. On Dec. 14, 1874, USG nominated Fagan as marshal, Western District, Ark. On Feb. 2, 1875, Luther C. White, Van Buren, Ark., wrote to USG. "I would not presume to write you without what I deem sufficient cause. The republican party in the Western Counties of Arkansas have almost to a unit Petitioned your Excellency though our Senators, to confer upon me the office of U. S. Marshall for Western District of Arkansas; presuming as a matter of course, that Gen. Fagan will be rejected by the Senate. I have not been in accord with our Senators in the late *Brooks-Baxter* imbroglio, and I presume they prefer another man. I have deemed it proper however under the circumstances, to call your attention to the fact that the party have united on me, because, first, I held the office under Mr Lincoln, and 2d because it is recognised as a fact that our party interest require that the late *groove* in which the office has been run must be rubbed out. Honest and influential men of the party have been writing private letters as well as petitions to our Senators for the last two months. I beg to say that I have nothing personally against Messrs Clayton and Dorsey, and I would like to be their friend; and above all I desire the success of the repub. party.... I have also taken the liberty to address the Atty General on this matter, and I assure you that this matter is assuming large proportions" ALS, DNA, RG 60, Letters Received, Ark. In a petition docketed Aug. 20, James E. Bennett *et al.* wrote to USG. "The undersigned, republicans, respectfully reccommend the Suspension or removal from office of James F. Fagan Marshal of the Western District of Arkansas, because they say that he is not only an ex-confederate, but a loud-mouthed democrat, and not in Sympathy with either the present federal administration, or with the strugling-downtrodden republicans of Arkansas, besides his reputation as a Government officer, for veracity, integrity and fair dealing is bad, and a disgrace to the administration of your Excellency, and respectfully but urgently request his removal and the appointment of an honest man and a republican in his stead, ..." DS (undated), *ibid.* On Aug. 25, Judge Isaac C. Parker, Western District, Ark., St. Louis, wrote to USG. "*Private*... I have learned that an effort is now being made to remove Gen Jas F Fagan Marshall of the Western Dis-

trict of Arkansas. I desire to say to you privately for your guidance in the premises that I think such a move ought not to be countenanced by you as I think Gen Fagan is making a good officer   I am satisfied he has made every effort that a man could make to conduct the office well and to perform its duty in such a manner as to entail the least ex[pe]nse possible upon the government. The office is the most difficult and dangerous in the whole country   The Stories carried to the Department against Fagan are either started by lawless desperadoes who fear a brave, determined man like Fagan or by parties who want his place or Subordinate places in his office   He in my judgement should be aided by the Department   The authrites should stand by him and say to the croakers and fault finders aid this man who is trying to enforce the law and bring security to the Indian country rather than try to pull him down   I state Mr President that Gen Fagan is a good officer   You will get none better and in my judgement you should retain him   He does his duty well and is an ardent friend of your administration   any thing you may hear to the contrary notwithstanding. I hope you will not listen to the croakers and fault finders   This letter is writen to you privately as it might be considered by some that as judge of the court I was takeing part in a political appointment. My excuse for writing this is that I feel a desire to see the court over which I preside well officered: And I know you may be desirous of hearing from one on this subject who has no interest but this" ALS, USG 3.

In [*June, 1876*], U.S. Senators Powell Clayton and Stephen W. Dorsey of Ark. wrote to USG. "Understanding that Genl James F Fagan contemplates resigning the position of United States Marshal for the Western District of Arkansas we the undersigned earnestly beg you to appoint Genl D P Upham Marshal for said District   General Upham is an active sterling republican of undoubted honesty and probity   His appointment to the position herein indicated would be hailed with delight by the Republican party of the state and is one which would give to the state an honest and efficient officer, and at the same time reflect credit on the administration making the appointment" LS (stamped June 22), OFH. On July 3, USG nominated Daniel P. Upham to replace Fagan.

To Hamilton Fish

———

Long Branch, N. J.
July 2d /75

DEAR GOVERNOR:

I have just been shown a Circular which it has been intended to distribute among Federal officials with the view of soliciting contributions (voluntary ones; for it does not contemplate that any one should be compelled to respond on pain of loosing his position) for the laudible purpose of maintaining the organization of the republican party. Money is necessary for this purpose, to buy & distribute documents, print tickets, send speakers into the field, &c. and I do not see that any parties are more directly interested in this than the office holders whose places yieald them a compensation of more than $1000 00 pr. annum. I understand it is to be distributed to none others.

You may say if you please to the balance of the Cabinet that my views on this subject are as here expressed.

> Very Truly
> your obt. svt.
> U. S. GRANT

HON. HAMILTON FISH SEC. OF STATE.

ALS, DLC-Hamilton Fish. On July 8, 1875, Secretary of State Hamilton Fish commented in his diary after showing USG's letter to cabinet members. ". . . The circular referred to by the President is from the Committee of which Zac Chandler spoke to me on July 1st; Chandler having gone to Long Branch immediatly after seeing me and the Presidents letter appears to me dated probably while Chandler was with him at Long Branch." *Ibid.*

To Edwards Pierrepont

> Long Branch, N. J.
> July 3d 1875

HON. EDWARDS PIERREPONT
ATTY. GEN.
DEAR SIR:

Will you be kind enough to examine the records in the office of Mr. Wolcott, recently suspended from the office of U. S. Marshal for the territory of Wyoming.

If injustice has been done him we may be able to correct it by giving the present incumbent—a most worthy man I believe—some other position.

> U. S. GRANT

ALS, DNA, RG 60, Letters from the President. An undated note is enclosed. "His record is satisfactory before the department: no existing charges against him: His management of court expenses, economical and of the penitentiary worthy of much praise." N, *ibid.*

On April 5, 1869, USG nominated Frank Wolcott as land office receiver, Wyoming Territory; on April 16, the Senate tabled the nomination. On Dec. 27, Benjamin H. Bristow, Louisville, wrote to USG. "Major Frank Wolcott of this state will be an applicant for the office of Surveyor General of Wyoming   Having known Major Wolcott most favorable for several years I have pleasure in commending him to your Excellency. He was among the first in Ky to volunteer in the Union Army and throughout the war bore himself most gallantly. He has been a consistent, working Republican and is, as I believe, fully competent to perform the duties of the office to which he aspires. His appointment would give pleasure to his late comrades in arms and to the Republicans of Ky." ALS, *ibid.*, RG 48, Appointment Papers, Wyoming Territory. James Speed, Allan A. Burton, E. Rumsey Wing, and Mortimer M. Benton also wrote to USG in support of Wolcott. *Ibid.* On Feb. 8, 1870, USG renominated Wolcott as land office receiver. On Dec. 20, 1871, John W. Kingman, Wyoming Territory Supreme Court, wrote to Silas Reed, surveyor gen., Wyoming Territory. ". . . I have understood that Major Wolcott and others associated with him, were attempting to jump the claims of the parties who had built their cabins and settled in the region of the Iron mountain; and that Major Wolcott was acting as the manager and general agent of the party." ALS, *ibid.*

On May 23, 1872, USG nominated Wolcott as marshal, Wyoming Territory. On May 28, Secretary of the Interior Columbus Delano wrote to USG. "I enclose two telegrams which have been received by me today, protesting against the appointment of Frank Wolcott as US Marshal for Wyoming. I will remark in this connection, that some time ago serious charges were preferred against him in his capacity of Receiver of the land Office at Cheyenne, and which had not been decided upon at the time of his nomination and confirmation by the Senate." LS, *ibid.*, RG 60, Records Relating to Appointments. On the same day, Reed and Herman Glafcke, secretary, Wyoming Territory, had each telegraphed to Delano. "Mysef and maj Glaficke feel great amazement at the deception practiced upon the President in the removal of Major Howe and the appointment of wolcott as marshall do try to have it undone at once   I vouch for Howe as one of the Presidents Strongest & most influential Supporters in the territories" "Personal   the reported appointment & confirmation of Wolcott as US Marshall for Wyoming is a surprise to republicans here take in consideration his course as receiver of the land office   It is a sad blow to our party organization & greatly regreted by a large majority of our substantial & influential republicans & of ardent supporters of the administration" Telegrams received, *ibid.* On June 13, J. H. Martin *et al.*, Cheyenne, wrote to USG. "The undersigned Citizens of Wyoming Territory without respect to party organization or political affitiation would respectfully petition your Excellency to remove from the office of United States Marshal for our Territory, Frank Wolcott—recently appointed by you to that position and who by his conduct while holding the position of Receiver of public monies in the US Land office in this city has rendered himself obnoxious to a large majority of our citizens—. . ." DS (31 signatures), *ibid.* On the same day, Reed wrote to Delano. "*Personal* . . . Wyoming affairs have for the past two years been managed in the interest of a Small Ring, composed principally of a part of our U. S. Officials—most of whom are very unpopular with the people of both parties. All this time I have remained *neutral*, & urged peace and harmony, in the honor & interest of Genl. Grant's Administration. I took no part & said nothing to the President because he did not ask my advice. I know it is more to the honor of an administration & a duty they owe the President, for its officials to act in *harmony*—and the good opinion of the people is all essential. This brings me to the case of Marshall Howe—a good officer—an active & earnest Republican, with a good Army record, as Genl F. A. Walker can testify—possessed of great energy & enthusiasm of character, & quite popular with our people, & has a large circle of influential friends in Massachusetts. Delegate Jones & Govr Campbell have struck him down now the 2nd time before the President—all from a personal feeling of rivalry. A man is put in his place who stands condemned in your Dept— for *Unofficer*-like conduct—and the feeling here would result in lynching him, if there were as few law officers as four years ago—partly because of his aiding an attempt to 'Jump' Squatter's claims. The first effect of his appt was so discouraging to the mass of our party that we feared it would pronounce for Greely. We have no Presidential vote, it is true, but we have an energetic—wide awake people, whose friends live in all the states east of us—and the *moral* effect might be to turn the scale against us in closely contested states. Majr. Glafcke, Judge Kingman & myself urged firmness & patience & advised a *ratification* meeting for *Grant & Wilson*, in which Howe united & gave most effective aid—It was a great Success—Nearly the whole party in the County was present—and at the close of the meeting voted a resolution by acclamation against Wolcott—& that the President had been deceived. . . ." ALS, *ibid.* See *PUSG*, 22, 58–65. On May 29, 1875, USG suspended Wolcott; on May 31, USG designated Gilbert Adams as marshal. See Endorsement, July 13, 1875.

To Nathaniel Carlin

———

Long Branch, N. J.
July 3d 1875

DEAR SIR:

I am sorry that your letters, and one from Gov. Jewell,[1] give no better account of farm opperations. You will have to get on the best you can until I can get out there some time this fall.

You should sell as you can every mare not used for farm work that does not breed, as soon as possible. I would also sell all horse colts that do not give promise when ever suitable offers are made. Even good colts I would sell for good prices, but all others I would force a little. Do you not think it advisable to breed the two filleys you have been driving yet this year? I would breed all the filley mares that do not give good promise of speed. The small black mare—of the pair—I would not sell if she will breed. You may also sell Hambletonian or exchange him for brood mares if you have a chance. Get rid of him.

In regard to the stock mares you sent an account of I can not purchase. I have not got the means. I hope the Knox mare may prove good. She cost me $800⁰⁰⁄₁₀₀ and would prove a loss if she were to sell now for a 1000. But if she will not breed sell her the best you can. She is to small and to expensive to keep for farm work. Bob Akers I intended as a name for Mr. A. and also after Jo Jeffersons character of "Bob Akers" in the play of "The Rivals."[2] I think it sounds well also.

In speaking of breeding this year the filleys you are driving I had forgotten that you said in one of your letters that they were giving a good deal of promise! If so you may exercise your judgement about breeding them.

Yours Truly

U. S. GRANT

ALS, OClWHi. On June 1, 1875, Levi P. Luckey wrote to John F. Long, St. Louis. "The President directs me to acknowledge the receipt of your letter of the 29th, and I enclose you his check for five hundred dollars ($500.) to apply on the bills you mention. He thinks that Carlin should have some money coming in by this time from the two horses so that he could pay these bills for feed, &c. The President wishes me to say in regard to the horse colt foaled on the 9th of May, from the mare 'Bell St. Joe,' which he purchased of Mr. Ackers, that, he spoke particularly to Carlin that in case it should be a horse colt he wanted it named 'Bob Akers.' Please have Carlin change the name 'Expectation' and comply with the President's wish in the matter. . . . P. S. The President says he would prefer to have Dr Sharpe's land enclosed and fenced in with his; that is, the way you suggest." Copy, DLC-USG, II, 2. On June 4, Long wrote to Nathaniel Carlin. "I am just in receipt of a letter from the President, Saying you must change the name of the colt, from the Akers Mare. He says it must be changed to '*Bob Akers*,' as he had intended from the first, *if a horse colt*. He also says (in sending me some money,) that the services of the *horses* ought to be bringing in money to buy feed &c. including Small bills. And again, that the Sharp tract may be enclosed in the general fence as asked by Mr Jackson—I suppose he means that part of Sharp's, south of the Barracks road,   Please advise Mr. Jackson of this . . ." ALS, OClWHi. On July 25, B. F. Akers, Lawrence, Kan., wrote to Carlin concerning horses and breeding prospects. ALS, *ibid.* See letters to John F. Long, April 4, July 13, 1875.

1. On June 20, Postmaster Gen. Marshall Jewell had visited USG's farm while in St. Louis on a postal inspection tour. See *St. Louis Dispatch*, June 19, 21, 1875. On June 28, Jewell telegraphed to Orville E. Babcock. "Are you going to Long Branch to night, and can you tell me if the President will be here this week or at what time. I have many things to say to him but shall keep them if I can learn when he will be here" Telegram received, DNA, RG 107, Telegrams Collected (Bound).

2. Joseph Jefferson III had played Bob Acres in Richard Brinsley Sheridan's eighteenth-century comedy, *The Rivals.* See *The Autobiography of Joseph Jefferson* (New York, 1890), pp. 150, 399–400.

To Hamilton Fish

———

Long Branch, N. J.
July 5th /75

HON. HAMILTON FISH;
SEC. OF STATE:
DEAR SIR:

If there is a German Consulate that can be given to Benj. H. Barrows, of Omaha, Neb, I think it will be advisable to confer it.

The application of Mr. B. is on file now in the Department of State, signed by the two Senators.

> Very Truly
> your obt. svt.
> U. S. GRANT

ALS, DLC-Hamilton Fish. On April 7, 1875, U.S. Senators Algernon S. Paddock and Phineas W. Hitchcock of Neb. wrote to USG. "We have the honor to recommend the appointment of Hon. Benjamin H. Barrows of Omaha Nebraska as Consul at Hamburgh, or Dresden, or Brussels, or at some consulate of like grade. Mr Barrows was recently a member of the Legislature, and at present Edits the leading Administration Organ in our state, at Omaha. . . ." LS, DNA, RG 59, Letters of Application and Recommendation. Related papers are *ibid.* On April 15, Paddock telegraphed to Orville E. Babcock. "Please bring up My Utah New Mexico Matter Also Benjamin H. Barrows as Consul before President goes" Telegram received, *ibid.*, RG 107, Telegrams Collected (Bound). On July 9, Secretary of State Hamilton Fish visited USG at Long Branch. "I refer to a telegram which he had sent respecting Barrows of Nebraska whom the two Senators from that State have been importuning me for months past to appoint to a German Consulate. I told him there was none vacant and I could not recommend the removal of any now in office unless possibly he wished to change the man at Dresden, he asked if there had not been some charges against him. I replied none of importance but that Gov Jewell had made a very informal report of it. He asked who was the consul at Hamburgh as that was the place they seemed particularly to wish and had told him the incumbent had been a long time in office. I mentioned Robinson's name adding that he was a very good consul and I could not recommend his removal for the appointment of a Nebraska man He inquires where he was from I told him I believed he was from Mass but that his father was a clergyman settled in New York." Fish diary (retrospective entry dated July 7), DLC-Hamilton Fish. See *ibid.*, May 3, 1875; *PUSG*, 24, 80–81. On Jan. 31 and Feb. 7, 1876, Fish recorded in his diary. "Senator Paddock is very much disturbed by the nomination of Meyer of Nebraska as Consul General at Shanghai; saying that while Myer is a respectable man he has no position and does not deserve an appointment to such an important post—His anxiety is to get Barrows some European Consulate . . . I speak to the President of my conversation with Paddock—He says he has no objection to putting Barrows in Wilson's place except that it would be giving Neb—more than its proportion of Consulates. He authorizes me to make any changes which I may think proper and will be glad if I can find a place of $1500 or 2000 for Barrows." "I suggested the transfer of Wilson from Bremen to Hamburg, and of King now at Dublin to Bremen and the appointment of Barrows of Neb to Dublin, but I am to see Cameron to ascertain whether any Pa interests will be brought in conflict with each other" DLC-Hamilton Fish. On Feb. 11, USG nominated Benjamin H. Barrows as consul, Dublin; Wilson King as consul, Bremen; and John M. Wilson as consul, Hamburg. On Feb. 15, Josiah King, Pittsburgh, wrote to USG. "It was owing to your personal interferance, some 3¼ years ago, that my son Wilson King was appointed to the *Dublin Consulate.* I hav[e] not ceased to be thankful for the favor, and upon enquiry about a year ago at the State Department, wa[s] told by the Chief Clerk Mr Brown, that my sons record was very satisfactory—I am in rect this a. [m.] of a cable dispatch from my son, in these words *'Why another Consul appointed here?'* I have no othe[r] intimation of his removal—If it be true that he is another has been appointed—May I not ask if it be not for some fault, that it may be *withdrawn or not Confirmed* If for a fault may I not ask what?—and if without a fault and removal is determined upon why not give him an oppt.y. to *resign* I regret to obtrude this matter upon your notice, but as it toutches my finest sensibilities I hope you will excuse me" ALS, DNA, RG 59, Miscellaneous Letters.

On April 29, 1875, Paddock, New York City, had telegraphed to USG. "I beg of you appoint Alonzo G, Paddock Marshal Utah   Maxfield [*Maxwell*] Make good Pension Agent for Western Territories," Telegram received, *ibid.*, RG 60, Records Relating to Appointments. Related papers are *ibid.* No appointment followed.

To Adam Badeau

———

Long Branch, N. J.
July 5th /75

DEAR GENERAL:

Your letter written a few days before you sailed for Liverpool was duly received and I should have answered it before you got away. What I wanted particularly to say—and now do say—is that I will not regard your declination of the Mission to Brussells for the present. I presume Jones will not return to Brussells, though under the letter which he received when his resignation was tendered he can do so. His household goods &c. were sent home in advance.[1] If he does not return the Mission will still be tendered to you, and I hope you with Mrs. Badeau, may enjoy it. Of course I can not know, or even surprise, why you did not wish Mrs. Wilcoxsin to accompany you; but I can very well understand how two sisters who had never been seperated for a whole day before the marriage of the second one should feel loth to part with the Ocean dividing them. But this will all be right very soon and I know you will then prefer a Mission to a Consulate.

I am not giving advice but doing what I think you will be glad of on second reflection. If I am mistaken you can decline the Mission when it reaches you.

My family, and your friends here at the Branch, are all well. Buck sails from Liverpool on the 8th inst. so that I hope you may meet him before he starts.[2]

Please remember me to Gn. Schenck & daughters.

Very Truly Yours
U. S. GRANT

GEN. A. BADEAU.

ALS, Munson-Williams-Proctor Institute, Utica, N. Y. On July 21, 1875, Secretary of
State Hamilton Fish recorded in his diary a cabinet exchange with USG. "He states that
he has not signed Badeaus Commission as Minister to Brussels but is awaiting Jones return. I told him that we had this morning received a telegram from Jones informing us that
he would sail on his return tomorrow." DLC-Hamilton Fish. On Aug. 20, John L. Cadwalader, asst. secretary of state, wrote to Adam Badeau conveying his commission as minister to Belgium. Copy, DNA, RG 59, Diplomatic Instructions, Belgium. On Sept. 20,
Badeau wrote to Fish concerning this commission. ". . . I regret to say that private reasons compel me to decline the honor which I highly appreciate, and had hoped to be able
to accept. . . ." ALS, *ibid.*, Diplomatic Despatches, Belgium. On Oct. 8, Fish wrote to Badeau acknowledging his declination. Copy, *ibid.*, Diplomatic Instructions, Belgium. Badeau
remained consul gen., London. See *Badeau*, pp. 476–77; first letter to Hamilton Fish,
July 14, 1875.

On Dec. 22, Badeau wrote to Fish. "I take the liberty of asking you to hand the enclosed letter to the President *in person*. I have been in the habit of sending under cover to
Babcock such letters as were intended for the President alone. I trust I need not say that
this like its predecessors, is on purely personal and unofficial subjects. Although you may
perhaps at times have thought other wise, I have been to you always *a thoroughly loyal subordinate*, especially during my last stay in America. Someday you may have proof of my assertion. Meanwhile I beg your pardon for the trouble I ask you to take, . . ." ALS, DLC-
Hamilton Fish. On Jan. 24 and July 11, 1876, Badeau wrote to USG. "Confidential . . . I
hope you will be glad to know that I begin to hope for some comfort in my family life.
Mrs. Wilcoxson is to be married on the 21st of February. Her cousin came over to see me
from Brussels, where he is Dutch Consul, (as well a very rich banker), and talked up affairs. He professed himself entirely satisfied with my course, and very angry at the behavior of the trustee in America; and said the only way out of the difficulties was for Mrs.
Wilcoxson to marry. He would take her to his house and present eight suitors to her, in
instalments of four, but out of the eight she must choose one. He told me he could promise me a brother in law in one month; and he has been as good as his word. Mrs. W. took
the second man presented, and her wedding dress is selected. Indeed, she determined on
her dress before she did on her man. Now, the French relatives and the husband elect want
us all four to return as soon as possible to America, and do exactly what you advised me
(you may remember) last summer; that is, sell every particle of the estate, and invest the
proceeds in government or other safe securities. I urged this in June; my wife (when sane)
has always wished me to manage her financial affairs; but Mrs. W. refusing so we came
away, leaving the estate very much entangled. I think it would be very much more advisable to wait until *after* the Centennial, as the value of real estate must then be greatly en-
hanced over its present price. I shall certainly endeavour to persuade my future brother-
in law of this; and as he is a man of sense and affairs, he will probably see the justice of my
view. But I could not afford to let him go to America without me; if he should insist on going soon, I hope it will not be impossible for me to obtain another leave. I dont want to go
home during the elections, as it will certainly be said that I went to electioneer; and if I
stay here and Mrs W. remains in Brussels, I shall probably have a quiet home, and finish
my book. Neither of the two husbands is likely to receive or abet the fugitive wife of the
other. For a month I have lived peaceably. I see by the papers that the Committee on Appropriations has reported a bill to remove the Consulate General for this Kingdom from
London to Liverpool. This has been tried twice before, since I have been here, but the manifest impropriety of the change prevented it. The reports which I requested the State Department to shew you a month or two ago, of themselves shew where the Consulate Gen-

eral should be. London has always returned more fees by thousands of dollars annually to the Government, than Liverpool; the variety and amount of general business done is vastly greater; and the fact that London is the capital is of itself a reason. I am obliged to have personal intercourse with the Minister two or three times a week; (as the Consuls are prohibited from corresponding direct with him); so also I must often see British officials personally; all of this business would be greatly delayed by the change proposed. Gen Fairchild wrote me at once when he saw the proposition to say that he opposed, that he thought London the place for the Consulate General; and he had so written to Gov. Fish. When Rome became the capital of Italy, and Berlin the capital of the new German empire, in both cases the State Department recommended the creation or removal of Consulates General at the new capitals. The idea I suppose is that Consuls have nothing to do except with ships, and that there is more American shipping at Liverpool than at London; but so there is more at Havre than at Paris and the shipping does not make one third of the business. I do not care so much about the proposed reduction of pay, if it is general; but the other change would be invidious, and both Gov. Fish and Mr. Cadwallader assured me personally when I was last in Washington of their complete satisfaction with my performance of my duties; and I have been officially complimented since my return   I hope you will be so good as to make it known to Senators that you disapprove and do not wish, this change. Of course that would settle the question. I beg you will not forget this. I have written officially and personally to Gov Fish, and told him I should write to you   Nellie and her husband were to have dined with us about this time, but the illness of her baby prevented her going to stay with the Schencks. We hope for the pleasure of receiving her later; unless my misfortunes are renewed. (But I do now have some hope for better domestic days.) I thank you very much for your goodness to my brother, which secured his retention in the post office at New York. Please, dear General, make my best compliments to Mrs Grant, and tell her the funny story of Mrs Wilcoxson and her eight suitors and that she selected her dress before she did her husband. Wishing you renewed good fortune, health and happiness in all your public and private relations, and begging you to beleive me most constantly grateful for all your kindnesses, . . ." "I have taken the liberty of giving my friend and brother in law, Mr. Amédée Wilbaux a letter of introduction to yourself. In all the terrible difficulties I have had to contend with, he has been my staunch supporter. He is in America to arrange the estate of his wife and mine, and likely to succeed. Mrs. Badeau is with him and her sister, but again penitent and most anxious to return to me; and although she has nearly ruined me pecuniarily, incurring debts for *thousands* of dollars, without my knowledge, for which I am legally responsible, I think when they return to Europe, I shall try once more to live with her. But I am obliged to retrench in every way, and even then I shall hardly avoid bankruptcy at the end of my term of office. I am just regaining some degree of health, and hope to have my literary work complete before the fourth of March. There is sure to be a great revulsion of feeling then in your favor among even your opponents, and if I can help to recall to the nation your great services, I shall consider that I have not lived in vain. Please remember me to Mrs. Grant and the family, . . ." ALS, USG 3. See Badeau to Fish, Jan. 26, 1876, DLC-Hamilton Fish.

On Oct. 26, 1875, Fish had recorded in his diary. "The President suggested the appointment of Mr Merrill of Natchez as Minister to Brussels—He does not remember his first name but says he was a man of large wealth before the war and of thorough Union principles throughout it." *Ibid.* On Oct. 31, U.S. Senator Henry B. Anthony of R. I., Providence, wrote to USG. "I am informed that Gen. Badeau has declined the Belgian mission. If this be correct, I would respectfully bring again to your attention the name of Henry S. Sanford, whose qualifications and services are attested by his record in the Department of

State, and whose character experience and circumstances eminently fulfill the conditions of diplomatic employment" ALS, *ibid.* On Dec. 9, USG nominated Ayres P. Merrill, Jr., a Miss. planter who also worked as a commission merchant in New York City, as minister to Belgium. On July 5 and 21, 1865, Merrill, Jr., New York City, had written to Badeau concerning his pardon under the amnesty proclamation and oath of allegiance. ALS, USG 3.

1. On March 19 and April 30, 1875, J. Russell Jones, U.S. minister, Brussels, wrote to Fish about shipping personal items to Philadelphia free of duty and his recall. ALS, DNA, RG 59, Diplomatic Despatches, Belgium. On July 13, Fish wrote to Jones concerning his resignation. ". . . your wishes in the matter having been made known to the President, I am directed to accept your resignation and at the same time to express to you the President's appreciation of the intelligence and discretion which has marked your service at Brussels. . . . On the receipt of your despatch indicating your wish to be recalled a letter was immediately prepared but owing to an intimation which had reached the President and by him communicated to me that you had desired to return to this country on leave and to resign after your return it was withheld. . . ." Copy, *ibid.*, Diplomatic Instructions, Belgium. On July 20, Jones cabled to Fish. "Sail twenty second State of Nevada to New York—Please provide for admitting our things." Cable received (on July 21, at 9:45 A.M.), *ibid.*, Diplomatic Despatches, Belgium. See Jones to Fish, Sept. 22, 1874, July 15, 20, 1875, *ibid.*; letter to Benjamin H. Bristow, [*Aug., 1875*]; letter to J. Russell Jones, Oct. 5, 1875.

2. On March 1, Orville E. Babcock had written to Fish. "The Presidents son Ulysses S. Grant Jr, purposes going to Europe and he would be pleased to have his Passport prepared and sent down." LS, DNA, RG 59, Requisition for Special Passports.

To Edwards Pierrepont

———

Long Branch, N. J.

July 7th /75

DEAR SIR:

If Marshal Dunn, of Del. has not resigned, or if his resignation has not been accepted or successor appointed I think, from the protests I receive against the change, it may be well to suspend action until more accurate information can be had of the real needs of the public good in respect to a change.

Very Truly Yours,

U. S. GRANT

HON. EDWARDS PIERREPONT, ATTY. GEN.

ALS, DNA, RG 60, Letters from the President. On July 8, 1875, Attorney Gen. Edwards Pierrepont telegraphed to USG, Long Branch. "Marshal Dunn has not resigned, but will remain until your further order." Copy, *ibid.*, Letters Sent to Executive Officers. See letter to Edwards Pierrepont, June 23, 1875.

On April 7, 1869, USG had nominated John M. Dunn as marshal, Del. On May 24,

1872, "one who knows and Suferd," Wilmington, Del., wrote to USG. "there is somting wrong In the Marshalls ofice in this Place   U. S Marshall John M Dunn gets the Baliffs of the courts to Sign Blank receits and bills them up and gave Two Men five Dollars for Watching Brandy they had received and charged the goverment with Month wages for A wachman   he is Not considerd A honest Man   one of Bailiffs received Eight Dollars the Last Pay he got from the Marshall By Signing A Blank   there is somtting whrong in the ofice of the Marshall" L, DNA, RG 60, Letters from the President.

On March 7, 1873, USG renominated Dunn; on March 21, the Senate rejected Dunn's nomination; on March 24, USG returned Dunn's nomination upon the Senate's request; on March 26, the Senate confirmed this nomination. On March 24, Henry F. Pickels, chairman, Del. Republican Committee, Wilmington, had telegraphed to USG. "Please not to make any appointments for Marshall of Delaware until our Congressman Can be heard from,   There are several first Class men who will be applicants. Please answer," Telegram Received, *ibid.*, Records Relating to Appointments. On Jan. 10, Edward T. Righter, Wilmington, had written to USG. "As I have worked hard for the purpose of giving you two terms in the Presidentall Chair, I think it nothing but right that you should reward me by confering some kind of an Office to me. as I have been in a great measure instrumental in Turning Little Delaware over to the Republicans.   if you can conveiently confer an Office on me I am not particular what kind it shall be. but I might mention that I should like to be U. S. Marshall of this place in place of John Dunn. who is not very well liked here. . . ." ALS, *ibid.* On March 22, Del. Senator Leander F. Riddle and William M. Field, Wilmington, wrote to USG. "Mr Dunn, the recently appointed U. S. Marshal for the District of Delaware, having failed of confirmation in the Senate, the office thereby becoming vacant, we take pleasure in recommending Mr Robert G. Frame—Attorney-at-law, of this city— for the office of Marshal. . . ." LS, *ibid.* Related papers are *ibid.* On April 21, 1869, Robert C. Fraim, New Castle, Del., had written to USG seeking a diplomatic appointment. ALS, *ibid.*, RG 59, Letters of Application and Recommendation. On March 24, 1873, David E. Buckingham, Wilmington, wrote to USG. "I write you soliciting the appointment of Marshall for the district of Del: I have no petition to present, as I am opposed to going around beging for signatures. I am an ex Soldier and my military history is the history of the 4th Del Inft having entered it at its organization and participated in every battle in which it was engaged untill the close of the war, . . ." ALS, *ibid.*, RG 60, Records Relating to Appointments. On Dec. 11, USG endorsed papers containing charges against Dunn. "Refered to the Atty. Gen. with the request that he examine into the charges against the Marshal of Del. and if satisfied, to name a successor." AES, *ibid.* Dunn remained in office. See *Wilmington Every Evening*, Nov. 13–15, 18–19, Dec. 2, 1873.

On July 1, 1876, Samuel M. Harrington, "Delaware Member of the National Republican Executive Committee," Wilmington, wrote to USG. "The undersigned respectfully requests the removal of John M. Dunn United States Marshal for the District of Delaware and the appointment of Samuel Barr of Wilmington in his stead, . . ." LS, *ibid.* No appointment followed.

On July 11, A. E. Davis, "on behalf of the Republicans of Wilmington," wrote to USG. "We perceive that Judge Fisher has asked to have his name withdrawn for the position of U S District Atty for Delaware, and that you have named J H Hoffecker Esq for the position. Mr Hoffecker is a first class christian gentleman, and a fair lawyer,   now Mr Higgins has been removed we trust Marshal John M Dunn, will be speedily required to step out. This man is a disgrace to the Republican Party here. That he has committed gross frauds against the U S. there can be no doubt,   this man was as poor as poverty when appointed Marshal   he now ownes several houses. and at this time is building himself a fine resi-

dence. he spends money very laishly. This cannot be done honestly out of the *legal fees* of the Marshals Office in Delaware. It can be proven that Dunn has had a great many vouchers signed *in blank* against the Government he paying $5 for such signatures   Three years ago, he was publically expelled from the membership of the city Republican Executive Committee for ballot box stuffing and charges were then prefered against him to Atty Gen'l Williams for frauds against the U S Government, affadavits were taken and forwarded *to Atty Generals Office at Washington*, but when the letters were called for at Washington they could not be found in the Office of Atty General   Mr Higgins, Marshal Dunn, Post Master Lewis (*since dismissed in disgrace*) with several other politicians of the same stamp went to Washington immediately, and represented to the Republican members of the Senate, that the charges against Dunn *were Democratic lies*, when they knew, (or should have known) that the charges could be sustained. And if the evidence had not been stolen from, or secreted in, Atty Gen'l Williams Office, there could have been no trouble to show Dunns guilt. Mr Bayard of Delaware made a full statement of Dunn's dishonesty, but unfortunately Mr Bayard was a Democrat, and his testimony did not have sufficient weight to prevent Dunn's confirmation. He should now be removed,   At the time and effort was made to prevent Dunns confirmation several prominent Republicans men of sterling worth, called on Robert C Fraim Esq, atty at Law of this city, and got his consent to accept the Office. Judge Fisher knowing Mr Fraim intimately, used his influnce on his behalf, but Mr Higgins being the District Atty had the influence of *Williams*, and by his efforts Dunn was retained. I am informed, that Mr Fraim would now accept the appointment, . . ."
ALS, *ibid.*, Letters from the President. Dunn remained in office.

To Edwards Pierrepont

Long Branch, N. J.
July 8th 1875.

DEAR JUDGE:

I am in receipt of your letter of yesterday speaking of the complaints against Judge Fisher, Dist. Atty. for the Dist. of Columbia. I have no doubt but the good of the service demands a change. You may notify Judge Fisher of the fact and give him an opportunity to resign. The change will be made whether he resigns or not. The complaints coming from three of the departments of the Govt.—exclusive of the department over the Dist. Atty.—the Court, and from many other sources there is no use in Judge Fisher attempting to get a stay of proceedings. It will be much better for his future success if he should voluntarily withdraw.

I know Gen. Wells well. He was Dist. Atty. of the Dist. of Va. and made an excellent record. No better man could be selected for the office.

Very truly yours

U. S. Grant

Hon. Edwards Pierrepont Atty. Genl.

Copy, DLC-USG, II, 2. On July 16, 1875, Attorney Gen. Edwards Pierrepont wrote to USG. *"Confidential* . . . I much regret that Judge Fisher did not take your kind suggestions and resign quietly—I wrote him a delicate note and instead of coming to me he hastened to Long-Branch and all the 'Papers' stated the fact and it had the appearance of an issue— The Judge has been to see me this morning and asks delay until you send for me—I will of course go to you at any hour which you desire—his unwise rush to Long-Branch has given rise to much opposition which would never have arisen if he had done as you so considerately advised—To day the follwig appears in the Republican . . . Not a suggestion for a newspaper has gone from my office—I have been *very* desirous that Judge Fisher should resign quietly and without damage to him—The Judge had scarcely left my office when a Lawyer came in and made the charge which I have had copied & herewith send—He says many worse will be sent about young Fisher—that he is interested in a gambling-house &c. In looking further I cut the enclosed from the Republican of to day—This is very unpleasant to me as I know & esteem Judge Fisher   But I see no way out of this matter but the way you suggested—Judge Fisher asks me to have delay—I told him that to say nothing of outside complaints, when three cabinet officers complain the matter cannot be overlooked—I told him that unless the Secretary of the Treasury and the Post-Master General (who are in town) will withdraw all complaints it is idle to ask a change of purpose He thinks they *will not* aid him—I know they will not. I advise you how it now stands" ALS, USG 3. Newspaper clippings concerning mail tampering cases and George P. Fisher's imminent removal as U.S. attorney, D. C., are *ibid.* Also enclosed is an affidavit dated July 16 charging Charles G. Fisher, asst. U.S. attorney, with demanding cash to fix cases. DS, *ibid.* On July 31, Pierrepont wrote to Secretary of State Hamilton Fish. "I am directed by the President to request you to issue a commission appointing Henry H. Wells, to be U. S. Attorney for the District of Columbia, to take effect on the 4th of September next, in place of George P. F[is]her, resigned." Copy, DNA, RG 60, Letters Sent to Executive Officers. See *PUSG*, 19, 158–59; *ibid.*, 20, 65; *ibid.*, 22, 51; letter to Edwards Pierrepont, July 17, 1875.

On Jan. 13, 1877, USG pardoned Charles G. Fisher, sentenced Jan. 3 in D. C. Supreme Court to eleven months in prison for "abstracting papers from the files in the office of the Clerk of the said Court," because he was "morally irresponsible for his conduct; . . . and inasmuch as his transfer from the District jail to the Government Hospital for the Insane is duly provided for." Copy, DNA, RG 59, General Records. On Jan. 18, Fisher escaped from the asylum. See *PUSG*, 18, 351; *Washington Evening Star*, Jan. 19, 1877; *New York Times*, Sept. 22, 1875, Aug. 5, 6, 1879.

To Sherman & Grant

Long Branch, N. J.
July 9th /75

DEAR SIR:

I have no doubt overdrawn my account this month, not more I trust however than Mrs. Grant & I together have in bank. I hope you will meet all my drafts that may be presented and should I inconveniently overrun notify me and I will make good.

Very Truly Yours
U. S. GRANT

SHERMAN & GRANT
BANKERS, WASHINGTON, D. C.

ALS, Mrs. Paul E. Ruestow, Jacksonville, Fla. On May 27, 1875, USG wrote to Secretary of the Treasury Benjamin H. Bristow. "I have to request that hereafter the warrants for my Salary may be issued to the firm of Sherman & Grant, Bankers of this city." LS, DNA, RG 56, Letters Received from the President. On the same day, USG wrote a similar letter to David W. Mahon, 1st auditor, Treasury Dept. Copy, DLC-USG, II, 2.

Endorsement

Respectfully returned to the Atty. Gen.   Gen. Brice is an officer (retired) who is not likely to speak as he does within unless he is sure of the truth of his statements. It may be well to get Mr. Adams record from the wWar Dept. I would approve the restoration of Walcott.

U. S. GRANT

JULY 13TH /75

AES, DNA, RG 60, Records Relating to Appointments. Written on a letter of June 2, 1875, from Benjamin W. Brice, former paymaster gen., Baltimore, to Attorney Gen. Edwards Pierrepont. "A sense of duty to the Country & to the Administration impels me to address you; a liberty which I am sure will be excused in consideration of its purpose & motive. My attention has been called to an associated press paragraph in the newspapers of yesterday, (Viz) 'The President to day signed the commission of *Gilbert Adams* to be U. S. Marshal for the Territory of Wyoming.' Now if this be (as I am advised it is) the Gilbert Adams, a former resident of Philadelphia, who was a Lieut. & Captain of Volunteers during the Late War, and who for a time served as A. D. C. on the staff of Brig. Gen. Lawrence P. Graham (Col L. P. Graham U. S. Army retired), and after the War became a sutler or trader connected with some military Post in Wyoming Ter. I wish to give you information of his character, his true character, of which of course the President & yourself are ignorant and about which you have doubtless been grossly deceived. I content myself for the present with a bare statement of the fact that I have had opportunities to know Adams well and am therefore able with positiveness to assure you that he is, without qualification or mitigation, an unscrupulous knave, swindler & liar, and, I scruple not to add (referring to one instance within my own cognizance) a corrupt forger. No public trust in his hands can be safe for a day, and none should be confided to him. Facts & specifications with proofs are available and can be supplied to the Department if required to establish what is here charged." ALS, *ibid.* On July 30, USG removed Gilbert Adams as marshal, Wyoming Territory.

On Dec. 4, Governor John M. Thayer of Wyoming Territory wrote to USG. *"Personal.* . . . I have forwarded to you, through Senator Hitchcock, my recommendation in favor of William F. Sweezey for Marshal of this Territory. I believe now that both Senators Hitchcock and Paddock will support it. As Governor of Wyoming, and as your friend and supporter, I am compelled to state that the appointment of the present incumbent of the Marshalship of this Territory, Frank Wolcot, is offensive to almost the whole people. of this If you knew what the feeling is towards him, as I see it and know it, you would not tolerate his appointment for a day. I have no feeling against Wolcot personally,—he has I am actuated by no motive save that of the public interests. Numerous petitions have been filed recently with the Atty General, asking for his removal, and the re-appointment of Adams, but I understand Adams is out of the question. You have been annoyed with the quarrels and squabbles here in Wyoming for years. I want to relieve you of them, and I am glad to be able to say that they are dying out. If the administration will take my advice in regard to appointments here, I am willing be to be held responsible. I cannot give my advice too strongly in favor of a new Marshal, and I know I am expressing the feelings of nine tenths of the people of Wyoming. I respectfully ask that you do not make a nomination of a chief justice here till I see you, which will be about the 20th inst. The term of the present incumbent, Judge Fisher, expires sometime this month. There is no need for haste in filling the vacancy. . . . I find no suitable person in the Territory for Marshal, who could take it." ALS, *ibid.* On Dec. 15, USG nominated William S. Sweezy as marshal, Wyoming Territory. See *PUSG*, 23, 248; letter to Edwards Pierrepont, July 3, 1875; Endorsement, Feb. 2, 1877.

On Dec. 17, 1875, USG renominated Joseph W. Fisher as chief justice, Wyoming Territory. On Jan. 18, 1876, Thayer and U.S. Delegate William R. Steele of Wyoming Territory, Washington, D. C., wrote to USG. "The undersigned, as Governor of Wyoming Territory, and its Delegate in Congress, feel compelled to unite in an urgent request, that you will withdraw from the Senate of the U. S, the nomination of Hon. Joseph W. Fisher, as Chief Justice of Wyoming Ty. It is very unpleasant to us to have to trouble you with this subject, but we feel it our duty to protest against an appointment that we cannot but think will be in the nature of a public misfortune to our Territory—It is no small Evil to have an incompetent man appointed Judge and placed over a people for four years to decide their most important rights—And Judge Fisher's legal Knowledge and Experience do not fit him for the duties of his high position—This request is not made upon personal grounds but solely for the reason that Judge Fisher, is weak and incompetent for so arduous and important a trust—" LS, DNA, RG 60, Records Relating to Appointments. Steele added an undated endorsement. "For myself I desire, to say, that being a Democrat, I neither ask nor expect the appointment of a political friend to the Judgeship, but expect that any gentleman appointed will be a Republican—All I ask; and that it seems to me I may properly do, is, that any man appointed Chief Justice of Wyoming Ty. shall be not only a lawyer of ability and experience, but an honest man. who will administer the law without fear or favor—" AES, *ibid.* Thayer also added an undated endorsement. "I beg, Mr President, you will not consider me officious. I did not want to interfere in these matters, but I have been pressed so much by people in the Territory to ask for changes, that I could not avoid this painful duty. Of course I shall cheerfully acquiesce in your decision in regard to Judge Fisher, whatever it may be. I would prefer this paper should not go on file, unless necessary." AES, *ibid.* Fisher was confirmed.

To John F. Long

Long Branch, N. J.
July 13th /75

DEAR JUDGE:

On my return from Washington yesterday I found yours of the 19th inst. asking instructions as to the payment of two bills for Merchandise certified to be correct by Carlin. I presume these to be purchases made by Carlin for his own use and should be paid by him. With all my efforts I have failed to get any account of farm receipts and expenses for ten months or more. I have finally made up my mind that my farming experiment is to wind up with a great loss, increasing as long as the experiment is continued. I will therefore execute the design indicated in my letter from Washington. The best plan probably will be to advertise for sale at private sale until a certain day and then every thing to be sold at auction. Terms should be cash for sums under fifty dollars, and six months credit, with i[n]terest, and good security, on all sums over.

I would like to retain something as a relic from the farm and would indicate the Ethan Allen Colt and any other one that Carlin may think the best. On these I would fix a price, say One Thousand $100[0]$^{00}/_{100}$ for Bob Acres, and the full value of the other, and unless they reach this let them be bought in for me. I got Jackson to move from Pa to go on my farm. Our contract however cannot be construed as binding for more than one year. I do not want to turn him adrift however to his loss. He might therefore continue with

AL (incomplete), MoSHi. See letter to Nathaniel Carlin, Aug. 24, 1875; letter to Edward F. Beale, Sept. 8, 1875.

On July 10, 1875, USG, Cape May, N. J., telegraphed to Julia Dent Grant, Long Branch. "Arrived after a beautiful Sail down the Delaware" Telegram received, USG 3.

To Hamilton Fish

———

Long Branch, N. J.
July 14th /75

Dear Governor:

I am in receipt of your letter of yesterday. The commissions which you have sent I will sign though it is possible Gn. Badeau may decline his. Should he do so I doubt if we could do better than to advance Gn. Fairchild to the Belg. Mission? In that case Wayne could still take Fairchilds place.

I am rather impressed with the objections urged against bringing Judge Russell from Venezuala[1] in a Naval vessel and accept the plan of a simple recall.

Very Truly Yours
U. S. Grant

Hon. Hamilton Fish Sec. of State.

ALS, DLC-Hamilton Fish. On Tuesday, July 13, 1875, Secretary of State Hamilton Fish wrote to USG, Long Branch. "I send, to day, the Commissions for the new Ministers to Brussells, the Hague, & Ecuador, as directed by you when I had the pleasure to see you at Long Branch. Also one for Mr Owen as Consul at Messina—he is recommended by the Senators & Representatives from Vermont to take the place of Mr Rankin, of that state, who declines the appointment—I delay writing to Govr Fairchild & to Gen Wayne feeling it my duty to write to you what I have heard since we parted—A Gentleman in whom I have very great confidence, who has within the last week returned from London & from the Continent, & whom I met on Saturday last, tells me that painful rumors of Genl Badeau's habits were Current on the Continent, & that in London they were a common topic of conversation—that he was there told, that, not long since, the General had invited some Company, to either dinner, breakfast, or supper (I am not sure which) & when the Company assembled, the General was not in condition to receive them, or to be seen—that the business of the Consulate is transacted entirely by the Vice Consul General—that parties calling & enquiring for the General are almost invariably told that he is 'engaged,' & are obliged to make their Communications to the Vice Consul General who, by the way is a very Competent & I believe a very upright officer, but is understood to be an English Subject—The gentleman who gives me this information does not profess to speak from any experience of his own, but to state what is currently talked of among Americans as well as forigners—he says that it is generally spoken of, & the common talk is that the reason why the General cannot be seen at the Consulate, is that is in a condition not to be seen—In addition to this Mr Robeson tells me that he was recently informed, that while the General was staying at the Fifth Avenue Hotel, on his late visit, he had been intoxicated for several days, & thereby confined to his room—It is with great pain that I make this communication, but I feel it my duty to lay before you the statements as they have reached me—I have laid your letter of July 2d respecting political contributions before each member of the Cabinet, now in Washington—all being here except the Secretary of War—To day, I have had a long interview with all of these Gentlemen on the Venezuelan business—All but the Post Master General, concurred in the propriety & necessity of withdrawing our Minister. I will prepare instructions accordingly—There was much discussion, & much doubt expressed, as to the propriety of sending a Vessel of war to bring him home, & the opinion seemed to be unanimous that it would be neither wise or expedient to keep a vessel on that coast after his withdrawal, that independent of the risk of yellow fever at this Season, it would be an exhibition of force, before a weak power, without the object of exerting force, & would have the appearance of a menace, without its reality—I find that the letters of recall to Mr Jones, although signed were not forwarded—they appear to have been withheld, at the time, in Consequence of an intimation that Mr Jones had expressed a wish to return to the United States on leave of absence, & to resign after reaching this Country, and it was supposed that he had been led to sending the request for a recall under a misapprehension of a reference to him in a private letter from me to Mr Washburne, which seemed to have been Communicated to him—I wrote to Washburne explaining that there was no desire for his resignation on my part, or on the part of the Government. When you mentioned to me his recent telegram to Genl Babcock, I did not, at the time, remember the circumstances, which have been recalled by the Correspondence &c of the Department—I telegraphed to him yesterday explaining the delay & authorising him either to return *on leave*, or to await the letters of recall which leave by to day's mail—He ought to receive the letters of recall by about the 25th of this month—I regret the delay, but hope that it may not subject him to inconvenience." ALS, USG 3. See following letter; letter to Adam Badeau, July 5, 1875.

On July 9, Fish spoke with USG at Long Branch. "I mention to him the nomination of Francis B. Stockbridge the recommendations of Ferry & Chandler for the Hague and that Wullweber of Iowa accepts the mission to Ecuador   He replies that was the place Harry Wayne was to have had in case the Iowa man did not take it. I express regret at Waynes dis appointment and a wish that he might have some other place and suggested the Marshalship of Georgia. He replies he would give him that if it were vacant, that he thought he would prefer the collectorship of Savannah which he also would give if vacant but that both offices were very well filled the Marshal by an officer of the Army who had been induced to resign his commission to accept this place at the request of the Governmt He remarked that he would make Gov Fairchilds Consul General in London   I ask if he had decided definitely to appoint Badeau to Brussels   He replied O yes! I promised it to him before he left   I then inquired whether he would be willing to give Wayne the Consulate at Liverpool in the event of Fairchilds preferring going to London. He said he wished to offer London to Fairchilds and added if he did not go to London I might offer that place to Wayne" Fish diary (retrospective entry dated July 7), DLC-Hamilton Fish. On July 17, Fish wrote to USG. "Govr Fairchild is one of the very best Consuls in the service, & I have no doubt would make a very excellent Diplomatic Representive, excepting to lose so admirable a consul from a very important Consulate, no selection for Brussels would be more acceptable to me. Pecuniarily, the Consulate is worth more than the Mission, and involves less necessity of expenditure. Before Badeau's decision, & before any committal to Fairchild I think it right to tell you that Senator Howe, is very anxious for the appointment of George E Hoskins of Wisconsin to a Diplomatic position—he has written me two very urgent letters, & indicates Columbia, & suggests that Scruggs be re-called   I do not know that he would urge him for Brussells, but both Fairchild & Hoskins are from Wisconsin, and possibly you might wish to gratify the Senator—I think that of the two probably Fairchild would make the better Representative at Brussels, but I would find it difficult to suggest a ~~name~~ person, who will discharge the duties of the Liverpool Consulate as Fairchild has done. I shall be gratified to have Harry Wayne provided for— but he must make a first rate Consul to maintain the character Fairchild has given to the Liverpool Consulate—" ALS (press), *ibid.* See Endorsement, Sept. 5, 1874; letter to Hamilton Fish, Aug. 3, 1875.

On June 5, U.S. Senator Thomas W. Ferry of Mich. and Zachariah Chandler, Grand Haven, had written to USG to recommend the appointment of Francis B. Stockbridge as minister to the Netherlands. LS, DNA, RG 59, Letters of Application and Recommendation. Related papers are *ibid.* On July 12, USG appointed Stockbridge. On Sept. 20, Stockbridge, Kalamazoo, Mich., wrote to USG. "On account of recent occurrences, I am compelled, against my preference—and for reasons beyond my control—to respectfully tender my resignation as Minister Resident of the United States to the Netherlands—" ALS, *ibid.*, Letters of Resignation and Declination. On Dec. 11, Ferry and U.S. Senator Isaac P. Christiancy of Mich. wrote to USG recommending James Birney to replace Stockbridge. LS, *ibid.*, Letters of Application and Recommendation. On Dec. 17, USG nominated Birney as minister to the Netherlands. In March and on June 21, 1869, Birney, Bay City, Mich., had written to USG. "During Mr Lincolns first term as President he offered me a Foreign Mission. My circumstances were such at that time, that I could not conveniently accept the offer. While in Washington a few weeks ago the Michigan members of the House of Representatives united in recommending my appointment as Consul General to Havana. There was a vacancy at this point, and I felt an interest in the questions soon to be determined there. I would be glad to serve you in carrying out your policy in regard to the Independence and Annexation of Cuba. If however before you receive this you have filled the place by the recommendation of another I would be pleased to have you regard the recommendation, as applying as well to several European points—as Liverpool London Havre, or Florence. Although I have served the Republican party of this state in several prominent positions I have never as yet received anything of the patronage of the Federal Government. Hoping that my application may receive your favorable consideration . . ." "If Michigan should be entitled to a Foreign appointment through the resignation of Hon W A Howard nominated to the China Mission, I would be pleased to be favorably considered in that connection. My recommendation unanimously Signed by the Michigan delegation, for a Foreign appointment is on file in the Office of the Secretary of State" ALS, *ibid.* On Sept. 28, 1870, Birney again wrote to USG. "The Michigan delegation have unanimously recommended me on more than one occasion for a foreign appointment. I am still desirous of going abroad. It has occurred to me that as Mr Morton and myself are graduates of the same University, and both western men, that I would be acceptable to him as Secretary of his Legation. . . ." ALS, *ibid.* On Nov. 8, 1873, Birney wrote to USG. "Having received reliable information that Hon. John M. Francis Minister Resident at Athens, is about tendering to you his resignation, Senator Chandler, Hon N. B. Bradley my representative, and others of the Michigan delegation, will make application to you in my behalf, as to the successorship. That you may give the application the most favorable consideration is the earnest wish of your habitual supporter." ALS, *ibid.*

On June 11, 1875, James Caplis, Detroit, wrote to USG. "I hereby make application to be appointed Minister Resident to Ecuador. My residence is & has been for sixteen years in the city of Detroit During the last thirteen years I have been a member of the Bar of the Supreme Court of Michigan. During that time also I have been an active member of the Republican Party. I have represented the 1st District—(Detroit) in the Legislature of Michigan. . . ." ALS, *ibid.* Related papers, including a letter from Governor John J. Bagley of Mich. to USG recommending Caplis as "one of our best Irish American Citizens," are *ibid.* No appointment followed. See *PUSG*, 24, 322–24.

On Jan. 4, 1873, U.S. Representative Luke P. Poland of Vt. had written to Fish. "Andrew E. Rankin Esq of St. Johnsbury Vt. my son in law, is very desirous to go abroad, and to enable him to do so wishes to obtain a Consular appointment. Mr. R. is a graduate of Middlebury College, and also of the law department of Harvard. A difficulty of his eyes prevented his entering upon his profession, and he accepted the Clerkship of the Courts in our County of Caledonia, which place he has held for nearly or quite ten years. The life is too sedentary for his health, as well as rather irksome for its monotony. . . ." ALS, DNA, RG 59, Letters of Application and Recommendation. On June 25, 1875, U.S. Representative Charles H. Joyce of Vt., Rutland, wrote to Fish. "I have been informed that Rankin would not accept the consulship at Messina Italy I am very anxious to have George H. Owen of Rutland appointed to that place—I hope you will hold it open until I can send you papers from our Congressional delegation for Mr Owen." ALS, *ibid.* On June 28, U.S. Senator George F. Edmunds of Vt., Burlington, wrote to USG recommending George H. Owen. ALS, *ibid.* Related papers are *ibid.* On Dec. 9, USG nominated Owen as consul, Messina.

1. On July 6, Fish, Garrison, N. Y., had written to USG. "Will you allow me to ask if you expect to be at Long-Branch during the remainder of this week, or whether you contemplate holding a Cabinet Meeting at Washington within the next ten days. There are some matters in our Foreign relations which will shortly need your decision—especially with regard to Venezuela, with which State our relations are very far from satisfactory, and very possibly may be thought to require the recall of our Minister and the breaking off of Diplomatic Intercourse—a serious step, the gravity and consequences of which, it has occurred to me, may be such that you would prefer to have it discussed in Cabinet. A decision should however be made before the next mail, which, I think will be on the 9th inst —Should you not be going to Washington, I will return thither, by the way of Long-Branch—Will you have the goodness to let me know, by telegraph, whether I shall do so, or whether you are going to Washington—The matter respecting which Mr Cass made a confidential Communication, is not likely to reach an early result—The present Government of Spain is too uncertain of its own tenure of power, to venture upon any thing in the direction suggested—I have not heard a word from Mr Cass, but Mr Sandford has seen him, and obtains no satisfactory information through him—Mr S. has however been very active and efficient in pursuing enquiries through other channels, the result of which seems to shew a strong and growing opinion among prominent Spaniards, that separation must be the final result, and that it cannot be very long deferred, but that it is unquestionably true that the present Government is not firmly enough established to attempt it, and that, at the present time, no political party has the courage to propose it." ALS (press), DLC-Hamilton Fish. On July 9, Fish met USG at Long Branch. "I carried with me a large bulk of correspondence, both instructions and dispatches between the Department and the Legation at Venezuela on the subject of claims awarded under the Treaty. On introducing the subject the President at once said that he was familiar with the whole question and thought it was clear what course we should pursue and that was to withdraw our Minis-

ter and he thought it would be well to send a vessel of war to bring him home and that the Secretary of the Navy should order another vessel to continue cruising on the coast of Venezuela during the summer, that perhaps it might be well to let Mr Dalla Costa, the Venezuelan Minister know that such would be the action of this Government. I advised against this until after the instructions to Judge Russell to return should have been forwarded   I propose to leave with the President the correspondence which I had with me, he declined saying that it was not worth while   I then asked if he did not think it advisable before coming to a definite conclusion soon to take the opinion of the members of the Cabinet. He desired me to convene them on my return to Washington and take their opinion   I then told him that we had no information from Mr Cass since he left the U. S. on the subject which he had communicated confidentially with regard to our arrangements with Spain with respect to Cuba. That Mr Sanford had seen him and had written to him but could get no information   he had however seen several parties of position and influence and the result was that there seemed to be a growing feeling in Spain that she cannot much longer retain the Island of Cuba but that the government is not strong enough to venture upon any measure in the direction of a severance of the present connection . . ." Fish diary (retrospective entry dated July 7), *ibid.* See letter to Hamilton Fish, Aug. 9, 1875.

On July 21 (Wednesday) and 23, Fish recorded in his diary. "The President enquires of the condition of affairs in Cuba; I tell him they are the same and that no confidence could be placed in these ~~affairs~~ reports published in the papers—both sides are equally inaccurate—. . . After Cabinet had adjourned I remained and read to him the confidential letter from Cushing received yesterday and dated June 26th referring to the relations of Cuba & Spain and asking whether the President would be ready to assume 'the responsibility and burden of mediation, intervention, guarantee and protection of Cuba if invited by Spain'   He enquires if I have heard anything from Sanford—I explain to him the purport of Sanfords recent letters and that the negotiation suggested by Lewis Cass appears to be futile. That Queen Isabella through whom Cass proposed the negotiation was without influence at Madrid and was still so unpopular that her son did not venture to allow her to visit him. I also read to him the project enclosed by Cushing as a basis for the settlement of the Cuban Question. . . . He remarked that he considered this the most hopeful thing with regard to Cuba and authorizes me to say to Cushing that if invited he will undertake the mediation on the general plan of the basis proposed   I then tell the President that if this is to be undertaken I must have the entire confidence and support of the Administration in all of its branches, that I cannot undertake it with the sinister and underhand influences which have been operating against me especially in connection with the Cuban Question, that the National Republican of this City professes to be a personal organ of the Presidents and has unvariably been thwarting the policy which he authorized me to pursue and which he has told me he approved. It has published several articles denunciatory of the State Department and of its policy on this question, had earnestly and violently advocated the recognition of belligerency or of Cuban Independence and that Murdock the Editor had told me and also Robeson that he had never published a word on that subject that had not been authorized from the White House   I knew the influences which operated on behalf of the White House and the motives of some of the persons who professed to speak in his name—further that several millions of dollars of Cuban Bonds had been distributed about Washington whose value were supposed to be dependent upon the granting of the U. S. to Cuba of either belligerency or independence that if he desired me to proceed in this negotiation I must be assured that these influences should be arrested and that the publications in the Republican on this subject should cease. He told me he would send word to Murdock not to publish anything without my approval." "In the Cabinet Meeting on Wednesday the Presiden[t] inquired as to the condition of affairs in Cuba   I immediately apprehended that the Cuban influence of Babcock, Casey, ~~Murdock~~tagh, & the rest of the thieves had suggested the inquiry hence in my conversation after the meeting I speak of the necessity of keeping those men quiet and silencing the Washington Republican   After obtaining from him the promise which he made I was surprised to find in the Republican of this morning the annexed article which evidently (the article) had been written before his arrival from Long Branch and he doubtless had forgotten to speak to ~~Murdock~~tagh. I therefore write him today calling his attention but I fear the thieves are too strong." DLC-Hamilton Fish. The clipping is *ibid.* Spanish government instability derailed this irregular diplomatic initiative. See Fish diary, July 26, Dec. 6, 1875, *ibid.*; *PUSG*, 24, 374–75; Fish to Caleb Cushing, U.S. minister, Spain, Feb. 6, 1874, Oct. 1, 1875, DNA, RG 59, Diplomatic Instructions, Spain (the first partially printed in *Foreign Relations, 1874,* pp. 859–63); Cushing to Fish, Sept. 14, 1875, DNA, RG 59, Diplomatic Despatches, Spain; Nevins, *Fish,* pp. 871–75.

To Hamilton Fish

Confidential

Long Branch, N. J.
July 14th /75

Dear Governor:

I do not receive the New York Herald in my house nor read it except when away from home; but to-day after receiving your letter giving the result of the Cabinet conference yesterday, on Venezuelan matters, I was told of the meeting, and the subject of consultation,— taken from the Herald of this morning—so substantially correct that it seems impossible to be guess work entirely. Of course the meeting could not be kept secret; but the subject under consideration could.—I do not know that any harm is done in this instance, but so many times matters are discussed that should not come before the public except at the proper time and in an official and proper manner. In fact all Cabinet discussions should be treat as entirely confidential until duly authorized to be given to the public.

I write to you my dear Governor as the head of the Cabinet, not only by virtue of representing the State Department, but also in length of service as a Cabinet Minister to lay this matter before your associates in such manner as you may deem most proper. If there is eavesdroping it should be corrected. If the result of pumping by correspondents they, (the corres[pon]dents) should be avoided.

Very Truly Yours

U. S. GRANT

HON. HAMILTON FISH SEC. OF STATE

ALS, DLC-Hamilton Fish. On July 14, 1875, Secretary of State Hamilton Fish wrote to USG, Long Branch. "I am much concerned, this morning, to find published in the newspaper, an account of the meeting held here yesterday, giving not only the facts of the meeting, (which Reporters would naturally have obtained) but also the subject discussed, & a detailed account of much that was said—The meeting was held with *closed* doors, in my office, no one being present except the five six members of the Cabinet (including myself) who are now in Washington—I carefully abstained from mentioning either the object of the meeting, or what took place, even to the assistant secretaries, or to my Confidential Private Secretary—& have not alluded to the subject in conversation with any person, other than the members of the Cabinet who were present—As this publication of what should be most confidential, exposes to Venezuela, the purpose & design of this Government, in advance of the opportunity of instructing our Minister, I desire in justice to myself, (as the matter affects the Department which you have entrusted to me) and as due to you, to state that by no possibility has this breach of confidence, occured through me, or any person connected with this Department—. . . PS. I enclose an extract from one of the Journals, shewing the minuteness of detail, in which the proceedings of the meeting have been made public—" ALS (press), *ibid.* See letter to Hamilton Fish, July 15, 1875.

On July 13 and 20, Fish recorded in his diary. "In accordance with the Presidents request to confer with the Members of the Cabinet on the Venezuela question I had invited those in Washington to meet at my office this day at noon. The Secretaries of War, Navy & Interior, PostMaster-General & Attorney General attended. . . ." "On the day after the meeting of the Cabinet last week on the Venezuela question the full detailed account appeared evidently communicated by some one who had been present   The annexed was cut from the N. Y. Herald July 14th . . . My impression as well as that of Bristow Pierrepont and Robeson rested upon Jewell who is very fond of having the newspaper reporters about him and often talks incautiously   Jewell protested however that he had given no information and had spoken to no one on the subject. During this evening with Robeson Bristow, Jewell Pierrepont, Cadwalader & myself being present: Pierrepont stated he had discovered who had given the information; he told me subsequently that it was Delano who had communicated the proceedings to Gobright who had given it to the Associated Press and to the reporters on newspaper row. Holland (Gobrights assistant) gave the information to Pierrepont which was afterwards confirmed by Clark of the American Press Association who had sent it to the Balimore Sun" DLC-Hamilton Fish. On July 21, Fish recorded in his diary a conversation with USG. "He refers to his letter to me of the 14th on the subject relating to the discussion in the Cabinet Meeting of the 13th and says that his suspicion had fallen on one Member of the Cabinet and his letter had been written for his benefit. He says that the allusion to newspaper correspondents was expressly for 'our friend Jewell' who he said with a smile 'is very leaky' and has furnished the Tribune and other liberal papers with a great deal of gossip. I tell him in this instance he must acquit Jewell, that I in common with others of the Cabinet had had the same suspicion but that the Attorney General had made an investigation and was satisfied that the information in this case came from Delano; he expresses some surprise and said that after reading my letter he had received one from Jewell the tenor of which made him think that he (Jewell) had been the Communicating Member of the Cabinet." *Ibid.*

To Columbus Delano

Long Branch, N. J.
July 15th 1875.

Dear Sir:

Enclosed I send you a letter addressed to you but sent to me from the Graphic Office.[1] Do you not think it advisable to discontinue the Photo Lithographing by or for the Patent Office until the whole subject of the law under which this work is done is investigated? I do not know both sides of the question at issue but it seems to me from the showing before me that the Commissioner of Patents[2] has not consulted the best interests of the public service in his course in this matter.

Very truly yours
U. S. Grant

Hon. C. Delano, Secty. of the Interior

Copies, DLC-USG, II, 2; DLC-John Russell Young. On July 16, 1875, Secretary of the Interior Columbus Delano wrote to USG. "I have your favor of the 15th., enclosing copy of a letter to the Secretary of the Interior from the Graphic Company, relative to the matter of a contract for back issues of patent drawings. I have given this subject very careful and patient investigation, in consequence of the questions involved, and of the deep interest felt in it by the parties, as well as by certain members of Congress who have been connected with the subject. I have arrived at the conclusion that the contracts made by the Patent Office for the photolithographing, in so far as they were made without advertising for bids, and in so far as it was attempted to continue them without advertising, were illegal and made in violation of law. This opinion was first announced to the 2nd of June, last, in a letter to the Comr. of Patents referring to the contract made with the Graphic Company, a copy of which is here enclosed, and on the 15th. of July I reiterated this opinion in the matter relating to the contracts and extention thereof, made by the Patent Office with Norris Peters, copy of which is also herewith. You will see; I think, by reference to these communications that I have arrived at the same conclusion which your mind seems to have reached, in regard to this subject. I have hastened my conclusions, as expressed in the letters here enclosed, as rapidly as I could, consistently with other public duties, but I have been compelled to hear many and long arguments by the parties interested, which has necessarily delayed my final decision. I enclose a letter just received from Hon. W. B. Allison, in reference to the Nebraska surveys, and also one from Mr. Waldo M. Potter, on the same subject." LS, USG 3. The enclosures concerning the disputed contract are *ibid*. On July 19, USG, Long Branch, wrote to Delano. "I am in receipt of yr. letter of the 16th inst with enclosure showing that as early as the 2nd of June, you decided against the legality of the Commissioner of Patents giving out work without advertising &c. I think the Commissioner should be requested to resign at once, and should be removed if he fails to comply," Copies, *ibid.*; DLC-USG, II, 3. See letter to Columbus Delano, July 28, 1875.

1. On Aug. 27, James H. Goodsell, Charles M. Goodsell, and John G. Moore, "Managers of the Graphic Co," Washington, D. C., wrote to USG. "We respectfully submit herewith a copy of our argument presented to the Commissioner of Internal Revenue to-day in the matter of our bid for imprinting Internal Revenue stamps, under the advertisement dated July 7, 1875. The concluding part of this argument contains certain legal questions which we asked the Commissioner of Internal Revenue to submit to the Attorney General in the event of a decision against giving us the contract. The Commissioner has decided against our claim and refused to submit the questions as requested. Moreover he proposes to take such action as would be a great injustice to us. We have the honor to request that you order that the questions raised by us be referred to the Attorney General for his consideration and decision." DS, USG 3. The enclosure is *ibid*. In Nov., the *New York Times* charged the Goodsells, publishers of the *New York Daily Graphic*, with unfair bidding practices in obtaining a revenue stamp contract. The *Times* later apologized. See *New York Times*, Nov. 20, 23, 24, 1875, Jan. 10, 1877.

2. John M. Thacher, employed in the Patent Office since 1864, had graduated from the University of Vermont (1859), studied law, and served as capt., 13th Vt. On Dec. 9, 1874, USG nominated Thacher as commissioner of patents.

On Dec. 30, 1875, Azariah Moore, Shellsburg, Iowa, wrote to USG concerning Thacher's mishandling of a patent application. ALS, DNA, RG 48, Miscellaneous Div., Letters Received.

To Hamilton Fish

Long Branch, N. J.
July 15th /75

DEAR GOVERNOR;

Your letter of yesterday in relation to the exposure of the proceedings of the Cabinet meeting of the day before was answered by my letter of last evening. One thing more however I wish to say. I know without your assurance that it was not exposed through your department. Not thinking about the meeting being at the State Department—I had not seen the paper giving the account of it—I supposed the meeting had take place in the usual place of meeting. Hence my allusion to the possibility of eavesdrop[p]ing!

Very Truly Yours
U. S. GRANT

HON. HAMILTON FISH SEC. OF STATE

ALS, DLC-Hamilton Fish. See second letter to Hamilton Fish, July 14, 1875.

To James G. Blaine

———

Long Branch, N. J.
July 15th /75

DEAR SIR:

Some time last week I received Mrs. Blaines & your kind invitation for Mrs. Grant & myself to visit you and to renew our attempt to reach Mt. Desert.[1] Mrs. Grant & I are both desirous of going but do not see how we can do so well without a much longer absence from Long Branch than we feel inclined to indulge in under present circumstances. My daughter, you are aware, is with us but will return to England soon after she is able to travel.[2] Before leaving Washington Mrs. Grant promised Mrs. Jewell to visit her for a few days this Summer. I also promised Burnside a day or two.[3] Beside these engagements I have long had a desire to make one deliberate trip through the White Mountains, and have already written to Gov.r Stearns—who has kindly volunteered to make all arrangements—that Mrs. Grant & I, with either Fred. & his wife, or my two youngest sons, would be ready to start any day week after next. We proposed to make the two former visits while out on this excursion. All this will take something over two weeks. However I will let you know from some point in the White Mountains if we can go. But do not put either yourself or Mrs. Blaine to any inconvenience, nor put off any other engagement to meet this rather unlikely one. I fear Mrs. Grant will be anxious to return to her grand son before the programme already laid down is carried out.

With kind regards for Mrs. Blaine & yourself,

Your obt. svt.

U. S. GRANT

HON. J. G. BLAINE

ALS, DLC-James G. Blaine. USG did not visit Maine or the White Mountains in 1875.
    On Feb. 4, Levi P. Luckey had telegraphed to Speaker of the House James G. Blaine.
"Does invitation to dinner to-night include President and Mrs. Grant?" Telegram
received, DNA, RG 107, Telegrams Collected (Bound). On the same day, Blaine telegraphed to Luckey. "Of course the President & Mrs Grant at seven (7) o'clock" Telegram
received, *ibid.*

    1. In Aug., 1873, USG had visited the Blaines in Maine. See *PUSG*, 24, 195–96.
    2. On July 17, 1875, Lucinda Morton, Indianapolis, wrote to Julia Dent Grant. "Your
despatch announcing the birth of your grandson, and the favorable condition of Nellie gave
me much pleasure, and the news will I am sure be receved with gratification by all your
friends. Nellie was so sweet in her disposition, so kind to all, so agreeable in her manners,
that she was beloved by all who knew her, and all will rejoice to hear she has come well
through her first trial. . . ." ALS, InHi. See letter to William W. Smith, April 6, 1875.
    3. See letter to Oliver Hoyt, Aug. 27, 1875; Ben: Perley Poore, *The Life and Pub-
lic Services of Ambrose E. Burnside, Soldier—Citizen—Statesman* (Providence, R. I., 1882),
pp. 320–21.

To Columbus Delano

Long Branch, N. J.
July 16th 1875.

DEAR SIR:

    Prof. Marsh of Yale College has addressed to me his complaints
in printed form against the management of Indian Affairs, particularly at the Red Cloud Agency. His charges are so specific as to dates
and facts that they must either be true or susceptible of undoubted
refutation. After reading the pamphlet carefully I am convinced that
Agent Saville[1] is wholly incompetent and unfit for his position or
that Prof. Marsh is an incompetent observer, easily led without his
knowledge to work the designs of bad and unscrupulous men. The
pamphlet enclosed has insinuations against the Secretary of the Interior and pretty direct charges against the Commissioner of Indian
Affairs.[2] This however should not prevent the Board appointed to

investigate the affairs at the Red Cloud Agency from having all the statements made by Prof. Marsh in regard to mismanagement at that agency before them for verification or contradiction.

Very truly yours

U. S. GRANT

HON. C. DELANO SECTY. OF THE INTERIOR.

Copies, DLC–USG, II, 2; DLC–John Russell Young. See following letter.

 On July 1, 1875, Edward P. Smith, commissioner of Indian Affairs, wrote to Othniel C. Marsh, Yale Scientific School, New Haven, Conn. "At the request of the Honorable Secretary of the Interior the Board of Indian Commissioners have nominated as a committee to investigate affairs at Red Cloud Agency, Hon, A, H. Bullock of Worcester, Mass, Hon, Thos. C, Fletcher, of St Louis, Mo, and Hon. Geo W, Lane, of the Chamber of Commerce, New York City; and it is understood that these gentlemen have accepted the service to which they have been invited. In preparing instructions for their guidance, I have not been able to furnish them your complaints against the Red Cloud Agency administration, except in a general way, as detailed to me by yourself at several interviews: but I have informed them of the request of the Secretary that you will reduce these complaints to a written statement to be accompanied with such proofs and suggestions as to reliable sources of evidence as will aid in securing a thourough investigation. I have also informed them of the appointment and purpose of this Commission, and of my intention to renew the request heretofore made by the Hon. Secretary that you will now furnish the said written statement, making the charges as specific, and furnishing evidence as much in detail, as possible; or if you are not prepared to do this, that you will, in any way most agreeable to yourself, make known in a definite form your impressions and views respecting Indian Affairs, as resulting from your personal observation while in the Indian country. I make this request of you in the belief that you can have no other desire in this matter than that the interests and rights both of the Indians and of the Government may be protected; and I desire to renew the assurance heretofore given you, that it is the sincere wish and purpose of the Department to prevent frauds as far as possible, and to omit no effort to discover them when perpetrated, and in all respects to bring the Indian service to the highest possible standard of humanity and strict integrity." Copy, USG 3. On July 3, Marsh, New Haven, wrote to Smith. ". . . I have as yet received no communication from the gentlemen named, but I will at once proceed to prepare a detailed statement embodying the evidence on this subject now in my possession, a copy of which I will with pleasure lay before the committee so soon as they inform me that they have organized and are ready to act." *New York Times*, July 5, 1875. See letter to Wayne MacVeagh, July 22, 1875; William H. Armstrong, *A Friend to God's Poor: Edward Parmelee Smith* (Athens, Ga., 1993), pp. 342–44, 349–50, 355–60.

 On July 17, Saturday, USG, Long Branch, wrote to Clinton B. Fisk, chairman, Board of Indian Commissioners. "I will be pleased to see Commissioner Smith when ever he calls, either to-morrow or Monday." ALS (facsimile), Robert A. Siegel Auction Galleries, Inc., Sale 764A, Dec. 10, 1994, no. 130. On July 28 and 29, a correspondent reported from Long Branch. "Seven of the ten members of the Indian Commission met at the West End Hotel to-day to hold the customary quarterly conference. . . . Later in the afternoon they called upon the President at his cottage, and arranged with him for a formal interview to-morrow. . . . The subject of the Marsh charges did not enter into the conversation with the

President, nor otherwise than casually into the deliberations of the commission. . . . There seems to be no fixed programme for to-morrow's interview with the President. It is only certain that a few changes in Indian management will be recommended, and improbable that the charges against Secretary Delano will be talked about unless the President asks for an expression of opinion. In that case, several of the Commissioners, if they talk to the same purport that they have in conversation to-day, will not speak well of the Secretary. Prof. Marsh's charges are more likely to be discussed. Secretary Delano and Indian Commissioner E. P. Smith have not arrived, the latter being absent, after a stay here of several weeks. . . ." "The Indian Commissioners kept their appointment for a conference with the President to-day. . . . The President has unqualifiedly uttered his confidence in the ultimate success of the existing policy of Indian management. Referring to the accusations of corruption in the administration of Indian affairs he said decisively that the truth should be ascertained and given to the public. Other than this no reference was made to the attack upon Secretary Delano and his department. Gen Fisk stated for the board the measures taken and contemplated to enforce an honest fulfillment of Indian contracts, to insure an entire delivery of the supplies paid for, and to better the moral and temporal condition of the various tribes. The President promised all the help asked for, and was more outspoken than is his habit. He talked about the difficulties in the way of dealing with the wilder Indians, such as the Sioux, but did not suggest any radical change of management. . . ." *New York Times*, July 29, 30, 1875.

On June 18, Ezra A. Hayt, Indian commissioner, Patterson, N. Y., had telegraphed to USG. "The board of indian Commissions respectfully request you to order the appointment of army officers to act as inspectors of Indians suppies at Kansas City, Sioux City & Cheyenne   in no other way can we get an honest & competent inspection. Immediate action is desirable" Telegram received, DNA, RG 94, Letters Received, 3273 1875. Related papers are *ibid*. Capts. Jeremiah H. Gilman, Charles McClure, and Richard I. Eskridge received the assignments. On Jan. 20, 1877, Hayt, New York City, wrote to USG. "Over two years and a half ago, I was recommended by the constituted authorities of the Reformed Church in America to fill a vacant place in the Board of Indian Commissioners—That selection was confirmed by your subsequent appointment, and I became the representative in the Board of one of the oldest and most respectable denominations in the Country. In the several imperfect and incomplete acts of Congress creating the Board of Indian Commissioners, there seemed to be the purpose to organize a body of reputable men intended to exercise joint control with the Secretary of the Interior over the disbursement of the appropriations made by the Act of 1869; to supervise all expenditures of money appropriated for the benefit of Indians in the United States; to inspect all goods purchased for said Indians, in connection with the Commissioner of Indian Affairs, whose duty it is to consult said Board in making purchases of said goods (Act of 1870); to examine vouchers and accounts of Contractors and others for supplies, goods, transportation, buildings or machinery furnished (Act of 1871); to visit Indian Agencies and inspect vouchers, books and papers thereof; and in this connection any member of the Board was empowered to investigate all contracts expenditures and accounts in connection with the Indian service, and to have access to all books and papers relating thereto in any government office (Act of 1872). The plain intention of the various acts was to create an independent body to supervise the Indian service generally, neither subject to, nor superior to the Secretary of the Interior, but accountable to the President, and intended to aid him in carrying out the humane policy he had instituted for the civilization and christianization of the various Indian tribes. In accordance with the various acts of Congress defining the duties of the Board, of which I have given a synopsis, the Board at its meeting in January 1875, adopted the following by-law: (Article VII). 'The Purchasing Committee must superintend all purchases of goods required for the Indian department, and contracts for transportation, and must take all necessary precaution to ensure the government against any fraud or peculation, any overcharge for goods, or against any deception by reason of delivery of goods inferior to sample. It shall also be the duty of the Committee to have goods properly examined before shipment of the same.' As chairman of the ᵽPurchasing Committee for the last two years, it has been my especial duty, and has occupied nearly the whole time that I could devote to the work, to look after the purchases made, the inspection after purchase, and the final delivery of the goods at the various agencies. Early in the year 1875 the report of Professor Marsh on the bad quality of certain supplies received at the Red Cloud Agency fixed the attention of the Country upon the method of supplying the Indians, and although his statements were made without sufficient examination and without any attempt at verification, the public generally were prepared to accept them as true. The Purchasing Committee gave the matter serious attention, and as a result determined to leave no means untried thereafter to secure the best goods possible for the money and trace the same to their destination. To this end they employed a competent clerk to follow the goods with invoices and bills of lading, and to check off the cases and quantities of goods on arrival. The work was thoroughly done at the Red Cloud and sSpotted Tail Agencies, and to day the evidence is conclusive that the identical goods purchased for those agencies and subjected to this scrutiny were delivered at the agencies, and it is needless to add that the care thus exercised is the best method of relieving the Indian Bureau from charges similar to those that made Professor Marsh famous for the time. This year the purchases of flour having been made deliverable at the agencies in the Indian Territory without any provision for its inspection until after it had reached its destination, and with no competent inspection possible there, it became necessary for the Purchasing Committee to send a trustworthy clerk to the Territory to take samples out of each lot delivered, and send them by mail to this City where a competent inspector could pass on their quality. I had previously pointed out to the Commissioner of Indian affairs the difficulties that would follow from sending flour to the agencies before inspection, namely: that if bad flour was sent there, it would be impossible to have it removed; that Indian agents were not experts and could not tell whether flour was up to grade or not; and that many times they would take poor flour for fear they would not get any other. The Commissioner under date of Sept 29th 1876, expressly approved of the sending of a clerk of the Board to do the work I have indicated. After an accurate test of samples forwarded to me, the highest authority on the Corn exchange in this city threw out about one quarter of the flour delivered at these agencies, as from ten to twenty per cent below the grade of XX flour which the contractors had agreed to deliver. The Clerk of the Board was also instructed to examine all supplies and annuity goods received at the agencies, and in the pursuit of this work he was met with a refusal to allow the examination and verification of the quantity of annuity goods. I appealed to the Commissioner of Indian Affairs and he declined to give his permission for this examination and verification, unless the Clerk should wait until the month of March next, when blankets and other annuity goods would be delivered to the Indians. Passing over the unwisdom of delivering blankets after the winter had passed, there is no good reason why the goods should not have been compared with the invoices, and thus the ability to prove that they were either right or wrong be placed within the power of the Committee. There should be no real diversity of interest between the Board and the Bureau in this matter. Both are supposed to want only what is right. This refusal of the Commissioner seems to have been the beginning of a difficulty, that developed very rapidly by the presence of the Chief Clerk of the Bureau in the Territory, and now I come to a matter personal to myself. On the ninth day of January current, I received a telegram, copy of which is sent herewith (marked "A") to which I replied (copy marked "B"), which brought me Commissioner Stickney's letter copy of which is enclosed (marked "C"). Mr Stickney's letter was received by me on the morning of the 10th inst, and on the afternoon of the same day, I received Mr Galpin's letter, a copy of which is sent herein (marked "D"). On the 11th I consulted with another member of the Purchasing Committee, and on the 12th wrote a letter to the Secretary of the Interior copy of which is enclosed (marked "E"). On the same date, Jan'y 12th without waiting to hear what I had to say in reply the Secretary mailed to me the letter (marked "F") The haste with which this indignity was thrust upon me, and the want of courtesy and absence of fairness displayed, is simply amazing. I am satisfied that, in the ordinary routine of business between the head of the department and yourself, a matter of this kind could only be brought to your notice by the Secretary; and any statement made by him must have been very imperfect, if it could lead you to demand my resignation, so near the close of your term of office and that of the Board. Even though the statements in Mr Galpin's letter are true, in regard to what Mr Leeds is reported to have said, it is unjust to connect me with them without a particle of evidence showing my complicity; especially when I entertain no such sentiments and have never made any such statements. Of course if a Clerk of the Board should speak disrespectfully of the Secretary or Commissioner it would be a sufficient reason for his recall, but it is no reason for launching an indignity at me. Having made this statement, as being due to myself in my personal and official vindication, I respectfully invite your candid consideration to it. And acting on the supposition that you still remain desirous of my retiracy from the Board, notwithstanding the ex parte and injurious prejudgment, without a hearing, to which I have been subjected, I hereby respectfully tender my resignation as a member of the Board of Indian Commissioners, in conformity with your request transmitted to me by the Secretary of the Interior." LS, *ibid.*, RG 48, Appointment Div., Letters Received.

1. On Aug. 31, 1875, John J. Saville, agent, Red Cloud Agency, Neb., reported to Smith. "This agency, situated on White Earth River in Northwestern Nebraska, was established August, 1873, at which time I took charge of it. . . . On arrival at this agency two years ago, with few exceptions, the Indians were wild and vicious; they could not be made to understand the necessity of regular issues of food, but insisted on their own lawless way of giving every man as much as he wanted. Every effort to bring the issues to a regular quantity was met by headstrong and even threatening opposition by every individual, from Red Cloud to the meanest loafer. . . . I determined, at whatever cost, to count them. By authority of the Department, I withheld rations and the annuity goods until they submitted to be counted. This raised a bitter opposition that at one time threatened an open outbreak. . . . This enumeration has enabled me to distribute food with more accuracy; but yet many difficulties exist from the disposition of the Indians to oppose any change, however trivial, and in the difficulty of teaching them anything like business habits, from their want of knowledge of the diversities of time and consequent want of valuation of time. The attack upon the Interior Department and Indian Bureau, making this agency the objective point, has done much to embarrass the work. When carried on, as it has been, by councils and advice from tools of designing men to arouse the suspicions of the Indians and dissatisfy them with all that is done for them, it has been a demoralizing influence that has been of incalculable disadvantage to the Indians. . . . Civilization carries with it a destruction of the Indian's polity, and necessitates a changed condition that is distasteful to the Indian. He would, therefore, be more than human did he not resist it and vent his dissatisfaction in complaints against those who are forcing this change upon him. Therefore, those who take the complaints of the Indians as evidence of wrong done by those who deal with them show their ignorance of the condition of things at the agencies. . . ." *HED*, 44-1-1, part 5,

I, 752–53. Saville resigned following investigation by a special commission. On Dec. 9, USG nominated James S. Hastings as agent, Red Cloud Agency. See *ibid.*, 43-2-1, part 5, I, 559–60; 44-2-1, part 5, I, 437.

2. Smith resigned in the aftermath of investigation. See letter to Oliver Hoyt, Nov. 4, 1875.

To Othniel C. Marsh

———

Long Branch, N. J.

July 16th /75

PROF. O. C. MARSH;

DEAR SIR:

I have rec'd and read carefully your letter and accompanying pamphlet, dated July 10th, and am taking stepts to verify or refute the statements you make in regard to the bad management of the Red Cloud Agency. The charges and statements you make are sufficiently explicit either to be substantiated or refuted—to prove fraud and bad management, or incompetant observation.

Assuring you of my earnest desire for an honest administration in every department of the Government, and willingness to ferret out and punish fraud wherever found, I am:

Very Truly

your obt. svt.

U. S. GRANT

ALS, CtY. Othniel C. Marsh, renowned paleontologist, had taught at Yale since 1866. On July 10, 1875, Marsh, Yale College, wrote to USG. "In the two interviews I have had with you on Indian Affairs, I was impressed with your earnest desire to do justice to the Indians, and with your broad and philanthropic views on the whole Indian Question. This must be my excuse, as a private citizen, for coming again to you, to lay before you a statement of wrongs committed on the Sioux Indians, mainly under my own observation, during a recent visit to their country. My visit to this region was wholly in the interests of Science, with no intention or wish to investigate Indian affairs. The frauds I observed were brought to my notice by Red Cloud, who refused to allow my party to enter the 'Bad Lands,' until I had promised to submit his complaints to you in person. Since my interview with you upon this subject, I have been informed by the Commissioner of Indian Affairs of the appointment of a committee to investigate affairs at the Red Cloud Agency, and invited to lay a statement of the facts before them. This I am quite ready to do whenever the committee request it. I must decline, however, to repeat [give] my statements to that [to the Interior] Department alone, for the following reasons: 1st. I have no confidence whatever in the sincerity of the Secretary of the Interior or the Commissioner of Indian Affairs,

when they publicly announce their wish and determination to correct the present abuses
in Indian management, because I have reason to know that they have long been aware of
these abuses, and have made no sincere effort to reform them. 2d. In all my intercourse
with these two officials, their object has manifestly been to find out, not so much what the
frauds actually were, as the extent of my information concerning them, so as to prevent,
by every means in their power, all publicity or exposure of them. 3d. The evidence now in
my possession reflects unfavorably on both Secretary Delano and Commissioner Smith.
For these reasons, I have thought best to lay before you, to whom, in accordance with my
promise to Red Cloud, I made my first communication, the accompanying statement in detail, in full confidence that the evidence presented will meet with the consideration its importance demands. In the Statement which accompanies this letter, I have given the results
of my investigation into the affairs of Red Cloud Agency, the largest and most important
in the West. These results clearly indicate both mismanagement and fraud, especially in
the following particulars: 1st. The Agent, J. J. Saville, is wholly unfitted for his position,
and guilty of gross frauds upon the Indians in his charge. 2d. The number of Indians at this
Agency has been systematically overstated, for ~~the~~ purpose[s] ~~of defrauding the Govern-
ment~~ [which can only contemplate fraud]. 3d. The last issue of Annuity Goods, which I
witnessed, was a suspicious transaction, and, in part, at least, fraudulent. 4th. The beef cattle given to the Indians have been very inferior, owing to systematic frauds practiced by
the agent and beef contractors. 5th. The pork issued to the Indians during my visit was
not suitable for human food. 6th. The flour was very inferior, and the evidence of fraud in
this article is conclusive. 7th. The sugar and coffee issued were not good, although better
than the other supplies. 8th. The tobacco observed was rotten, and of little or no use to the
Indians. 9th. In consequence of fraud and mismanagement, the Indians suffered greatly
during the past winter for want of food and clothing. 10th. The contract for freight from
Cheyenne to Red Cloud Agency was fraudulent, as the true distance is 145 miles, while the
contractor was paid for 212 miles. I would especially call your attention to the evidence of
fraud in beef cattle, as presented in the accompanying statement. This subject I investigated with much care, as beef is the principal article of food of the Sioux Indians, and the
frauds I observed have caused great suffering among them, as well as great pecuniary loss
to the Government. The statement I have prepared is supported in all its essential parts
by the testimony of officers of the Army, who were with me on my expedition, or at the
Red Cloud Agency. Among these officers are several personally known to you, and all are
gentlemen of high character. Should any part of my statement be seriously questioned, I
trust you will allow these gentlemen ot be heard. If the commanding officers of all posts
near Indian Agencies, or other equally trustworthy and disinterested observers there,
could likewise testify, I think it would be found that I have but faintly indicated the corruption pervading Indian affairs. I have purposely confined myself in this statement to a
single agency, and mainly to the time of my visit, without reference to much other testimony, which has come to me incidentally in the prosecution of my inquiries, showing
frauds of equal magnitude at other points. This corruption, which is a constant source of
discontent and hostility among the Indians themselves, is, in my judgment, a natural result of the present [loose and] irresponsible system of furnishing the Indians with goods
and supplies, a system that tends directly to invite fraud. I do not believe that anything but
a radical change in this respect will prevent the continued demoralization of the Indian
Service. You alone have the will and the power to destroy that combination of bad men,
known as the Indian Ring, who are debasing this service, and thwarting the efforts of all
who endeavor to bring to a full consummation your noble policy of peace." O. C. Marsh, *A
Statement of Affairs at Red Cloud Agency*, . . . (n. p., n. d.), pp. 3–6; bracketed text was hand-
written and printed in a later version of this pamphlet. Marsh's statement of the same date

is also addressed to USG. "In November last, while on a geological expedition to explore the 'Bad Lands' south of the Black Hills, I was obliged to pass near Red Cloud Agency, and was detained there several days by the opposition of the Sioux Indians. In endeavoring to propitiate the Indians, and obtain their permission to proceed with my party, I held several councils with Red Cloud and his principal chiefs, saw the issue of Annuity goods, and provisions, and had other opportunities of seeing the actual state of affairs at this important Agency. I found the Indians in want of food and clothing, greatly dissatisfied with their agent, J. J. Saville, and strong in their belief that they were systematically defrauded of the goods and supplies sent them by the government. In one council, attended by nearly all the prominent chiefs, Red Cloud made specific charges of fraud against the agent and contractors, and urged me to make this known to the Great Father, and to carry to him samples of the rations the Indians were then receiving. Mainly to gain consent for my expedition to proceed, I made Red Cloud the promise he desired. Soon after, he gave me samples of flour, sugar, coffee, and tobacco, to show to you, assuring me that they were the rations he himself was using, and fair samples of those lately issued to his people. In consequence of the promise thus made to Red Cloud and his associates, their immediate opposition to my proposed explorations ceased. Other difficulties were successively overcome, the expedition at last reached its destination, and fully accomplished its purpose, notwithstanding great suffering from cold, and open hostility of the Indians around us. When about to return, we escaped a large war party of Indians in consequence of warning and assistance sent by Red Cloud. This act of kindness led me on my return to the Agency to make further investigations there, especially in the directions indicated by the chiefs, and I soon found reason to believe that their statements of mismanagement and fraud were essentially true. The information I received also from officers of the Army, and other trustworthy observers familiar with the subject, fully confirmed this, and proved, moreover, that affairs at this Agency had long been in the same condition. On my return to the East, my professional duties prevented me for some time from fulfilling the promise made to Red Cloud; but in April last, as you will remember, I gave you his message, showed you the sample of rations he had entrusted to me, and received from you the assurance of your wish to do full justice to the Indians, and correct any abuses in their management. I then regarded my mission at an end. As a matter of courtesy, I showed to the Commissioner of Indian Affairs the same samples, and told him of various things I saw at the Red Cloud Agency that indicated a bad state of affairs there; naturally supposing that such information, from a disinterested observer, would be kindly received, and existing wrongs be prevented in future. I regret to say that the information I ventured to offer to this official was far from acceptable; the inferior rations I exhibited were plausibly explained, and the damaging facts I had observed were considered of little consequence. Commissioner Smith's manner of receiving this information naturally deterred me from giving him many other facts of a similar nature then in my possession, and I have since deemed it best to withhold them. Subsequently, I met the Board of Indian Commissioners in New York, at their request, and gave them a more full account of the condition of things at Red Cloud and other Agencies that I had visited. . . . While the Sioux delegations were in Washington, in June last, I had the honor of meeting, personally, on his invitation, the Honorable Secretary of the Interior. He informed me that he had long taken a deep interest in the Indians, and had had great experience in the management of their affairs. He was especially interested in the efforts to Christainize and civilize these wards of the nation, and he earnestly entreated me to aid him in the enterprise. His appeal in behalf of this noble work—of which so much is said in the East, and so little seen in the West—moved me deeply; but having no time and little inclination for such professional philanthropy, I was obliged to decline. The state of affairs at Red Cloud Agency in November last, to which I directed his attention, he declined to discuss; but, in the most solemn manner, assured me that if I would give him all my information on this point, he would at once see that the abuses, if any existed, were officially removed. He manifested great sorrow that I had not brought Red Cloud's samples directly to him—a service which Red Cloud himself, who knew the Honorable Secretary, did not ask me to perform. In reply to the urgent request of the Honorable Secretary for the information in my possession about Indian affairs, I informed him, that whenever the Commission he intended to appoint, or any other Commission empowered to ascertain the whole truth, should be ready, I would cheerfully co-operate with it in every way in my power. . . . The results of my investigation into the affairs of Red Cloud Indian Agency are embodied in the following statements, arranged for convenience under distinct heads:—I. *The Indian Agent at Red Cloud's Agency.* In the first conversation I had with Red Cloud, when Gen. L. P. Bradley and Col. T. H. Stanton were present, he complained bitterly of his agent, J. J. Saville, who for the past two years has had charge of his Agency. Red Cloud's specified charges were, that his Agent was incompetent, weak and vacillating, having no influence over the Indians; and especially that he was in league with the contractors to defraud the Indians of the food and clothing sent them by the Government. I regret to say that all I saw myself at the Agency, and all I learned from trustworthy observers, and official records, has convinced me that these charges were well-founded. . . . That a chief of such note and ability as Red Cloud should be subjected to the caprices of such an agent, is in itself a gross indignity and ill-calculated to inspire him or his people with respect for the advantages of civilization. . . . The incompetence and true character of Agent Saville was well known to the Interior Department before my visit, as is shown by an official report made by United States Indian Inspector J. D. Bevier, Oct. 21, 1874. In this report, the Inspector exposed a fraudulent contract made privately by Agent Saville with hls father-in-law, A. R. Appleton, by which the Government would have been largely a loser. Inspector Bevier states, moreover, that while investigating the contract, Agent Saville made false representations to him, and Mr. Appleton endeavored to bribe him to silence. Other special Commissioners of the Interior Department had, likewise, reported unfavorably of this Agent and affairs at the Agency. And yet this man has for the past two years, with the full approval of the Department, had charge of the most important Agency in the West, where nearly half a million of dollars annually passes through his hands. In all his official relations Agent Saville has proved himself a weak man, and he should never have been placed in so responsible a position. If honest when appointed, as some good men believe, he fell an easy victim to the wiles of beef and freight-contractors of the Indian Ring, as many stronger men, agents and high officials, have done before him. II.—*Number of Indians at Agency Over-estimated.* There is good reason to believe that the number of Indians supplied with provisions at Red Cloud Agency has been largely over-estimated, resulting in extensive losses to the Government. . . . The number of Indians actually at Red Cloud Agency, when I was there in November last, could not have been more than 1,200 lodges, or 8,400 individuals. Judging from all the information I could obtain, I doubt if this number has been exceeded within the last two years. Some observers, best qualified to judge, placed the number lower, and among these was Jules Ecoffe, of Fort Laramie, whom I have known for several years. He was with me at the Agency, acted as my interpreter in one council, and is personally acquainted with nearly all the Indians there. The statement of the Agent, that, on October 1st, there were at the Agency over 15,000 Indians, no disinterested person, familiar with the facts, believes for a moment, especially as at that time the wilder Indians had not commenced to return to the Agency for the winter. III. *Issue of Annuity Goods.* I was present at the Red Cloud Agency at the annual issue of Annuity goods, November 12, 1874, and personally observed nearly all that were delivered. I saw the entire issue of blankets, and carefully examined the quality of those delivered. The number of bales of blankets I did not count as they were issued, but, soon after all were given out, my attention was called to the number of these by the chief Red Dog, who stood near me in the warehouse during the issue. He strongly asserted that the issue was fraudulent, and that the number of blankets issued was much less than the Indians were entitled to; and that the number issued to him for his own band was not more than half what he should have had. This earnest protest on the part of the chief, who is next in rank to Red Cloud, called my attention particularly to the amount issued; and on recalling the exact circumstances of the delivery, which I had witnessed a few minutes before, I felt reasonably certain that not more than twenty bales were issued, and that the number could not possibly have exceeded twenty-five bales. One of the persons whom I then saw assisting the agent in issuing the blankets was Louis Richard (or, as the name is usually pronounced and written at the Agency, Louis Reshaw), whom I knew personally, and subsequently employed as interpreter by the advice of General L. P. Bradley, who had previously employed him as guide, and spoke in high terms of his faithfulness and reliability. I subsequently met Louis Richard in Washington with J. S. Collins, Esq., of Fort Laramie, now secretary of the Special Sioux Commission, who had brought him on from the Red Cloud Agency as a trustworthy interpreter, and who spoke highly of his truthfulness. On conversing with Mr. Richard about the affairs of Red Cloud Agency, with which we were both conversant, I learned incidentally that he had carefully counted all the bales of blankets that were issued on November 12, 1874, when he assisted in the distribution which I witnessed. He assured me that the number of bales of blankets then issued was eighteen, each bale containing fifty pairs of blankets, . . . On subsequently examining the Property Returns of Agent Saville for the 4th quarter, 1874, at Red Cloud Agency, which he had rendered to the Indian Bureau, and were on file in the Interior Department, I was surprised to find that he had certified to the issue, on Nov. 12th, 1874, of no less than thirty-five bales of blankets, and had furnished a paper purporting to be a receipt of the Indian Chiefs for that number. In a recent communication from the Indian Bureau, I learn that the true number of bales shipped to Red Cloud Agency in 1874 was thirty-seven, or 1,850 pairs. Hence it would appear that the Indians at this Agency received less than one-half the number of blankets for which the the government paid. The blankets actually issued were bitterly complained of by the Indians, for two reasons—the first being their small sizes, which were not adapted to men as large as the Sioux braves, and were only fitted for women and children. The second and most serious objection, however, was the fact, that the brand U. S. I. D. on each blanket had been put on with some material which rotted or burned the cloth, and after a short wear this brand was replaced by holes, . . . IV.—*Frauds in Beef Cattle*. The frauds perpetrated in supplying the Red Cloud Agency with beef cattle have been so gigantic, and so long and systematically continued, that it is well worth while to show how they are accomplished, and who is responsible for the outrage. The contract for furnishing cattle to this and other Sioux Agencies for the last fiscal year was given to J. K. Foreman, of Omaha, and was signed by Indian Commissioner Smith, July 14th, 1874. . . . There is abundant evidence that this contract was not made in good faith. The contract was not filled by the party to whom it was given, but (like too many Indian contracts) was transferred for 'a valuable consideration' a few days after it was signed, to W. A. Paxton, of Omaha. As this assignment could not take place, by the terms of the contract, 'without the written consent of the Secretary of the Interior,' the full responsibility of this transfer rests with him. This contract was nominally in force at the time of my visit to Red Cloud Agency. The real beef contractor, however, whom I found supplying this Agency, was the well known Bosler, notorious for frauds in previous contracts, and for this reason excluded by the published regulations from any participation in future contracts. This second virtual transfer of the contract to him was well known to every one at the Agency, and in that region, and must have been equally well known to the Interior Department. . . . On the morning of November 14th, while I was at the Red Cloud Agency, Mr. Bosler, one of the contractors, brought to the Agency a herd of several hundred head of Texas cattle, the first that had been received for some weeks previous. This lot was accepted by the agent, and receipted for, but he only weighed a portion of the herd. These cattle, I saw and carefully examined. Major A. S. Burt of the 9th Infantry, who commanded the escort to my expedition, was with me at the time, and also examined them with care. They were the poorest lot of Texas cattle I have ever seen during all my experience in the West, where I have seen many hundreds of herds, at various points between this Agency and Southern Kansas, and have myself purchased many animals for the use of my expeditions. All the cattle in this herd were wretchedly gaunt and thin, and the majority of them were small, many being yearlings. A large number were of the kind known among cattle-men as 'scallawags,' and not a few were weak and decrepid. I noticed the character of these cattle particularly, because the beef issued at this Agency had been the subject of several conversations between Red Cloud, Gen. Bradley, and myself, and I was desirous of knowing with certainty whether the statements of the chief on this point were true. . . . In this region, the cattle should be in good condition at this season of the year, if ever, yet the cattle of this herd were so wretchedly poor that even the contractor, Mr. Bosler, deemed it necessary to apologize for them. In explanation of their condition, he informed me that he had been obliged to overdrive them, so as to reach the agency in time for the issue. I subsequently learned that this was a standing excuse, when persons not directly interested in Indian affairs witnessed a cattle delivery. . . . I was not prepared, however, for the evidence which I found in the Second Auditor's office of the Treasury Department, where the receipts are filed as vouchers for the payment to the contractor. I there ascertained that Agent Saville had given a receipt for this same herd of 701 head of diminutive cattle, in which he certified that their actual weight as weighed by him was 731,485 pounds, *which would make the average exceed* 1,043 *pounds per head*. More than this, I found that according to Agent Saville's receipts, all the cattle received during the same quarter of 1874 had reached nearly the same average, or more than 1,040 pounds each. . . . In other words, this large herd of cattle which no one could fairly estimate at a greater average weight per head than 750 pounds, and which both the agent and contractor apologized for as being much inferior to their regular issues, and which Agent Saville only claimed to have weighed 850 pounds, were charged to the Government by that official as weighing more than 1,043 pounds each, and the contractor actually received pay at that rate! . . . These various beef transactions took place under the contract assigned to W. A. Paxton, well known to be merely the agent of Bosler, who personally filled the contract. Although this contract had been violated in all its important features, and shameful frauds practiced in its fulfillment, Commissioner Smith did not call on the bondsmen of the contractor for satisfaction, as the law required him to do, but, on March 17th, 1875, privately made a new contract with the same W. A. Paxton (or in reality with Bosler), to supply beef for the same Red Cloud Agency at a much higher price ($3.00 per 100 pounds) than this contractor had originally bound himself to do. This contract was illegal, as it was given by the Commissioner without advertising for proposals. . . . V. *Pork issued at the Agency*. Major A. S. Burt and myself were at the issue of provisions, November 15, 1874, and, among other things, saw and examined the pork that was delivered. . . . The Indians received this pork ration with evident disgust. Most of them merely cut off the outer thin layer of fat, and threw the rest away on the spot. In one of the recent Councils in Washington, Red Cloud earnestly complained of the pork issued to him and his people, and said that he thought some of the children had died from eating it. After this particular issue, the Indians so strongly objected to the quality of this pork that the fact was reported by the Agent to the Department in Washington. The contract under which this wretched pork was furnished to the Indians was given to J. W. L. Slavens, of Kansas City—well known as a favorite contractor of the Interior Department—and was signed by Commissioner Smith, July 11, 1874. . . . VI. *Flour issued at the Agency.* My attention was called to the flour rations at this Agency by Red Cloud himself, and this was one of the samples he gave me to take to Washington. A few days afterward, I saw the issue of provisions at the Agency, and my attention was again attracted to the subject by seeing a sack of flour, which an Indian woman had just received and was carrying away, burst open, and part of its contents fall on the ground. This flour was dark in color, and adhesive to the touch, although it had not been wet, and inferior in quality. . . . I have recently received a portion of the original sample of the flour on which the contract was based for the last fiscal year, 1874–75. This is a totally different article in appearance from the flour I saw issued to the Indians at the Agency, and in use in the lodges, and no one could mistake the one for the other. This sample of flour is the only sample, of all the supplies purchased last year, that the Department retained, by which to compare the supplies actually delivered to the Indians, and thus prevent fraud. The reason why this natural precaution against frauds has not been taken, remains for the Department of the Interior to explain. . . . The responsibility for all this mismanagement and fraud should rest with Secretary Delano and Commissioner Smith, who have long known of the abuses at Red Cloud Agency. No less than five special Commissioners, or other officials, appointed and paid by the Department of the Interior, had personally investigated this agency before my visit, and given that Department information indicating the bad state of affairs there. A portion of the responsibility for the inferior goods and supplies purchased last year should perhaps attach to Messrs. F. H. Smith, N. J. Turney and J. D. Lang, of the Board of Indian Commissioners. These gentlemen assisted in making the purchases, retained no samples by which the character of their purchases could be subsequently tested, and published no report of their action, as previous Purchasing Committees of the Board had done. In conclusion, I have only to say, that having been, while engaged in my professional duties, incidentally made the bearer of Red Cloud's message to you, and having endeavored, when the justice of his complaints was questioned by those responsible for the management of the Indian Affairs, to ascertain the truth, I now leave the whole subject in your hands, in perfect confidence that the facts I have presented will lead to good results." *Ibid.*, pp. 7–38. On July 20, Marsh, New York City, testified on these subjects. *Report of the Special Commission Appointed to Investigate the Affairs of the Red Cloud Indian Agency, July, 1875* (Washington, 1875), pp. 21–57. On Aug. 12, 13, 23, and 24, John J. Saville, agent, Red Cloud Agency, Neb., rebutted Marsh's charges. *Ibid.*, pp. 380–453. On Aug. 12, Nelson J. Turney, Circleville, Ohio, wrote to USG. "Failing health and a pressure of private business compells me to tender my Resignation as a member of the Indian Commission—. . ." ALS, DNA, RG 48, Appointment Div., Letters Received. See previous letter; *New York Times*, May 24, 1875.

On Sept. 9, Marsh, Washington, D. C., testified. ". . . My statement was finished July 10, and it was my intention to have taken it to the President on that day, but having ascertained that he was absent at Cape May, I awaited his return until the 13th, and then started to present it in person, but uncertain whether he had really returned, I mailed it to him from New York, so as to reach Long Branch that afternoon. Subsequently, but the same day, I gave copies of the pamphlet at the same time to the only two New York papers that had asked for it, namely, the Tribune and Evening Post; but no part of the document was published by either of these papers until next day. Having ascertained definitely on the 14th that the President had returned to Long Branch, I went there and called on him the same evening, to explain to him my statement more fully, and to state why I had not brought it in person. I would say here that in none of the three interviews which I have had with the President on Indian affairs has the Secretary of the Interior been mentioned.

Hence, the statement that the President told me to go to Secretary Delano with my complaints is totally false. . . . I went first of all to the Interior Department on the 23d of April, and made complaint to the Commissioner of Indian Affairs, whom I then regarded, and still regard, as the proper person to receive such information. How unwelcome the facts I presented were, and how uncivilly received, I have already stated before the commission. My promise to Red Cloud to carry his message to the Great Father, I fulfilled the next day; and my reception by the President was in marked contrast to that given me at the Department, . . . Is it strange that under the circumstances I should doubt the sincerity of Secretary Delano and Commissioner Smith, when they publicly announce, as is done in the Commissioner's letter to me, 'That it is the sincere wish and purpose of the Department to prevent frauds as far as possible, and to omit no effort to discover them when perpetrated?' I think the result fully justifies me in so doing. . . ." *Report of the Special Commission*, pp. 58–61. On Sept. 13 and 14, Marsh testified at greater length. *Ibid.*, pp. 62–113. On Sept. 15 and 16, Edward P. Smith, commissioner of Indian Affairs, rebutted Marsh's charges. *Ibid.*, pp. 657–727. On Sept. 17, Secretary of the Interior Columbus Delano testified similarly. *Ibid.*, pp. 753–59. See letter to George W. Atherton, Oct. 16, 1875; Charles Schuchert and Clara Mae LeVene, *O. C. Marsh: Pioneer in Paleontology* (New Haven, 1940), pp. 139–66.

To Edwards Pierrepont

Long Branch, N. J.
July 17th 1875.

DEAR JUDGE:

I forward you further papers in the matter of the District Attorney for the Dist. of Columbia. You may withdraw for the present the request for the resignation of Judge Fisher. I do not feel so well satisfied as I did that a change will be necessary, and even if such a change should be necessary in the end I do not wish to contribute to the triumph of the enemies that are no assailing the Judge—the Sun, the Tribune &c

Very truly yours
U. S. GRANT

HON. EDWARDS PIERREPONT, ATTY. GENL.

Copies, DLC-USG, II, 2; DLC-John Russell Young. On July 24, 1875, Attorney Gen. Edwards Pierrepont wrote to USG. "I enclose the resignation of Judge Fisher done in a frank and manly way like a true gentleman and honest man as he is. I do not doubt the necessity; the office thro' his wild son, was in such repute that nothing but a complete change could possibly restore the necessary confidence—I am sure that he has taken the right course and I wish to say that in all the numerous complaints not one has ever touched his integrity—I made his acquaintance in the Surratt trial where I saw his character tested. I found him brave where others cowered and my estimate of him as a gentleman, and as a judge and as a man of uprightness and honor is very high. It is impossible for the father in official place not to be injured by a wayward son so closely connected with his office and in the hope of reforming him you and I can see why the Judge retained him, but the public *will not so see it*. I sorely regret, while I firmly believe in the necessity of the change made. Judge Fisher, as you know, has the manners the bearing and the education which will fit him for a foreign place, which he tells me that he desires, and which I sincerely hope may be opened to him . . . P. S. Judge Fisher tells me that after conference with Mrs Fisher he would much prefer a Judicial place and asks that of Judge Durell in La—I find that the court here begins Sept 20th   I therefore suggest that Gov. Wells commission take efft on that day—I will so send it unless I hear to the contrary from you—" ALS, USG 3. On July 20 and 23, George P. Fisher, Washington, D. C., had written to USG. ". . . I place my resignation upon the true ground, that complaints have been made against me, that certain criminal cases sent from some of the Departments for prosecution have not been conducted to their satisfaction; although my own conscience and the judges of the Supreme and Police Courts of the District have stamped the seal of their approval, upon the record of all my official acts. Had I anticipated, when the office was so kindly and gracefully tendered me, by Your Excellency, that dissatisfaction, with my discharge of its onerous duties, was likely to arise, on the part of any person, whose good opinion was worth the prizing, I should never have accepted; and now, for a similar reason, and because, I fear that the complaints, to which I have alluded may possibly in somewise embarrass you, if I should not step forward and relieve the trouble by my resignation, I have, thus, cheerfully tendered it. In so doing I beg to assure you, that so long as my life and memory last, I shall not cease to appreciate, the inestimable services which you have rendered your country and mine, in the cabinet as well as in the field or abate, in the slightest measure my gratitude for the great personal kindness to myself which you have ever manifested." ALS, DNA, RG 60, Letters Received, D. C. "*Confidential* . . . I have placed my letter of resignation, in the hands of my good friend Judge Pierrepont to be forwarded to you. It is made to take at a future day and I have left a blank, which I desire you to fill with the day that shall suit your own wish in that behalf. I would prefer to turn over the office to my successor (who I presume will be Governor Wells) on the first day of the next quarter since I think that would be better in respect to the accounts of the office which are rendered quarterly and indeed in all respects: yet I shall not be disposed to object to any day with which you may fill the blank. It will afford me the greatest pleasure to lend any aid I can render to Governor Wells when he shall be inaugurated both because it is right and because he is your friend. I believe he has never practised much, if any, before the courts of this district; and therefore, however gifted and well versed, in the law generally, he will, at first, probably, experience some difficulty, in consequence of the peculiar system of laws, by which this district is governed. I was enabled to avoid this trouble by reason of my seven years experience upon the Bench. There will be no Criminal Court or Grand Jury in session here until the 20th day of September and it will require some six or eight days after that for the Grand Jury to finish the business which I have already in hand for it. And now, my dear General, may I not venture a word for myself? I am now approaching the completion of my eight and fiftieth year. I have worked hard all my life endeavoring always to perform every duty in good faith relying only on the strength of my own right arm and the promise of that Good Being who instructed me, in early life to 'seek first the Kingdom of God and his righteousness and that all else needful should be added,' until kind friends, like yourself, took me warmly by the hand and led me on to higher hopes and aspirations. Nearly all my life, since my early manhood, has been spent in the public service and still I

have very little of this worlds goods. I have filled many official positions, without complaint or accusation even from my political opponents; and now for the first time in my
public career I am smitten in the house of my friends wrongfully, I know, but as they,
doubtless, believe, for good cause. Still I have an unshaken confidence, in Him, who 'is too
wise to err and too good to be unkind' and a firm reliance on your stern sense of justice
and high generosity for my final triumphant vindication; and therefore, I shall cherish the
hope, that now, that the weight of years is coming on me and my, once, vigorous constitution has been impaired, by long and unremitting public labors, you will, by bestowing on
me some foreign appointment or some judicial position at home, afford me the opportunity, to retire from my present position to one less laborious; so that, while I may, under
Heaven's blessing regain my health, I may at the same time wipe off from my escutcheon
the unseemly blurs flung against it by the self-styled 'independent press'—your enemy
and mine and of all good and true men   Should you be inclined as, I am quite sure, you are
to comply with the suggestion of such an appointment, which I made to you last week at
Long Branch may I ask that you will signify the same to myself or to Judge Pierrepont, at
as early a day as may be convenient?" ALS, USG 3. See letter to Edwards Pierrepont,
July 8, 1875; Hamilton Fish diary, July 20, 21, 1875; *New York Tribune*, July 16, 17, 1875.

On Oct. 21, James R. Lofland, Milford, Del., wrote to USG. "I take great pleasure in
according my testimony to the honesty, uprightness and integrity of Hon Geo. P. Fisher
late U. S. District Attorney. I have known Mr Fisher long and intimately—in fact I esteem
it an honor to include him among my most intimate and valued friends. In all my intimacy
and acquaintance, I have never known an act which would cast the least suspicion of a
doubt upon his honor as a man or a gentleman. I know him so well that I would risk my
reputation or life upon his integrity and uprightness. He is worthy of all trust and
confidence, and his friends and the Republican party in this State are unshaken in their
faith in him. They would rejoice at some mark of your favor, which would lift him out of
the abuse and vituperation which has been so wantonly and cruelly heaped upon him by an
unbridled and licentious press. They think that after a man has given his best years to the
party and the public, he ought not to be hounded down by every disappointed or malicious
Scribbler whose chief business seems to be, to defame and slander better men. Any recognition you may bestow on Mr Fisher, will be most gratifying, to his many friends in this
State and to the Republican Party, and to none more than myself so well do I know him
and his whole life." ALS, DNA, RG 60, Letters from the President.

On May 20, 1876, Fisher, Milford, wrote to USG. "Now that the clamor and excitement raised against my poor, unfortunate boy, by the miserable conspirators, who, for base
purposes, have endeavored to fasten the crimes of others upon him, have subsided, I hope
you will not suffer his misfortune to be, any longer, an obstacle in the way of your carrying out your wishes, respecting my self, expressed to Judge Pierrepont, last summer, and
by him repeated to me. A letter, received from Mr Luckey, last winter, conveyed an intimation that, although you still entertained for me, the same kindly feeling as you did, when
you appointed and reappointed me, to the office of U. S. Attorney, yet you were restrained
from sending me before the Senate, by the apprehension that I might be rejected by that
body. I have never entertained any apprehension of that; and I would be willing to risk
my confirmation upon the votes of our democratic Senators from this state, who have
known me well, for more than a quarter of a century. If you could only know the bitter anguish, I have suffered, from the reflection, which my invited resignation and the malignant slanders of a diabolical press cast upon me; and could understand how I was made
the innocent victim of a foul conspiracy, embracing in its circle some, in whom I had placed
implicit confidence, I am very sure, you would not longer delay my vindication from the

wrongs, I have suffered, without a knowledge, until recently, of the real authors of them." ALS, *ibid.*, Records Relating to Appointments. On June 22, USG wrote a note. "Apt. Geo. P. Fisher Dist. Atty. for Delaware vice Higgins to be removed." AN, OHi.

On June 26, John D. Rodney, Georgetown, Del., wrote to USG. "In the announcment made to the public of the Appointment of Judge Fisher to supersede A M Higgins Esq as District Attorney the Republicans of this State are taken very much by surprise and generally express great regret. It was hoped by the party that all officers of the Government now in Office would be permitted to remain at present until after the Campaign was over. It is a fact that the Rep party in this State is divided and has been so but under the nomination of Hays & Wheeler we can all go to work, but if it is to be uncertain whether removals are to be made it will cause us much trouble and Certainly revive old dissentions and more especially in this case. In my opinion the carrying out of this removal will work injuriously to the party in this state and in the Country: I have never believed that Mr Fisher was privy to the malpractices of those engaged in the Offices under him in Washington but many do and the Country at large more or less hold him accountable for them and to place him in the position of District Attorney will work serious injury to the party. I was in Phil when I saw first the fact and find so far as any expression was made it was strongly condemnatory of the appointment. I feel that Mr Higgins ought not to be removed unless there was some charge alledged against him And if such charges are made then I would not be willing to see Judge Fisher appointed. I was not favourable to the Appointment of Mr Higgins at first, but now I do most sincerely protest against his removal—" ALS, DNA, RG 60, Letters Received, Del. Related papers are *ibid.* On June 28, Monday, John S. Prettyman, collector of Internal Revenue, Del., Milford, wrote to USG. "I was at Washington on Saturday last to see you in relation to the recent nomination of Hon. Geo. P. Fisher to be District Attorney for Delaware; but failing to see you I send this on the subject by the hands of my Son Harry H. Prettyman who can give you any other information that you may desire in relation to Delaware politics. The nomination of Mr. Fisher is not agreeable news to your friends in this State, and while they know that your motive in appointing him was a good one, they will be highly gratified if you can see your way clear to withdraw it. They do not desire to oppose the confirmation because it has the appearance of putting them in opposition to you. They have stood firmly by you in all your administration and intend to do so to the end, confident that your motives are always right though like all that are human, you may be liable to make mistakes; and especially so from over confidence in the representations of those whom you believe to be your friends. If you can do this you will highly gratify all your real friends in this State. Pardon the liberty I have taken . . ." LS, *ibid.*, Records Relating to Appointments. On the same day, Howard M. Jenkins, editor, *Wilmington Daily Commercial and Delaware Weekly Tribune*, wrote to USG. "PERSONAL, . . . Having visited Washington for the purpose of seeing you in relation to the U. S. Attorneyship for Delaware, on Saturday, and found you absent, I beg to present, in this note, the suggestions which I desired to offer personally. The nomination of Fisher causes sincere regret, here, amongst the Republicans of the State, and not less with those who have always been your warm personal friends than those of other classes. If we were to concede his fitness, and to assume that nothing that occurred in and about his Washington office, while U. S. Attorney for the District of Columbia, was chargeable to him, it yet is true that his appointment would do great damage to the Republican party of Delaware, and would be a heavy price to pay for his personal advantage and elevation   The reason for this is that Mr. Fisher has long stood charged here with undue interference in the U. S. appointments, while he was a resident of Washington and not entitled to dispose of places in this State. The ill-feeling that grew out of this is widespread, deep-seated, and sensitive, and when the impression was given out, in addition to this, that gross scandals had attached to his official service as Attorney, forcing him out of his place, the public opinion of this State settled down against him, and his selection, now, for any place of confidence and trust in this State will demoralize the party here to the most distressing extent. There are additional reasons, too, why, just at this moment, Mr. Fisher could not represent the Government, with fitness. He was the special friend and patron of Dr. W. D. Nolen, recently Collector of Customs, whom the Government has been obliged—after removing him—to prosecute for withholding over $5000. of duties, collected in the autumn of 1872, and never paid over. It is declared here that Mr. Fisher was a party to this with-holding—that he advised Dr. Nolen to it. Certainly, he could not represent the United States in the prosecution, (which is to be tried in October.) Further, I regret that any change should be made in the Attorneyship. Mr. Higgins, whom you appointed in 1869, is an excellent officer, . . ." ALS, *ibid.* On July 7, Samuel M. Harrington, "Del. Member of the National Republican Executive Committee," Wilmington, wrote to USG. "Judge Fisher having requested that his nomination as Attorney of the United States for the District of Delaware be withdrawn, I hereby recommend the appointment of James H. Hoffecker Jr for that position." ALS, *ibid.* On July 8, USG withdrew Fisher's nomination. See Endorsement, July 20, 1876.

On April 25, Anthony Higgins, U.S. attorney, Wilmington, had written to USG. "I would respectfully recommend Hon: Lewis Thompson of the City of Wilmington as Collector of Customs for the District of Delaware in the vacancy about to occur in that office—Mr Thompson is a man of integrity & capacity of the highest standing in this State. He was one of the organizers of the Republican Party in the State, has several times represented his County in the Legislature, & has always been an advanced and Sterling Republican. Mr Thompson's appointment would give general satisfaction here and is one in every way proper to be made" ALS, DNA, RG 56, Collector of Customs Applications. Related papers are *ibid.* On April 26, USG nominated Lewis Thompson as collector of customs, Del., to replace William D. Nolen. On Dec. 11, USG pardoned Nolen, convicted of embezzlement and sentenced to six months in prison and "a fine of $4997.65 and costs," upon solicitation "by many of the most respectable citizens of Delaware, who represent that he is of advanced age (63 years,) and had always, before the said charge of embezzlement, borne a good character in the said State, . . ." Copy, *ibid.*, RG 59, General Records.

On June 25, 1875, USG had suspended Prettyman as collector of Internal Revenue, Del. On July 2, Secretary of the Treasury Benjamin H. Bristow wrote to USG, Long Branch. "Your telegram received   The Commissioner of Internal Revenue has taken steps to inquire as to the propriety of the changes in Delaware." Copy, *ibid.*, RG 56, Letters Sent to the President. On July 7, Bristow wrote to USG. "Referring to your dispatch directing the suspension of your order for the removal of Mr. J. S. Prettyman, Collector of Internal Revenue for the State of Delaware, and the appointment of Mr. James R. Lofland, I have the honor to hand you herewith a letter from the Commissioner of Internal Revenue in reply to my inquiry as to the propriety of making the change. I concur in the opinion expressed by the Commissioner that a change is not desirable." LS (press), DLC-Benjamin H. Bristow. On July 1, 1876, Harrington wrote to USG. "The undersigned respectfully requests the removal of John S. Prettyman Collector of Internal Revenue for the District of Delaware and the appointment of James R. Lofland of Milford Delaware in his stead. . . ." ALS, DNA, RG 56, General Records. Prettyman continued as collector of Internal Revenue.

Endorsement

————

Refered to the Sec. of the Int. for his suggestion & advice. I have serious doubts whether the removal of Mr. Clarke was not unjust to him, and have had such doubts before the receipt of this letter.

U. S. GRANT

JULY 22D /75

AES, DNA, RG 48, Appointment Div., Letters Received. Written on a letter of June, 1875, from Rufus L. B. Clarke, Washington, D. C., to USG concerning his suspension as an examiner-in-chief in the Patent Office with the concurrence of John M. Thacher, commissioner of patents. ". . . Mr. Secretary Delano has assured me that no conversation was had between himself & your Excellency subsequent to my interviews. Undoubtedly the matter escaped your mind, or opportunity did not present. . . . As I understood from your Excellency, the final Suspension was had upon an issue made by the Commissioner 'that *he or I must leave the Office*'! Without stopping to consider by what right or authority he makes & forces such an issue upon *me*,—Allow me to suggest that a proper consideration of the qualifications, situation & past services of the parties might well have resulted in a different determination. The qualifications should have been left to the Official Conduct & acts of the two—fully recorded in the Books of the Office; And to the Opinions & judgment of those most interested & Conversant with the business of the Office—*inside* & *out*—including ALL the Ex-Commissioners. As to Situation—*He is a young Bachillor*! I have a family—four of whom are in their studies. To you, who have so long known Washington, it is unnecessary I should say more. You know the usual result of a sudden cutting off of supplies. I leave it then to your understanding, & save myself the humility of dwelling upon it. . . . When your Excellency considers all the facts & peculiar circumstances of this case—the secret & treacherous & false conduct of my accusers; the spontaneous protest & testimony of the whole Bar & others—the considerate action of the Senate—the strong remonstrace & earnest appeal of my friends, embracing the entire Delegation of Iowa, & at least two Members of your Cabinet, & other prominent & leading men in the Republican Party—Must you not come to the conclusion that one of the most graceful & politic acts of your popular administration would be to do me the prompt & simple justice of countermanding the Order of Suspension, & thus re-instating me in my position. There is nothing in the situation of things in the Office to prevent this. If there is a Will, there is a Way. Or should it be deemed advisable, on account of any embarrassment; not to make this re-instatemt, Might not your Excellency even more fully vindicate me, & wipe out the disgrace which my enemies have caused me, by an appointmt to a position of a still higher grade—an appointmnt which would be hailed—inside the Office & outside—as 'poetic Justice'—& one to which I am entitled by right of Seniority in regular promotion, over the present Commissioner & his Assistant!" ALS, *ibid.* On April 28 and May 12, Clarke had written to USG on the same subject. ALS, *ibid.* Clarke endorsed the second letter. "President Grant will not consider me wanting in respect in not waiting longer a summons to his presence after sending in my card. I am obliged by another appointmt to leave. Senator Allison told me last Eveng that he should see you this Morning & I drew this up to hand to him to be presented to your Excellency   I missed of seeing him, & now respectfully request you will read it over your cigar at leisure. Pardon my great earnestness & persisting. To me it is a matter of honor & justice & 'I shall fight it out on this line if it takes all summer'" AES, *ibid.*

On March 22, Grace Greenwood (Sara Jane Clarke Lippincott), New York City, had written to USG. "I venture to appeal directly to you against the summary decapitation of my brother—Mr. Clarke, Examiner in Chief of the Patent Office. It was brought about secretly and by ways and means which you are too brave and honorable to have approved of—had you understood al[l.] I am the more troubled, about this matter from fearing that ill-will against me had something to do with it[.] I have heard that Ex-Commissioner Leggett wrongly ascribes to me certain articles against him, which appeared in a Washington journal. I never write anything about anybody to which I dare not set my name. This false impression may have caused Mr. Leggett's unfriendliness to me. Soon after his appointment, I had the honor of bearing a note from you, to him—requesting him, if consistent, to give a clerical position to a friend of mine—a lady. This he positively promised to do,—he not only failed to keep his word—but two years later, denied to my face having made such a promise. I do not think that a *gentleman* ever gave me the lie before—still, *because* of this personal grievance, I carefully abstained from all criticism of Mr. Leggett, in my 'Times' articles. I trust you will do justly by my brother, who has ever been loyal to you. God knows he is an honest man—inflexibly, watchfully honest in his judicial position—and 'that's what's the matter.'" ALS, DLC-USG, IB. On March 29, U.S. Senator William B. Allison of Iowa, New York City, telegraphed to USG. "I hope you will not remove Clark Examiner of Patents until I can see you in about three 3 weeks, I can give good reasons I think why it should not be done," Telegram received, *ibid.* On March 31, George W. Childs, Philadelphia, wrote to USG. "I am asked by some friends of Judge Clarke, who are also very dear friends of mine, to write in behalf of Judge Clarke's retention in the office of Examiner in the Patent office. I know many who are well calculated to form a just and correct opinion, and from their judgment I feel warranted in asking his continuance in the office he has filled so creditably." ALS, DNA, RG 48, Appointment Div., Letters Received. On April 28, U.S. Representative George W. McCrary of Iowa, Keokuk, wrote to USG. "I wish most earnestly to protest against the removal of R. L. B. Clarke Esqr from the position of Examiner in Chief in the Patent Office. I know him to be a competent and honest officer. He has ability as a lawyer and integrity as well as great *firmness.* His position being *judicial* he must often decide against, and may have offended, one or two leading patent attorneys, but this fact, if true, should I think induce the administration to sustain him. Col Clarke practiced law many years in this district and I know him well." ALS, *ibid.* Related papers are *ibid.*

On [*Aug.*] 18, Marcus S. Hopkins, chairman, Patent Office Board of Appeals, telegraphed to USG, Long Branch. "There is a vacancy Caused by the Death of Judge Nolaen. of the Patent office Board of appeals. There is a scramble for it by some who are not legally qualified but are supported by Political influence in the absence of the secy and commissioner and in view of the important judicial character of the Office & of my own interest in the appointment to be made I venture to invitite your attention to the statute which requires that the examiners in Chief shall be persons of competent Legal knowledge and scientific ability Permit me to urge that none but a Lawyer and one experienced in patent matters be appointed" Telegram received, *ibid.* On Aug. 19, John Dane, Jr., Washington, D. C., telegraphed to USG. "J. D. Stockbridge Esq who is named as candidate for one of the Examiners in Chief is a †Lawyer of ability member of the bar for three years principal examiner & now Judge of Interferrences in patent office his appointment will avail much for th public interests" Telegram received, *ibid.* On Sept. 8, Orville E. Babcock wrote to Secretary of the Interior Columbus Delano. "The President return by todays mail the Commission for Virgil D Stockbridge of Me. to be Examiner in chief in the Patent Office—he will be pleased to have R. L. B. Clark—late Examiner—appt to the vacancy created by the promotion of Mr. Stockbridge." Copy, DLC-USG, II, 3. On Dec. 8, USG nominated Virgil D. Stockbridge to replace George A. Nolen as one of three examiners-in-chief in the Patent Office.

On May 28, U.S. Senator William Sharon of Nev., San Francisco, had written to USG. "Mr James Newlands, now principal Examiner of the Patent Office, is an applicant for the position of Examiner in Chief of that office. He is a gentleman of liberal Education, fine ability and large experience in the business of the Patent Office. His appointment would be received by his Associates with entire satisfaction and would be confer a personal favor on me." LS, DNA, RG 48, Appointment Div., Letters Received. On the same day, Sharon also wrote to USG recommending James Newlands "to any vacancy which may occur in the Appeal Board" in the Patent Office. LS, *ibid.* On Sept. 4, U.S. Senator Aaron H. Cragin of N. H., Lebanon, wrote to USG recommending Newlands. ALS, *ibid.* No appointment followed.

On Aug. 19, Samuel F. Miller, U.S. Supreme Court, had written to USG. "The death of Mr Nolan one of the board of appeal in the Patent office creates a vacancy for which I take the liberty of recommending Mr. A. G. Wilkinson. The great number of litigated patent cases which come before the Judges of the Supreme Court authorizes me to say that the duties of that place are delicate and important and require both integrity and a high degree of scientific attainmts   Mr. Wilkinson in the latter respect has no superior in the department, and his honesty is vouched by all who know him. . . ." ALS, *ibid.* On the same day, U.S. Representative Henry H. Starkweather of Conn., Norwich, wrote to USG recommending Ahab G. Wilkinson. ALS, *ibid.* On Aug. 24, Wilkinson, U.S. Patent Office, wrote to USG. "I would most respectfully beg leave to file my application for the position of Examiner-in-Chief of the Patent Office to fill the vacancy caused by the recent death of Mr G. A. Nolen, and to file with it a letter kindly offered me by Judge Miller of the Supreme Court   I have reason to suppose that Secretary Jewell will personally confer with you upon the matter and that Mr Starkweather in whose Congressional District I belong has already written   In addition to my fitness for the placed as vouched for in my letters alluded to above, may I be allowed to add that I have served for ten years as an Examiner in this Office and for the last six of them as Principal Examiner (the grade next below the one I now seek) while my presumed competitors for the position have served but a part of this time having been more recently appointed Principal Examiners." ALS, *ibid.* On Aug. 25, Wilkinson again wrote to USG drawing attention to additional recommendations. ". . . I am the more anxious that your Excellency should see the letters, inasmuch, as my course has been for ten years as an Examiner, such, as not to conciliate the large body of Washington Attorneys, who will make such representation, as to lead the Commissioner of Patents to hesitate to make my nomination." LS, *ibid.* Related papers are *ibid.* No appointment followed.

On Aug. 19, William Read, Washington, D. C., had written to USG, Bristol, R. I. "Mr Nolen, one of the examiners-in chief of the U. S. Patent office died yesterday, leaving a vacancy in that body to be filled by you—In 1853. I was appointed an examiner in the U. S. Patent office, and for years had charge of the grant of patents in different classes of invention. During the past year, I have been soliciting patents for the firm of Chipman, Hosmer & Co of this city, arguing their cases before the examiners, examiners-in chief, and Commissioner of Patents, and from my varied experience both in and out of the office, I believe that I am fully capable of fill- the position of examiner-in chief in the patent office—. . ." ALS, *ibid.* No appointment followed.

On Sept. 26, U.S. Senator Oliver P. Morton of Ind., Indianapolis, wrote to USG. "I am informed that the friends of James M. Blanchard, Esq formerly of Indiana, will present his name for the vacancy on the Board of Examiners at the Patent Office. He is a practical mechanic, intelligent an his integrity is unquestioned—He has had fourteen years experience as an Examiner in the office or as a Patent Solicitor—He will reflect credit upon the position and I earnestly hope you may be able to give him an appointment—" LS, *ibid.* No appointment followed.

On Nov. 1, Allison, Dubuque, telegraphed to USG. "I would like Very Much to have Judge Woodward Made an examiner in chief in the patent office   I am told there is a vacancy" Telegram received (at 8:15 P.M.), *ibid.* On Nov. 10, Wilkinson wrote to USG. "In the matter of the appointment of Examiner in Chief of the Patent Office, may I ask of your Excellency, a single favor. So far, the representations in favor of my Competitor, (Mr Woodward), have been entirely 'ex parte.' I would most respectfully beg you before deciding adversely upon my case, to get from the Patent Office, the record of Mr Woodward for the past year, to see whether he was, or was not aiding in the removal of Judge Clarke, whom you re-instated; and whether he was not nominated for the Appointment for which I was urged by Messrs Jewell, Buckingham, Hawley and Starkweather of Connecticut, upon the sole grounds of his availability to defeat Judge Clarke; also, whether after an experience of some months as Examiner in Chief, his record was such as you would consider as warranting a re-appointment, and whether the Patent Office in at once giving him his old place at $2500. and his young Son an Assistant Examinership at $1600. (there being already one Iowa man upon the Board of three) did not fully requite him for his disappointment. Genl Cowen, and Genl Spear, Ass't Comr of Patents, are familiar with these facts, and Genl Spear with my record for eleven years as Examiner. I believe myself fully warranted in saying that Mr Duells choice (so far as you may deem it proper for him to exercise it) falls strongly upon myself. I have been urged personally and by letter, by Judge Miller, Secretaries Jewell, Bristow, Asst Sec'y Burnam, and the Connecticut delegation, some members from Rhode Island and Mass. and Mrs Wilkinson's Missouri friends and members." L, *ibid.* On Nov. 13, a correspondent reported from Washington, D. C. "The President to-day appointed T. C. Woodward, of Iowa, to be Examiner-in-Chief of the Patent Office, vice Hopkins, resigned. There has been a strenuous contest for this position on the part of several candidates. The successful applicant was supported by Secretary Belknap." *New York Times*, Nov. 14, 1875.

To Columbus Delano

Confidential

Long Branch, N. J.
July 22d /75

DEAR SIR:

On reflection yesterday I concluded not to mention in Cabinet the subject you & I had spoken of in our interview before the meeting.

My judgement rather was that that there was no necessity of consultation further than between ourselves.

As soon as I hear again from Senator Morrill, and get an answer from McVeigh, I will telegraph you so that you may inform them where to go, when, and what to do.

Very truly yours,

U. S. GRANT

HON. C. DELANO SEC. OF THE INT.

Typescript, OFH. See following letter.

To Wayne MacVeagh

Long Branch, N. J.

July 22d /75

HON. W. MCVEIGH,
DEAR SIR:

I have asked Hon. T. O. Howe, Hon. Lott Morrill, and now ask you, to serve on a commission to examine into the conduct of the Red Cloud Indian Agency. Senator Howe accepts and Senator Morrill responds that his acceptance will depend on the time and place of meeting. I have replied that the meeting would be soon and at the Red Cloud Agency, about two days stage travel North of Chienne, Wyoming Territory. This is only day travel. Please answer.

Very Truly Yours

U. S. GRANT

ALS, PHi. On Aug. 30, 1875, USG, Long Branch, telegraphed to Secretary of the Interior Columbus Delano. "I think it advisable that senator Howe should be relieved from ~~serv~~ serving on the sioux treaty Commission as he should join the red cloud Commission in preparing & signing their reports." Telegram received (at 10:10 P.M.), DNA, RG 75, Letters Received, Dakota Superintendency. On Sept. 15, Edward P. Smith, commissioner of Indian Affairs, testified before the special commission to investigate the Red Cloud Agency concerning that commission's creation. ". . . Professor Marsh was invited before the Board of Indian Commissioners, to whom he gave a much more extended account of his Red Cloud observations and inferences; upon which statement the board immediately took action by appointing a committee of their own number to investigate and report the facts. This committee, not being ready to proceed at once to the investigation, the Secretary of the Interior requested the chairman of the Board of Indian Commissioners to name suitable persons to form a commission to take the whole matter into inquiry, and report. Much time was consumed in the composition of this commission, owing to the inability of persons invited to serve. Among those who thus declined were Hon. H. A. Bullock, of Massachusetts; G. W. Lane, of the Board of Trade of New York; Senator Stevenson, of Kentucky; Senator Washburn, of Massachusetts; Professor Seely, of Amherst College; and Senator Morrill, of Maine. . . ." *Report of the Special Commission Appointed to Investigate the Affairs of the Red Cloud Indian Agency, July, 1875* (Washington, 1875), p. 658. USG added U.S. Senator Timothy O. Howe of Wis. and George W. Atherton to the original commission— Thomas C. Fletcher, Benjamin W. Harris, Charles J. Faulkner—selected by the Board of Indian Commissioners. See *ibid.*, pp. xv–xvi.

On Aug. 10, Fletcher spoke at a council with Sioux chiefs at Red Cloud Agency, Neb. "We come here to see you and to talk with you, and we were selected for that purpose by the Great Father in Washington, not with the intention of making any treaties or bargains with you, or of getting you to agree to anything with us, but simply to talk with you. There are four of us here. Another, (Senator Howe,) a great white man, was to have been with us, but has not joined us yet; why we do not know. We were sent here to talk with you and learn from you if any person has ill-used you in any manner. If the agent or any of the contractors who have been employed by our Government to furnish you goods and supplies have cheated you, we want to find that out. And if we find that anybody has cheated you, given you bad rations, or not given you enough, or has done any wrong, we will have him punished for it by our law. We want you to talk with us as good friends, and tell us all about how you have been getting on and how you have been treated. The white man is very smart, you know; he will not only cheat Indians, but he will cheat white men too, and we want you to tell us all about what has been done here. But it is only a few bad white men that would wrong you; the great body of the white men want you treated right, and we are here to represent them. You are men and so are we, and we want you to talk with us not only in council, but as one man talks to another about his affairs. The Great Father and the white men want you to do well, want you to be happy, want you to be rich some time or other. You must learn the ways of the white man. . . ." *Ibid.*, p. 296. Red Cloud responded. ". . . When I went to see the Great Father in Washington this summer, he told me that twelve months' rations and twelve months' annuity goods were sent to us. I believe this myself, but I don't believe whoever the Great Father has to buy these goods and provisions to forward to us here sends them out. I think there is something wrong about that. . . . I tell you now, and I have said it before, that we don't want any Army officer as an Indian agent. There are plenty of men in the country that you can get for agents besides military men. We want a man close to our Great Father's place—a good man, not an officer. We want some person who has the confidence of the Great Father in Washington. We don't want as an agent any man who wants to come out here to get rich. We don't want a poor man as an agent. . . . What I have been telling you to-day they questioned me upon the same subject in Washington, and I told my Great Father then what I have told you here to-day. And he asked me if I had come with the intention of getting another agent. I kept still and did not say a word, and he repeated the question to me, and then I spoke to him and I told him this: 'My Great Father, you are sitting here with your people; and I am here with my people. You have told me before when I came here that if my agent did not do right, and I did not like him, and the nation did not like him, you had plenty more, and you would give me another. You told me these words when I was in Washington before this. The reason why I have come here is that the agent we have got, it seems, and myself don't succeed in getting the necessaries for my people, and that is why I have come here to tell you, so that you can decide what to do about it.' Then he told me, 'I will give you a father who will be ahead of all the fathers you have ever had.' When he said that we shook hands together, and all was right. It was the Commissioner of Indian Affairs I had this conversation with. I told him, 'My father, I don't want a soldier as agent, and I don't want a preacher as agent; but I want an old man about your age or a little younger, who has got a little gray hair on his head. That is the kind of man I want.' He said, 'All right, Red Cloud; go home, and in about thirty days there will be an agent at your place.' Now, the question I want to ask, is, How is it? I am not a child. I am looking for that agent to come, and I hope my Great Father is not going to deceive me. . . . Now as to those Black Hills. Our great Father has got a great many soldiers, and I never knew him when he wanted to stop anything wih his soldiers but he succeeded in it. The reason I tell you that is, that the people from the States who have gone to the Black Hills are stealing gold, digging it out and taking it away, and I don't see why the Great Father don't bring them back." *Ibid.*, pp. 297–99. See also *ibid.*, pp. 832–39. Other Sioux remarks, including appeals for John J. Saville's retention as agent, are *ibid.*, pp. 294–95, 300–308, 377–78, 502–10. On Aug. 12, the special commission met in council with Arapahoes and Cheyennes. *Ibid.*, pp. 375–77. Other Cheyenne remarks are *ibid.*, pp. 378–80. See letter to George W. Atherton, Oct. 16, 1875; William H. Armstrong, *Edward Parmelee Smith: A Friend to God's Poor* (Athens, Ga., 1993), pp. 361–69.

To Hamilton Fish

Long Branch, N. J.
July 27th /75

HON. HAMILTON FISH,
SEC. OF STATE;
SIR:

I return herewith the letter of Gen.l Foster, our Minister to Mexico, with approval of the appointment of Secretary recommended by him.

In regard to the apt. of Consul to Zanzibar I have no objection to Riley having the place.

Very Truly
your obt. svt.
U. S. GRANT

ALS, DLC-Hamilton Fish. On Friday, July 23, 1875, Secretary of State Hamilton Fish wrote to USG, Long Branch. "A vacancy in the Secretaryship of Legation in Mexico has arisen by the death of Mr Willett—I enclose a letter from Mr Forster on the subject of the succession, & the qualifications which he thinks necessary—I know nothing of Mr Daniel S. Richardson named by Mr Forster—There are several applicants for Secretaryships, but none specially for Mexico, & none so far as I can judge who has the qualifications which Mr Forster deems requisite—Shall a Commission issue to Mr Richardson? The Consulate at Zanzibar is again vacant—A person is recommended by the House in New York, which does a large business in Ivory with that place, and is also recommended by the Boston representatives of the same House, & by several of the Massachusetts Representatives & Senators—On the other hand, there are remonstrances by some respectable parties against the appointment of any person interested in, or connected with the House referred to—alleging that the last two Consuls have been appointed on the recommendation of that House, and have used the Consulate to the disadvantage of rival Houses, by giving information as to invoices, &c to their disadvantages   They have not asked the appointment of any one in their own interest—In the mean time Mr W. G. Riley of Virginia, who was appointed Consul at Laguayra, but was not confirmed by the Senate, applies for the place—the salary is $1.000—I am not aware of any other applicant—Please give me your instructions—Allow me to ask your attention to an article in the Republican of this morning—I am by no means sanguine of result from the letter which I read you on Wednesday—but an article like that in the Republican, which claims to be on friendly terms with the administration, is likely to produce the impression that the administration is not in the impartial attitude toward both sides, to *mediate* between them—A weak and feeble nation, whose power and influence are rapidly fading, is apt to be sensitive and jealous, & suspicious—It is such Articles as that referred to, which do no good, in the way of forming or enlightening public sentiment, that keep alive suspicions & mistrust in Spain, and diminish our influence in effecting a settlement—With my respectful regards to Mrs Grant . . ." ALS (press), *ibid.* An editorial "Shall Cuba Be Free?" urged U.S. support for Cuban independence from Spain. *Washington National Republican*, July 23, 1875. On July 28, USG appointed Daniel S. Richardson as secretary of legation, Mexico. For William G. Riley, see *PUSG*, 24, 467–68.

On July 7, John M. Kollock, Philadelphia, had written to USG. "I have the honor to ask that I be appointed, Secretary of Legation to mexico, and that my letters on file in the Department of State asking for the appointment of U S minister to Ecuador, be placed with this application." ALS, DNA, RG 59, Miscellaneous Letters. On May 31, Kollock, Washington, D. C., had written to USG. "Having failed in procuring a personal interview with you, I have taken the liberty of thus addressing you, asking the appointment of U S minister to Ecuador. . . . If letters were necessary, I could send scores of them to you,   I am endorsed, and warmly supported by at least three of our (Philadelphia) papers, and by the whole body of the Commercial Exchange, of our city. You know my connections with Dr Dalton (deceased) in the Establishment and maintaing of the 'Depot Field Hospitals' at city Point Va. . . . If it is not in your power to give me the appointment above can I ask one, where the climate will be beneficial to the health of my wife, and thereby *save her life*. You may remember her as Miss Mitchell, at 'Cavalery Corps Hospital' city Point Va   I am no Politician, and know you do not care for such recommendations. I ask it for former services, and for the *life* perhaps of my wife." ALS, *ibid.*, Letters of Application and Recommendation. No appointment followed.

On May 18, 1874, George Ropes, Boston, had written to USG. "I beg liberty to address you in behalf of a man absent from the Country. On February 4th 1874 you were so kind as to nominate Charles Edwin Ballard to be Consul at Zanzibar. He was pleased to receive the appointment as the salary One thousand dollars per annum would be a help to him and the distinction something and having an agreement with me to be my Agent at Zanzibar he sailed February 7th for Zanzibar where he arrived April 8th as I know by a Cable message received from him. The appointment was made on recommendation of Genl Butler his representative in Congress. Opposition was made to his confirmation on the ground that the former Consul who had been absent from his post a year had never resigned and wished to return. April 13th Gov. Boutwell reported in favor of Ballard's confirmation & he was confirmed but on the following day at the request of Genl Butler Gov. Boutwell entered a motion to reconsider the action of the Senate and nothing has since been done. I suppose that the ground on which Genl Butler was urged to request this was that the former Consul had sailed for Europe April 10th as represented by his friends to resume his duties. But his friends now admit that he was unable to proceed and will soon return from Europe and have withdrawn his name. They now urge upon Genl Butler to recommend another man—born in Boston they say—but who has to my knowlege always been employed by a New York house and last resided in Brooklyn, New York. They do this from feeling against me as they have little or no acquaintance with their candidate & recommend the New Yorker because being located in Salem they do not wish to incur the odium of taking the Consulship from Ballard for their own Agent. Mr. Ballard was born & bred in Salem, his father and Grandfather the latter 86 years of age now live there all highly respected. He has lived five years in Zanzibar is perfectly acquainted with the language of the country and though but Twenty two years of age, is of unusual prudence, tact and energy and also integrity and entirely equal to the duties of the Consulate. His friends are all warm supporters of your Administration *every one* a gentleman told me today. His papers were signed by Geo. Peabody & many others of Salem & many influential men there and here are interested in his behalf. His friends are indignant at the form the opposition to him has taken, now that all conflict with the former Consul is removed and a friend of mine who has the honor to know you, Mr. Hoyt, urges me to write you and assures me that your feelings & sympathy with his parents will prompt you to speak that one word to Gov. Boutwell which will induce him to withdraw the motion to reconsider and secure the young man his Commission." ALS, DLC-Benjamin F. Butler. USG endorsed this letter. "Forward to Senator Boutwell" AE (undated), *ibid.* On May 20, George M. White, Salem, Mass., wrote to USG. "At the request of my Grandfather, Mr. James Ballard, whose advanced age of eighty six years will not allow him to address you personally, as he desires; I write a few words relative to the nomination and confirmation of Mr. C. Edwin Ballard as Consul at Zanzibar. . . ." ALS, *ibid.* On June 1, George Ropes wrote to Fish advocating Charles E. Ballard as consul, Zanzibar. ALS, DNA, RG 59, Letters of Application and Recommendation. Related papers are *ibid.* On June 16, U.S. Senator Zachariah Chandler of Mich. withdrew his motion of April 15 to reconsider Ballard's appointment. On June 19, Francis R. Webb, Salem, wrote to USG. "I have had the honor to represent the United States at Zanzibar as Consul and Vice Consul for several years during your administration and in March of this year was obliged to leave my post of duty on account of dangerous illness. On my departure I appointed Mr F. M. Cheney to act as Deputy Consul until the pleasure of the Government was made known. On my arrival here last week I learned that the friends of a young man named Ballard had made application on his behalf for the Office of Consul at Zanzibar. The strong desire which I have that the Government should be worthily represented at a place where I have resided for many years emboldens me to respectfully request that Mr Cheney, whom I selected as the most suitable of our countrymen to leave in charge of the Consulate, may be commissioned as Consul. He is the eldest and longest resident American at Zanzibar, is known and respected by every one in the place, served in the Union Army during the rebellion, and would I am confident fill the position worthily and with dignity. On the other hand Mr Ballard is very young and I am of opinion that there is a strong objection to his holding the Office in the fact that when he was at Zanzibar before, the house which he represented and with which he was identified failed for nearly $100.000. and of the losers many entertain no friendly feelings regarding him as I know by personal observation. Of the two candidates Mr Cheney would I know be most acceptable to the Sultan of Zanzibar." ALS, *ibid.* Related papers are *ibid.*

On Nov. 4, U.S. Representative Benjamin F. Butler of Mass. wrote to Fish about Ballard's death, recommending Stephen Cloutman as consul, Zanzibar. LS, *ibid*. Related papers are *ibid*. On Dec. 8, USG nominated Cloutman. On Sept. 25, 1875, John J. Coker, Salem, wrote to USG. "I would most respectfully request of you the appointment of Consul at Zanzibar, an office recently made vacant by the death of the incumbent. I would state that I have resided in Africa more or less for nearly twenty eight years as Agent for merchants of Salem, . . ." ALS, *ibid*. On Sept. 29, Mass. Senator George B. Loring, Salem, wrote to USG. "I would respectfully recommend the appointment of Mr Coker to the Consulship which he desires. He is eminently fitted for the position." ALS, *ibid*. A related letter is *ibid*. On July 10, 1875, and May 30, 1876, Edward D. Ropes, Salem, wrote to Fish. "On the 27th ulto: news was received, by Cable, of the death, by apoplexy, on the 12th of June, of Capt. Stephen Cloutman, . . . His position as Agent for the firm of Mess. Arnold, Hines & Co, of New York, is to be filled by Capt. William Hollingsworth Hathorne, of this City, who leaves for Zanzibar on the 14th inst., and for whom we would respectfully ask the appointment of Consul. . . ." "Having received advices from our resident Agent in Zanzibar, that Mr. W. S. Riley is coming home, and has appointed Capt. W. H. Hathorne, Vice-Consul, I would respectfully urge his appointment as full Consul. . . ." ALS, *ibid*. Related papers are *ibid*. On July 21, USG authorized Fish to name a replacement for Riley, who had resigned. Hamilton Fish diary, July 21, 1876. On July 22, USG nominated William H. Hathorne as consul, Zanzibar.

To Columbus Delano

———

Long Branch, N. J.
July 28th /75.

Hon. C. Delano
Sec. of the Int.
Dear Sir:

In regard to the delay in receiving the resignation of Com. Thatcher and withdrawing the request therefor I see no reason for the former nor objection to the latter. There are no charges against Mr. Thatcher. I know your opinion of him and I have no reason to differ with you. Mr. T. can send in his resignation now, to take effect say the middle of August. Nothing has been said yet in the public prints about it. If there is delay it is most likely that it will become a newspaper removal which will prove unpleasant to all parties. In regard to the change you propose of Asst. Sec. I have only this to say: My general impression of Gen. Cowen has been favorable.[1] He is your Assistant and the choice was not dictated by me. I have always held that Cabinet Ministers should be permitted to have their own confidential assistants. If they do not suit they should be allowed to change them. In this matter exercise your judgment.

[*U. S. GRANT*]

Copy, DLC-USG, II, 3. On Aug. 5, 1875, John M. Thacher, commissioner of patents, wrote to USG. "I regretted that I was unable to obtain a personal interview with you last week when at Long Branch. I thank you, however, for the conclusion you have reached, which the Secretary has communicated to me. You shall be relieved from all embarrassment on my account as soon as possible. I am a poor man, however, dependent on my salary until I can arrange for other business; but in no event do I intend to remain in office later than the first of November next, when, if not before, I shall tender my resignation to take effect at the end of the month, so that the name of my successor may be sent in immediately upon the meeting of Congress." ALS, USG 3. See letter to Columbus Delano, July 15, 1875.

On Dec. 8, USG nominated R. Holland Duell as commissioner of patents. On April 12, U.S. Senator William Windom of Minn. had written to USG. "It affords me great pleasure to unite with the friends of Hon R. H Duell in presenting his name for Assistant Atty General. I served with judge Duell in the 36th and 37th Congresses and from my personal knowledge of him I can speak confidantly of his qualifications for said position. I am sure his appointment would secure the services of a most competent and valuable officer and give great satisfaction to the many friends with whom he served in Congress." ALS, DNA, RG 60, Applications and Recommendations. Related papers are *ibid*. See *Calendar*, Sept. 22, 1875.

On Aug. 31, U.S. Representative Charles B. Farwell of Ill., Chicago, wrote to USG. "I am informed that Mr Thatcher contemplates resigning his position of Commissioner of Patents—If this should take place I take great pleasure in naming to you for his successor Hon L. L. Bond of this city.—Mr. B. has had great experience as a patent lawyer, . . ." ALS, DNA, RG 48, Appointment Div., Letters Received. On Sept. 4, Norman B. Judd, collector of customs, Chicago, wrote to USG. "I am informed that the present Commissioner of Patents has resigned, and I desire to recommend the appointment of Hon. Lester L. Bond, of Chicago, to this position. I have known Mr. Bond as a private citizen and public man intimately for nearly a quarter of a century. He is an able lawyer and has filled offices of responsibility and trust with marked ability, and to the satisfaction of his constituents. He has been a member and President of our Common Council, acting Mayor of the city of Chicago; served several terms in the Illinois State Legislature, and was one of the Presidential electors who had the honor of casting the vote of this state for you in the election of 1872. . . ." LS, *ibid*. Related papers are *ibid*.

On Sept. 7, William Wheeler Hubbell, Washington, D. C., wrote to USG. "If agreeable to your Excellency I will be very glad of the appointment of Commissioner of Patents. Probably you may remember of me: that I invented the Explosive Shell Fuzes of the Navy, and Army, Both the time & impact of the Navy & the percussion of both—so decided by the Court of Claims, and over two millions of them were used in the War.—I was admitted to practice at the U. S. Supreme Court Bar in 1850—Am now 54 years of age, and in science & law well qualified by experience to fulfil the duties of the Office. It perhaps may be proper for me to mention that Congress has not yet fully settled with me for the Shell Fuzes:—Of these inventions I bore the great expense of development and of a long suit to determine my title, in my favor,—And I really need the Salary of the Office for a living. If permitted I refer your Excellency to your friends—Hon Simon Cameron, Hon John Scott (ex senator) Hon John P. Jones of Nevada. Hon John A Logan, Hon John Sherman, Hon Roscoe Conkling. Hon A. H. Cragin, All personal friends of mine." ALS, *ibid*.

On Dec. 27, 1876, Duell wrote to USG resigning as commissioner of patents. ALS, *ibid*. On Dec. 28, a correspondent reported from Washington, D. C. "The resignation of Judge Duell is a repetition of the universal course of affairs in the Patent Office for many years. He leaves the position[,] which pays but a small salary, to engage in patent law business, for which he has become specially qualified by experience in the office, and which offers unusual compensation. . . . Among the persons mentioned for the successorship are Congressman H[o]skins, of New-York; Hon. R. L. B. Clark, at present a member of the Appeal Board of the Patent Office, and W. H. Doolittle, at present Assistant Commissioner of Patents. . . ." *New York Times*, Dec. 29, 1876.

On Dec. 30, Alex. McMillan, Genoa, Ohio, wrote to USG. "I would like the position of Commissioner of Patents if found worthy, and the place is not already filled. My credentials will be signed by Ex Gov. Cox Member Elect to Congress from this district and also by our own Gov. Hayes. I apply thus dirrect, and (perhaps informally,) to save time, should you consider My application favorably. Please reply at once—" ALS, DNA, RG 48, Appointment Div., Letters Received. No appointment followed.

On Jan. 17, 1877, USG telegraphed to Secretary of the Interior Zachariah Chandler. "If Genl Speer does not accept Commissionership see me before offering it elsewhere." Telegram sent, *ibid*., RG 107, Telegrams Collected (Bound). On the same day, a correspondent reported from Washington, D. C. "Congressman MacDougall, of New-York, has declined the position of Commissioner of Patents, which was tendered to him by the President. The place has been offered to Mr. Ellis Spear, of Maine, late Assistant Commissioner, and it is understood that he has accepted. . . ." *New York Times*, Jan. 18, 1877. On Jan. 18, Chandler telegraphed to USG. "Genl Spear had accepted the offer of appointment and his nomination had gone before I received your telegram yesterday He is highly recommended." Telegram received, DNA, RG 107, Telegrams Collected (Bound). On the same day, U.S. Representative Clinton D. MacDougall of N. Y. telegraphed to USG. "I have reason to believe the appointment of spear is not a proper one to make. I send a private note by messenger." Telegram received, *ibid*. Also on Jan. 18, USG nominated Ellis Spear as commissioner of patents.

1. On Feb. 14, 1876, Benjamin R. Cowen had written to USG. "I have the honor to tender my resignation of the position of Ass't Sec'y of the Interior, to take effect on the 14th proximo, until which time I respectfully request leave of absence. I take this Step because of the condition of my business in Ohio which requires my personal attention, and which cannot be longer neglected without Serious loss. . . ." ALS, *ibid*., RG 48, Appointment Div., Letters Received. On March 3, USG nominated Charles T. Gorham as asst. secretary of the interior.

Endorsement

Refered to the Sec. of the Treas. This was intended as a private letter for my information, and contained many extracts from St. Louis papers not deemed necessary to forward. They are obtainable and have no dougbt been all read by the federal officials in St. Louis. I forward this for information and to the end that if it trows any light upon new parties to summons a̶t̶s witnesses they may brought out. Let no guilty man escape if it can be avoided—Be specially vigilant—or instruct those engaged in the prosecutions of fraud to be— agains all who insinuate that they have high influence to protect, or to protect them. No personal consideration should stand in the way of performing a public duty.

U. S. GRANT

JULY 29TH /75

AES, CSmH. *HMD*, 44-1-186, 485. Written on a letter of July 19, 1875, from William D. W. Barnard, Kirkwood, Mo., to USG. "*Confidential* . . . Writing Genl Sherman in my behalf in 1864, you done me the high honor to close with, 'Mr Barnard, has been a sincere friend of mine, when I wanted friends and when there was no apparent possible chance of him ever deriving any benefit from it, you may trust Mr B, with the assurance that he will betray no trust' Valueing these assurances of your high regard and confidence.—I need hardly tell you, how assiduously I have striven to prove worthy of, and maintain same— or refer to history for the re-occuring evidence of the many-fold intricaces of polished inuendo and intrigue, indulged in, around Power—instigated by Place, Jelousy, Unfriendliness, Revenge, &C, &C—From evidence in my possession, I feel that I have not escaped the efforts of such; to place us in antagonism—But I am rewarded by the conciousness of your generous feelings of old—If, there ever was a time, when, your true admirers should exert themselves, in this section, to correct the inferences, sought to be created, against you, by your political adversaries and unworthy parties here, who have occupied place and dastardly outraged confidence—with others yet in office—It has been, the past three months—The 'clips' enclosed, from the Republican and Times of to day—marked 'A' and 'B'—show some of the many efforts, to tarnish your great name—by implication—that from the Republican, it is intimated, beares the 'ear marks' of John. B. Henderson—assisting in the prossecution of cases before the Grand jury—the closing of which is simply infamous—and I fear, aided in his old animosity, by a report whispered around, since Casey left the city, by the apologists of the 'ring', that he said, 'Mr Bristow had deceived you and would not retain the Tres'y portfolio thirty days'—I have denied this assertion, when made in my presence and have written him what has been said—Neither Henderson and Dyer like a bone in your body—they will do what generality of lawyers consider their duty—nothing more—and both inspired with political asperations, will take good care to advance what they may regard their own, or friends interest—Feeling thus, I can not but think, that the interest of the Government and your own past record, should be protected by aditional counsel,—known to be actuated by the highest sense of duty and fielty— regardless of the prospective influence of Press—Party—or self angrandisement—Atty Eaton is a mere stick and had it not been for high family and social influences, it is pretty well understood, would have been impeached in his Bankruptcy office sometime since— Again, as I have had occasion to say to Mr Newcomb himself, I do not believe there will be a conviction of the indited, whilst he retains the Marshalship—convinced of this, of what I know has occured and occuring, I can not but state it to you—the reasons for which would make this communication too lengthy although I premise, who the velveted hand is, that holds him in power—and why McKee of the Globe, it has been generally understood for years, has been head and ears cognisant of—an abettor—and participant of the 'ring swag'—as far back as 71, it is stated and believed that he asserted your being con-

sulted and consenting to the ring—received two portions of the divide—with the understanding among the initiated, that one part was for the lamented Ford—not one cent of
which I am confident was ever proffered—did he get—or would have taken—I am creditably informed that these facts could have been brought out, but for interviews with and
influences brought to bear upon a witness and a seeming studdied effort to shield him
(McK under the audacious assertion that his inditement, would lead to exposures that
would strike so high, as to distroy the Party of the Republic—McKee should be called before the Grand Jury and probed to the quick—but parties herein named, with Benton,
Blow, Walsh (endorsers on Democrat purchase) Maguire, Newcomb and others, do not
want it—an inditement could and should be had, but may not take place, from influences
exerted and will be continued, *to save him*—And in after time, will be said, would have been,
but for protecting others—and this by some of the very men herein named—Col
Normeile prosecuting Circuit Atty—McDonal and Joyces confidential friend, asked me
Saturday 'how far matters were going to be pushed towards them'—said, I thought until
the last man made restitution to his utmost ability to pay and were punished to the extent
of the law—if local officers done their duty—He replied that both had told him, that day
when seeking bail—'that you could not give them up, or Babcock was lost'—(this is the
kind of talk indulged in and frequently by the 'Globe claquers' speaking as openly of you—)
I said, they, or anyone, who talks that way, little knew the stuff of which you are made—
let the blow fall upon whom it may, you would see that the honor of the Government was
guarded and the laws enforced—It is truly painful to write thus—but viewing the great
stake—the means—the ways—the desperation—to thwart justice—even by dragging
in their shameful schemes—the names of innocent and dead—Duty requires that you be
kept advised—even at the expense of tireing—" ALS, CSmH. *HMD*, 44-1-186, 484–85.

On July 30, Secretary of the Treasury Benjamin H. Bristow wrote to USG. "Mr
Barnard's letter with your indorsment was received this morning. There is much in Mr
Barnards letter confirmatory of what has come to me from other sources, and worthy of
serious consideration. I have little doubt that the Marshal, Newcombe, is so far complicated by his relations with members of the 'ring,' and their friends that he cannot do his
whole duty fearlessly and impartially, and am satisfied that a change in that office would
be wholesome. As to what he says of Dyer and Henderson and their alleged unfriendliness
to you I hope he is mistaken, though I cannot say positively, as I do not know either of them
personally, nor have I any information on the subject one way or the other. You will remember that there was much difficulty in getting suitable counsel to represent the Government in these prosecutions in St Louis. Mr Dyer, as you will recollect was named by
the Secty of War, who has confidence in him. Henderson was employed by the Attorney
General upon the recommendation of Dyer, after several other eminent lawyers had declined. So far as I am able to see Dyer has done his duty well, though he reports that he
has encountrd the most serious obstacles in his investigation before the Grand Jury, and
expresses the opinion that he has not got to the bottom of the frauds. He thinks, however
he will be able to do so at the next term of the Court   In view of the character of your indorsment on Mr Barnards letter I ought perhaps to say that the most persistent efforts
have been made both here and in St Louis to create the belief that there is a want of harmony between you & myself touching these prosecutions. Of course I know how utterly
false all such statements are, and have taken pains to contradict them in every proper way,
but it cannot be denied that the frequent repetition of them by parties who *profess* to have
your confidence has done some mischief. For this reason I would like to have your permission to make public the substance of your indorsment on Mr Barnards letter. Of course I
do not mean to give out any of the statements of the letter, but simply the substance of
your indorsment—or what would be better still, I would be glad to give to the public a

brief letter from you instructing me to have the local officers in St Louis make thorough investigation of the whisky frauds and prosecute rigorously every one of the guilty parties without regard—to their station or personal friendships. This would place you right, and would silence your enemies, at least on this subject. I submit for your consideration whether it is not well to do this. I am at liberty to say that the Attorney General and Secretary of the Navy concur in this suggestion   I propose to leave here tonight for Ky, but will return next week—say Thursday or Friday. . . . P. S. A few days ago I received a note from you requesting me to do something for Col P. B. Foulke, who was continued as a Special Inspector of Customs. Yesterday facts come to my knowledge which show conclusively that he has formed connection with the St Louis whisky ring for the purpose of defeating the prosecutions. For this reason I have directed him to be dropped from the roll, as I know you would not wish him retained." ALS, USG 3; press, DLC-Benjamin H. Bristow. On July 27, 1876, Bluford Wilson, former solicitor of the treasury, testified concerning USG's endorsement before a select committee of the House of Representatives appointed to investigate revenue fraud involving distilleries in St. Louis and Milwaukee. "Q. Was this indorsement of which you have spoken voluntarily given by the President of the United States, or was it the result of any advice or urgency upon the part of the Secretary of the Treasury or yourself?—A. We had long sought for a sign from the President which in some emphatic way would be a warrant to us and a guarantee of his sympathy and support in our efforts to bring to punishment the guilty parties, whoever they might be. . . . Q. Did not the Secretary of the Treasury go down to Long Branch, where the President was summering, for the purpose of obtaining from the President some such declaration as that which was indorsed upon that letter, or did he not go for that and other purposes?—A. I cannot state positively that the Secretary visited the President at Long Branch for the specific purpose referred to in your inquiry, until after the receipt of the indorsement from the President. He then did visit the President upon an understanding between the Secretary and myself that the publication of that indorsement was due alike to him and to myself, and was the best answer which it was in our power to give to the enemies of General Bristow, the members of the whisky ring, notably McDonald and others, who were then already busy in Saint Louis in their efforts to break down his character and sully his fair fame. . . . Q. What was the result of the interview which the Secretary had with the President in reference to the publication of that indorsement?—A. I was authorized by the Secretary of the Treasury to give it to the public press, . . ." *HMD*, 44-1-186, 357. See *New York Times*, Aug. 17, 1875.

On April 1, David P. Dyer, U.S. attorney, Eastern District, Mo., had testified before the committee. ". . . The evidence discloses the fact that in 1871 a man of the name of Megrue, who had been formerly an assessor in Cincinnati under Mr. Johnson's administration, went to Saint Louis, at the instance of Joyce, a revenue-agent, who was then in the supervisor's office in Saint Louis, and there an arrangement was made that these distillers were to go into the manufacturing of illicit whisky, and that the tax of seventy cents on the gallon was to be divided between the officers and the distillers. Embraced in that arrangement were the supervisor, this man Joyce, the collector of the district; then Charles W. Ford; William McKee, now one of the proprietors of the Globe-Democrat, and Fitzroy, making five. They kept an account at the distillers' of all the illicit whisky that was made, and the gaugers and store-keepers were paid from one to two dollars a barrel for each barrel that was turned out; they kept an account of the illicit whisky made at the distillers', and every Saturday reported to the collector for the ring the amount of crooked whisky, and either the distiller or the gauger paid the money over as the case might be. The arrangement between the distiller and the rectifier was that thirty-five cents, the distiller's half of the seventy cents, was divided between him and the rectifier; that division was made by the distiller selling crooked whisky at, say, seventeen cents a gallon less than the market-price. That is how the rectifier got his share of the amount retained by the distiller. The amount paid to the officers was on each Saturday evening taken to the office of the supervisor of internal revenue and there divided into various packages and distributed among them. . . ." *HMD*, 44-1-186, 31.

On Feb. 4, 1875, Levi P. Luckey had written to Bristow. "The President directs me to say that he desires that the circular order transferring Supervisors of Internal Revenue be suspended by telegraph until further orders." ALS, DNA, RG 56, Letters Received from the President. On Aug. 2, 1876, Alexander P. Tutton, former supervisor of Internal Revenue, testified before the committee. ". . . That order transferred me to Saint Louis, and transferred all the supervisors from one place to another—I believe there were ten of them. Supervisor McDonald was to come to Philadelphia, and Supervisor Munn was to come to New York, I think. That order was made and promulgated in the latter part of January, to take effect on the 15th of February. . . . I went up to the President and said substantially this to him: that I was satisfied that this course would not reach these frauds if they existed, and that I had suggested to the Secretary what I thought would be a much better plan—to send some men out without its being known, and let them investigate and find what those people were doing—whether they were stealing, and to what extent. I suggested Mr. Brooks as the best man I knew for that purpose. The President, after thinking over the matter, said, 'I believe you are right. I do not believe this transfer of supervisors will accomplish the end, and I will have the order suspended for the present.'. . . Q. Do you know that Mr. Henderson in his argument in the Babcock case took occasion to censure the President severely for countermanding that order?—A. Yes; it looked so to me in reading Mr. Henderson's speech. The inference I took from it, as I understood it, was that he charged Babcock first with being in complicity with the whisky ring at Saint Louis, and then charged him with having influenced the President to revoke that order in the interest of the ring, and that the President had done it from improper motives, to favor Babcock; that is the way I understood the speech. Q. Do you know of your own knowledge that this charge of Henderson's was false?—A. I was satisfied that Mr. Babcock had had nothing to do with the changing of the President's mind, for when I first went to see him he had no idea of changing that order at all. He said that something ought to be done, that the Secretary thought great frauds were being committed, and they should be got at in some way; that while he did not himself think that any of these officers at Saint Louis or Chicago were in collusion with the distillers, yet his impression was that they had got accustomed to the routine way of doing things which the officers there had, and that they knew exactly how to evade or escape them. . . . I remember he said that he found that to be the case in the Army—that officers whom he considered good men, and men who intended to do their duty, would get into the habit of doing things in a certain routine way, and that people who wanted to get around them could do so. He said, 'I believe that may be the case with these revenue-agents, and by making a change the parties that come in anew can do things in a different rut, and by that means run against the thieves.' I remember saying to him, (although when testifying about this matter before I did not think of it,) 'Do you suppose if I had any arrangement with the distillers in Philadelphia or Baltimore, now that I have notice that I am going to be sent away and that Mr. McDonald is coming to Philadelphia with his revenue-agents, I would not go to work and bury that thing so deep that nobody could find it?' He rather laughed and says, 'Of course you would.' 'Well,' said I, 'if there is anything wrong out there, they will do the same thing.' Then he said he would suspend that order and I left him. Q. Did he say or did you say anything about making the order of suspension as public as the order for the transfer had been made?—A. I said to him this: that if this order of transfer of supervisors were rescinded now, and that rescission made public, those people, if they were committing frauds, as the Secretary said or supposed they were, would be emboldened by the rescission and would think the coast all clear and keep on committing frauds, and that this would be just the time to send a man like Brooks right in among them, quietly, to see what they were doing. I said they would be running things pretty lively, and they could be found out at once. . . ." *HMD*, 44-1-186, 438–39. On Aug. 7, Wilson testified before the committee. ". . . Q. Do you not know that the very plan carried out by you in sending secret agents into the field to ferret out these frauds was suggested to the President by Mr. Tutton, and that on that ground the order transferring supervisors was rescinded?—A. I do not know that Mr. Tutton had anything to do, either directly or indirectly, nearly or remotely, with the plans adopted by the Secretary of the Treasury and myself for the detection of frauds on the revenue. The statement that he had is utterly absurd and untrue. . . ." *Ibid.*, pp. 480–81. See *ibid.*, pp. 84–85; John McDonald, *Secrets of the Great Whiskey Ring* (Chicago, 1880), pp. 121–25.

On March 18, 1875, John McDonald, supervisor of Internal Revenue, St. Louis, had written to Orville E. Babcock. "From the Associated Press Dispatch, I perceive, that some party or parties seem to take especial pains to make it appear that the local revenue officers at points now undergoing investigation, are in a measure antagonistic to the Honorable Secretary of the Treasury, and the respective investigating officers, and that (they the local officers) impeded rather than assisted in such investigations. I desire to state, that so far as my district is concerned, every facility and courtesy that could be reasonably expected, has been granted by the revenue officers of this district. I have taken pains to ascertain this fact particularly. It cannot be denied, but that business-men, fellow citizens, and personal friends of some thirty years standing, have expressed themselves freely upon the peculiar manner in which the investigation here was begun, without either my knowledge or co-operation, but beyond that, nothing has been done or said. I trust however that the result will justify the mode of proceedure. So far as I am individually concerned, I have tendered to Supervisor Hawley, and his corps of assistants every possible courtesy and facility as they will testify. With regard to so much of this matter as pertains to my district, I have to say, that it is simply the culmination of the old fight, long and persistently kept up by a circle of blackmailers who were dismissed by me from the service here some two years since, for suspected complicity with certain distillers, but so far as I am personally concerned I deny, and defy any, and all imputations of connivance with a 'whiskey ring', or any party, or parties for fraud of any kind. In the investigation now progressing one's actions will speak for themselves, as against any defamation by perjured blackmailers. 'Will fight it out on this line if it should take a life time'   Col. Joyce is out of town, have not seen him since the 1st inst. My picture of the General has not yet come to hand" ALS, ICN. In 1874, according to McDonald, USG had endorsed a letter written by John A. Joyce, Internal Revenue agent, St. Louis, to William O. Avery, chief clerk, Treasury Dept., concerning a possible investigation into revenue collection at St. Louis. "Joyce and McDonald are reliable and trustworthy. Let them have the information they want." *Secrets of the Great Whiskey Ring*, p. 94. On Dec. 3, Joyce telegraphed to Babcock. "Has Secretary or Commissioner ordered any body here?" Copy, DLC-Benjamin H. Bristow. *Secrets of the Great Whiskey Ring*, p. 105. See letter to Adolph E. Borie, Sept. 25, 1874, note 1.

On April 18, 1875, Bluford Wilson wrote to James H. Wilson. ". . . Yesterday I had a long talk with Bristow on all the points of my conference with Porter, and the daily data [re]ceived from my agents operating in St Louis, Chicago Milwaukee Louisville and elsewhere against the Whiskey ring. In view of my report from Porter he declared he would resign May 1st—I told him he could not until the 'ring' thieves were crushed and then read him my reports. He was thoroughly aroused, and will go at the President with a straight issue on his return—I said to him to demand an honest Commissioner—Mc-

Donald and Munn's removal on the facts furnished by me, and then if the President failed him, to resign. . . ." ALS, WyU.

On April 23, "Grit" [*Joyce*], St. Louis, telegraphed to Babcock. "Tell Mc to see Parker of Colorado, and telegram to Commissioner, Crush out the St Louis enemies." Copy, DLC-Benjamin H. Bristow. *Secrets of the Great Whiskey Ring*, p. 150.

On May 4, John W. Douglass wrote to USG resigning as commissioner of Internal Revenue. ALS, DNA, RG 56, Letters Received from the President. On July 24, Douglass, Washington, D. C., wrote to [Babcock]. "As a general thing I don't notice newspaper false-hoods, but the enclosed is so *d——d a lie*, from beginning to end, that I step over my usual habit to say so—You of course know that nothing of the kind ever occurred between the President & me at the White House & I can assure you that the scene pictured at the Trea-sury did not occur—" ALS, ICN. The enclosed clipping described a meeting between Douglass and Bristow, followed by a summons to the White House. ". . . When Douglass arrived the President demanded of him a more explicit statement of the reasons of his fail-ure to have the laws obeyed. The Commissioner again referred to the personal friends of the President who held official positions in St. Louis, who, he claimed, were obstructing the due execution of the Revenue laws. The President did not relish this direct thrust, and proceeded to unburden his mind in a very emphatic way. So far as his personal friends were concerned, he did not have any whom he intended to uphold if they engaged in the busi-ness of defrauding the Government. He knew how to dispose of them, and it was, to say the least of it, a piece of impertinence on the part of the Commissioner to even suppose for a moment that he (the President) would sustain any official who resorted to corrupt prac-tices. He then concluded by informing Douglass that as he had to make a beginning, he was ready at once to receive the resignation of the Commissioner of Internal Revenue. The manner of the President was so emphatic that no other course was left open to Douglass but to hand in the little document which retired him from official life. . . ." *Ibid.* On May 5, Bristow, Philadelphia, had telegraphed to USG. "I think it would be well to offer Douglas sixth auditorship but any delay in change would be unwise I have urged Pratt to come on at the earliest practicable day & he has fixed the fifteenth the public interest requires that the change be consummated at once" Telegram received (at 6:22 P.M.), DLC-USG, IB. For-mer U.S. Senator Daniel D. Pratt of Ind. replaced Douglass. For James H. Wilson's bid to replace Douglass, see letter to George H. Williams, April 28, 1875; Bluford Wilson to James H. Wilson, March 31, 1875, ALS, WyU.

On May 7, Babcock wrote to McDonald. "Your letter at hand—I shall send the pho-tograph in a day or two, and will try to get Gen Belknaps. Sorry your assistants have re-signed it must keep you quite busy I have delivered your messages. Hope the bird was a good traveller Your friend is doing the best he can you can I believe rely upon him. The new Commissioner takes his place on the 15th, and change generally will take place at that date, though your services will be needed till the first of June—All well here but busy Regards to Mrs McD, Joyce and wife and other friends" Facsimile, *Secrets of the Great Whiskey Ring*, p. 162.

On May 8, John F. Long and Henry C. Wright, St. Louis, telegraphed to USG. "Un-derstanding that Constantine Maguire has tendered his resignation as Collector of Int Rev Conditionally we ask that it be not accepted believing it would affect political affairs here, he makes a good officer & his past record is above suspicion" Telegram received, DLC-USG, IB. On the same day, U.S. Senator Stephen W. Dorsey of Ark., St. Louis, telegraphed to USG. "I incidentally learn that Genl McDonald has offered his resignation I trust it will not be accepted. he is an able & honest officer a devoted friend of the administration & a republican whose labors have been felt throughout his district" Telegram received (at 8:10 P.M.), *ibid.* On May 12, Bristow wrote to Constantine Maguire that his resignation had

been accepted. Copy, DNA, RG 56, Letters Sent. On May 22, Bristow wrote a similar letter to McDonald. Copy, *ibid.* Also on May 22, Secretary of State Hamilton Fish recorded
in his diary. "Bristow tells me that Babcock is as deep as any in the Whiskey Ring that he
has most positive evidence he will not say of actual fraud but of intimate relations and
confidential correspondence with the very worst of them. That a man (whose name I did
not catch) appointed at St Louis on Babcocks recommendation was the center pin of the
plot; that when speaking to the President about the frauds the President had said, referring to this man, that there was one honest man upon whom they could rely as he was an
intimate acquaintance & confidential friend of Babcocks; whereupon Bristow told the
President that he was the head center of all the frauds that he was at this time in New York
with $160 000 of money fraudulently obtained ready to take a steamer on the first indica-
tion of any effort to arrest him" DLC-Hamilton Fish.

On May 20, Lindsay Murdoch, Marble Hill, Mo., had written to Babcock. "Under
consideration of the uniform courtesey with which I have been treated by yourself on former occasion I make bold to write to you as an applicant for a position in one of the many
vacancies which apparently present developments in the whiskey ring will compell in my
section,   I base my claim on the fact that I was removed from my position of Collector of
2nd Dist Missouri because I would not cooperate with officers of the government (my superiors) to defraud the government,   in proof of this I enclose a copy of a sworn statement
and accompanying letter which I forwarded to the President on the 7th of June 1873, that
I believe I have been an object of persecution by the whiskey ring,—While in Office I honestly discharged my duties, and being removed by improper influences I ask that I receive
some appointment as a vindication of my past course,   I have been a consistent Republican and at present am a member of the Republican State central committee. I have uniformly supported President Grant and have for him feelings of regard and consideration,
and fully appreciate the delicate position he is sometimes forced to occupy.—I will state in
making my application that should circumstance require the removal of the supervisor of
this district I respectfully make application for that position, and should a vacancy occurr
I will esteem it a great favor if you will have my claims considered before an appointment
is made   In fact I will say that my circumstance are such that an appointment of any sort
would be more than acceptable at present,   should I not hear from you unfavorably and
should contingencie warrant I will make a personal application to the President with recommendations from leading Republicans for any position that may be available.—In regard to the parties implicated I will say I have no vindictive feelings toward them and have
no desire to carry matters any further than is absolutely necessary out of consideration for
the good name of the Republican party,   To prevent misunderstanding I will say I sent a
copy of enclosed affidavit to Secretary Bristow last week—Hoping I may have an early and
favorable response . . ." ALS, ICN. Murdoch enclosed a copy of a letter to USG, dated
June 6, 187[3]. "Having failed to get any satisfactory explanation for my sudden removal
from the office of Collector 2d dist Mo I am forced to the conclusion it must have been accomplished by the Supervisors office for interested motives of the worst character,   I have
made a statement under oath, which I respectfully submit for your Excellencys consideration—I have held the matter strictly private and any action you may take in the premises
need not be burthened with publicity" Copy, *ibid.* In the enclosed affidavit, also dated
June 6, Murdoch swore that Joyce had described the arrangement with the distillers and
urged him to participate. Copy, *ibid.* On April 11, 1876, James O. Brodhead testified before
the committee. "Q. Were you one of the special counsel of the United States in the recent
whisky trials in Saint Louis?—A. Yes, sir; I was retained by the Government a short time
prior to the trial of McKee, as attorney in that case and the Maguire case and the Babcock
case. . . . Q. Were there any letters used upon the trial of the Babcock case written by Ford

to the President, speaking of the character of McDonald?—A. Yes, sir; there was a letter written by the collector for the southeastern district of Missouri, Lindley Murdock; a letter written by Lindley Murdock, a certified copy of which we had from the Treasury Department, complaining of McDonald and bringing certain charges against him. I don't recollect exactly the purport of the letter. Murdock, I think, was removed by McDonald's instrumentality about that time. Q. You say that letter was addressed to the President or to Mr. Ford, and forwarded?—A. The letter was addressed to the President; there was also a letter of Mr. Ford's which was directed to the President, and which Concannon produced to us, in Ford's handwriting, addressed to the President and telling him what kind of a man he thought McDonald was, . . ." *HMD*, 44-1-186, 89, 94. See *PUSG*, 20, 149–50; *ibid.*, 22, 462–63.

On May 21, 1875, John M. Krum, St. Louis, telegraphed to USG. "Norman Cutter is Strongly recommended for Supervisor internal revenue" Telegram received (at 4:15 P.M.), DLC-USG, IB.

On June 3, William S. Harney, St. Louis, wrote to USG. "Mr Sturgeon whom you know perfectly will, & whom you know to be one of the noblest works of God, is desirous of getting the appointment of United States Collector of Internal Revenue of this City.— Now, my dear General, it is useless for me to say anything to you of his fitness for the appointment in *every respect* & I know that every one would be happy to learn of his being appointed—As to myself General, I would take it as the greatest favor I ever received in my life & I do hope and beg you to give it to him, you will never have cause to regret it & you may just set me down as your Slave for life. May Prosperity attend you always . . ." ALS, Gilder Lehrman Collection, NNP. On June 5, Edwin O. Stanard, St. Louis, wrote to USG. "I learn there is some doubt about Mr. Lightner accepting the position of Collector of Internal Revenue in this City and if this is so, I take great pleasure in recommending Hon. Isaac H. Sturgeon of St. Louis for the place,   I dont think there is a man in our midst better qualified and that would render more general satisfaction to the people and that would please the Department in the discharge of the duties of the office better than Mr. Sturgeon.—I hope he may be appointed." Copy, DLC-Benjamin H. Bristow. On the same day, D. P. Rowland, president, and George H. Morgan, secretary, Merchants' Exchange of St. Louis, wrote to USG recommending Isaac H. Sturgeon. Copy, *ibid*. On June 8, Bristow wrote to USG. "Referring to the matter of the Collectorship of Internal Revenue at St. Louis, I have to advise you that Mr. Lightner has concluded to decline the place, and it becomes necessary to make another selection. Among the persons named, it seems to me that the appointment should be given either to Isaac H. Sturgeon or Stephen D. Barlow. I am inclined to think from all I can hear, that Mr. Sturgeon would be the most satisfactory appointment. I do not know Mr. Barlow, but he is strongly recommended by Commissioner Eaton, who was consulted about the former appointment. Supervisor Hedrick telegraphs me from Milwaukee this morning that he has unearthed several hundred barrels of fraudulent whiskey concealed in an old brewery in that city. He says the fight with the whiskey ring is becoming more intense and exciting—to use his own words 'it is just now getting red hot'." LS (press), *ibid*. On June 10, USG appointed Sturgeon as collector of Internal Revenue, 1st District, Mo., to replace Maguire. DS, MoSHi.

On June 25, Dyer wrote to Bluford Wilson. "In accordance with a suggestion made while you were here, I procured a Subpoena duces tecum for certain correspondence by telegraph between certain parties here and at Washington, and beg to enclose for your information copies of such dispatches as tend to prove collusion between parties here and at Washington and would be glad to receive your suggestions touching further inquiry. We are getting along slowly but I think very surely and satisfactorily in our examination. The evidence seems to be abundant. I am waiting patiently for Conduce G. McGrew who holds the key to the ring. I have sent a capias for him to the District Attorney at Washington and also to New York." LS (press), DNA, RG 118, Letters Sent, U.S. Attorneys, Eastern District, Mo.

On July 14, Babcock, Long Branch, wrote to McDonald. "Confidential . . . I enclose you a—newspaper article—which you have undoubtedly seen—I want to say that I have not seen the correspond who wrote this in 8 or ten weeks—and I have never made any statements that could be construed into this. I do not suppose it is necessary for me to write this, but I do it to assure you that I do not believe in joining in abuse of you and Joyce (Who have always been kind to me) now that you are in trouble—When that matter is all disposed of—and you gentlemen are vindicated—as I believe you will be—if I have any complaints—to make I will make them to you and not to newspaper correspondents   Unless I know something very different from anything that I know now I shall have no complaints to make, for I am not aware that I have ever received anything but kindness at the hands of either you or Joyce—Please remember me to Mrs McD—Joyce and Mrs J—. . . P. S. I thought I had the newspaper article. It was from the Chicago Tribune—and represented that you had abused the confidence of the Sectys of the Presd with whom you had corresponded &c &c.   as I said before I have never said such a thing—. . . P. S. 2 I have seen Joyces manly card in the paper   When are you coming East" ALS (facsimile), *Secrets of the Great Whiskey Ring*, p. 185.

On July 18, Conduce G. Megrue, Washington, D. C., wrote to Babcock. "You dobtless have not only seen but heard many reports through the press & otherwise in connection with myself St Louis, &c &c. I write you this to assure that instead of in anyway throwing dirt upon you or the President, I had an opportunity while in St Louis to fully give my opinion as to the course taken by McDonald & Joyce wherein they had done you both injustice, & especially did I shew the Dist Attorney & Jury why they had so freely used your names &c &c. I write this in justice to myself, & that neither of you may believe the many lies you see instigated by the press & especially Genl Boyington of the Cinti Gazett. You will pardon me when I say that when Mr Luckey whom I do not know, & certainly have never used his name in any way, could be better employed than running around attempting to Slander me—As to Wm O. Avery I hope he may get simply what is due him Certain is it that no Gentleman can be benefitted by ~~by~~ his association. He is a contemptible dog—As I have always said, I am your friend & whenever in my power would serve you. McDonald Joyce, Avery &co to the contrary notwithstanding" ALS, ICN. On July 27, an anonymous person at Washington, D. C., wrote to Babcock, Long Branch, demanding money and a patronage position in return for withholding damaging information from the press. L, *ibid.*

On July 20, Bristow wrote to USG. "I hand you herewith copy of a message received this morning by Mr Pratt from Supervisor Hedrick giving the result of the investigation of whiskey frauds by the Grand Jury at Oshkosh Wisconsin. You will perhaps recollect that Hedrick was temporarily transfered from Iowa to Missouri for the purpose of making seizures and instituting such other proceedings as the facts might justify. He has done his duty well and has shown himself to be a fearless, competent and discreet officer. I have no official advices from St Louis as to what parties are indicted. I only know that the Grand Jury has adjourned after having returned a large number of indictments" ALS (press), DLC-Benjamin H. Bristow.

On July 26 (Monday) and Sept. 17, Fish recorded in his diary after conversations with Bristow. "He called at the Department today and spent more than an hour with me; he appears very much worried and threatens to resign   I remonstrate but he alludes to the uncomfortable position & to the enormous influence both monied and political which is arrayed against him in his efforts to expose the Whiskey Frauds He refers to his statement made at the Cabinet on Wednesday last when he had read a number of telegrams passing between Washington and the parties in St Louis engaged in the Whiskey Trade and refers to one signed Sylph which the Assistant District Atty in Mo had supposed to have been written by Avery the Chief Clerk of the Treasury that he had obtained the original despatches from Washington, of which the prosecution in Mo had copies, from the telegraph office and he had stated to the President in Cabinet that the despatches signed Sylph were not in Averys hand writing. He asked me if I had noticed his statement with regard to these despatches I told him that I had and had noticed he had twice repeated it. He said he had done so intentionally for he should have stated had he been asked and then added that it was in Babcocks and that to be sure of evidence on that point he had caused it to be photographed and showed me a copy of the proof. I do not doubt but that it is Babcocks writing he says that those familiar with it and the experts in the Treasury Department all say it is. It is a telegram to McDonald of I think December 12th informing him that he had succeeded and the parties would not go. The parties referred to were detectives or experts who were ordered to St Louis and other points west to look into the Whiskey Frauds McDonald who was an especial friend of Babcocks and implicated in the fraud had been in to Washington to prevent investigation On a former occasion he had succeeded but Bristow had induced Douglass the Commissionr of Internal Revenue to appoint his agents; that Douglass remonstrated and told him he would strike people at the White House but he still insisted on their appointment Early in December last McDougall [*McDonald*] come on again and passed most of his time at Babcocks and on Dec 12 the day McDougall left the order for sending the agents to St Louis was revoked without his knowing it and on the 13th this telegram signed sylph was sent to McDougall He further stated that McDougall had since admitted to him the existence of great frauds but said if they were going to pull him down they would have to strike some persons bigger than he, that were at the White House. He states that indictments have been found against a large number of the parties; named McDougall, Joyce, & Avery (Chief Clerk of the Treasury) among the number and that they had gotten over the two principle witnesses and that with money and political influence it was difficult to meet the ends of Justice" "he stated that he had had a conversation with Genl Babcock and had told him that the District Attorney of Missouri had the telegram to MacDonald signed Sylph and was in possession of all the facts with regard to it. Babcock admitted he had written it but denies that it was in connection with the Whiskey business, connecting it with some matter which Bristow said had occurred two months previously He told Babcock he felt it was his duty to the President to bring the matter before him; which he had since done, the President said the sylph telegram did not refer to the Whiskey business but to a supposed order of the transfer of Supervisor Bristow replied that unfortunately that transfer did not take place until Feb—while the telegram was dated December. Bristow says that he thinks Babcock will be indicted and had told him so and that the Grand Jury was to meet in November. Some of Babcocks friends he says wish him to get a position on the Elevated Rail Road in NewYork and he Bristow had suggested to Porter to advise Babcock to resign which however Porter declined to do Bristow thinks that his friends consider Babcock stronger as the Presidents Private Secretary in case of indictment than otherwise." DLC-Hamilton Fish. See letter to Edwards Pierrepont, Oct. 18, 1875; Nevins, *Fish*, pp. 762–69, 786–89; Ross A. Webb, *Benjamin Helm Bristow: Border State Politician* (Lexington, Ky., 1969), pp. 187–212; David P. Dyer, *Autobiography and Reminiscences* (St. Louis, 1922), pp. 151–70.

Order

Washington 31st July. 1875.

It becomes the painful duty of the President to announce to the people of the United States, the death of Andrew Johnson, the last survivor of his honored predecessors, which occurred in Carter County, East Tennessee, at an early hour this morning.

The solemnity of the occasion which called him to the Presidency, with the varied nature and length of his public services, will cause him to be long remembered, and occasion mourning for the death of a distinguished public servant.

As a mark of respect for the memory of the deceased it is ordered that the Executive Mansion, and the several Departments of the government at Washington, be draped in mourning, until the close of the day designated for his funeral; and that all public business be suspended on that day.

It is further ordered that the War and Navy Departments cause suitable honors to be paid on the occasion to the memory of the illustrious dead.

U. S. GRANT

DS, DLC-Executive Orders. On July 31, 1875, John L. Cadwalader, act. secretary of state, telegraphed to USG, Long Branch. "Information received of Death of andrew Johnson in East tennessee early this morning   on the death of Mr Buchanan and Mr filmore an executive Order was issued Draping Executive Mansion & Departments in mourning and suspending public business on the Day of the funeral. If you so direct order in usual form Can be sent to you by messenger for signature" Telegram received, DLC-USG, IB. On the same day, USG telegraphed to Secretary of State Hamilton Fish. "PLEASE HAVE ISSUED THE USUAL ORDERS TO THE MEMORY OF EX. PRESIDENT JOHNSON." Telegram received, DNA, RG 59, Miscellaneous Letters.

On Aug. 1, Sunday, Augustus H. Pettibone, asst. U.S. attorney, Greenville, Tenn., telegraphed to USG. "Johnsons funeral tuesday Eleven am   will you attend   answer" Telegram received, DLC-USG, IB. USG did not attend this funeral.

Endorsement

Will the Sec. of State please submit this to such of the Cabinet as may be in Washington to enable those concerned in the appointments or appointees refered to to enquire into the charges made, and give their opinion as to what action should be taken, if any, on these resolutions.

U. S. Grant

Aug. 2d /75

AES, DLC-Hamilton Fish. Written on an undated memorandum from Alfred Morton, Richmond. "The Executive Committee of the Republican Party of Virginia convened for the purpose of taking into consideration the iniatory steps in the opening of an important state campaign, involving the very existence of our party in this state, and to prepare as far as practicable the organization of the party for the Presidential and Congressional campaign of next year, having reviewed and maturely considered the sources which ought to contribute to the organization, strength and character of the Republican Party in Virginia, are disheartened to to find that a source from which they have a reasonable right to expect such aid—i. e. the National Civil Officials in Virginia, with few exceptions have become indifferent to party obligation, and are more available to and beneficial to the Democratic or Conservative, than to the Republican Party. As an illustration of this condition of affairs they cite this the Metropolitan District. Two out of the three Inspectors in the office of Collector of Customs—Messrs Vaden and Gwathney are Democrats. The Collector and the rest of the office, excepting the janitor and watchman, having lost political interest and identity. The office of Collector of Internal Revenue has for one of its heads a member of the Confederate and more recently of the Democratic state government, and a corps of employees utterly indifferent and wholly uninfluential and injurious to the party. The Post Office, which if controlled by an honest and capable Republican, would reflect more credit upon the administration, and very materially aid in saving Richmond City and the 3d Congressional Dist. to the Republican Party, is in charge of an aged and excentric lady, most offluently rewarded by the Administration, but allured by the specious flattery of the Democrats, controls her office in their interest. A majority of its employees are Democrats and aliens. . . ." DS, *ibid.* See *PUSG,* 19, 337–39.

In Dec., William Hays, chairman, Republican congressional committee, 1st District, Va., and five others, wrote to USG. "We most cordially endorse, and most earnestly solicit the appointment of Mr Nash as Collector of Customs at Tappahannock Va. Mr Nash has been closely identified with the Republican party from its organization in Va. is known throughout the district as a hardworking and influential Republican. We believe he will prove a capable & efficient officer which will reflect credit on the Administration & the republican party. The character of some of the federal appointees in this the first Congressional district is such that the party has become most sadly demoralized and many of the most worthy supporters have become disgusted and alienated. We most earnestly entreat that the positions may be filled by honest capable Republicans wide awake workers for the principles they believe to be right and who commands the confidence & respect of the party." LS, DNA, RG 56, Collector of Customs Applications. Ephraim Nash wrote an undated letter to USG. "We regret to trouble you but circumstances makes it necessary, and in behalf of the Republicans of the 1st district of Va, we ask that the control of the patronage be rescued from J. B. Sener, whose record in Congress is doubtless remembered by you as voting with the Democrats, on all party & political questions. And he was correctly stigmatized the Judas Iscariot of the party. . . ." ALS, *ibid.* A petition with numerous signatures, dated May 18, recommending Hays as collector of customs, Tappahannock, is *ibid.* On Feb. 16, 1876, USG nominated John T. Hoskins as collector of customs, Tappahannock, to replace Edward M. Sandy.

On Aug. 4, William Green, chairman, and Charles Whittle, secretary, Richmond, wrote to USG. "We, the bearer of this Memorial and Colleagues, have the honor to transmit to Your Excellency in writing the humble wishes of the Republican people, assembled in different meetings at different places within the 3thd Congressional District of Va, to wit: Whereas, We, the Republican people do earnestly believe, that we are greatly wronged in our Rights at the last elections held in Richmond and the different counties and thereby were unjustly overpowered by the Democratic party, and, Whereas we believe and are convinced, that these Democratic victories were achieved solely by the mismanagement of our Party-leaders, which to a great deal is to be attributed to an unfortunate spirit of some of the Party-leaders to quarrel amongst themselves, partially for ambition sake and in the most instances for selfish purposes, . . . The main charges against Dr C. Mills & his Subordinates and Joseph Cox & his Subordinates are: that they are conspiring with the Democratic Tilden & Hendricks Clubs, now existing all over the Districts, Believing, that by so doing they will retain their Offices under Democratic Rule, if the Democratic party should be victorious! Praying, that Your Excellency will comply with the earnest wishes of all the Republican Voters and at once remove those above named Officers and nominate in place of Dr C. Mills another highly respected citizen, C. Burton, who enjoys the full confidence of all loyal Republicans, . . ." LS, *ibid.*, Letters Received from the President. On Jan. 30, 1877, USG renominated Charles S. Mills as collector of customs, Richmond. See *PUSG*, 20, 345–47; *Calendar*, June 9, 1874.

In an undated note, USG wrote. "Refer to the Collect[or] of the Port of Richmond to know if place can be given this applicant." AN, Wayde Chrismer, Bel Air, Md.

To Marshall Jewell

Long Branch N. J.
August 2nd 75,

Dear Sir,

Your letter of the 29th of July asking an intimation from me as to whether I will attend the exercises to take place on the opening of the new Postoffice Building in N. Y. City about the last of this, or the first of next month was duly received. The intimation that you do not see how invitations to the four or five Editors of leading City papers can be helped is sufficient to enable me to answer positively that I will not be present   It never came within my comprehension why a slanderer who promulgated his lies to millions of people should be regarded with so much more favor than the man who only communicates it to the few people with whom he comes in contact

I think there should be no formal opening of the New York City Postoffice if Postmaster James [1] feels the least obligation to invite the Editors of Either of at least three of the leading New York daileys

Yours very truly
U S GRANT

Copy, DLC-John Russell Young.

1. Born in 1831 in Utica, N. Y., Thomas L. James, a Whig journalist, joined the customs service and moved to New York City, where he rose to deputy collector. On March 17, 1873, USG nominated James as postmaster, New York City.

To Elizabeth King

————

Long Branch, N. J.
Aug. 2d /75

MY DEAR MRS. KING:

Your very kind invitation for Mrs. Grant & I to visit you, and Georgetown again this Summer, was duly received. I am much obliged to you for the invitation, and hope yet that at least I will be able to visit my old home, and boyhood friends, before time makes further havoc among them. But this Summer I cannot go. My daughter sails for England about the last of this month, and neither Mrs. Grant or myself feel like any protracted absence while she is still with us. Later I must go to St. Louis where my private business calls ~~calls~~ me.

Give my kindest regards to all my old Georgetown friends and say how much I desire to see them again, and how often I run over the names of my old school-day acquaintances. Commodore Ammen and myself have had a plan for several years of going together to our old homes to visit; but unless we do it this year, or next, I will not be able to *command* his time, though I will my own. Now he is subject to my orders: now I am subjected to the call of the country, but then will be free, while the Commodore will only be transfered to another *superior officer*—superior in rank only for he has but few superiors.

Mrs. Grant joins me in kindest regards to yourself & family.

Yours Very Truly

U. S. GRANT

MRS. E. KING,

ALS, DLC–USG, IB.

To Hamilton Fish

———

Long Branch, N. J.

August 3d 1875

HON. HAMILTON FISH,

SEC. OF STATE;

DEAR SIR:

I find that there is some anxiety felt among our friends in New York for the appointment of Nathan I Newwitter[1] as Consul to Hamburgh, vice another New Yorker who I understand has been there for some time. The application, and recommendations, of Mr. N. are on file in the department. From the name I took him to be a German and objected to the appointment on the ground of the rule we have established of making no foreign appointments of naturalized citizens to the Country of their nativity. But I was informed that Mr. Newwitter was born in Albany and is therefore a native American. Unless there be special reasons for the retention of the present incumbent the appointment may be made.

Very Truly

your obt. svt.

U. S. GRANT

ALS, DLC-Hamilton Fish. On Aug. 4, 1875, Secretary of State Hamilton Fish, Garrison, N. Y., wrote to USG, Long Branch. "Mr Cadwalader has forwarded to me your letter respecting Mr Newwitter & the Consulate at Hamburgh—Mr Robinson, the present Consul at Hamburgh, is one of the very best & most accomplished consuls in the service—He is moreover the Despatch Agent of the Department—this is a position of confidence, & of responsibility, & I should regret very much to be obliged to dispense with the services of one who understands the business, & has experience, & who has by long service gained the

confidence of the Department, & be obliged to take a new person of whom I know nothing except from the recommendation signed by about a dozen or fifteen gentlemen in
Newyork—No doubt he may be a very worthy & a competent person—the signatures to
his recommendation are very respectable but are all of one set of gentlemen—those connected with the Newyork Custom House—While I should regret displacing Mr Robinson, or losing his services at Hamburgh—I do not object to the appointment of Mr
Newwitter to some other place—The Consulate at Kingston, Jamaica, is worth two thousand dollars & is held by a Newyorker who has twice left his post without leave—If desired, Mr N. might be appointed there without any injury to the Service—" ALS (press),
ibid. Papers related to Edward Robinson, consul, Hamburg, are in DNA, RG 59, Letters of
Application and Recommendation. See letter to Hamilton Fish, July 5, 1875.

On July 5, U.S. Senator Timothy O. Howe of Wis., Green Bay, had written to USG.
"I am afraid I shall want a little help before I get our family settled for the 'falls work' The
republican press of this State does not improve. The Gazette of this place is Edited by a
thorough republican—a cultured & vigorous writer. But he has been unfortunate in business—is now in bankruptcy—has a family to gather daily bread for, which his Newspaper
will not provide He cannot Sit down to Editorial work—There is another man here who
can do that, & will, do it, if I can provide for Mr George E. Hoskinson the present Editor.
If you want a Surveyor General or Secy. for a territory Mr Hoskinson would supply you
admirably—I asked Mr Fish if Scruggs Could not be withdrawn from Bogata—I believe
he is still there—Nursing republicanism in Ga. is much like Cultivating the tea plant in
N. H.—*It wont pay*—I write the Secretary again, to day. I hope he will talk with you—If
Scruggs has no value Except his worth in Georgia politics—I shd think you would do well
to Exchange him for Mr H." ALS, USG 3. On Aug. 8, George E. Hoskinson, Green Bay,
wrote to USG. "In departing from the usual Etiquette in such matters as I wish to treat of
I beg it may not be charged up to inordinate greed of office, but to the wish to frankly confer with you as Chief of the Republican Party, and as one friend with another, although,
personally, I am a stranger to you. I desire the position of Minister Resident at Columbia,
and wish to present one or two considerations why I have thought it proper in my self to
make a personal application and present my claim for a hearing. I am now and have been
since 1869 Editor of the State Gazette—a journal which has given your Administration a
warm and zealous support, and has been at all times radical and pronounced Republican. I
have labored six years without any reward or hope of reward till now. I have never sought
any office—but On the contrary have always steadily declined to be considered a candidate when urged to become one. In the panic of '73 my moderate fortune was swept away
and the U. S. Circuit Court at Milwaukee is now settling my Estate for the benefit of cred-
itors. In this state of affairs I believe I am justified in asking something from the party I
have faithfully served. Judge Howe, a personal friend, has Endeavored to assist me. He
wrote me, last winter, that the Surveyor-Generalship of Arizona was likely to soon become
vacant and asked me how it would suit. I gladly accepted the possibility, and my recommendation, endorsed by the Entire Wisconsin delegation in Congress is, I think, now on
file in the Secty of Interior's office. But nothing came of it. In June, the Judge and I, in canvassing the possibilities, concluded to request of you the appointment I now refer to. The
Judge wrote to you, and to Sec'y Fish. In due time he heard from Mr. Fish, and showed me
his letter. From this it appears he has no objection to the change. Up to the time the Judge
went West on the Sioux Commission he had not heard from you. That he will be absent
so long is the excuse for this my personal appeal to you. The office is a political one, and I
feel the less compunctions in asking it at your hands from the fact that the State which Mr
S—s represents (Georgia) is so hopelessly Democratic. I am 39 years of age: can translate
Latin: read, write and speak French, and with the help of these cognate languages could

speedily acquire Spanish. I would beg as early a reply as the nature of the subject, and your own convenience will admit of, and, whether favorable as I earnestly hope it may be, or unfavorable I shall ever remain A warm political friend and admirer" ALS, DLC-Hamilton Fish. A favorable endorsement from USG to Fish is *ibid.* On Dec. 17, USG nominated Hoskinson as consul, Kingston, to replace James G. Grindlay.

1. On March 27, 1869, Nathan J. Newwitter, New York City, had written to Fish seeking a consulship in Germany. ". . . My father has been a merchant in this city and Albany, for over thirty years   My character as a merchant and citizen, in all my antecedents, can bear the strictest investigation—and my political career, has been for the support of the Goverment, and its fundamental principles. Although but twenty-four years of age, I am considered as having exerted considerable influence, for the carrying out, and advocating measures which I believed essential for the benefit of my country. . . ." ALS, DNA, RG 59, Letters of Application and Recommendation. On Sept. 5, 1875, Newwitter wrote to USG. "I beg herewith with your permission to accept of the consulship at Osaka & Hioga (Japan), which you were kind enough this morning to offer me through the kindness of Mr. Lewis J Phillips. Thanking you for the courtesy extended and the honor conferred, which shall be filled with my best efforts to the credit of my country and your administration, . . ." ALS (written on stationery of the West End Hotel, Long Branch), *ibid.* On Sept. 7, USG endorsed this letter. "Refered to the Sec. of State. Mr. N. may be commissioned according to his request." AES, *ibid.* Related papers, including an undated petition signed by George Opdyke, Horace Porter, Thomas Murphy, and others, recommending Newwitter as consul, Hamburg, are *ibid.* On Dec. 9, USG nominated Newwitter as consul, Osaka and Hiogo. On Nov. 7, 1872, Newwitter, New York City, had written to USG. "The overwhelming endorsement you have received from the American people, sustaining your successful administration; unparelled in the history of our country, prompt me dear President to congratulate you most sincerely. With the kindest assurance of my regard and the sincerest wishes for your future health and prosperiety, . . ." ALS, USG 3.

Endorsement

Refered to the Sec. of War. The writer of the enclosed slip is right if his premises are right—that the flag of the Pope was saluted ~~by~~ officially. Please have enquiry made as to occurrence and authority for it.

U. S. GRANT

AUG. 5TH /75.

AES, DNA, RG 94, Letters Received, 4379 1875. Written on a letter of Aug. 3, 1875, Tuesday, from Lewis R. Dunn, pastor, Halsey Street Methodist Church, Newark, N. J., to USG. "My attention was called to the fact referred to in the enclosed communication on Monday of this week. I at once penned this article for the Newark Daily Advertiser. I feel that the matter is one of very much importance & significance, and have taken the liberty of calling your attention to it—I am well satisfied that our government is not prepared to recognize the Papal hierarchy—and yet this act of the Commandant of Fort Tompkins *does* recognize that hierarchy & its flag—Hoping that you will give this matter your early attention. . . ." ALS, *ibid.* See clipping, *ibid.*; *New York Tribune*, Aug. 2, 1875. On Aug. 14, Maj. Horatio G. Gibson, Fort Wadsworth, N. Y., endorsed papers on this subject. ". . . On the morning of the departure of the Papal Delegation from the port of New-York, Father Goodwin, the Priest of St Mary's Parish at Clifton S. I. waited upon me, and requested me, to fire a gun or two as the steamer conveying the distinguished embassy passed the Narrows. Seeing no impropriety in granting a request to do a slight honor to a representation which had conferred an unusual and distinguished honor upon our country, I directed the fire of five guns, and they were accordingly fired. I will add, that I am no Roman Catholic, and by birth, education and prejudice as much opposed to the papal hierarchy, as the writer of the communication to the President of the United States, and that if requested, I should have done the same honor to a representation of any other great church of the Christendom." ES, DNA, RG 94, Letters Received, 4379 1875. A delegation led by Monsignor Caesar Roncetti had arrived in April to install Archbishop John McCloskey of New York City as the first U.S. cardinal. See *New York Times*, April 7, 1875. On May 27, USG spoke to the delegation at the White House. "I beg, Monseigneur, that you will convey to the Pope my thanks for his kind expressions of regard and good wishes for the country and for myself, and I am happy to reciprocate your own kind expressions for me." *Washington National Republican*, May 28, 1875.

To Benjamin H. Bristow

Long Branch N. J.
Aug. 7th /75.

DEAR SIR:

The enclosed statement of Mr. John M Mueller in relation to the report of Commissioners to examine and report upon the new Chicago Custom House building has been with me for some time.[1] I have deferred sending it to the department until the publication of the report of the Chicago builders who have examined the same building, and subjects reported upon by the former Com. That report is now published and contradicts the former in almost every particular.— There may be reasons why the Chicago builders are prejudiced in favor of having the present building stand and the work progress. But is there more evidence of partiality on their part for the present structure, material, &c. than there is of prejudice on the part of the former Commission against all these? It looks to me very much as though the present supervisor of the building has exerted himself unduly to have the building condemned, and to prejudice the public against it. He is charged directly with leaving the present incomplete structure exposed so as to increase existing defects, and to create new ones. I would suggest first, that Genl Holman[2] be transferred elsewhere, and a successor be placed over the building who has no prejudices in the matter, that the new superintendent be instructed to take proper precautions to preserve the work already done, until it is decided what is to be done with the building.

I could further suggest that a further commission of seven persons be selected, without consultation with the supervising Architect of the Treas, to examine and report upon this work. In selecting the new commission, I would take three Architects, all from different cities, and men eminent in their profession, two builders & two civil engineers of like character, with the report of such a commission we could at least go before Congress prepared to recommend definitely whether work should progress on the present building or not

Very respectfully
Your obt svt
U S. GRANT

HON B H BRISTOW
SEC OF THE TREAS.

Copy, DLC-USG, II, 3. On Aug. 11, 1875, Wednesday, Secretary of the Treasury Benjamin H. Bristow, Saratoga, N. Y., telegraphed to USG, Long Branch. "Your letter about the Chicago Custom House was forwarded to me here and I concur fully in all your suggestions. I have telegraphed the Acting Secretary to transfer General Holman and put some impartial man in charge, and will select such Commission as you suggest. The trouble is to find the right men. Can you not suggest names of Commissioners. Mr Whitestone of Louisville, formerly of Cincinnati, is a thoroughly educated architect, and, I think, was Mullett's instructor and subsequently one of his subordinates. He is the only Architect whom I know personally as entirely competent and impartial. I will be here until Friday morning." Copy (press, telegram sent), DLC-Benjamin H. Bristow. On the same day, USG telegraphed to Bristow. "I would be at a loss to appoint such a commission as suggested without some inquiry. For one of the architects however I would, I would say Mr. Whitstone & for the engineers Genl Harry Wilson NewYork City & Genl Wm B Franklin of Hartford Conn   I will try to suggest other names tomorrow" Telegram received (at 8:55 P.M.), *ibid.* USG and Bristow appointed James H. Wilson, William B. Franklin, John McArthur, Jr., Henry Whitestone, Nathaniel J. Bradlee, Andrew Kennedy, and Richard J. Dobbins to a new commission to investigate the Chicago Customhouse. On Sept. 23, this commission recommended completing the unfinished structure with modifications. See Endorsement, May 26, 1875; letter to Benjamin H. Bristow, Sept. 27, 1875; *HED*, 44-1-2, 622, 650–51; *Chicago Tribune*, Aug. 22–23, 25, Sept. 4–5, 7, 10–11, 27, 1875.

On Aug. 7, A. G. Mills, former chief clerk for Alfred B. Mullett, Long Branch, had written to Orville E. Babcock. "CHICAGO CUSTOM HOUSE . . . Allow me to add a few words to what I said to you orally. From the enclosed slip which I send to show the reported opinions of Judge Drummond, Genl. Webster, Genl. McArthur & others, you will see that the 'Times' still (but it is now the only paper) continues the cry of fraud & collusion between Mullett and Mueller which was inspired by telegrams from Washington, and yet I have, during the present week, conversed freely with the correspondents of all the Chicago papers in Washington & they admit that they have no evidence of any fraud or collusion and dont know of any. Potter has repeatedly made the same admission to me. Mr. Bristow I have never spoken to on the subject, but as the several challenges to produce any evidence he may have have failed to elicit anything, I apprehend that Mullett's detractors will be obliged to fall back on a few defective stones in the building to deduce an inference to support their baseless calumnies. Potter has claimed that he was not actuated by hostility to Mullett in the Chicago matter, but was anxious to proceed with the building if it could be done safely, yet instead of honestly searching for light in the unanimous report made by the Chicago Commissioners, three of whom he has heretofore strongly endorsed, he has made haste, as soon as their report arrived in Washington, to publicly brand them as ignorant, as will be found by the Washington dispatches of the Chicago papers published yesterday. When Mr. Bristow arrived in Washington, yesterday, he said he should not regard the report of the Chicago Architects, that it was predetermined & he knew all along that it would be favorable, and yet three of that Commission are quoted in the Treasury Commission's report to give weight and authority to certain statements therein made, and Mr. Chesbrough was added to the Chicago commission at the written suggestion of Mr. Bristow, contained in his letter of June 27th, published in the Chicago papers on the following day. All the suggestions made by the Secretary in that letter have been fully complied with, & notwithstanding the predictions confidently made in the Treasy that there would be a disagreement, the report is unanimous and does not admi[t] a shadow of a doubt as to the feasibility of resuming work on the building immediately. Mr. Bristow also reiterated his statement made on July 14th, that he would read the report of the Chicago Commission 'if he had time.' I learned of these statements made by Mr. Bristow yesterday from correspondents of the Chicago press who said they would appear in the Chicago papers of today. Charges of fraud & collusion can certainly be investigated by the Dept, or by Congress without interrupting work on the building. I have no right to speak for the people of Chicago on this subject; They have spoken & are speaking distinctly & unanimously through their press, by petition [&] by all the methods open to them, but I do assert that with the building season fast slipping away, the building open & exposed to the elements, it will, if left in the hands of hostile agents & turned over to the tender mercies of a hostile House of Representatives, be used as a case of mismanagement & waste of the public money such as the Opposition will search elsewhere for in vain throughout the record of the present administration." ALS, USG 3. Enclosed clippings are *ibid.* A separate commission of Chicago architects had completed an investigation that found the customhouse sound and fit for further construction, contrary to the view of William A. Potter, supervising architect. See *Chicago Tribune*, July 14, 25, 31, Aug. 3–4, 6–7, 1875; Mills to Babcock, Aug. 16 and 23, 1875, USG 3.

On Aug. 24, Emery A. Storrs, Chicago, wrote to Babcock, Long Branch. "I have been told that both yourself and Mr Campbell have taken an active and intelligent interest in the matter of the Chicago Custom House for which you can rest assured every citizen of chicago will feel very greatful—and the time has now come when I desire to say a few words to you personally, I doubt whether there is to day a single intelligent and unprejudiced man in the city of Chicago who does not beleive that the Stoppage of that work was entirely unnecessary; and who has not a suspicion, if he has not an absolute beleif, that the work was stopped for the purpose of gratifying and promoting some personal schemes The first Commission Organized by the Secretary of the Treasury was so unfairly Constructed, and its report was so grossly untrue and unjust; that on behalf of Mr Mueller as you probably know and also on behalf of many Citizens of Chicago I Called upon the President and asked permission to lay before him a Statement of the facts, so far at least as Mr Mueller was Concerned, and to reply to that report.   with his usual fairness the President consented to receive and consider such St[atemen]t, and it did not take me long to discover that whatever might be the Situation of Other Officers—the President had no private Axes to grind, and was disposed to see fair play;—to hear all the facts, and not to be Concluded by the report of the Commission. Mr Muellers statement was accordingly prepared and submitted. In the meantime a Committee of Chicago Architects had been appointed by the Mayor and Common Council of this City. The reccommendation of such Committee Came from our best Citizens; and it is needless to say that no one in Mr Muellers interest had the slighest hand in it,   They proceeded with their works, expending a great deal of time in its prosecution; and finally reached a Conclusion directly the reverse of the report of the government Commission. Apprehending that the Chicago Architects would Expose the absurdity of the report made by Patters Committee; Every Conceiveable Agency was resorted to—to frighten or flatter them into a different course; These having all failed; no course was left—except to abuse the Chicago Comittee . . ." ALS, *ibid.* A related newspaper clipping is *ibid.* Earlier, Storrs, as John M. Mueller's counsel, had spoken with USG at Long Branch concerning the Chicago Customhouse. See *Chicago Tribune*, July 11, 1875.

In a communication docketed Aug. 7, 1876, three men "representing a majority of the working Men of the City of Washington, D C.," petitioned USG concerning "an earnest and respectful Memorial, signed by 700 of our number, praying that the appointment of Supervising Architect of the Treasury Department, now vacant, may be tendered to the Honorable A. B. Mullett, who formerly occupied that position; and we trust that you, in whom we have at all times recognized a zealous, and valuable friend to the working Man, will use your good offices to promote that appointment—an appointment, which, we are assured, will, not only contribute to the best interests of the working Men of this city, but will be regarded with much satisfaction by the working Men in all sections of the country." DS (undated), DNA, RG 56, Letters Received from the President. On Aug. 11, Secretary of the Treasury Lot M. Morrill appointed James G. Hill as supervising architect. *New York Times*, Aug. 12, 1876. On Aug. 18, Mullett, Washington, D. C., wrote to USG. "I have been informed by my friends that you have expressed a purpose to give me employment as Architect in connection with the completion of the public buildings designed by me. I feel very grateful for this proof of your confidence: and desire to say that such employment would be very gratifying and acceptable to me. The building season is however far advanced, and the work on some particularly Chicago is in such a condition that immediate action is necessary to preserve the design. Trusting you may be able to make an early decision . . ." Suzanne Mullett Smith and Daisy M. Smith, eds., *A. B. Mullett Diaries &c. . . .* (Washington, 1985), p. 111. Hill objected to Mullett's appointment and prevented him from completing designated duties. See *ibid.*, pp. 110–12, 127.

1. Mueller supplied stone for the Chicago Customhouse considered by some as unsuitable. He wrote to USG defending the stone and attacking the report that urged demolition of the building. *Chicago Tribune*, July 30, 1875.

2. Bvt. brig. gen. vols. for service as col., 1st U.S. Colored Inf. (1863–65), John H. Holman, architect and builder, earlier had superintended construction of the Knoxville Customhouse. Samuel Hannaford replaced Holman as superintendent of the Chicago Customhouse.

To Silas Reed

———

[*Long Branch. N. J.*
Aug. 7th /75.

DEAR SIR:

Your letter of resignation of the 30th ult. was duly received, but has not been acted upon until now. I have this day fowarded it to the Sec of the Int. with instructions to accept it to take effect on the 10th of sept.] or as soon thereafter as your successor may qualify.

In accepting your resignation allow me to say that I know of no reason to be dissatisfied with your administration of the office of Surveyor General. On the contrary I believe it has been efficiently and advantageously to the Govt. filled during your entire administration.

With sincere wishes for your welfare, and assurances of my personal friendship, I am,

Very Truly, Your obt. svt.
U. S. GRANT

DR. SILAS REED,
SURV. GN. W. T.

ALS (partial facsimile, bracketed text not in USG's hand), R. M. Smythe & Co., Inc., Sale No. 145, Nov. 30, 1995, no. 172; copies, USG 3; CtY. *HRC*, 44-1-794, VII, 4. On July 30, 1875, Silas Reed, Cheyenne, had written to USG. "You will recollect that after my reinstatement in the office some two years ago, I voluntarily stated to you that it was not my desire to hold the office any great length of time, and that when the circumstances should be favorable I would tender my resignation. That time has now arrived—my multiplied private affairs demanding my constant attention. I therefore herewith place my resignation in your hands. Thanking you for your long and continued kindness, . . ." ALS, DNA, RG 48, Appointment Papers, Wyoming Territory; ADf, CtY. On Aug. 7, USG endorsed this letter. "Refered to the sec. of the Int.   Surveyor Gen. S. Reed's resignation may be accepted to take effect on the 10th of Sept. or as soon thereafter as his successor may qualify." AES, DNA, RG 48, Appointment Papers, Wyoming Territory. See *PUSG*, 24, 170–74; Lewis L. Gould, *Wyoming: A Political History, 1868–1896* (New Haven, 1968), pp. 50–51.

On Aug. 21, USG, Long Branch, telegraphed to Secretary of the Interior Columbus Delano. "The appointment of Edward C David as surveyor General of wyoming Territory should be sent at once to enable him to qualify by the tenth of sept the date of acceptance of Dr. Reids resignation" Telegram received (at 2:10 P.M.), DNA, RG 48, Appointment Papers, Wyoming Territory.

In May, 1884, and in [*1884–85*], Reed wrote to USG, New York City. "I came out of the Utah Mountains 10 days ago—In taking a survey of the political field I feel quite hopeful that you will have found enough in the (the now Silent) Chicago Convention to ~~cause~~ effect your nomination after the prominent forces have clashed and exhausted themselves. I hope ~~your~~ the friends with a mutual understanding will remain quiet, until the opportune moment arrives" "Please permit me to introduce to ~~his~~ your favorable acquaintance, the bearer of this note, Mr Wm H. Macomber, an esteemed young friend of mine whose people ~~are~~ reside in Bostonians—He has resided in China 15 yrs—& ~~before returning there~~, now desires to see & take by the hand the ~~great~~ Conquirer of the great Rebellion. He is applying for the Position of Tea ~~at in~~ Inspector under the U. States, for which duty he is Specially well fitted by experience & good character   He has passed a creditable Examinatn before the Civil Service Commission, being one of 4 whose names have been referred to Secy. McCulloch for appointment. He is in hopes that ~~that~~ you m~~ay~~ight be able & willing to offer him Some advice or Suggestions that would aid him in ~~securing the appoint~~ his purpose. . . . P. S. Congress will yet do you Justice by the passage of a proper bill for your retirmt as General" ADf, CtY.

To Hamilton Fish

———

Long Branch, N. J.
August. 8th /75.

DEAR GOVERNOR:

I know of no reason why Baron Blanc should be objected to as the representative of Italy to this country, unless it is that we are very sorry to part with Count. Corti who has proven himself so acceptable to the American people. You may if you please inform the present Sec. of Legation in your own way, our appreciation of the former representative of his country here, and give assurances that his successor will find nothing to apologize for, or regret, in the services of his predecessor while holding the position of Minister to the United States.

Faithfully yours,
U S GRANT

HON. HAMILTON FISH SEC. OF STATE

Copy, DLC-USG, II, 3. On Aug. 5, 1875, Secretary of State Hamilton Fish, Garrison, N. Y., wrote to USG. "The Italian Charge writes by instruction of his Government to ask if you have any objection to receive Baron Blanc, as Envoy Extraordinary &c from Italy—he says that he has been Under-Secretary of State & at present is Italian Minister at Brussels. He is represented to be an accomplished Gentleman—The Consul at Osaca in Japan, has recently died.   the salary is (I think) three thousand dollars—he has Judicial functions—if

Mr Newitter is a lawyer, possibly this place will suit him—The Consul at Port-said (Egypt) is also dead—the salary there, is, I think two thousand dollars—I have but a moment to catch the mail, but thought that one or other of these place, just become vacant, might please Mr Newittr" ALS (press), DLC-Hamilton Fish. For Nathan J. Newwitter, see letters to Hamilton Fish, Aug. 3, 27, 1875. On Nov. 12, Albert Blanc presented his credentials to USG as minister from Italy.

On June 21, Fish, Garrison, had written to USG, Long Branch. "I leave here tomorrow for Washington, intending to stop in Philadelphia to attend Miss Cadwaladers wedding—Count Corti is about to return home, having been transferred to the Mission to Constantinople—He desires an audience to present his letters of recall. As he proposes to sail in the Russia on the 30th of this month, I have promised to take your instructions as to the audience—& whether you will receive him at Long Branch, & if so when it will be Convenient to you. Will you have the goodness to let me know (by letter to Washington) what will be most convenient & agreeable to you—It has been intimated to him, that it is not necessary to make a formal address on leave taking—but as the Count has rendered very valuable services, as umpire on the Joint Claims Commission, it occurs to me that possibly you might think proper to make his case somewhat exceptional, & to say something which he might have in writing, as a recognition of appreciation of his services—Please let me know what you prefer in this respect—If you think proper to mark his services by a reply, I will forward a copy of the address which he proposes to make, & a suggested form of reply for your approval—" ALS, CSmH. On June 25 and 26, Fish again wrote to USG about the departure of Count Corti as Italian minister. ALS (press), DLC-Hamilton Fish.

Endorsement

Refered to the Sec. of the Treas. and the Sec. of War, approving the application of Mr. Eads for the services of the Govt. officers named within.

The work undertaken by Mr. Eads is of such National importance that the request within should be granted even if attended with inconvenience.

U. S. GRANT

AUG. 9TH /75

AES, DNA, RG 77, Letters Received. Written on a letter of Aug. 5, 1875, from James B. Eads, New York City, to USG. "Charged by act of Congress with the execution of a public work of great national importance, involving engineering problems of peculiar delicacy, with renumeration depending wholly upon the realization of stipulated results by works to be constructed at my own expense, I naturally desire the aid and counsel of eminent engineers who have bestowed especial study upon this subject. As an engineer myself I should not of course have undertaken this great enterprise without full confidence in my own plans for its execution, nor perhaps without knowing that my own views were, on the whole, approved by other engineers of great experience and ability. Nevertheless I feel that the personal responsibility I am under, and the high national importance of attaining the most thorough and substantial success, demand that no possible means be neglected on my part to insure the desired result, and that I should therefore obtain the views of the most competent engineers known to me, upon the proposed location and construction of the contemplated works. With their experience and foresight I would be safer from error, and with their concurrence, additional assurance would be given that the plans adopted are judicious and reliable. In selecting this professional counsel, circumstances clearly indicate those whose opinions would be most valuable   A great public improvement very similar in character has been recently executed with the most complete and permanent success by Sir Charles A Hartley of England with whom I have had an extended correspondence regarding this work, and whose advice in prosecuting it I have already secured. Genl Barnard. U. S. Engrs. was the president of the board convened in 1873 to consider the question of a ship canal, or the alternative of deepening the mouth of one of the passes. He has given to this subject profound study and I feel that his counsel will be of great value. Beside these two distinguished gentlemen I am plainly directed to the eminent engineers selected by Your Excellency under the act of June 23d 1874 and constituting a commission whose special function was to decide between the two different methods of improvement recently under discussion by Congress and the public. I am desirous of inviting as counsellors in this work, all of the members of this commission and thus constituting an advisory Board of nine of the ablest and most thoroughly informed engineers upon this question, that can probably be selected in the world. Five of these gentlemen are officers of the government 'namely' Genls Barnard, Wright, Alexander, and Comstock Engrs U. S. A. and Prof. Mitchell C. E., of the U S Coast survey. I assume that some authorization or approval by Your Excellency will be necessary and proper to enable these gentlemen to thus co'operate with me should they consent to do so. The assistance required by me will not take them long nor often from their stations, and no expense will be incurred by the Government as their compensation for this special service and their expenses will be cheerfully borne by myself. I am encouraged to hope that the desired authorization will be promptly granted in view of the great national importance of securing the best possible results from the works; a consideration which I am sure is fully appreciated by Your Excellency." LS, *ibid.* Related papers are *ibid.* On Aug. 26, Secretary of the Treasury Benjamin H. Bristow wrote to USG. "A copy of the letter of Captain Eads, of the 5th inst., addressed to you, with a copy of your endorsement thereon, directing compliance with his request, was received at this Department in my absence, and by Mr. Conant, Assistant Secretary, referred to Captain Patterson, Superintendent of the United States Coast Survey, with instructions to assign Professor Mitchell to perform the duties requested by Mr. Eads, in accordance with your direction. Captain Patterson has addressed to me a letter in reply which contains statements such as I deem necessary to bring to your attention, and, therefore, have the honor to transmit herewith Capt. Patterson's letter with enclosures. Awaiting your further direction in the matter, . . ." LS (press), DLC-Benjamin H. Bristow.

On March 3, USG had signed legislation granting Eads a contract "to construct such permanent and sufficient jettees, and such auxiliary works as are necessary to create and permanently maintain, as hereinafter set forth, a wide and deep channel between the South Pass of the Mississippi River and the Gulf of Mexico." *U.S. Statutes at Large*, XVIII, part 3, p. 463. See Proclamation, July 3, 1874; *HED*, 43-2-114. On June 1, USG approved the reservation of land "bordering on the Passes of the Mississippi River, and extending twelve miles on both sides of the river above the Passes," for military purposes. Copies,

DNA, RG 77, Letters Received; *ibid.*, RG 94, Military Reservation Div.; *ibid.*, RG 107, Letters Sent, Military Affairs.

On June 26, Eads, New Orleans, wrote to USG. "I have the honor to inform your excellency that under the authority granted to me by the president and congress of the United States, I commenced on the fourteenth of this month the construction of permanent works at the bar of the South pass of the Mississippi, designed to create and maintain a wide and deep channel between that river and the Gulf of Mexico. The contractors, Messrs. James Andrews & Co., to whom I have intrusted a large portion of the construction, have already extended provisional works from the land's end seaward on the line of the east jetty fully one thousand feet, and are progressing at the rate of two hundred feet per day. They have about two hundred mechanics and laborers engaged on the work, with four pile-driving machines, two steamboats, and a number of barges, and have a large quantity of stone and other materials ready for use. Additional machinery and accommodations are being rapidly prepared, and in a short time the force will be largely increased. Telegraph communication has been established between this city and the head of the pass, and the line is being continued to the works at the mouth of the pass. I desire to assure your excellency that no effort will be spared to meet the public expectation and secure deep water between the river and the gulf at the earliest possible date." *St. Louis Post-Dispatch*, June 29, 1875.

On July 14, Henry T. Crosby, chief clerk, War Dept., wrote to Orville E. Babcock, Long Branch. "I have the honor to transmit herewith, in the absence of the Secretary of War, for the approval or otherwise, of the President, a draft of the regulations prepared by the Chief of Engineers for the protection of the public interests connected with the improvement of the South Pass of the Mississippi river, now being prosecuted under the direction of Captain James B. Eads, under the Act of Congress approved March 3d 1875. Will you please submit the same to the President, and return the papers to this Department with his action endorsed thereon." Copy, DNA, RG 107, Letters Sent, Military Affairs. On July 27, USG signed orders regulating the use of materials from public lands in jetty construction. Copy, *ibid.* *HED*, 44-1-1, part 2, II, part I, p. 977. See *SED*, 44-1-5.

On Nov. 3, [*1876*], USG wrote a note. "~~Will the Adj. Gn.~~ [The Pres. directs me to ask you to] inform ~~me~~ [him] whether, before the Sec. of War left Washington, he ordered a board of Eng. Officers to examine and report upon Capt. Eads work at the mouth of the Miss." AN (bracketed material not in USG's hand), Wayde Chrismer, Bel Air, Md. In his Nov. 20 annual report, Secretary of War James D. Cameron wrote to USG that a commission had investigated a contract dispute over targeted channel depth. *HED*, 44-2-1, part 2, I, 17. Upon achieving the target depth, Eads was to be paid either with funds appropriated by Congress or with interest-bearing bonds issued by the Treasury Dept. On Jan. 30, 1877, the House of Representatives voted to appropriate the money; on Feb. 8, the Senate voted to postpone the House bill indefinitely. See *CR*, 44–2, 1305–8, 1340–47; *HED*, 44-2-28; *SRC*, 44-2-632. On Feb. 9, USG wrote to Charles F. Conant, asst. secretary of the treasury. "Since the action of the Senate yesterday in the matter of Capt. Eads claim for work done at the mouth of the Miss. river I think there should be no delay on the part of the Treas. in giving him the bonds due in payment." ALS, Houlé Gallery and Bookshop, Los Angeles, Calif.

On April 5, 1880, Eads spoke about the jetties at a New Orleans banquet honoring USG. ". . . From the first inception of the enterprise, the man whom all the nations of the world have so recently, so unprecedentedly, and so justly honored, was its earnest and faithful friend. . . ." Estill McHenry, ed., *Addresses and Papers of James B. Eads, together with a Biographical Sketch* (St. Louis, 1884), pp. 357–58. See E. L. Corthell, *A History of the Jetties at the Mouth of the Mississippi River* (New York, 1880), pp. 92–93, 266–74; Florence Dorsey, *Road to the Sea: The Story of James B. Eads and the Mississippi River* (New York, 1947), pp. 167–200; John M. Barry, *Rising Tide: The Great Mississippi Flood of 1927 and How It Changed America* (New York, 1997), pp. 67–92.

To Hamilton Fish

Long Branch, N. J.

Aug. 9th /75

DEAR GOVERNOR;

Your letter of the 7th inst. with inclosures, suggesting the appointment of further Commissioners to the Chilian Fair is received. I see no objection to the appoint of any reasonable number of reputable persons on such commission as may be requested by Americans interested in the exhibition.

You are authorized to call upon the Sec. of the Navy for a vessel to visit the Haytian waters.

Of course the payment of our claim by the Venezuelan Government will obviate the necessity of recalling Judge Russell, our minister to that country.

Very Truly Yours

U. S. GRANT

HON. HAMILTON FISH, SEC. OF STATE.

ALS, DLC-Hamilton Fish. On Aug. 7 and 25, 1875, Secretary of State Hamilton Fish, Garrison, N. Y., wrote to USG, Long Branch. "I enclose a paper addressed to me by some Gentlemen interested in the Chilian Exhibition, requesting the appointment of additional Commissioners—you will remember that Genl Vickers was appointed a Commissioner without compensation, *to examine & report.* I understand that many Americans propose to exhibit articles there, & the field is worth cultivating, & if it meet your views I think that these Gentlemen might be allowed to suggest two or three names (the character of the Gentlemen who sign the letter, is a guarantee that they will suggest worthy persons) as Commissioners to look after the interests of the Exhibiters—who might either be *associated* with Genl Vickers, or constitute an entirely distinct Commission, as you shall think best—of course there being no appropriation they could receive nothing from the Government—If you will have the goodness to let me know your wishes in this matter, I will make answer to the gentlemen who have written me—May I ask the favour of the return of the enclosed papers. A dispatch just now received from Mr Russell says that the President of Venezuela, has promised him to pay the money which has been withheld—it was to be paid, *without condition*, within a day or two after the date of Mr Russells despatch—Mr Bassett (in Haiti) writes that some Haytians have sought Asylum in his legation, & that Haytian troops are watching & surrounding the Legation to arrest these parties if they leave his House—Bassett disregarded his instructions in allowing these Refugees to take Asylum in the Legation—possibly, they h may have got in without his assent, but as he has always advocated the granting of asylum (in opposition to the instructions & the policy of this Government) I fear that he encouraged them to come to him—If it prove so, I shall be inclined to recommend his recall, but at present am not prepared to judge him—heretofore he has been a very intelligent & official Minister—But whatever *his* fault may be, the watching & surrounding his legation with a military force, seems an indignity which cannot be allowed—I have therefore caused Mr Preston to [*be*] informed that the United States cannot allow this, & that it must *immediately* cease—& that a vessel of war will be sent there, unless he can give assurance of the immediate cessation of the apparent menace & force surrounding our Legation—If this meet your approval, I shall be glad to have your authority to request the Secretary of the Navy to send a vessel down   I think it will be adviseable to send the vessel, whatever assurances Mr Preston may give—" "I have much satisfaction in advising you of the payment by Venezuela of the amount heretofore withheld by that Govt, of the indemnities due under our Convention—I am in the receipt of drafts on London amounting to £12,366. 18s 6d at 90 days sight—The Haytian questions are not yet satisfactory disposed of. I feel however a reasonable confidence that they will be adjusted without any serious complications. But Mr Bassett has embarassed us, and on the settlement of the pending questions, will need a *very severe* rebuke, if not an absolute recall." ALS (press), *ibid.* The Chilean Exhibition opened at Santiago on Sept. 16. For the diplomatic controversy with Venezuela involving claims payments, see first letter to Hamilton Fish, July 14, 1875; Thomas Russell, U.S. minister, Venezuela, to Fish, May 31, June 15, Sept. 4, 1875, DNA, RG 59, Diplomatic Despatches, Venezuela (the first partially printed in *Foreign Relations, 1875*, II, 1374–75); Fish to Russell, June 4, July 23, 1875, DNA, RG 59, Diplomatic Instructions, Venezuela (the first partially printed in *Foreign Relations, 1875*, II, 1375–77); *ibid.*, pp. 1369, 1372, 1378–84.

On Aug. 20, Benjamin Silliman, Jr., New Haven, Conn., had written to USG. "PERSONAL.... You were good enough, at my request, at least in part, to appoint HON. E. D. BASSETT to the position of *Minister Resident at Haiti.* He has proved himself worthy of the trust imposed in him and as I am happy to learn has the confidence of his Government. Lately he has communicated to me by a trusty messenger, verbally, his distressing situation growing out of his extending the *Rights of Asylum* to GENERAL CANAL a General of the Haitian Army, procribed by reason of his popularity with the people. Since May 3d Mr Bassett's premises have been surrounded by an army of native soldiery, armed with Henry rifles, to prevent the escape of Canal to whom a decree of exile is denied. Another General, who at the same time sought Right of Asylum, *with the English Consul,* has been permitted a decree of exile and has escaped death by flight. Meantime the American Minester's residence is practically in a state of seige. His family are permitted to come and go by day, but at night only at the risk of life. I sent out Mr Bassett's family to him in June at his request. But it was in the conviction that before their arrival this duress would be removed. Their wrectchedness at being under the survillience of these semibarbarous soldiery, practically prisoners in their own house and deprived of all quiet and peace of mind, can readily be imagined and is simply intolerable. Mr Bassett has, with a delicate sense of etiquette, refrained from writing these details to me. But I know it is his earnest wish that this distressing condition of things so derogatory to our national honor, should be brought to your personal notice. No doubt the State Department are in possession of full communications from Mr Bassett setting forth all his official acts   But he is not the man to make known, in that way, his personal sacrifices or the sufferings of his family. Hence I take the liberty of making, for your consideration, this unofficial statement; beleiving you will see that an honorable solution is found for the deliverance of a zealous and faithful officer from difficulties growing out of the discharge of his duties   I understand that the *Right of Asylum* has always been extended to political refugees in Haiti, and is respected even in the most lawless times. But it is certainly derogatory to our Flag that the American Minister in the exercise of this hospitality should be punished by the indignities under which Mr Bassett has suffered for nearly four months past. . . . Postscript Aug 25   I am this moment in receipt of a letter from Mr Bassett of which the following is a copy   Port au Prince Haiti August 16, 1875   PROF B SILLIMAN   My dear Sir   I have barely time and strength to acknowledge the receipt of your last favor, and to thank you for its interesting contents. I suppose you have seen Mr Bushnell whom I charged to see you and give you some particulars. I may add that the difficulty sore and trying about my refugees still continues. Its issue is still involved in doubt. All this causes me very much inquietude and anxiety. My health has become quite unsatisfactory. I am unable often to come to my office, and am part of the time in bed. My little son U. S. Grant is down with fever. Mrs Bassett who kept up surprisingly well all through July, has become somewhat indisposed these past few days, though I think she may not become sick entirely. How trouble and anxiety accumulate sometimes. Loaded with anxietyies and troubles and enfeebled by continued indisposition, I am yet inspired by confident hope, . . . EBENEZER D. BASSETT" LS, DNA, RG 59, Miscellaneous Letters.

On Sept. 22, Fish wrote to Ebenezer D. Bassett, U.S. minister, Port-au-Prince, requesting an explanation of his communications with Silliman. Copy, *ibid.*, Diplomatic Instructions, Haiti and Santo Domingo. On Oct. 12, Bassett wrote to Fish. ". . . I have never at any time intentionally acted in contravention of that feature in our law which forbids diplomatic agents to correspond on public affairs with unofficial persons, . . . An American gentleman Mr Bushnell has been living as an agreeable guest in my house here for more than four years. His home is Clinton, Connecticut. When he was about to leave this city for his home in June last, it was decided between us that, as Clinton is so near New Haven where my family then were, he should call to pay his respects to them and fulfill some personal missions with which I charged him for them. At the same time, as Professor Benjamin Silliman, as well as his father before him, was the earliest and best friend of Mrs Bassett's family, and was charged with many personal interests of mine, I could not fail to give him a line to that gentleman. The note which I gave him was simply an ordinary one of introduction. I wanted Mr Bushnell to explain to Professor Silliman why I had not fulfilled and could not then fulfill certain purely personal arrangements which I had made with the latter. This was all. Mr Bushnell, though a most intimate and valued friend in my family these many years, knew nothing whatever from me or through me in any way, of my official correspondence with you or with this government. He could not therefore possibly have given to my most esteemed friend Professor Silliman anything more than his impressions of it from what he and every one else here knew of my perilous personal situation growing out of the affair of the refugees. . . ." ALS, *ibid.*, Diplomatic Despatches, Haiti. On Nov. 20, Fish wrote to Bassett. ". . . The letter which the President referred to this Department showed that information had been communicated to the writer, which was of a nature that a Diplomatic Representative of the Government should not have communicated to private citizens, however high their personal and social position. In the belief that the embarrassments arising from the difficulty to which the communication referred to have been happily disposed of, and bearing in mind the personal inconveniences to which your according of asylum to the Refugees, appears to have subjected you, the Department accepts your assurance that you did not intentionally violate the law which prohibits your correspondence with private persons on the relations of your government or your Legation with the Government to which you are accredited." Copy, *ibid.*, Diplomatic Instructions, Haiti and Santo Domingo. See Fish diary, June 3, Aug. 12, 18, 1875, DLC-Hamilton Fish; *Foreign Relations, 1875*, II, 686–748; *Foreign Relations, 1876*, pp. 320–22.

To William W. Belknap

DATED, LONG BRANCH N J [*Aug.*] 11 [*1875*]
TO SECTY OF WAR WASHN
Cadet Geo P Scriven may be restored to the military academy with reprimand & on the grounds that others equally guilty in the Hazing for which he has been dismissed have not been detected punished he will be confined to the guard tent performing all his military duties for the balance of the encampment & to his room in arrest performing in like manner all his duties during the ensuing academic year unless sooner relieved by excutive orders.

U. S. GRANT

Telegram received, DNA, RG 94, Correspondence, USMA. On Aug. 4, 1875, Col. Thomas H. Ruger, superintendent, USMA, wrote to Secretary of War William W. Belknap. "I have the honor to report that on the 28th of July, ulto:, Cadet *George P. Scriven* of the 3rd class, with others whose names I am not at present able to report, was engaged in molesting and assaulting a New Cadet Sentinel at the Cadets Encampment, in violation of Par; 135. Regulations for the Academy. I would respectfully recommend that Cadet George P. Scriven be summarily dismissed." LS, *ibid.* On Aug. 12, Lt. Gen. Philip H. Sheridan, Chicago, wrote to USG. "I feel a great interest in Cadet Scrivener, just dismissed from the Academy for hazing a pleb. He stands very high in all his studies, in fact, among the first, with only 12 demerit for the year, and if anything can be done for him, it would be very gratifying to me. If he could be restored with heavy punishment, or even if his dismissal could be changed to suspension, it would perhaps with what has happened to him be sufficient for an example. If you can consistently do anything to help him I will feel very grateful." Copy, DLC-Philip H. Sheridan. George P. Scriven graduated USMA in 1878.

On Sept. 3, Henry T. Crosby, chief clerk, War Dept., wrote to Ruger. "The following order has been received from the President, endorsed upon the Court Martial proceedings of Cadet Captain Henry D. Borup, U. S. M. A: 'Sentence approved; but mitigated so far as dismissal is concerned. Cadet Borup will be reduced to the ranks, and he, and all his class engaged in the meeting referred to in the testimony accompanying the proceedings, and in sending the note to Cadet Robinson, will be reprimanded. All other Cadet officers so engaged will be reduced to the ranks, and the privates of the 1st Class engaged with them, will be placed in arrest for sixty days, not to be excused thereby, however, from any military or Academic duty. If there be no members of the 1st class qualified to fill the offices of said Class, or an insufficient number of them, their places will be supplied by Cadets of the 2nd Class, as Acting Cadet Officers.' I herewith enclose a copy of the Court Martial order in Mr. Borup's case, and have the honor to request that you will take the necessary measures to carry out the instructions of the President above communicated. The order to the Class to be announced at the same time as that of Cadet Borup." Copy, DNA, RG 94, Letters Sent, USMA. For Henry Dana Borup, see *PUSG*, 21, 404. Charles M. Robinson, admitted to USMA in 1874, did not graduate.

On Feb. 2, U.S. Representative Thomas Whitehead of Va. had written to USG. "I nominated for appointment as a Cadet to the Military Academy Jos H Martin of Lynchburg Va in my district   The selection was made after a competitive examination Mental & Physical: He Martin was pronounced perfect by a Medical Examiner of official standing & on a University of Va examination he stood 484 with 500 as highest   He was 17 years old vivacious sprightly & mischievous   He was charged with 'hazing' another 'Pleb' & dismissed not on the complaint of the party hazed or of officers but upon information of some unknown informer & some time after the alleged offence   I applied to the Secry of War to reduce his sentence from dismissal to suspension. . . . I now respectfully ask that I may be permitted to renominate him for examination next June and I take leave here to say that I am thus importunate on account of his mother & will promise for him that this shall be a lesson preventing him hereafter from violating the smallest rule" ALS, DNA, RG 94, Correspondence, USMA. Admitted to USMA in 1874, Joseph H. Martin did not graduate.

To Roscoe Conkling

Long Branch, N. J.
Aug. 12th 1875

MY DEAR SENATOR:

Your kind invitation for me to visit you on the 15th of Sept. on the occasion of the re-union of the Society of the Army of the Cumberland, is received. I will gladly do so if this side of the Miss. river at the time. My private affairs in Mo. are in such sad condition that I must visit there soon and at least cut off the heavy expenses my farm is putting me to.[1] If not compelled to go earlyer than the time of the Army meeting[2] I will go by the way of Utica and spend a day or two with you. In that case we will have broken up here and sent baggage & servants to Washington, and Mrs. Grant will be with me.

Nellie leaves on the 28th of this month to return to England.[3] Jesse will be returning to Cornell about the middle of Sept. so there will be no family but Mrs. Grant and myself unless I should take Fred. and his wife that way on their way west. But in that case their accompanying us would make no difference for they would expect to stop at the hotel.

For other guests either of the gentlemen named by you, or any others in their ~~in their~~ stead who would be agreeable to you would be so to me.

Please present the kindest regards of Mrs. Grant, Nellie & myself to Mrs. Conkling & Miss Bessie.

Very Truly yours
U. S. GRANT

HON. ROSCOE CONKLING U. S. S.

ALS, DLC-Roscoe Conkling.

    1. See letter to Edward F. Beale, Sept. 8, 1875.
    2. See Speech, Sept. 15, 1875.
    3. Ellen Grant Sartoris, her husband, and their infant son sailed from New York City for Liverpool on the *Baltic.*

To AG Edward D. Townsend

Long Branch, N. J.
Aug. 23d 1875.

GEN. E. D. TOWNSEND,
ADJ. GEN. U. S. A.
SIR:

    Edmund R. Williams may be examined immediately for the position of 2d Lt. U. S. Inf.y, and if he passes be assigned with rank from the same date of those already appointed.

Respectfully &c
U. S. GRANT

ALS, DNA, RG 94, ACP, 4086 1875. On Aug. 24, 1875, AG Edward D. Townsend wrote to USG, Long Branch. "Your order of the 23d inst relative to the exn of Ed~~ward~~mund R Williams with view to his appt as 2d Lt. of Inftry has been received; and instructions have been given for him to appr before the Bd of Exn ~~at~~ in this City" ADf (initialed, undated), *ibid.*; copy, *ibid.*, Letters Sent. On Aug. 7, USG had written an endorsement for Edmund R.

Williams. "Referred to the Adjt. Gen. of the Army who will please acknowledge receipt of Mr. Williams application and answer whether his request can be granted, the answer to be sent to Mr. W. himself. If his record is as stated I would be glad to see him get an appointment." Copy, *ibid.*, ACP, 4086 1875. On Aug. 11, Townsend wrote to USG. "I have the honor to acknowledge your reference of the application of Mr. E. R. Williams for a clerkship, and respectfully enclose herewith a copy of the reply sent to Mr Williams—" Copy, *ibid.*, Letters Sent. On Aug. 30, USG wrote to Townsend. "The question of age in the case of Mr. Ed R. Williams may be waved, he having prepared and passed an examination long before he become of the age fixed by regulation as the extreme limit of for admission to the Army as a Commissioned officer." ALS, *ibid.*, ACP, 4086 1875. Williams never served as 2nd lt.

On July 3, Orville E. Babcock, Long Branch, had written to Henry T. Crosby, chief clerk, War Dept., conveying USG's instructions to appoint Charles H. Ingalls, Homer W. Wheeler, Basil N. Waters, James H. Lane, Bernard A. Byrne, Charles T. Manning, and James D. Nickerson as 2nd lts. ALS, *ibid.*, ACP, 3019 1875. On the same day, Babcock again wrote to Crosby. "(Personal.). . . Gen. Ingalls can give the State & P. O. address of the Ingalls to appt 2d Lieut. in the Arty. Lane is the son of Ex Senator Lane of Kansas and there are papers on file for him, from which you can get his address. Wheeler is a nephew of mine—and is the post Trader at Fort Wallace. I do not know that he will accept. If he does can you not have him examined at Fort Leavenworth and have Gen. Robt. Williams, A. A. G. and Col. Dunn on the board. I send to day Gen. Popes letter recommending him. I shall be pleased if this can be done. If he accepts, I may ask a few weeks leave to close out his tradership—But I can secure that if he accepts, so need not bother you with it. The President approves the sentence of Court Martial in case of Moroney, retired. You can issue this and there will be a place to put Nichols,—so that Brodhead and others can be apptd at once. . . . P. S. Basil Norris's address is Baltimore, Md." Copy, *ibid.* Related papers are *ibid.* On July 6, USG remitted the portion of retired 1st Lt. Patrick H. Moroney's court-martial sentence stipulating imprisonment for drawing double pay. Copy, DLC-Charles Ewing. Moroney was dismissed and compelled to refund his overpayment. See DNA, RG 94, Letters Received, 2626 1875; William M. Dunn, asst. judge advocate gen., to Crosby and Crosby to Babcock, July 7, 1875, *ibid.*, RG 107, Letters Sent, Military Affairs. James W. Nicholls resigned as maj., paymaster, as of July 23. On March 5, John M. Brodhead, second comptroller, U.S. Treasury, had written to USG. "If you have not decided absolutely on the list of new Paymasters, I hope you will put on my brother. His commission as Paymaster was presented by Secty Stanton to President Johnson, for his signature, just about the time they became hostile, & the President declined to sign it though Mass. was entitled to more. My brother is recommended by two or three Governors & Ex Governors of the State and the M. C's from Mass. as well as by the former & present Paymaster General. But I know well the embarrassment that the multitude of applications may cause you, and if you can not oblige me in the matter, I shall have no fault to find, . . ." ALS, *ibid.*, RG 94, ACP, 2621 1875. On June 2, Levi P. Luckey wrote to Secretary of War William W. Belknap. "The President directs me to say that, believing that no promise is as yet made for the appointment of Paymaster for the next vacancy, you may enter the name of Col. Josiah A Broadhead, Boston, Mass, to be favorably considered for the next vacancy." ALS, *ibid.* Related papers are *ibid.*; *ibid.*, 2840 1875; *ibid.*, 3350 1875. On Dec. 6, USG nominated Josiah A. Brodhead as maj., paymaster, to date from July 25. On July 17, Nickerson, "Corporal Gen'l. Service," St. Paul, had written to AG, Washington, D. C., acknowledging his appointment as 2nd lt. pending passage of the required examination. ALS, *ibid.*, 3506

1875. Wheeler, Waters, Lane, Byrne, Nickerson, and Ingalls served as 2nd lts.; Manning never served.

In Jan., 1875, Governor Thomas A. Osborn of Kan. *et al.* had petitioned USG. "The undersigned, Judges, State Officers and members of the Legislature of the State of Kansas, respectfully and earnestly recommend the appointment of James H. Lane to the position of second Lieutenant in the regular army. Mr. Lane is the son of the late Hon. James H Lane, who served this country with distinction in the war with Mexico and in the Free State struggle in Kansas, and as United States Senator and is a young man of fine ability, and good Character and we are confident would fill a position in the army with honor to himself and the Government. The appointment of Mr. Lane would be universally regarded by the people of Kansas as an act of justice; a recognition of the memory and services of his distinguished father and would meet with their cordial approval" DS, *ibid.*, 3756 1875. This petition was signed by Vice President Henry Wilson, Speaker of the House James G. Blaine, and many other members of Congress. Related papers are *ibid.*

On May 24, Manning, Baltimore, wrote to USG. "I respectfully solicit from you an appointment as Second Lieutenant in the Army—in any arm of the Service   My education, training and active life has been in the field with civil engineers—I was born in Cumberland, Md—in 1853 so that I am now nearly twenty two years of age, well grown, and sound in mind and body—I am son of Col. Charles P. Manning, well known as a civil engineer, and grandson of the late general Chas. M. Thruston of Cumberland, . . ." ALS, *ibid.*, 4011 1875. Supporting letters include one of May 17 from Charles Gilpin, surveyor of customs, Baltimore, to USG vouching for the family's loyalty "in a community where disloyalty was the rule and loyalty the exception at the commencement and during the entire war," and subsequent financial hardship. ALS, *ibid.* On May 24, USG endorsed these letters. "Refered to the Sec. of War. Let special attention be called to this application when appointments are next made to the Army." AES, *ibid.*

On June 24, Waters, Washington, D. C., wrote to Belknap. "I have the honor to apply for appointment as Second Lieutenant in the U. S. Army. I was born in Baltimore Maryland, 25th of May, 1850: and have been employed in the United States Signal Service since 24th day of July 1873. I respectfully refer to Surgeon Basil Norris, as my friend and relative." ALS, *ibid.*, 3905 1875. On July 3, USG endorsed this letter. "Refered to the Sec. of War. Let special attention be called to this application when apts. are made." AES, *ibid.*

On June 29, Brig. Gen. John Pope, Fort Leavenworth, Kan., wrote to USG. "It is with great pleasure that I avail myself of the opportunity to present to your favorable consideration for an appointment in the Army, Mr Homer Wheeler at present Post Trader at Ft Wallace Kansas—Mr Wheeler is a young gentleman of great force of character & energy & has more than once rendered valuable service to the Army on the Frontier as a Volunteer—He was particularly distinguished in this way in the fight of Lt Henely 6th Cavalry with Indians on the 20th of April last in which fight it is hardly too much to say that much of the credit was due to Mr Wheeler's energy and courage. I think his appointment would be an excellent one & would furnish the Army with a young officer of a kind much needed" ALS, *ibid.*, 4633 1875. Related papers are *ibid.* On May 16, Wheeler, Fort Wallace, Kan., had written to Babcock. "Since I wrote you last we have been having considerable excitment about the Indians. I went out with a party of men under the command of Liut Austin Henly, Fourty all told, after some Indians that corralled Four of my men on the 15th of last Month. . . ." ALS, ICN. On March 27, 1874, Wheeler had written to Babcock. "You will see by enclosed affidavits I have been indicted by the Grand Jury for purchasing Goverment stock that had been stolen   I shall have to attend trial the 13th of April as I am under

$2000,00 bonds   the U. S. Marshal allowed me to sign the bond. I should like to have you get the case dismissed if possible. . . . I know there is no dainger of convicting me, but I can not stand the expense as I am very hard up for money. . . ." ALS, DNA, RG 60, Letters Received, Kan. The enclosures are *ibid.* See Homer W. Wheeler, *Buffalo Days: Forty Years in the Old West* . . . (New York, 1925).

On July 13, 1875, Luckey wrote to Belknap. "The President directs me to say that he will be pleased to have Mr. George Frederick Cooke of D. C. appointed a second Lieutenant in the army." Copy, DLC-USG, II, 2. On July 27, Babcock, Long Branch, wrote to Crosby. "The President will be pleased to have you send Mr Barnard down with the list of persons recommended for Lieuts in the Army, and tell him to bring those marked special or otherwise" Copies, *ibid.*, II, 2, 3. On July 29, Crosby wrote to Townsend concerning 2nd lt. applicants and vacancies. LS, DNA, RG 94, ACP, 3366 1875. On July 31, William T. Barnard, act. chief clerk, War Dept., wrote to Townsend. "The President has directed me to request you to appoint, William H. C. Bowen, of Nebraska, Henry Johnson, of California, R H. R. Loughborough, of Virginia, William B. Pratt, of Missouri, William W. Schipman, of the Army, Stephen T. Seyburn, of Kansas, and Louis Wilhelmi of Pennsylvania, Second Lieutenants, to fill existing vacancies in the Army, and order them before a Board for examination. He also directs me to say, it is his intention that Alfred B. Johnson, of Minnesota, a former appointee, shall be ordered before a Board for examination, in the same manner as other appointments to the army from civil-life." LS, *ibid.*, 4510 1875. George F. Cooke, Alfred B. Johnson, William H. C. Bowen, Henry Johnson, Jr., Robert H. R. Loughborough, Sgt. William W. Shipman, Stephen Y. Seyburn, and Louis Wilhelmi served as 2nd lts.

On Dec. 19, 1874, A. J. Sypher, New Orleans, had written to USG. "It is with pleasure that I recomend Stephen Y Seyburn for appointment as 2d Lieutenant in U. S. Army, he is the Son of Capt I D Seyburn late of the U. S. N. and in every way worthy of the position,   If consistant with the Service I hope he will be appointed . . . *I was with you* from Ft Henry to vicksburg" ALS, *ibid.*, 3720 1875. Related papers are *ibid.* On Aug. 2, 1875, Babcock wrote to Barnard. "Please send me a list of the appts of Leuts made by the President when you were here. I am sorry you did not telegraph me the day you would be here. I should have remained at home—If the gentleman referred to in this telegram from Gen Williams was not included in the list. the President says his name can be added to the list." ALS, *ibid.*, 2864 1875. On Aug. 4, Barnard telegraphed to Babcock. "S. Y. Seyburn, ~~recomm~~ (not Sciburn) recommended by Genl Pope, Genl Williams and others was appointed Second Lieutenant. List by mail" ALS (telegram sent), *ibid.*, RG 107, Telegrams Collected (Bound).

On July 15, U.S. Representative Charles O'Neill of Pa. had written to USG. "I hope you will pardon my intrusion but my personal feeling in the desired appointment of Louis Wilhelmi as a 2nd Lieutenant in the Army is offered as an apology. Some months ago I filed in the War Department the application and recommendations of Mr Wilhelmi. He had been in the Class of 1872 at West but left invalided by Sunstroke or something like it after he had been some 15 months I think at the Academy. For two years nearly he has been constantly improving in health and there is on file with his papers the Certificate of one of the eminent Surgeons of Philadelphia declaring that he is entirely well and fit for any duty. . . ." ALS, *ibid.*, RG 94, ACP, 5121 1875. On May 23, O'Neill, Philadelphia, had written to USG on the same subject. ALS, *ibid.*

On July 22, Secretary of the Treasury Benjamin H. Bristow wrote to USG. "I beg to present to you Mr A. B. Johnson, son of my friend Genl R. W. Johnson, and to Commend him to your favorable regard. He is a most excellent & worthy young man." ALS, *ibid.*,

3620 1875. On July 26, USG endorsed this letter. "The Sec. of War. Mr. A. B. Johnson may be appointed a 2d Lt. in the Army." AES, *ibid*. On July 27, 8:00 P.M., Alfred Johnson, Washington, D. C., wrote to Crosby. ". . . I have just arrived in the City from Long Branch where I got the President's endorsement—. . . I am the son of Genl R. W. Johnson U. S. A (retired) of the class of 1849—. . ." ALS (on Willard's Hotel stationery), *ibid*. On May 31, Richard W. Johnson, St. Paul, had written to USG concerning his son. ". . . I need hardly say, that after a service of 26 years, (part of which was past under your command), that I have no political influence and must rely upon you for the appointment   You have always shown your friendship for the old officers of the army and I feel that I shall not appeal to you in vain. My son 22 years old and a College graduate and well fitted for the position" LS, *ibid*.

On July 31, Barnard telegraphed to USG. "Wm B. Pratt recommended by General Logan and Governor T. C Fletcher of missouri and appointed second Lieutenant yesterday gives his age over Thirty three years and Consequently Cannot be appointed without violating the Department Regulation which fixes the limit of age at Thirty years   shall the Regulation be waived in his Case." Telegram received, *ibid*., IB; telegram sent, DNA, RG 107, Telegrams Collected (Bound). On the same day, USG, Long Branch, telegraphed to chief clerk, War Dept. "MAKE NO EXCEPTIONS TO RULES IN REGARD TO AGE OF APPOINTEES TO THE ARMY." Telegram received, *ibid*., RG 94, ACP, 3398 1875. In an undated letter, John F. Long, surveyor of customs, St. Louis, had written to USG recommending William B. Pratt, former capt. and bvt. maj., 31st Mo., for appointment as paymaster. ALS (docketed April 22), *ibid*. William H. Benton and John M. Krum favorably endorsed this letter. AES (undated), *ibid*. Related papers are *ibid*. For another aspirant excluded by age, see Louis Y. Mitchell to USG, Aug. 14, 1874 (*ibid*., Applications for Positions in War Dept.) and July 22, 1875 (*ibid*., ACP, 3425 1875).

On Aug. 27, Townsend wrote to USG, Long Branch. "Your order of the 25th inst, relative to the examination of George E. Andrews, with view to his appointment as 2d Lieutenant U. S. Army, has been received, and instructions have been given for him to appear before the Board of Examination in this city." Copy, *ibid*., Letters Sent. George E. Andrews never served as 2nd lt.

On Aug. 30, USG telegraphed to Townsend. "Is a board now in Session in Washn for the Examination of persons appointed Second Lieutenants in the Army," Telegram received, *ibid*., ACP, 3804 1875. On the same day, Townsend telegraphed to USG. "A Board is now in Session in Washington to examine Second Lieutenants. Ten persons invited before it, and nine more before Boards at other points—Leavenworth St Paul San Francisco, Omaha." Telegram sent, *ibid*., RG 107, Telegrams Collected (Bound).

On Sept. 16, Bowen, Omaha, wrote to USG after passing his examination. "On the 27th of last July, I called upon you, requesting an appointment in the Regular Army. . . . I would most respectfully request your excellency to have my commission forwarded as early as possible, as all I can depend on for my substance, is, or will be, my pay as 2d Lieutenant." ALS, *ibid*., RG 94, ACP, 3792 1875. Related papers are *ibid*.

On April 12, Harry Tiffany, Washington, D. C., had written to USG. "I have the honor to respectfully petition that I may be commissioned as a 2d Lieutenant of the United States Army. I served in the Regular Army, 4th Cavalry, from August 9th 1869 to August 9th 1874 and was Sergeant Major from February 20th 1872 till date of discharge, serving under the name of Harry Thompson. On the 1st day of January 1875 I enlisted in Company "H" 3d U. S. Infantry, as Harry Thompson, and was appointed Corporal March 15th 1875, which grade I now hold. I have the honor to invite your attention to the enclosed letters from the Officers under whom I have served, who testify as to my services, also my fitness for the position asked for. Trusting that your Excellency will favorably consider my application, . . ." ALS, *ibid.*, 3624 1876. The enclosures are *ibid.* In [*May*], Otis H. Tiffany, Chicago, wrote to USG that Harry Tiffany "is the grand son of the late Hon Louis McLane of Md. being the son of Mr. Henry Tiffany now of N. Y. who married Miss Sallie McLane. The young man is by education & experience competent for a Lieutenancy—Enlisted under the assumed name of Thompson because of his family, and now desires to resume his own name & be promoted,   he will furnish testimonials & I earnestly request that you will gratify all his friends by giving him a vacancy." ALS (docketed May 8), *ibid.* On Aug. 11, 1876, USG nominated Tiffany as 2nd lt., 11th Inf. See *New York Times*, Dec. 29, 1878.

On May 5, 1875, N. Johnson, Washington, D. C., had written to USG. "I have the honor to apply for the appointment of my son William V W. Reily, as Lieut. in one of the Regiments of Cavalry. U S. Army. His Father was an officer in the U S. Navy. & was lost with the U S. Brig Porpoise—while in the discharge of his duty." ALS, DNA, RG 94, ACP, 4087 1875. On Sept. 4, Babcock, Long Branch, wrote to Crosby. "The President will be pleased to have Wm. V. W. Riley appointed a second Lieut. in the army and ordered before the board for examination in Washington D. C." ALS, *ibid.* On June 25, 1876, 2nd Lt. William V. W. Reily, 7th Cav., died at the Little Big Horn.

On Aug. 4, 187[5], Townsend had telegraphed to USG, Long Branch. "The following is submitted for instructions. Jackson mississippi Augst Third Eighteen Seventy five. Hon W W Belknap secretary war   we recommend andrew E Kilpatrick for appointment as second Lieutenant in the army & Earnestly request that you authorize him to appear before the board of Examination now in session in Washington for examination   Mr Kilpatrick is twenty three years old & is now assistant professor of mathematics in the university of mississippi   if considered favorably by telegram   Adelbert Ames Governor mississippi B R Bruce U S Senator L. Q C Lamar m C First District miss Alexander Stewart Chancellor university of mississippi" Telegram received, *ibid.*, 4013 1875. On the same day, USG telegraphed to Townsend. "YOU MAY APPOINT ANDREW E. KILPATRICK OF MISS. LIEUT." Telegram received (at 4:46 P.M.), *ibid.* On Dec. 6, USG nominated Andrew E. Kilpatrick as 2nd lt., 17th Inf., to date from Oct. 15.

On Aug. 5, George W. Patten, USMA 1830, Poughkeepsie, N. Y., had written to Babcock. "I respectfully solicit through you, the attention of the President to the following representations   In the early part of last month, my son, Williams S. Patten, made an application, through the War Department, for one of the vacant positions of PayMaster in the Army. This application fortified by a letter from myself and by certificates of competency from some of the most influencial persons in Poughkeepsie, was lodged by Mr Ketchum, one of the Commissioners for the District of Columbia, with the Chief clerk of the War Department, but the Secretary being absent I have reason to think that the application, not having as yet been seen by him, has never been referred to the President . . . His age is twenty three years and should a paymastership not be available he would gladly accept any other suitable position either civil or military which the Executive might be pleased to bestow on him" ALS, *ibid.*, 4039 1875. On Aug. 10, USG endorsed papers related to William S. Patten. "Refered to the Sec. of War. Mr. Patten may be nominated for a Second Lieutenancy and sent before the board now examining Candidates for admission into the Army." AES, *ibid.* On Sept. 9, USG telegraphed to Belknap. "W S Patton may be assigned to the 1st artillery if he has passed as satisfactory examination" Telegram received (at 1:35 P.M.), *ibid.* On Dec. 6, USG nominated Patten as 2nd lt., 18th Inf., to date from Oct. 15.

On Aug. 11, John B. Blake, Washington, D. C., had written to USG. "Understanding

that there are a number of appointments of Second Lieutenants soon to be made in the
army I respectfully recommend my young friend, Mr Wm J. Nicholson of this District, as
peculiarly fitted for that branch of the public service, especially cavalry, possessing as he
does a fine physique, great activity, a liberal education and promising talents. He is a son
of Capt. S. Nicholson of the Navy and a nephew of Mr W. W. Corcoran, who I am satisfied,
but for his absence from the city, would cordially unite with me in this application. His
grandfather, the late Dr Wm Jones, was my preceptor and partner, and hence I feel a pa-
ternal interest in young Nicholson and will esteem a compliance with my request as a *personal* favor. I place this application on personal grounds because of the confidence you manifested in me by tendering me an appointment on the board of public works for this
District, which, however unfortunately it eventuated for me, I shall ever hold in proud and
grateful recollection." ALS, *ibid.*, 3662 1876. On Aug. 11, 1876, USG nominated William
J. Nicholson as 2nd lt., 7th Cav.

On Aug. 11, 1875, Jonathan Drake Stevenson, Jr., San Francisco, had written to USG.
"The undersigned most respectfully solicits an appointment as 2nd Lieutenant of Infantry, in the Army of the United States, and confidently, refers to accompanying recommendations as evidence of his worth, and fitness, for the appointment he asks." ALS, *ibid.*,
4649 1875. On July 9, Gen. William T. Sherman, St. Louis, had written to USG. "It give
me pleasure to recommend to your special notice, the Claims of J. D. Stevenson Jr. of
San Francisco, to an appointment as 2nd Lieut of Infantry, for which he is already an applicant, endorsed by many persons competent to judge of his qualifications. I remember
him only as a Child and base my recommendation on the Services of his Father Capt M R.
Stevenson, and of his Grand Father Colonel J. D. Stevenson. His mother is the daughter of
Mr Kennerly of Jefferson Barracks well known to you, and his Father was Capt M. R
Stevenson U. S. Army, but who was one of the Captains of the Regiment of Volunteers
Commanded by his Father J. D. Stevenson, which Sailed around Cape Horn in 1846, and
occupied California till the end of the Mexican War. From representations made to me I
am satisfied that young Stevenson has all the Physical & Mental Qualifications needed
for the Commission sought for, but I ask a consideration of his Case in compliment to the
Services and Character of his Grand Father Colonel J. D. Stevenson of California." ALS,
ibid. On Aug. 6, Eliza K. Stevenson, San Francisco, wrote to USG. "Yours, is the power to
gladden the hearts of a widow, and Orphan of one of your companion in Arms, and I, having rendered his Son very miserable by my opposition to his entering West Point, appeal
to you in his behalf, & trusting to your sympathy in my remorse, I beg you will favorably—
and speedily—consider his application for a position in the Army. From childhood to the
present day, his ambition has been to become a 'distinguished' Soldier. Indeed so great is
his infatuation—and my reproach for his unhappiness, that I would be tempted to sacrifice pride so far, as to yield my consent to his enlistment, rather than he should endure the
disappointment, your declining to appoint him—would produce   *All* who *know* my Son
would attest his qualifications as to Morals, principle, temperance, and his unselfish devotion to me. Notwithstanding his great disappointment—which frequently renders him
painfully despondent—and the numerous obstacles with which he has had—and still
has—to contend—he has since he was Sixteen years of age supported—not only me—
but has assisted in the care of others. dear to us. I feel as do all who know his character that
he would be a credit to the position he solicits. And I will await with much anxiety the receipt of your reply which is to render me the, happiest, or most miserable of Mothers. Let
me beg it may not be the latter. We have endured *so* much! Remember me very kindly to
Jule—. . ." ALS, *ibid.* On Sept. 8, Babcock wrote to Crosby. "The President will be pleased
to have J D Stevenson Jr. appt a 2nd Lieut in the army. The appointment can be sent to

Genl W T Sherman—" ALS, *ibid*. Related papers are *ibid*. Stevenson, Jr., never served as 2nd lt.

On Sept. 16, Commander Edward P. Lull, "Comdg late *Panama* & late *Nicaragua* Expeditions," Washington, D. C., wrote to USG. "I respectfully beg leave to recommend for appointment as second Lieutenant in the U. S. Army, Mr. John E. Buck, of Hartford, Conn, late Commander's clerk, U. S. Navy. Mr. Buck served in two of the Interoceanic Canal Expeditions and showed so much intelligence, zeal and endurance, and is so thoroughly a gentleman, that I desire most earnestly to express my appreciation of his merits. Though holding the appointment of clerk, Mr. Buck served constantly in the field." ALS, *ibid*., Applications for Positions in War Dept. On Sept. 25, Commodore Daniel Ammen favorably endorsed this letter. AES, *ibid*. On Sept. 16, Majs. Simeon Smith and Charles M. Terrell, paymasters, Omaha, wrote to USG recommending N. J. Vedder, pay dept. clerk and "son of Major Nicholas Vedder Paymaster," for appointment as 2nd lt. LS, *ibid*. On Sept. 22, Charles E. Sears, Oakland, Calif., wrote to USG. "Having been honored by the recommendations of my friends to the Hon. C. B. Curtis, and being additionally honored by having my name placed on a list to be submitted to you for appointment (as per date of enclosure) may it please you to grant me the order to appear before the board that is to be convened in San Francisco in the early part of October of this year. I have been anxiously waiting and studying for nearly two years. I can pass the examination and can refer to my admission to the Cornell University in 1868 as to my ability. *Please* give me the opportunity to be examined (preferring the Cavalry service) and I shall not be afraid of the result. Neither will the service ever have cause to be ashamed of me—I have had nearly three years experience of Nevada life." ALS, *ibid*. Related papers are *ibid*.; *ibid*., RG 59, Letters of Application and Recommendation. John E. Buck, Vedder, and Sears never served as 2nd lts.

On Sept. 23, Belknap wrote to U.S. Senator Aaron A. Sargent of Calif., San Francisco. "Yours of September 4th concerning Mr. Charles Jansen for a Second Lieutenancy has been received. During my absence over twenty Lieutenants were appointed by the President, and he has signified his intention of making no more appointments until the class which graduates next summer at West Point, is assigned to duty; as there are not at present, enough vacancies for that class. Mr. J's. name was brought to the attention of the President, with two or three hundred others, at the time the last selections were made. When additional appointments are made I shall with great pleasure see that Mr. Jansen's name is again brought to his attention." Copy, *ibid*., RG 107, Letters Sent, Military Affairs. No appointment followed.

To Elihu B. Washburne

Long Branch, N. J.
Aug. 23d /75

Dear Washburne;

I have been intending for a long time to write to you, but I have so got out of the way of writing social letters that I have not now left a single correspondent—not even in my own family—except on official business. I have nothing now special to say further than that I am always glad to hear from you. In political matters you keep posted through the press, and are no doubt struck with the chronic, annual scare of the ~~Democratic~~ Republicans lest the Democrats should get into power. Just now the Ohio election is frightening them. They seem to feel as though the loss of Ohio this fall would insure a Democratic victory next year, and lead to inflation of the currency, repudiation, the undoing of all that has been accomplished by the War and Republican Administrations in the way of re-construction, and National disgrace. I take a much more hopeful view of the situation. I am anxious of course to see the republicans carry Ohio. But if they should not I should not feel in the least dis-couraged. The fact is that while Ohio is sound ~~in Ohio~~ by one hun-dred thousand majority on the financial issue, and the republicans have out a sound platform on that issue, and the democrats a very unsound and dishonest one, if Ohio is lost in this election it will be on this question alone. So much time elapses between nominations and election that the democrats will all be whipped into line on the ground that the question now at issue is only which of the two par-ties they would rather see controll the state. They are not voting for an Executi[ve] of the Nation, nor for law-makers who can legislate on the subject of National finances. In the republican ranks there are very many men who are in debt, or whos business has slackened, that think an abundent currency would help them out of their difficulties, and who will not vote; or if they do vote it will be against their party. I believe that if the democratic party carries Ohio this fall it will give the repudiationests—for inflation means repudiation—such a pres-tige in the nominating convention next year that the hard money men of the party—including all from the pacific coast, all New En-gland, New York, New Jersey, Delaware, Maryland, Texas and some from other states—that they will split and put up two tickets as they did in /60. If so the race in /76 will be an easy one. With a contrary result there will probably be but two tickets, both on a moderately sound financial platform.

I did not think of writing so much of a political letter as I have done, but it may interest you to hear private views on this subject.

On the question of candidates for next year there seems to be nothing definate to base a prediction upon as to who will be the standard bearers.[1]

Jones and family have returned, and gone on to Chicago after spending a few days here. I gave him Butcher Boy[2]—the horse that set him out of the buggy so suddenly as to cause some lameness—to hack about with in his old age—Jones old age—B B is only eighteen an[d] as good as ever. Old Bucephelus has killed off all my old sto[ck] of carriage horses and is better now himself than when you drove him. He has got now to be dangerous to drive single, and double, or four in hand, he requires an extra severe bit to manage.

My family are all well and join in kindest regards to you, Mrs. Washburne and the children.

Very Truly Yours

U. S. GRANT

ALS, IHi.

1. On Dec. 22, 1874, Elihu Washburne, Paris, wrote to [*Orville E. Babcock*]. "You must agree to the wisdom of what I wrote you awhile ago, that if matters went much further I ought to put an effectual quietus on all that foolish and absurd talk about my being a candidate for the Presidency. There is a chance that I may be struck by lightning, but that I should be a candidate for the Presidency is, as *you know*, far beyond the reach of human possibility. The only result of the talk is to have me hounded by all the press for the next two years. This slip is a vile specimen. I never said anything of the kind and no such letter was ever written from Paris. It was got up by some scoundrel at Washington, equally the enemy of the General and myself, hoping to disturb our friendship" AL (incomplete), Babcock Papers, ICN. A clipping asserting that Elihu Washburne would not support USG for a third term is *ibid.*

2. On Aug. 12, 1875, USG, Long Branch, wrote a note. "Mr. Nat. Carlin, Supt. of Stock on White Haven Farm, Mo. will please deliver to the order of the Hon. J. R. Jones, of Chicago, Ill. my gray gelding Butcher Boy." ANS, CSmH. On Sept. 29, J. Russell Jones, Chicago, wrote a note. "Please deliver 'Butcher Boy' to the bearer & oblige" ANS, DLC-USG, IC.

To Nathaniel Carlin

Long Branch, N. J.
Aug. 24th /75

DEAR SIR:

By the same mail that takes this I have written to Judge Long and to Mr. Jackson, discontinuing the services of the latter, and directing the terms of sales &c. You will hear from Judge Long in a few days.

Mr. J. will turn over every thing to you and discharge all his hands except such as you choose to keep. I want you now to go to work with every energy and get in all the wheat & grass you possibly can. The public sale will take place on the 11 October.[1] No farm work can be done after that. Between now and day of sale dispose of all the stock you can at private sale. I have instructed that Claymore and the best of the mares and colts may be bought in if they do not bring reasonably fair prices for the times. You may take all the horses you can get to winter, and if you do not get sufficient to use up the feed you may sell the balance.

Yours Truly
U. S. GRANT

NAT. CARLIN, ESQR

P. S. Mr. J's wages were to be $600 00

Enquire for letter for Mr. Jackson when you get this and send it to him.

U. S. G.

ALS, ICarbS. See letter to Edward F. Beale, Sept. 8, 1875.

On Sept. 9, 1875, Orvil L. Grant, Washington, D. C., wrote to William S. Oliver, Little Rock. "I would like to have a good fast horse and might buy one if I could get it at a bargain. Col A P Curry has called my attention to your black horse Prince. If you desire to sell him what is your very bottom price? I can not afford to buy unless I can do it at a moderate price. Also state his speed—age and qualities" ALS, OClWHi. On Sept. 14, A. P. Curry, Little Rock, wrote to Nathaniel Carlin. "I have just recd the enclosed letter from Genl Grants brother and answered him by this mail telling him that he could have Black Prince for Seven hundred dollars and told him to write to you please read his letter and return it to me think you can Sell him Prince and know he will Suit him for he would be king bee in Washington" ALS, *ibid.*

1. Actually Sept. 30.

To Columbus Delano

_____

Long Branch, N. J., Aug. 26, 1875

My Dear Mr. Sec.,

With this I send the acceptance of your resignation. There is no
need of publicity until about the time I shall want to name your successor. At this time I have thought of but two names for the place.
One is the present Commissioner of Int. Rev., the other is Mr. Wayne
McVeigh of Pa. I think now of starting west about the 12th of Sept.
Should I do so I will not return to Washington—after that time—
until about the middle of October. I may go down for a day just before that time, and should I do so I would want to consult with the
Cabinet about your successor. Should I not go to Washington before
going West you might meet me some place in Ohio, and take that occasion to give the fact of your resignation to the public. I could then
either announce the name of your successor, or could send a letter to
the Sec. of State submitting different names that I would ask the
opinion of the Cabinet about, and get an answer in time to name your
successor so as to have him qualify by the first of October. . . .

The Collector, No. 842 (1975), I-687; Paul C. Richards Presidential Catalogue [1982], no.
172. In 1875, Secretary of the Interior Columbus Delano wrote to USG concerning his
resignation and the "geographical position" of his replacement. William Evarts Benjamin,
Catalogue No. 42, March, 1892, p. 9. See letter to Hamilton Fish, Sept. 10, 1875; letter to
Columbus Delano, Sept. 22, 1875.

To Edwards Pierrepont

_____

Long Branch, N. J.
August 26, 1875

. . . Mr. Bennett may be all very well (for chief justice of Utah) but
his endorsements are against him . . . It looks to me as if what are
known in Utah Territory as "Jack Mormons" were making a "dead-
set" to get in one of their men.

Of the men named for the place so far I would give the prefer-

ence to Judge White, of Ala. or Judge Crozier[1] of Kansas. I am very
desirous to do something for Judge White, and I look upon him as a
very upright man, and one possessed of considerable ability . . .

Charles Hamilton Auction No. 5, Oct. 8, 1964, no. 84. On Aug. 9, 1875, David P. Lowe, Fort
Scott, Kan., wrote to USG resigning as chief justice, Utah Territory. ALS, DNA, RG 75,
Letters Received, Utah Territory. On Aug. 21, Orville E. Babcock, Long Branch, wrote to
Attorney Gen. Edwards Pierrepont. "I enclose to you a letter from Judge Lowe, the Pres-
ident says you may appoint Hon Alexander White, of Selma Alabama, Ex Member of Congress." ALS, *ibid.*, RG 60, Letters from the President. The enclosure is *ibid.* On April 19,
John Coburn, Indianapolis, had written to USG. "When in Washington, a few days ago, I
was too much occupied to call on you before you left for Concord. I had intended to call
& say a word of approval as to the application of Judge White of Alabama for the office of
Assistant Attorney General. He served in the House with me and I know of his ability
as a lawyer. . . ." ALS, *ibid.*, Applications and Recommendations. Related papers are *ibid.*
On July 21, U.S. Senator George E. Spencer of Ala., New York City, wrote to Babcock.
"On my return here last evening; I found the enclosed letter from Hon. Alex. White. I wish
you would read it, and if you think best, read it to the President. There is no man in the
country abler or more deserving than Col. White. There is no better or more eminent
lawyer in the Country. I have served the Administration faithfully, and have asked and
received very few favors. I do not often annoy the President with applications for offices,
but have received some very hard blows; notwithstanding which, I am not, nor have I been
sore-headed. There is a rumor that there will soon be a vacancy in the Board of Commissioners of the District of Columbia. Why cannot this place be tendered to Col. White?
Now, my dear General, if you will take a personal interest in this matter, and aid me in securing Col. White a position commensurate with his character and abilities, you will place
me under obligations I will not soon forget. Please make a memorandum of my prophecies
of yesterday, and then tell me, a year hence, whether I am or am not a false prophet. The
President spoke yesterday in the highest terms of Col. White, and expressed an earnest
desire to provide for him in a substantial manner. Trusting that you will not forget this
matter, . . ." ALS, USG 3. The enclosure is a letter of July 18 from Alexander White, Talladega, Ala., to Spencer concerning a promised patronage appointment. ". . . If there are
difficulties in the way of your seeing the Prest let me know. You know I am not in the habit
of talking imprudently. As things now are in this state it is necessary for me to know fully
your plans and views; The Democratic press and a portion of our own party are damning
us together as the Spencer White & Sheats ring. You are away, and I have to bear the burden of it, for it is against me more than Sheats. their most malignant attacks are directed. . . ." ALS, *ibid.* On Aug. 5, Spencer again wrote to Babcock. "*Confidential* . . . I enclose you a very able political letter from the Hon. Alexander White, of Alabama, which I
think should be communicated in full to the President. . . ." ALS, *ibid.* The enclosure is a
letter of July 31 from White to Spencer assessing 1876 presidential prospects. "Confidential . . . There is no one ~~else~~ who ~~can~~ as Pres't ~~Grant~~ can, keep down this rising spirit of
rebellion at the South, except Gen Grant. He is not only the terror of the Secesh, but he
has the confidence of all Union men. I have given you in part and only in part my reasons
for believing that the fate of this country depends upon the renomination of Gen Grant. I
believe that Grant has the sagacity to see it himself, and the lofty patriotism which would
enable him to form a just conclusion with regard to it and I do not believe he would decline a nomination . . ." ALS, *ibid.* White, former C.S. soldier and Republican U.S. Repre-

sentative from Ala. (1873–75), served only a few months on the Utah Territory Supreme Court.

On March 16, USG had nominated Oliver A. Patton as land office register, Salt Lake City. In 1867, Patton, who served in the C.S. Army, had married Rachel E. Tompkins, a daughter of USG's Aunt Rachel. On Dec. 9, 1874, Patton, Charleston, West Va., wrote to USG. "I beg to submit my application for a nomination to a position on some branch of the public service to which your excellency may deem me suited, though were I permitted to choose I should in view of the critical condition of my daughters health pray the appointment to the Corps diplomatique of some southern latitude, and particularly do I ask the nomination to the vacancy occasioned by the decease, of Mr Wing late *Minister to Equador, S. A.* Will your excellency encourage me to hope for it? to the end that I may present my self with my credentials to your excellency. Trusting that my character and political antecedents, when understood, will sustain and justify my ambition for this mark of your excellencys distinguish[in]g favor, . . ." ALS, DNA, RG 59, Letters of Application and Recommendation. Related papers are *ibid.* On Aug. 20, 1875, Patton, Salt Lake City, wrote to USG. "Thanking your Excellency for the kind consideration which prompted my appointment to a position in a country which has proven pleasant to my family and myself— as well as highly conducive to the health of my wife and not desiring to absorb the time so necessary to preserve you for the arduous labors, before you, will take the liberty of suggesting to you, in view of your appointment of a Chief Justice for Utah, to succeed Judge Lowe, that if it does not please your Excellency to restore Judge McKean (which permit me to say would be gratifying to all parties here) that *no appointment be made from Utah* as it would create a faction against the administration, and thereby damage our cause in utah. Please accept for yourself and family the profound affection of us all,   Genl. Sheridan reached here last night." ALS, *ibid.*, RG 75, Letters Received, Utah Territory. On Oct. 16, 1876, Patton telegraphed to USG. "For the Sake of my family Honor without instantly acting Secty Gorhams Order Suspending me Send an honest man to Investigate this Office M. M. Kaighn has been intimate only with Mormons Sutherland is their Attorney—" Telegram received (at 6:39 P.M.), DLC-USG, IB. On Nov. 2, Rachel E. Patton, Salt Lake City, telegraphed to USG. "Do justice   require immediate investigation for my sake Will you" Telegram received, *ibid.* On Jan. 9, 1877, USG nominated Barbour Lewis as land office register, Salt Lake City, to replace Patton. On May 18, Oliver Patton wrote to U.S. Representative James A. Garfield of Ohio. "Upon an occasion of a visit to my relative, the late president at his office in Washington I enquired of him if any charges had been made against me as Register, (of the U. S. Land Office at Salt Lake) to which he smilingly answered 'Yes, Disloyalty and intemperance' both of which I regarded as too silly for any notice whatever. I have been informed that some person living at Salt Lake has forwarded to you a book with marginal notes alleged to have been written by me and reflecting desrespect to you and disloyalty to the goverment. I now have an interpretation of Genl Grants remark, and I pronounce the general charge and the specification—if my suspicion is correct, utterly false and emenating from a depraved heart wickedly bent on mischief to myself officially and personally and a design by such base means to reach the official position to which president Grant had assigned me here. . . ." ALS, DLC-James A. Garfield.

On Feb. 7, 1876, Moses M. Bane, Washington, D. C., had written to USG. "I have the honor to apply for the appointment of Judge of the United States Court in either of the Territories of Dakota or Utah but would prefer the latter." LS, Morristown National Historical Park, Morristown, N. J. Favorable endorsements are *ibid.* On April 6, Bane, Quincy, Ill., wrote to USG. "When Senator Oglesby and myself called on you in February, to consult you relative to my appointment to a judicial position in one of the territories, you

thought a vacancy would Soon occur in both Dacota & Utah, and that I Should have a position. I write to ask you if you think you will be able to give me an appointment during
the Spring or Summer?—Please excuse my anxiety for I am needing the position very
much. If any further endorsement is required, by notifying either Oglesby or Logan, or either of the republican congressmen from Illinois it will be furnished—" ALS, DNA, RG 60,
Records Relating to Appointments. A petition to USG stamped March 15, recommending
W. M. Zearing of Princeton, Ill., for a territorial judgeship, had been endorsed by Thomas
J. Henderson. "I cheerfully sign the above recommendation with the understanding that it
is not to interfere with a recommendation heretofore made of Gen Bane of Illinois—" AES,
ibid. On March 1, Bane had written to Secretary of War William W. Belknap on the same
subject. ALS, *ibid.*, Letters from the President. On June 10, 1874, Governor John L. Beveridge of Ill., Champaign, had written to USG. "I take pleasure in recommending Genl
M. M. Bane of Quincy. Ills. as U. S. Minister to Bolivia. . . ." ALS, *ibid.*, RG 59, Letters of
Application and Recommendation. Related papers are *ibid.* On May 18, 1876, USG nominated Bane as secretary, Utah Territory. On Jan. 8, 1877, USG nominated Levi P. Luckey
in place of Bane; on Jan. 9, USG nominated Bane as land office receiver, Salt Lake City.

On March 20, 1876, USG had nominated John M. Coghlan as chief justice, Utah Territory. On April 19, USG noted: "Michael Schoeffer, Ill. for Chief Justice of Utah." AN,
OHi. On the same day, Culver C. Sniffen wrote to Pierrepont. "The President directs me
to say that he will have no objection to the appointment of Michael Schoeffer of Illinois, as
Chief Justice of Utah." ALS, DNA, RG 60, Letters from the President. Also on April 19,
USG nominated Michael Schaeffer to replace Coghlan, who had resigned to accept nomination as U.S. attorney, Calif.

On Jan. 13, U.S. Senator Thomas W. Ferry of Mich. had written to USG. "Understanding that there is an effort now being made to impeach the integrity of General
George R. Maxwell, United States Marshall of the Territory of Utah, charging him with
certain malfeasance in office, We the undersigned Senators and Representatives of the
state of Michigan would state that we have known, Genl Maxwell personally and by reputation for many years, as a soldier, and an ardent defender of the Union during the late
civil war. From the same source we are acquainted with his personal reputation, and believe him to be in every respect upright honest and honorable. And having understood that
charges have been preferred against him by ~~irresponsible~~ parties in Utah, looking to his
removal from office as said United States Marshal of Utah, we are of the opinion that said
Maxwell has been an efficient and faithful officer of the Government, and that these
charges have been preferred against him for malicious and unworthy purposes, and that
said Maxwell should be sustained and protected by the Executive in his present official position" ALS, *ibid.*, Letters Received, D. C. Favorable endorsements are *ibid.* On Jan. 14, U.S.
Senator John Sherman of Ohio wrote to USG. "Edmund Wilkes, of Salt Lake City, a son
of Admiral Wilkes, comes strongly recommended to me by a personal acquaintance in
whom I have great confidence and I have no hesitation in recommending Mr. Wilkes for
appointment to the marshalship of Utah Territory with the assurance that he will be faithful, honest and capable." LS, *ibid.*, Records Relating to Appointments. A related letter is
ibid. On Feb. 2, U.S. Senator Timothy O. Howe of Wis. wrote to Pierrepont. "I saw the
President this morning. He concedes there must be a new—Marshall in Utah—& said he
had spoken to you of Mr Wm Nelson of LaCrosse—He is the Gentleman on whose behalf I wrote the note which you could not read   Knowing your *limited attainments* I will
write no more now, than to say it is my deliberate belief that Mr Nelson will furnish you
as good an officer as you are likely to get and his appointment will help Wisconsin more
than the appointment of any other man can help any other State" ALS, *ibid.* On Feb. 14,

C. P. Lyford, Methodist pastor, Salt Lake City, wrote to USG. "I ask the privilege of adding my testimony to that of others as to the integrity; uprightness and moral worth of Gen'l. Geo. B. Maxwell—U. S. Marshall for this Territory. We consider it fortunate for the cause of law and good government as well as for the safety and well-being of society that the duties of that responsible office devolv[e] upon him. It would be a pleasure to say this at any time, but it is doubly so now, when as I understand, his enemies, and especially the enemies of Americanism in Utah are seeking his overthrow. I feel assured that I not only express my own opinion but also that of the christian people with whom I am associated in church relations." ALS, *ibid.*, Letters Received, D. C. A related petition from the bar of Salt Lake City and Utah Territory is *ibid.* On Feb. 17, USG nominated William Nelson as marshal, Utah Territory, to replace George R. Maxwell.

On April 23, Robert T. Lincoln and fifteen others, Chicago, wrote to USG. "The undersigned respectfully recommend for appointment to the position of United States Marshal ofor the Territory of Utah or one of the other Territories, Mr Charles E. Scharlan, of the City of Chicago. Mr Scharlan served during the entire late war in the 57th Regiment Ills. Infty, with great credit to himself, and at the close of the Rebellion he was honorably discharged from the service   He has served four years as Deputy Sheriff of Cook county to the entire satisfaction of the people. By his personal efforts and great personal influence among his countrymen—(the German Americans) he added probably not less than fifteen hundred votes to the Republican cause in the election of 1874, and during the campaign of 1875—(November last) he travelled over the entire county, speaking in German every evening. His ability to fill the position acceptably is unquestionable, and his character for integrity and honesty is above reproach,   Trusting that you may find it consistent with the good of the public service to give him the position he desires, . . ." LS, *ibid.*, Records Relating to Appointments. No appointment followed.

On April 12, U.S. Senator Timothy O. Howe of Wis. had written to USG. "Pursuant to promise I send you two brief papers & ask that you will read them for the *sole* purpose of removing, so far as they may, the impression wh. you have recd that Whitney is anti republican & in sympathy with Mormons." ALS, USG 3. On April 1, Governor George W. Emery of Utah Territory had written to Howe. "I write you at the request of Geo. E. Whitney Esq. of this City, who feels that he has been misrepresented in Washington, and desires to put himself right before his friends in that City. I know Mr. Whitney well and have ever since I came to the Territory, and know how he is regarded by the people here, and take pleasure in stating that he is a gentleman of most excellent character, a good Lawyer with a good practice, a thorough Republican and a friend of the Administration. The only offense I ever heard him accused of, was his opposition, to what is known here, the Mc-Kean faction or ring. To day I am confident ⅞ of all business men and all the Federal officials here, with *one* exception—(the Sec. of Territory) agree with Mr. Whitney concerning that faction, and the unnecessary trouble it is constantly creating here in Utah. This McKean faction seem to have no other object or purpose but to abuse the President and his friends, and to keep up a difficulty generally. Till recently there has been but one Daily paper (Gentile) here, in Salt Lake City, and that Judge McKean's mouthpiece, in comparison to which the 'New York Sun' is tame. I say this in behalf of Mr. Whitney, whose offense, if it be an offense, is worthy of praise" ALS, *ibid.* On March 31, Judge Philip H. Emerson, Utah Territory Supreme Court, and eight others had petitioned Pierrepont in behalf of George E. Whitney. ". . . As the Acknowledged Author of the 'Poland Bill' so called he deserves the sincere good wishes of friends of reform in Utah." DS, *ibid.* No appointment followed.

On Jan. 28, Oliver Patton, Maxwell, and two others had visited USG. "The interview had relation particularly to obtaining some definition of polygamy, so that the crime can be reached in the courts. . . . They also desire a remodeling of the suffrage laws so that the ballot may be strictly secret in fact, it being only nominally so at present, and affording freedom to Mormons who would, if permitted by the sentiment of their churches, vote with the Gentiles. It is desired as well that the Mormon women be not allowed to vote, and that female suffrage, which to that extent exists in the territory, be set aside. The President expressed his sympathy for any movement tending to alleviate the present condition of matters in Utah, and the evils spoken of by the delegation, and assured them of his aid in all laws passed towards that end." *Washington Evening Star*, Jan. 28, 1876.

1. Robert Crozier served as U.S. attorney, Kan. (1861–64), Kan. chief justice, (1864–67), and Republican U.S. Senator (1873–74). On Nov. 5, 1874, Brig. Gen. John Pope, Fort Leavenworth, Kan., had telegraphed to USG. "The mission to Ecuador vacant by death, will you think of Judge Robert Crozier Ex Senator from Kansas for the post," Telegram received, *ibid.*, RG 59, Letters of Application and Recommendation. No appointment followed.

To Adolph E. Borie

Long Branch, N. J.
Aug. 26th /75

MY DEAR MR. BORIE:

I think some of making a trip to Colorado this fall. If I do I would like very much to have you & Mrs. Borie accompany us. The plan and route will be about this. About the 11th of Sept. we will leave here and go to Ithaca, spend a day there and go to Utica and remain with Senator Conkling until the 16th thence to Niagara Falls for a day or two. You and Mrs. Borie could join us at Niagara from which point, or Erie Pa we will be fitted out with special cars that will take us to Denver and return. I should expect to spend a week in Colorado and visit the points of interest.

I will know in a few days if this plan can be carried out, and will ~~let you~~ advise you in time. Our party will consist of Fred & wife & Buck, beside ourselves.

Mrs. Grant's & my kindest regards to Mrs. Borie.

yours Truly
U. S. GRANT

ALS, PHi. See letter to Adolph E. Borie, Sept. 8, 1875.

Endorsement

————

Refered to the Sec. of State. If there is a South American Consulate Mr. Browne can have I have no objection to his appointment

U. S. GRANT

AUG. 27TH /75

AES, DNA, RG 59, Letters of Application and Recommendation. Written on a letter of June 23, 1875, from U.S. Senator Richard J. Oglesby of Ill., Decatur, to USG. "Rev Dr Edward B M Browne of Peoria Ills a Native of Hungary who has been a citizen of the U S. for several years a gentleman of high scientific and literary attainments now suffering from disease of the Eyes and for that reason compelled to desist from the pursuit of professional life. desires to find such employment in the public service as to afford him change of climate and such reasonable compensation as to pay ordinay expenses—he is highly recommended to me by Hon O P Morton. and by members of the Jewish church of this State. I Therefore feel at liberty to recommend him to your favorable consideration—and to request of you for him some appointment in the U S. or to foreign Nations and would feel personally gratified at his success." ALS, *ibid.* On Aug. 23, Rabbi Isaac M. Wise, Cincinnati, wrote to USG. "Permit me, to call your attention to the bearer, Rev. Dr. Browne of Peoria, Ills. whose prominent talents and learning are well appreciated by a large number of our people. He begs a particular favor of you in his time of distressing sickness, which, if granted, would make a very favorable impression on very many of your zealous friends, and also many of your political opponents   Permit me, Mr. President, to express to you my utmost respect for your many virtues as the chief magistrate of our blessed country." ALS, *ibid.* Born in 1844 in Hungary, Edward B. M. Browne studied in Cincinnati under Wise, completed a medical degree at the University of Cincinnati (1869) and a law degree at the University of Wisconsin (1871), and served as rabbi for temples in Milwaukee, Evansville, Ind., and Peoria. See *PUSG*, 22, 397; Steven Hertzberg, *Strangers Within The Gate City: The Jews of Atlanta 1845–1915* (Philadelphia, 1978), pp. 62–64.

On Sept. 7, 1875, Browne, Peoria, wrote to Secretary of State Hamilton Fish. "It is absolute necessity that impelled me to this importunity and I claim the full amount of your charity in my behalf, which I hope you will exercise in accordance with the hight of your personal & official station.—As per enclosed slip from the Chicago Times you will learn of my misfortune. Senator Morton of Indiana was kind enough to espouse my cause which resulted in letters of recommendation to His Excellency the President requesting of him my appointment to some foreign office. On the 27th ult. I visited the president at Long Branch and he informed me that there is no vacancy in the foreign service at present, but he would refer the matter to Your Honor—and he did so at once—to nominate me for some consulate as soon as vacant. I then desired to go to Europe, but there being no probability of a European vacancy I wanted one in South America in preference to any other, and I am looking anxiously for your favorable consideration to wrest me from the grasp of possible blindness.—To-day a friend called my attention to the fact that the Hon John H. Goodenow Consul in Turkey had resigned, and I come now before you with prayers and supplications to remember me graciously and nominate me for said office.—Permit me to add, that while I come to you without a plea, still I do not claim the favor as a *mere gratuity*. I am recognized as one of the finest lecturers & stump speakers in the Country, am known in every Jewish family throughout the U. S. am not without some influence abroad & especially in my own state. I have lived for three years in the South and am posted in the history of our politics. Allow me therefore to state *confidentially* that I have promised to come back next year in time to 'stump' the United States both in the English & German languages for the Republican party & I can amply repay the favor now to be bestowed upon me, besides your charitable deed will find its due reward.—" ALS, *ibid*. The enclosure is *ibid*. On Oct. 16, 1875, and July 25, 1876, Browne, Evansville, again wrote to Fish. "Your favor of the 25th ult, has been forwarded to me to this place where I spend a short vacation, and will you kindly accept the gratitude of a man in misfortune? You were pleased to inform me that no vacancy of the kind to suit me was existing at present, but you would send me a list of such inferior consulates in South America as are not filled thus far. Will you then be so kind to forward that list to my address in *Peoria Ills* so that I may select, no matter how small the income, so that I can travel and save myself from impending blindness. Should something better have turned up of late or in case it occur in future, then I hope you will remember me in your kindness.—I will look forward with anxious eyes even to the list of Consulates you spoke of and thanking you for your favor thus far, . . ." "On receipt of your favor dated Oct 29th 1875 addressed to me in Peoria Ills, and offering me a number of consulates to select the most convenient, I upon consulting my friends Senator Oglesby among them I ascertained that neither of these offices would suffice to support me even without my family Hence I had to decline and wrote accordingly November the 4th. . . ." ALS, *ibid*. No appointment followed.

To Hamilton Fish

———

Long Branch, N. J.
Aug. 27th /75

DEAR GOVERNOR:

Your letter stating what Consular vacancies existed that might be tendered to the Albany gentleman—whose name I have forgotten—has been mislaid so that I cannot put my hand upon it. Will you be kind enough to re-state them, and add whether the Leipsig consulate[1] is vacant. He would, I understand, be pleased with that and I am a good deal pressed on the subject.

Very Truly
your obt. svt.
U. S. GRANT

HON. HAMILTON FISH, SEC. OF STATE.

ALS, DLC-Hamilton Fish. On Aug. 30, 1875, Secretary of State Hamilton Fish wrote to USG, Long Branch. "The vacant Consulates of which I recently wrote are Port Said, salary $1000 & Osaca (in Japan) salary $2000, both are caused by death, the latter has judicial powers, & should be filled by a person with some capacity in that line. I also mentioned Kingston, (Jamaica) salary $2,000, now filled by a Newyorker who has *twice* left his post without leave, & who might, for that reason, be superceded. . . ." ALS (press), *ibid.* See letters to Hamilton Fish, Aug. 3, 8, 1875.

On Jan. 31, 1876, U.S. Representative John D. White of Ky. wrote to Fish. "Since the President informed me that I might name a consul for a place in Egypt, I have looked around for a suitable person; and, now, recommend to you for appointment Capt. A. E. Adams of Piketon, Pike co., Ky   Hoping that he can be appointed without delay as it will require two weeks to notify him and have him come, . . ." ALS, DNA, RG 59, Letters of Application and Recommendation. On Feb. 7, USG nominated Alexander E. Adams as consul, Port Said. See telegram to Alphonso Taft, Aug. 31, 1876.

1. On Dec. 6, 1870, USG had nominated John H. Steuart as consul, Leipzig, in place of Michael J. Cramer. Steuart retained his position.

To Oliver Hoyt

————

Long Branch, N. J.
Aug. 27th 1875

My Dear Mr. Hoyt;

Your very kind favor, and accompanyments, come duly to hand, and allow me to thank you for both. I have not tried the segars but I know they are all right.[1] Allow me to assure you tho that I highly appreciated your company during the entirely pleasant trip from Jersey [City to Bris]tol, and only regreted [that we did] not have you with us on the fishing excursion which followed. We drew up some twenty-five fine cod, the first I had ever seen caught.

> With great respect,
> your obt. svt.
> U. S. Grant

ALS (partial facsimile), Superior Galleries, Feb. 6, 1993, no. 106. Born in 1823 in Stamford, Conn., Oliver Hoyt prospered as a leather merchant in New York City, helped raise money presented to USG after the Civil War, served as Republican presidential elector (1872) from Conn., and contributed generously to Methodist Episcopal causes. See letter to Oliver Hoyt, Nov. 4, 1875.

After visiting Fairpoint, N. Y., on Aug. 14 and 15, 1875, USG, Ulysses S. Grant, Jr., and Orville E. Babcock traveled via train to Bristol, R. I., arriving on Aug. 17. See *New York Times*, Aug. 15–18, 1875. On Aug. 19, a correspondent reported from Providence, R. I. "This morning President Grant and party went out to the Coggeshall Ledge cod-fishing, the party meeting good success. The President hauled out several fine fish. At 2 o'clock this afternoon the cutter Grant ran into the harbor of Block Island, and the President, Secretary Bristow, Secretary Robeson, Attorney General Pierrepont and others of the party landed at the new pier, inside of the Government break-water. Here the President was met by Senators Anthony and Burnside and Gen. Woodruff, of the Lighthouse Board, and was enthusiastically greeted by nearly the whole resident and visiting population of the island, which never before was visited by a President of the United States. President Grant proceeded to Ball's Ocean View Hotel, near the landing, where he held a reception for an hour or two, and afterward dined. The cutter left the island with the Presidential party at 5 o'clock this afternoon for Long Branch." *Ibid.*, Aug. 20, 1875.

1. On April 24 and June 17, 1876, Hoyt, New York City, wrote to USG. "I send you by Adams Express this day, A Box containing one thousand Segars, which I beleave are of good quality. I trust they will reach you safely, and afford you A little comfort." "I Send you this day, by Adams Express, A Box containing one Thousand Segars, which I hope will reach you safely, and prove satisfactory. I have so much faith, in the vendor, that I have allowed him to pack them, it is possible, that he may not send, the ones that I have bought, If you do not find them A no. one please let me know, so that I can correct any mistake. I presume you are pleased, with the nominations at Cincinnatti, I beleave the choice will be ratified by the People." ALS, DLC-USG, IB.

To William W. Smith

Long Branch, N. J.
August 30th /75

Dear Smith:

Mrs. Grant and I will go west about the 20th of Sept. and return by the way of Washington, Pa and spend a few days with you before going to the Capital. We will probably reach Pittsburgh about the 10th of Oct. and remain until say the 16th. If you wish to be away at that time do not hesitate to say so and we will make our visit at some other time.

The family are all well & join in much love to you all.

Yours Truly
U. S. Grant

ALS, Washington County Historical Society, Washington, Pa.
On Nov. 8, 1875, William W. Smith, Washington, Pa., wrote to USG. "I have been requested by a number of prominent citizens to forward to you the enclosed application. I heartily endorse all that is said in favor of Rev Mr. Fraser. His appointment will give great satisfaction to his friends here" ALS, DNA, RG 94, Applications for Positions in War Dept.

The enclosure, a letter of Oct. 9 recommending George Fraser as post chaplain, is *ibid.* No appointment followed.

To Benjamin H. Bristow

[*Aug., 1875*]

DEAR MR. SECRETARY;

I send you a letter just received from Gen. Webster. I have know Webster slightly for many years, and intimately since /61. He was on my staff during the early part of the War, and until I put him in charge of Southern rail-road management, which I did because I knew his honesty, energy & capacity could be relied on.—I send you this letter not to be put on file, but that you may show it, or such parts as you choose, to the Atty. Gen. & Postmaster Gen. whos representatives—as well as yours—in Chicago are somewhat implicated by its statements. I judge that so far as Dist. Atty goes the employment of Hunter, ~~to~~ or some man like him, to assist the Dist. Atty. in prossecuting the Whiskey ring is as much as he means to imply. Ward[1] I have been inclined to look upon as a true man. He may have been somewhat disqualified for his present trying position by having been elected to Congress for one term, and to ~~dob~~be so elected feeling constrained to accept the kind of services Gen. W. describes as controlling politics in Chicago.

Please save Gen. Websters letter to return to me in Washington the coming fall.

Yours Truly
U. S. GRANT

ALS, DLC-Benjamin H. Bristow. On Aug. 9, 1875, Secretary of the Treasury Benjamin H. Bristow, New York City, wrote to Bluford Wilson, solicitor of the treasury, concerning the need for secrecy about sensitive evidence recently uncovered in the investigation of revenue frauds. ". . . P. S.—Ask Webster to write the President fully his views about the Chicago customhouse and the whisky ring. He has great confidence in Webster, and it is going to require the utmost watchfulness of his real friends to prevent his being misled by men who profess friendship for him, but who are acting treacherously. Tell Webster to write strongly and give him the plain truth, and to mark his letter 'confidential.'" *HMD*, 44-1-186, 363. On May 7, Wilson and Bristow had met with USG to discuss revelations of widespread revenue fraud. ". . . It was agreed by both the Secretary and the President that changes should be made in all the more important offices; that the supervisors, the revenue agents, and the collectors were to go out, and the names of their successors were canvassed and determined upon. The President said that as to Saint Louis, he would himself look after the proper persons to be appointed to fill the vacancies, and names were suggested by him and discussed. He stated that McDonald had been a friend of his, and had grievously betrayed, not only that friendship, but the public. As to the others, including Munn of Chicago, and the collector at Saint Louis, he said they were either knaves or fools, and in either case should go out. As a successor for Munn he himself suggested the name of his old and trusted friend, General James D. Webster, then assistant treasurer in Chicago. The Secretary was directed to write to General Webster, and, in confidence, to offer him Munn's place, and the President said that the matter should be kept to ourselves, and the whole matter settled before the politicians, Logan and others, obtained any knowledge of our purpose. . . . I suggested to the President that General Webster had a position worth $5,000 a year; that he was an old man, and not familiar with revenue affairs, and that he probably would not be inclined to make the change. The President said to the Secretary then, 'Say to General Webster that I will take it as a personal favor if he will accept the office.' Other names and other kindred matters were discussed, and we arose to go. The President stopped me by the inquiry, 'Wilson, there is something in what you say about Webster. If he will not take it, do you know anybody out in Illinois that would make a competent supervisor? I told him I did; that while it would perhaps subject me to unfriendly criticism and misrepresentation, on his request I would be glad to give him the names of the parties. He said, 'You give me the names, and I will take care of you.' I then named Col. A. C. Matthews, then collector of the ninth district of Illinois, and after him Col. Jonathan Merriam, collector of the Springfield district of Illinois. I added, to the President, that they were both experienced, honest, and capable officers of high character; Matthews perhaps known to himself, having been a soldier with us as colonel of the 99th Illinois during the Vicksburgh campaign, and Merriam as lieutenant-colonel of the 117th; . . . When General Webster declined the office of supervisor of internal revenue, the Secretary of the Treasury, as I understand and believe, with the approval of the President, directed me to tender the appointment to Colonel Matthews. . . ." Wilson testimony (July 27, 1876), *ibid.*, p. 356.

On June 7, Bristow wrote to USG. "On my return to the Treasury Department I find that nothing has been heard from Mr. Wadsworth in response to the request for his resignation, except through the newspapers. There appears to be a determination on the part of the *Inter Ocean* to make the impression that the request for Wadsworth's resignation is a mere whim of mine, and that I am actuated by personal and selfish motives. You will remember that when I submitted the matter to you I told you the removal of Wadsworth would probably be resisted and would make some trouble politically. I am not surprised at what has followed the request for his resignation. On reconsideration of the matter I am still of opinion that Wadsworth should retire. It is impossible to look over the records of his office in connection with the late Whiskey frauds in that District, without coming to the conclusion that there has been at least the grossest carelessness in the office. Some of your best friends in Chicago strongly advise a change in the Collectorship. So far as I am concerned, I have no personal choice as to Mr. Wadsworth's successor, but I have no doubt that General Webster, who was named by you for the place, would make a most excellent officer. I have the greatest confidence in his integrity, ability and faithfulness to you and your Administration. I think it would be a serious mistake to permit Mr. Wadsworth to remain after what has occurred. It would be accepted at once as an evidence of weakness on the part of the Government which would greatly encourage those who have been engaged in the frauds on the revenue. I am glad to say that I have very encouraging accounts from St. Louis. The new District Attorney has taken hold in earnest, and has already procured indictments against a number of persons for frauds on the revenue and promises to have many more. It does not seem probable that we will be able to try any of the cases before the summer vacation of the Courts, unless we can force trials in Wisconsin. I hand you a slip from the *Inter Ocean* merely to show you how the correspondent of that paper is endeavoring to make the impression that there is a want of harmony in your Administration touching the prosecution of whiskey frauds and the collection of the revenue. It would not be at all difficult to show such a state of facts as would fully justify the removal of Mr. Wadsworth, but I have had no disposition, nor have I yet any desire to do him an injury, and hope it will not become necessary to make any publication of the actual facts as they have been ascertained from the records of his office." LS (press), DLC-Benjamin H. Bristow. On June 9, Bristow wrote to Philip Wadsworth, Chicago. "Your telegram to the Commissioner of Internal Revenue, and letter to the President both dated the 2nd instant, tendering your resignation as Collector of Internal Revenue for the 1st district of Illinois, have been received, and by direction of the President the same is hereby accepted, to take effect upon the appointment and qualification of a successor. In this connection I am directed by the President to say that no formal charges have been made affecting your personal or official integrity: but in view of the recent developments relative to the collection of the revenue in your district, a change in the collectorship is deemed important to the proper administration of the law and collection of the revenue in future." Copy, DNA, RG 56, Letters Sent. Joseph D. Webster replaced Wadsworth as collector of Internal Revenue, 1st District, Ill. See *Chicago Tribune*, June 1–3, 6, 1875.

On June 8, Webster, asst. treasurer, Chicago, had written to USG. "In case of my appointment as Collector of Int. Revenue, the question of my successor in *this* office naturally comes up. I have felt very reluctant to make any recommendation or request in that connection; but at the request of my cashier, Mr. W. C. Nichols, I wish to say that that gentleman's designation as my successor would undoubtedly meet the approval of many of the best men of the Republican party here as well as of the Bankers and business men generally. He would at once and with out difficulty secure the necessary *bonds*. He is thoroughly conversant with the duties of the office which he has discharged for two years at a salary considerably *below what services of the same kind secure* in business life. He is in every way worthy of this consideration at the hands of the government. His integrity is above suspicion, and I should be much pleased personally with his appointment. It would be a little out of the usual course, and none the worse for that—" ALS, DNA, RG 56, Asst. Treasurers and Mint Officials, Letters Received. On June 10, Charles G. Hammond, Clifton Springs, N. Y., wrote to USG. "Having been this moment informed that Genl J D Webster has presented the name of William C Nichols as his successor in the office of United States Assistant Treasurer at Chicago, I beg to add my testimony to the worth and high character of Mr Nichols—For years Mr Nichols had charge under my immediate supervision of the Millions that Came into the hands of the Chicago 'Relief & aid Society' in Consequence of the fire of 1871. . . ." ALS, *ibid.* On June 12, Bristow wrote to Orville E. Babcock. "Your note of the 10th Inst received. I have no one to suggest for Assistant Treasurer at Chicago, but am content to follow Mr Campbell's suggestion   Can you give me Burley's full name? We tried a case against some distillers at Evansville Inda yesterday & got a conviction. This is the first blood, and is in the most doubtful case we had. I have instructed all officials to go slow & make no seizure that cannot be certainly sustained in Court. I wrote the President a few days ago about the appointment of a sixth Auditor. Since then I have heard some allegations against McGrew which seem to require investigation in a quiet way. I have withdrawn my acceptance of the Boston invitation & will stay here until I go to N. Y. to see my family off for Europe on the 23d   All well here & weather pleasant   My regards to the President" ALS, USG 3. On June 28, Samuel B. Gookins, Chicago, wrote to USG.

"I have the honor to transmit herewith a letter just received from Hon D. D. Pratt, Commissioner of Internal Revenue, which will sufficiently explain my object in sending it to you. If I can receive the appointment of Assistant Treasurer at Chicago, without entering into a contest with other candidates, as I suppose is usually done in such cases, I shall be pleased to render the required service according to the best of my ability. Having known Mr Pratt intimately for many years, I do not deem any further endorsement, as to my qualifications for those duties necessary" ALS, DNA, RG 56, Asst. Treasurers and Mint Officials, Letters Received. On June 29, Bristow twice telegraphed to USG, Long Branch. "Mr. Burley declines Assistant Treasurership at Chicago. Bradley telegraphs recommendation of Nichols the present Chief Clerk and Deputy. Who shall be appointed? It is desirable to make the appointment at an early day as Webster wants to take possession of the other office at once." "Since my message of this morning I have received the following by telegraph. 'Shall we recommend an assistant Treasurer at Chicago' (signed) 'C. B. FARWELL R. H. CAMPBELL.'" Press copies (telegrams sent), DLC-Benjamin H. Bristow. On June [29], USG telegraphed to Bristow. "YOU MAY APPOINT NICHOLS A[SST.] TREAS. AT CHICAGO." Telegram received, DNA, RG 56, Asst. Treasurers and Mint Officials, Letters Received.

On June 7, B. W. Raymond, Chicago, had written to USG. "A good work has been done in Revenue Dept of Chicago. *But* you have not completed your work untill you requre the Resignation of Mr N. B. Judd I was in the Custom House 5 Months under him I know the workings of that office and *I know* the buisness is not well done. Goods are often smuggled into this Port there is no vigilence. Drinking Lager Beer runing saloons and being a foreigner is requisite for a place in his Department It is a gross outrage on this community that he is retained he could get no place at the hands of the people *Again* The Comr in Bankruptcy is a fraud and is the nucleus of a ring Mr Hibbard the Comr & his pet & partner Jenkins will retire worth half Million They are robing the Estates of Bankrupts Phil Hoyne is Another of the same stamp & Is not fit for the favours he obtains from the Govt. Messrs Webster & Ward are good men & true These statements I and hundreds besides will attest Judd has kept one man one year that was not at his post but 3 times in 5 months He is now out of the service He has one man now who has kept a mistress in the House with a Daughter 8 Years and never had any occupation but selling Whiskey & this same man was placed by the recommendation of Philip Wadsworth who I am happy to know has his orders to leave If you will continue the good work you will receive the approbation of *the best classes* here I told Erwin for Col of Rev that a certain man under him was a fraud. He took no notice the man Died last Oct and it turns out he made and spent a good deal of money started a saloon in the City & other investments was a single man & Drunk on an average 3 times a week I beg of you not to Stop now We have good men and Mr Judd has had his share You will find no whiskey bloats reccommended by Genl Webster I do know much about the Post Office but I met a *Drunkard* yesterday who said he was in the P. O. You may put your own estimate on this it is free *truth*" ALS, *ibid.*, Letters Received from the President.

On Sept. 9 and 16, Bristow wrote to USG. "After the most careful consideration I am persuaded that a change should be made in the office of Collector of Customs at Chicago. It is of the utmost importance to have the moral support at least of every officer of the Treasury Deptmt in our efforts to punish the perpetrators of frauds, and to collect the revenues. I am quite satisfied that Mr Judd is not in sympathy with the Govmt in the movement against the Whisky ring in Chicago. 'He that is not for us is against us.' I have taken pains to get the opinions of some of our best men in Chicago on this matter, and I think there can be no doubt that a change should be made. Judge Drummond and others suggest the appointment of Honble J Russell Jones, whom I do not personally know, but for whom I have high regard   However I need not tell you anything of Mr Jones for I doubt not you know him well. I would be glad to have him succeed Mr Judd, if you think proper to direct it. I suppose it would be well enough to give Mr Judd an opportunity to resign, and with your approval I propose to invite him to do so. I will submit to you in a few days the name of a successor to Mr Ham appraiser at Chicago. I hope to find, a competent and trustworthy person, who will attend to his duties and not give his time and energies to the abuse of this Department, and opposition to its efforts to enforce law." "I hand you herewith an order suspending Mr. Ham, Appraiser at Chicago, and also a commission for Mr. Adolph Schoeninger. Mr. Schoeninger is strongly recommended by General Webster, Mr. Bradley, and Mr. Campbell. They all speak of him as a man well qualified for the place, and a German whose standing and character will give strength to the party in Chicago. I have written Mr. Judd privately, requesting his resignation and expressing the hope that it would suit his convenience to turn over the office by the first of October; but have heard nothing from him as yet." ALS and LS (press), DLC-Benjamin H. Bristow. On Sept. 17, Norman B. Judd, collector of customs, Chicago, wrote to USG resigning his office. LS, DNA, RG 56, Collector of Customs Applications. On Sept. 20, Bristow telegraphed to USG, Long Branch. "I have received Judd's resignation to take effect on the thirtieth inst. For whom shall I have commission made and where will it reach you?" Press copy (telegram sent), DLC-Benjamin H. Bristow. On Tuesday, Sept. 21, Bristow wrote to USG. "I have received Mr Judd's resignation to take effect on the 1st proximo, and as I learn through the morning papers that you are to start west on Thursday I send Mr Martin, Appointment Clerk of this Deptmt, to you with a commission in blank for Judd's successor. I have no one in my mind but Mr Jones, but leave the blank to be filled with any name you may prefer. I send by Mr Martin, also an Executive order suspending Ham, Appraiser at Chicago, and a Commission for Reiner C. Feldkamp who is recommended by Genl Webster, Mr Campbell and Mr Bradley. Wishing you a pleasant trip, and safe return . . ." ALS (press), *ibid.* On Sept. 23, Bristow telegraphed to J. Russell Jones, Chicago. "The President has signed a Commission for you as Collector of Customs at Chicago. Mr Judds resignation takes Effect the thirteenth instant   I beg to Express my Earnest wish that you will Consent to accept the office and Enter on the duties on the first proximo. I send a blank bond today by mail." Telegram received, ICHi. Jones accepted the appointment. See letter to J. Russell Jones, Oct. 5, 1875; *Chicago Tribune*, Oct. 1–2, 1875; Ross A. Webb, *Benjamin Helm Bristow: Border State Politician* (Lexington, Ky., 1969), pp. 208–11.

On Sept. 25, George W. Jones and four others, Dubuque, wrote to USG, "Expected at DesMoines." "The undersigned your old acquaintances & unwavering friends take occasion to present to your Excellency the name of Captain Orrin Smith, now of Chicago, but formerly of Galena, as a suitable one for the appointment of Collector of Customs at Chicago Illinois which, we perceive, is about to be vacated by the present incumbent. It is scarcely necessary to say anything to you, Mr President, recommendatory of Capt Smith as, we doubt not, that you, like all other persons who have lived as long as you have in the West cannot but be aware of the peculiar qualifications which our friend posses for the position referred to. Nor can there be any doubt, whatever, as to the gratification to the whole people of the west which such an appointment would give. Captain Smith came to these Lead Mines in the year 1824, passed with distinguished credit through two Indian Wars & did as much to reclaim & build up the Country as almost any man who ever resided in our country; & as a pioner & as Sheriff of Jo Daviess County, President of the Galena Packet Company & otherwise won the confidence, respect & heartfelt esteem of the masses, it mattered not of what party, sect or creed. Dame Fortune in latter years has not cast her favors at his feet & as he is now possessed of but little of this world's wealth and is now, as he has ever been, too self denying to ask for himself we, wholly unknown to him, voluntarily make this appeal to your Excellency in behalf of himself & his most estmable family. . . ." LS, DNA, RG 56, Collector of Customs Applications. The docket is endorsed: "Too late" *Ibid.*

1. Jasper D. Ward, Chicago lawyer and Republican, had served as Ill. senator (1862–70) and U.S. Representative (1873–75). On March 19, 1875, U.S. Senators John A. Logan and Richard J. Oglesby of Ill. telegraphed to USG. "We hope you will send J. D. Ward's name in today" Telegram received, DLC-USG, IB. On the same day, Levi P. Luckey telegraphed to Logan. "J. D. Ward's nomination was signed before the receipt of your telegram." ALS (telegram sent), DNA, RG 107, Telegrams Collected (Bound). On March 11, Benjamin H. Campbell, William H. Bradley, and Burton C. Cook, Chicago, had telegraphed to Orville E. Babcock. "B C Cook says he on behalf of Mr Glover dist atty had a full understanding last week with Hon J. D Ward & Hon C B Farwell. that Mr Glover would resign June first unless completely recovered & that Mr Ward who was recommended as Mr Glovers successor will confirm this statement   under these circumstances Is Mr Glovers resignation insisted on before Mr Wards return & an interview with him can be had" Telegram received (at 7:10 P.M.), DLC-USG, IB. On March 12, Babcock drafted a reply. "The President has no objection to the delay you gentlemen ask." ADf (initialed), *ibid.* On March 19, USG nominated Ward as U.S. attorney, Northern District, Ill., in place of Joseph O. Glover. See *Chicago Tribune,* March 20, 1875.

Wilson later testified that despite allegations of Ward's involvement in whiskey frauds, USG had refused to remove him "until he was confronted by evidence, on the 3d of December, which showed that Mr. Ward was a partner in the Powell distillery, and had improper relations with Jacob Rehm, which statement was made to the President by Hon. Burton C. Cook." *HMD,* 44-1-186, 364. On Dec. 3, Wilson wrote to Bristow. "Mr. Cook was just in to see me, with some startling news. He saw President Grant after he met you, and was assured by the President that he would remove Ward promptly, and to that end he would ask Webster at once to name his successor; but what was especially noteworthy was a letter to Cook, from a reliable friend in Chicago, attributing Logan's illness to sheer fright, and which charges that he is in it, and that the atmosphere is full of rumors about Ward's connection with the ring, his relations with Distiller Powell, &c. The inclosed, from Brooks, may interest you. The Lord give you wisdom." *Ibid.*, pp. 364, 516. See *ibid.*, pp. 477–79. On Dec. 10, a correspondent reported from Washington, D. C. "The Hon. Mark Bangs, of Lacon, Marshall County, it was decided at the Cabinet meeting to-day, is to be appointed United States District Attorney for the Northern District of Illinois, to succeed Jasper D. Ward. Bangs was the second choice of the six Congressmen from Northern Illinois, who presented the names of Lathrop, of Rockford, Bangs, of Lacon, and Canfield, of Aurora. Lathrop declined the place. The Congressmen who recommended him are very much pleased that the President appointed him. They had all thought that Hunter, of Chicago, would be appointed. H. H. Honore telegraphed an elaborate dispatch advocating Hunter. Fred Grant, his special friend, spoke a good word for him, but the President yielded to the Congressmen. John B. Hawley, of Rock Island, tried hard to get the place. . . ." *Chicago Tribune,* Dec. 11, 1875. On Dec. 13, USG nominated Mark Bangs as U.S. attorney, Northern District, Ill. See *ibid.*, Dec. 7–9, 12, 1875.

On Dec. 12, a correspondent reported from Washington, D. C. "Mr. C. B. Farwell . . . authorizes the following statement: That he (Farwell) and Gen. Logan endeavored at one time to have Bluford Wilson, Solicitor of the Treasury, removed: that thereby they incurred the deadly enmity of said Wilson; that they worked to have Glover removed from the office of District Attorney, and Ward appointed, and succeeded, and thereby secured the enmity of Burton C. Cook; that, in the course of events, Wilson went to Chicago, and demanded of Ward that he have Farwell indicted by the Grand Jury, and in answer to Ward's inquiry on what evidence Wilson said it made no difference, to indict him, and the evidence could be got afterwards. . . ." *Ibid.*, Dec. 14, 1875. Ward denied this allegation. *Ibid.* On Dec. 15, Wilson, St. Louis, wrote to USG. "Pardon me for troubling you to read the inclosed clipping from yesterday morning's Chicago Tribune. I might, under ordinary circumstances, be quite content to let the matter rest where Mr. Ward's explanation leaves it, and to permit that gentleman and the Hon. C. B. Farwell to settle their own differences in their own way. In view, however, of the many misstatements in relation to myself that have reached you, and of the fact that I did not care to go into the matter with the reporter, I wish to say to you that the whole story of Mr. Farwell, as it relates to me, is utterly and unqualifiedly false. Even as a joke, a poor one at best, it is wholly without foundation or warrant in any word or act of mine in reference to any case of any human being either in-side or outside of the whisky-ring suits. If it comes in your way, I will be obliged if you will show this to Mr. Farwell. If he has been at you with his complaint against me, I will take it as a favor if you will call his attention to my answer. The situation here and at Chicago seems to be satisfactory. I return to Washington to-night." *HMD*, 44-1-186, 365. See let-ter to Edwards Pierrepont, July 29, 1876.

To J. C. Bancroft Davis

———

Long Branch, N. J.
Sept. 5th 1875.

Hon. J. C. B. Davis:
U. S. Min. Plen,[1] &c.
Dear Sir:

This will introduce to you Mr. Archibald Alexander, son of Mr. H. Alexander, of the law firm of Alexander, Green & Co of New York City.

Mr. Alexander, although very young, graduated this year at Princeton, taking very high honors in his class—second I think—and now visits Berlin for the purpose of continuing his studies in that Capitol for a year or two. His father I claim as one of my best friends, and the young man himself I feel perfectly secure in endors-ing to you as one who will prove a credit to his country both for his capacity & learning, and also for his high moral character. Any thing that you can do to facilitate his progress will be received as a per-sonal favor to me, and will be appreciated by Mr. Alexander.

With great respect,
your obt. svt.
U. S. Grant

ALS, DLC-J. C. Bancroft Davis.

On March 31, 1876, Henry M. Alexander, Alexander & Green, New York City, wrote to USG recommending José de Carricarte, Spanish banker. "You may recollect that I spoke to you in the cars last June on the subject of the appointment of a consul at Coruna, Spain when you told me to make the application. . . ." ALS, DNA, RG 59, Letters of Application and Recommendation. Related papers are *ibid.* No appointment followed.

1. On June 10, 1874, USG had nominated J. C. Bancroft Davis as minister to Germany. On March 12, George Bancroft, U.S. minister, Berlin, had written to USG. "When I received a commission as minister to Berlin, it afforded me the greatest satisfaction to receive the very friendly letter in which you gave the appointment your hearty approval. Still more have I cause to be gratified by the uniform support which I have received from your administration since your accession to the Presidency. Many reasons conspire to make me wish to retire from the employment about the first day of October next; and I ask your consent to my retirement at that time. The intervening months will enable me to finish such business as I have been specially instructed to transact. At the same time I beg leave to ask, that alike from motives drawn from the public welfare & from justice resting on particular considerations, Col. Bliss may be retained in his position as Secretary of this Legation. . . . P. S. Col. Bliss is the Son-in-law of our common friend Mr Wm. J. Albert of Baltimore." LS, USG 3. On April 15 and May 5, Fish recorded in his diary. "*President*: . . . Asked when Bancrofts' resignation took effect and spoke of his successor, commented on the non receipt of Bliss' resignation and said that Mr. Albert, his father-in-law about a fortnight since asked if he could not be continued and was told No, that he had been appointed solely on Mr. Bancroft's account and now that Mr. Bancroft is to return he wishes the place vacant." "He requested me to prepare nominations for Nicholas Fish as Secretary of Legation at Berlin vice Bliss resigned, and Chapman Coleman, of Maryland as 2d Secretary there vice Fish promoted. Asked if I had anything as to when Jay is expected back—and inquired whether J. C. B. Davis would not like that position. I told him there were reasons why it might not be agreeable to make him the successor of Jay. He laughed and said they are making Bancroft Davis responsible for everything now: they say he wrote my veto message" DLC-Hamilton Fish.

Endorsement

Refered to the Sec. of State. I was called upon by Mr. Merchant, the son of an old Army officer, and brother of a classmate of mine,[1] in the interest of Mr. Delmege for this Commercial Agency. Mr. M. seemed to attach much importance to American Commercial interests in having such an agency established. If it is proper Make the appointment and the Sec. of State sees no objection to it, I have no objection to Mr. Delmege being appointed.

U. S. GRANT

SEPT. 7TH /75

AES, DNA, RG 59, Miscellaneous Letters. Written on a letter of Sept. 1, 1875, from S. L. Merchant, New York City, to USG. "I have the honour to apply to you for the appointment of Mr E. T. Delmege as Vice Commercial Agent at the port of Point-de-Galle, Island of Ceylon. While the United States is represented by a Commercial Agent at the port of Colombo in that Island I desire briefly to give my reasons for this application in behalf of Mr Delmege. Galle is situated at the extreme Southern point of Ceylon. All tonnage whether steam or sail passing to and from the China Seas and the East Indies to ports in the United States, South America, Great Britain or Continent of Europe seek this placeort as a place of call either for supplies or to receive orders respecting their future destination. Its importance is more appreciated by the Commercial than the political interests. Every Nation, without exception, with any maritime strength has its representative at that port. . . . Mr Delmege it is true is a British subject but as there are no american residents at the port and his character and position have already been highly endorsed by some of the first merchants and other Foreign Consuls, (This recommendation can be found already filed at the State Dept) I can see no objections on account of his nationality to his representing American interests particularly as other Govts do not hesitate to avail of the services of competent and reliable foreign subjects. . . . In conclusion I may add—there are no emoluments connected with the Office and that it is sought by Mr Delmege for the honor which it confers—hence the Govt can be honourably and efficiently represented and its interests protected with credit to the nation and your Administration which so thoughtfully provides for the interests of its citizens without any expense whatever to the State. I might add for your information that Mr Delmege is full consul for Portugal and vice-consul for Spain a magistrate and one of her Majesty's Justices of the Peace. Trusting that under the above circumstances I I may have the pleasure shortly of communicating to this gentleman the information that you have been pleased to confer upon him the high honor which he solicits . . ." ALS, *ibid.* On the same day, Merchant again wrote to USG concerning E. T. Delmege, marked "To the President—*personal.*" ". . . He is a man of large means and therefore can [h]ave no sordid purposes in view but seeks the [a]ppointment for the honour which it brings him. . . ." ALS, *ibid.* Francis Newman, U.S. consul, Ceylon, opposed a commercial agent at Point de Galle. D, *ibid.* On June 3, 1873, S. L. Merchant & Co. had written to Secretary of State Hamilton Fish recommending Delmege for appointment as commercial agent at Point de Galle. L, *ibid.*, Letters of Application and Recommendation. Point de Galle did not receive a commercial agent.

1. Merchant's father and brother were Charles S. Merchant (USMA 1814) and Charles G. Merchant (USMA 1843).

To Levi P. Luckey

Long Branch, N. J. ~~Washington~~ ~~D C~~. Sept 7th *1875*
To L. P. LUCKEY
SECRETARY, EX. MANSION, WASHINGTON, D. C.
Submit despatch from Miss. to Attorney General and ask for his advice and answer to Gov. Ames as to whether proclamation of last year is still in force and telegraph [me] advice
U. S. GRANT

Copy, DNA, RG 60, Letters from the President. On Sept. 7, 1875, Governor Adelbert Ames of Miss. telegraphed to USG, Washington, D. C. "Domestic violence in its most aggravated form exists in certain parts of this State. On the evening of the first Inst. unauthorized and Illegal armed bodies overthrew the Civil Authorities of Yazoo County and took forcible possession of said County from which the Sheriff the Peace Officer of the County was compelled to flee for Safety and is still a refugee, the Sheriff of this, Hinds County, reports that since the fourth Inst. he has been unable after every effort to maintain the peace and protect right. He reports various murders by unauthorized armed bodies who are scouring the County. Warren County is also reported as being in a state of terrorism from the demonstrations of still other unauthorized armed bodies, and a feeling of insecurity pervades in other Counties of the State. After careful examination of all reports I find myself compelled to appeal to the General Government for the means of giving that protection which every every aAmerican citizen is entitled. I do not make formal application under the Provisions of the Constitution of the United States but telegraph you to know if you can and will regard the proclamation issued by you in December last on the application of the Legislature of this State ias still in force. The necessity of immediate action cannot be over stated. If your proclamation is not in force I will at once make a formal application in accordance with Provisions of the Constitution of the United States." Copy, *ibid.* On Sept. 6, William H. Harney, sheriff, Hinds County, Jackson, Miss., had written to Ames. "I proceeded yesterday, the 5th inst., to summon a posse of citizens to quell the riotous proceedings now going on at Clinton and vicinity, and to protect the lives of citizens. My posse went to Clinton and found the town quiet, the lives of citizens in town were being protected by a patrol of citizens, under the command of the mayor of that town. Several innocent, unarmed, and peaceable colored citizens were shot down within the town limits yesterday morning. Detached squads of white men were scouting through the country, murdering and driving the colored people from their homes. . . . As I write men are coming in telling of the fearful slaughter. The colored people are unarmed and defenseless. As the peace-officer of the county, I appeal to your excellency to use what means there is at your command to stop this slaughter of an innocent and defenseless people. I am powerless to stay the carnage, and no man knows where it will end if your excellency cannot give aid to a death-stricken people." *SRC*, 44-1-527, II, Documentary Evidence, 40–41. On Sept. 8, Attorney Gen. Edwards Pierrepont telegraphed to USG, Long Branch. "The proclamation of December last is not now in force. I have so advised and Mr Luckey will thus telegraph Governor Ames." Copy, DNA, RG 60, Letters Sent to Executive Officers. On the same day, 10:30 A.M., Levi P. Luckey telegraphed Pierrepont's determination to Ames. *New York Times*, Sept. 9, 1875. See *ibid.*, Sept. 8, 1875; Blanche Butler Ames, comp., *Chronicles From the Nineteenth Century: Family Letters of Blanche Butler and Adelbert Ames*... (1957), II, 156–57, 159–60, 163–64, 165–67; Proclamation, Dec. 21, 1874; telegram to AG Edward D. Townsend, Sept. 8, 1875.

On Aug. 23, "Nelson Care of Mrs Scanlon," Grenada, Miss., had telegraphed to USG. "Send men to help me here from and send pass right off   I can go to see you." Telegram received (at 4:47 P.M.), DLC-USG, IB.

On Sept. 7, E. C. Walker, Jr., Macon, Miss., wrote to USG. "I will take Pleasurer of Writing you afew Lines   This County Is now in up Raw and Pres., I Have Wrote the Hon Governor Two (2) Letters and Pres., I know you Have it in To your Powder To Stop White Peopels from Killing Black Peopels . . . now Pres I will ask To your Hon Doant the 13 & 14 & 15 Demenments Gives the (Cold) Peopels the Same Rights and the voice to the Balord Box as it Do the Whites   Dear Sir if it Do The White Peopels Says that If the negro Doant voat the Din: Ticket the will not 1 of them Get Heomes next year and Pres Do for Gord Sake Stand by thes Poor (Cold) Peopels   I ask you Pres in Gord.s name in Gord name Help us If it Is in your Powder and Pres I know that it is in your Powder To Help the Poor (Cold) Peopels in this County for we all ar Hear on the White Peopels Land With out Land or With out arms and With any thing To Pertect our Self With and Pres I Do think that you Have it in to your Power To Deman us Arms To Pertect our Selvs With . . . President I under stand That you Says that you Doant Want the President office any Longer and A. D. 1876. O, Pres What Will become of We Poor Black Peopel.s When you Steap out of that office   The (Cold) Peopels Says You Shall not Come Out of that office and I Say So too" ALS, DNA, RG 60, Letters Received, Miss. See *SRC,* 44-1-527, II, Documentary Evidence, 71–72.

On Sept. 8, Charles Gray and three others, "colored citizens," Vicksburg, telegraphed to USG. "The telegrams of ~~g~~Governor Ames to you stating that a reign of terrorism prevails in this county is without a shadow of truth." Telegram received (on Sept. 9), DLC-USG, IB.

To Joseph W. Vance

———

Long Branch, N. J.
Sept. 7th 1875,

DEAR SIR:

Your note of the 23d of August inviting me to attend a reception & banquet to be given in Paris, Ill. on the 21st of Oct. by the members of my old 31st[1] Ill. Vols. was duly received. I do not know a reception that it would be more gratifying for me to attend than this. But I must forego the pleasure. My private interests compel me to be in St. Louis about the end of this month, and it will be impossible for me to extend my visit so late as to the 21st of August.

I hope you will have a most gratifying re-union, and only regret that so many that composed the regiment when I ceased to be ~~your~~

its immediate commander can not be with you. They offered up their lives in a just & patriotic cause, & I hope due notice will be paid to their memory at your Banquet.

Faithfully Yours

U. S. GRANT

CAPT. J. W. VANCE COR. SEC.

ALS, Gilder Lehrman Collection, NNP. Joseph W. Vance served as 1st lt., 21st Ill., during USG's brief service as col. in 1861.

On Aug. 26, 1875, Horace M. Woolley, Oakland, Ill., wrote to USG. "you may think it strange to hear from me, one of your 21st boys I was your *Private Orderly*, while you was Colonel of the 21st.   you will remember me I guess I hope so at least for you have always been esteemed as a friend by me.   our Regt has a Reunion at Paris Edgar Co on the 21st day of Oct. 1875 in Commeration of the battle we were engaged in at F[r]edrickstown Mo in 1861. I have not been in very good health since the War. I was young when I went into the service. I think *Fred* and I are about the same age. Camp life was rather to hard for me but I went through three years all right but have been broken down Ever since. I havent been able too do a days work for over Eight Months. about 5 years ago I made application for Pension and have been Ex twice by the Govt Surgeons made out affidavits by Regt Surgeon & Co officers and witnessed by five of my Co companions, and all the nessesary papers have been sent too Pension Dept 3 months ago, and no tidings yet. . . . I will send you my Photo, before long, so you Can see if you have lost all rememberance of me. you used too Call me *Hod*—my best regards too you. give my respects to Fred your family also" ALS, DNA, RG 48, Miscellaneous Div., Letters Received.

1. 21st.

To AG Edward D. Townsend

LONG BRANCH NJ. SEPTR. VIIITH. [*1875*]
ADJ. GEN. U. S. A. WASHINGTON DC.
YOU MAY INSTRUCT COMMANDING OFFICER OF TROOPS IN MISSISSIPPI THAT HE MAY ASSIST THE GOVERNOR IN MAINTAINING ORDER AND PRESERVING LIFE IN CASE OF INSURRECTION TOO FORMIDABLE FOR HIM TO SUPPRESS BEFORE TELEGRAPHING YOUR ORDER SUBMIT IT WITH THIS DISPATCH TO THE ATTY. GENERAL TO SEE IF IT IS ENTIRELY LEGAL INFORM GOV. AMES OF ANY INSTRUCTIONS YOU GIVE.

U. S. GRANT.

Telegram received (at 9:30 P.M.), DNA, RG 94, Letters Received, 4676 1875. On Sept. 8 (9:30 P.M.) and 9 (3:00 P.M.), AG Edward D. Townsend telegraphed to USG, Long Branch. "Your despatch of this date concerning Mississippi is just received and will be obeyed." "Pending decision of question of Proclamation by Attorney General, I have early this morning telegraphed General Augur to be ready to furnish aid. He replies there are troops enough in the State & they only need to be distributed where necessary" ADfS (telegrams sent), *ibid.* On Sept. 8, 5:30 P.M., Governor Adelbert Ames of Miss. had telegraphed to USG, Washington, D. C. "Domestic violence prevails in various parts of this State beyond the power of the State authorities to suppress. The Legislature cannot be convened in time to meet the emergency. I therefore, in accordance with Sec. 4, Article 4, of the Constitution of the United States, which provides that 'The United States shall guaranty to every State in this Union a republican form of government and shall protect each of them against invasion; and on application of the Legislature, or of the Executive (when the Legislature cannot be convened) against domestic violence,' make this my application for such aid from the Federal Government as may be necessary to restore peace to the State, and protect its citizens" ALS (press, telegram sent), Ames Letterbook, Miss. Dept. of Archives and History, Jackson, Miss.; *New York Times*, Sept. 9, 1875. On the same day, Ames wrote to his wife Blanche Butler Ames. "Today I made an application to the President of the U. S. for troops to keep the peace and preserve life. We must have them, or the colored voters of the state will be deprived of their rights and liberties, which the amendments of the Constitution expressly stipulate to maintain. My telegram went this afternoon, and I await confidently a favorable reply. . . ." Blanche Butler Ames, comp., *Chronicles From the Nineteenth Century: Family Letters of Blanche Butler and Adelbert Ames . . .* (1957), II, 167.

　　Also on Sept. 8, "WE COLORED CITIZENS," Vicksburg, wrote to Adelbert Ames. "The rebles turbulent; are aiming themselves here now to-day to go to Satartia to murder more poor negros. Gov., aint the no pertiction? This [C]onfedrate military all ovr the State, now call Granger. They are better prepared now for fighting than they was before the war. They read yr proclamation to-day and dam you and proclamation too; thy intend to hang yo, ore get some secret scoundral to kill you. We heard that the Vicksburg banditts offered $10,000 to any man, or body of men, if thy would kill you. Gov., they say we rads shan't have no meeting, no hold no ellection. . . . The rebs are riding around all through this county now, at night, taking arms from the colored folks daring to ever leave home." *SRC*, 44-1-527, II, Documentary Evidence, 89. On April 27–29, 1876, Adelbert Ames, Washington, D. C., testified before a select committee investigating the 1875 Miss. election. *Ibid.*, I, 1–46.

　　On Sept. 9, 1875, Levi P. Luckey wrote to Secretary of State Hamilton Fish. "The President directs me to furnish you and the Attorney Genl with the enclosed copy of a despatch received last evening from Gov. Ames, of Miss, and also of the despatches sent to the Adjutant General of the Army; and to say that, if you and the Attorney General deem it necessary a proclamation may be issued in accordance with the call of the Governor of Miss" ALS, DNA, RG 59, Miscellaneous Letters. The enclosures are *ibid.*

　　On Sept. 9 and 11, James Z. George, chairman, Miss. Democratic Executive Committee, telegraphed to Attorney Gen. Edwards Pierrepont. "There are no disturbances in this State, and no obstructions to the execution of the laws. There has been an unexpected conflict at a political meeting, and some subsequent disturbance, but everything is quiet now. The Governor's call for United States troops does not even pretend that there is any insurrection against the State Government, as required by the revision of United States Statutes of 1873, pages 10 to 34. Peace prevails throughout the State, and the employment of United States troops would but increase the distrust of the people in the good faith of the present State Government." *New York Times*, Sept. 10, 1875. *SRC*, 44-1-527, I, 382.

". . . Offers are freely made to the governor of assistance to preserve the peace should danger of disturbance occur. The people of Mississippi claim the right of American citizens to
be heard before they are condemned. I re-assert that perfect peace prevails throughout the
State, and there is no danger of disturbance unless initiated by the State authorities, which
I hope they will not do." *Ibid.* On Sept. 10 and 11, Pierrepont telegraphed to USG, Long
Branch. "No proclamation issued, and no troops ordered out. I think the war in Mississippi—over from the information received. Expect telegram soon from the Governor
more specific. Will then communicate." "I have no dispatch from Governor Ames, although I have this morning repeated my telegram; but I have just received a dispatch from
Senator Pease, stating that there is no difficulty in putting down the riot, and that the
sending of Federal troops would do great mischief. I am satisfied that the war is over. Governor Alcorn is now present while I write this, and he has full confidence in the dispatch
of Senator Pease." Copies, DNA, RG 60, Letters Sent to Executive Officers. On Sept. 10
and 11, Pierrepont had telegraphed to Ames. "The United States forces have been put in
readiness. No orders have yet been given them to move, and no proclamation has been issued. Everything is ready. Is there such an insurrection against the State Government as
cannot be put down by the State military forces, aided by all the other powers of the State
Government and the aid of the true citizens?" "To my dispatch of yesterday morning, in
which I mentioned that the troops were held in readiness, and asked whether the situation
of the insurrection was such against the State authorities that the State Government and
the aid of loyal citizens could not put it down. I have received no reply." *New York Times*,
Sept. 13, 1875. On Sept. 11, Ames telegraphed to Pierrepont. "The necessity which called
for my dispatch of the 8th inst. to the President still exists. Your question of yesterday, repeated to-day, asks for information which I gladly give. The violence is incident to the contest preceding the pending election. Unfortunately, the question of race, which has been
prominent at the South since the war, has assumed magnified importance at this time in
certain localities. In fact, the race feeling is so intense that protection for the colored
people by the white organizations is despaired of. A political contest made on the white
line forbids it. The history of the colored people since reconstruction, and its bearing on
the situation at this time, and a detailed statement of the troubles here, cannot be con-
densed in a telegram. This State has been opposed to organizing a Militia of colored men.
It has been believed by them that it would develop a war of races, which would extend beyond the borders of this State. The organization of whites alone, where the issue is one of
race, would be equally ineffectual. The most complete protection would be found in the
strict non-interference of the whites. Contradictions will be numerous, as they were last
December, [*b*]ut the report of the Congressional Committee proves the correctness of my
assertion. I am aware of the reluctance of the people of the country to national interference
in State affairs, though if there be no violation of the law there can be no interference. Permit me to express the hope that the odium of such interference shall not attach to President Grant or the Republican Party. As the Governor of the State I made a demand which
cannot well be refused. Let the odium, in all its magnitude, descend upon me. I cannot escape the conscious discharge of my duty toward a class of American citizens whose only
offense consists in their color. I am powerless to protect." *Ibid.*, Sept. 21, 1875. Also on
Sept. [*11*], Blanche Ames, Lowell, Mass., wrote to Adelbert Ames. ". . . The papers Saturday brought me the news of Grant's dilatory shilly-shally conduct, and my indignation was
without bounds. It is shameful. . . ." Ames, *Chronicles From the Nineteenth Century*, II, 171.
See *ibid.*, pp. 169, 172, 174–75, 179; *New York Times*, Sept. 11, 1875; letter to Edwards
Pierrepont, Sept. 13, 1875.

On Sept. 12, a letter with return address H. K. Gordon, "Lunatic Asylum," Hinds
County, Jackson, Miss., was written to USG. "We have seat our selves with the pleasure of

congratulate you of our state at large. Hon. Sir we are sorry to say to you that we Col. People of the south are in a very bad condition at the present time. And has been for the Last Twentyfour months. We will say so for as the state of mississippi is consern there has been over a 400. people Kill in it lest time than Two year. We do hope that you will take and action upon it for us yoor people." L, DNA, RG 60, Letters from the President.

On Sept. 23, Sarah A. Dickey, Clinton, Miss., wrote to USG. "Allow a humble woman to address your Excellence in behalf of the poor oppressed colored people of the Southern states and especially of this State. Seeing, as I do, that thousands of them are just on the eve of being sacrificed at the hand of the assassin, I cannot hold my peace. Whoever says to you that our troubles in Miss. are slight and that we do not need assistance from the Federal Government is an enemy to the colored people and sanctions their slaughter. I have been laboring in the capacity of an educator, either directly or indirectly, for the freed-men, in this State ever since Dec. 1863. Have been at Clinton nearly five years. During this time I have made the acquaintance of quite a number of the white people, and have learned their sentiments in reference to the colored people and the, so called, carpetbaggers. *I know* that they are a desperate people: I *know* their 'hearts are deceitful above all things.' I *know*, too, that the white people of this state, and I believe also of all the other Southern States, have united almost to a man to keep up this killing of colored men until they shall have succeeded in killing off all of the *leading* men, and as many others as possible. All they want is to see them dead on the ground. They will avail themselves of every apparent opportu-nity and make every pretext that they possibly can to commit these bloody deeds until they shall have satiated their thirst for the blood of these innocent people. I was at the republi-can mass meeting, held at this place (Clinton) on the 4th inst., myself. Was on the ground early and I saw enough with my own eyes to convince any honest person that the repub-licans went there for nothing but peace, profit and pleasure, and that the democrats, who were on the ground, went there for the express purpose of creating a disturbance and of killing as many as they could. The Southern white people are just as deceitful and as wily as men can be. I know that the Authorities of our Government are doing and will do all that they can, so far as they understand the necessities of the case, to stay the sheding of innocent blood: but I feel that with the certain knowledge which I have, it would be inhu-man in me to remain quiet. I feel sure, I MAY be mistaken, yet I do feel very sure that to arm a militia of colored men is simply to usher them into the jaws of death. If a *war* of *races* or of *parties* should ensue then you would know just what course to take; but I fear that the white people would take a course which would be equally if not more disastrous to the col-ored people and which would be much harder to meet by the general government. I think they would only make it another pretext to slaughter colored men not only here but all over the State.... I know that these Southern people are simply carrying on a kind of gur-rilla war and I know that they are planning to continue in this course until they shall have succeeded in killing thousands of colored men and of reducing the remnant to a condition of slavery. You hear a great deal about the massacre at Clinton, but you do not hear the worst. It cannot not be told. Hoping God's blessings may attend these earnest thoughts... P. S. Do not understand me to say that Gov. Ames is not doing all in his power to allay these difficulties. I believe he is." ALS, *ibid.* See Helen Griffith, *Dauntless in Mississippi: The Life of Sarah A. Dickey 1838–1904* (1965), especially pp. 81–83.

To Edward F. Beale

Long Branch, N. J.
Sept. 8th /75

DEAR GENERAL:

My farming opperations at so great a distance from my own supervision have proven so expensive that I have determined to break
it up. My entire stock is advertised for sale on the 30th inst.[1] Among
it is one very superior 2d Hambletonian Stallion, 6 years old, that
took the first premium at the St. Louis Fair last fall.[2] His colts are
said to be promising without a single exception. There are also a few
thoroughbred mares stinted to this horse. The times are such that I
have no idea that this stock will bring twenty-five per cent its value.
Knowing that you are just starting a stock farm—that you can over-
see yourself—it occurred to me that you might want some of the
pick of this stock? If you do you can have it before the sale, at your
own price, or have a bidder on hand, or if you choose you can have
some of the best of the stock sent to your place as mine and make any
satisfactory arrangement for keeping or disposal afterwards.

I will be here, with the exception of a few days, until about the
23d. Then I will go to St. Louis to remain a few days. I will not be
there at the sale.

My kindest regards to Mrs. Bealle & the young ladies.

Yours Truly
U. S. GRANT

GN. E. F. BEALLE

ALS, DLC-Decatur House Papers. Born in Washington, D. C., Edward F. Beale graduated
from the U.S. Naval Academy (1845), served during the Mexican War, and resigned from
the navy (1850) to enter business in Calif. He held appointments under President Millard
Fillmore as Indian superintendent and President Abraham Lincoln as surveyor gen., purchased Decatur House (1871) across from the White House, and gained social and political prominence. In 1875, Beale bought Ash Hill, an estate near Hyattsville, Md. Mary E.
Beale, his wife, was the daughter of former U.S. Representative Samuel Edwards of Pa. See
Gerald Thompson, *Edward F. Beale & The American West* (Albuquerque, 1983), especially
pp. 194–98.

On Sept. 9, 1872, USG, Long Branch, had written to Beale. "Mrs. Grant & I will be
pleased to have you dine with us, socially, this after-noon at Two O'Clock. Please return verbal answer by the bearer." ALS, DLC-Decatur House Papers. On Nov. 6, Admiral

David D. Porter, Washington, D. C., wrote to U.S. Senator Simon Cameron of Pa. concerning USG's reelection. "... I was at the Presidents last night and after all the news came in we sat down to a handsome supper. the President bore the result in his usual quiet way. but no doubt his heart was glad—what a rebuke to his detractors—Rumours are afloat that Mr Robeson is going abroad—, now has it ever struck you—what a splendid secretary of the Navy. Cousin Edward Beale would make, he is devoted to General Grant and the President likes him very much—The latter owes a good deal to Penna, and yourself, which he acknowledged to me; and if such a thing could be brought about it would be a good thing for all concerned, ..." ALS, DLC-Simon Cameron. On Nov. 30, 1873, Sunday, USG wrote to Beale. "Mrs. Grant and I will take pleasure in dining with you any day this week, after Tuesday, that may best suit you, unless Mrs. Grant should be detained by company which she is now expecting. I can accept for myself without conditions." ALS, DLC-Decatur House Papers. In 1873, Beale wrote to USG sending Vancouver salmon and cooking instructions. William Evarts Benjamin, Catalogue No. 42, March, 1892, p. 4. On March 17, 1874, USG and Julia Dent Grant invited Beale's daughters to dinner for March 18. D, DLC-Decatur House Papers. On Aug. 5, USG, Long Branch, wrote to Beale. "May Mrs. Grant & I have the pleasure of the Company of yourself, Mrs. Beall and daughters at dinner to-day at three O'clock?" ALS, *ibid.* Another dinner invitation for March 24, 1875, is *ibid.* On Oct. 22, Orville E. Babcock wrote to Beale. "The President will be pleased if you can find time to drop in and see him about 3 pm today." ALS, *ibid.* On April 12, 1876, Culver C. Sniffen wrote to Beale. "The President directs me to say to you that if it is pleasant tomorrow and you are going out to your farm he would like to drive out with you at about one o'clock." ALS, *ibid.* On May 23, USG wrote to [Sniffen]. "Make out nomination of Ed F. Beall of the District of Columbia" AN, OHi. On May 24, USG nominated Beale as minister to Austria-Hungary.

On Feb. 28, Robert M. Kelly, *Louisville Commercial*, had written to USG. "Understanding that Mr. John B. Bowman, Regent of Kentucky University is an applicant for the mission to Vienna, I have the honor to recommend his appointment in the strongest terms. He is a gentleman of the best culture and capacity and as minister would reflect credit on the diplomatic service. In his efforts to build up a great University in this state—a work to which without compensation he has given his life—he has been hindered and harassed extremely on account of his persistent devotion to the cause of the country and because of his connection with the Republican party...." ALS, DNA, RG 59, Letters of Application and Recommendation. John M. Harlan, Louisville, and U.S. Representatives James G. Blaine of Maine and James A. Garfield of Ohio also wrote to USG recommending John B. Bowman. ALS, *ibid.* On May 6, Bowman, Philadelphia, telegraphed to USG. "Please remember my application for Austrian mission   testimonial filed with you & Secretary Fish" Telegram received, *ibid.* See *DAB*, II, 520–21.

On April 12, Adolph E. Borie, Philadelphia, had written to USG. "Do what I can, I am obliged to trouble you every now and then. The enclosed must speak for itself and I can only add that Genl Post made a most excellent impression on us all when at Vienna in 1872, both as a perfect gentleman, and a very intelligent Official" ALS, DNA, RG 59, Letters of Application and Recommendation. On March 21, Philip Sidney Post, consul gen., Vienna, had written to Borie. "Mr. Orth, having been nominated for Governor of Indiana, expects to reach Washington about the middle of May and will then resign his position as Minister at this place. If he is consulted with reference to his successor he will strongly recommend my appointment...." ALS, *ibid.* Related papers, including favorable endorsements from Gen. William T. Sherman and Lt. Gen. Philip H. Sheridan, are *ibid.* Post continued as consul gen.

1. On Sept. 30, 1875, a correspondent reported from St. Louis. "The sale of President Grant's blooded stock took place at his farm, 10 miles from this city, to-day, according to advertisements. The day was not very propitious and the attendance slim. The stock went at exceedingly low prices. Young Hambleton, 7 years old, a stallion, was knocked down for $300. A fine double team sold for $680, said to have been bid in for the President. The trotting mare Bessie Knox, for which the President paid $1,000, brought $200. Another trotting mare, Belle of St. Joe, was bid in for General Grant for $1,000. The mare Vicksburg, ridden by General Grant at Vicksburg, was knocked down for $56. About a dozen brood mares, mostly thoroughbreds, sold from $45 to $85. . . ." *Chicago Tribune,* Oct. 1, 1875. For more detailed accounts of the sale, see *St. Louis Globe-Democrat* and *St. Louis Dispatch,* Oct. 1, 1875. See also letter to John F. Long, July 13, 1875.

On Nov. 20, Ed Harkness, St. Louis, wrote to USG. "At your sale of horses at your farm in September last, my brother bought for me a dark brown mare, named 'Virginia' & claimed to be thoroughbred. As Messrs Lanham & Long said you would furnish any information in regard to the stock, I take the liberty of requesting you to send me her pedigree, if you have it, or any information by which it could be traced, it would be a great favor as I desire to place her on record. Hoping for an early answer, . . ." ALS, USG 3.

2. See letter to Adolph E. Borie, Sept. 25, 1874, note 1.

To Adolph E. Borie

Long Branch, N. J.
Sept. 8th /75

MY DEAR MR. BORIE,

My letter of yesterday answers yours of same date with the exception of the question of the probable time of our return. I think we will be in Pittsburgh about the 12th of October. Unless unexpectedly called to Washington I will remain there, or rather in Washington, Pa until the 16th or 18th. Mr. Smith with whom we will stay has a large house, will be glad to have you & Mrs. Borie stop also. But if you can not spare the time you would reach Phila say about the 13th.

Yours Truly
U. S. GRANT

HON. A. E. BORIE.

ALS, PHi. On Sept. 7, 1875, USG, Long Branch, wrote to Adolph E. Borie. "My plan for starting on a western trip has been changed on account of change of day for the sale of my stock in St. Louis . . . Mrs. Bo[*rie*] and you will be delighted with the Rocky Mountain scenery, climate and accommodations . . . P. S. Take with you the parapharnalia for a full game of Boston." Swann Galleries, Inc., Sale No. 1374, May 31, 1985, no. 111.

On Sept. 9, USG wrote to Borie. "Will you be kind enough to allow some one from your office purchase for me—and send by Ex—the value of the enclosed in 'Yellow Cord' for lighting cigars in the wind?. . . P. S. If I knew where to send I would not trouble you with this commission." ALS, James F. Ruddy, Rancho Mirage, Calif.

To Columbus Delano

————

Long Branch N. J.
Sept 9th 1875.

DEAR SIR:

Enclosed I send you dispatches from Gen. Pope. & Gen. McKenzie which show a laxity somewhere in getting supplies to the reserve Indians about Fort Sill. I understand from Col. Grant,[1] who has just returned from an inspection tour in that country, that there has been a great deal of distress among the Indians by reason of negligence in getting their supplies to them.   we are probably indebted to the discretion of Gen. McKenzie and the dread the Indians have of him— for the comparative peace so long maintained. The Agt. there is highly spoken of for his integrity and interest in his business. I think it would be well if the Sec. would a personal examination of the amt. of supplies purchased & paid for for these Indians in the last six months how many of such supplies have reached them, where the fault lies, and apply the remedy. In six weeks from now bad roads may be expected to set in, when the means of supply will become precarious if the provisions are not in store at the point of destination.

Very respectfully
U. S. GRANT

THE SEC. OF THE INT.

P. S. Since the 1st of July to the 2d of Sept. not one pound of supplies of any discription has reached Fort Sill except beef.

Copy, DLC-USG, II, 3. On Aug. 31, 1875, Brig. Gen. John Pope, Fort Leavenworth, Kan., wrote to Gen. William T. Sherman, St. Louis. "The following copies of telegrams from Colonel Mackenzie, commanding Fort Sill, are respectfully transmitted. I have so often been obliged to report such failures on the part of the Indian Department that I am reluctant to report farther on the subject, but the emergency is pressing and unless these Indians are fed and the obligations of the Indian Department to them be fulfilled, we may expect, certainly, a stampede of the Kiowas and Comanches from their reservations. I am constrained, therefore, to ask the consideration of the War Department of this subject, as through that Department alone, it seems, we must expect anything like a strict fulfillment of the obligations the Government has assumed toward the Indians." LS, DNA, RG 94, Letters Received, 4608 1875. On Aug. 23 and 27, Col. Ranald S. Mackenzie, 4th Cav., Fort Sill, Indian Territory, had telegraphed to Asst. AG, Dept. of Mo., Fort Leavenworth. ". . . The Interior Department at this place has habitually been without various parts of the Indian ration, ever since my arrival in March. They are now out of sugar and coffee, but expect it very soon. If the Secy of the Interior will reimburse will it not be well to direct me issue to Agent on his receipts at any time that I can. It might sometimes save suffering in the winter and improper annoyance to Indians at any season." "The Indian Agent here is now out of sugar, coffee and salt, He has only flour enough for two (2) weeks, Cannot I be authorized to issue to the Agent. There is very bad management in supplying the Agent at this place, which is not his fault but which is the fault of some superior, whom, I do not know. It is unpleasant to be expected to make Indians believe (behave?) themselves who are unjustly dealt with. The Interior Department has, I am informed, plenty of money to feed these Indians, so there can be no excuse on that score." Copies, *ibid.* On Sept. 1, Sherman endorsed these papers to Secretary of War William W. Belknap, "inviting prompt attention to the real danger, that Starvation may compel the Kioways & Comanches to break away from the reservation in Search of food" AES, *ibid.* See *HED*, 43-2-91.

On Sept. 20, James M. Haworth, agent, Kiowa and Comanche Agency, Indian Territory, reported to Edward P. Smith, commissioner of Indian Affairs. ". . . Among the serious hinderances we have had to contend with was the failure of wagon transportation to transport our supplies from the railroad in proper time. We were compelled to live from 'hand to mouth,' sometimes not knowing where the rations for the coming issue-day would be had from. . . . I have received many kindnesses from General Mackenzie and his subordinate officers; he has been especially obliging in furnishing me subsistence to issue to my Indians when my supplies have been short. My observation leads me to suggest that at agencies where troops are regarded as necessary, white troops should be employed in place of colored, as the influence is far less demoralizing with the white than colored. In concluding my report, I desire to say that my experience of nearly three years with these people causes me more than ever to admire the wisdom of his Excellency the President in inaugurating the present pacific mode of governing his 'red children;' and could lawless white men be kept from among them, and their subsistence department kept properly supplied, I believe his most sanguine expectations would be realized, and only a few years pass before they would cease to be a burden to the Government, or a source of revenue to bad men. . . ." *Ibid.*, 44-1-1, part 5, I, 777. See *ibid.*, pp. 770–76, 790–91; Burritt M. Hiatt, "James M. Haworth, Quaker Indian Agent," *Bulletin of Friends Historical Association*, 47, 2 (Autumn, 1958), 80–93.

On Sept. 20 and 27, Smith wrote to Secretary of the Interior Columbus Delano recommending selective cooperation with the army to supply Indians near Fort Sill. Copies, DNA, RG 94, Letters Received, 4608 1875. Related papers are *ibid.* Indian provisions remained a problem in that vicinity. See *HED*, 44-2-1, part 5, I, 450–57, 468–70.

1. On Sept. 2, Col. Richard C. Drum, asst. AG, Chicago, had telegraphed to USG, Long Branch. "Colonel Grant left Fort Sill yesterday for Chicago." LS (telegram sent), DNA, RG 393, Military Div. of the Mo., Letters Sent (press); copy, *ibid.*, Letters Sent.

To AG Edward D. Townsend

Long Branch [*Sept.*] 9th [*187*]5

Genl Townsend,
Adj Genl, Washn,

Please inform me the number of vacancies at large now Existing at West Point

U. S. Grant.

Telegram received, DNA, RG 107, Telegrams Collected (Bound). On Sept. 10, 1875, AG Edward D. Townsend telegraphed to USG, Long Branch. "Your despatch of ninth 9 delivered this morning. On inquiry in the Secretary's office where records of West Point are kept, the chief clerk states he thinks there are three 3 in excess of number at [*large*] allowed by law. There is doubt as to [constr]uction of law. The Secretary will be at Saint James Hotel, New York, tomorrow, and chief clerk thinks he will know whether vacancies exist, as he personally directs [busin]ess of Military Academy." LS (telegram sent), *ibid.* On the same day, USG telegraphed to Townsend. "Can you tell me the number of vacancies at large at West Point," Telegram received, *ibid.* On Sept. 11, Townsend telegraphed to USG. "Your two 2 despatches of the tenth 10 concerning west Point, are received. The war Office [c]lerk who keeps the records of the Secretary has gone to New York to meet him and the chief clerk is not familiar with them. [*I* s]ent you by last night's mail a list [of n]ames, arranged by classes, of the cadets [appo]inted at large as appears by the records. [*The* l]ist contains forty-three 43 names. [*There*] therefore seems to be no vacancy. [*I*] regret not having been able to give [y]ou a definite answer at first, but the [*records*] of the Academy are managed by the [Secreta]ry, and not through this Office. I therefore [h]av[e n]o means of knowing personally." LS (telegram sent), *ibid.*

On July 1, Henry T. Crosby, chief clerk, War Dept., had telegraphed to Orville E. Babcock, Long Branch. "Barnard will see you at Long Branch to-morrow and give all information about cadetships at large." LS (telegram sent), *ibid.* On July 13, the War Dept. prepared memoranda on USG's USMA appointments, a matter complicated by a change in the law. D, *ibid.*, RG 94, Correspondence, USMA. See Robert H. Hall, USMA AG, to William T. Barnard, clerk, War Dept., Aug. 25, 1875, *ibid.*; *CR*, 43–2, 1254; *U.S. Statutes at Large*, XVIII, part 3, pp. 466–67. On March 1, U.S. Representative Moses W. Field of Mich. had written to USG. "My amendment to the West Point Mil,y Academy Bill having been agreed to by the Senate and the House having concurred therein—authorizing the President to fill any vacancies at the Academy of the Cadets appointed by him 'at large,' I beg to call your attention to the application of *Albert Blackstone Scott grandson of General Whiteley U. S. Army* for Executive appointment to the Military Academy. I refer to my former Communication as to his qualifications and respectfully recommend the appointment." LS, DNA, RG 94, Correspondence, USMA. Related papers are *ibid.* Albert B. Scott graduated USMA in 1880.

On July 28, 1875, Crosby had written to USG. "I have the honor to report that the application of J. H. Burns (Cadet at large) for reinstatement at the Military Academy, which was referred by your direction to the Academic Board, has been considered by that body, and their report is to the effect that no sufficient reason exists for recommending his restoration. Mr. Burns had failed in Mathematics at the late examination, and was reported as having but little aptitude, not studious and very inattentive to regulations. Mr. Burns' letter of application was dated Long Branch July 1st, and he has been informed of the action of the Board by letter to that address." Copy, *ibid.*, Letters Sent, USMA. Joel H. Burns had entered USMA in 1874.

On Aug. 27, 1875, Babcock wrote to Crosby. "The President will be pleased to have John McLean appointed an alternate on the list of Cadets to be examined next month. Mr McLean will be appointed to his place at the foot of the alternates already appointed, and will be examined in case he is reached on the list. Mr McLean will appear at West Point at his own expense." ALS, *ibid.*, Correspondence, USMA. On Sept. 4 and 8, Crosby wrote to USG. "I have the honor to inform you that a telegram received from West Point, announces that John C. Dent and Frederick Dent Sharp, have been rejected by the Academic Board; and that Alternates John B. Barnadeau and J. S. Culbertson have both been rejected, the former by the Medical Board, and the latter by the Academic Board." "I have the honor to report, in addition to the rejection of Messrs. Dent. Sharp, Bernadeau and Culbertson, the Department has been notified that Wm A. Nichols and Jno. McLean have also failed in their examination. Edward J. Winslow—who has not yet reported—is the only remaining Alternate on the list for 1875; John B. Marcou and Leonard C. Couch having declined their appointment. Messrs. Lugenbeel, Garesché, Huse, Reynolds, and Bingham have been admitted. As the Examining Board will adjourn in a few days, it will, perhaps, be impracticable to make any further appointments this year. . . . P. S.:—Since the foregoing was written the following telegram has been received from Col. Robt. H. Hall Adjutant U. S. M. A. dated Sept. 8th. 'Following message received last Evening: "Cedar Rapids, Iowa, Sept. 7th The Supt. Military Academy. Edward J Winslow will be unable to report for examination, because of sickness. Signed—E. F. Winslow."'" Copies, *ibid.*, Letters Sent, USMA. Louis Garesché did not graduate USMA. For John G. Lugenbeel, William B. Reynolds, and Frederick Dent Sharp, see *PUSG*, 24, 429–30, 471; telegram to Henry T. Crosby, Sept. 2, 1874.

On June 16, 1873, Darius N. Couch, Norwalk, Conn., had written to USG. "I have the honor to apply for the appointment 'at large' of my only son Master Leonard C. Couch to a Cadetship at West Point for the year 1875. I trust Mr President that you will take into consideration my faithful services during the war with Mexico as well as the Rebellion and grant this request . . ." ALS, DNA, RG 94, Correspondence, USMA.

On Jan. 8, 1874, Charles W. Eliot, president, Harvard University, had written to USG. "Mrs Jane (Belknap) Marcou tells me that she proposes to ask of you an appointment at the Military Academy for her son John Belknap Marcou. I am not personally acquainted with the young man, but I know his father and mother well, and so feel that I have some trustworthy knowledge of him. His father is a man of science, eminent as a geologist. Although Mr Marcou is of foreign birth, his children are brought up in this country and are thorough Americans. Mrs Marcou comes of a sturdy New England stock which might well produce a soldier. I trust that her petition may receive your favorable consideration." ALS, *ibid.* Related papers are *ibid.* John B. Marcou graduated from Harvard in 1876.

On Jan. 14, 1874, Lt. Col. Frederick T. Dent, Fort Trumbull, Conn., had written to USG. "I have the honour to request the appointment of my Son John C Dent as a cadet of the U S Mily Academy when the next appointments are made—he will be seventeen years old on the 6th of next August" ALS, *ibid.* On Aug. 11, 1876, USG nominated John C. Dent as 2nd lt., 20th Inf. See *ibid.*, ACP, 3113 1876; *New York Times*, Dec. 12, 1933.

On July 28, 1874, Jessie Benton Frémont, "Pocaho near Tarrytown," N. Y., had written to USG. "You have been so kind to me personally that I offered Guy Huse this personal letter to you. He has been for five years intimately with my children—they were together in Dresden, and he is often as at present with me here—and I know him to have every quality needed in an officer. I recognize the disability his Father's part in our war makes, and while, personally, it would not influence you yet officially it may have to do so. But knowing Guy as I do, knowing he is loyal, and that he has give me his word always to remain so, I will not leave a chance untried for him. For I have seen and honored this young soldier in his fighting a harder battle than swords and bullets can make—that hard fight with poverty which tries a young nature to its uttermost. He has done his steady best in this—cheerfully too—but the panic has stopped all the employment he could get, although to work he is not ashamed, and would do any honest work that brought pay. My son is now well again and goes back in a month to West Point. It is a question however whether after such serious hemorrhages his lungs can stand the winter there. If he has to leave, this time it must be to resign completely and try for life in a softer climate than this. If the many applications fill your short number of appointments already, this would give an unexpected vacancy. It would soften the pain of Frank's lost career, to know that it had helped Guy to a position he can fill with honor and fidelity—and with deep gratitude to yourself. I think we should leave to Divine Justice to visit the Sins of the Fathers upon the children, and I have had enough to suffer for being loyal to give my opinion weight individually. It is only that way that I can offer it to you who cannot go by your own feelings only—which I have proved to be generous—but must be governed by what is due to the public. In this case, it would tell most soothingly on an imme[n]se circle of the best Southern families." ALS, DNA, RG 94, Correspondence, USMA. Related papers are *ibid.* USG endorsed these papers. "Place on list of supernumeraries for /75 next below those already designated." AE (initialed, undated), *ibid.* Guy E. Huse, who graduated USMA in 1879, was the son of Caleb Huse, USMA 1851, who served as C.S.A. purchasing agent in Europe.

On Oct. 5, 1874, Speaker of the House James G. Blaine, Augusta, Maine, had written to USG. "Mr. Theodore Bingham at present a student at Yale College in his Junior year—son of Rev. J. F. Bingham of Portsmouth N. H.—is very anxious to enter the West Point Military Academy—. . ." ALS, *ibid.* On Nov. 4, USG endorsed this letter. "Refered to the Sec. of War. Let special attention be called to this application when Cadet appointments are made. Should vacancies occur in the class of /75 beyond those already promised Mr. Bingham may be appointed to fill one." AES, *ibid.* Related papers are *ibid.* Theodore A. Bingham graduated USMA in 1879.

On Dec. 4, 1874, Edward F. Winslow, St. Louis, had written to USG. "I take the liberty of requesting the appointment of my nephew Edward F. Winslow, eldest son of Henry E. Winslow of Oakland, California, as cadet to the United States Military Academy. His father was an officer of volunteers and all his family were loyal to the Government during the Rebellion. I respectfully request the favorable consideration of this application on my own behalf, believing that the youth is in every way worthy of it, and feeling assured that he will do credit to his family and to the Academy." ALS, *ibid.* Related papers, including favorable endorsements from James H. Wilson and Horace Porter, dated Dec. 5, New York City, are *ibid.* Edward F. Winslow's nephew did not attend USMA.

On July 8, 1875, James L. Lardner, Jr., Philadelphia, had written to George W. Childs. "The President (authorized by Act of Congress) made eleven additional appointments to West Point for this June to fill up the vacancies that had occurred in the four classes there, so as to keep the number of the cadets appointed by him, up to forty at all times. Next June (1876) there will to all probabilities be at least three vacancies from the same reason i. e. from cadets at large in the four classes failing to pass the next January examination and the alternates at large failing this September. If the President would appoint me in place of one of these I would be very grateful, study hard . . ." ALS, *ibid*. On July 9, USG endorsed this letter. "The Sec. of War. If young Lardner, son of Adm.l Lardner can be appointed to the Mil. Academy in Sept. without interfering with those already designated let him be appointed." AES, *ibid*. On March 19, Rear Admiral James L. Lardner, Philadelphia, had written to USG on the same subject. ALS, *ibid*. Adolph E. Borie and Childs favorably endorsed this letter. AES (undated), *ibid*. Related papers are *ibid*. Admitted to USMA, Lardner, Jr., did not graduate.

On July 24, USG, New York City, telegraphed to Col. Thomas H. Ruger, superintendent, USMA. "I will be at West Point this evening on Steamer Mary Powell Please be kind enough to engage three rooms at Hotel" Telegram received, USMA. On July 25, William A. Nichols, West Point, N. Y., wrote to USG. "I have the honor to request that my name may be placed amongst the applicants for appointment 'At Large' to a Cadetship at the U. S. Military Academy. I am the son of the late General W. A. Nichols U. S. Adjutant General's Department and the Grandson of the late General R. E. DeRussy U. S. Engineers. I am now 19 years and 2 months of age. My residence is Fort Leavenworth Kansas. I respectfully request that my application may be considered, for September of this year should a vacancy occur at that time." ALS, DNA, RG 94, Correspondence, USMA. On July 26, Maj. Alfred Mordecai, USMA instructor, wrote to Babcock. "The President saw here yesterday Wm Nichols the youngest son of the late Genl W. A Nichols Adjt Genl's Dept. The young man is an applicant for appointment 'At Large' here—The President told him that he felt quite sure his name had not appeared before him on his list from which to nominate, and that the best he could do now would be to give him an 'alternate' for this September & then for next June As I understood it to be the desire of the President that the name of young Nichols should be placed on his list, an application has been made out which I forward herewith. Will you under the circumstances be kind enough to take it in hand and see that the proper thing is done with it.—" ALS, *ibid*. On July 29, USG endorsed this application. "Refered to the Sec. of War. If there should be a vacancy, 'At Large' at West Point in Aug. next, after giving a chance to all those already designated as 'Alternates' Mr. Nichols may be appointed." AES, *ibid*. Related papers are *ibid*. On July 27, 1876, Brig. Gen. John Pope, Fort Leavenworth, telegraphed to USG. "Second Lieutenant E. D. Nichols Twenty Third Infantry Son of Mrs W A Nichols died in Omaha on Sunday last. May I not beg that you will now give her last son and only child W A Nichols the appointment of Second Lieutenant. I would be grateful for a telegraphic reply" Telegram received (at 1:56 P.M.), *ibid*., ACP, 1913 1877. USG directed a reply. "Will see if it is possible" E (undated), *ibid*. Related papers are *ibid*. Nichols was appointed 2nd lt., 23rd Inf., as of May 7, 1877.

On Aug. 26, 1875, Sgt. Thomas McEnaney, West Point, had written to USG. "I have been a Soldier of the Regular Army for the past twenty four years, and can therefore only apply to you for this favor. I desire to ask of you, the opportunity to place my son William at the Academy as a Cadet, And while I can not ask for a direct appointment knowing that you have so many to provide for; still dare hope that you will give him the chance of an alternate next year. He is now eighteen years of age and he is in every way worthy and capable of passing his examination and graduating in the four years. I am Sergeant in Co. E Battalion of Engineers stationed at West Point, and can refer to the officers on duty at the Academy as to my worthiness." ALS, *ibid*., Correspondence, USMA. On Aug. 27, USG endorsed this letter. "Refered to the Sec. of War. If more vacancies should occur next year than is already provided for at West Point this application may be considered." AES, *ibid*. Designated the seventh alternate for 1876, William McEnaney did not attend USMA.

On Oct. 22, 1875, Luckey wrote to George H. Sharpe, surveyor of customs, New York City. "Both your letters with enclosures of Dr. Forsyth were duly received and read by the President. He says he hopes and expects to appoint your boy but they figure here at the Department that he has no more appointments now and has put in one or two too many as it is. I have no doubt it will soon work around all right." Copy, DLC-USG, II, 3. On Jan. 22, 1876, USG directed the "appt of Henry G. Sharpe as Cadet at Large for 1876—" N, DNA, RG 94, Correspondence, USMA. Sharpe graduated USMA in 1880.

To Hamilton Fish

Long Branch, N. J.
Sept. 10th /75

MY DEAR GOVERNOR:

In June last the Sec. of the Int. tendered his resignation.[1] I did not like the nature of the attack upon him, nor the people who made it. For these reasons I defered action until recently. The time before the meeting of Congress shortning so rapidly, and feeling that whoever comes in his place should have a reasonable time before in which to prepare his report to accompany the Message, I, some three weeks since, accepted his resignation, to take effect on the 1st day of Oct. With the letter accepting I sent a private note saying that the Sec. might take his own time, and select his own manner of promulgating the fact to the public; saying however that if I should go to Washington before making my visit West that I should want to consult with the Cabinet about his successor. Should I not visit Washington before going West he might see me as I passed through Ohio and make that the occasion of giving to the public the fact of his resignation.

Now I have determined not to go to Washington before the middle of October. I will start West about the 22d of this month. Unless you should hear from me again on this subject in the mean time, I wish you would lay the matter of a new Sec. of the Int. before the Cabinet as soon as you know I have passed Columbus, O.

The names that have suggested themselves to my mind are Ex Senator Scott, of Pa Wayne McVeigh, Pa G. Dawson Coleman, Pa (I would take no one from Ohio) Ex Senator Pratt, Ia & L. S. Felt, Ill.

I would not go East of Pa for another member of the Cabinet, and I do not know one who would suit the place either in the South or on the Pacific. There may be ~~plenty~~ many of them, but their names do not suggest themselves to me now.

Coleman & Felt are rather unknow to the public, but they are both men of fortune, and of fine business qualifications. The latter would be fully equal to the position of Sec. of the Treas. and the only thing against his appointment would be that the public would have to learn this fact after he took office.

I will be in St. Louis until about the 28th of Sept. The sale of my stock takes place on the 30th and I want to be away before that takes place. I wish the cabinet would canvass these names,—and any others that suggest themselves,—in time to communicate to me the result while ~~in St. Louis~~. there.

This letter shows the territory from which I would like to make the selection. I am not particular as to the state, only excluding those states already represented in the Cabinet, Ohio, and the New England States which have one representative.

Very Truly

your obt. svt.

U. S. GRANT

HON. HAMILTON FISH SEC. OF STATE.

ALS, DLC-Hamilton Fish. On Monday, Sept. 13, 1875, Secretary of State Hamilton Fish wrote to USG, Long Branch. "Your letter of 10th reached me late on Saturday Evening. I leave here for Washington tomorrow—& will say nothing of the subject of your letter until your passage by Columbus is Announced—& will immediately advise you by mail, at St Louis of the Conclusion reached. Would it not be well for Genl Babcock to have some cipher by which communication may be made by telegraph—for if you do not leave Long Branch until 22d—your passing Columbus would not allow a consultation before 24th—& but little margin will be left for mail communications to St Louis by the 28th   Mrs Fish desires to be most affectionately remembered to Mrs Grant—& yourself" ALS (press), *ibid.* See letter to Hamilton Fish, Sept. 14, 1875.

On Sept. 24 and 26, Fish wrote to USG, St. Louis. "Assuming that you had passed Columbus—I requested those of my Colleagues who are in the City, to meet me to day, & laid before them your letters of 10. & 13th inst. The Secretary of the Treasury, & Post Master General alone are here—the Secretary of War having left last night, & the Attorney General, yesterday mornig—the Secretary of the Navy has not yet returned. The three members of the Cabinet present were entirely agreed upon each of the following points. I. that, in view of the near approach of the Presidential election, & the great importance of the immediately impending Elections, it would be of doubtful expediency, if not a dangerous experiment to bring, at this time, into the Cabinet any gentleman, not sufficiently known to the public, that they would have to learn his competence after he takes office—II. that the great financial question, is at this time predominant, and that it seems essential that any one now to be brought into the Cabinet, should ~~notbe~~ not ~~only~~ only sound, on the financial question, and fully in accord with the Hard money doctrine in which you have planted the Administration, but that his record on this paramount question should be such as to preclude criticism. III. that, although all of the Gentlemen named in your letter of the 10th were not personally known to all three of us, we are satisfied that an association with either would be personally agreeable—each of us, as to those he knows personaly, having pleasure in the acquaintance, & entertainig a full confidence, that official intercourse would prove as pleasant as the acquaintance has been. Governor Jewell desired it to be stated that he personally knows Mr Felt & has entire confidence in his ability and integrity—but he adheres to the *first* point stated. The view taken in the *first* point, if accepted, would reduce the names suggested to three. The controlling importance attached to the *second* point and the fact that two of these three names had recently been in the Senate, led to an examination of some of the debates, & proceedings in the Senate, on the financial and currency questions. It appeared that on the vote in the Senate on April 28, 1874, on the passage of the Bill, over your veto which gave hope & laid the foundation of a restored credit, & a sounder Currency, one of these Senators voted to override the veto—the other (Scott) voted to sustain it—Should this reduce the number to two Gentlemen from Pennsylvania, we are not prepared to entertain any preference between them—personally either would be acceptable, and the intricacies of Pennsylvania politics are too deep to justify us in venturing to solve any questions resting wholly on sectional divisions within the party in that State. It was with great hesitancy that we approached your request that other names than those mentioned in your letter, which might suggest themselves should be canvassed—but the confidence implied in the request, & the importance of the appointment to be made, & its effect upon the public mind, led to a ~~determination~~ consultation, from which we almost withdrew in hesitancy not knowing how far the suggestion of John B. Henderson's name might fail to be personally acceptable to you—my own acquaintance with him, is comparatively slight—but Genl Bristow & Govr Jewell know him more intimately, & unite in attributing to him high character, and very eminent qualifications—my own slight acquaintance with him inclines me to concur in their estimate—" ALS (press), DLC-Hamilton Fish. "Should a vacancy occur in the Secretaryship of the Interior, the Assistant Secretary may act, until the appointment of a Successor—but the Statute also says that a vacancy by death or resignation must not be temporarily filled (under the Section which thus Authorises the Assistant to act temporarily) *'for a longer period than ten days'*— you will remember that this same question arose at the time of Genl Rawlins death—It occurs to me therefore that you will wish to sign the Commission of whomsoever you will appoint, before you go to Colorado—I therefore enclose a Commission *in blank*, that the appointee may qualify, and enter upon the duties of the office, if necessary, before your return to Washington—I presume that the new appointee must qualify & enter upon the office, by the Eleventh of October, if Mr Delanos resignation takes effect on the first—I do not think that I can be mistaken in my construction of the Statutes—but as I am the only member of the Cabinet in town, I have none of my colleagues to advise with—" ALS, MoSHi.

On Oct. 1 and 4, a correspondent reported from Washington, D. C. "There is still no official news concerning Delano's successor, and the fact occasions much surprise. It is certain that the position was tendered to Coleman, but the delay suggests the possibility of his declining. . . . Secretary Fish and Gen. Jewell have no knowledge as to who has been selected. The names from which the choice was made are said to have been Coleman and

McVeigh, of Pennsylvania; Felt, of Galena, Ill.; Pratt, of Indiana; and Judge Taft, of Ohio." "There is no official news as to the new Secretary of the Interior. The friends of Assistant-Secretary Cowen state to-night that Cowen expects and hopes to receive the appointment. The latest Pennsylvania name that has been mentioned is that of John H. Ewing, of Washington, Pa. He was formerly in Congress." *Chicago Tribune*, Oct. 2, 5, 1875. On June 29, Attorney Gen. Edwards Pierrepont had written confidentially to Alphonso Taft, care of Benjamin Silliman, Jr., New Haven, Conn. "As soon as you possibly can go to Long Branch, See the President *at once*. Give him your full views upon Ohio matters The condition of the canvass &c. Talk with him, becom acquainted with him and let him become acquainted with you. The great importance of carrying Ohio is your reason for seeing him and for taking his suggestions. Do not mention that anything beyond your own desire to confer sent you" LS, DLC-William Howard Taft. See letter to J. Russell Jones, Oct. 5, 1875.

1. See letter to Columbus Delano, June 20, 1875.

To Adolph E. Borie

Long Branch, N. J.
Sept. 10th /75

MY DEAR MR. BORIE:

By all means invite Miss. Sallie to accompany us. She is not so big but we can hang her to the bell rope if we are crouded. Instead of an officers car as we had before we are, I think, to have a Pullman sleeper which will give abundance of sleeping room for our small party.

Yours Truly
U. S. GRANT

P. S. Tell the Admiral that I think I can appoint his son in the Army, but fear that the place in the Marine Corps, may be promised.[1]

U. S. G.

ALS, PHi. See letter to Adolph E. Borie, Aug. 26, 1875.

1. On Oct. 19, 1875, USG wrote to Secretary of the Navy George M. Robeson. "I shall be pleased to have Mr. Steedman, son of Admiral Steedman appointed to fill the next vacancy in the Marine Corps." Copy, DLC-USG, II, 3. On Oct. 20 and 25, Orville E. Babcock wrote to Otis H. Tiffany, Chicago. "The President directs me to say in regard to the application to appoint E. D. Holbrook to the army that he finds there is no vacancy in the marine Corps, so he cannot appoint Steedman to the Marine Corps. I am sorry as this will disappoint you." "I have your favor. I wrote you just what the President told me to write, and supposed you understood it. The President had appointed as many Lieutenants in the Army as he could and he must leave vacancies enough for the graduating class who will

have to go home if there are no vacancies to which they can be assigned. Now Steedman
has an appointment in the Army but prefers the Marine Corps and the President ~~says~~ said
the exchange could be made, supposing there was a vacancy, but found there was none.
Have I made it plain this time? I supposed the President had spoken to you of Steedman."
Copies, *ibid.* On Jan. 10, 1876, USG nominated Richard R. Steedman as 2nd lt., 7th Inf.
Charles Steedman, retired rear admiral, was Adolph E. Borie's close friend. See DNA, RG
94, ACP, 5521 1875; Amos Lawrence Mason, ed., *Memoir and Correspondence of Charles
Steedman . . .* (Cambridge, Mass., 1912), p. 436.

To Edwards Pierrepont

———

Long Branch, N. J.
Sept. 13th /75

Hon. Edwards Pierrepont,
Atty. Gen. U. S.
Dear Sir:

Your report upon the Mississippi revolt, by Special Messenger,
is received, and I have just read it. I am somewhat perplexed to know
what directions to give in the matter. The whole public are tired out
with these annual, autumnal outbreaks in the South, and there is so
much unwholsome lying done by the press and people in regard to
the cause & extent of these breaches of the peace that the great majority are ready now to condemn any interference on the part of the
government. I heartily wish peace and good order might be restored
without the issueing of a proclamation. But if it is not the proclamation must be issued; and if it is I shall instruct the Commander of the
forces to have no childs play.[1] If there is a necessity for ~~m~~Military interference there is justice in such interference as to deter evil doers.

I start to-morrow for Utica.[2] If a proclamation becomes necessary it can be given to the press at once, and take date from its publication, and be sent to me there for signature. I believe this will be
proper? If it is not the publication will have to await my signature.

I do not see how we are to evade the call of the governor, if made
strictly within the Constitution and acts of Congress there under. If
the Executive is to be the judge when such insurrection or invasion
exists as to warrant federal interference the Constitutional provision

refered to in your report may become a dead letter even under a well meaning but timid executive. The so called liberal and opposition press would then become the power to determine when, or whether, troops should be used for the maintanance of a republican form of government.

I think on the whole a proclamation had better be prepared and sent to me for signature. It need not be published, nor the public made aware of its existence without telegraphic advice. In the mean time I would suggest the sending of a dispatch—or letter by private messenger—to Gen. Ames urging him to strengthen his position by exhausting his own resorces in restoring order before he receives govt. aid. He might accept the assistance offered by the citizens of Jackson and elsewhere. I am fully aware that the proffered assistance might prove dangerous. It might prove the offer of the wolf to the Shepherd to take charge of the sheepfold. But Governor Ames, and his advisors, can be made perfectly secure. As many of the troops now in Miss. as he deems necessary may be sent to Jackson. If he is betrayed by those who offer assistance he will be in a position to defeat their ends and punish them. I will wait to hear what you, and such members of the Cabinet as you may choose to consult, have to say to these suggestions. If you wish to send any dispatch to me that you do not wish opperators to read give it to Mr. Luckey and he will put it in Sipher.

Very Respectfully
your obt. svt.
U. S. GRANT

ALS, CtY. On Sunday, Sept. 12, 1875, Attorney Gen. Edwards Pierrepont wrote to USG. "I report upon the Mississippi disturbance in the order of events. I received your directions on the 9th; forthwith I advised the Adjutant General to order General Augur to hold his troops in readiness and to advise Gov. Ames of the fact. I caused a proclamation to be made in duplicate. I telegraphed to Gov. Fish at his Country place, but received no reply until the next day by reason of an accident which he has explained. Meanwhile I received the following, . . . These are all the dispatches received since you referred the matter to me. Before that I learned from the United States Attorney at Jackson in reply to my dispatch that there were grave disturbances but that there was no resistance to any United States authority. After all the delay Gov. Ames does not answer my question, which I regret. I made it specific quoting from the Statute in order to bring his call if possible within the lette[r] of the law. It is not strictly so now but in a great emergency I do not think it well to be too stiff about words   the real substance is what we are to look to and that is my perplexity. I do not think that the Constitution & the laws now invoked were intended for a case where the State authorities were supported by a very large majority of the people and where the State government was not found inadequate to the emergency after some effort to quell the riot. This seems to me a matter of much gravity. The Secretary of State will be here to-morrow, Secretaries Bristow & Delano are now here and the Postmaster General will be here on Tuesday. I send this by special messenger and await your further instructions . . ." Copy, DNA, RG 60, Letters Sent to Executive Officers. See telegram to AG Edward D. Townsend, Sept. 8, 1875. On Sept. 14, Pierrepont twice telegraphed to USG, care of U.S. Senator Roscoe Conkling of N. Y., Utica. "I have sent telegraphic dispatch to Governor Ames and private dispatch als[o.]   For greater caution I send you a paper to sign, and to be sent back here. I do not think it will be needed but I think it should be ready. Please keep me advised of where telegram will reach you from time to time. Your letter is in full accord with my own views and with those of Secretary Bristow the only one of the Cabinet whom I have been able to see. It contains the best suggestions possible and their substance has been sent in private dispatch to Governor Ames. Until I hear from you there is no occasion for solicitude." "I changed my communication to Governor Ames; and, as changed I send it you by next mail—differing somewhat from the copy sent you." Copies, DNA, RG 60, Letters Sent to Executive Officers. On the same day, Pierrepont had telegraphed to Governor Adelbert Ames of Miss. "This hour I have had dispatches from the President. I can best convey to you his ideas by extracts from his dispatch. . . . You see by this the mind of the President with which I and every member of the Cabinet who has been consulted are in full accord. You see the difficulties;—you see the responsibilities which you assume. ~~The proclamation I have sent for the President's signature; it will be issued if you say so, but the troops will not be ordered out for 'child's play.'~~ We cannot understand why you do not strengthen yourself in the way the President suggests, nor do we see why you do not call the ‖Legislature together and obtain from them whatever powers and money and arms you need. . . . You make no suggestion even, that there is any insurrection against the government of the State, or that the legislature would not support you in any measures you might propose, to preserve the public order. I suggest that you take all lawful means, and all needed measures to preserve the peace by the forces in your own State, and let the country see that the citizens of Miss. who are largely favorable to good order, and who are largely Republican, have the courage and the manhood to *fight* for their rights and to destroy the bloody ruffians who murder the innocent and unoffending freedmen. Every thing is in readiness;—be careful to bring yourself strictly within the Constitution and the laws, and if there *is such resistance to your State authorities as you cannot, by all the means at your command, suppress*, the President will swiftly aid you in crushing these lawless traitors to human rights. Telegraph me on receipt of this, and state *explicitly* what you need." DfS (telegram sent), *ibid.*, Letters from the President. On Sept. 16, Pierrepont telegraphed to USG, Utica. "No proclamation needed. Mississippi delegation in writing request to publish letter to Ames containing the extracts from yours to me. Bristow & Jewell urge the same. They all say it will produce quiet   shall I do it" Telegram received (at 9:35 A.M.), DLC-USG, IB; copy, DNA, RG 60, Letters Sent to Executive Officers. USG telegraphed permission to Pierrepont. Charles Hamilton Auction No. 79, July 24, 1974, no. 8. On Sept. 24, James Z. George and eight others, Jackson, Miss., telegraphed to Pierrepont. ". . . The undersigned, members of democratic State committee, assembled here to-day from every part of the State, take pleasure in assuring you that everywhere throughout the State the most profound peace and good order prevails." *SRC*, 44-1-527, I, 385. On Sept. 30, Ames wrote to USG. "Your letter and Atty. General Pierrepont's have produced marked improvement in the condition of affairs here. The white-liners, whose only policy is intimidation, are themselves somewhat intimidated. I am organizing militia, and will fight them if necessary. One thing we all deem highly important, and that is a change in two or three Federal officials. The time of election is near and our party ask immediate action; the removal of J. L. Lake, U. S. Marshall Southern District, and G. W. Wells, U. S. Dist. Att'y Northern District. Lake will not act—is incompetent, physically and morally. Wells is running for Congress, backed by white-liners. Pease you know. Neither of the above named is in accord with the Republican party. The misrepresentations of men like Wells and Pease, holding positions by your appointment, embarrass us, and give heart to murderous white-liners. We pray you for some quick blow at such men. It is believed that white-liners will delay violence till one or two days before election." LS (press), Ames Letterbook, Miss. Dept. of Archives and History, Jackson, Miss. On Oct. 17, Sunday, a correspondent reported from Washington, D. C. "Ex-Senator Pease had a long interview on Saturday with the President on the subject of Mississippi including the causes of the difficulties, the presen[t] condition of affairs and the remedies. The President talked freely, and said that he was much gratified that the two political parties had effected an amicable adjustment, by which a fair election would be held and peace maintained in the State. Efforts have heretofore been made by Senator Bruce and friends for the removal of four Federal officers in Mississippi, but Mr. Pease has assurances that no removals would be made in that State for mere partisan reasons. Attorney General Pierrepont assured him that no one coming under his department would be disturbed." *Baltimore American and Commercial Advertiser*, Oct. 18, 1875. See *New York Times*, Sept. 17, Oct. 9–10, 1875; Blanche Butler Ames, comp., *Chronicles From the Nineteenth Century: Family Letters of Blanche Butler and Adelbert Ames . . .* (1957), II, 177–217.

On Sept. 15, George M. Buchanan, "Sheriff Marshall Co Missi & Nominee Republican Party for State Treasurer," and four others, Washington, D. C., had written to USG. "The undersigned a Committee appointed by the Republican State Exutive Committee of Mississippi for the purpose of visiting Washington andto lay before the National Administration the Condition of Affairs in Our State, would most respectfully reccomend, that the following changes be made in the 'Federal Offices' in our State, believing that the Same will tend to promote peace, subserve the interest of the National & State governments and materially assist in administering justice and the protection of the people. To Wit, Virgil. B. Waddell to be U. S. District Attorney for the Northern District, in place of G. Wiley Wells present incumbent. Edward. P. Hatch to be post Master at Holly Springs. Missi in place of Dewitte Stearns present incumbent. Frank. A. Clover to be United States Marshal for the Southern district of Mississippi in place of John. L. Lake Jr present incumbent. John. B. Raymond to be Post Master at Vicksburg Missi in place of Henry. R. Pease present incumbent" LS, DNA, RG 60, Records Relating to Appointments. On Oct. 18, Alexander Warner, Jackson, telegraphed to USG. "The changes as suggested by the state Ex Committee are very Important notwithstanding the recent peace arrangements   what may we expect   messrs Pease & Co do not represent the republican of this state" Telegram received (at 9:03 P.M.), *ibid.* On July 15, 1876, Warner, Washington, D. C., testified before a select committee investigating the 1875 Miss. election. "Question. Where are you now living?—Answer. In Madison County, Mississippi. . . . Went into the Federal Army from Connecticut. After the close of the war I settled in Mississippi; bought property there in 1865—bought a plantation. . . . Q. Were you in any way in 1875 connected with the republican organization in any official capacity?—A. Yes, sir. . . . I was chairman of the republican State executive committee. . . . I became satisfied that the will of the people could not be expressed at the polls; and I will state to the committee that I came to Washington in company with other gentlemen to see the President and the heads of the Departments, to see what protection our people could have. . . . It was not for me to dictate or recommend to the Administration what to do. I so told the heads of the Departments; I so told the President, that a committee had come to give the situation of the State of Mississippi; to tell him precisely what was going on down there and see what, if anything, could be done. . . . I thought they ought to give us good men for office, and so I told General Grant. He says, 'Have you anybody to recommend?' I said, 'Neither my friends nor myself have anybody to recommend; we are not here in anybody's interest; we are here to secure a fair and honest election.'. . . The President asked about certain individuals down there— officers. We did not go to him to ask for the removal of any one; we wanted to give him the situation of the State, to see what he would advise us to do among ourselves. He asked us about the officers down there. . . . Q. Did you want military aid?—A. I did, I am frank to say, sir. . . . Q. Who came with you, General Warner?—A. Senator Bruce, Major Howe, Hon. James Hill, and Captain Buchanan, who was candidate for State treasurer on the re- publican State ticket, and Capt. John B. Raymond. . . . We met in New York, where Gen- eral Grant was on his way to attend some meeting at Utica, and we saw him in New York. . . ." *SRC,* 44-1-527, I, 960–62, 968–69.

On April 21, 1874, Lt. Governor Alexander K. Davis of Miss. had written to USG. "The object of this Communication is to present the name of Col. G. Wiley Wells to Your Excellency for reappointment to the position of U. S. Atty for the Northern Dist of this State with my hearty Endorsement—. . ." LS, DNA, RG 60, Records Relating to Appoint- ments. On May 29, A. P. Shattuck, collector of Internal Revenue, 1st District, Brookhaven, Miss., wrote to USG. "I have the honor to recommend the reappointment of Col. G. W. Wells U. S. Dist. Attorney for the Northern Dist. of Miss. Col Wells is a lawyer of ac- knowledged ability and occupies an enviable position in his profession. In his official du- ties he has manifested an untiring devotion to the interests of the government. The abil- ity and fearlessness which at the risk of personal safety he displayed in the prosecution and conviction of the Ku Klux of North Miss. has won for him the gratitude of the loyal people of that District and entitles to the favorable consideration of the government. He is an ac- tive republican and an earnest supporter of the administration. I am satisfied that it is the wish of the republicans of his district that he should be reappointed and I earnestly rec- ommend it" LS, *ibid.* Related papers are *ibid.* On the same day, USG nominated G. Wiley Wells to continue as U.S. attorney, Northern District, Miss. On Nov. 10, 1875, Richard McAllister, Washington, D. C., wrote to Pierrepont. "I take the liberty to enclose you a let- ter (just received and I am sure intended for no eye but my own) from B. W. Lee Esqr Asst U. S. Atty: for the Northern Dist. of Mississippi. This letter is an honest expression from an honest and promising young republican in your own Department and will show you the exact state of things in the 2nd Congressional Dist in the State of Mississippi where your U. S. Attorney has just been elected to Congress over Maj: Howe the late M. C. by over 8000 maj. You will see that Col Wells has carried the great body of the Republican voters and that in one of the largest Counties Howe had only 6 votes. Some evil designed persons have impressed the President with the idea that Col Wells was false to the Repub- lican party and under this erroneous impression the President has been induced to remove two of Col Wells best friends Ex Senator Pease and Judge Stearns, the latter the P. M. at Holly Springs where Col Wells resides and to appoint his bitter enemies E. P. Hatch and John Raymond in their places. I feel certain that the President will reverse this Action when he comes fully to understand all the circumstances. They will doubtless soon be laid before him in due form by the proper parties from Mississippi. There are no better Re- publicans living than Col Wells, who was a gallant Federal officer from the State of New- York, Pease from Connecticut and Stearns from Iowa. I was formerly upon Genl Grant's staff and was his fast friend in the darkest hours of his military history. After reading this letter and the enclosed if you will hand them to the President upon his return from New- York you will much oblige . . . *P. S.* I feel sure that you must be well posted in Mississippi affairs as you heard both factions and had your own agents in the State to advise you. The course of non-intervention which you advised, if now strictly adhered to in all things, will as certainly make Mississippi a Republican State next year as that the sun will rise tomorrow. The result this year is not a democratic victory but a stern protest from the whole people against bad and imbecile government. Ames course had disgusted every decent man in the State. *Ames himself arranged by treaty with the Democrats* for a peaceable election and the result is that he is overwhelmingly repudiated." ALS, *ibid.*, Letters from the President. The enclosure is a letter of Nov. 6 from B. W. Lee, Holly Springs, Miss., to McAllister. ". . . The State has gone democratic in nearly every county and the state ticket headed by Buchanan was defeated by 30,000. It is not considered as a *democratic* triumph, but as a *peoples* victory over corruption and bad government for which the honest men of *both parties united,* Ames power is broken and now the Republicans of the state will reorganize under an honest leadership, ~~and~~ put their best men forward and in 1876 redeem the state by as large a majority as the one which elects the democratic ticket this year, This is *certain* and allready steps are being taken for this purpose, . . . The Republicans are all jubilant as well the conservatives, and none feel disheartened except the bad leaders who have been over thrown. We all feel free now to choose new and honest leaders," ALS, *ibid.* See *SRC*, 42-2-41, part 12, II, 1147–67.

On Nov. 15, B. G. Lawrence, Holly Springs, wrote to USG. "Though unknown to you personally I venture an appeal in my own behalf—circumstances generally Directs the course to be persued owing to the unprecedented whorle in our political affairs I am inclined to place my name before you as an applicant for the appointment of District Attorney for the Northern District of Mississippi in place of G Wiley Wells . . . I have been a resident of this county for 30 years my course through the past is too well known for Doubts in comment" ALS, DNA, RG 60, Records Relating to Appointments. On Dec. 4, Henry B. Whitfield, Columbus, Miss., wrote to USG. "I have the honor to make application, through the office of the Attorney General, for appointment as United States District Attorney, for the Northern District of Mississippi, whenever the resignation of Hon. G. Wiley Wells, the present incumbent of that office, shall be accepted. In regard to my character as a man, my capacity and standing as a lawyer, and fitness to discharge the duties of the position sought, I beg leave respectfully to refer you to the recommendations herewith filed. Other testimonials will be presented, if desired." ALS, *ibid.* On Oct. 8, Whitfield, Macon, Miss., had written to Ames. "Private and confidential. . . . A conflict is imminent almost every day; and, in my deliberate judgment, we cannot and will not have a fair, free, or full election unless we have such positive intervention of Government authority, *either directly, or in such shape that the people will believe it, see it, and feel its power.* We are very anxious to hear directly from you in this section of the State, as to your views of what can and will be done. . . ." *SRC*, 44-1-527, II, Documentary Evidence, 72. See *ibid.*, pp. 53–54, 56. On Dec. 15, USG nominated Whitfield as U.S. attorney, Northern District, Miss., to replace Wells. On Jan. 3, 187[6], Thomas Norvell, Aberdeen, Miss., wrote to USG. "I was a soldier in Co. A. 20. Ills Regt during the late war, and have resided since in this State. Sometime ago I placed my claim for bounty under act of 1865, in the hands of Henry B. Whitfield for collection, and I have every reason to believe that he has collected it, but he refuses to pay me any part of it. My reason for stating this is because I learn that you have nominated him to the Senate for U. S. district atty for the Northern district of Miss. and I want you to know the character of the man. Senators Bruce and Alcorn know him to be wholly unreliable in every respect, without any reputation for truth or honesty, and unworthy of any public trust. and in giving him this position you put him in a place where he may swindle others as he has me out of my bounty money." LS (misdated 1875), DNA, RG 60, Records Relating to Appointments. On April 25, USG nominated Thomas Walton as

U.S. attorney, Northern District, Miss., to replace Whitfield. On May 4, Walton, Washington, D. C., concluded lengthy testimony before the committee. ". . . I also desire to say, that what I have said about my want of influence with colored voters, does not show that I am not indebted to colored men for support. Indeed, they have often extended to me a most generous personal support; notably in a late instance where Senator Bruce started, and Mr. Lynch, the colored member of Congress, and Mr. Hill, the colored secretary of state in Mississippi, all of whom I value very highly, strongly supported a recommendation for my appointment as United States district attorney by President Grant, and succeeded in procuring such appointment." *SRC*, 44-1-527, I, 66. See *ibid.*, p. 1002.

On March 3, 1875, USG had nominated Henry R. Pease as postmaster, Vicksburg. On Nov. 13, Postmaster Gen. Marshall Jewell telegraphed to Orville E. Babcock. "Senator Pease wants an interview with the President and I think it but fair that he should have one. Will you ask the President if he will see him and at what time" Telegram received, DLC-USG, IB. On the same day, Babcock telegraphed to Jewell. "He says he cannot see him to day, as he has so many engagements" ANS (telegram sent), DNA, RG 107, Telegrams Collected (Bound). On Dec. 4, 1876, Rose W. Pease, Vicksburg, wrote to USG. "President of the United States. And I thank God for that. for out of the depths of this 'Inferno' our only hope rests in you. My husband (Ex Senator Pease) is in daily danger of life and limb. My children can not attend school for they are unsafe on the streets, to so great an extent ~~are~~ is the bitterness of these people carried. Even the children imbibe it; and woe to the little yankee unable to protect herself. The feeling against my husband is particularly bitter, because he is a Republican leader and a northern man, and worse than this in the estimation of these southern democrats, he spent two months during the recent struggle canvassing in the north. He made forty nine speeches for our Republican Nominee, and these people know their atrocities and barbarisms were fully exposed.   they are exasperated against him and I am in a state of constant terror: I begged him not to return here at all, but he would not hear me. He has been in this country since 1861. In Vicksburg since 1866. Assisted in the reconstruction of the State. Has thoroughly canvassed the State at every election held since. It is now a matter of *pride* with him not to be *driven* out, and is also a matter of *necessity*. Each campaign has drawn heavily upon him and all we have left is here. If we leave it we leave *all* and must begin at the bottom of the ladder again. He hopes to struggle through here and escape the Assassin. but every day new dangers threaten, until thoroughly terror stricken and almost crazed with fear, without the permission or knowledge of my husband, I write to you, to beg you to appoint him to some position that will not be beneath him to accept, where we can live in peace. Something that will enable him to support his family until he can arrange his business and settle him self again at his profession (That of Law.) You may think, now that the election is over the danger is passed, but this Congressional district will be contested, and he is actively assisting the republican nominee. Some witnesses from Louisianna on their way to New Orleans in the Ouachitas Parish case, had to flee this City for their lives. He helped them to escape. When this becomes known, as it is already suspicioned, his danger will be increased. Thus every day some thing arises for a worker to do. In 1862 his life was in danger from the Ku Klux, now it is in double danger from the Bull-dozers. The only thing that protects him is being an officer of the United States. And for *this I thank you.* During the opposition to him here last Fall (1875.) you sustained him in his Office. Just after the recent election I called upon you to express my gratitude to you in person. You were not recieving, being engaged with your message. The salary recieved from his present position is now his only income. In his profession he would recieve nothing.   the pressure is so great that no man would dare employ a republican Lawyer. My Sister will bear this letter to you and I pray it may recieve your kind consideration   She can tell you many things I can not write. but you are one of the few great men who appreciates the situation down here, and any thing more is unnecessary from me. Again thanking you for your past kindness . . ." ALS, *ibid.*, RG 60, Letters from the President.

On Feb. 20, 1874, Wells, Holly Springs, had written to Ames. "I have the honor to recommend to you for reappointment as Chancellor for the Ninth (9th) Chancery District, De Witt Stearns. I would respectfully state, that Judge Stearns is one of the few Republican Judges of this state, who has at all times been an ardent supporter of yourself; His position in the Republican party has never been of a doubtfull character, but has always been positive. In the last campaign he did valuable work for the party, and before the nominations were made, was at work in this County, Benton Yalobusha and Calhoun, for you; He has always supported the nominees of our party, except that at the last election, he with nearly every white Republican in this County, did not support Geo Buchannan, and his reasons for not supporting him, were, that he beleived with all of us that Geo Buchanan was not at heart a Republican; that, he, Buchanan, was a Powers man until he found that Powers could not be nominated,   A large number of Republicans, and in fact the leading ones of this County, knew that Buchanan attended Powers secret meetings through an invitation from Powers, and on passes forwarded by him, (Powers); therefore Judge Stearns with myself and many others, refused to support Buchanan, and I know personaly that while he did not vote for Buchanan, he did not vote for any person for sheriff, . . ." ALS, *ibid.*, RG 59, Letters of Application and Recommendation. On Aug. 3, 1876, Dewitt Stearns, Washington, D. C., wrote to USG. "I am informed that a vacancy exists in the Consular service, Viz: Consul at Trinidad de Cuba. I have been urged by many of my friends to make application for the position, yielding in a great measure to their good judgment I hereby signify my willingness to accept the same and trust that if appointed I shall be able to discharge the duties incident to the position in a manner to reflect credit and honor upon the Government." ALS, *ibid.* Related papers are *ibid.* On Aug. 6, Ulysses S. Grant, Jr., wrote to Secretary of State Hamilton Fish. "The President asks that you will please send the over the nomination of Mr Stearns for Consul to Satiago de Cuba. The Mississippi delegation agree—Senator Bruce alone not recommending though not objecting." ALS, *ibid.* On Aug. 15, USG appointed Stearns as consul, Trinidad de Cuba.

On Oct. 15, 1875, a correspondent had reported from Washington, D. C. "The President arrived here this morning, and this being the regular Cabinet day a session was called at 12 o'clock. . . . The Attorney General stated at the Cabinet meeting that he is in receipt of information, which he deems authentic, to the effect that both parties in Mississippi have agreed to terms which will prevent further trouble in that State, and a peaceable election is confidently anticipated." *New York Times*, Oct. 16, 1875. On Nov. 4, John B. Raymond, Jackson, telegraphed to U.S. Senator Blanche K. Bruce of Miss. "Democrats carried all but ten counties,   democratic Congressmen probably all elected,   the election a complete farce." Telegram received (at 3:31 P.M.), DLC-USG, IB. On March 31, 1876, Bruce spoke in favor of a resolution for senatorial investigation of the 1875 Miss. election. ". . . The civil officers of the State were unequal to meet and suppress the murderous violence that frequently broke out in different parts of the State, and the State executive found himself thrown for support upon a militia partially organized and poorly armed. When he attempted to perfect and call out this force and to use the very small appropriation that had been made for their equipment, he was met by the courts with an injunction against the use of the money, and by the proscriptive element of the opposition with such fierce outcry and show of counter-force, that he became convinced a civil strife, a war of races, would be precipitated unless he staid his hand. As a last resort, the protection provided in the national Constitution for a State threatened with domestic violence was sought; but the national Executive—from perhaps a scrupulous desire to avoid the appearance of interference by the Federal authority with the internal affairs of that State—declined to accede to the request made for Federal troops. . . . It has been suggested, as the popular sentiment of the country, that the colored citizens must no longer expect special legislation for their benefit, nor exceptional interference by the National Government for their protection. . . . But I allege that we do not seek special action in our behalf, except to meet special danger, and only then such as all classes of citizens are entitled to receive under the Constitution. We do not ask the enactment of new laws, but only the enforcement of those that already exist. . . ." *CR*, 44–1, 2101, 2103. On the same day, after debates over previous weeks, the resolution passed. *Ibid.*, p. 2119–20. See *ibid.*, 233–39, 494–99, 2064–76, 2105–19; *ibid.*, Appendix, 17–25; *SRC*, 44-1-527; George S. Boutwell, *Reminiscences of Sixty Years in Public Affairs* (New York, 1902), II, 279–82; Ames, *Chronicles From the Nineteenth Century*, II, 217–33, 242–51; *New York Times*, Oct. 18, 1875; John R. Lynch, *The Facts of Reconstruction* (New York, 1915), pp. 137–55; William C. Harris, *The Day of the Carpetbagger: Republican Reconstruction in Mississippi* (Baton Rouge, 1979), pp. 616–21, 650–90; Endorsement, Sept. 27, 1875.

On Nov. 6, 1875, Hiram R. Revels, Holly Springs, had written to USG. "In view of the results of the recent election in our State, I have determined to write you a letter canvassing the situation and giving you my views thereon. I will premise by saying that I am no politician, though having been honored by a seat in the United States Senate. I never have sought political preferment, nor do I ask it now, but am engaged in my calling—the ministry—and feeling an earnest desire for the welfare of all the people, irrespective of race or color, I have deemed it advisable to submit to you for consideration a few thoughts in regard to the political situation in this State. Since reconstruction, the masses of my people have been, as it were, enslaved in mind by unprincipled adventurers, who, caring nothing for country, were willing to stoop to anything, no matter how infamous, to secure power to themselves and perpetuate it. My people are naturally republicans and always will be, but as they grow older in freedom so do they in wisdom. A great portion of them have learned that they were being used as mere tools, and, as in the late election, not being able to correct the existing evil among themselves, they determined, by casting their ballots against these unprincipled adventurers, to overthrow them; and now that they have succeeded in defeating these unprincipled adventurers, they are organizing for a republican victory in 1876; that we will be successful there cannot be a doubt. There are many good white republicans in the State who will unite with us, and who have aided us in establishing ourselves as a people. In almost every instance these men who have aided us have been cried down by the so-called republican officials in power in the State. My people have been told by these schemers when men were placed upon the ticket who were notoriously corrupt and dishonest, that they must vote for them; that the salvation of the party depended upon it; that the man who scratched a ticket was not a republican. This is only one of the many means these unprincipled demagogues have devised to perpetuate the intellectual bondage of my people. To defeat this policy, at the late election men irrespective of race, color, or party affiliation, united and voted together against men known to be incompetent and dishonest. I cannot recognize, nor do the masses of my people who read recognize, the majority of the officials who have been in power for the past two years as republicans. We do not believe that republicanism means corruption, theft, and embezzlement. These three offenses have been prevalent among a great portion of our officeholders; to them must be attributed the defeat of the republican party in the State if defeat there was; but I, with all the lights before me, look upon it as an uprising of the people, the whole people, to crush out corrupt rings and men from power. Mississippi is to-day as much republican as it ever was, and in November, 1876, we will roll up a rousing majority for the republican candidate for President, whoever he may be. The great masses of the white people have abandoned their hostility to the General Government and republican principles, and to-day accept as a fact that all men are born free and equal, and I believe are ready to guarantee to my people every right and privilege guaranteed to an American citizen. The bitterness and hate created by the late civil strife has, in my opinion, been obliterated in this State, except, perhaps, in some localities, and would have long since been entirely obliterated, were it not for some unprincipled men who would keep alive the bitterness of the past and inculcate a hatred between the races, in order that they may aggrandize themselves by office and its emoluments to control my people, the effect of which is to degrade them. As an evidence that party-lines in this State have been obliterated, men were supported without regard to their party affiliations, their birth, or their color by those who heretofore have acted with the democratic party, by this course giving an evidence of their sincerity that they have abandoned the political issues of the past, and were only desirous of inaugurating an honest State government and restoring a mutual confidence between the races. I give you my opinion, that had our State administration adhered to republican principles and stood by the platform upon which it was elected, the State to-day would have been on the highway of prosperity. Peace would have prevailed within her borders, and the republican party would have embraced within its folds thousands of the best and purest citizens of which Mississippi can boast, and the election just passed would have been a republican victory of not less than eighty to a hundred thousand majority; but the dishonest course which has been pursued has forced into silence and retirement nearly all of the leading republicans who organized and have heretofore led the party to victory. A few who have been bold enough to stand by republican principles and condemn dishonesty, corruption, and incompetency, have been supported and elected by overwhelming majorities. If the State administration had adhered to republican principles, advanced patriotic measures, appointed only honest and competent men to office, and sought to restore confidence between the races, bloodshed would have been unknown, peace would have prevailed, Federal interference been unthought of; harmony, friendship, and mutual confidence would have taken the place of the bayonet. In conclusion, let me say to you, and through you to the great republican party of the North, that I deemed it my duty, in behalf of my people, that I present these facts, in order that they and the white people (their former owners) should not suffer the misrepresentations which certain demagogues seemed desirous of encouraging." *SRC,* 44-1-527, I, 1019–20; *SMD,* 44-2-45, 594–95. On June 22, 1876, Revels, Jackson, testified. "Q. You were elected to the Senate of the United States by the legislature of Mississippi, in what year?—A. In 1870. . . . I think for an unexpired term of about one year and one month. . . . At present I am professor of theology in Shaw University. Last January I ceased to be the pastor of my church there. . . . Q. Did you take part in the political canvass of the year 1875?—A. To some extent, in behalf of Colonel Wells for Congress. . . . Q. Did you publish a letter after the election in 1875, giving your views as to the course of the administration of Governor Ames in this State and its effect upon the election in that year?—A. I did. . . . The object of my writing that letter was simply this: I believed then, as I do now, that certain imprudent men, so-called republicans, had broken our party down, and that after the defeat they rushed to Washington and were trying to mislead the President and throw the blame on the pure republican party of the State and the innocent old white citizens. As I have said in one or two Christian papers in explanation of my reason for writing that letter, I felt it my duty as a Christian man, as far as my humble influence would go, to defend both the old white citizens and the innocent republican party against their attempt to throw the results of their faults upon them. Another reason was this: I am a republican in every sense, and I was not only trying to have fair play done all the people here, but I was working for the future good of the republican party, and for this reason I believed that if these men succeeded in deceiving the President and the national republican party into recognizing them, they would on the strength of that recognition come back and force themselves upon us as leaders and kill our party forever. . . ." *SRC*, 44-1-527, I, 1015–19.

On Nov. 15, 1875, Hannibal C. Carter, Jackson, had written to USG. "I have felt compelled, from a sense of duty as a citizen of the State and a member of the republican party, to write to you in relation to the condition of affairs in Mississippi, and present a few leading facts as to the causes which have led to the recent defeat of the republican party in this State. You will please pardon any seeming egotism when I say that I am prepared to form a correct judgment upon the condition of our political affairs and the causes which led to the defeat at the late election, having been actively engaged in organizing and building up the party from the beginning of its existence in the State. I have been a member of the legislative branch of the government, and have contributed in my humble way something toward incorporating republican principles in the legislation of the State. I have the honor of having drawn, introduced, and secured the passage of a bill protecting colored men in their civil rights. I am identified by ties of race with the colored people of the country, and am therefore prepared to appreciate the principles of republicanism and the necessity for their maintenance. I was also one of the presidential electors in 1872 and voted for you. I do not propose to go into a detailed statement of the condition of things in our State, for it would be trespassing upon your valuable time. Unfortunate as the defeat of our party may seem to be to those unacquainted with the true state of affairs, I am happy to be able to say that it is by no means a hopeless case—very far from it. It might most properly be denominated a signal repulse and not a defeat, and this repulse is not without value to the party in the future. It has taught us the importance of unity of action, and the necessity of wise counsel and judicious management of the State administration and the exercise of caution in the conduct of our party affairs. And last, but not least, it has enabled us to get rid of many bad men—political adventurers—who have contributed largely to demoralize the party by their disgraceful conduct. The main cause of our defeat was the want of proper leadership. Governor Ames, to whom we very properly looked for leadership, most signally failed, as the sequel most clearly shows. The whole matter may be summed up in a few words: It was the inordinate ambition of the governor to be re-elected to the United States Senate. Had he gone forward and administered faithfully the duties of his office, looking to the highest interests of the State, inaugurating reforms, seeking the material and social welfare of the people, sought the counsel of good, patriotic men, instead of surrounding himself, as he has, with a class of men notoriously corrupt, demagogues of the worst type, and through whose advice and counsel he has prostituted the high office of the chief magistracy of the State to promote their personal schemes—had he been content to let the office of United States Senator seek him instead of seeking it, the condition of the party would have been far different to-day; its supremacy would have been maintained with an increased popular sympathy and support. The truth is, Mr. President, Governor Ames has, during his entire administration, bent all his energies, used all the power and patronage of his office, in an attempt to build up a personal party, and, like his predecessor, Governor Alcorn, who made a similar attempt, has utterly failed and forfeited the confidence of many who have heretofore been his personal friends as well as the confidence of the party in his ability as a leader. A great misapprehension exists as to the real sentiments of the colored people in relation to their future. They are represented as being utterly demoralized and discouraged, while the contrary is true; they are quiet and hopeful, full of confidence in the ultimate triumph of republican principles. Especially are they encouraged by the indications that the General Government will be controlled under the auspices of the republican party for another presidential term. It is also represented that the republicans of Mississippi have lost confidence in you and your administration because of your refusal to declare martial law at the request of Governor Ames. Several of our most distinguished men, whose fealty to the party cannot be questioned, have been severely censured by Governor Ames and his few friends for sustaining your policy of non-intervention—such men as Ex-Senators Pease and Revels, Ex-Governor Powers, Congressmen McKee, Niles, Wells, and many others. They have been charged with having sold out the party to the opposition, and I am informed that a committee, pretending to represent the sentiments of the republican party of this State, have complained to you that Senator Pease and others had betrayed the party, and demanded his removal from office. Permit me to say, from my knowledge of the position taken and the sentiments entertained by Pease and others complained of, that such representations, if made to you, are unqualifiedly false. The truth is, Mr. President, that a large majority of the republican party fully indorse your action in relation to Federal intervention, and clearly comprehend the wisdom of the course pursued by the gentlemen above referred to, in sustaining your policy. Any other policy would have resulted in revolution, forced the General Government to have interfered, and the democratic party would have then raised a clamor against your administration, charging the republican party with using the Federal bayonet for partisan purposes, and inevitably resulted in the defeat of the party in the recent elections in the Northern States, and the final overthrow of the party in 1876. There is no question but that the party in this State can be rallied again next year, and re-organized on a higher and better basis, and cast her electoral vote in 1876, as she did in 1872, for U. S. Grant for President. Of course much depends upon the policy pursued from this time onward. In conclusion, allow me to say that any intervention in the use of Federal patronage in the interests of Governor Ames and his few friends, who have proven themselves wholly incompetent to lead the party or manage its affairs, or, indeed, to be used in the interest of any particular faction or clique, will, in my judgment, prove disastrous in the extreme—destroy all hope of a harmonious re-organization of the party for victory in 1876. In this connection, permit me to express my settled conviction that the removal of Ex-Senator Pease and Judge Stearns, who are known to be strong advocates of your re-election, will be construed as an indorsement of Governor Ames and his reckless follies; an indorsement of a policy that has well-nigh ruined the party and the State government; an indorsement of those who are utterly powerless to do anything toward re-establishing the party, and who are known to be opposed to you personally and the policy of your administration toward toward the south. It can result in no good, but, in my judgment, will prove a most disastrous blow upon the party. The worst feature of the case, however, is the appointment of John B. Raymond to succeed Senator Pease. It is unquestionably the most unfortunate appointment that could be made. He is notoriously unscrupulous and corrupt   He is known to have corruptly procured legislation in his own interest as State printer for several years past. The indorsement by the national administration of such men as Raymond will wipe out the last ray of hope entertained by the honest and true men of the party. I undertake to say that his appointment alone, establishing, as it will be held, the future policy of the party in this State, will utterly defeat all attempts to harmonize the party and restore that confidence which is needed to bring back the fifteen thousand white men who have heretofore, and until the last election, voted the republican ticket, for without their support the party is irretrievably lost." *Ibid.*, II, 1083–84. See *ibid.*, pp. 1342–43.

On Nov. 24, George E. Harris, Miss. attorney gen., wrote to USG. "Mississippi with a Republican majority two years ago, of 24,000 has just gone Democratic by an overwhelming majority say 30,000. This was no less astonishing to the Democracy, than it was Sad to the Republicans and in as much as many have undertaken to account for our defeat and contradictory statements have been made, as to the real cause, I think it proper to write & give you a plain and unvarnished statement of affairs here, and while it is painful

to give the whole truth yet it will in some degree relieve me as legal advisor from the responsibility of many of the fatal blunders of the present State administration and at the
same time give the real causes of our defeat.—Governor Ames was inaugurated in January 1874 under the most favorable auspices. His address promised economy and reform
and was well received by the whole country, even our political opponents in a state of disruption, many of them having voted for him, expressed a willingness to support him in all
that he had promised and advised but instead of encouraging every indication of returning friendship, his cold indifference drove them at once into a direct antagonism. He
seemed to contract his views and narrow his circle of friends to a few confidential advisors, as it were a close corporation of mercenary men, who knew but little of the wants of
the people of the state, and cared less, men who have no identity of interest, or sympathy
in common with the people of the state, and to deal plain, I must call names, such men as
John B Raymond, A T Morgan A R Howe and a few lesser lights if possible. . . . Thus it
will be seen that the party in this State has been governed and controlled by a few men not
to exceed a half a dozen including the Governor who have persistently violated the constitution and the most sacred pledges that the party had made in its platform. Then in two
~~cases~~ instances he approved two Bills on the same day which contradicted each other, and
this with a few other unpardonable blunders caused the calling of an extra Session of the
Legislature in July last without any extraordinary occasion, thus giving us three (3) Sessions in eight (8) months instead of one in two years as we had promised. Then comes the
Canvass for the November election 1875. The State convention was held (with Morgan as
chairman)   It not only failed, but positively refused to indorse the National Administration. Senator Pease insisting on it, but before the delegation started to Washington to ask
for the removal of several of the Government officers, they called the Central Executive
Committee together, and they endorsed your administration and added it as Section 20,
and then started to the Capitol to ask the removal of Senator Pease, Judge Stearns and
Capt Lake to make room for some of their friends. I presume that the reason of the refusal
to endorse the national administration was this, the Governor had complained that he had
'been snubbed by the administration at Washington.' The Governor had commenced his
fight on Senator Pease, doubtless because he thought Pease would be in his way for the
United States Senate—He and Howe fought Col. Wells because they thought Wells would
be in Howe's way for re-election to Congress, and it seems now that he was. You will perceive that there is some difference ~~in~~of opinion among Republicans here, as to what is true
and genuine Republicanism—The adherents of the State administration who have pursued a Suicidal policy on the one hand, and on the other, those of us who advocate and defend the national administration and insist upon honest and economical State Government. As a further evidence of the effect produced by their course of conduct in the recent
Canvass, there was not a man in the State who would so Stultify himself as to undertake
to defend the record made by the party in the last two years, and we were under the dis-
agreable necessity of discussing men instead of measures, and no one could meet the Democrats in joint discussion as formerly. Senator Pease Genl McKee Judge Stearns and myself made a few Speeches for Wells, against Howe, the friend of Ames and for this offence
we were called Democrats by Howe and others. That was a falsehood too infamous to require contradiction. Now I think the real cause of our defeat is obvious. The Democrats, at
all times ready to use any and all means, fair or foul to succeed, seized upon this as a favorable time when our record could not be defended, to produce terror and to intimidate
the colored voters, which they did. Whether there was real danger or not, the colored
people believed it and many thousands of them either remained at home or voted the Democratic ticket, and hence the peaceable and quiet election and our defeat. Another cause.
The Governor a short time before the election commenced organizing the State militia

this led the colored people to believe that there was real danger, and that Ames was their best friend, and that he would protect them, but a few days before the election, there came among us a strange man (I think they called him Governor Chase) I never met him, who took charge of the Peace department, as it was called and made a compromise with the Democracy, and Governor Ames disbanded his militia, and now his record having driven almost every white man from the party, the colored men had no moral support and they dispaired of success and the party was an easy prey to the political enemy. But whilst they thought they ~~thought~~ had protection, they had nominated, in some of the colored counties, tickets that would disgrace Mexico or San Domingo, and this too served to exasperate the Democracy and thus it is seen that our defeat was caused by the Democrats taking advantage of the Shameful imbecility and base corruption of our State administration and a few adherents   As to the complaints against Senator Pease, the head and front of his offending, is his bold and fearless manner of defending the national administration in the course you have taken in Mississippi affairs, and his fair exposure of corruption in this state. Col Wells is called a Democrat by the wreckers, because he beat Howe for Congress, and had the temerity to speak the truth concerning affairs here. He was the regular Republican nominee for congress, Howe was the issue of a bogus, and bolting convention. The Democracy had no candidate, they preferred Wells to Howe, and voted for him, and so he received the ~~vote~~ support of both parties, and hence his large majority. He is a ~~staunch~~ true Republican and staunch supporter of the national administration as I am sure his course in Congress will prove and this I regard as a good test of a true Republican. . . . Now for the future. what is the course. we want to carry this State next year in the Presidential Election. We cannot do it as we now stand. We must have honest men in the front, those who have scuttled the Ship of State must take back seats. We must have men, in whose promises the people can rely, men who will give character and moral support to the party, otherwise the white people will be against us, and the Colored people will never again rally to us, we will be again defeated, and the architects of our ~~own~~ ruin will leave the State like rats leave a sinking ship. I believe we can carry the State next year by proper management and an honest course. Thousands are against us now who fear to trust the Democracy, and will go with us under favorable auspices, and if our State administration had pursued the proper course for the last two years, The democrats could never have beaten us. I know the people of the State having resided among them for the last thirty three (33) years. The Government appointees here we think are good men and true Republicans   We need no changes made for political purposes and no troops, leave the management of these matters here to your real friends. I am sure that affairs here have been misrepresented to you by designing men for their selfish ends. I think I can take a fair and impartial view of the situation, having no aspirations for place or position, but have the temerity to speak the plain unvarnished truth in these matters. This letter though of some length has given but a bare outline of the character and conduct of a few would be leaders who have wrought our sad defeat, but should they choose to deny anything I have said of them I will not only prove it, but strike them at other points that are equally salient" ALS, DLC-Thomas F. Bayard. *SMD,* 44-2-45, 590–94. See *ibid.,* pp. 793–824.

On Dec. 16, O. W. Cole, Memphis, telegraphed to USG. "The way that the colored people were abused in coahama County Miss please forward this to chief emigrant office at Cohoma of about one thousand persons wants to emigrant" Telegram received (at 8:00 P.M.), DLC-USG, IB.

On Dec. 24, Michael Shaughnessy, collector of Internal Revenue, Jackson, telegraphed to Daniel D. Pratt, commissioner of Internal Revenue. "My deputy W. B. Redmond has been driven from his office and home and from county to county in his division, while discharging his official duty, by armed bodies who publicly defy the authority of the

United States and threaten to resist it. Redmond cannot discharge his duties without military assistance. Instruct me in the premises" Copy, DNA, RG 94, Letters Received, 6467 1875. Pratt endorsed this communication to Secretary of War William W. Belknap for USG's consideration. AES (undated), *ibid.* USG endorsed these papers. "Instruct Sec. of War to direct protection to be given" AE (undated), *ibid.* Related papers are *ibid.*

1. On Sept. 27, William A. Alcorn, sheriff, Tallahatchie County, Charleston, Miss., had written to Ames. "Yours of the 22nd inst. to hand; contents noted. In reply will say, that I think it would be very unwise to organize the militia in this county. It would undoubtedly cause bloodshed. The people of this county are more quiet now than they have been during the last five months. President Grant's letter, 'I will instruct the commander of the forces to have no child's play,' I think has caused the calm that now exists. I do not wish to organize the militia, but hope to get more able protection if necessary." *SRC*, 44-1-527, II, Documentary Evidence, 81. See *ibid.*, pp. 82–83.

2. See Speech, Sept. 15, 1875.

To Hamilton Fish

Long Branch, N. J.
Sept. 14th /75

DEAR GOVERNOR,

I wrote you a letter a few days since on a subject to be kept confidential until after I pass Columbus, O. on my way West. Did you get it? I presume so, though having one from you of a later date, and making no mention of the fact I was afraid it might have miscarried.

Yours Truly
U. S. GRANT

HON. HAMILTON FISH, SEC. OF STATE

ALS, DLC-Hamilton Fish. On Wednesday, Sept. 15, 1875, Secretary of State Hamilton Fish telegraphed to USG, care of U.S. Senator Roscoe Conkling of N. Y., Utica. "Letter of Friday received on Saturday Evening—and answered on Monday—It will be strictly observed—" ADfS (press), *ibid.* On Sept. 11 and 16, Fish wrote to USG, Long Branch. "I am glad to be able to announce another successful result, in one of our long contested questions with the Government of Columbia. We have obtained an award of thirty thousand dollars, in the case of the 'Montijo', which you will remember was seized, in the early days of your Administration, by one of the contending factions, in some of the ever-occuring commotions of those countries. Columbia, denied our claim, & finally, reluctantly yielded to an Arbitration, which has resulted in the Award referred to. Little by little, we seem to be picking up the old claims, & settling outstanding questions—all goes well except with Spain, whose government, at present, is too weak to act, and not quite weak enough for a desperate venture—I shall return to Washington on Tuesday. The Attorney General telegraphs me that he considers the Mississippi troubles as at an end—" "I enclose a letter of introduction, by Genl Badeau, to you of Lord Houghton, formerly Mr Monckton Milnes, long a Member of Parliament, of liberal tendencies, and the proclaimed friend of this Governmt, during the Rebellion. He called here to day, and expressed a great desire to see you, proposing to go to Long-Branch for that purpose, at the close of next week, enquiring whether you would then be there—on hearing that you propose to go to St Louis (whence he has just returned) next week, he requested me to forward the letter to you with the expression of regret not to have been able personally to deliver it—but expressing the hope that he may be able to return here, in October, after your return—From some expressions of his, I ascertained that he would be gratified to receive from you, some recognition of the receipt of the letter of introduction, and in view of his high character as a Poet, a Scholar, & Statesman, and of his warm support of our cause during the rebellion, perhaps, (as I hope) you may feel inclined to make his call an exceptional one, and either write, or authorise some kind recognition—Your letter of 10th (last Friday) was postmarked at Long Branch on the *11*th & reached me *late* in the Evenig of that day. My letter to you had then been mailed & despatched—On Monday I wrote in acknowledgment of your Confidential letter of 11th   I think a good selection can be made—from the list submitted— Either would make a good officer, possibly questions of geography will be the main test —" ALS (press), *ibid.* On Nov. 13, Lord Houghton called on USG and Julia Dent Grant at the White House. *New York Times,* Nov. 14, 1875. See letter to Hamilton Fish, Sept. 10, 1875; *Foreign Relations, 1871,* pp. 230–41; *Foreign Relations, 1875,* I, 427–29.

Speech

[*Sept. 15, 1875*]

Ladies and Gentlemen of Utica, and Comrades of the Army of the Cumberland:

It affords me very great pleasure to be here this evening, and if there was any one drawback to it it was the consciousness that I would possibly be called upon to say a few words. Now, I would like to write all that I think about this, and have you read it, for you know it is not one of my gifts to stand up before you and say what I wish to say. I can take two or three of you in a private room and say all I like to say on an occasion of this sort, but there are others to follow me who are not troubled with my diffidence.

Society of the Army of the Cumberland, Ninth Reunion, Utica, N. Y.: 1868–1875 (Cincinnati, 1876), p. 53. Joseph Hooker, vice president, Society of the Army of the Cumberland, presided over the reunion. See letter to Roscoe Conkling, Aug. 12, 1875; letter to Adolph E. Borie, Aug. 26, 1875; *New York Times,* Sept. 16, 1875.

On Oct. 5, Gen. William T. Sherman, St. Louis, wrote to Conkling, Utica. ". . . I doubt if Genl Grant will or ought to record what he said at Utica openly and undisguisedly, in

your presence, and at Gov Seymour's   I believe he will do so at some future time, if occasion offers, but meantime, I would like to have you write me simply what he said to us in
the Carriage, as you drove me up to Judge Hunts. My memory is that addressing me he
said that at first he was disturbed by the criticisms of my recently published Memoirs, but
that when he reached Long Branch, he sat down with a blank card & pencil to note Errors,
that he Carefully read the two Vols and his card was blank—that the criticisms were unfair, though he might have advised certain omissions for the Sake of prudence—but added
—'while you were about it I wish you had pricked another bubble, the Battle of Hooker
above the Clouds' which he proceeded to do. He then spoke of Hooker in much stronger
terms than I had used, adding that on the Stage he had purposely passed him because in
California he (Hooker) had spoken of him (Grant) in a manner that freed him of all delicacy. I do not wish to use any letter you may make in answer to this, but to hold it, simply
till he General Grant will speak out sentiments which I believe he has long Entertained,
or as vouchers to my own memory should I pass away suddenly. . . ." ALS, DLC-Roscoe
Conkling. On Oct. 15, Conkling wrote to Sherman. *"Private.* . . . I have your letter asking
me to write out what the President said in my carriage last month in this City about your
'Memoirs,' etc. My recollection of his words is somewhat blended with what he said the
same morning at breakfast much more at large—but I will most cheerfully comply with
your request, unless we should be taking a questionable liberty in setting down on paper
a private conversation without the permission of the person whose conversation it was. . . ."
ALS, DLC-William T. Sherman. See Sherman to Conkling, Nov. 1, 1875, DLC-Roscoe
Conkling; Conkling to Sherman (incomplete), Jan. 12, 1876, DLC-William T. Sherman;
letters to William T. Sherman, Jan. 29, 1876.

To Edwards Pierrepont

———

[*Elizabeth, N. J.*,[1] *Sept. 21, 1875*]
. . . I do not know of any lawyer in the Circuit to whom to tender the
position unless it should be Senator Edmunds, and he I should dislike to see leave the Senate. But you are well acquainted with the Bar
in that Circuit, and its wants, and can no doubt suggest the right
man for the place. If you will send me a commission . . . either filled
up or the name blank, with suggestions as to the best man I will sign
and return it.

Charles Hamilton Auction No. 7, March 25, 1965, no. 86. On Oct. 13, 1875, a correspondent reported from Washington, D. C. "Senator Edmunds, of Vermont, has been tendered
by the President the appointment of United States Circuit Judge for the Second Judicial
Circuit, made vacant by the death of Judge Woodruff. He arrived here this morning to consult with the Attorney-General and others in respect to the matter. Edmunds says he has
by no means decided to accept the place, but, on the contrary, is disposed to decline it. He
thinks the salary is inadequate, and he is already in a position which satisfies his tastes and
ambition. . . ." *Chicago Tribune*, Oct. 14, 1875. On Dec. 15, USG nominated Alexander S.

Johnson as judge, 2nd Circuit, to replace Lewis B. Woodruff. See *New York Times*, Dec. 31, 1873, Sept. 26, 1874.

1. On Sept. 21, USG and Frederick Dent Grant visited the N. J. State Fair at Waverly. See *Ibid.*, Sept. 22, 1875.

To Columbus Delano

LONG BRANCH, N. J., Sept. 22, 1875.

DEAR SIR: Your letter of the 5th of July, tendering your resignation of the office of Secretary of the Interior, was duly received, and has been held by me until this time without action because of the continued persecution which I believed, and believe, was being unjustly heaped on you through the public press.[1] I only now take action because the time is rapidly approaching when the Secretary of the Interior will have to commence his labors preparatory to rendering his annual report to accompany the Executive Message to Congress.

I therefore accept your resignation, to take effect on the 1st day of October, leaving a little more than two months from the induction of your successor until the assembling of Congress.

In accepting your resignation I am not unmindful of the fact that about the time of the meeting of Congress, one year ago, you stated to me that you felt the necessity of retiring from the Cabinet, and asked me whether I would prefer your resignation so as to have your successor confirmed by the Senate during the last session, or whether I would prefer it in vacation. My answer was, that I would prefer not having it at all. That was my feeling at the time, and I now believe that you have filled every public trust confided to you with ability and integrity.

I sincerely trust that the future will place you right in the estimation of the public, and that you will continue to enjoy its confidence as you have done through so many years of public and official life. With continued respect and friendship I subscribe myself, very truly, your obedient servant,

U. S. GRANT.

HON. C. DELANO, SECRETARY OF INTERIOR.

New York Times, Sept. 27, 1875. On July 5, 1875, Secretary of the Interior Columbus Delano wrote to USG. "I have the honor to transmit with this note my resignation of the office of Secretary of the Interior. You have been aware for some time of my earnest desire to retire from public life, and you have understood the reasons connected with my private business and domestic afflictions which have produced and intensified this desire. Last Fall, in November, I requested you to accept my resignation. You asked me not to insist upon it, and expressed a desire that I should remain in your Cabinet until the end of your Administration, or as long as I found it agreeable to do so. At your request and solicitation I declined then to insist upon your acceptance of my resignation, assuring you, however, that I must resign during the early part of the ensuing Spring. When that period arrived, and during the months of April and May, you advised me again not to resign, which advice agreed with my own judgment. The reasons for this conclusion need not be stated here. Since you were called by your fellow-citizens to perform the duties of Chief Magistrate you have invited me, without the solicitation of myself or friends, so far as I know and believe, to take charge of two important and responsible public trusts—the Internal Revenue Bureau and the Interior Department. I was Commissioner of Internal Revenue from March, 1869, to November, 1870, a period of one year and eight months. The results of my administration you know, and they are not, I trust, entirely unknown to my fellow-citizens. The difficulties of this position, and the diligence, care, and labor required of me in discharging its duties you also understand, and of these I trust the public has some correct appreciation. I assumed the duties of the Interior Department in November, 1870, and have discharged them to the best of my ability for a period of four years and eight months. They have been laborious, difficult, and delicate. They have embraced the supervision of the General Land Office, the Indian Bureau, the Pension and Patent Offices, the Bureau of Education, and a mass of miscellaneous business unknown to any except those connected with the public service. The business of the Land Office is very extensive, and involves the adjudication and settlement of legal questions growing out of railroad grants liberally and profusely made a few years since, and Mexican and Spanish grants made before we acquired California and New-Mexico, and also, those growing out of our mineral laws and large mining interests, to say nothing of those that arose under our homestead and pre-emption systems. These cause the head of the department a vast amount of judicial labor and responsibility which is not generally understood. The Indian Bureau, as you know, is full of intricate, delicate, and vexatious questions, growing out of numerous Indian treaties and the imperfectly-defined relations existing between the Government and the Indian races. The execution of this service is already greatly embarrassed by the remoteness of the localities where much of it has to be performed, thus preventing contact and personal supervision over the persons employed, as well as by the want of salaries large enough to command talent, character, and capacity equal to the duties and responsibilities of the positions. Many of the important duties of the head of the department are connected with the material and pecuniary interests of individuals. These interests are often large in amount. The Secretary, in deciding, must necessarily reject the claim of one of the parties, and thereby not unfrequently finds himself assailed by the misrepresentations and falsehoods of the defeated claimants. I feel confident that a thorough and impartial examination into the present condition of the public service connected with each and all of the bureaus attached to the Interior Department will show to all candid and fair-minded men that it has never been in a more prosperous or better condition than it now is; and I feel sure that the most scrutinizing examination will sustain the opinion here expressed, and that it will also lead to the conviction that great improvements have been made under your policy in the service connected with the Indian Bureau. I allude to these matters briefly, to remind you of the exhausting labor which fidelity to my duties during the last six years and four months has demanded of me, and to show you in part that one of my age requires rest and recuperation. During all these years of toil I have had your support, your sympathy, and, as I believe, your entire confidence. Had it been otherwise I should have long since retired. As I have said, your political favors have come unsolicited, and, therefore, have been highly appreciated. You have always lightened my burdens by cheerful, prompt, and cordial co-operation. When our official relations are severed, I shall always continue to cherish for you the highest regard, founded, as it is, upon my unqualified confidence in your unselfish patriotism, in the accuracy and solidity of your judgment, and in the high sense of justice which has always characterized you, and from which, in my judgment, nothing can tempt you intentionally to deviate." *Ibid.* On Sept. 22, Delano visited USG at Elizabeth, N. J., to urge acceptance of his resignation. *Ibid.* See letter to J. Russell Jones, Oct. 5, 1875.

1. See letter to Benjamin H. Bristow, June 28, 1875.

On Aug. 11, William Welsh, Philadelphia, had written an open letter to USG. "I invite your attention to an overt act by your representatives at the head of the Department of the Interior which, with its attendant circumstances, reveals the lamentable moral condition of that department and demands prompt action by you. I refer to a libellous attack on Mr. Samuel Walker, the confidential clerk of your original Board of Indian Commissioners on account of official services performed by him in detecting and exposing frauds under the authority and direction of that Board. This libel, I have good reason to believe, was concocted and published by General B. R. Cowan, the Assistant Secretary of the Interior, with the cordial approval of Secretary Delano. . . . This is the culmination of a series of covert attacks by Secretary Delano and General Cowan on an officer of a co-ordinate branch of the government, because he exposed frauds that it was the duty of the Interior Department to check. . . . I am not among those who have censured you so strongly for refusing to remove Secretary Delano when he became justly liable to evil report. You allowed him to leave the Department of the Interior in charge of subordinates for months together, that he might canvass the country and secure your re-election to the Presidency. His efficient services entitled him, under the rules of all political parties, to claim a continuance of office unless he committed some gross misdemeanor or possibly some criminal act. You have intimate friends in Philadelphia, such as Messrs. Borie, Childs, Drexel and Stuart, who are entitled to the confidence of their fellow citizens, and through their co-operation you can be relieved from the charge of violating party rules. At your request I am sure that they would examine the papers in my possession, and if they become satisfied that Secretary Delano and Assistant Secretary Cowan are guilty of a criminal libel when acting in their official capacity, you certainly will not allow them to remain in their present position. It requires much boldness for a private citizen to make this public statement, when he knows the fearful power exerted in Congress and elsewhere by those who adroitly use the patronage of the Department of the Interior. Under its influence I have seen private citizens quail, and some of our most reliable Senators and members of the House of Representatives become very passive in measures of reform. Before they had received favors they were my most efficient helpers. It is not my purpose at this time to show how, through the Land Office and other offices of the Interior Department, an almost irresistible power can be wielded by such adroit manipulators as Secretaries Delano and Cowan. . . . It is my intention to give still further public statements of such facts in regard to their management of the Indian Office as have come under my observation, as a thorough reform is decreed by the people. I desire here, as before, to make my public acknowledgment of your merciful, prompt and effective aid rendered in the Indian service, when you were at the head of the army and since you have become President. Every suggestion I ever made to you was promptly responded to, save only the investigation of frauds allowed by your appointees. Even this lamentable trait I believe springs from a distorted virtue. Your protection of General Parker when he was convicted of misfeasance, or malfeasance, as Commissioner of Indian Affairs, and of those who now control that office, seems wholly unaccountable, except on the hypothesis that love in you is blind. It may seem strange to others that I should have written this open letter, but necessity was laid upon me to write, and I could not, with proper self-respect, address you in any other way, as you have in every instance closed your mind to evidence that must have convinced any other man." *New York Herald*, Aug. 13, 1875 (reprinted from the *Philadelpia Evening Telegram*, Aug. 12, 1875).

Endorsement

Respectfully referred to the Atty General who will please examine the matter submitted and report to me his opinion thereon.

U. S. GRANT

SEPT 23D 1875

ES, DNA, RG 60, Letters from the President. Written on a letter of Sept. 11, 1875, from William Dennison, John H. Ketcham, and S. Ledyard Phelps, D. C. commissioners, to USG concerning D. C. bonds. "The accounts of most of the work in progress on the streets and avenues, and sewers of the District of Columbia, are, under the act of Congress of June 20, 1874, audited by the Board of Audit created by that statute and composed of the First and Second Comptrollers of the United States Treasury, and are settled by certificates of that Board convertible into what are known as 3–65 bonds of the District. Any undue depreciation of these bonds produces dissatisfaction on the part of the contractors and causes some embarrassment in the completion of the work. In one important instance it was at one time apprehended that the contractors might abandon the work; and in general if the bonds become unduly depreciated it is likely that the contractors may be less inclined to efficient performance of their contracts. In order, therefore, without litigation, to secure proper accomplishment of such work, it is to the interest of the District that the bonds shall maintain a fair market value. The debt represented by the bonds remains the same whether they are depreciated or not. The market value of the securities in which the District is in this way interested depends, to a great extent, upon the existence or absence of a pledge on the part of the United States to provide payment of the interest and create a sinking fund for the payment of the principal, and upon the degree of public confidence in the existence of such a pledge. The relation of the United States towards the bonds was the subject of an opinion by the late Attorney General whose examination of the subject led him to the conclusion that by congressional enactment the faith of the United States is pledged to provide the revenue necessary to meet the interest as the same becomes due, and to create a sinking fund for the payment of the principal. . . ." LS, *ibid.* On March 13, Attorney Gen. George H. Williams had written to USG affirming federal government liability for principal and interest on these bonds. Copy, *ibid.*, Opinions. *Official Opinions of the Attorneys-General*, XIV, 545–47. On March 15, Orville E. Babcock wrote to the D. C. commissioners. "I am directed by the President to transmit herewith the opinion of the Hon. Attorney General on the subject of the District 3–65 Bonds—in connection with the recent act of Congress appd. Feby. 20th 1875" Copy, DLC-USG, II, 2. On May 6, Henry D. Cooke, Washington, D. C., wrote to USG. "Will you kindly furnish me with an authentic copy of the opinion of the Attorney General, in relation to District of Columbia bonds, commonly known as Three-Sixty five (3.65) Bonds? This is needed, to reply satisfactorily to inquiries which are made in relation thereto, both in New York and London." ALS, DNA, RG 60, Letters from the President. On the same day, Williams wrote to USG. "In compliance with your request I have the honor to transmit herewith a certified copy of the opinion rendered to you on the 13th of March last, relative to the District of Columbia bonds." Copy, *ibid.*, Letters Sent to Executive Officers. See message to Congress, June 20, 1874; *HMD*, 43-2-35; *SRC*, 43-2-588; *HED*, 44-1-1, part 7, pp. 10–11, 29–31.

On Oct. 22, Attorney Gen. Edwards Pierrepont wrote to USG. "The question submitted by the President to the Attorney General, is whether 'the faith of the United States is pledged to provide for the payment of the interest and principal of the 3–65 District Bonds.' That the faith of the United States is so pledged I have no doubt whatever: and I respectfully suggest that the contrary opinions which have been given by some eminently respectable lawyers have resulted from a hasty and superficial examination of the question. . . ." LS, DNA, RG 60, Letters from the President. *Official Opinions of the Attorneys-General*, XV, 56–60. On Oct. 26, Babcock wrote to D. C. commissioners transmitting this opinion. Copy, DLC-USG, II, 3.

On March 1[4], 187[6], USG wrote to Secretary of the Treasury Benjamin H. Bristow. "I have this day signed the Joint Resolution, directing the Commissioners of the District of Columbia to pay the interest on the bonds issued in pursuance of the Act of Congress, approved June 20, 1874. &c, &c, of which the enclosed printed bill is a true copy." LS (misdated), DNA, RG 56, Letters Received from the President. The enclosure is *ibid.* Continued doubt over authority and funds to pay interest on these bonds had prompted the D. C. commissioners to seek a joint resolution from Congress, provoking extensive debate on D. C. finances. See *CR*, 44–1, 595–98, 708–19, 757–69, 787–99, 818–35, 853–66, 1682–87. On April 19, USG wrote to Congress transmitting the final report of the board of audit. Copy, DNA, RG 130, Messages to Congress. *HED*, 44-1-160.

To James B. Howell, George W. McCrary, et al.

St. Louis, Mo., Sept 25th, 1875.

To Hon. J. B. Howell, Hon. Geo. W. McCreary, and others—GENTLEMEN: It would afford me great pleasure to accept your very cordial invitation to visit Keokuk and attend the Iowa State Fair on my way to Des Moines. My personal business matters which have called me to this city,[1] compel me to remain here so long that I am obliged to forego the pleasure an acceptance would afford me. I am glad of an opportunity though to visit your great State, and to meet again so many of her brave soldiers.[2]

Thanking you again for your very kind invitation, I am truly yours,

U. S. GRANT.

Iowa State Register, Sept. 29, 1875. U.S. Representative George W. McCrary of Iowa, who entered Congress in 1869, had been a lawyer in Keokuk and state legislator; James B. Howell was a Keokuk newspaper editor. On Sept. 18, 1875, Secretary of War William W. Belknap telegraphed to Orville E. Babcock, Long Branch, asking whether USG could attend the Iowa State Fair in Keokuk if supplied with a special train from Des Moines on Sept. 30. ALS (telegram sent), DNA, RG 107, Telegrams Collected (Bound).

1. See letter to Edward F. Beale, Sept. 8, 1875. On Sept. 23, USG, Columbus, Ohio, telegraphed to Gen. William T. Sherman, St. Louis. "Much obliged for your invitation but my party is so large and I shall be so busy during my stay in St. Louis that it will be better to stop at the Hotel—" Telegram received (at 6:40 P.M.), DLC-William T. Sherman.
2. See Speech, [*Sept. 29, 1875*].

To Benjamin H. Bristow
———

St. Louis, Mo.
Sept. 27th /75

HON. B. H. BRISTOW,
SEC. OF THE TREAS.
DEAR SIR:

I see published in the morning papers the report of the last Commission to examine the Chicago Custom House building, and your indorsement & instructions thereon. In view of the lateness of the season, and the almost certainty that there will be a Congressional investigation of the matter the coming winter do you not think it advisable to limit the instructions to strengthening the foundations, as recommended by the Commission, and preserving the work from the weather until work can be resumed in the Spring? I do not write this as absolute, but ask you to think if this might not be better than to change the plans and destroy work already done before the impending investigation. My whole desire is "to be sure we are right and then to go ahead."

Very Truly Yours
U. S. GRANT

ALS, DLC-Benjamin H. Bristow. On Sept. 29, 1875, Charles F. Conant, asst. secretary of the treasury, endorsed this letter to Secretary of the Treasury Benjamin H. Bristow. "Mr. Potter will make his first order to day—and base it upon the above suggestions. He ~~can~~ will then issue further orders as you may direct." AE (initialed), *ibid*. See letter to Benjamin H. Bristow, Aug. 7, 1875; *Chicago Tribune*, Oct. 5, 22, 1875.

On Oct. 20, Emery A. Storrs, Chicago, telegraphed to Orville E. Babcock. "There is a wide spread impression here that Potter's treatment of the Custom House will result in its destruction. This is the opinion of some of our best architects,　I am urged by many of our best men to Call your attention to the imminence of the danger so that it may be averted,　Must that great building Endangered to gratify the whims & wounded vanity of Mr Potter　There is no difference of opinion in this city concerning Potter's course and I tell you it is very positive and the feeling is very bitter and it is not wise to disregard it,　our citizens have no hope Except in the President," Telegram received (on Oct. 21), DLC-USG, IB. U.S. Senator John A. Logan of Ill. added to this telegram. "Have read this despatch,　The matter should be looked into," *Ibid*.

Endorsement

Refered to the Atty. Gen. If there be appropriation out of which such services as Gov. Ames asks can be paid I think it might be advisable to grant this request.

U. S. GRANT

SEPT. 27TH /75

AES, CtY. Written on a letter of Sept. 25, 1875, from Governor Adelbert Ames of Miss. to USG, St. Louis. "This will be presented you by Mr. W. W. Dedrick, U. S. District Att'y, who visits you to obtain an order from you on the departments for detectives to visit this State, to penetrate the schemes and plots of the white-liners, who are preparing to deprive the colored men of their civil and political liberties by violence. The necessity of the presence and co-operation of such officers in Mississippi, at the present time, cannot well be overstated," ALS, *ibid*. In 1875, George K. Chase wrote to Attorney Gen. Edwards Pierrepont requesting an appointment as investigator. Charles Hamilton Auction No. 79, July 24, 1974, no. 8. Chase, who suffered bankruptcy in 1868, went as a detective to Miss. On Oct. 16, 1875, Ames wrote to Pierrepont. "Through the timely and skillful intervention of Mr. G. K. Chase, a bloody revolution has been averted. The condition of affairs which preceded the Clinton riot grew worse from day to day, and soon attained gigantic proportions under the feeling of hostility to the Militia I was organizing. The danger became apparent to all, and in the interest of peace and a fair election, an understanding was had to this effect. The opposition was to do all in their power to preserve the peace. I have faith in their honor and implicit confidence that they can accomplish all they undertake. Consequently I believe we will have peace, order, and a fair election. I write this letter chiefly to thank you for sending here a gentleman who has succeeded in inspiring us all with confidence, and who by his wisdom and tact has saved the state from a catastrophe of blood. Personally I feel under the greatest obligations to him." Blanche Butler Ames, comp., *Chronicles From the Nineteenth Century: Family Letters of Blanche Butler and Adelbert Ames* . . . (1957), II, 236–37. On Oct. 23, Pierrepont wrote to Ames. "Yours of the 16th came duly, and yesterday I presented it to the President, who read it to Senator Bruce; and I also presented it to the Cabinet. I delayed answering it until the meeting of the Cabinet, and I have to say that the course you have taken meets the approval of the President and of the Cabinet, and that they are each and all much gratified that your judicious course in making this settlement and producing peace without bloodshed proves that you have acted wisely. I sincerely hope that those with whom you have negotiated will keep their agreement, and that you will have a peaceful election. You may be assured that to produce this result without the necessity of calling out the Federal troops will redound greatly to your credit throughout the entire North. You will be advised of the preparations made to aid you in case the opposition violate their honor and break their faith. You may feel assured that this department will always be ready to aid you in any lawful way to preserve order and to give the right to every citizen to vote as he pleases." James Wilford Garner, *Reconstruction in Mississippi* (1901; reprinted, Gloucester, Mass., 1964), p. 389. About Oct. 27, Chase communicated to Pierrepont. "I deem it my duty to give you facts relative to the situation in Mississippi to-day. It is impossible to have a fair election on November 2nd without the aid of U. S. troops. The peace pledges of the leading citizens and democratic conservatives will be kept so far as they can. The determination by the democrats throughout the State is to carry the election; and to that end they have so intimidated the negroes, by the hanging of several leaders and other lawless parties, that they dare not put out a ticket in Yazoo County, which has two thousand republican majority. In other counties they have to put out a compromise ticket, through fear of violence. The governor is powerless to protect the republicans. Refugees are daily coming in, and many complaints by mail are received. An invasion from Alabama is imminent. To have a fair election, troops must come. If that is not desired, peace can be had, and the State will be democratic. Please inform me secretly as to how I shall advise the governor. Use the governor's cipher." *SRC*, 44-1-527, II, Documentary Evidence, 92. On Nov. 5, Blanche Butler Ames, Lowell, Mass., wrote to her husband Adelbert Ames. ". . . I want to write you my opinion of Mr. Chase. You have always spoken of him most kindly. But I believe him to be like his chief, an unreliable trickster, with no conception of propriety or the dignity of the Government, he has tried to represent.—If a Catholic, a good Jesuit. . . . I wonder if our worthy President has received backbone enough to attend to his affairs, and has yet found nerve enough to do what is right, instead of what is politic. I am glad I am not a *man* of that stamp, forever sacrificing what is right to what is expedient. No doubt you will say 'Oh, no Blanche, you misjudge Mr. Chase.' I only want to put myself on record against him and his director, that is all. I am always suspicious of middlemen, and I take it that Mr. Chase has been acting in that capacity lately. . . ." Ames, *Chronicles From the Nineteenth Century*, II, 251–52. See *ibid.*, pp. 230, 235–36, 239–41; *New York Times*, Dec. 8, 1868; letter to Edwards Pierrepont, Sept. 13, 1875.

On July 12, 1876, Chase, Washington, D. C., testified before a select committee investigating the 1875 Miss. election. ". . . At present I am agent of the Department of Justice. Q. How long have you resided in the city of New York?—A. Thirty-eight years, sir; born there, and always lived there. Q. Did you go to the State of Mississippi last fall?—A. I did, sir. . . . About the 1st of October, I think it was the 1st to the 5th, I went to the State of Mississippi at the request of Hon. Edwards Pierrepont, Attorney-General, for the purpose of ascertaining the true condition of affairs there, and, if possible, to quiet the political excitement in that State. . . . About that time I became acquainted with General George, whom I found to be the recognized leader of the opposition. We had a long conference. I told him that I was from Washington; that the Attorney-General had sent me to Mississippi to ascertain the true condition of affairs there, and I wished to know what could be done to insure peace and quiet throughout the State. He stated that he could do nothing without the consent of Mr. Barksdale; that while he was the chairman and recognized head of the opposition in the State, he had no authority to act, to make any compromise or pledges, without the consent of Mr. E. Barksdale; and he desired me to meet him. I consented. . . . Then, after a long conference between George and myself, it was agreed that he (George) would get a number of the prominent citizens, and they would go to the governor, and they (the democratic citizens) would pledge him peace and a peaceful election; that there should be no more killing or no more outrages if he would disband the militia. . . . The next day we had a peace meeting, of General George and prominent citizens, at the governor's mansion, in which the citizens pledged themselves to keep the peace and to have a peaceable election; that a republican ticket should be put up in all the counties, and that they should not be molested or interfered with in any way. I was present at that conference with the governor, simply as a spectator, . . . There was a perfect understanding, and everything between the governor and the democrats fixed, as I thought. It continued so for several days, then the outrages began again. . . . So it went on until I thought it was my duty to report to the Attorney-General that there was no chance for a fair election without the aid of United States troops. I did so, and the order was issued for troops to prevent actual bloodshed. . . . My agents told me that they said they intended to carry the election peaceably if they could, forcibly if they must; that was the determination of the white democratic people; that they preferred to do it peaceably, to use quiet intimidation with the negroes, which they did to a great extent, and if it became necessary, if there was a troublesome nigger among them, then they must kill him, if he should interfere in politics. . . . Q. Did you make a report in writing to the Attorney-General?—A. I wrote a number of letters, private and confidential letters, to the Attorney-General; I made no regular report. . . . He had known me well for a number of years, and knew I was a business man and that I had some capacity for managing men and things. Q. Had you ever been in Mississippi before?—A. Never. Q. Did you know anything about the people there?—A. Not at all. . . . Q. Was your appointment verbally from the Attorney-General?—A. I think it was, sir. Q. What was your pay?—A. It was $6 a day. . . . I was authorized to get the information and pay for it, if necessary. Q. How many persons did you employ?—A. Two persons. . . . I took one from New York and one from here. Q. Were they persons previously known as detectives?—A. One of them was. . . . Q. You stated, Mr. Chase, that you relied largely on a reliable source in Jackson for information?—A. Yes, sir. Q. That, perhaps, is a secret with you, and I would not ask you who it was, but I will ask you whether or not it was Governor Ames?—A. No, sir, it was not Governor Ames, it was a prominent democrat; and I would not, could not, give his name under any circumstances; but he is a very reliable man, and gave me these facts in the interest of law and order entirely. . . ." *SRC*, 44-1-527, II, 1801–4, 1807–11, 1819. For Ethelbert Barksdale's related testimony, see *ibid.*, I, 447, 473–74.

On Nov. 13, 1875, Pierrepont had written to USG. "I send this written charge agt. Major Allen mentiond yesterdy . . ." ANS, DNA, RG 94, Letters Received, 5644 1875. On Nov. 12, Chase, Washington, D. C., had written to Pierrepont. "I reduce to writing the verbal report which I made to you in relation to the course of Major Allen in Mississippi. About two weeks before the election, the Democratic Committee called upon Major Allen, commanding the United States troops at Jackson, and obtained from him a fine brass cannon belonging to the United States. They then dressed up democratic citizens in artillery uniform, manning this cannon, upon which 'U. S.' was prominently painted, and with mules took it around the country and in the adjacent counties, carrying at the same time the United States flag, night and day firing it, and firing it very many times in succession, calling it a national salute. The negroes were made to believe that this was permitted by the United States, and that the United States were going back upon them, to reduce them again to servitude. They were greatly terrified, and many fled to the woods and concealed themselves in various ways. This was continued until the day before the election; and produced great consternation and demoralization with the colored Republican voters. I personally (after consultation with Governor Ames) spoke to Major Allen, in command of the troops, and told him that this was *an outrage*, and ought not to be permitted. He laughed, and evidently not sympathizing with our side of the question, replied that 'he would have lent it to the Republicans in the same way if they had asked for it, but they did not ask for it.' He made *no effort* to stop it, and expressed no *dissatisfaction* with it. I deem it my duty as the Agent whom you sent to Mississippi to make a truthful report of this matter; and I have thus reduced it to writing because you required my reports to be reduced to writing, in addition to the verbal reports which I have made. My more full reports upon other matters will be soon prepared." LS, *ibid.* Capt. Arthur W. Allyn, 16th Inf., was court-martialed and acquitted on charges of improperly loaning a cannon to Miss. Democrats. See General Court Martial Orders, No. 1, Dept. of the Gulf, New Orleans, Jan. 11, 1876, *ibid.*; *SRC*, 44-1-527, II, 1814.

To Edwards Pierrepont

———

Sept. 27th *1875*

DEAR SIR:

Herewith I forward papers relating to the U. S. Marshalship of this district of Mo. It might be well to get the views of the Sec. of the Treas. as to whether he thinks a change should be made. If so a simple request to the present Marshal, Judge Newcomb, to resign would be sufficient. He has voluntarily stated to me that he had no intention of retaining the office much longer under any circumstances, and that to go out a littler earlier would be no disappointment to him.

Truly Yours
U. S. GRANT

HON. EDWARDS PIERREPONT ATTY. GEN.

ALS, DNA, RG 60, Records Relating to Appointments. Written on stationery of the St. Louis post office. On Sept. 29, 1875, Carman A. Newcomb, U.S. marshal, St. Louis, wrote to Attorney Gen. Edwards Pierrepont. "It was my intention at the close of the last fiscal year to retire from this office, but in consequence of the recent prosecutions against the St Louis Whiskey ring I determined to defer doing so for reasons which you can appreciate. I now feel at liberty to carry out my original intention, and hereby tender my resignation to take effect at the pleasure of the President." ALS, *ibid.*, Letters Received, Mo. See Endorsement, July 29, 1875; letter to Edwards Pierrepont, Oct. 18, 1875.

On Sept. 7, Newcomb had written to USG, Long Branch. "I have this day recieved a letter from our mutual friend Hon: H. T. Blow, and have his permission to use any part of it in writing to the Attorney General or yourself. In detailing a conversation had with you, He says, 'The President was in New York yesterday, and in conversation with him, I found that he is deeply in earnest regarding the frauds of Office holders, and determined to put an end to every Spicies of dishonesty on their part (as well as an end to them). He has been confiding, and slow to believe that the men he has honored and trusted, would prove false to their oaths and duties, but the facts seem to be so conclusive, that just now, his highest obligations, are the discharge of his own duty, under the circumstances. He said in speaking of the dishonesty of officials in St Louis that, it had been represented and strongly, that your Sympathy was with the odious Ring, and that therefore any Jury empannelled by you would be favorable to the Ring.' The representation was made and urged and I inferred really embarrassed him' et. Permit me Mr President to say, That it is quite impossible for me to quiet the fears of those who have expressed to you doubts as to my being able to so far divest myself of personal feeling as to select an impartial Jury for the trial of the accused persons in the matter of the violation of the Revenue laws now pending in the Courts of this District. I will say however generally that I dont believe there is a *good responsible* man of any party in this city who believes I am in Sympathy with the Whisky ring, or any one connected therewith. My expressions, My demeanor and my feelings, would all lead me to the opposite extreme. I will inform you how Juries are selected. In the U. S. Circuit Court the Marshal is required to furnish to the Clerk of said Court a list of two hundred names, the Clerk writes each name on a slip of paper, and puts them in a box and after they are mixed up, 36 slips are drawn out by the Marshal without knowing whom he is drawing. These 36 constitute the Jury for one term. The same process is repeated each time. The names constituting the list are taken from the body of the District, not more than one tenth from any one County. Such is the order of Court. I write to some good responsible man in each County, who furnishes me the names. I hardly ever know one in ten of the Jurors selected. In the District Court I choose the men myself who compose the Jury, and am therefore more directly responsible, observing the above rule not to take more than one tenth from any one County. and depending largely upon others for the names. So you see if the Marshal were disposed to pack a Jury the opportunity to do so would be very remote. It is a delicate duty to select a Jury to try important cases, and one that no Marshal would voluntarily choose, and perhaps where so much feeling exists in a community as we have had here, it will be quite impossible to satisfy every one, indeed if it can ever be done, but so concious am I of the rectitude of my intentions, that I do expect to select a Jury, composed of men who will be satisfactory to all fair minded men. I believe the Jury just drawn for the Circuit Court is such an one. Col. Dyer and Hon: John B. Henderson are the direct representatives of the Government here, and are personally professionally and officially interested in the success of cases now pending in this District, and I am perfectly willing they shall be the Judges of my conduct touching these matters. I have a perfect history of every man drawn on the Jury for the next term, written by the best men in the several counties from which they are taken, as to their intelligence, their general character, pecuniary standing, and habits of life, and dont fear to leave them to stand on their own merits. It is my intention to select for Jurors the very best men in the communities where they reside, Men of intelligence and good character, after I have done this my duty ends, the balance devolves on others. It is not the business of the Marshal to select a Jury to try any particular case, but to furnish Jurors in the several Courts of such known character as that any and all cases may be safely committed to them, and whose verdict will carry such weight that it cant be impeached for want of character in the Jurors. After I have done this much no more can be expected. Mr President I am not writing this letter as a plea to be [contin]ued in office, but I am exceedingly anxious that you shall be satisfied that *I have not and will not violate the trust you have committed to me*. And I am determined that all doubt shall be removed, and that you shall have no embarrassment on my account. I will forward you the views of the United States District Attorney on these matters soon as he returns to the city." ALS, DNA, RG 60, Letters Received, Mo. On Sept. 9, John F. Long, surveyor of customs, St. Louis, wrote to USG. "Madam Rumor with her thousand tongues says unfavorable reports touching the official conduct of our U. S. Marshal Judge Newcomb, in connection with the great Whiskey frauds of our state, have reached your ears, and unless those rumors are contradicted, evidently injustice would be done to an upright honest and conscientious public officer, who we believe has been faithful to that Government, whose laws he had sworn to honestly administer, in his official capacity.—the truth is, Mr. President, no public officer, however true and faithful to his government, is free from the petty malice and assaults of the vicious, the sneaking inuendos of secret enemies, who becoming jealous of his position, seek to make capital out of imaginary wrongs or unfounded evils. . . ." LS, *ibid*. On the same day, Isaac H. Sturgeon, collector of Internal Revenue, and Alton R. Easton, pension agent, St. Louis, each wrote to USG in support of Newcomb. ALS, *ibid*. On Sept. 14, USG endorsed these papers. "Refered to the Atty. Gen. with request that the Sec. of the Treas. be shewn these papers." AES, *ibid*.

On Aug. 10, Chester H. Krum, St. Louis, had written to John McDonald. "*Private*. . . . I think, that matters are about ripe for an interview with U S. G. Avery leaves to-night and is going to Long Branch. A friend of his here, will write strongly as to matters before the Grand Jury. Newcomb will be within reach, I think, by [t]he [l]atter part of this week. If you think it adviseable for me to go on, telegraph me 'Broke my leg this morning, cannot come,' and I will meet you at the Palmer House in Chicago. I shall register as Henry B. Gordon. Don't make any arrangements about my going on unless it will do some good & get all of your facts in shape." AL (initialed, facsimile), John McDonald, *Secrets of the Great Whiskey Ring* (Chicago, 1880), p. 191. Krum served as attorney for McDonald, former supervisor of Internal Revenue. On Sept. 21, Ferdinand Meyer, supervisor of Internal Revenue, St. Louis, wrote to USG. "The course of Internal Revenue business lately, has brought me very much in contact with C. A. Newcomb, United States Marshal in this City, who personally has always shown me great courtesy and consideration whenever I have had occasion to see him. I wish, however, very respectfully to draw your attention to the state of inefficiency prevailing among his deputies, none of whom appear to be qualified to properly discharge the important duties connected with their position. This inefficiency often leads to great delay in the execution of writs, involving on the part of those in charge of cases much unnecessary trouble and needless annoyance in prompting the deputies to a more speedy performance of their duty. Marshal Newcomb has also appointed persons of notoriously bad character to important positions as watchmen of property under seizure,—persons who have been heard to express sentiments opposed in the strongest manner to the action and policy of the present administration, particularly in regard to the violations of Internal Revenue law lately brought to light in this City. It is almost unnecessary to observe that the greatest care ought to have been exercised in the selection of persons in whose custody, property of such considerable value had to be placed. In friendly communication with the deputy-marshals, on the street, as well as in the marshal's office, may be seen men, over whom hang many grave and serious criminal charges, and who at present are under indictment in the United States Courts. In short, the character of the persons who may be observed in the marshal's office, the tardy and inefficient manner in which business is conducted, all point to a lack of personal interest in his duties and supervision of those of his deputies, and I cannot but think that the ends of justice and the interests of the government would be subserved by the removal of Marshal Newcombe from office." LS, DNA, RG 60, Records Relating to Appointments. On Sept. 25, William D. W. Barnard, St. Louis, wrote to USG. "I herewith charge C. A. Newcomb Marshal of the United States for the eastern district of Missouri with unofficial conduct in his office, and specify the following facts as constituting such unofficial conduct. 1st That John A. Joyce was on the complaint of the United States indicted in the District Court of the United States for the Western district of Missouri on the 14th day of September 1875. That a capias was issued by the said Court on the 15th day of September 1875, and was on the 17th day of September 1875 received by said Newcomb, on the morning of that day, and was only served on the said Joyce on the 21st day of September 1875, by the said Marshal, by causing the arrest of said Joyce by virtue thereof, and that the residence of said Joyce from the 17th to the 21st of September 1875 inclusive was well known to the said Newcomb to be at the Planters House in the City of St Louis. That such arrest after the receipt of the Capias, was delayed to enable the said Joyce to apply, as he did apply, on the said 21st day of September 1875 for Habeus Corpus, and is still under the protection of the last named writ. 2d That in guarding the property of a distiller seized, a large amount, say \$1.600.—was charged for such service, when not more than \$600.—was paid to the watchman. 3d That attorneys and clients having business in the Courts for the said eastern district of Missouri, have had presented to them and paid by them, fee bills, or items of costs, unusual and illegal, as I am informed from the Marshals office. 4th That on the 6th day of August 1875 there appeared in the Globe-Democrat, a paper silent in regard to the whisky frauds, a list of Petit Jurors for the trial of the then pending indictments against officials, distillers and rectifiers, drawn on the 5th day of August 1875 which publication was unusual and suggestive. 5th That on the 10th day of November 1874 a judgment in favor of the United States vs Peter Curran for the sum of \$3.244.09 was obtained in the United States Court for the eastern district of Missouri. That on the 6th day of March 1875, an execution was issued on said judgment and placed in the hands of the said Marshal and returnable at the May term of said Court 1875. That the said Curran, while the said execution was held by said Marshal, had property sufficient out of which to satisfy the amount thereof, but on the exposure of the whisky frauds and while the Grand Jury in the United States Court was in session at the May term 1875, he was approached by two citizens well known and and interested, to prevent indictment and informed that if he, the said Curran would not appear before the said Grand Jury and testify, the judgment described in the said execution would be satisfied by other parties. That said proposition was rejected by said Curran, and that he said Curran did appear before the Grand Jury on behalf of the Government. That immediately thereafter the said Newcomb levied upon the property of the said Curran to satisfy the judgment aforesaid. That the said execution has never been paid, and that on the 8th day of July 1875 the same was returned by the said Newcomb with the following endorsement made by him thereon 'Levy made and released by District Attorney'. I have reason to believe that said Curran, being a distiller, has formerly paid the 'ring' a large amount of money, exceeding as I understand, One Hundred Thousand dollars. . . . 10th That among the persons summoned as Grand Jurors at the May term 1875 were three persons resident of St Louis and notoriously sympathising with the whisky ring, who were discharged by the Court from service on the said Grand Jury, and were not discharged at their own personal request. 11th That Deputies of the said Marshal had knowledge of frauds against the Government under the Revenue laws, and that they associated notoriously with the persons engaged in the lines of business from whence the United States Revenue tax was payable, manifestly in the pretended discharge of their official duties, more interested in courting the friendship of parties now under indictment, than in protecting the interests of the Government. 12th That the said Newcomb as Marshal illegally appointed persons to make service of subpoena upon witnesses needed by the Government. That upon such illegal appointment, and sevice, parties so served were attached for non-appearance, and that upon their appearance upon attachment for contempt of Court, the question was raised by their counsel whether such service of Subpoena was legal, and the Court, (Hon Judge Treat Presiding,) held that the appointment by said Newcomb of the person making such service was illegal, and without authority of law, and reprimanding the said Marshal for his gross, negligent and illegal performance of duty, dismissed the witness at the costs of said Newcomb. 13th That during the long session of the May Grand Jury, covering a period of ~~six~~ 12 weeks, the parties interested in the whiskey ring were better posted about the daily doings of the Grand Jury than the friends of the Government.—" LS, *ibid.* On Oct. 25, Chauncey I. Filley, postmaster, St. Louis, wrote to USG. "I am informed by a responsible & reputable person now at my elbow, that Peter Curran one of the distillers who gave such valuable ~~testimony~~ information to Supervisor Hawley and who was before the Grand Jury & could have implicated McKee & Maguire—but was not questioned even to the information he had previously given Hawley—is of the impression that Dyer does not desire to implicate McKee or Maguire, as he Curran proffered Dyer to make a statement ~~to that effect~~ to Bluford Wilson, when he was recently here, relating to McKee & when Dyer, Wilson & Curran were in the same room together, which proffer Dyer declined to use, saying to Curran that Wilson had not time to listen to it. I have had important information from this same channel before, and I know it is reliable, and I dont care who knows it. Curran afterwards sought & had an interview with Wilson, through a letter to Secy Bristow from Coloney spl Rev Agt—saying Curran could impart valuable information to (Wilson or) Secy Bristow relating to McKee. Wilson said that he would write to him a week ago last Saturday—& Curran has had no letter. This is the Statement and it has an air of singularity at least— that some encouragement is not given to secure testimony & information on that direction" ALS, USG 3.

On March 27, 1876, Newcomb wrote to USG. "Will you pardon me for Inquiring if it would interfere with your arrangements, to designate me, as one of the visitors to West Point this year? If I should conclude to be a candidate for Congress, I think some such nominal recognition by you, would be a great advantage to me, and will so be appreciated. I will be in Washington soon and wish to confer with about some other matters." ALS, DNA, RG 94, USMA, Board of Visitors. No appointment followed and Newcomb did not run for Congress.

Speech

————

[*Des Moines, Sept. 29, 1875*]

COMRADES &c.

It always affords me much gratification to meet my old comrades in arms of 10–14 years ago,[1] and to live over again the trials and ~~hard ships~~ of those days hardships imposed for ~~the~~ in the preservation & perpetuation of our free ~~government~~ institutions. We believed then, and believe now that we had a government worth fighting for, and, if need be, dying for. How many of our comrades of those days paid the latter price for our preserved Union　Let their ~~memories be~~ heroism & sacrifice be ever green in our memory.

Let not the results of their sacrific~~eds~~ be destroyed. The Union & free institutions for which they fell should be held more dear for these sacrifices.

We will not deny to any of those who fought against us any privilege under the government which we claim for ourselves. On the contrary we welcome all ~~of them~~ such who come forward in good faith to help build up the waste places, and perpatuate our institutions against all enemies as brothers in full interest with us in a common heritage. But we are not prepared to apologise for the part we took in the great struggle. It is to be hoped that like trials will never befall our country. In this sentiment no class of people can more heartily join than the soldier who submitted to the dangers, trials & hardships of the camp & the battle field, on which ever side he may have ~~been found~~ fought. No class of people are more interested in guarding against a recurrence of those days. Let us then begin by guarding against every ~~danger~~ enemy threatning the perpetuity of free republican institutions. I do not bring into this assemblage politics, certainly not partizan politics: but it is a fair subject for the deliberation of soldiers to consider what may be necessary to secure the prize for which they battled. In a republic like ours where the citizen is the sovreign and the official the servant, where no power is exercised except by the will of the people, it is important that the sovreign—the people—should possess intelligence. The free school is the promoter of that intelligence which is to preserve us as a free nation. If we are to have another contest in the near future of our national existence I predict that the dividing line ~~is not to~~ will not be Mason & Dixons but between patriotism, & intelligence on the one side & superstition, ambition & ignorance on the other. Now in this centennial year of our National existence I believe it a good time to begin the work of ~~preparing~~ strengthening the ~~house to stand which~~ foundation of the house ~~erected by our~~ commenced by our patriotic forefathers. ~~com commenced to build,~~ one hundred years ago at Concord & Lexington.[2] Let us all labor to add all needful guarantees for the more perfect security of Free Thought, Free speech, a Free Press, Pure Morals, Unfettered Religious sentiment, and of Equal Right & Privileges to all men irrespective of ~~race~~ Nationality, Color or Religion. Encourage free schools and resolve that not one dollar of money appropriated to their support no matter how raised, shall be appropriated to the support of any sectarian school. Resolve that either the state or Nation, or both combined, shall support institutions of learning ~~that will~~ sufficient to afford to every child growing up in the ~~Nation~~ land the opportunity of a good common school education, unmixed with sectarian, pagan or atheistical tenets. Leave the matter of religion to the family circle, the church & the private school support[ed] entirely by private contribution   Keep the church and state ~~separate~~ forever separate,   With these safeguards I believe the battles which created us "the Army of the Tennessee"[3] will not have been fought in vain

ADf, IaHA. Katherine Gue Leonard wrote that USG had drafted this speech at her "father's desk in the U. S. Pension office Des Moines." AES (undated), *ibid.* In Sept., 1875, Benjamin F. Gue served as pension agent, Des Moines. On Sept. 29, USG delivered this speech at the reunion of the Society of the Army of the Tennessee. On Oct. 7, Thursday, a correspondent reported from Des Moines. "No speech of the President has excited so much comment as that he delivered here on Wednesday last, and the speculations as to the motive for it are as various as the papers which make them. Some say it is a bid for a third term; others, that it is to influence the election in Ohio; others, that it is to precipitate the contest which he warns people to beware of; others, that it has been long premeditated, and was a master-stroke of policy. The fact is, it was almost an impromptu speech. During the afternoon, the President had given a reception to the school-children, in the Opera-House, when a scene met his gaze which would have awakened enthusiasm in the heart of any American citizen. From the Opera-House he took a carriage for a drive through the city. By his side sat Judge Cole, of the Supreme Bench, who has great pride in the Capital City, and the culture and refinement of her citizens, and especially in her public schools, which are really worthy the pride of every citizen. During the drive, in which the school-buildings were viewed, the topic of public schools was discussed by the party, after various political question[s] had been talked over. The President expressed himself very earnestly upon the subject, and seemed anxious to impress his views upon those with him. The wish was expressed that he would give them to the public. The President replied that, if he had time, he would prepare them and present them at the reunion that evening, as he expected to be called on to say something, and he knew of no subject more impressed upon his mind just then. The drive was cut short, and the President taken to Judge Cole's residence at half-past 5; and, during the thity minutes preceding supper, on four sheets of commercial note-paper he hastily penciled the speech which has set the nation agog. . . ." *Chicago Tribune*, Oct. 9, 1875. For another account of USG's composition of this speech, see Will Porter, *Annals of Polk County, Iowa, and City of Des Moines* (Des Moines, 1898), p. 896. A garbled version of USG's speech, widely disseminated through newspapers, led to the belief that USG had criticized public funding for higher education. See *Report of the Pro-*

ceedings of the Society of the Army of the Tennessee, at the Ninth Annual Meeting, . . . (Cincinnati, 1877), pp. 370–85; *Chicago Tribune*, Oct. 1, 1875; L. F. Parker, "President Grant's Des Moines Address," *Annals of Iowa*, Third Series, III, 3 (Oct., 1897), 179–92; L. F. Andrews, *Pioneers of Polk County, Iowa* . . . (Des Moines, 1908), I, 305–7; Tyler Anbinder, "Ulysses S. Grant, Nativist," *Civil War History*, XLIII, 2 (June, 1997), 128–39; Ward M. McAfee, *Religion, Race, and Reconstruction: The Public School in the Politics of the 1870s* (Albany, N. Y., 1998), pp. 192–96; letter to Samuel J. Kirkwood, Nov. 17, 1875.

At the reunion banquet on Sept. 30, Gen. William T. Sherman toasted the president. USG responded. "GENTLEMEN OF THE ARMY OF THE TENNESSEE, LADIES AND GENTLEMEN:— It has always been understood that this toast was to be drank standing, and in silence, and no response was to be expected. But I thank the Society of the Army of the Tennessee very gratefully for the reception which they have given to this toast, and I will beg of you to excuse me from making any further remarks." *Report of the Proceedings of the Society of the Army of the Tennessee*, p. 398. On Sept. 20 (Monday) and 21, Secretary of War William W. Belknap had telegraphed to Orville E. Babcock, Long Branch. "I leave ~~here~~ on Saturday night for Des Moines. If possible before you go please telegraph me ~~the~~ a list of the persons who will accompany the President to Des Moines so that I can notify the Committee, but in any event before leaving Saint Louis for Des Moines I wish that you would telegraph to Hon. C. C. Cole Chairman of reception Committee there ~~a list~~ their names so that the proper arrangements can be made—" "Ayers has been transferred. Leave on Saturday night with ten or twelve others for Des Moines" ALS (telegrams sent), DNA, RG 107, Telegrams Collected (Bound). On Oct. 4, Sherman, St. Louis, wrote to Ellen E. Sherman. ". . . If Belknap Came to Des Moines to displace me in the Society his failure was absolute. We never had a more Enthusiastic meeting, and to me personally the demonstration was so open that Even Grant noticed it. The Crowd in the Theater called for me before Grant, and it was with difficulty I could still the Call, and Explain that as Presiding officer, I would Close the Exercises.—Also at the Banquet I had the toast of the March to the Sea—Grand in Conception—Fortunate in its leader, and Glorious in results—In my response I reaffirmed the truth of my account—& Called on Grant who sat by me, as a witness—. . ." ALS (incomplete), InNd.

On Oct. 1, Babcock, Des Moines, had telegraphed to Mayor James Cushing of Dubuque. "The President does not expect to be able to visit Dubuque. He will notify you in time if he is able. Please thank the citizens for their cordial invitation." *Chicago Tribune*, Oct. 2, 1875. Also on [*Oct. 1*], USG, Omaha, spoke to students at the public high school. "I am pleased to stand beneath the shadow of this building, which is so well calculated to prepare you for useful occupations and honorable stations in life. His Honor, the Mayor, has said that I am in favor of free speech, and therefore I want other people to do the talking." *New York Times*, Oct. 10, 1875. Mayor Champion S. Chase of Omaha had introduced USG as "the hero-soldier, the friend of free men, free speech, and free press, and last, but not least, the friend of free schools." *Ibid.*

On Oct. 2, USG stopped at Cheyenne, Wyoming Territory, for a reception and brief tour. *Salt Lake City Herald*, Oct. 3, 1875. On the same day, U.S. Delegate George Q. Cannon of Utah Territory, and two others, Salt Lake City, telegraphed to USG. "Upon learning of your intention to visit Utah, the City Council of Salt Lake City passed resolutions, extending the hospitalities of the city to yourself and party. A special train will leave here in the morning to meet your Excellency at Ogden. The civil and military officers of the government, the officers of the Territory and city, and other citizens, are invited to form the party." *Deseret News*, Oct. 6, 1875. On Oct. 5, a local reporter described USG's visit to Salt Lake City on Oct. 3 (Sunday) and 4. ". . . The presidential party, consisting of the President and Mrs. Grant, Colonel Fred. Grant and wife, General O. E. Babcock, ex-Secretary of the Navy Adolph E. Borie, wife and daughter, and Governor Thayer, of Wyoming, arrived in the city Sunday afternoon, and after spending twenty-six hours here, took their departure last evening for Denver. . . . While at Ogden the president cordially received the representatives of our city council, who were presented to him, and said in reply to Hon. George Q. Cannon, who tendered him the hospitality of the city in behalf of the municipality, that he had accepted an invitation of the governor of the territory to be his guest; that he could only remain in Utah until Monday afternoon, and would be happy to avail himself of any courtesies at the hands of the city that he might have time to accept. He expressed his obligations for the attention paid him by the municipal authorities. Other Utah gentlemen were then introduced. As the train was moving out of Ogden, President Young stepped from the car of the Utah Central upon the platform where the president was standing, and was presented to President Grant by Mr. Cannon, both gentlemen uncovering. President Young said: 'President Grant, this is the first time I have ever seen a president of my country.' President Grant nodded, and after a few enquiries and compliments, President Young was conducted to the interior of the car, and presented to Mrs. U. S. Grant, Mrs. Col. Fred. Grant, Mrs. Borie and the other ladies and gentlemen of the party. Mrs. Grant entered into a familiar conversation with President Young, which was prolonged for about half an hour, when the latter took his leave of the ladies and of President Grant, saying a few words to the president as he passed upon his return to the Utah Central train. During the entire trip from Ogden to this city President Grant occupied the platform of his car with Governor Emery and Delegate Cannon, the latter being kept engaged in conversation by the president in regard to the various points of interest in the territory. The president asked a good many questions which showed a keen interest in the material resources of the country and the industries of various kinds. Indeed he appeared to be far more impressed with these things than he did with the people whom he met. . . . At the station in this city the president and party were taken in charge by the Federal court house committee and conveyed in carriages to the Walker House. Many thousands of people had assembled at the depot, and from there to East Temple, on both sides of the street, were arranged the city Sabbath school children, with their teachers. The president and Mrs. Grant and Governor Emery rode up in an open barouche, behind four handsome greys. The president, as he passed along, waved his hat to the crowds, who saluted him without boisterous demonstration. During the afternoon the president remained at the hotel, where he received calls from many officials and leading citizens. A large crowd had also gathered in front of the Walker house, and to gratify their desire to see the president, Grant stepped out upon the balcony, and was introduced to the multitude by Gov. Emery, who stated that the president was suffering from a Rocky Mountain cold, was very hoarse, and it would therefore be difficult for him to respond to the calls for a speech. Early Monday morning, the president, in an open buggy with Gov. Emery, was driven to the Temple block, when he went into the tabernacle, and looked at the foundation walls of the temple. He was next driven to the north bench, where he obtained a fine view of the city; and afterwards went to Camp Douglas. . . . After spending a brief time in Douglas the governor drove the president a short distance up Emigration cañon, and then returned to the city and his hotel, where a public reception was held, when several hundred citizens, ladies and gentlemen were presented to the president. . . ." *Salt Lake City Herald*, Oct. 5, 1875. For the extensive arrangements to greet USG, see *ibid.*, Oct. 3, 1875. See also *Julia Grant*, pp. 184–85; Dean C. Jessee, ed., *Letters of Brigham Young to His Sons* (Salt Lake City, 1974), pp. 223–24; Leonard J. Arrington, *Brigham Young: American Moses* (New York, 1985), pp. 373–74.

On Oct. 4, Lt. Gen. Philip H. Sheridan, San Francisco, wrote to Babcock. "Tell the President to take my Judgmt & Come ~~out fo~~ here if only for two days. He will be fully repaid in Evy way for the short time spent & the Rail Road will bring him quickly   It will only Consume five or six days of his valuable time & will be *a happy visit*" ADfS, DLC-Philip H. Sheridan. On Sept. 29, Babcock, Des Moines, had telegraphed to Governor John L. Routt of Colorado Territory. "Shall visit Denver on our return east. Will notify you." *Denver Times*, Sept. 29, 1875. Between Oct. 5 and 9, USG and party visited Denver and other places in Colorado Territory. *Ibid.*, Oct. 6–9, 1875. On Oct. 15, USG returned to Washington, D. C., after a western trip that also included a stop in Kansas City, Mo. See *Chicago Tribune*, Oct. 12, 1875. On Oct. 19, USG wrote to Silas H. H. Clark, gen. superintendent, Union Pacific Railroad, Omaha. "I avail myself of the first leisure since my return to thank you for the many courtesies extended to me and my party while passing over the road under your charge. The kind attention shown us by the officials of your road added much to the comfort and pleasure of the trip, which I assure you was very much enjoyed by the entire party." Copy, DLC-USG, II, 3. On the same day, USG wrote similar letters to Edward H. Rollins, secretary, Union Pacific Railroad, Boston, and Thomas A. Scott, president, Pennsylvania Railroad, Philadelphia. Copies, *ibid.*

On Sept. 29, E. S. Sullivan, San Francisco, had written to USG. "Allow me to congratulate you on your excellent speech at 'Des Moines' As usual you struck the nail right on the head. Please remember me to Mrs Grant . . . My daughter Mrs Jones says 'send my love to the President' which I hereby do." ALS, USG 3. On Sept. 30, William B. Ely, Hartford, wrote to USG. "Your Excellencys speech at Des Moines Iowa Sep 30th is as 'Apples of Gold in Pitchers of silver', Glorious words, from a Glorious Man, so says one of the Yeomanry of the Union," ALS, *ibid.* On the same day, Edward W. Whitaker, Washington, D. C., wrote to USG. "I have just read the telegraphic report of your words to the old army of the Tennessee, and respond AMEN. Have not heard any thing so good since some of the orders to 'advance along the whole line' during the war. To tell the truth, I have (of late), been feeling that we had no leader, that our sacrifices in the war were for naught, that the 'pocket-books' were running the country and ~~determined~~ proposed to crush all spirit of freedom in the people." ALS, *ibid.* Clippings from Boston newspapers commending USG's speech are *ibid.* Also on Sept. 30, Sophia F. Porter, Chicago, wrote to USG. "I write, to thank you for the noble words spoken at the Reunion of the Army of the Tennessee, on the subject of Sectarian Education. Allow me respectfully to assure you that, as you follow out this 'line' of policy, you will win the gratitude of every true patriot in our land, and will bring gladness into the heart of every Christian, North and South, East and West.—I have ventured to express my own sentiments, to you in this manner, Since I remember that my Father, Chester Gurney—(now dead) labored most earnestly, in the cause of liberty—political social, and religious—He drew up the document, styled the 'Platform of the Republican Party:' at the Convention in Detroit, where originated the party that placed you in the Presidential Chair—but was an occasion of loss, to *him*.—As his daughter, I thank you, for thus carrying out the principles *he* loved so well, and labored for, so untiringly. Perhaps it may be well to add, that your correspondent is 'Church Visitor'—(commonly termed, 'missionary') of the 1st Congregational Ch. of this city, (of which, also, the wife of Joseph Medill Esq. is a member.)" ALS, *ibid.*

On Oct. 1, James A. Briggs, Brooklyn, wrote to USG. "You will allow one whose orphan head in boyhood drew from the Public Treasury of the State of Vermont, one dollar and a half a year, as a Scholar in her Public Schools, to thank you Most heartily for your *good words*, spoken at the Evening Session of the Army of the Tennessee, at deMoines, yesterday, in favor of Free Schools. For this speech you deserve the thanks of every man, woman & child in our broad land, who wishes, that our Civil & religious liberties & our excellent Institutions may be handed down to all coming generations. *'Encourage Free Schools' 'Keep the Church and the State forever Separate.'* Glorious declarations these, from one who was born in Ohio, the eldest of the daughters of the Ordinance of 1787! Your

words 'are like apples of gold in pictures of Silver', and will fall like sunshine on the nation's heart. In this country 99. out of 100 of children and Youth can only be educated in
our Common Schools, and they are the caskets that contain the jewels of our land. Our Pil-
grim Fathers established free Schools, that their children might learn to read the word of
God. Let it be our duty & pleasure to perpetuate them, that *'Intelligence* may ever triumph
over *ignorance.*'" ALS, *ibid.* On Oct. 14, Samuel A. Goddard, Birmingham, England, wrote
to USG. "I have read with intense interest your Speech on the Educational question as reported by the Telegraph   This in my opinion is the most important question in its bearing upon the permanence of American institutions that has presented itself, since the suppression of the rebellion and the abolition of Slavery. Your views on this subject as
expressed in this speech should form the text and the rallying point for the nation, and I
think nothing more valuable could have been offered. Were public schools to degenerate
into seminaries for the teaching of Creeds and dogmas, there would soon be an end to re-
ligious-freedom, and the Glory of America in a most important respect would have departed. I believe your Speech taken as a text, and acted upon, will be as important to the
nation as Washingtons farewell address. The great interest I take in this question is offered as an excuse for the liberty taken in writing this letter . . . We have, today, accounts
of the Elections in *Ohio, Iowa* & *Nebraska,* and greatly rejoice." ALS, *ibid.* On May 24, 1869,
U.S. Senator Henry Wilson of Mass., Natick, had written to USG. "I send you some papers in behalf of Mr Goddard who desires the Consulship at Sheffield. He has rendered
good service to the country and is worthy & able. His friends are among our best citizens
and your warmest friends. Will you look at the case and have Mr Fish examine into it?"
ALS, DNA, RG 59, Letters of Application and Recommendation. On April 6, 1872, Goddard wrote to USG. "I take the liberty of addressing your Excellency ion a subject personal to myself. During the whole period of the Rebellion and for about two years afterward, I devoted full one half of my time to the defence of the Union, with the great object
of preventing the acknowledgment of the Rebels by Great Britain. I hold that I wrote more
in defence of the Union and to greater effect, than all the Americans in Europe besides, and
this at a time when the support of my family depended on my daily exertions. It is held by
many, that but for Mr Brights speeches and my exertions, Gt Britain would certainly have
acknowledged the Rebels. That would probably have cost the United States Govt One
Thousand Millions of dollars more. . . . The War nearly destroyed my business. I am now
seventy five years of age: too old to attempt another business, and with a family dependant
upon me for support, *but for which facts,* I should not have the honor of addressing to your
Excellency this letter. . . ." ALS, *ibid.* Related papers are *ibid.* No appointment followed.

On Oct. 18, 1875, Benjamin Van Riper and two others, Jersey City, wrote to USG.
"Thousands of our Fellow Citizens have read your speech at the late re union of the Army
of Tennessee and deem it an act of moral heroism unequalled by any President of this Republic   they realize that its utterance at this time upon the closing of our Centennial year,
is worthy of your Patriotism, and they feel confident that when the impartial historian
shall write the record of mens devotion to Religious freedom, civil law, and equal rights,
to all, no name will fill a brighter page than yours. . . ." L, Smithsonian Institution.

On Oct. 19, William L. Ellsworth, New York City, wrote to USG. *"Personal* . . . I enclose you a copy of the Resolutions passed at the recent meeting of the Grand Council of
this State, of which I have the honor to be a member of the Committee on Resolutions—I
will simply add that I concur with them in every particular & hope to see you renominated
for the position you now occupy—I have no doubt but that you can count on the American Vote in convention & otherwise—" ALS, USG 3. Enclosed are resolutions of the
American Political League, Grand Council of the State of New York, dated Oct. 16. ". . .
Resolved that the American Public School system of this Country is one of the elements of

its glory & strength, & must not be interfered with by demagogues or Prince in the interest of any foreign religious Potentate   Resolved, That we have entire confidence in the fidelity & patriotism of the President of the United States, Ulysses S. Grant, recognizing in him the valorous Soldier whose services in the field culminated in crushing the recent gigantic rebellion—and whose impartial exercise of the duties imposed upon him as the head of this Government, and during a season of general business stagnation and financial embarrassment, entitle him to the thanks of every American Citizen . . ." Copy, *ibid.* On Dec. 1, 1876, Ellsworth, chief secretary, American Alliance, Philadelphia, wrote to USG. "'Hold the Fort' untill a new Election for President. Call upon the loyal States for assistance (if nescessary) to maintain order. You will be supported by the people and the American Alliance favor this action   I have the honor to heartily Concur as I ever have in your reelection. Call upon me in any way in the cause. . . . My regards to Genl Ingalls." ALS, *ibid.*

On Oct. 28, 1875, Peter Cooper, New York City, had written to USG. "Your speech given to the Army of the Tennessee at Des Moines on the 30th of September, has just come to my notice. The sentiments which I find expressed in it, are so just, so patriotic, and so worthy of the chief magistrate of a great Republic, that I feel impelled to ask you to accept my thanks. It is well said by a soldier who contributed so largely to emancipate his country from a perpetual war against chattel slavery, 'that if we are to have another contest in the near future for our national existence, I predict that the dividing line will not be Mason's and Dixon's, but between patriotism and intelligence on the one hand, and superstition, ambition, and ignorance on the other.' These are foes which the sword alone can never put down. Hence it is a matter of great importance that our rulers should have the intelligence and patriotism that can cope with these enemies of our Republic. These are times that call, in an eminent degree, for that fidelity to truth, and knowledge of affairs in the administration of the public trusts, which alone can stem the superstition that would invade our education, resist the ambition that would overthrow our liberties, and enlighten the ignorance that would darken the councils of the nation. Permit me again to thank you for the excellent sentiments of your address, and for the patriotism and intelligence which dictated your whole speech on so worthy an occasion. . . . P. S. I herewith send you a pamphlet on the all-important question of the currency, to which I respectfully call your attention." LS, *ibid.* On Oct. 30, Theodore Bourne, corresponding secretary, American Common School League, New York City, wrote to USG. "*Private . . .* I should have addressed you before but have been so busy with the great work before us—But I must pause a moment to express here great gratification I derived from perusing your address before the Army of the Tennessee, Sept 30 especially that portion which relates to the Common Schools and the Bible as the foundation of our free Institutions   The very day your address was delivered I was engaged in perfecting the organization of the American Common School League copies of the prospectus & Constitution of which I forward—It had occurred to me, in July, that such an Association was needed and when the Republican Party adopted the Resolution number 9 of the Platform at Saratoga they evinced both wisdom and courage, and I determined to carry out the plans I had formed—. . . You can better imagine than I describe how I felt when after my *preliminary work* was ended, by assembling those who consented to act with me on the 1st October I read your speech in defence of our Schools—Surely Divine Providence is directing our Nation to a better destiny than to bow down to the Minions of Rome or truckle for the Irish Roman vote   I look upon your address as having been like the *blast of a trumpet* to startle our MOUSING POLITICIANS. It *will be of great service in this campaign*—In fact that *address*; the Ninth Resolution of our Platform and the 'American Common School League' will I believe give the Republican Party the victory here in Novr. With sincere hope that the Divine blessing will be with and shield you, and bless our united efforts for His cause . . . P. S. I also enclose some new songs by Wm Oland Bourne formerly Editor of the 'Soldiers Friend & Grand Army of the Republic' which are stirring the hearts of thousands: All our Methodist Churches are red-hot with enthusiasm as well as the other sects but they are *several degrees* below the *Methodists*." ALS, *ibid.* The enclosures are *ibid.* In Oct., James F. Simmons, Troy, N. Y., wrote to USG. "The words You spoke at the Soldiers Reunion Des Moines, has thrilled Many Loyal Hearts throughout the Union   And if at any future time, the hated Jesuitas should dare to show their hands, You have to only speak the word, and the Grand Army will rally around You, Phenix like from its own ashes." ALS, *ibid.* Probably in Oct., Thomas M. Kennedy, Rockford, Ill., wrote to USG seeking a consular position. ". . . Regardless of consequences I have Since I became a Citizen thought it my duty to Support the Republican party and Shall never change as long as the Institution is conducted as it is now. I am entirely opposed to any change in the present School System of the Country in as much as I know that it would be the ruin of many children who are now doing well, in fine were such tolerated the children of Calic Parents would be as unfit for business as if they came direct from any foreign country   I know that Americans and especially the enlightened Republican Party has been our best friends—I am Married and two Bright children going to School and I Must Say they not only have learned well but they are Polite and respectful. . . ." ALS (docketed Oct. 19), DNA, RG 59, Letters of Application and Recommendation. Related papers are *ibid.* No appointment followed.

On Nov. 11, Carl H. Horsch, proprietor, Pine Grove Mineral Springs, Dover, N. H., wrote to USG. "Your truly sublime and prophetic words uttered at Des Moines, thrill every fibre and attribute of a developed liberal body and soul! You manifest, that you are also a General in this struggle which is going on even now, and if you fight the battles as well and successfully, as you did in our late contest, you will do more for the maintainance and the promotion of the principles unfolded in the Declaration of Indep. and the Constitution, than any other man has been able to do thus far. But before we can enjoy the ripe fruit of that beautiful blossom 'All men are created free and equal' and have in reality 'free speech, a free press, pure morals, unfettered religious sentiments and equal rights and privileges to all men irrespective of nationality color or religion, the separation of Church and State must be complete. No protestant's or any other dictated fast days. No ordered or enforced religious services sustained by the government. No exemption from taxation of ecclestiastical property. No formal judicial oath (:That will be the free citizen land where an oath is given by the shaking of hands!:) Equal rights to both sexes, and true religion. Our contest will be: To free us from the stil remaining ecclestiastical favoritism, egotism and pretensions. With the hope and the sincere wish, that you may live long, and labor for and with us for the promotion of those principles expressed in your speach, and we may with all mankind enjoy Universal Liberty." ALS, USG 3. On Nov. 16, Henry O. Wagoner, Denver, wrote to USG. "My dear Man, that Speech at Des Moine, as I thought at the time, Struck the Key-Note to the American people. Like Sampson of old, you then and there felt the pillars of the National temple. 'Third term and Caesarism' have about spent their force. One Man in the right, with God upon his side, is a Majority against the Universe. Pardon this intrusion in the midst of Message labors—" ALS, *ibid.*

On Feb. 21, 1876, Thomas Royall, Louisville, wrote to USG. "*Personal:* . . . As an Englishman, and a resident in the Australia for upwards of 20 years, and a correspondent for one of the largest journals at Sydney, New South Wales: I take pleasure in clipping from my late files, & enclosing you—your words uttered at 'Des Moines' I'oa last year, upon the subject of Education,   I had these inserted in the papers at Sydney, & since that time numerous Editorials and comments have appeared in the columns of the press commending the pregnant wisdom therein displayed: for every word therein stated is strictly in consonance with the Education Act, *now in force in the Aust: Colonies* & for which the Colonists, have stoutly fought, and opposed the influence of [th]e 'Roman Catholic Church,' [*who*] very bitterly traversed the liberal measures enacted by Parliament of New South Wales. we have now in force there, one of the most liberal measures, ever passed into Law in any land, upon the Education question; & one constantly quoted, by the leading Statesmen of Her Majesty's (Queen Victoria's) Parliament. I shall take plasure in sending you a copy thereof at no distant period." ALS, *ibid.* The enclosure is *ibid.*

    1. On Sept. 22, 1875, USG had written to John C. Smith, former col. and bvt. brig. gen. "Your letter of the 14th inst. extending an invitation to me to attend the reunion of the 96th Regiment, Illinois Volunteers, was duly received. I regret that public duties will prevent my acceptance, but I hope you will have a most agreeable meeting, and that you may all live to have many more such, and that at some time in the future, it may be my good fortune to be with you." *Reception to the Ninety-Sixth Regiment, Illinois Infantry Volunteers, . . .* (Chicago, 1890), p. 77. This reunion took place at Waukegan, Ill., Sept. 28–29.

    2. See letter to Joseph A. Harwood, April 27, 1875.

    3. On Aug. 28, Levi P. Luckey had written to Lewis M. Dayton, recording secretary. "The President directs me to enclose you four dollars the amount of the receipt you sent a day or two since for dues of the Society of the Army of the Tenn." Copy, DLC-USG, II, 3.

To J. Russell Jones

Denver, Colorado, Oct. 5th *1875*

DEAR JONES:

    I have just signed a commission for Sec. of the Int. and forwarded to Mr. Luckey, private Secretary in Washington, with instructions to fill your name in if you accept, which I hope you will do.

    On receipt of this I wish you would telegraph me your decission saying "I accept" in case you do; and in case you do not telegraph enquiring when my party will be in Chicago.

    Mr. Delano's resignation took effect on the first of Oct. By the revised Statutes the place should be filled within ten days, in this case by the eleventh of this month. I hope therefore you will take the first train for Washington after this reaches you and qualify. You may then return to Chicago and say good buy to the people.

                          Respectfully yours

                          U. S. GRANT

HON. J. RUSSELL JONES, CHICAGO, ILL.

ALS (on Grand Central Hotel stationery), George Jones, Chicago, Ill.; copy (in Orville E. Babcock's hand), USG 3. On Oct. 8, 1875, J. Russell Jones, collector of customs, Chicago, telegraphed to USG. "When will Your Party be in Chicago? where will a letter reach You" Telegram received (at 4:30 P.M.), *ibid*. On Oct. 9, Jones wrote to USG. "I have written Babcock fully why I was compelled to decline the secretaryship of the Interior, and he will hand you the letter. It was the tightest position I was ever placed in. If I had not felt sure that my wife could not have survived two winters at Washington, and did not my pecuniary condition imperatively demand that I should turn my attention to getting out of debt, it would have been the happiest event of my life to have availed myself of your great kindness, for which I hasten to express to you my profound gratitude. I hope to live long enough to be able to prove to you that I fully appreciate this new proof of your kindness to me, and that I am not now, and shall not hereafter be lacking in devotion to you and your interests. If I could have known a little sooner what was in store for me I could have shaped matters so that by leaving Mrs Jones here I could have accepted, but, with a debt of over $60.000 hanging over me, I dare not leave. It will keep me pegging away for several years—with good luck, to work out of debt. I earnestly hope that my action has not occasioned you serious inconvenience, and—with kind regards to Mrs Grant, . . ." ALS, *ibid*. Probably in Sept. or Oct., [Bluford Wilson], solicitor of the treasury, wrote to his brother James H. Wilson. "The succession to the [In]terior Department seems difficult of satisfactory solution. Fish is against Jones . . ." AL (damaged), Wy-Ar. Another damaged letter acknowledging "the good news about Jones" is *ibid*. See also *Chicago Tribune*, Oct. 14, 1875.

On Oct. 10 and 14, Secretary of State Hamilton Fish recorded in his diary. "Anxious as I have been for nearly a fortnight to go to New York but detained by the uncertainty of the Presidents wish and intention with respect to filling the vacancy in the Interior Department I request Mr Brown to go today after church to the White House and ascertain if any information had been received there Between one & two oclock he came to my house accompanyed by Mr Sniffin Assistant Private Secretary to the President who had a blank commission signed by the President (the same which I forwarded to him a fortnight ago today and which had been returned together with my letter written two weeks ago) without any name inserted. He said a name was to be sent by telegraph and thought I might sign it in blank and allow the name subsequently to be filled in I did not feel that I was authorized to do this and being anxious to go to New York tonight I ask that should a telegraph be received before 6 'oclock it should be brought to me with the commission which I would then sign; but I fear that we will hear nothing further of it" "Going to Newark to attend the wedding of John Davis I met Secretary Robeson in the cars who tells me that he has seen Horace Porter the evening before who had informed him that the Secretaryship had been offered to Russell Jones who had declined the offer; and that the President since had offered it to Zack Chandler who would accept. He states that the President and Chandler would be in Washington probably this day or tomorrow." DLC-Hamilton Fish.

On Oct. 15, a correspondent reported from Washington, D. C. "Upon the arrival of the President this morning notice was sent to members of the Cabinet to meet him in council at noon. . . . The President announced the name of Secretary Delano's successor, and enjoined secrecy until the gentleman who has been tendered the place can be heard from. . . ." *New York Times*, Oct. 16, 1875. On Oct. 18, Saturday, another correspondent reported from Washington, D. C. "It can be positively stated that ex-Senator Chandler, of Michigan, had not, to 11 o'clock to-night, been offered the position of Secretary of the Interior, as has been announced, but it is pretty certain that he will have an interview with the President to-morrow morning, . . . There is not much doubt that the position had been previously offered to ex-Senator Pratt, Commissioner of Internal Revenue, who, for personal and other reasons, has declined to accept it. Ex-Gov. Dennison, of Ohio, was also offered the office, but he declined it, last Saturday. . . ." *Chicago Tribune*, Oct. 19, 1875. On

Oct. 19, correspondents again reported from Washington, D. C. "Ex-Senator Chandler held a long interview with the President this morning and accepted the appointment of Secretary of the Interior. The commission was made out immediately, . . ." *New York Times*, Oct. 20, 1875. "It would be difficult to describe the effect produced here by the appointment of ex-Senator Zach Chandler to the Cabinet position of Secretary of the Interior. . . . The appointment is said to be 'Grant all over,' and shows that at this ticklish period of the career of the republican party the President is not afraid to intimate afresh his cherished belief that he is stronger than his party, . . . There is bad blood between the President and Simon Cameron. It seems that on last Saturday the ex-Secretary of War came down from Pennsylvania to get the Secretaryship for ex-Congressman Scofield, of Erie. The President, who was in no humor to see him, much less to listen to the demand, snubbed him. . . ." *New York Herald*, Oct. 20, 1875. In 1875, George H. Williams wrote to USG praising Zachariah Chandler's appointment. William Evarts Benjamin, Catalogue No. 42, March, 1892, p. 23. See letter to Hamilton Fish, Sept. 10, 1875; *New York Times*, Oct. 12, 1875; *New York Tribune*, Oct. 19, 20, 1875; *Chicago Tribune*, Oct. 20, 1875; Harry James Brown and Frederick D. Williams, eds., *The Diary of James A. Garfield* (East Lansing, Mich., 1967–81), III, 168–69; Nevins, *Fish*, pp. 778–80; Mary Karl George, *Zachariah Chandler: A Political Biography* (East Lansing, Mich., 1969), pp. 241–44.

To John F. Long

Chicago, Oct. 12th *1875*

DEAR JUDGE

I am just in receipt of your letter saying that Carlin claimed to have written authority to remain on the farm and keep stock until Spring! I have no recollectio[n] of giving such authority and certainly do not approve of it. I wish you would proceed as you had proposed to do and free me from all responsibility for debts contracted by others.

We have had a delightful trip to the Mountains and are now hurrying back to Washington to commence the labors of the Winter.

Sincerely Yours

U. S. GRANT

JUDGE J. F. LONG

ALS, Goodspeed's Book Shop, Inc., Boston, Mass. Written on stationery of the Palmer House. On Oct. 13, 1875, John F. Long, St. Louis, wrote to Nathaniel Carlin. "I am just in receipt of Presidents Grant's Letter of the 12th inst. in which he directs me to carry out his instruction given me in my office on the 26th ult:—to close out all his personal property on the farm, and to rent or lease out the Farm—and to give possession upon perfecting the Lease. Hence I advise you that I shall sell all remaining property on the farm (included in the schedule you furnished the Prest.) on Tuesday next the 19th inst. And that from the 20th inst your Services on the farm will cease. Your personal services will be paid for to that date." ALS, CSmH. On Oct. 16 (twice) and 19, Levi P. Luckey wrote to Long. "I see by your letter of Oct. 6th to the President that you ask when Mr. Carlin's salary commenced. I asked him if he answered the question and he said he did not remember. By his direction I send you the accounts sent by Carlin from the time he commenced up to about June 1st last year since which time he has sent none. I suggested that as you were going to settle with Mr. Carlin that you should have these accounts." "The President directs me to write and say that in any leases you may make of part of the farm to date them the 5th of November. His idea is that he wishes to be without loss & to have the reservation till that date in case he should conclude to make another arrangement." "The President has executed the Power of Attorney in your name and directs me to enclose it to you" Copies, DLC-USG, II, 3. See letter to John F. Long, Nov. 29, 1874.

On April 5, 1876, Culver C. Sniffen wrote to Long. "The President directs me to acknowledge the receipt of your letter of the 27th ult. & to say that all necessary fencing on his farm may be made, to be paid for by the tenants and to be deducted from their rent. The fence may be a post & rail or any other that you will approve." Copy, DLC-USG, II, 3. On May 26, Ulysses S. Grant, Jr., wrote to Long. "Your letter of the 20th received—The President directs me to say that the renewal of insurance on the buildings is all right—He was glad to know that you had attended to the matter—" Copy, *ibid.*

To John F. Long

—————

Oct. 15th /75

Dear Judge,

Mr. Frank Wells has arrived with the eight horses in his charge, in fair condition with the exception of one of them which was bit by the other horses. Nothing serious however.

I wish you would be good enough to get for me the pedigree, of the six sent to me, and that you also get the same of Claymore for Gov. Hunt.[1]

We just arrived here this morning, all well after a most delightful trip.

Very Truly Yours
U. S. Grant

Judge J. F. Long

ALS, Williams College, Williamstown, Mass.

1. USG presented the stallion Claymore to former Governor Alexander C. Hunt of Colorado Territory. See *PUSG*, 19, 357; letter to Adolph E. Borie, Sept. 25, 1874, note 1;

Julia Lipsey, *Governor Hunt of Colorado Territory: His Life and His Family* (Colorado Springs, 1960), p. 16.

On Jan. 20, 1876, Levi P. Luckey wrote to Hunt, Denver. "The President directs me to write you and say that while in the Territory he stated that he would take $5000 00 bonds in the D. P. & R. narrow gauge rail road. After his return he received a letter from Gen. Palmer suggesting that he should take seven bonds of $1000 each, which at $750. made $5,250. to be paid in monthly installments of $1,050, and asking whether he should draw for the money or whether the President would pay in an other manner proposed in the letter. The President answered to draw monthly at sight. The draft was presented and paid for November, but since that time he has heard nothing. Please advise him in regard to this matter and either have the money paid returned or the bonds delivered where they may be had when the last payment is made." Copy, DLC-USG, II, 3. On Oct. 25, 1875, Orville E. Babcock had written to William J. Palmer, Denver & Rio Grande Railway Co., Philadelphia. "The President directs me to say in reply to your favor of the 20th inst. that he will take the seven bonds $5250. and that you can draw on him for the money as it becomes due. He says you need not hold the other subject to his order any longer." Copy, *ibid.* On Jan. 31, 1876, Luckey wrote to Palmer. "The President directs me to say that he is unable to find the certificate for the first installment of 20%, which he paid in November, on his subscription to the stock of the D. & R. G. Ry. Co. and thinks it must have been destroyed and thrown in his waste basket as he does not remember of seeing it. Will you be good enough to have a duplicate issued and sent to him, and very much oblige him." Copy, *ibid.* On Dec. 15, Palmer, New York City, wrote to Ulysses S. Grant, Jr. "In response to your favor of 13th Inst—I would say—that there were issued to the President—the following securities for the $5250. paid in. $7000 in Bonds of the Denver & Rio Grande Rw. Co. $7000 in Stock of the Denver & Rio Grande Rw. Co. $2100 in Stock of The Southern Colorado Coal & Iron Co. The Coupons of the Bonds—due Nov 1. last—are payable by Mess Rutten & Bon[n]—52 Exchange Place New York—By depositing the Coupons in Bank at Washington they will be placed to your credit. The previous interest—to May 1. 1876 (7% gold per annum on $7000. Bonds—was paid to the President direct—by My check May 1. When the developement of the trade of the Country, and of the Coal Mines near Trinidad, enables dividends to be paid upon the stocks (which were issued as a bonus to the subscribers)—you will be advised. Please give the President my kindest regards," ALS (tabular material expanded), USG 3. See John S. Fisher, *A Builder of the West: The Life of General William Jackson Palmer* (Caldwell, Idaho, 1939); Robert G. Athearn, *Rebel of the Rockies: A History of the Denver and Rio Grande Western Railroad* (New Haven, 1962).

To George W. Atherton

Oct. 16th /75

DEAR SIR:

I shall be out this evening, probably as late as eleven Oclock, too late to receive the Copy of the report of the Red Cloud investigating Committee which I will be glad to receive as well as to see you in person. If you do not leave the city before Monday[1] evening I will be glad to receive it at any hour on Monday, or, if you choose, any hour to-morrow after one O'clock p. m.

Very respectfully

your obt. svt.

U. S. GRANT

PROF G. W. ATHERTON,

ALS, Pennsylvania State University, University Park, Pa. George W. Atherton served as 1st lt., 10th Conn., graduated from Yale, and accepted a series of professorial appointments. On Oct. 16, 1875, Atherton, Rutgers College, New Brunswick, N. J., wrote to USG. "I have the honor herewith to transmit a copy of the report of the Red Cloud investigating commission, together with a printed copy of the accompanying testimony. Referring to your telegram of appointment of July 27, 1875, and the letter of instructions of July 30, 1875, received from you through the Secretary of the Interior, I have the honor to state that immediately on receipt of your telegram I proceeded to Cheyenne, where I joined Messrs. Fletcher, Harris, and Faulkner on the 31st of July. They had already taken testimony in New York, Omaha, and Cheyenne, which they placed at my disposal, and from that time onward I have fully participated in all their work, including the preparation of the report now submitted. The commission has acted throughout as a single body, and the conclusions reached are the result of our joint deliberations, and express our unanimous judgment. For this reason I have, at the request of the three members nominated by the Board of Indian Commissioners, joined them in signing the report which they have addressed to that body, of which the one herewith transmitted is a copy. It may be proper to say, however, that in case my conclusions had differed on any important point from those of the other members of the commission, I should have deemed it my duty to submit to you a separate report, but the course which I have adopted seemed more in accordance with the spirit of your instructions, and I trust it will meet your approval. The Hon. Timothy O. Howe, to whom, jointly with myself, your letter of instructions was addressed, has been present with the commission during a small part of its investigations. He was not present at any time during the preparation of the report, and his name consequently does not appear among the signers." *Report of the Special Commission Appointed to Investigate the Affairs of the Red Cloud Indian Agency, July, 1875* (Washington, 1875), p. LXXVII. On the same day, Thomas C. Fletcher, Benjamin W. Harris, Charles J. Faulkner, and Atherton issued a report that disputed or modified many of Othniel C. Marsh's allegations concerning fraud in the Red Cloud Agency. See *ibid.*, pp. XV–LXXV; letter to Othniel C. Marsh, July 16, 1875; letter to Wayne MacVeagh, July 22, 1875; *New York Times*, Oct. 5, 19, 1875; Roger L. Williams, *The Origins of Federal Support for Higher Education: George W. Atherton and the Land-Grant College Movement* (University Park, Pa., 1991); William H. Armstrong, *A Friend to God's Poor: Edward Parmelee Smith* (Athens, Ga., 1993), pp. 370–74.

On Nov. 1 and 2, a correspondent reported from Washington, D. C. "Several Pastors in this City, of different denominations, who were apprehensive that the Government was about to abandon its peace policy toward the Indians, called upon the President to-day to express their conviction that such a course would greatly disappoint Christian people in all parts of the country, and be a blow to the cause of Christianity throughout the world. The President, with great promptness and precision, replied that he did not regard the peace policy a failure, and that it not only would not be abandoned while he occupied that place, but that it was his hope that during his administration it would become so firmly established as to be the necessary policy of his successors. . . ." "Secretary Chandler, accompanied by Assistant Secretary Cowen, called at the Executive mansion to-day and had a long talk with the President, mainly in regard to Indian affairs. Secretary Belknap and Gens. Sheridan and Crooke participated in the conference, and gave expression to their well-known opinions concerning the Indian question, besides furnishing much information respecting the practical administration of the peace policy within the limits of their past and present commands." *New York Times*, Nov. 2, 4, 1875.

1. Oct. 18.

To Edwards Pierrepont

Oct. 18th /75

DEAR JUDGE:

By reference to the Star of this evening I see that Bonner has been appointed Marshal of the E. district of Mo. I recollect that you told me that the resignation of Newcomb, and the endorsements for Bonner[1] had come in such a way that you supposed it was with my knowledge and approval, and that you had therefore made out his commission. I presume it has been put beforme me, and that I have signed it without looking at it. I hope it is not to late to stop it before it reaches Mr. Bonner's hands. Either St Gem[2] or Leffingwell[3]—I think the former—should be appointed.

Very Respectfully
Your obt. svt.
U. S. GRANT

HON. EDWARDS PIERREPONT ATTY. GEN. U. S.

ALS, DNA, RG 60, Records Relating to Appointments. On Oct. 11, Attorney Gen. Edwards Pierrepont wrote to Secretary of State Hamilton Fish requesting a commission for Benjamin R. Bonner as marshal, Eastern District, Mo., in place of Carman A. Newcomb. Copy, *ibid.*, Letters Sent to Executive Officers. See letter to Edwards Pierrepont, Sept. 27, 1875.

On Nov. 5, John B. Henderson, St. Louis, wrote to Bluford Wilson, solicitor of the treasury, concerning the marshalship. ". . . In August last, you remember, I made no positive recommendation in the conversation on the subject with General Pierrepont, General Bristow, and yourself. In September, however, a letter came from General Pierrepont to Colonel D., asking him to consult me, and that we join in a recommendation of some fit person. We consulted, and agreed on Benjamin R. Bonner, of this city. I naturally supposed that the appointment would at once be made; but owing, I presume, to the President's absence, it was delayed till telegrams came announcing the appointment of Bonner, and finally until other candidates found out by some means that Colonel Dyer and myself had recommended Bonner. Thereupon, divers persons from this city, who seem to know more about the duty of the Government attorneys than they do themselves, proceeded to Washington and most kindly informed the President that I was a most bitter and relentless enemy of his, both personally and politically, and that the appointment of Bonner was a scheme devised to aid in the purposes of my malevolence. They further urged him to think, as I have reason to believe, that the developments here as to his secretary, General Babcock, were nothing but a put-up job to strike the President himself by aspersions and calumnies upon persons occupying confidential relations with him. These things were said, not because they had one particle of foundation in truth, but simply to effect the defeat of Bonner and the appointment of their own favorites. These things so long delayed the appointment that Newcomb had already been compelled to summon both grand and petit jurors for the term. After this was done, it was exceedingly doubtful whether it would be politic to change officers until after the court, and this conviction was the more strongly impressed upon my mind by the antecedents of some of those who might be appointed. How easy for the incoming man to practice treachery and place the responsibility of our failure on the shoulders of the outgoing officer who summoned the juries; hence, with a double view, one in the interest of the public service here, and the other to thwart a political trick which its projectors expected to accomplish through falsehood to the President and injustice to me, I telegraphed to General Pierrepont to postpone the change of marshals, but in the course of ten days after that dispatch signed by Eaton and myself, I became satisfied that the present marshal should not be retained on my responsibility, and Eaton seemed to feel equally the necessity of divesting himself of all responsibility in that behalf. . . . To conclude on this subject, the Department has my recommendation of Mr. Bonner for that place, and I do not and shall not change it, and still believe he should be appointed. Circumstances are such as to make it impossible for me to intimate that Mr. Newcomb should remain. . . ." *HMD*, 44-1-186, 401. Henderson, former U.S. Senator from Mo., assisted U.S. Attorney David P. Dyer in prosecuting the whiskey ring cases. See Endorsement, Dec. 3, 1875. On Nov. 10, Wilson, St. Louis, telegraphed to USG, New York City. "Public interests imperitively demand a change in the Marshalls Office here; George W. Fishback is strongly recommended by our friends, and I have no doubt will make a good officer." Copy, DLC-Benjamin H. Bristow.

On May 22, William D. W. Barnard, St. Louis, had written to USG. "I write in the interest of Hon. Robt C Allen of this County, who is an applicant for the Marshalship of this District—Judge Allen was a thorough and uncomprising friend of the Gov't from the start—a pronounced Republican, of action—was in the army during the entire war; I am informed, and has been since its close, one of our County Judges and an active member of our State Cenl Rep. Committee—a man of mature judgement, fearless and upright; whose integrity is beyond reproach—and party fealty unquestioned—. . ." ALS, DNA, RG 60, Records Relating to Appointments. Related papers are *ibid*. On Sept. 30, Lucien Eaton, St. Louis, wrote to Pierrepont. "*Confidential* . . . The fact of the resignation of the Marshal of this District is published tonight. Among the aspirants for the place is Robt. Allen one of the Justices of our County Court—an administrative & not judicial body. He has been obtaining recommendations for months. I desire to say that he ought not to be appointed for all the reasons that made the present incumbent's resignation desirable. One or two thoroughly good men have been thought of but I do not wish even to recommend a man till I *know* he would accept if appointed" ALS, *ibid*. Letters recommending Lyne S. Metcalf, Wrenshall Fielding, Hiram W. Snyder, and Edwin Ticknor to replace Newcomb are *ibid*.

1. On Sept. 21, Bonner, St. Louis, had written to USG. "There is a prevailing rumor that the U S Marshall for the Eastern District of Mo will retire from that office at an early day. *Assuming this to be true* I respectfully solicit your favorable consideration of my application for the office, and trust you will regard my appointment as consistant with the public good. I am authorized by *Hon Robt Campbell,* Col. *A R Easton* and *Genl A G Edwards* to say that should you be pleased to refer to them for information they will cheerfully recommend me for the position. It will be my pleasure to administer the office with the *strictest fidelity* in *the honor* and *integrity* of the government." ALS, *ibid.* On Oct. 22, Jacob S. Merrell, chairman, Republican Central Committee, St. Louis County, telegraphed to USG. "I have known B R Bonner intimately for twenty years   would recommend & prefer him for marshal to any other living man   will write explaining former telegram" Telegram received (at 4:32 P.M.), DLC-USG, IB. On the same day, Merrell wrote to USG. "Yesterday I signed a Telegram to your Honor, stating Mr. St. Gem would be acceptable to the Republicans of this city as U. S. Marshall. The motive I had in signing that was that I was informed the appointment lay between Mr. St Gem and Mr. Leffinwell.   the latter I felt verry decided ~~would~~ was not the proper man for the position, and at the same time I stated I considered Mr. B. R. Bonner the best man for the place, and today when I learned the choice did not rest between St. Gem & Leffinwell, I Telegraphed you my views. There is no man I believe better qualified, or more acceptable to the Republicans or Administration party of this state than the Hon. B. B. Bonner, and I feel it a pleasant duty to endorse him, and to explain the Telegram I signed yesterday" ALS, DNA, RG 60, Records Relating to Appointments. Related papers are *ibid.* On Oct. 26, Bonner telegraphed to USG. "Will you hold open appointment of marshal until I can reach Washn'" Telegram received (at 5:05 P.M.), *ibid.*

2. Descended from French settlers of St. Genevieve, Mo., Gustavus St. Gem engaged in lead mining, served as capt., 47th Mo., and moved to St. Louis, where he sold real estate. On Oct. 11, Chauncey I. Filley, St. Louis, had written to Pierrepont. "I would most respectfully submit to your attention and consideration as a proper and in every qualified person to fill the Vacancy in the office of U S Marshal of the Eastern District of Missouri Gustavus St Gem of St Geneveive Mo. Col St Gem was an out and out Unionist from the commencement of the War and prior thereto. He has been an upright and thorough Republican and one of the organizers of the party in Missouri   He is in accord with the true Republicans of the State. Has been elected and served in the Legislature and Constitutional Convention of 1865 which abolished Slavery. He is a fluent German speaker and also French   He is well known throughout the State and knows the State   He has never bolted a convention and has been a delegate to every Republican State Convention. He was a delegate to the last Philadelphia National Convention. He has no connection nor never had, with any rings—and the Administration and the prosecution of the cases at St Louis cannot find a truer man to represent its interests." ALS, *ibid.* On Oct. 18, Daniel T. Jewett, St. Louis, telegraphed to USG. "If there is no Show for Ramsey Colonel St-Gem would give full satisfaction to the true republicans   dont want Bonner" Telegram received (at 4:00 P.M.), *ibid.* On Oct. 25 and 26, Filley wrote and telegraphed to USG. "Herewith find reccommendation from Hon Amadee Valle who is well calculated to speak for the old French people   Hon Isidor Bush who is a representative Israelite. Judge John H Fisse who is a leading & honored German   Judge John Grether Same kind and Biebinger of 4th nat Bank   I have met with no square Administration Republican who knows of St Gems application but think it a most fitting one to be made. . . . The majority of, & every man approached ~~by~~of the Republican County Committee reccommend St Gem Earnestly which paper will be forwarded" "Forwarded last evening recommendations of leading French German & Israelite citizens for Stgem   the majority of, and every one seen of the county

republican Committee endorse him in the face of all the known applicants,   The latest ru-
mored appointment is not favorably received. If Stgem has no show as between Stevenson
& Leffingwell would prefer latter though dont think either would give satisfaction to the
party friends   the selection of a tried republican & thoroughly competent person from the
interior of the state free from any combinations or complications whose character habits
& ability past & present presents a guarantee for future fitness and credit to the administration and office such Stgem is looked upon and thus remove the acrimony & rivalry existing among the many city applicants   there can be no honest objection made to him by
the public & his appointment would be received with general satisfaction" ALS and telegram received, *ibid.* On Oct. 29, R. J. Wilkinson *et al.*, St. Louis, telegraphed to USG. "In
behalf of the Colored citizens of the City we would respectfully recommend Col St Jem as
one known to have been tried & true & whose appointment would give our people increased confidence & satisfaction." Telegram received, *ibid.* Related papers are *ibid.*

        3. Born in 1809 in Mass., Hiram W. Leffingwell settled in St. Louis in 1843 and pur-
sued a career in real estate and as a surveyor, laying out the city's Grand Avenue and Forest Park. On Dec. 15, USG nominated Leffingwell as marshal. See *PUSG*, 20, 77; letter to
Alton R. Easton, Nov. 21, 1875.

To Adolph E. Borie

————

Nov. 4th /75

My Dear Mr. Borie:

        Can you not come down to-morrow and spend Saturday & Sun-
day with me? Bring Drexel or Childs, or both with you. We may succeed in wining a few more shares of the Ledger.

        New York & Pa did splendidly yesterday.[1]

Yours Truly
U. S. Grant

ALS, PHi.

        1. On Tuesday, Nov. 2, Republicans had carried state and local elections in N. Y. and
Pa. See Speech, Nov. 6, 1875.

To Oliver Hoyt

———

Nov. 4th 1875.

DEAR SIR:

Both the new Sec. of the Int. and myself believe that public opinion demands a change of the present Commissioner of Indian Affairs,[1] and I feel disposed, in this instance, to listen to its demand. I
will state however that my confidence in the integrity and zeal of the
present incumbent is not in the least degree shaken. But I think a
[change will answer (insure) the public interest—so much by way of
prelude. The real object in my writing to you now, is to ask if you
will accept the position. It is one of considerable labor, and respon-
siblity, but at the same time it is a position where a person may do a
great deal of good—I hope you will see your way clear to accept it.
May I ask an early reply to this, and ask at the same time that you do
not communicate the substance of this until a commissioner is appointed if you should decline. With high regard,

Your obt. svt.

U. S. GRANT.]

OLIVER HOYT, ESQ STAMFORD, CONN.

AL (partial facsimile, bracketed material not in USG's hand), Superior Galleries Manuscript Auction, Part I, May 29, 1993, no. 287; copy (incomplete), DLC-USG, II, 3. USG did
not nominate Oliver Hoyt as commissioner of Indian Affairs. See letter to Oliver Hoyt,
Aug. 27, 1875.

On Nov. 16, 1875, Robert Campbell, St. Louis, wrote to USG. "I have the honor to acknowledge receipt of your Telegram of 13th inst asking if I would accept the position of
Commnr of Indian affairs, to which I replied on 15th respectfully declining   My private
business requires my personal attention and I could not possibly go to Washington to fill
any office, and it would be doing a wrong to you, to accept an office without giving all the
time and my best ability to discharge the duty faithfully   The matter will be kept confidential   Accept my thanks for your kind confidence" ALS, USG 3. See *New York Times*,
Nov. 17, 1875; William H. Armstrong, *A Friend to God's Poor: Edward Parmelee Smith*
(Athens, Ga., 1993), pp. 374–75.

On Nov. 27, Secretary of the Interior Zachariah Chandler telegraphed to Orville E.
Babcock. "Has the Boston man been heard from?" Telegram received, DLC-USG, IB. On
Nov. 27 and 29, a correspondent reported from Washington, D. C. "The appointment of
a Commissioner of Indian Affairs in place of Mr. Smith has been tendered to Edward S. Tobey, of Boston. Mr. Tobey is here to-night at the request of the President and the Secretary of the Interior. . . ." "Mr. E. S. Tobey, of Boston, informed Secretary Chandler this afternoon that he feels obliged to decline the position of Commissioner of Indian Affairs,

tendered him by the President, as private business, and especially a large trust recently confided to him, will require his personal attention at home. . . . Mr. Tobey is President of the American Missionary Association, and a retired merchant of the highest standing. . . ." *New York Times*, Nov. 28, 30, 1875. On Nov. 29, Edward S. Tobey, Washington, D. C., wrote to USG. "In compliance with your request I have carefully reviewed the grounds of my declination of the office of Commissioner of Indian Affairs, as tendered to me in your communicat[i]on received in Boston more than a week since. My experience for three years as a member of the Board of Indian Commissioners has served to deepen my conviction of the importance and practical character of your humane and energetic policy toward the Indian tribes of our country, and that the department of the Government to which you have kindly invited my services affords no ordinary opportunity of usefulness to one who is in cordial sympathy with your purposes, and who is prepared to give that undivided and assiduous attention which shall secure a faithful and efficient administration of the affairs of the Indian Department in their minutest detail. As such service the Government and people emphatically demand, and they ought not and will not be satisfied with anything less, to fulfill these conditions, were I to accept the position, would require a transfer of my residence to Washington, and oblige me to seriously prejudice interests which cannot properly be delegated to others at the present time. I am therefore reluctantly brought to my original decision, that it is incompatible with existing duties and obligations to accept the position which you have offered me   Allow me to express the sincere hope that you will be able to accomplish your well-known purpose of obtaining the services of an able and faithful officer, whose established character will be a pledge that his duties will be fearlessly discharged, above and beyond all mere political influence or considerations. I have the fullest assurance and confidence that such an officer will have the cordial and energetic cooperation of the Honorable Secretary of the Interior, and those working harmoniously and in mutual sympathy with the Board of Indian Commissioners, under the sanction of your authority and influence, will doubtless secure a continued progress in protecting the rights of both the Indian tribes and of the people of the United States. I beg you to accept the assurances of my appreciation of the confidence implied in your invitation, . . ." *Ibid.*, Dec. 1, 1875. On Dec. 9, 1873, Tobey, Boston, had written to USG. "I regret that the condition of my health prevents me from continuing to give that attention to the duties of a member of the 'Board of Indian Commissioners which fidelity to that important trust demands. I therefore respectfuly tender my resignation. Permit me to express my sincere appreciation of the honor conferred by your appointment, as well as the privilege of being associated with the distinguished gentlemen, whose great devotion to the responsible and arduous duties devolving on them have done so much to demonstrate the wisdom and success of your policy towards the Indian tribes." ALS, DNA, RG 48, Appointment Div., Letters Received.

On Nov. 30, 1875, Marcus L. Ward, Washington, D. C., wrote to USG. "I have carefully considered the question of the Indian Commissionership. I appreciate better than I can state the honor of being thus connected with an Administration which, with just people, is now and in history will be so distinguished for ability and patriotism; but, having been engaged in a detail of business for many years until weary of it, I hesitate taking upon me the toil incident to the administration of the Indian Bureau, and finding my family, who sometimes judge better of our duty than ourselves, unwilling that I should assume the labors of the position, I am constrained to decline. Thanking you for this mark of confidence, . . ." *New York Times*, Dec. 6, 1875. The ALS is listed in William Evarts Benjamin, Catalogue No. 27, Nov., 1889, p. 10. On Dec. 3, Chandler telegraphed to Babcock. "Has anything been heard from the Jersey man." Telegram received, DLC-USG, IB. On the same day, Babcock telegraphed to Chandler. "Nothing heard from him.   am informed that he is in town." ALS (telegram sent), DNA, RG 107, Telegrams Collected (Bound).

On Dec. 2, George H. Stuart, Philadelphia, had written to USG. "In my hastily written reply to your telegram, I did not have time to express the deep interest I feel in the Indian policy adopted by you. As you are aware I was conversant with some abuses and mismanagement and having confidence in your sincerity and desire to carry out your Indian policy successfully, Mr Campbell Mr Brunott and myself did not hesitate to call upon you at Long Branch, and personally call your attention to these abuses. Subsequent investigation by yourself and the Hon Ex Secretary of the Interior has proven all the statements then made to you, to have been well founded. But, my dear Mr President, I want to say, that I still have the most firm conviction that your Indian policy is a success. While we had most decided objection to two or three agents whom we did not think proper men to be in the Service,—I say most unhesitatingly that the present system of appointment has brought a class of men into the Service as Indian Agents, vastly superior to any before in it, and those whom under circumstances of peculair temptation I believe are as faithful and honest as any class of men in the government Service. The policy is doing what was never before really attempted,—it is teaching the Indians civilization and Christianity,—giving them books, schools, Homes and Churches, and the result of following it up, will be in a few years the settlement of the Indian question, and they will be as the colored people now largely are, able to take care of themselves. As Mr Tobey has finally declined the position of Commissioner of Indian Affairs I would recommend *Mr Thomas. K. Cree*. He has the confidence of the old members of the Board, is a personal friend of *Senator Scott*, and has the confidence of the entire business community in Pittsburgh where he was engaged in business prior to his connection with our Board. In Philadelphia Mr Cree numbers among his personal friends many of our most prominent men, well known to *Mr Borie & Mr Childs*. He stands well with the Press of our City, having come into contact largely with them during the past few weeks. He possesses an acquaintance with Indian matters, such as probably no other person not connected with the service, possesses. His executive ability and business qualifications, to my own personal knowledge are of a very high order. I cannot say however that Mr Cree would accept the position if tendered him. May I not venture to suggest to you again that you recommend that the Indian Bureau be made a separate department, as is the Agricultural & Education Bureaus. By so doing you could hold the head of it, personally responsible for the conduct of the department, and would secure the same honesty in its administration as has been secured in other branches of the government service. Any other transfer of the department would be deprecated by all the friends of your Indian policy and by many of your personal friends." LS, *ibid.*, RG 48, Appointment Div., Letters Received.

On Dec. 7, U.S. Representative James A. Garfield of Ohio learned that Chandler had telegraphed to John Q. Smith offering nomination as commissioner of Indian Affairs. Harry James Brown and Frederick D. Williams, eds., *The Diary of James A. Garfield* (East Lansing, Mich., 1967–81), III, 195. On Dec. 8, USG nominated Smith. See *New York Times*, Dec. 9, 1875.

On Nov. 30, A. D. Lynch, Indianapolis, had written to USG. "I respectfully ask your consideration of my name for the appointment—of 'Commissioner of Indian Affairs.' If you will Entertain the application I can present the Endorsement of Senator Morton, our Representatives, Hon D D Pratt, Hon J. C New Hon Jas. Tyner—Hon John Jay Knox and others. Your own personal knowledge of me—as the son of Rev Thomas H. Lynch may be sufficient. May I ask that my name be presented to Secty Chandler." ALS, DNA, RG 48, Appointment Div., Letters Received. On Nov. 6, 1872, Thomas H. Lynch, Indianapolis, had written to USG. "I must congratulate you on the result of the election yesterday.—It is most gratifying to your political and personal friends   I have now voted at twelve Presidential elections and at none with more pride and hope than at that of yesterday—May your second term be as wise and happy as your first one has been for the welfare of the country—" ALS, USG 3.

On Dec. 2, 1875, J. D. Burke, "Choctaw Indian," Washington, D. C., wrote to USG. "I desire most respectfully to call your attention to the appointment of Dr. William Nicholson, of Belvidere, North Carolina, as a suitable person to receive the position of Commissioner of Indian Affairs. This gentleman is well known to be deeply interested in the welfare of the Indians, and you would do great honor to the State of North Carolina, and to the interest of the Indians, by appointing him to that position. . . . Dr. Nicholson is stopping at Ebbitt House." ALS, DNA, RG 48, Appointment Div., Letters Received.

On Dec. 7, George W. Atherton, Rutgers College, New Brunswick, N. J., wrote to USG. "If it will not be considered intrusive, I should be glad to suggest to your consideration the name of ex-Gov. Newell, of Allentown, in this State, for the office of Com'r. of Indian Affairs. He has been in the House of Representatives three terms, and was Governor of New Jersey from 1856 to 1859. He is a man of decided vigor and force of character, of unsullied integrity, & of wide and honorable reputation. I believe he would make a most capable and efficient officer, and one entirely in accord with your views of administration. The appointment would be of excellent effect also in one of our doubtful Congressional Districts; and I am sure it would be generally received by the Republicans of the State as a fit recognition of a deserving public man. Whatever consideration you may give to this suggestion, I trust you will accept my assurance that my only motive in making it is the good of the public service." ALS, *ibid.* A related letter is *ibid.*

In a letter docketed Dec. 14, A. M. Sarringar, Lamb's Corners, N. Y., wrote to USG. "I notice that no one is willing to take the position of Indian commi Comisioner in place of com Smith   now i. Should be pleased to take the position if it would be in accordance with your wishes to appint me or have me appointed.   now now it may Seem Strange that i Should write you not being personaly acquainted or perhaps have not heard much from of me   now I will give you a little history of myself   i am A Son of Californy Joe who was Sharp Shooter in the army. . . ." ALS (undated), *ibid.* For California Joe, see Capt. C. A. Stevens, *Berdan's United States Sharpshooters in the Army of the Potomac 1861–1865* (1892; reprinted, Dayton, 1972), pp. 49–51.

In an undated letter, "A warm friend of the present Administration," Kalamazoo, Mich., wrote to USG. "I would recommend to your notice as Indian Commissioner Gen Dwight May of this village as being honest and in every way capable of the trust. He served his country during the entire Late war and went for the coton Thieves lively. May seen to it, *every man had is right in the district where he had command.* I refer you to Judge Wells President of the Alabama Claim, who has known May from boyhood all the way to the present time. I was with May as an under Officr nearly the whole of the war and know him well. I will not give my name lest you may think I want some Office for myself. May dont know any thing about this. Please ask Judge Wells about him. He is too good a man not to be used in some way for the Government." L, DNA, RG 48, Appointment Div., Letters Received.

On July 20, 1876, Thomas Foster, Washington, D. C., wrote to USG. "I formally apply for the post of Commissioner of Indian Affairs, in which, I understand, there will soon be a vacancy, by the removal of the present incumbents for incompetency. You may possibly remember—(multitudinous as are the calls upon your memory)—that I was once before an applicant for this position; and that I was strongly pressed for it by (then) Senator Ramsey, and the whole Minnesota Delegation. Though not appointed on that occasion, it was some consolation, that you gave the position to so entirely competent a man as Edward Payson Smith—your advisers, in his case, certainly did not impose upon you a logger-head, . . . As for my own qualifications for the position I seek, they are, briefly— that since 1849 I have been a diligent student of Indians, their manners, customs, disposition, languages and traditions—that I have lived, in ~~an~~ official capacities, amongst several tribes; that I understand, or know, their several histories, in the past and present; and that I have been reputed to possess office application and administrative faculty. I have, for the past two or three years been engaged in the preparation of an Encyclopaedia of Indian Affairs and of the Race, . . . The Minnesota Delegation will credit me with mainly contributing, by my editorial conduct, of the leading daily at St Paul, to the political revolution of the State in 1859–60. More recently, I endeavored to establish a Republican press to *advocate your administration* in Fairfax County, Virginia, and still more recently, with that view, I revived *'The National Intelligencer'* in this city: so that I may be said to have a claim, not only in a general party sense, but upon *yourself personally*: and you have the reputation of not forgetting your friends. . . . P. S. Should it not be deemed best for me to receive the Indian Commissionership, I suggest that Indian Inspector Vandevere might make a good one; and in case of his appointment I should like to be Indian Inspector in his place, as it would afford me facilities for collecting 'Data' for my Indian Encyclopaedia: besides, I am posted in all the wiles of Indian agencies, having lived at them, though not as an agent: in one case, amongst the Winnebagoes, in the capacity of Superintendent of their Manual Labor Schools, and in the other I was Government Physician amongst the Sioux" ALS, *ibid.* No appointment followed.

1. Edward P. Smith served as commissioner of Indian Affairs until Dec. 11, 1875. On Jan. 24, 1876, Smith, New York City, wrote to USG. "The American Missionary Association represents and is supported by the Congregational churches of the United States. Hon. E. S. Tobey of Boston is its President. It was organized with special reference to the Welfare of the Negro race and is now carrying on an extended industrial and educational work among the colored people of the South. The officers of the Association are endeavoring to connect with their work in the United States an enterprise of a similar nature in some portion of Africa and their attention has been especially directed to the negroes of the Soudan in the region of the upper Nile within the Kingdom of the Kèdive of Egypt— The base idea of the proposed work is Christian Civilization to be inaugurated largely through the means of Industrial Schools similar to that established by the Association at Hampton, Virginia and with marked success under the direction of General Armstrong. The Association has honored me with a Commission of inquiry & report upon the feasibility of such an enterprise and if possible not only to procure permission for the experiment from the Kèdive, but to enlist his interest in it and secure his endorsement of it as a promotor of civilization among his subjects. In accordance with your kind permission granted at an interview with which I was honored on the 14th Inst I venture to request from your hand a letter of introduction to His Highness the Viceroy of Egypt, commendatory of the proposed object of my visit; and, so far as the facts and your acquaintance will warrant, of myself as a reliable representative of such an enterprise. It may not be improper for me to add that my appointment on this mission, as appears from the minutes of the meeting, was deemed suitable on account of my long service in duties of a public, philanthropic and religious Character, as Field Secretary of the U. S. Christian Commission during the war and afterwards as Field Secretary of the Association in charge of its Southern Schools, and of late as Commissioner of Indian Affairs—In behalf of the Association

which I represent and deeply grateful for the many kindnesses I have received at your hands . . ." ALS, *ibid.*, RG 59, Miscellaneous Letters. Levi P. Luckey favorably endorsed this letter to Secretary of State Hamilton Fish. ES (undated), *ibid.* Smith died in Africa on June 15. See Armstrong, *A Friend to God's Poor*, pp. 379, 387–90, 396–401.

Speech

[*Nov. 6, 1875*]

GENTLEMEN: I am very glad to meet you on this occasion, and to congratulate you on so good a cause for rejoicing to the entire country over the elections of last Tuesday. While the Republican majorities were not great, they were sufficient to accomplish the purpose. The "rag baby"[1] has been entirely suppressed, and the people now know what kind of money they are to have in the future, and I think we have an assurance that the Republicans will control this Government for at least four years longer.[2]

New York Times, Nov. 7, 1875. USG spoke to serenading Republicans from the White House portico.

1. Cartoonist Thomas Nast first used a "rag baby" to symbolize inflationary paper money in the Sept. 4, 1875, issue of *Harper's Weekly.* See Albert Bigelow Paine, *Th. Nast: His Period and His Pictures* (New York, 1904), pp. 313–15.
2. In [*Dec.*], Governor Daniel H. Chamberlain of S. C. wrote to USG. "I am induced by recent extraordinary circumstances occurring in this State to address you by this communication, as the head, in a certain sense, of the republican party. The General Assembly of this State on the 16th inst. elected W. J. Whipper and F. J. Moses, Jr., as Judges of the Circuit Court of this State, the former for the Circuit embracing the city of Charleston and constituting by far the most important circuit of the State in point of population, wealth and business. The character of F. J. Moses, Jr., is known to you and to the world. Unless the entirely universal opinion of all who are familiar with his career is mistaken, he is as infamous a character as ever in any age disgraced and prostituted public position. The character of W. J. Whipper, according to my belief and the belief of all good men in this State, so far as I am informed, differs from that of Moses only in extent to which opportunity has allowed him to exhibit it. The election of these two men to judicial offices sends a thrill of horror through the State. It compels men of all parties who respect decency, virtue or civilization to utter their loudest protests against the outrage of their election. They have not even the poor qualification of such a degree of legal learning as to qualify them for the intelligent discharge of any judicial duty. The least of all the evils inflicted on the people of this State by their election is the fact that it compels all republicans who love or honor the principles of their party to refuse to countenance or tolerate such representatives. . . . To try to save the seven electoral votes of South Carolina at the price of silence under this infliction will cost us, in my judgment, many times that number of votes elsewhere. We want your moral and political support in this struggle with political iniquity in

its worst forms. It is as suicidal to give countenance to Whipper and Moses here as it would be to give countenance to the whiskey thieves in St. Louis. The party feal[t]y of such men is disastrous to the party. I have written earnestly. I cannot do otherwise. Let no man convince you that I am anything but a republican until common decency compels me to be something else. Give us your countenance as you have given it, as I believe, in the past, and if we cannot save South Carolina to the party we can prevent our party here from becoming a thousandfold greater burden to the national republican party than it has ever been before. We propose to declare war on this Whipper-Moses gang. We propose to ask the national republican party to sustain us, and we know that you and all true republicans will bid us God speed when you know the depths of degradation to which these men are plunging us. This letter is, of course, addressed only to you, but you can make any use of it you see fit, and I remain your sincere friend and fellow republican," *New York Herald*, April 4, 1876. See *New York Times*, Jan. 3, 1876; Peggy Lamson, *The Glorious Failure: Black Congressman Robert Brown Elliott and the Reconstruction in South Carolina* (New York, 1973), pp. 220–25.

To Lt. Col. Frederick T. Dent

————

Nov. 10th /75

DEAR FRED.

I have had no further word from the Hall Safe Manufacturing Co.[1] in relation to the purchase of the farm. It is not probable that the sale, if it is effected, can give anything before the first of Jan.y, and possibly not before March. Then, if sold, the payment is to be 25 pr. ct. down, balance on time. I do not think therefore that you can count anything from this sourse for the present.

Yours Truly

U. S. GRANT

GN. F. T. DENT

ALS, ICarbS. Written on stationery of the Fifth Avenue Hotel, New York City. On Dec. 18, 1875, a St. Louis correspondent reported on the possible sale of USG's farm. ". . . It will be remembered that some negotiations were first on foot with the Pullman Palace Car Company. These have fallen through, and now the Hall Patent Safe Company, of Indianapolis, are negotiating for the land, on which to build their works in the vicinity of the Gravois Creek. The company want 1,000 acres, and General Grant, for his 793 acres, has made a proposition to sell at the rate of $300 per acre, including all the improvements and appurtenances on the farm. This would realize the sum of $237,900. The Safe Company, it is understood, do not object to the price, but couple its acceptance with a proposition to General Grant that he take $50,000 of the company's stock, which proposition he is considering; and this is as far as the pending negotiations have progressed. . . ." *New York Herald*, Dec. 19, 1875. On Dec. 27, Gen. William T. Sherman, St. Louis, wrote to Lt. Col. Frederick T. Dent. ". . . I have no doubt one of these days you will all drift back to Old St Louis, which is spreading all over the Country, so that it may be when you next come you will find your Farm in town. I saw the President a few days ago in New York, and he said he was negotiating for the Sale of the Farm at $300. an acre. This is a better price than I supposed was possible in these hard times. My best love to Mrs Dent." ALS, ICarbS.

1. Joseph L. Hall founded the Hall Safe & Lock Co. in Cincinnati in 1867. On Dec. 21, Levi P. Luckey wrote to the co. "The President wishes me to write you and say that he received a letter from you shortly after his return from the West, but that he has not received any word from you since relative to the proposition regarding his farm at St. Louis" Copy, DLC-USG, II, 3.

To Edwards Pierrepont

[I wish the Atty. Gen. would hear Gen. Negley in regard to the case where he has been indicted by the Grand Jury of this Dist. In hearing his explanation it seems to me] there should be a suspension of action against indicted parties—giving full security for their appearance when wanted—until the real criminal has been tried. But of this you will be better qualified to judge, after hearing, than I.

U. S. GRANT

Nov. 13TH /75

ALS (partial facsimile), Swann Auction Galleries, Sale No. 1912, Nov. 1, 2001, no. 210. A Pittsburgh native, James S. Negley served in the Mexican War and the Civil War, where he won promotion to maj. gen. vols. after the battle of Stone's River, but lost command after Chickamauga. After three terms in Congress (1869–75), Negley lobbied on behalf of Julius Witowski, who claimed reimbursement for supplies seized by federal forces in La. An investigation of this claim and another led to indictments for fraud and a shakeup in the Treasury Dept.; Negley ultimately avoided prosecution. See letter to John M. Brodhead, Dec. 31, 1875; *Washington National Republican*, Oct. 14, 1875; *New York Times*, Oct. 14, 1877; *HRC*, 50-1-632.

To Samuel J. Kirkwood

November 17th 1875.

[Hon. SAMUEL J. KIRKWOOD]
IOWA CITY, IOWA.
DEAR SIR:

Your letter of the 4th instant was received about the time I was starting for New York City, one week ago yesterday. I expected to answer it immediately on my return,[1] but, permitted the matter to escape my mind until this time.

What I said at Des Moines was hastily noted down in pencil and may have expressed my views imperfectly. I have not the manuscript before me as I gave it to the Secretary of the Society.[2] My idea of what I said is this: "Resolve that [th]e State or Nation, or both combined shall furnish to every child growing up in the land, the means of acquiring a good common school education" etc.

Such is my idea and such I intended to have said.

I feel no hostility to free education going as high as the State or National government feels able to provide—protecting however every child in the privilege of a common school education before public means are appropriated to a higher education for the few.

Yours truly.

U. S. GRANT

LS, State Historical Society of Iowa, Iowa City, Iowa; Df, USG 3. On Nov. 4, 1875, Samuel J. Kirkwood, Iowa City, wrote to USG. "Permit me to call your attention to an extract from your speech in DesMoines Iowa that has attracted so much attention, in these words. . . . We have in this State, a State Agricultural College, a state University and many High Schools all of which are supported to a greater or less extent by the State—Some of our people oppose the policy of State aid to these institutions and claim that in the extract above, you intended to express the opinion that such policy is wrong. Others claim that your intention was only to denounce the policy of giving State Aid to schools of any grade, in which 'sectarian, pagan, or atheistical tenets' are taught—The State Agricultural College, the State University and our High Schools are strictly non-Sectarian and are open to all without distinction of race color or sect, or sex—Those who oppose the policy of granting State Aid to these institutions are using your speech in the press of the State to influence public opinion against granting to them further aid by the State—Will you be kind enough to inform me ~~whether~~ precisely how you desire to be understood? I may desire to use your answer publicly." ALS (clipping omitted), *ibid*. Kirkwood, Republican governor of Iowa (1860–64) and U.S. Senator (1866–67), had been elected to another term as governor in Oct., 1875. See Speech, [*Sept. 29, 1875*]; Annual Message, Dec. 7, 1875.

On Dec. 2, James S. Clarkson, editor, *Iowa State Register*, and postmaster, Des Moines, wrote to Orville E. Babcock supporting him against Whiskey Ring allegations and commenting on USG's visit. "*Personal*. . . . The President made friends of all our people by his quiet & unostentatious coming, his readiness to meet all who wished to see him, & especially by his speech. I have yet to find a person, outside of the Catholic Church, who did not like the speech, & indeed many of the more intelligent Catholics endorse it heartily. I refer to this more especially because I have been told that one of the most prominent politicians of our State has written the President criticizing the positions taken in his speech, & stating that it was injuring the party here in Iowa. If this be true, I cannot divine the purpose in any man in writing a letter so far from the real facts. For the speech has met with well-nigh universal favor in Iowa, in both parties & in all classes, & so far only two papers in the State, aside from the Catholic church papers, have attacked it, & they democratic papers. Instead of injuring the Republican party here it has very greatly strengthened the party throughout the State, as I am sure it has throughout the nation. I know it has gained the President many thousands of friends & supporters among our Iowa people who never have supported him before, while it has also recalled to him many of the Republicans who went off from the party in 1872. I shall be glad, at any time, to serve you, in any way that I can." ALS, USG 3.

On Jan. 27, public school superintendents attending a National Educational Association convention in Washington, D. C., had visited USG at the White House "to thank him for the encouragement he had given in recommending the cause of national education in his messages to Congress. The President said that education was one of the best reconstruction measures, and he therefore felt a great interest in it, and had recommended the cause to Congress; and would give every measure in aid of education his hearty support. As the execution of the laws depended on the masses, and as the laws should be executed intelligently, it should be the duty of all to earnestly urge onward the cause of popular education." *Washington Evening Star*, Jan. 27, 1875.

1. On Nov. 8, USG went to New York City with Julia Dent Grant and Babcock; on Nov. 11, he returned to Washington, D. C.

2. Lewis M. Dayton, recording secretary, Society of the Army of the Tennessee.

To Abel R. Corbin

———

Nov. 19th /75

My Dear Mr. Corbin:

Mrs. Grant showed me your letter of Wednesday.[1] I will be very glad to have you come down say the Saturday[2] before the meeting of Congress, when my message will probably be compledted. In the mean time if you have written anything on the school question which you would like me to see send it directed to Mrs. Grant   I will not hesitate to use anything my judgement approves of.

We are all quite well. Would like to have Jennie come with you if she can.

Yours Truly
U. S. Grant

ALS, Nellie C. Rothwell, La Jolla, Calif. See Annual Message, Dec. 7, 1875.

1. Nov. 17, 1875.
2. Dec. 4.

To Alton R. Easton

Nov. 21st /75

Dear Colonel:

Your letter of the 19th inst. recd. The names of the three persons best recommended for Marshal of the Eastn District of Mo. were submitted, as you suggest, by the Atty. Gen. to you, Long & Wright—I suggested the postmaster, Filley, also—to advise which of the three would probably be the most satisfactory. On receipt of your dispatch a commission was filled and signed for Stevenson. Just then, before the commission had gone out, such reports were rec'd by both the Atty. Gn. and myself as to create at least a doubt as to whether it should go out atall. While waiting for further information a dispatch was received from the Dist. Atty. saying that is was important that a new Marshal should be appointed without delay. It was then given to Leffingwell against whom nothing had been said.

Of course no disrespect was intended to either of the parties consulted. The intention was to appoint either of the three who you might suggest. But we believed that your recommendation would be withdraw immediately on the information rec'd here.

Yours Truly
U. S. Grant

Col. A. R. Easton

ALS, MoSHi. On Nov. 4, 1875, John F. Long, surveyor of customs, St. Louis, wrote to USG. "On the 19th ult. Atty. Genl. Pierepont, dispatched to Cols. Easton & Wright and myself for information touching the fitness of men for U. S. Marshal. '*Which* will make the better marshal, of Mr. Leffingwell, Genl. J. D. Stevenson Mr. St. Gem' We promptly responded 'John D. Stevenson.' *signed*—A. R. Easton, J. F: Long, & H. C. Wright.' Genl. Stevenson now goes to Washington to ask a settlemt of the matter. And we are still of the opinion that the appointment of Gel. S. will be a good one for the Govermt. and meet the wishes of those here, who demand an honest discharge of the duties devolving on a Govt. Officer. . . . P. S. Col. Easton is absent." ALS, DNA, RG 60, Records Relating to Appointments. Also on Nov. 4, Thursday, John D. Stevenson, St. Louis, telegraphed to Orville E. Babcock. "Say to the President I will be in *Washn* Saturday with letters & testimonials from his personal & political friends here that I think will be entirely satisfactory to him" Telegram received (at 4:26 P.M.), DLC-USG, IB. On the same day, Roderick E. Rombauer, St. Louis, wrote to USG. "Information reached me to day that interested parties are opposing the appointment of Gen. John D. Stevenson, to the position of Marshal of the eastern district of Missouri on the ground that the appointment does not give satisfaction to our citizens—As a resident of St Louis for more than twenty two years, during the greater part of which time I have moved in public life, and occupied public positions, I claim to be familiar with public men in this City & State, and do cheerfully say, that the appointment of Gen. Stevenson is in my opinion not only well merited by the appointee by long continued and valuable services, to the State and to the cause of the union,—but also one which gives great satisfaction to our citizens, owing to the merits of the appointee & his fitness for the position" ALS, DNA, RG 60, Records Relating to Appointments. Related papers recommending Stevenson are *ibid.*

On Nov. 5, William D. W. Barnard, St. Louis, telegraphed to USG. "Have undeniable evidence of Stephenson's irregularities and deficit as land agent and Attorney of Missouri Pacific R. R. which will present in a few days" Telegram received (at 2:10 P.M.), *ibid.* On Nov. 10, Pierrepont telegraphed to USG, New York City. "News from St. Louis makes it absolutely necessary to change the Marshal forthwith. I wish to get the commission ready to be signed at your first return. Shall it be Bonner, Fox, Metcalf, Leffingwell, Ramsay, St. Gem or who?" Copy, *ibid.*, Letters Sent to Executive Officers. See letter to Edwards Pierrepont, Oct. 18, 1875.

Proclamation

———

Washington, November 22d 1875.

It is with profound sorrow that the President has to announce to the people of the United States, the death of the Vice President, Henry Wilson, who died in the Capitol of the Nation, this morning.

The eminent station of the deceased, his high character, his long career in the service of his State, and of the Union, his devotion to the cause of freedom, and the ability which he brought to the discharge of every duty, stand conspicuous and are indelibly impressed on the hearts and affections of the American People.

In testimony of respect for this distinguished citizen and faithful public servant, the various Departments of the Government will be closed on the day of the funeral and the Executive Mansion and all the Executive Departments in Washington will be draped with badges of mourning for thirty days.

The Secretaries of War and of the Navy will issue orders that appropriate military and naval honors be rendered to the memory of one whose virtues and services will long be borne in recollection by a grateful Nation.

U. S. GRANT

DS, DLC-Executive Orders. On Nov. 22, 1875, Orville E. Babcock wrote to Secretary of State Hamilton Fish. "The President will be pleased to have you meet him at his office at half past ten this morning for conference relative to the decease of the Vice President which occurred this morning at 7.20 oclock." LS, DLC-Hamilton Fish. Babcock sent similar letters to other cabinet officers. LS, DLC-Benjamin H. Bristow; copy, DLC-USG, II, 3. Vice President Henry Wilson had been confined to his room at the capitol following a Nov. 10 stroke. On Nov. 16, Col. Jedediah H. Baxter, chief medical purveyor, wrote to USG. "In consequence of having sat up too long—eight hours yesterday—the Vice President did not rest as well last night as heretofore, and is this morning somewhat more nervous. This condition, however, is only temporary, and will yield to rest and quiet." *New York Herald*, Nov. 17, 1875. See *PUSG*, 24, 187; Richard H. Abbott, *Cobbler in Congress: The Life of Henry Wilson, 1812–1875* (Lexington, Ky., 1972), pp. 255–57. On Nov. 26, USG and cabinet attended Wilson's funeral in the Senate Chamber.

On Nov. 22, U.S. Senator Thomas W. Ferry of Mich., Grand Haven, had telegraphed to USG. "I received with profound sorrow the information of the death of Vice President Wilson & share with you in this great loss to the country, & mourn with his personal friends" Telegram received (at 1:04 P.M.), DNA, RG 59, Miscellaneous Letters.

On Nov. 23, Secretary of the Navy George M. Robeson, Philadelphia, telegraphed to USG. "Am detained here by sickness of my wife   hope to be home tomorrow." Telegram received (at 6:40 P.M.), DLC-USG, IB.

On Nov. 24, Wednesday, Postmaster Gen. Marshall Jewell, New York City, telegraphed to USG. "Unless you desire me to be in Washington friday I shall remain and attend the funeral of senator Ferry   A telegram to Hartford will find me" Telegram received (at 10:20 A.M.), *ibid.* U.S. Senator Orris S. Ferry of Conn. had died Nov. 21.

On Nov. 24, Edward B. Pickett, president, Tex. constitutional convention, wrote to USG transmitting a resolution eulogizing Wilson. LS and DS, DNA, RG 59, Miscellaneous Letters.

To William L. Burt

Nov. 29. 1875.

DEAR SIR:

Having satisfied mysilf in the matter in controversy between you and the Postmaster General in favor of the latter, it becomes my duty, to say so to you, and to add, that if your resignation as Postmaster of the city of Boston is received between this, and the meeting of Congress, I will accept it.

Very respectfully
your obt svt
U. S. GRANT

MR. W. L. BURT P. M. BOSTON MASS.

Copies, DLC-USG, II, 3; DLC-John Russell Young. On Oct. 21, 1875, William L. Burt, postmaster, Boston, wrote to USG. "In my various conversations with Mr. Jewell on the 21st, 22nd, 23rd, 24th, of Sept. he made certain statements which as a friend to you and those around you I deem it my personal duty to report. I have already stated to you in conversation the substance of these statements and giving them as they occurred in connection with my history of the official complaints I have to make. I have now separated them that you may use them separately if you desire. For the purpose of impressing upon me as I suppose the fact that neither Gen'l. Babcock nor yourself could render me any assistance, Mr. Jewell said that 'we are getting out bad men every where, they were the President's friends'; Gen'l. Babcock tried to protect them, he (Babcock) was a friend of bad men and protected them   He then named two prominent men in Washington who he said were corrupt and Babcock was shielding them. He said that the President had had them all around him and referred by name to Gen'l. Porter   He said we are gradually getting hold of these bad men but the President stuck to them and finally he said we take them right from his hands and land them in States Prison. I expressed astonishment at his statements and he said they would prove themselves true in cases that he then knew of and I would find it so. He referred two or three times to this influence of the President and his personal staff at the White House. I was impressed that some great calamity was impending or such uncalled for statements of men whom I knew well would not be made to me under such circumstances. At another time the same style of conversation, he spoke of Mr. Delano then Secretary. He siad Delano has got to go, I don't know whether he is honest or not. President Grant can't save him. The newspaper press is down on him and thier judgment is the judgment of the world. He nor no one else can stand against it. I told him that I thought Secretary Delano was an upright and long tried man, and ought to be sustain him, and he had better have left before. He said that the President had hurt himself by standing by Delano when the public demanded that he should go out, he said it was so that th Interior Department would have been broken up if he had to be kept there. He said the President was hurting himself all over the country by sustaining and standing by bad men, and whether they were bad or not he ought to let them go and build up his administration. In this connection another person was referred to in connection with Gen'l. Babcock but it did not make the same impression upon my mind as the name of Gen'l. Babcock did, but it was in relation to matters in Washington and St. Louis. The substance of these statements was made in different forms but all with the same ideas. I did not know at the time and do not now know to what Mr. Jewell referred as to the special complaint against any of these men, but he referred to Gen'l. Porter, Gen'l. Babcock, and Capt. Luckey and the President in a manner that there could be no mistake as I certainly had no previous intimation of this kind, and the charges I have stated were forced upon me step by step in the conversation. If Mr. Jewell desired to impressed upon me his own great power and influence in these matters and that was his object it entirely failed as I was wholly occupied with the idea of the great misfortune that might befall at any time the President and his friends. Please reagrd this as private and I trust it will not be necessary to a full understanding and appreciation of the matters contained in my official communication." TLS, USG 3. On Dec. 8, USG nominated Edward S. Tobey to replace Burt, who had resigned.

On March 1, Postmaster Gen. Marshall Jewell had telegraphed to Orville E. Babcock. "Please ask the President if he has any news in regard to the Postmaster at Boston and if he wants me to make up Quarter Appointment or to do anything about ~~two~~ it as I expect to come up about two o'clock and await his orders. I hear nothing about it one way or the other   Also about the Montgomery Ala. case. I have not heard from Mr Sheets whether he will take the office or not" Telegram received, DLC-USG, IB. On the same day, Babcock telegraphed to Jewell. "The President says leave those two matters for the Extra session. He goes to the Senate about two." ALS (telegram sent), DNA, RG 107, Telegrams Collected (Bound). On March 4, Jewell telegraphed to Babcock. "I have the following telegram from Boston.   please state if you wish any action in regard to it. I would suggest an interview with the President so that we shall authorize Judge Hoar or some person of that class to listen to any statements that may be made. I do not know what it means. 'From Boston 4th HON. MARSHALL JEWELL Post Master Genl. Mr Lewin who stands high as an honest man & has been at the head of the mailing Dep't of Boston Post Office for some twenty eight years says he as well as others can make startling developments, as to its management should the Post Master Genl. authorize some one to question them J. H. CHADWICK'" Telegram received, DLC-USG, IB. On March 8, USG renominated Burt; on the same day, USG nominated John J. Martin as postmaster, Montgomery, and Charles C. Sheats as 6th auditor, Treasury Dept., in place of Martin.

Endorsement

The Sec of War may convene the Court of Enquiry asked for.

U. S. GRANT

DEC. 3D 1875.

AES, DNA, RG 94, Letters Received, 6074 1875. *HMD*, 44-1-186, 495. Written on a letter of Dec. 2, 1875, from Orville E. Babcock to USG. "On the 29th. ultimo, in the trial of W. O. Avery before the U. S. Court at St. Louis, Mo., one of the prosecuting Attorneys Hon. J. H. Henderson introduced certain telegrams alleged to have been sent by me to Messrs. McDonald and Joyce recently convicted of complicity in the Whisky frauds, and is reported in the St. Louis Globe-Democrat as having used the following language. . . . Upon being informed of this charge I telegraphed to D. P. Dyer, U. S. District Attorney at St. Louis, as follows, on the 30th ult.:—'I am absolutely innocent, and every telegram which I sent will appear perfectly innocent the moment I can be heard—I demand a hearing before the court: When can I testify.' And received upon the same day the following telegram:—'The evidence in the Avery case is closed. The next case involving the question of conspiracy is set for the fifteenth of December. DAVID P. DYER—Dist. Atty.' The opportunity to answer the charges contained in the above speech having been thus denied me, and being left without any opportunity to vindicate myself, I respectfully demand a Court of Enquiry and request that an immediate investigation be ordered." LS, DNA, RG 94, Letters Received, 6074 1875. *HMD*, 44-1-186, 493–95. An enclosed clipping reported a courtroom exchange between John B. Henderson, special U.S. counsel, and Chester H. Krum, defense attorney, during the trial of William O. Avery, former Treasury Dept. clerk, charged with conspiracy in the whiskey frauds. Krum argued that telegrams implicating Babcock had been inappropriately introduced as evidence in order to connect the White House to the Avery case. Henderson responded. ". . . It is very far from the opinion of myself or any of my associates that the President of the United States knew anything about the Ring. I desire to enter, right here, my protest against any such declaration on the part of Judge Krum, or anybody else. If Judge Krum wants my opinion, I will give it to him very frankly, and that is that the President of the United States has been grossly deceived and imposed upon by men who professed to be his friends, here and in Washington. And, sir, I do enter a solemn declaration, now in the beginning, that, in my judgment, the President of the United States knew nothing at all of what was going on in the Ring. It is the opinion of all my associates, and these dispatches do not in the least implicate the President of the United States. So far from implicating, they exculpate him, in the language of my associate. They show that he had nothing to do with it—not only negatively, but affirmatively; that he knew nothing of these gross and outrageous impositions upon his confidence in men. Now, in reference to another point. We did not intend to offer these dispatches at all, and if any responsibility attaches, it attaches to my friend, who objected to the testimony of Mr. Douglass. We, sir, had made up our minds not to introduce the dispatches, but the gentleman has imposed, under the ruling of the court, the absolute necessity upon us unwillingly to connect the name of General Babcock with the matter. I asked the witness who interfered or asked him to do away with the order transferring the Supervisors and Revenue Agents through different districts, the only way which could have effectually broken up the frauds throughout the country. . . . I asked who interfered to prevent it. He simply said that General Babcock came to him and said it couldn't be done. . . . Let us introduce enough to satisfy the jury that General Babcock performed his part, and we will rest there. I do now repudiate forever the idea that we are attacking the President of the United States or bringing scandal on that name. We desire no such thing, and these very dispatches which we propose to offer not only proves that the President knew nothing of it, but that he has been deceived throughout the whole affair. And the fact that John McDonald or Joyce or Babcock was his friend, proves nothing against the good name of the President; . . ." *St. Louis Globe-Democrat*, Nov. 30, 1875. See Endorsement, July 29, 1875.

On Nov. 28, John F. Long, St. Louis, wrote to Babcock. "The President being engaged upon his Annal Message, I do not hear from him as usual. And not wishing to disturb him untill he has leisure, I refrain from writing to him now. The 'Whiskey Trials' are still in progress,—the testimony Sometimes interspersed with the names of 'O. Grant' 'Genl. Babcock,' 'Judge Long' and even 'Secrety Bristow.' But the Genl's Telegram of the 27th inst. to atty. Dyer, put a quietus upon the croakings of political demagogues, and the street gossips of cramped intelects, as far as *he* was concerned, and has in a degree stoped their *guessing lies* about you and O. Grant. I settled Hutchings of the Times, and I am persuaded he will drop—*by accident*, yours, O. Grant's and my name from his vilianous—speculations about 'Whiskey Frauds' &c . . . I have watched closely the trials and have yet to hear aught of even a suspicion of guilt, against that old *War-horse Secy Bristow*, whose towering height above the villians is conspicuous, and whose solid foundation upon justice to his country and to men, are so far beyond the reach of little, weak, cowardly and base minds,—warped by ignorance and political prejudice; their idle rumers do not reach him, in the minds of intelligent men. And I think I may say the same of you and O. Grant, and Col. Dent.—For myself, I am at all times ready, and when that great and good man,—President Grant, shall find, that I (as an officer) have abused his confidence and have knowingly violated the Laws of a country that has used me kindly and given me an honest living,—I want him to,—I *expect* him to take off my official head close to the shoulders,—and when the sentence is read, before decapitation, I shall say '*Bully for President Grant.*' If you have a little time drop me a few lines to relieve the monotony. My regards to the President, to Secy. Bristow and to Geo. W. Dent" ALS, ICN. On Nov. 8, David P. Dyer, U.S. attorney, St. Louis, had written to Attorney Gen. Edwards Pierrepont. ". . . Of course there has been no evidence nor the shadow of evidence against the President's brother or brother-in-law, both of whom were mentioned in this paper as being implicated—The object was to start the report and then in case no indictments were presented to cry out against the prosecution &c. Of course the purpose in all this is well understood here—. . ." ALS (press), DNA, RG 118, Letters Sent, U.S. Attorneys, Eastern District, Mo. On Nov. 27, Secretary of the Treasury Benjamin H. Bristow telegraphed to Dyer denying rumors that he had invested in a Louisville distillery. *St. Louis Globe-Democrat*, Nov. 28, 1875.

On Nov. 29, Dyer wrote to Bristow. "Enclosed herewith you will find copies of certain telegrams sent by Joyce to Babcock. They explain themselves and need no word of comment from me. 'Let no guilty man escape.'" ALS (press), DNA, RG 118, Letters Sent, U.S. Attorneys, Eastern District, Mo. On the same day, Dyer telegraphed and wrote to Pierrepont. "I send you by mail copies of original telegrams in my possession addressed to ~~Sylph~~ Babcock and all in the hand writing of Joyce. They are important and as they strike me, without explanation." "You will find herewith copies of eight telegrams, the originals of which are in my possession. These dispatches reached me yesterday on a *subpoena duces tecum*. Acting upon what I consider sufficient testimony to connect Babcock with the conspiracy to defraud the revenue in this District, or at least with having a guilty knowledge thereof, I shall prepare and lay before the Grand Jury a bill of indictment against him. It is painful to me as it should be to every good citizen of the country that the President of the United States should be betrayed by those so close to him as Gen Babcock. I know that there is no one more anxious than the President himself to see the plunderers of the public Treasury punished, but how ever this may be I have marked out for myself a plain path to follow in these prosecutions, and that I shall follow to the end. Where the testimony is sufficient let neither place, position or wealth shield the guilty party   I should like to have your impressions after reading these dispatches." ALS (press, telegram sent) and LS (press), *ibid.*; telegram received (at 10:57 A.M.), *ibid.*, RG 60, Letters Received, Mo. On March 22, 1876, Pierrepont testified before the select committee to investigate whiskey frauds. "Q. Who brought the subject of General Babcock's complicity in those frauds before the Cabinet in the early part of November or early in December, as you have stated?— A. Well, probably to have it clearly understood, I should state this: One day in the Cabinet prior to the time to which you allude, Mr. Bristow came into the Cabinet, having copies of some of [t]hose telegrams, which at that time I had not seen, and showed them to me in the Cabinet aside, and we talked the matter over, and thought it was a matter of such apparent seriousness that we would stay after the Cabinet meeting, and bring it to the knowledge of the President, and we did so. . . . They were some of the telegrams that were sent to him. I think one was known as the 'Sylph' telegram, and there were two or three others; I think I have copies of them here. . . . To General Bristow and myself this looked like a very serious matter. Of course we did not understand anything about the circumstances of it, and when we brought the telegrams to the President at the time I mention, the President called General Babcock into the room before us and asked him what it meant. General Babcock then commenced an explanation of these telegrams, and turning in this way to the President said: 'You know when Joyce was here;' so, so; 'You know about the letters that Joyce wrote, and you know when we were out there;' so, so—I cannot repeat what he said—'and you know what was said about the change of supervisors after Mr. Ford's death,' and the like. Well, as this was a matter which had occurred long before I was in the Cabinet, and about which I had no information whatever, the explanation gave me no light at all, but it seemed to be a satisfactory explanation to the President. The Secretary of the Treasury and I then both insisted that this was a matter so serious that if he could give an explanation which, as he said, was complete and perfect, and if he was perfectly innocent, as he said he was, he should go out there and make an explanation; and we pressed it as a thing that he ought to do on the spot, and the President fell into the view that we expressed. We were urgent about it. General Babcock said he would do it, and he then wrote a telegram to some one out there, demanding that he might come and have an explanation. . . ." *HMD*, 44-1-186, 2–3. See *PUSG*, 24, 232.

On Dec. 2 and 3, 1875, Secretary of State Hamilton Fish had recorded in his diary. "I received a note from the President requesting that I call upon him at 4 o'clk which I did and found the Cabinet present. . . . The President alluded to the Revenue Fraud suits progressing in St Louis and read a letter addressed to him by Genl Babcock demanding a Court of Inquiry which he said he had been unwilling to assent without submitting the question to the Cabinet. The precise effect and scope of a Court of Inquiry was not known to most of us and questions were asked in that direction. Genl. Belknap was not able posatively to answer all questions that were asked but it was understood and so represented that a Court of Inquiry when asked by an Officer against whom serious charges were pending was a matter of equitable right, that it would have no effect on proceedings pending before the civil tribunals   It was therefore conceded by all that Genl Babcock was entitled to a Court of Inquiry and the Attorney General was requested by the President to telegraph to the District Attorney in St Louis the fact that he had made such request." "The question of the Court of Inquiry in the case of Babcock was again considered The President enquired of the Attorney General whether he had any reply from St Louis and whether indictments had been found   Pierrepont then read a telegram from the District Attorney stating that no list of indictments had been returned and that he did not know what conclusion the Grand Jury would come to in the facts before them. Belknap read some authorities on the organization and power of a Court of Inquiry and it was decided that the Court be ordered and the President named Genls ~~Sherman~~ Sheridan Hancock & Terry, stating that he would have named Sherman but there was no precedent for assigning the Commander in Chief as Judge of a Court. Secretary of War reminded him that Genl Sherman while Commander in Chief had been detailed as presiding officer on the Court of Inquiry of Genl Howard. The President appeared to have forgotten this, but when it was brought to his recollection he made no change but left Sherman out and ordered it to convene in Chicago on the 9th instant   The Attorney General was directed to inform the District Attorney in St Louis of the order and to direct him to furnish the court with any documents and facts which they might require. On leaving the Cabinet Pierrepont remarked that he would let the prosecuting Attorney understand that this order would not suspend or interfere with the pending criminal proceedings at St Louis, to interfere with which he said would be ruinous to Babcock the President and the Administration" DLC-Hamilton Fish.

On Dec. 3, Dyer telegraphed to Pierrepont. "Your dispatch saying that General Babcock on account of the charges appearing against him in the public journals has made a formal demand as an officer of the army for a court of enquiry was received by me this morning. No bill of indictment has been returned against him as yet. I am not able to say whe[ther] the Grand Jury will make a [presentment] or not. Do you [understand] that if a [court of enquiry] is ordered that that supercedes an enquiry before the court here. Please give me your views and opinion." ALS (press, telegram sent), DNA, RG 118, Letters Sent, U.S. Attorneys, Eastern District, Mo.; telegram received (at 11:55 A.M.), *ibid.*, RG 60, Letters Received, Mo. On Dec. 6, Monday, Pierrepont wrote to Dyer. "The President informs me that the Court of Inquiry convenes at Chicago next Thursday, that Genl Babcock starts to-night to meet his trial, that Colonel Gardner is the Judge Advocate to whom at Chicago you will please send any documentary evidence bearing upon the case and the names and the residence of any witnesses whose testimony you judge important to make the investigation thorough. If there is any evidence in addition to that sent me please forward it and communicate with the Judge Advocate at Chicago by messenger or otherwise as you deem most safe, to the end that this important inquiry which will attract the attention of the country may be complete in every respect. I repeat what I have so often said that we wish no innocent man tarnished and no guilty one to escape." Copy, *ibid.*, RG 94, Letters Received, 6074 1875. *HMD*, 44-1-186, 5.

On Dec. 3, Henderson had presented closing arguments to the jury in the Avery case. ". . . What business had Babcock to go to Douglass? He is put there for what purpose? To watch the revenues of the country, to collect them honestly, and see that they are honestly paid out. That is his whole duty. What business has Babcock with it? What business has he to interfere with the discharge of those duties? None whatever, sir. When an official goes into office he ought to be free and independent except where the law binds (upon) him. He should know no master except the law, and if he knows any other master our Government is tumbling down. What right has the President? He has the right to turn this officer out, if he wants to, and put in another; but what right has he even, (though there is no evidence that he ever attempted it, I believe.) What right has the President to interfere with the honest discharge of the duties of a Secretary of the Treasury? None whatever. What right has he to interfere with the discharge of the duties of Commissioner Douglass? None. The law tells Douglass what to do. Douglass only showed a lamentable weakness of character in listening to Babcock or any other mortal man. . . . Gentlemen, why does this man bend the supple hinges of the knee? Why does he yield to presidential interference, or to the interference of the secretary of the honored President? It was none of their business. It belonged not to Grant, it belonged not to Babcock, it was Douglass's own business. He stood responsible. . . ." *Ibid.*, p. 70. See *St. Louis Globe-Democrat*, Dec. 4, 10, 1875. On Dec. 7, Lucien Eaton, special U.S. counsel, St. Louis, telegraphed and wrote to Pierrepont. "As parties in sympathy with the unconvicted members of the Whiskey ring here are assiduously dissemminating the idea that Gen Henderson criticised the President in his argument of the Avery Case it is simple justice to say his speech which was wholly unpremeditated in form does not bear any such interpretation in my judgment   none of the newspapers report him accurately   he intended no criticism as I know privately heard all he said & did not so understand him   a sworn copy from official Stenographer officers notes will be mailed you by me tonight   Henderson took occasion to say in the trial that the despatches exonerated the President & I know he meant it" "Personal & confidential. . . . In compliance with my telegram of today I enclose you sworn report of what was said by Senator Henderson in the argument of the Avery case in supposed criticism of the President. You see he says expressly there was no interference by the President, but by Gen. Babcock, and his whole reference to the President was purely theoretical—addressed to the principle & not to the act—for there was none. The most frantic efforts of guilty parties toin charging any of the prosecuting officers here with being inimical to the president must fail, I think, for the charge is wantonly false. At all times and everywhere we have assiduously sought to show that the President was not implicated in the remotest degree." Telegram received (at 3:35 P.M.) and ALS, DNA, RG 60, Letters Received, Mo. Also on Dec. 7, Fish recorded in his diary. "Judge Pierrepont calls my attention to the report of a speech said to have been made by Mr Henderson in St Louis at the trial of Avery in which he indulged in severe personal abuse of the President   I had not seen the speach but had seen a newspaper statement of it and agreed with Pierrepont that some notice should be taken of it and that in case the speach was as reported it was an outrage which could not be overlooked. At about the same time, whether he heard our conversation or not I do not know, the President read an extract from the Cincinnati Inquirer, stating that it was a hostile paper and that possibly the remarks actually made might differ from the report; but that he was satisfied that Henderson was a personal enemy of his and was disposed to abuse him when opportunity offered. The indecency of a Counsel specially designated by the President abusing him was severely denounced by all the Cabinet. Pierrepont & Bristow explained, as they had previously done, how Henderson came to be appointed. Pierrepont suggested that he be directed to write to Dyer calling attention to the report of the speach and requesting that he send correct report of what Henderson had said." DLC-Hamilton Fish. On Dec. 9, Pierrepont wrote to Dyer. "Evidence has reached here that on the trial of Avery, Mr. Henderson took advantage of his position as special counsel for the Government to assail the President *who was not on trial*. His efforts in that line will be *no longer paid for* by this Department. You will give a copy of this dispatch to Genl. Henderson" Copy, DLC-USG, II, 3. Culver C. Sniffen noted on this letter. "President returned verbal answer by messenger that he 'heartily approved' " AE (initialed), *ibid.* Also on Dec. 9, William D. W. Barnard, St. Louis, telegraphed to USG. "The grand jury have presented an indictment against Genl Babcock for conspiracy and fraud against the United States." Telegram received, DNA, RG 60, Letters Received, Mo. On the same day, Dyer thrice telegraphed to Pierrepont. "The information which you say you have that Mr Henderson in the trial of Avery assailed the President is utterly unfounded. Shall I inform him that he is discharged as special Counsel of the Government in the Revenue cases in this district?" "The grandjury to-day returned a true bill for conspiracy to defraud the revenue against Orville E. Babcock. I have a dispatch from the Judge Advocate of the Court of Inquiry at Chicago asking for charges and evidence against Gen. Babcock. I know of nothing which can be called charges except this indictment and what transpired in the legitimate discharge of duty by the attorneys of the government in the trials of John McDonald and Wm O. Avery. Shall I order copies of the stenographic reports of those trials for the Judge Advocate? Is it expected that documentary evidence brought into the District Court of the United States for this District by its process and which is constantly needed in the pros[ecution of] cases pending before it and before the Circuit Court of this District shall be transmitted by me to Chicago beyond their jurisdiction? I respectfully suggest that I have no power to do so without contempt of this court. I also suggest that the government is now ready to enter upon the trial of the indictment, and for that purpose I am sending to Chicago a copy of the indictment and a capias for General Babcock" "The speech of Mr Henderson was extemporaneous and the stenographic reports alone can determine the correctness of your information. Mr Eaton sent you the portions relating to this subject. Please examine them and answer at once." ALS, LS, and ALS (press, telegrams sent), *ibid.*, RG 118, Letters Sent, U.S. Attorneys, Eastern District, Mo.; telegrams received (at 2:20, 2:24, and 5:17 P.M.), *ibid.*, RG 60, Letters Received, Mo. *HMD*, 44-1-186, 5. On April 1, 1876, Dyer testified before the select committee. "Q. Did you send the documents, evidence, and list of witnesses to Colonel Gardner, as directed by the Attorney-General?— A. I never furnished him any list of witnesses or anything else. . . . I made up my mind that I would not send it to him, and I did not. In the first place, I could not have sent it to him without being in contempt of the court, by sending testimony out of the jurisdiction of the court, and in the next place, if the grand jury was going to find a true bill against Babcock, I did not propose that Asa Bird Gardner or anybody else should have the looking over of that testimony in court, and make it public to the world before I should try the case." *Ibid.*, p. 40. See *ibid.*, pp. 57, 63; Dyer to Asa B. Gardiner, Dec. 9, 1875, DNA, RG 118, Letters Sent, U.S. Attorneys, Eastern District, Mo.

On or before Dec. 9, Elias W. Fox and eighteen others, St. Louis, wrote to USG. "The undersigned, late United States Grand Jurors for the Eastern District of Missouri, in the discharge of their sworn duty, have found it imperative upon them to present to the United States Court of said District the names of many officials and other persons connected with conspiracy to defraud the Internal Revenue of the United States. As citizens of our common country, sincerely desiring to uphold the hands of the Chief Executive in securing an honest collection of the public revenue, we cannot refrain from thus testifying to our estimation of the moral support which we have leaned upon, as imparted in your notable instructions to the Secretary of the Treasury, *'Let no guilty man escape.'* With this, all good citizens can contribute their share in aiding the Government, and in sustaining your administration in its endeavors to conduct it with purity and fidelity. We, individually and collectively, tender to you our highest considerations of esteem and confidence, and an assurance of our appreciation of the wisdom, patriotism and independence displayed in directing the measures necessary for detecting and correcting the gigantic frauds which have so lately preyed upon the public revenues." *St. Louis Globe-Democrat*, Dec. 10, 1875. On Nov. 3, Dyer had written to Barnard. "I am in receipt of your favor of the 2d inst in which you say that you are creditably informed that the Gov't's interest demands the dropping of Messrs E. W. Fox and Henry Griffin from the present Grand Jury on the grounds of their intimate personal relations with some of the parties implicated in the revenue frauds—I am obliged to you for the information, but you know or ought to know that I have no power to drop any man from the panel of my own motion—. . . I will therefore be obliged to you if you will give me the name of your informant, so that I may take the proper steps to procure his affidavit to be presented to the Court, . . ." ALS (press), DNA, RG 118, Letters Sent, U.S. Attorneys, Eastern District, Mo. On April 1, 1876, Dyer testified concerning Fox. ". . . I am now perfectly convinced that there was a man upon that grand jury who disclosed every fact that was testified to there in reference to Babcock. He came here to Washington in January, and I am satisfied that he knew all that occurred in the grand-jury room and made use of it. . . . Q. You refer to things that he said to the President about you, do you not?—A. Yes, sir; there was a matter about me—that I understood he said that I had brow-beaten the grand jury into finding an indictment against Babcock, and had sworn myself as a witness in the case. The fact was this: when the question came before the grand jury as to whether the Sylph dispatch was in Babcock's handwriting I became a little impatient and told them that there had never been any question about that; that the Secretary of the Treasury and the Attorney-General both had told me that General Babcock admitted the dispatch; and Fox asked if I was under oath, and then I was sworn and testified that I had been so informed. . . . I see it announced in the papers that William C. Fox, who I understand to be a son of E. W. Fox, has been recently appointed to a consulship at some German state. Fox is a man that was formerly a collector of the port at Saint Louis, and a smart, shrewd fellow he is. . . . Q. How is it that you know that he represented these things about what had transpired in the grand-jury room concerning yourself?— A. . . . The Attorney-General remarked to me that there was a grand juror here, and he said he found that so far as any information that came to him was concerned, it was known by the President before it was known by him; that he had gone over intending to tell the President of the statements I had made about Grimes, and the President volunteered to tell him about it, and he spoke of a grand juror, and I knew Fox had been here. . . . The trouble in Saint Louis all the time has been from a set of self-constituted advisers who undertake to know more about a man's business than he does himself, and who are always running to the President and talking about an attempt being made to throw mud on him. . . . Another man who, I think, has given most of the information is W. D. W. Barnard, a banker in Saint Louis. He is a brother-in-law of John Dent, who is a brother-in-law of General Grant, and Fox would go and tell Barnard, and he would write to the President. There has been a continual effort from the first to make a misunderstanding. Q. What was the evidence of Grimes that was communicated by the President?—A. It was that General Babcock had written to John McDonald, under cover to Grimes, three letters, and that

Grimes had delivered the letters to McDonald after his (McDonald's) indictment." *HMD*, 44-1-186, 40–41. On July 12 and 13, Fox testified concerning a Jan. conversation with USG. "I said to the President that I thought that Dyer's action before the grand jury was unprofessional, and that his general talk was of such a character that I checked him two or three times, and told him that I thought he was going beyond his duty. He volunteered statements to such an extent that I interrupted him and demanded that he be sworn. . . . Q. Are you prepared to swear that you did not go to the President of the United States and detail the facts which had appeared before the grand jury?—A. I am. . . . Q. If the President told Attorney-General Pierrepont that you did tell him over the evidence given before the grand jury, did he or did he not tell the truth?—A. I do not know what he told the Attorney-General. . . . I may have stated some facts that occurred before the grand jury, but I did not state it as communicating it, because it was all published. If there was any fact that I stated in connection with it, and you will call my attention to it, I will tell you whether I said it or not. I claim I had a right to speak to the President as much as I would to Mr. Dyer, and would have no hesitancy in doing so, but it was a short interview, and I do not recall any special point. I do not think the President would lie about it. If he has made any representations to the Attorney-General that I said a certain thing, I have no doubt he told the truth." *Ibid.*, pp. 337, 339, 341–42. See John McDonald, *Secrets of the Great Whiskey Ring . . .* (Chicago, 1880), pp. 206–10; letter to Elias W. Fox, June 5, 1874.

On Dec. 9, 1875, James H. Wilson, New York City, had written to USG. "Confidential . . . On the 8th day of November I received a private letter from my brother Maj Wilson now Solicitor of the Treasury enclosing a letter dated Novr 7th addressed to you, giving you a summary of the case agnst Gen'l Babcock. The Major requested me to deliv[e]r this letter to you in person unless I should perceive some good reason why I should not do so, and I write now to say that while I approve heartily of the idea of laying the whole case before you, I failed to deliver the letter because I regarded it as the duty of the Attorney General and the Secretary of the Treasury and not of the Solicitor to communicate directly with you upon such grave affairs, and advised the Solicitor to that effect. I may add that I heard shortly afterwards that this idea had been adopted, and I thought no more abt. the letter addressed to you. Permit me to say one [*word*] more Mr President and that is that if all the other officers of the government had served you with the unshaken unselfish fidelity, and personal devotion that I know has actuated Gen'l Bristow, & Maj. Wilson, in every thought, word and deed, you would have had far less cause for feeling annoyed than you have had. They have not only done their duty by you fearlessly and well, but I am sure they have striven to so conduct themselves in the trying situations they have held as to avoid not only evil itself but every appearance of evil. In closing this note, I cannot refrain from expressing the earnest hope that you will, hereafter as heretofore, give them your confidence unreservedly and fully, permitting no officious interference between you and them, no matter what source it may come from, and I express this hope in the strong conviction that no one can intermeddle but to your common detriment and annoyance, and from interested motives alike injurious to you and the honor of your name and administration—Thanking you for the patient and courteous hearing you gave Maj. Wilson yesterday, and trusting that you will pardon the liberty I have taken in writing to you at such length, . . ." ALS (press), DLC-James H. Wilson. On Sept. 24, Solicitor of the Treasury Bluford Wilson had written to Henderson, St. Louis. "This will introduce to you William H. Herr, an agent of the secret-service division of the Treasury Department, who is sent to you for special duty in connection with the cases of the United States against McDonald and Joyce for conspiracy and violation of the internal-revenue laws. It seems especially desirable, in view of the importance of those cases, that the defendants should be placed under strict surveillance for the next ten days or two weeks, in order to anticipate any

move on their part to escape, and to keep yourself apprised as far as possible of their asso-
ciations, movements, and plans with reference to the charge of conspiracy. Referring to my
conference with you when here, I need not remind you that it is every way important that
you should neglect no fair precaution to reach the very bottom or *top* of the conspiracy in
its ramifications. Perhaps the opportunity to obtain information may be got during the
next ten days. It will be well for you to put in with Herr some man of your own choice. The
latter has orders to follow your instructions in everything." *HMD*, 44-1-186, 488. On
July 27, 1876, Bluford Wilson testified. ". . . It turned out that this letter of mine was taken
from among the papers of General Henderson while he was engaged in a law argument in
the courts at Saint Louis; that McDonald or Joyce got possession of it, and, to support the
charge that I was putting spies on the President, after the word 'top,' in my letter, the capital letters 'W. H.' were forged therein. The forgery was apparent on comparison with the
letter-press copy, which I was lucky enough under the circumstances to have retained in
my letter-book, and that fact doubtless saved me from instant removal. . . . General Horace Porter, a warm friend of General Babcock's, and at that time of my own, was that Sunday in the city. In going down for my letter-book I met him somewhat disturbed about the
matter. . . . After my interview with General Porter I supposed that the matter of the forged
letter was settled, and gave no more attention to it until I was sent for by the President.
The President said to me, in substance, that it seemed to him that I was endeavoring to involve him in frauds. I expressed my surprise, and asked him upon what ground. He said,
'You wrote a letter to Saint Louis to General John B. Henderson, a copy of which I have
seen, in which you tell General Henderson that he must go to the very bottom and top of
the W. H. It was written to General Henderson during my visit to Saint Louis, about the
time I left Long Branch, and the time which you therein seemed to indicate as necessary
for extra vigilance was the ten days, or about the time that it was understood I was to remain there.' He asked me what explanation I had to make of it, stating that Mr. Dyer and
Mr. Henderson were personal enemies of his, and that it was important to him to know just
what attitude the prosecution meant to assume with reference to those trials. He expressed
to me his confident belief in General Babcock's innocence. . . . I told the President that we
would let the matter rest there until I could go and get my letter-books, and my record as
contained in my private memoranda in connection with the whole Babcock matter, and he
consented to that. I got my letter-press book. I got his Barnard letter. I got all the other
memoranda which I thought would throw any light upon my connection with General
Babcock's case and went back. I showed the President in the first place the Barnard letter, . . . I read to the President of the United States the concluding sentences in his letter
in which he said, 'Be especially vigilant, or charge those in authority to be, against all those
who claim to have high authority to protect or to protect them,'. . . and I said to him,
'Mr. President, what I have done in the premises touching General Babcock I have done
under the warrant and in full pursuance of your own instructions to the Secretary of the
Treasury and to myself.' He said, 'Certainly. I had Babcock and Jim Casey in mind when I
made that indorsement, and I expected you to do your duty.'. . . I showed him my letter-
book containing the original and showed him the forgery, and on that he expressed himself as entirely and wholly satisfied. I explained to him that it was General Babcock that I
meant in the letter, and not himself; . . . The President was not satisfied with Mr. Henderson nor with Mr. Dyer; he referred to Mr. Henderson's acts of hostility to him and also to
Mr. Dyer, (he said he did not mind Dyer so much,) and stated that when they were appointed he had acquiesced in it, but had not taken any active part. He said, however, that
he was entirely satisfied with my explanation of my conduct in the premises, and gave me
a hearty greeting when I went away. Q. You have stated in your examination that during
an interview which you had with General Horace Porter the subject of the 'Sylph' dispatch

was discussed; that General Porter undertook to explain that dispatch by stating that the word 'Sylph' referred to a lewd woman with whom the President of the United States had been in intimate relations; did you call the attention of the President of the United States to this statement . . . and, if so, what did the President say in relation thereto?—A. I did, and in doing so said to the President that my justification for going on after my interview with General Porter was in the fact that the explanation he made to me was not satisfactory. I said to the President that he was put, by General Porter, in the attitude of having been the subject of McDonald's kind offices in connection with a lewd woman named Sylph. Q. What did the President say?—A. The President expressed his surprise that the general should have made such a statement, and said there was not one word of truth in it; brushed it out of his way in this way, [illustrating by a contemptuous gesture,] and went on. . . . Q. Do you not believe, and did you not at the time believe, that this explanation of General Porter's of the 'Sylph' dispatch was intended to deter you from doing your duty in the prosecution of General Babcock?—A. Most undoubtedly I did, and do." *Ibid.*, pp. 358–62 (brackets in original). Wilson testified that this meeting with USG had taken place on Dec. 8, 1875. See *ibid.*, p. 364. See also McDonald, *Secrets of the Great Whiskey Ring*, pp. 113–20, 193–202.

On Dec. 10, Fish recorded in his diary. "General Henderson's speech at St. Louis, in his summing up in the prosecution against Avery was read from a sworn copy of the notes taken by the Stenographer; as also telegrams from Dyer and Henderson. Without dissenting opinion it was agreed that the speech was an indecency and an outrage upon professional propriety, and the Attorney General was instructed to prepare a telegram discontinuing his employment; which he did and read to the Cabinet while in Session." DLC-Hamilton Fish. Pierrepont wrote to Dyer. "The sworn report of Mr Henderson's speech forwarded by Mr Eaton, and refered to by both you and Mr Henderson in your dispatches of yesterday as a *correct* report, was read in full cabinet to-day; and it was regarded by every member as an ~~gross~~ outrage upon professional propriety thus to reflect (without a shadow of reason) upon the President by whom ~~your~~ his employment by this Department was sanctioned in order that no impediment might be placed in the way, of bringing to speedy punishment every defrauder of the revenue at St Louis—you will ~~forthwith~~ advise Gen. Henderson of his discharge from further service and secure in his place the aid of the most able and efficient counsel you ~~whatever~~ can find without regard to his politics ~~or religion~~" ADfS (undated), USG 3. *HMD*, 44-1-186, 5–6. See letter to Edwards Pierrepont, Dec. 13, 1875.

On Dec. 13, Alexander P. Tutton, supervisor of Internal Revenue, Downington, Pa., wrote at length to USG. "I observe that ex-Senator Henderson, in the trial of the case of the U. S. vs. Avery (if his speech is correctly reported), charges General Babcock, your private secretary, with having some connection with the 'St. Louis Whisky Ring,' and in their interest, having improperly influenced you to revoke the order of the Secretary of the Treasury, transferring Supervisors, dated January 27th, 1875. As I have claimed the credit of having influenced you to revoke that order, I feel it my duty now to assume the responsibility and receive whatever odium, if any, attaches thereto. And with this in view, I beg leave to remind you of the facts as they recur to me. . . ." *Philadelphia Public Ledger*, Dec. 17, 1875. For Tutton's later testimony on this point, see Endorsement, July 29, 1875; see also Deposition, [*Feb. 12, 1876*].

On Dec. 12, Babcock, Chicago, had written to USG. "Since my request for a Court of Inquiry as the only appearent means open to me at the time of refuting the charges made against me at St Louis, a bill of indictment has been found in the U S Court and I shall consequently be afforded a means of vindication before that tribunal. I therefore respectfully suggest that the order convening the ~~e~~Court of Inquiry be revoked, as I trust that my case may be reached at an early day in the U S Court." ALS, DNA, RG 94, Letters Received, 6074 1875. On Dec. 15, AG Edward D. Townsend issued orders disbanding the court of inquiry. ADS, *ibid.* On Dec. 21, Fish recorded in his diary. "The subject of the Whiskey Frauds in Chicago and St Louis, more especially the prosecutions at Chicago, occupied most of the time. The question of compromise proposed with some of the indicted parties at St Louis on condition of their disclosing the opperations of the whole ring were talked of but it was deemed advisable to let the law take its course with out any intervention or stipulation with reference to any party   The Secretary of War read a long paper addressed to him by Major Gardiner, the Judge Advocate General detailed on the Babcock Inquiry complaining of Dyer the District Attorney of Saint Louis   The tone of this paper made a very unpleasant impression on my mind at least as to the object and expectations of results from that Court. Belknap narrated a long statement made to him by Gardiner of Genl Hancocks course on the opening of the Court   The statement was throughout that of a partisan and seemed to evince the loss of opportunity for some purpose which I do not wish to speculate upon." DLC-Hamilton Fish. See Nevins, *Fish*, pp. 790–92.

On Aug. 1, 1876, Sniffen wrote to U.S. Representative Harris M. Plaisted of Maine. "In connection with the subject of General Babcock's application (copy herewith) on the 2nd of December last for a Court of Inquiry, I am directed by the President to state that that application was, with the exception of the Secretary of the Navy, submitted to the entire Cabinet on the day of its presentation and answer to it was deferred until the following day, Friday December 3rd (and the day of the regular meeting of the Cabinet) when the order was given to convene the Court of Inquiry without a dissenting word from any Member. Before the Court of Inquiry proceeded to take testimony an indictment was found against General Babcock by the Grand Jury then in session in St. Louis and the Court of Inquiry adjourned without further action." Copy, DLC-USG, II, 3. On Aug. 5, Plaisted telegraphed to Sniffen. "Please send me certified copy of Babcock's application for court of inquiry, a complete copy   Send to me at Judiciary room" Telegram received, DNA, RG 107, Telegrams Collected (Bound). On Aug. 7, Plaisted, a Republican member of the select committee, questioned Bluford Wilson. "If the Secretary of the Treasury, in Cabinet meeting on the 2d and 3d of December, assented to the proposition of General Babcock in his application for a court of inquiry, or did not then and there object to the court of inquiry, was it fair and honorable on his part to represent to the district attorney his settled purpose to see that the proceedings before the civil tribunal should not be postponed, delayed, or embarrassed by the military tribunal?" Wilson responded: ". . . I have stated that, in my judgment, the Secretary of the Treasury had no objection to forty courts of inquiry so long as they did not interfere by taking away the evidence from the civil tribunal. That was the point of difficulty, and not the mere fact of the court of inquiry itself." *HMD*, 44-1-186, 492.

Annual Message

———

To the Senate and House of Representatives:

In submitting my seventh annual message to Congress, in this centennial year of our national existence as a free and independent people, it affords me great pleasure to recur to the advancement that has been made from the time of the colonies, one hundred years ago. We were then a people numbering only three millions. Now we number more than forty millions. Then industries were confined almost exclusively to the tillage of the soil. Now manufactories absorb much of the labor of the country.

Our liberties remain unimpaired; the bondmen have been freed from slavery; we have become possessed of the respect, if not the friendship, of all civilized nations. Our progress has been great in all the arts; in science, agriculture, commerce, navigation, mining, mechanics, law, medicine, &c.; and in general education the progress is likewise encouraging. Our thirteen States have become thirty-eight, including Colorado, (which has taken the initiatory steps to become a State,) and eight Territories, including the Indian Territory and Alaska, and excluding Colorado, making a territory extending from the Atlantic to the Pacific. On the south we have extended to the Gulf of Mexico, and in the west from the Mississippi to the Pacific.

One hundred years ago the cotton-gin, the steamship, the railroad, the telegraph, the reaping, sewing, and modern printing machines, and numerous other inventions of scarcely less value to our business and happiness, were entirely unknown.

In 1776, manufactories scarcely existed even in name in all this vast territory. In 1870, more than two millions of persons were employed in manufactories, producing more than $2,100,000,000 of products in amount annually, nearly equal to our national debt. From nearly the whole of the population of 1776 being engaged in the one occupation of agriculture, in 1870 so numerous and diversified had become the occupation of our people that less than six millions out of more than forty millions were so engaged. The extraordinary effect produced in our country by a resort to diversified occupations has built a market for the products of fertile lands distant from the seaboard and the markets of the world.

The American system of locating various and extensive manufactories next to the plow and the pasture, and adding connecting railroads and steamboats, has produced in our distant interior country a result noticeable by the intelligent portions of all commercial nations. The ingenuity and skill of American mechanics have been demonstrated at home and abroad in a manner most flattering to their pride. But for the extraordinary genius and ability of our mechanics, the achievements of our agriculturists, manufacturers, and transporters throughout the country would have been impossible of attainment.

The progress of the miner has also been great. Of coal our production was small; now many millions of tons are mined annually. So with iron, which formed scarcely an appreciable part of our products half a century ago, we now produce more than the world consumed at the beginning of our national existence. Lead, zinc, and copper, from being articles of import, we may expect to be large exporters of in the near future. The development of gold and silver mines in the United States and Territories has not only been remarkable, but has had a large influence upon the business of all commercial nations. Our merchants in the last hundred years have had a success and have established a reputation for enterprise, sagacity, progress, and integrity unsurpassed by peoples of older nationalities. This "good name" is not confined to their homes, but goes out upon every sea and into every port where commerce enters. With equal pride we can point to our progress in all of the learned professions.

As we are now about to enter upon our second centennial—commencing our manhood as a nation—it is well to look back upon the past and study what will be best to preserve and advance our future greatness. From the fall of Adam for his transgression to the present day, no nation has ever been free from threatened danger to its prosperity and happiness. We should look to the dangers threatening us, and remedy them so far as lies in our power. We are a republic whereof one man is as good as another before the law. Under such a form of government it is of the greatest importance that all should be possessed of education and intelligence enough to cast a vote with a right understanding of its meaning. A large association of ignorant men cannot, for any considerable period, oppose a successful resistance to tyranny and oppression from the educated few, but will inevitably sink into acquiescence to the will of intelligence, whether directed by the demagogue or by priestcraft. Hence the education of the masses becomes of the first necessity for the preser-

vation of our institutions. They are worth preserving, because they
have secured the greatest good to the greatest proportion of the population of any form of government yet devised. All other forms of
government approach it just in proportion to the general diffusion of
education and independence of thought and action. As the primary
step, therefore, to our advancement in all that has marked our progress in the past century, I suggest for your earnest consideration,
and most earnestly recommend it, that a constitutional amendment
be submitted to the legislatures of the several States for ratification,
making it the duty of each of the several States to establish and forever maintain free public schools adequate to the education of all the
children in the rudimentary branches within their respective limits, irrespective of sex, color, birthplace, or religions; forbidding the
teaching in said schools of religious, atheistic, or pagan tenets; and
prohibiting the granting of any school-funds, or school-taxes, or
any part thereof, either by legislative, municipal, or other authority,
for the benefit or in aid, directly or indirectly, of any religious sect or
denomination, or in aid or for the benefit of any other object of any
nature or kind whatever.[1]

In connection with this important question, I would also call
your attention to the importance of correcting an evil that, if permitted to continue, will probably lead to great trouble in our land
before the close of the nineteenth century. It is the accumulation of
vast amounts of untaxed church-property.[2]

In 1850, I believe, the church-property of the United States which
paid no tax, municipal or State, amounted to about $83,000,000. In
1860, the amount had doubled; in 1875, it is about $1,000,000,000.
By 1900, without check, it is safe to say this property will reach a
sum exceeding $3,000,000,000. So vast a sum, receiving all the pro-
tection and benefits of government, without bearing its proportion
of the burdens and expenses of the same, will not be looked upon ac-
quiescently by those who have to pay the taxes. In a growing country, where real estate enhances so rapidly with time as in the United
States, there is scarcely a limit to the wealth that may be acquired by
corporations, religious or otherwise, if allowed to retain real estate
without taxation. The contemplation of so vast a property as here al-

luded to, without taxation, may lead to sequestration without constitutional authority and through blood.

I would suggest the taxation of all property equally, whether church or corporation, exempting only the last resting-place of the dead, and, possibly, with proper restrictions, church-edifices.

Our relations with most of the foreign powers continue on a satisfactory and friendly footing.

Increased intercourse, the extension of commerce, and the cultivation of mutual interests have steadily improved our relations with the large majority of the powers of the world, rendering practicable the peaceful solution of questions which from time to time necessarily arise, leaving few which demand extended or particular notice.

The correspondence of the Department of State with our diplomatic representatives abroad is transmitted herewith.

I am happy to announce the passage of an act by the General Cortes of Portugal, proclaimed since the adjournment of Congress, for the abolition of servitude in the Portuguese colonies. It is to be hoped that such legislation may be another step toward the great consummation to be reached, when no man shall be permitted, directly or indirectly, under any guise, excuse, or form of law, to hold his fellow-man in bondage. I am of opinion also that it is the duty of the United States, as contributing toward that end, and required by the spirit of the age in which we live, to provide by suitable legislation that no citizen of the United States shall hold slaves as property in any other country or be interested therein.

Chili has made reparation in the case of the whale-ship Good Return, seized without sufficient cause upward of forty years ago. Though she had hitherto denied her accountability, the denial was never acquiesced in by this Government, and the justice of the claim has been so earnestly contended for that it has been gratifying that she should have at last acknowledged it.

The arbitrator in the case of the United States steamer Montijo, for the seizure and detention of which the Government of the United States of Colombia was held accountable, has decided in favor of the claim. This decision has settled a question which had been pending for several years, and which, while it continued open, might more or less disturb the good understanding which it is desirable should be maintained between the two republics.

A reciprocity treaty with the King of the Hawaiian Islands was concluded some months since. As it contains a stipulation that it shall not take effect until Congress shall enact the proper legislation for that purpose, copies of the instrument are herewith submitted, in order that, if such should be the pleasure of Congress, the necessary legislation upon the subject may be adopted.

In March last an arrangement was made, through Mr. Cushing, our minister in Madrid, with the Spanish government, for the payment by the latter to the United States of the sum of eighty thousand dollars in coin, for the purpose of the relief of the families or persons of the ship's company and certain passengers of the Virginius. This sum was to have been paid in three installments at two months each. It is due to the Spanish government that I should state that the payments were fully and spontaneously anticipated by that government, and that the whole amount was paid within but a few days more than two months from the date of the agreement, a copy of which is herewith transmitted. In pursuance of the terms of the adjustment I have directed the distribution of the amount among the parties entitled thereto, including the ship's company and such of the passengers as were American citizens. Payments are made accordingly, on the application by the parties entitled thereto.

The past year has furnished no evidence of an approaching termination of the ruinous conflict which has been raging for seven years in the neighboring island of Cuba.[3] The same disregard of the laws of civilized warfare and of the just demands of humanity which has heretofore called forth expressions of condemnation from the nations of Christendom has continued to blacken the sad scene. Desolation, ruin, and pillage are pervading the rich fields of one of the most fertile and productive regions of the earth, and the incendiaries' torch, firing plantations and valuable factories and buildings, is the agent marking the alternate advance or retreat of contending parties.

The protracted continuance of this strife seriously affects the interests of all commercial nations, but those of the United States more than others, by reason of close proximity, its larger trade and intercourse with Cuba, and the frequent and intimate personal and social relations which have grown up between its citizens and those of the island. Moreover, the property of our citizens in Cuba is large, and is rendered insecure and depreciated in value and in capacity of production by the continuance of the strife and the unnatural mode of its conduct. The same is true, differing only in degree, with respect to the interests and people of other nations; and the absence of any reasonable assurance of a near termination of the conflict must, of necessity, soon compel the states thus suffering to consider what the interests of their own people and their duty toward themselves may demand.

I have hoped that Spain would be enabled to establish peace in her colony, to afford security to the property and the interests of our citizens, and allow legitimate scope to trade and commerce and the natural productions of the island. Because of this hope, and from an extreme reluctance to interfere in the most remote manner in the affairs of another and a friendly nation, especially of one whose sympathy and friendship in the struggling infancy of our own existence must ever be remembered with gratitude, I have patiently and anxiously waited the progress of events. Our own civil conflict is too recent for us not to consider the difficulties which surround a government distracted by a dynastic rebellion at home, at the same time that it has to cope with separate insurrection in a distant colony. But whatever causes may have produced the situation which so grievously affects our interests, it exists, with all its attendant evils operating directly upon this country and its people. Thus far all the efforts of Spain have proved abortive, and time has marked no improvement in the situation. The armed bands of either side now occupy nearly the same ground as in the past, with the difference, from time to time, of more lives sacrificed, more property destroyed, and wider extents of fertile and productive fields and more and more of valuable property constantly wantonly sacrificed to the incendiaries' torch.

In contests of this nature, where a considerable body of people, who have attempted to free themselves of the control of the superior government, have reached such point in occupation of territory, in power, and in general organization as to constitute in fact a body politic, having a government in substance as well as in name, possessed of the elements of stability, and equipped with the machinery for the administration of internal policy and the execution of its laws, prepared and able to administer justice at home, as well as in its dealings with other powers, it is within the province of those other powers to recognize its existence as a new and independent nation. In such cases other nations simply deal with an actually existing condition of things, and recognize as one of the powers of the earth that body politic which, possessing the necessary elements, has, in fact, become a new power. In a word, the creation of a new state is a fact.

To establish the condition of things essential to the recognition of this fact, there must be a people occupying a known territory, united under some known and defined form of government, acknowledged by those subject thereto, in which the functions of government are administered by usual methods, competent to mete out justice to citizens and strangers, to afford remedies for public and for private wrongs, and able to assume the correlative international obligations, and capable of performing the corresponding international duties resulting from its acquisition of the rights of sovereignty. A power should exist complete in its organization, ready to take and able to maintain its place among the nations of the earth.

While conscious that the insurrection in Cuba has shown a strength and endurance which make it at least doubtful whether it be in the power of Spain to subdue it, it seems unquestionable that no such civil organization exists which may be recognized as an independent government capable of performing its international obligations and entitled to be treated as one of the powers of the earth. A recognition under such circumstances would be inconsistent with the facts, and would compel the power granting it soon to support by force the government to which it had really given its only claim of existence. In my judgment, the United States should adhere to the policy and the principles which have heretofore been its sure and safe guides in like contests between revolted colonies and their mother country, and, acting only upon the clearest evidence, should avoid any possibility of suspicion or of imputation.

A recognition of the independence of Cuba being, in my opinion, impracticable and indefensible, the question which next presents itself is that of the recognition of belligerent rights in the parties to the contest.

In a former message to Congress I had occasion to consider this question, and reached the conclusion that the conflict in Cuba, dreadful and devastating as were its incidents, did not rise to the fearful dignity of war.[4] Regarding it now, after this lapse of time, I am unable to see that any notable success, or any marked or real advance on the part of the insurgents, has essentially changed the character of the contest. It has acquired greater age, but not greater or more formidable proportions. It is possible that the acts of foreign powers, and even acts of Spain herself, of this very nature, might be pointed to in defense of such recognition. But now, as in its past history, the United States should carefully avoid the false lights which might lead it into the mazes of doubtful law and of questionable propriety, and adhere rigidly and sternly to the rule, which has been its guide, of doing only that which is right and honest and of good report. The question of according or of withholding rights of belligerency must be judged, in every case, in view of the particular attending facts. Unless justified by necessity, it is always, and justly, regarded as an unfriendly act, and a gratuitous demonstration of moral support to the rebellion. It is necessary, and it is required, when the interests and rights of another government or of its people are so far affected by a pending civil conflict as to require a definition of its relations to the parties thereto. But this conflict must be one which will be recognized in the sense of international law as war. Belligerence, too, is a fact. The mere existence of contending armed bodies, and their occasional conflicts, do not constitute war in the sense referred to. Applying to the existing condition of affairs in Cuba the tests recognized by publicists and writers on international law, and which have been observed by nations of dignity, honesty, and power, when free from sensitive or selfish and unworthy motives, I fail to find in the insurrection the existence of such a substantial political organization, real, palpable, and manifest to the world, having the forms and capable of the ordinary functions of government toward its own people and to other states, with courts for the administration of justice, with a local habitation, possessing such organization of force, such material, such occupation of territory, as to take the contest out of the category of a mere rebellious insurrection, or occasional skirmishes, and place it on the terrible footing of war, to which a recognition of belligerency would aim to elevate it. The contest, moreover, is solely on land; the insurrection has not possessed itself of a single sea-port whence it may send forth its flag, nor has it any means of communication with foreign powers except through the military lines of its adversaries. No apprehension of any of those sudden and difficult complications which a war upon the ocean is apt to precipitate upon the vessels, both commercial and national, and upon the consular officers of other powers, calls for the definition of their relations to the parties to the contest. Considered as a question of expediency, I regard the accordance of belligerent rights still to be as unwise and premature, as I regard it to be, at present, indefensible as a measure of right. Such recognition entails upon the country according the rights which flow from it difficult and complicated duties, and requires the exaction from the contending parties of the strict observance of their rights and obligations. It confers the right of search upon the high seas by vessels of both parties; it would subject the carrying of arms and munitions of war, which now may be transported freely and without interruption in the vessels of the United States, to detention and to possible seizure; it would give rise to countless vexatious questions, would release the parent government from responsibility for acts done by the insurgents, and would invest Spain with the right to exercise the supervision recognized by our treaty of 1795 over our commerce on the high seas, a very large part of which, in its traffic between the Atlantic and the Gulf States, and between all of them and the States on the Pacific, passes through the waters which wash the shores of Cuba. The exercise of this supervision could scarce fail to lead, if not to abuses, certainly to collisions perilous to the peaceful relations of the two states. There can be little doubt to what result such supervision would before long draw this nation. It would be unworthy of the United States to inaugurate the possibilities of such result, by measures of questionable right or expediency, or by any indirection. Apart from any question

of theoretical right, I am satisfied that, while the accordance of belligerent rights to the insurgents in Cuba might give them a hope and
an inducement to protract the struggle, it would be but a delusive
hope, and would not remove the evils which this Government and
its people are experiencing, but would draw the United States into
complications which it has waited long and already suffered much to
avoid. The recognition of independence, or of belligerency, being
thus, in my judgment, equally inadmissible, it remains to consider
what course shall be adopted should the conflict not soon be brought
to an end by acts of the parties themselves, and should the evils
which result therefrom, affecting all nations, and particularly the
United States, continue.

In such event, I am of opinion that other nations will be compelled to assume the responsibility which devolves upon them, and
to seriously consider the only remaining measures possible, mediation and intervention. Owing, perhaps, to the large expanse of water
separating the island from the peninsula, the want of harmony and
of personal sympathy between the inhabitants of the colony and
those sent thither to rule them, and want of adaptation of the ancient
colonial system of Europe to the present times and to the ideas
which the events of the past century have developed, the contending
parties appear to have within themselves no depository of common
confidence, to suggest wisdom when passion and excitement have
their sway, and to assume the part of peace-maker. In this view, in the
earlier days of the contest the good offices of the United States as a
mediator were tendered in good faith, without any selfish purpose, in
the interest of humanity and in sincere friendship for both parties,
but were at the time declined by Spain, with the declaration, nevertheless, that at a future time they would be indispensable. No intimation has been received that in the opinion of Spain that time has
been reached. And yet the strife continues with all its dread horrors
and all its injuries to the interests of the United States and of other
nations. Each party seems quite capable of working great injury and
damage to the other, as well as to all the relations and interests dependent on the existence of peace in the island; but they seem incapable of reaching any adjustment, and both have thus far failed of

achieving any success whereby one party shall possess and control the island to the exclusion of the other. Under these circumstances, the agency of others, either by mediation or by intervention, seems to be the only alternative which must, sooner or later, be invoked for the termination of the strife. At the same time, while thus impressed, I do not at this time recommend the adoption of any measure of intervention. I shall be ready at all times, and as the equal friend of both parties, to respond to a suggestion that the good offices of the United States will be acceptable to aid in bringing about a peace honorable to both. It is due to Spain, so far as this Government is concerned, that the agency of a third power, to which I have adverted, shall be adopted only as a last expedient. Had it been the desire of the United States to interfere in the affairs of Cuba, repeated opportunities for so doing have been presented within the last few years; but we have remained passive, and have performed our whole duty and all international obligations to Spain with friendship, fairness, and fidelity, and with a spirit of patience and forbearance which negatives every possible suggestion of desire to interfere or to add to the difficulties with which she has been surrounded.

The government of Spain has recently submitted to our minister at Madrid certain proposals which it is hoped may be found to be the basis, if not the actual submission, of terms to meet the requirements of the particular griefs of which this Government has felt itself entitled to complain. These proposals have not yet reached me in their full text. On their arrival they will be taken into careful examination, and may, I hope, lead to a satisfactory adjustment of the questions to which they refer, and remove the possibility of future occurrences, such as have given rise to our just complaints.

It is understood also that renewed efforts are being made to introduce reforms in the internal administration of the island. Persuaded, however, that a proper regard for the interests of the United States and of its citizens entitle it to relief from the strain to which it has been subjected by the difficulties of the questions, and the wrongs and losses which arise from the contest in Cuba, and that the interests of humanity itself demand the cessation of the strife before the whole island shall be laid waste and larger sacrifices of life be

made, I shall feel it my duty, should my hopes of a satisfactory adjustment and of the early restoration of peace and the removal of future causes of complaint be, unhappily, disappointed, to make a further communication to Congress at some period not far remote, and
during the present session, recommending what may then seem to
me to be necessary.

The Free Zone, so called, several years since established by the
Mexican government in certain of the States of that republic adjacent to our frontier, remains in full operation. It has always been materially injurious to honest traffic, for it operates as an incentive to
trades in Mexico to supply without customs-charges the wants of
inhabitants on this side the line, and prevents the same wants from
being supplied by merchants of the United States, thereby, to a considerable extent, defrauding our revenue and checking honest commercial enterprise.

Depredations by armed bands from Mexico on the people of
Texas near the frontier continue. Though the main object of these
incursions is robbery, they frequently result in the murder of unarmed and peaceably-disposed persons; and in some instances even
the United States post-offices and mail-communications have been
attacked. Renewed remonstrances upon this subject have been addressed to the Mexican government, but without much apparent effect.[5] The military force of this Government disposable for service in
that quarter is quite inadequate to effectually guard the line, even at
those points where the incursions are usually made. An experiment
of an armed vessel on the Rio Grande for that purpose is on trial, and
it is hoped that, if not thwarted by the shallowness of the river and
other natural obstacles, it may materially contribute to the protection of the herdsmen of Texas.

The proceedings of the joint commission under the convention
between the United States and Mexico of the 4th of July, 1868, on
the subject of claims, will soon be brought to a close. The result of
those proceedings will then be communicated to Congress.

I am happy to announce that the government of Venezuela has,
upon further consideration, practically abandoned its objection to
pay to the United States that share of its revenue which some years

since it allotted toward the extinguishment of the claims of foreigners generally. In thus reconsidering its determination that government has shown a just sense of self-respect which cannot fail to reflect credit upon it in the eyes of all disinterested persons elsewhere.
It is to be regretted, however, that its payments on account of claims
of citizens of the United States are still so meager in amount, and
that the stipulations of the treaty in regard to the sums to be paid
and the periods when those payments were to take place should have
been so signally disregarded.

Since my last annual message the exchange has been made of the
ratification of a treaty of commerce and navigation with Belgium,
and of conventions with the Mexican Republic for the further extension of the joint commission respecting claims; with the Hawaiian Islands for commercial reciprocity, and with the Ottoman Empire for extradition; all of which have been duly proclaimed.

The Court of Commissioners of Alabama Claims has prosecuted
its important duties very assiduously and very satisfactorily. It convened and was organized on the 22d day of July, 1874, and, by the
terms of the act under which it was created, was to exist for one year
from that date. The act provided, however, that should it be found
impracticable to complete the work of the court before the expiration of the year, the President might, by proclamation, extend the
time of its duration to a period not more than six months beyond the
expiration of the one year.

Having received satisfactory evidence that it would be impracticable to complete the work within the time originally fixed, I issued
a proclamation (a copy of which is presented herewith) extending
the time of duration of the court for a period of six months from and
after the 22d day of July last.[6]

A report made through the clerk of the court (communicated
herewith) shows the condition of the calendar on the 1st of November last, and the large amount of work which has been accomplished.
Thirteen hundred and eighty-two claims have been presented, of
which six hundred and eighty-two had been disposed of at the date
of the report. I am informed that one hundred and seventy cases were
decided during the month of November. Arguments are being made

and decisions given in the remaining cases with all the dispatch consistent with the proper consideration of the questions submitted. Many of these claims are in behalf of mariners, or depend on the evidence of mariners, whose absence has delayed the taking or the return of the necessary evidence.

It is represented to me that it will be impracticable for the court to finally dispose of all the cases before it within the present limit of its duration. Justice to the parties claimant, who have been at large expense in preparing their claims and obtaining the evidence in their support, suggests a short extension, to enable the court to dispose of all of the claims which have been presented.

I recommend the legislation which may be deemed proper to enable the court to complete the work before it.

I recommend that some suitable provision be made, by the creation of a special court or by conferring the necessary jurisdiction upon some appropriate tribunal, for the consideration and determination of the claims of aliens against the Government of the United States which have arisen within some reasonable limitation of time, or which may hereafter arise, excluding all claims barred by treaty-provisions or otherwise. It has been found impossible to give proper consideration to these claims by the Executive Departments of the Government. Such a tribunal would afford an opportunity to aliens other than British subjects to present their claims on account of acts committed against their persons or property during the rebellion, as also to those subjects of Great Britain whose claims, having arisen subsequent to the 9th day of April, 1865, could not be presented to the late commission organized pursuant to the provisions of the treaty of Washington.

The electric telegraph has become an essential and indispensable agent in the transmission of business and social messages. Its operation on land, and within the limit of particular States, is necessarily under the control of the jurisdiction within which it operates. The lines on the high seas, however, are not subject to the particular control of any one government.

In 1869, a concession was granted by the French government to a company which proposed to lay a cable from the shores of France to the United States. At that time there was a telegraphic connection between the United States and the continent of Europe, (through the possessions of Great Britain at either end of the line,) under the control of an association which had, at large outlay of capital and at great risk, demonstrated the practicability of maintaining such means of communication. The cost of correspondence by this agency was great, possibly not too large at the time for a proper remuneration for so hazardous and so costly an enterprise. It was, however, a heavy charge upon a means of communication which the progress in the social and commercial intercourse of the world found to be a necessity, and the obtaining of this French concession showed that other capital than that already invested was ready to enter into competition, with assurance of adequate return for their outlay. Impressed with the conviction that the interests, not only of the people of the United States, but of the world at large, demanded, or would demand, the multiplication of such means of communication between separated continents, I was desirous that the proposed connection should be made; but certain provisions of this concession were deemed by me to be objectionable, particularly one which gave for a long term of years the exclusive right of telegraphic communication by submarine cable between the shores of France and the United States. I could not concede that any power should claim the right to land a cable on the shores of the United States, and at the same time deny to the United States, or to its citizens or grantees, an equal right to land a cable on its shores. The right to control the conditions for the laying of a cable within the jurisdictional waters of the United States, to connect our shores with those of any foreign state, pertains exclusively to the Government of the United States, under such limitations and conditions as Congress may impose. In the absence of legislation by Congress, I was unwilling, on the one hand, to yield to a foreign state the right to say that its grantees might land on our shores, while it denied a similar right to our people to land on its shores; and, on the other hand, I was reluctant to deny to the great interests of the world and of civilization the facilities of such communication as were proposed. I therefore withheld any resistance to the landing of the cable on condition that the offensive monopoly feature of the concession be abandoned, and that the right of any cable which may be established by authority of this Government to land upon French territory, and to connect with French land-lines, and enjoy all the necessary facilities or privileges incident to the use thereof upon as favorable terms as any other company, be conceded. As the result thereof the company in question renounced the exclusive privilege, and the representative of France was informed that, understanding this relinquishment to be construed as granting the entire reciprocity and equal facilities which had been demanded, the opposition to the landing of the cable was withdrawn. The cable, under this French concession, was landed in the month of July, 1869, and has been an efficient and valuable agent of communication between this country and the other continent. It soon passed under the control, however, of those who had the management of the cable connecting Great Britain with this continent, and thus whatever benefit to the public might have ensued from competition between the two lines was lost, leaving only the greater facilities of an additional line, and the additional security in case of accident to one of them. But these increased facilities and this additional security, together with the control of the combined capital of the two companies, gave also greater power to prevent the future construction of other lines, and to limit the control of telegraphic communication between the two continents to those possessing the lines already laid. Within a few months past a cable has been laid, known as the United States Direct Cable Company,[7] connecting the United States directly with Great Britain. As soon as this cable was reported to be laid and in working order, the rates of the then existing consolidated companies were greatly reduced. Soon, however, a break was announced in this new cable, and immediately the rates of the other line, which had been reduced, were again raised. This cable being now repaired, the rates appear not to be reduced by either line from those formerly charged by the consolidated [co]mpanies.

There is reason to believe that large amounts of capital, both at home and abroad, are ready to seek profitable investment in the advancement of this useful and most civilizing means of intercourse and correspondence. They await, however, the assurance of the means and conditions on which they may safely be made tributary to the general good.

As these cable telegraph lines connect separate states, there are questions as to their organization and control, which probably can be best, if not solely, settled by conventions between the respective states. In the absence, however, of international conventions on the subject, municipal legislation may secure many points which appear to me important, if not indispensable for the protection of the public against the extortions which may result from a monopoly of the right of operating cable-telegrams, or from a combination between several lines:

I. No line should be allowed to land on the shores of the United States under the concession from another power, which does not admit the right of any other line or lines, formed in the United States, to land and freely connect with and operate through its land-lines.

II. No line should be allowed to land on the shores of the United States which is not by treaty-stipulation with the government from whose shores it proceeds, or by prohibition in its charter, or otherwise to the satisfaction of this Government, prohibited from consolidating or amalgamating with any other cable telegraph line, or combining therewith for the purpose of regulating and maintaining the cost of telegraphing.

III. All lines should be bound to give precedence in the transmission of the official messages of the governments of the two countries between which it may be laid.

IV. A power should be reserved to the two governments, either conjointly or to each, as regards the messages dispatched from its shores, to fix a limit to the charges to be demanded for the transmission of messages.

I present this subject to the earnest consideration of Congress.

In the mean time, and unless Congress otherwise direct, I shall not oppose the landing of any telegraphic cable which complies with and assents to the points above enumerated, but will feel it my duty to prevent the landing of any which does not conform to the first and second points as stated, and which will not stipulate to concede to this Government the precedence in the transmission of its official messages, and will not enter into a satisfactory arrangement with regard to its charges.

Among the pressing and important subjects to which, in my opinion, the attention of Congress should be directed are those relating to fraudulent naturalization and expatriation.

The United States, with great liberality, offers its citizenship to all who in good faith comply with the requirements of law. These requirements are as simple and upon as favorable terms to the emigrant as the high privilege to which he is admitted can or should permit. I do not propose any additional requirements to those which the law now demands. But the very simplicity and the want of unnecessary formality in our law have made fraudulent naturalization not infrequent, to the discredit and injury of all honest citizens, whether native or naturalized. Cases of this character are continually being brought to the notice of the Government by our representatives abroad, and also those of persons resident in other countries, most frequently those who, if they have remained in this country long enough to entitle them to become naturalized, have generally not much overpassed that period, and have returned to the country of their origin, where they reside, avoiding all duties to the United States by their absence, and claiming to be exempt from all duties to the country of their nativity and of their residence by reason of their alleged naturalization. It is due to this Government itself and to the great mass of the naturalized citizens who entirely, both in name and in fact, become citizens of the United States, that the high privilege of citizenship of the United State should not be held by fraud or in derogation of the laws and of the good name of every honest citizen. On many occasions it has been brought to the knowledge of the Government that certificates of naturalization are held, and protection or interference claimed, by parties who admit that not only they were not within the United States at the time of the pretended naturalization, but that they have never resided in the United States; in others, the certificate and record of the court show on their face that the person claiming to be naturalized had not resided the required time in the United States; in others, it is admitted upon examination that the requirements of law have not been complied with; in some cases even, such certificates have been matter of purchase. These are not isolated cases, arising at rare intervals, but of common occurrence, and which are reported from all quarters of the globe. Such occurrences cannot, and do not, fail to reflect upon the Government and injure all honest citizens. Such a fraud being discovered, however, there is no practicable means within the control of the Government by which the record of naturalization can be vacated; and should the certificate be taken up, as it usually is, by the diplomatic and consular representatives of the government to whom it may have been presented, there is nothing to prevent the person claiming to have been naturalized from obtaining a new certificate from the court in place of that which has been taken from him.

The evil has become so great and of such frequent occurrence that I cannot too earnestly recommend that some effective measures be adopted to provide a proper remedy and means for the vacating of any record thus fraudulently made, and of punishing the guilty parties to the transaction.

In this connection I refer also to the question of expatriation and the election of nationality.[8]

The United States was foremost in upholding the right of expatriation, and was principally instrumental in overthrowing the doctrine of perpetual allegiance. Congress has declared the right of expatriation to be a natural and inherent right of all people; but, while many other nations have enacted laws providing what formalities shall be necessary to work a change of allegiance, the United States has enacted no provisions of law, and has in no respect marked out how and when expatriation may be accomplished by its citizens. Instances are brought to the attention of the Government where citizens of the United States, either naturalized or native-born, have formally become citizens or subjects of foreign powers, but who, nevertheless, in the absence of any provisions of legislation on this question, when involved in difficulties, or when it seems to be their interest, claim to be citizens of the United States, and demand the intervention of a government which they have long since abandoned, and to which for years they have rendered no service, nor held themselves in any way amenable.

In other cases naturalized citizens, immediately after naturalization, have returned to their native country; have become engaged in
business; have accepted offices or pursuits inconsistent with American citizenship, and evidence no intent to return to the United States
until called upon to discharge some duty to the country where they
are residing, when at once they assert their citizenship, and call upon
the representatives of the Government to aid them in their unjust
pretensions. It is but justice to all *bona-fide* citizens that no doubt
should exist on such questions, and that Congress should determine
by enactment of law how expatriation may be accomplished, and
change of citizenship be established.

I also invite your attention to the necessity of regulating by law
the status of American women who may marry foreigners, and of
defining more fully that of children born in a foreign country of
American parents who may reside abroad; and also of some further
provision regulating or giving legal effect to marriages of American
citizens contracted in foreign countries. The correspondence submitted herewith shows a few of the constantly-occurring questions
on these points presented to the consideration of the Government.
There are few subjects to engage the attention of Congress on which
more delicate relations or more important interests are dependent.

In the month of July last the building erected for the Department
of State was taken possession of and occupied by that Department. I
am happy to announce that the archives and valuable papers of the
Government in the custody of that Department are now safely deposited and properly cared for.

The report of the Secretary of the Treasury shows the receipts
from customs for the fiscal year ending June 30, 1874, to have been
$163,103,833.69, and for the fiscal year ending June 30, 1875, to
have been $157,167,722.35, a decrease for the last fiscal year of
$5,936,111.34. Receipts from internal revenue for the year ending
the 30th of June, 1874, were $102,409,784.90, and for the year end-
ing June 30, 1875, $110,007,493.58; increase, $7,597,708.68.

The report also shows a complete history of the workings of the
Department for the last year, and contains recommendations for reforms and for legislation which I concur in, but cannot comment on

so fully as I should like to do if space would permit, but will confine myself to a few suggestions which I look upon as vital to the best interests of the whole people—coming within the purview of "Treasury"—I mean specie resumption.[9] Too much stress cannot be laid upon this question, and I hope Congress may be induced, at the earliest day practicable, to insure the consummation of the act of the last Congress, at its last session, to bring about specie resumption "on and after the 1st of January, 1879," at furthest. It would be a great blessing if this could be consummated even at an earlier day.

Nothing seems to me more certain than that a full, healthy, and permanent reaction cannot take place in favor of the industries and financial welfare of the country until we return to a measure of values recognized throughout the civilized world. While we use a currency not equivalent to this standard, the world's recognized standard, specie, becomes a commodity like the products of the soil, the surplus seeking a market wherever there is a demand for it.

Under our present system we should want none, nor would we have any, were it not that customs-dues must be paid in coin, and because of the pledge to pay interest on the public debt in coin. The yield of precious metals would flow out for the purchase of foreign productions and leave the United States "hewers of wood and drawers of water" because of wiser legislation on the subject of finance by the nations with whom we have dealings. I am not prepared to say that I can suggest the best legislation to secure the end most heartily recommended. It will be a source of great gratification to me to be able to approve any measure of Congress looking effectively toward securing "resumption."

Unlimited inflation would probably bring about specie payments more speedily than any legislation looking to redemption of the legal-tenders in coin. But it would be at the expense of honor. The legal-tenders would have no value beyond settling present liabilities, or, properly speaking, repudiating them. They would buy nothing after debts were all settled.

There are a few measures which seem to me important in this connection, and which I commend to your earnest consideration:

A repeal of so much of the legal-tender act as makes these notes

receivable for debts contracted after a date to be fixed in the act itself, say not later than the 1st of January, 1877. We should then have
quotations at real values, not fictitious ones. Gold would no longer
be at a premium, but currency at a discount. A healthy reaction
would set in at once, and with it a desire to make the currency equal
to what it purports to be. The merchants, manufacturers, and trades-
men of every calling could do business on a fair margin of profit, the
money to be received having an unvarying value. Laborers and all
classes who work for stipulated pay or salary would receive more for
their income, because extra profits would no longer be charged by
the capitalists to compensate for the risk of a downward fluctuation
in the value of the currency.

Second, that the Secretary of the Treasury be authorized to redeem say not to exceed two million ($2,000,000) dollars monthly
of legal-tender notes, by issuing in their stead a long bond, bearing
interest at the rate of 3.65 per cent. per annum, of denominations
ranging from $50 up to $1,000 each. This would in time reduce the
legal-tender notes to a volume that could be kept afloat without demanding redemption in large sums suddenly.

Third, that additional power be given to the Secretary of the
Treasury to accumulate gold for final redemption, either by increasing revenue, curtailing expenses, or both—it is preferable to do
both; and I recommend that reduction of expenditures be made
wherever it can be done without impairing Government obligations
or crippling the due execution thereof. One measure for increasing
the revenue—and the only one I think of—is the restoration of the
duty on tea and coffee. These duties would add probably $18,000,000
to the present amount received from imports, and would in no way
increase the prices paid for those articles by the consumers.[10]

These articles are the products of countries collecting revenue
from exports, and as we, the largest consumers, reduce the duties,
they proportionately increase them. With this addition to the revenue, many duties now collected, and which give but an insignificant
return for the cost of collection, might be remitted, and to the direct
advantage of consumers at home.

I would mention those articles which enter into manufactures of all sorts. All duty paid upon such articles goes directly to the cost of the article when manufactured here, and must be paid for by the consumers. These duties not only come from the consumers at home, but act as a protection to foreign manufacturers of the same completed articles in our own and distant markets.

I will suggest, or mention, another subject bearing upon the problem of "how to enable the Secretary of the Treasury to accumulate balances." It is to devise some better method of verifying claims against the Government than at present exists through the Court of Claims, especially those claims growing out of the late war. Nothing is more certain than that a very large percentage of the amounts passed and paid are either wholly fraudulent or are far in excess of the real losses sustained. The large amount of losses proven—on good testimony according to existing laws, by affidavits of fictitious or unscrupulous persons—to have been sustained on small farms and plantations are not only far beyond the possible yield of those places for any one year, but, as every one knows who has had experience in tilling the soil, and who has visited the scenes of these spoliations, are in many instances more than the individual claimants were ever worth, including their personal and real estate.

The report of the Attorney-General, which will be submitted to Congress at an early day, will contain a detailed history of awards made, and of claims pending of the class here referred to.

The report of the Secretary of War, accompanying this message, gives a detailed account of Army operations for the year just passed, expenses for maintenance, &c., with recommendations for legislation to which I respectfully invite your attention. To some of these I invite special attention:

First, the necessity of making $300,000 of the appropriation for the Subsistence Department available before the beginning of the next fiscal year. Without this provision troops at points distant from supply production must either go without food or existing laws must be violated. It is not attended with cost to the Treasury.

Second, his recommendation for the enactment of a system of annuities for the families of deceased officers by voluntary deductions from the monthly pay of officers. This again is not attended with burden upon the Treasury, and would for the future relieve much distress which every old Army officer has witnessed in the past —of officers dying suddenly or being killed, leaving families without even the means of reaching their friends, if fortunate enough to have friends to aid them.

Third, the repeal of the law abolishing mileage, and a return to the old system.

Fourth, the trial with torpedoes under the Corps of Engineers, and appropriation for the same. Should war ever occur between the United States and any maritime power, torpedoes will be among, if not the most effective and cheapest auxiliary for the defense of harbors, and also in aggressive operations, that we can have. Hence it is advisable to learn by experiment their best construction and application as well as effect.[11]

Fifth, a permanent organization for the Signal-Service Corps. This service has now become a necessity of peace as well as war, under the advancement made by the present able management.

Sixth, a renewal of the appropriation for compiling the official records of the war, &c.

The condition of our Navy at this time is a subject of satisfaction. It does not contain, it is true, any of the powerful cruising iron-clads which make so much of the maritime strength of some other nations, but neither our continental situation nor our foreign policy requires that we should have a large number of ships of this character, while this situation and the nature of our ports combine to make those of other nations little dangerous to us under any circumstances.

Our Navy does contain, however, a considerable number of iron-clads of the monitor class, which, though not properly cruisers, are powerful and effective for harbor defense and for operations near our own shores. Of these all the single-turreted ones, fifteen in number, have been substantially rebuilt, their rotten wooden beams replaced with iron, their hulls strengthened, and their engines and machinery thoroughly repaired, so that they are now in the most efficient condition and ready for sea as soon as they can be manned and put in commission.

The five double-turreted iron-clads belonging to our Navy, by far the most powerful of our ships for fighting purposes, are also in hand undergoing complete repairs, and could be ready for sea in periods varying from four to six months. With these completed according to the present design, and our two iron torpedo-boats now ready, our iron-clad fleet will be, for the purposes of defense at home, equal to any force that can readily be brought against it.

Of our wooden navy also, cruisers of various sizes, to the number of about forty, including those now in commission, are in the Atlantic, and could be ready for duty as fast as men could be enlisted for those not already in commission. Of these, one-third are in effect new ships, and though some of the remainder need considerable repairs to their boilers and machinery, they all are, or can readily be made, effective.

This constitutes a fleet of more than fifty war-ships, of which fifteen are iron-clad, now in hand on the Atlantic coast. The Navy has been brought to this condition by a judicious and practical application of what could be spared from the current appropriations of the last few years, and from that made to meet the possible emergency of two years ago. It has been done quietly, without proclamation or display, and though it has necessarily straitened the Department in its ordinary expenditure, and, as far as the iron-clads are concerned, has added nothing to the cruising force of the Navy, yet the result is not the less satisfactory, because it is to be found in a great increase of real rather than apparent force. The expenses incurred in the maintenance of an effective naval force in all its branches are necessarily large, but such force is essential to our position, relations, and character, and affects seriously the weight of our principles and policy throughout the whole sphere of national responsibilities.

The estimates for the regular support of this branch of the service for the next year amount to a little less in the aggregate than those made for the current year; but some additional appropriations are asked for objects not included in the ordinary maintenance of the Navy, but believed to be of pressing importance at this time. It would, in my opinion, be wise at once to afford sufficient means for the immediate completion of the five double-turreted monitors now undergoing repairs, which must otherwise advance slowly, and only as money can be spared from current expenses. Supplemented by these, our Navy, armed with the destructive weapons of modern warfare, manned by our seamen, and in charge of our instructed officers, will present a force powerful for the home purposes of a responsible though peaceful nation.

The report of the Postmaster-General, herewith transmitted, gives a full history of the workings of the Department for the year just past. It will be observed that the deficiency to be supplied from the General Treasury increased over the amount required for the preceding year. In a country so vast in area as the United States, with large portions sparsely settled, it must be expected that this important service will be more or less a burden upon the Treasury for many years to come. But there is no branch of the public service which interests the whole people more than that of cheap and rapid transmission of the mails to every inhabited part of our territory. Next to the free school, the post-office is the great educator of the people, and it may well receive the support of the General Government.

The subsidy of $150,000 per annum given to vessels of the United States for carrying the mails between New York and Rio de Janeiro having ceased on the 30th day of September last, we are without direct mail facilities with the South American states. This is greatly to be regretted, and I do not hesitate to recommend the authorization of a renewal of that contract, and also that the service may be increased from monthly to semi-monthly trips. The commercial advantages to be gained by a direct line of American steamers to the South American states will far outweigh the expense of the service.

By act of Congress approved March 3, 1875, almost all matter, whether properly mail-matter or not, may be sent any distance through the mails, in packages not exceeding four pounds in weight, for the sum of sixteen cents per pound. So far as the transmission of real mail-matter goes, this would seem entirely proper. But I suggest that the law be so amended as to exclude from the mails merchandise of all descriptions, and limit this transportation to articles enumerated, and which may be classed as mail-matter proper.

The discovery of gold in the Black Hills, a portion of the Sioux

reservation, has had the effect to induce a large emigration of miners to that point. Thus far the effort to protect the treaty rights of
the Indians to that section has been successful, but the next year will
certainly witness a large increase of such emigration. The negotiations for the relinquishment of the gold-fields having failed, it
will be necessary for Congress to adopt some measures to relieve the
embarrassment growing out of the causes named. The Secretary of
the Interior suggests that the supplies now appropriated for the sus-
tenance of that people, being no longer obligatory under the treaty
of 1868, but simply a gratuity, may be issued or withheld at his
discretion.

The condition of the Indian Territory,[12] to which I have referred
in several of my former annual messages, remains practically unchanged. The Secretary of the Interior has taken measures to obtain
a full report of the condition of that Territory, and will make it the
subject of a special report at an early day. It may then be necessary to
make some further recommendation in regard to legislation for the
government of that Territory.

The steady growth and increase of the business of the Patent-
Office indicates, in some measure, the progress of the industrial activity of the country. The receipts of the Office are in excess of its
expenditures, and the Office generally is in a prosperous and satisfactory condition.

The report of the General Land-Office shows that there were
2,459,601 acres less disposed of during this than during the last year.
More than one-half of this decrease was in lands disposed of under
the homestead and timber-culture laws. The cause of this decrease is
supposed to be found in the grasshopper scourge and the droughts
which prevailed so extensively in some of the frontier States and
Territories during that time as to discourage and deter entries by
actual settlers. The cash receipts were less, by $699,322.23 than dur-
ing the preceding year.

The entire surveyed area of the public domain is 680,253,094
acres, of which 26,077,531 acres were surveyed during the past year,
leaving 1,154,471,762 acres still unsurveyed.

The report of the Commissioner presents many interesting suggestions in regard to the management and disposition of the public domain [13] and the modification of existing laws, the apparent importance of which should insure for them the careful consideration of Congress.

The number of pensioners still continues to decrease, the highest number having been reached during the year ending June 30, 1873. During the last year, 11,557 names were added to the rolls, and 12,977 were dropped therefrom, showing a net decrease of 1,420. But while the number of pensioners has decreased, the annual amount due on the pension-rolls has increased $44,733.13. This is caused by the greatly increased average rate of pensions, which, by the liberal legislation of Congress, has increased from $90.26 in 1872 to $103.91 in 1875 to each invalid pensioner, an increase in the average rate of fifteen per cent. in the three years. During the year ending June 30, 1875, there was paid on account of pensions, including the expenses of disbursement, $29,683,116, being $910,632 less than was paid the preceding year. This reduction in amount of expenditures was produced by the decrease in the amount of arrearages due on allowed claims, and on pensions, the rate of which was increased by the legislation of the preceding session of Congress. At the close of the last fiscal year there were on the pension-rolls 234,821 persons, of whom 210,363 were Army pensioners, 105,478 being invalids and 104,885 widows and dependent relatives; 3,420 were Navy pensioners, of whom 1,636 were invalids and 1,784 widows and dependent relatives; 21,038 were pensioners of the war of 1812, 15,875 of whom were survivors and 5,163 were widows.

It is estimated that $29,535,000 will be required for the payment of pensions for the next fiscal year, an amount $965,000 less than the estimate for the present year.

The geological explorations have been prosecuted with energy during the year, covering an area of about forty thousand square miles in the Territories of Colorado, Utah, and New Mexico, developing the agricultural and mineral resources, and furnishing interesting scientific and topographical details of that region.

The method for the treatment of the Indians, adopted at the beginning of my first term, has been steadily pursued, and with satisfactory and encouraging results. It has been productive of evident improvement in the condition of that race, and will be continued, with only such modifications as further experience may indicate to be necessary.

The board heretofore appointed to take charge of the articles and materials pertaining to the War, the Navy, the Treasury, the Interior, and the Post-Office Departments, and the Department of Agriculture, the Smithsonian Institution, and the Commission of Food-Fishes, to be contributed, under the legislation of last session, to the International Exhibition to be held at Philadelphia during the centennial year 1876, has been diligent in the discharge of the duties which have devolved upon it; and the preparations so far made with the means at command give assurance that the governmental contribution will be made one of the marked characteristics of the exhibition. The board has observed commendable economy in the matter of the erection of a building for the governmental exhibit, the expense of which it is estimated will not exceed, say, $80,000. This amount has been withdrawn, under the law, from the appropriations of five of the principal Departments, which leaves some of those Departments without sufficient means to render their respective practical exhibits complete and satisfactory. The exhibition being an international one, and the Government being a voluntary contributor, it is my opinion that its contribution should be of a character, in quality and extent, to sustain the dignity and credit of so distinguished a contributor. The advantages to the country of a creditable display are, in an international point of view, of the first importance, while an indifferent or uncreditable participation by the Government would be humiliating to the patriotic feelings of our people themselves. I commend the estimates of the board for the necessary additional appropriations to the favorable consideration of Congress.

The powers of Europe, almost without exception, many of the South American states, and even the more distant eastern powers, have manifested their friendly sentiments toward the United States and the interest of the world in our progress by taking steps to join with us in celebrating the centennial of the nation, and I strongly recommend that a more national importance be given to this exhibition by such legislation and by such appropriation as will insure its success. Its value in bringing to our shores innumerable useful works of art and skill, the commingling of the citizens of foreign countries and our own, and the interchange of ideas and manufactures will far exceed any pecuniary outlay we may make.

I transmit herewith the report of the Commissioner of Agriculture, together with the reports of the commissioners, the board of audit, and the board of health of the District of Columbia, to all of which I invite your attention.

The Bureau of Agriculture has accomplished much in disseminating useful knowledge to the agriculturist, and also in introducing new and useful productions adapted to our soil and climate, and is worthy of the continued encouragement of the Government.

The report of the Commissioner of Education, which accompanies the report of the Secretary of the Interior, shows a gratifying progress in educational matters.

In nearly every annual message that I have had the honor of transmitting to Congress I have called attention to the anomalous, not to say scandalous, condition of affairs existing in the Territory of Utah, and have asked for definite legislation to correct it. That polygamy should exist in a free, enlightened, and Christian country, without the power to punish so flagrant a crime against decency and morality, seems preposterous. True, there is no law to sustain this unnatural vice, but what is needed is a law to punish it as a crime, and at the same time to fix the status of the innocent children, the offspring of this system, and of the possibly innocent plural wives. But, as an institution, polygamy should be banished from the land.

While this is being done, I invite the attention of Congress to another, though perhaps no less an evil, the importation of Chinese women, but few of whom are brought to our shores to pursue honorable or useful occupations.

Observations while visiting the Territories of Wyoming, Utah, and Colorado, during the past autumn, convinced me that existing laws regulating the disposition of public lands, timber, &c., and probably the mining laws themselves, are very defective, and should be carefully amended, and at an early day. In territory where cultivation of the soil can only be followed by irrigation, and where irrigation is not practicable the lands can only be used as pasturage, and this only where stock can reach water, (to quench its thirst,) cannot be governed by the same laws as to entries as lands every acre of which is an independent estate by itself.

Land must be held in larger quantities to justify the expense of conducting water upon it to make it fruitful, or to justify utilizing it as pasturage. The timber in most of the Territories is principally confined to the mountain regions which are held for entry in small quantities only, and as mineral lands. The timber is the property of the United States, for the disposal of which there is now no adequate law. The settler must become a consumer of this timber whether he lives upon the plain or engages in working the mines. Hence every man becomes either a trespasser himself, or, knowingly, a patron of trespassers.

My opportunities for observation were not sufficient to justify me in recommending specific legislation on these subjects, but I do recommend that a joint committee of the two Houses of Congress— sufficiently large to be divided into subcommittees—be organized to visit all the mining States and Territories during the coming summer, and that the committee shall report to Congress at the next session such laws, or amendments to laws, as it may deem necessary to secure the best interests of the Government and the people of these Territories who are doing so much for their development.

I am sure the citizens occupying the territory described do not wish to be trespassers, nor will they be if legal ways are provided for them to become owners of these actual necessities of their position.

As this will be the last annual message which I shall have the honor of transmitting to Congress before my successor is chosen, I will repeat or recapitulate the questions which I deem of vital importance, which may be legislated upon and settled at this session:

First. That the States shall be required to afford the opportunity of a good common-school education to every child within their limits.

Second. No sectarian tenets shall ever be taught in any school supported in whole or in part by the State, nation, or by the proceeds of any tax levied upon any community. Make education compulsory, so far as to deprive all persons who cannot read and write from becoming voters after the year 1890, disfranchising none, however, on grounds of illiteracy who may be voters at the time this amendment takes effect.

Third. Declare church and state forever separate and distinct, but each free within their proper spheres; and that all church-property shall bear its own proportion of taxation.

Fourth. Drive out licensed immorality, such as polygamy and the importation of women for illegitimate purposes. To recur again to the centennial year, it would seem as though now, as we are about to begin the second century of our national existence, would be a most fitting time for these reforms.

Fifth. Enact such laws as will insure a speedy return to a sound currency, such as will command the respect of the world.

Believing that these views will commend themselves to the great majority of the right-thinking and patriotic citizens of the United States, I submit the rest to Congress.

U. S. GRANT.

December 7, 1875.

Foreign Relations, 1875, pp. III–XVII. On Nov. 22 and Dec. 3, 1875, Secretary of State Hamilton Fish recorded in his diary. "I handed to the President the suggestions from the State Department for his message excepting as regards Spain, Mexico & Venezuela (the part with regard to Spain is not yet prepared) The parts with regard to Mexico and Venezuela were written some time since but recent disturbances have occured on the Mexican border which make necessary a redraft of the whole passage and that about Venezuela was written before receiving from Judge Russell a despatch stating that Venezuela had again suspended payment. I called his attention to the fact that there were two blanks with regard to dates, one of a telegraph line, and the other with regard to the number of cases decided in the Alabama Court of Commissions during the month of November which I would supply as soon as I could find out. Various subjects for the Message and probable action of Congress were discussed among them the Court of Claims. The Attorney General stated that he is preparing his report to Congress and will recommend some changes with regard to the Court; that there are now claims pending before it to an amount of $571.000.000; that cases are pending which have been there for 15 or more years; that parties wait until all possibility of obtaining testimony on behalf of the Government is lost; that the testimony taken is ex parte; that it is made up often as is suspected, on the main of persons who do not exist; and by others who are reckless and swear falsely: that it is impossible for the government to be fairly represented or to rebut an exaggerated statement: that with the best intention the court must pass upon the evidence before them. I suggested to Judge Pierrepont that he submit his report to the President before sending it and that the President make in his message a similar recommendation which would strongly enforce his own—He promised to do so" "The President read the draft of his Message He introduces the subject of St Domingo with a discussion and argument of considerable length in support of his policy of annexation and in justification of his Treaty of 1869. He stated that he had never alluded to the subject since the rejection of the Treaty. I told him he was mistaken for he had presented it in his Annual Message of 1870 very much in the same line of argument as that now used. He had forgotten all about it and questioned my recollection of the fact I obtained a copy and read the passage on that subject. It recalled to him the fact and he said he now remembered writing it but that till now it had entirely escaped him . . . The passages relating to Finance and Currency were discussed as read; at the conclusion of the reading attention was directed to some verbal alterations and to some occasional passages" DLC-Hamilton Fish.

On Dec. 8, S. Ledyard Phelps, D. C. commissioner, wrote to USG. "I desire to express to you the great gratification with which I have read your 'Message' which appears to me the ablest and best of such papers, I have ever perused, and I congratulate you earnestly upon the manner in which it is being received throughout the country." ALS, Ford Collection, NN.

On Dec. 9, Aaron F. Perry, Cincinnati, wrote to USG. "I have read your Message with attention and pleasure. I believe some of the topics will arrest the profoundest attention of the country and command broad and earnest sympathy. I believe it to be suggestive of a direction to public affairs wholesome for the country." ALS, USG 3.

On Dec. 15, Rev. D. W. Jacobson, Buffalo, wrote to USG. "Father of our country!—Ruler and Governor over the soil of our land America! our Lord! President Grant shall increase his glory, and his rule shall be extended over all, and throughout all the days of his life shall his horn be exalted on high! on high!! In the depth of my heart did I exult with joy and gladness at the voice of the sound of the harp—and at the brightness of the fruit of his pen, laid before the whole world—the brightness of his cogitations to Congress, in which he makes no distinctions of nationality and tongue, but is magnanimous and impartial unto all!" LS (in Hebrew), USG 3; translation, *ibid.* The translator noted: "The rest of the letter is not quite so clear, as it abounds with Chaldee words and expressions, not easily decipherable. It is, however, an invocation of God's blessings upon the President, and an expression of gratitude to the Almighty for giving the American people so good a man for their Chief Magistrate." *Ibid.*

1. On Dec. 9, *"Vivat Respublica,"* Philadelphia, had written to USG. "Your able and statesmanlike message has been read by the American People, and is endorsed by an overwhelming majority. Thank God you have expressed yourself so firmly and clearly on such views as must command the applause of every Patriot in the Land. Your suggested Amendment to the Constitution relating to the Public Schools, is offered *none too soon.* Keep on in the goodwork, The Keystone state, for *one,* stands by you." L, *ibid.*

On Dec. 10, Isaac B. Gara, Erie, Pa., wrote to USG. "I trust it will not be deemed improper in me to communicate to you the pleasure and satisfaction derived from a careful perusal of your last Annual Message. It is a sound, sensible, patriotic document, replete with suggestions and recommendations worthy of serious consideration and cordial approval. On the great currency question—the question of the hour—it gives no uncertain sound, and the discussion of the various other subjects which form the paper is characterized by a spirit of enlightened practical wisdom. Especially do I commend that feature wherein you dwell upon the need of amendments to the Constitution providing that the States shall be required to afford a common school education to every child within their limits; that education shall be made compulsory so far as to deprive all persons who cannot read and write from becoming voters after 1890; that no sectarian tenets shall ever be taught in the common schools; and that Church and State shall forever be declared separate and distinct. Upon the whole, the Message reflects credit upon your head and heart, and is calculated to strengthen public confidence in you as the head of the nation. The consciousness that you are by many unfairly and unjustly criticized has prompted me to write this letter, and this is my apology for sending it to you." ALS, *ibid.*

On Jan. 14, 1876, Norris W. Cuney, president, and James P. Ball, secretary, "Convention of the Colored Citizens of the State of Texas," Houston, petitioned USG. "We your Petitioners would respectfully represent that the present Constitution of the State of Texas provides that Free Schools shall be maintained in this State for, at least, four months in each year; and that by the therms of the Act of Congress permitting Texas to resume the exercise of the rights and priviliges of a Sate in the Union she is forbidden to abrogate that article in her Constitution. And your Petitioners would further represent that; notwithstanding the solemn and binding nature of the *Compact* thus entered into between the Goverment of the United States on the one hand; and the State of Texas on the other, the present State Government has, by nonfeasance, practically destroyed our system of Free Schools. And your Petitioners would further represent that the proposed new Constitution, now pending for adoption in this State silently ignores the existence of a Compact between the General Government a the State of Texas in relation the subject of education; and fails to make provision for an efficient system of Free Schools. And your Petitioners would further represent that; in addition to other funds, the new Constitution proposes to appropriate that portion of the Public Domain granted to the State Texas for the purpose of establishing an Agricultural College to an Institution to used for the education of the white youths of this State *exclusively*: Wherefore; to the end that a sacred and benificent compact made in the interest of Civilization and good government may not be wantonly and presumptiously violated and that we may be protected in our rights as citizens of the United States we pray your Excellency will enforce that Law of the United States which binds the State of Texas to the maintainence of Free Schools for all her citizens. And we your Petitioners will ever pray" DS, DNA, RG 60, Letters from the President.

On Feb. 25, James C. Campbell, St. Louis, wrote to USG. "Allow me to congratulate and most kindly thank you in my own name and thousands of others, For your kind mention and surport of the *American, Free, public, Schools,* In your last *Message* I send you our *platform of principles* on that subject, If you wish to correspond with me on that subject or any other at anytime, I will be very much pleased to do so" ALS, ICN.

2. On Dec. 2, 1875, Fish had recorded in his diary. "The President stated he had not finished his message but had it in contemplation to recommend an amendment to the constitution to prohibit donations by a state towards any religious body, and to subject all church and college property, with possibly the exception of cemeteries, to taxation He stated in 1850 the valuation of property held by religious bodies was $83.000 000 it had since grown to about $1.000 000 000 and that at this rate of growth and the exemption from taxation it would probably reach $4 000 000 000 by the end of the century that by that time there would be such an amount of popular indignation as to lead to its confiscation. But that besides all this the exemption of so large an amount of property from taxation threw an unjust burden upon others and should be restricted." DLC-Hamilton Fish.

On Dec. 8, Norman McLeod, Chicago, wrote to USG praising the annual message ". . . and in particular, the part of it which applies to our public Schools in all our united States. Sir let you & congress attend to it at all risks, also your part Set forth as to taxing every thing, but burial grounds, and that Should be free to all kinds of people, and let no man or Set of men, nor no corperation have no control over the ground for the dead, But free to all—all church property Should and ought to be taxed.   look at france every fifth acre belongs to the ~~cha~~ catholic church   Yes Sir I thank thank you and 20 of my friends joins me with thanks to you for ever . . . P. S. my dear Sir   few words more to you   See & order that every dishonest man woman or any one, who dont perform his honest duty be attended to & honest ones put in there places—and all who commit frauds in any departments be prosecuted to the bitter end, and if you do this, I am Sure that wee must & will have you for a third term (as mark the loyal people will not hear to anything that is disloyal or no insults to the flag that gave us our birth right—please write to me few words just So I will know that you have got this from a man who wishes you every Success in all your under takings   May god bless you & yours" ALS, USG 3.

On Dec. 17, John A. Dix, New York City, wrote to USG. "I do not trust too much to the accuracy of newspaper reports of interviews with distinguished men; but if the following extract from a letter in the *New York Herald* of this morning is correct, it would seem that you are under a misapprehension—not, perhaps, an uncommon one—in supposing that the property of Trinity Church in this city is not taxed: '*Taxation of Church Property*. Dr. Newman asserted that the President was misunderstood if he was believed to be inimical to any sect or denomination. Since the Message was written Methodist callers at the White House had upbraided him for so severe a blow at his own Church, the census of 1875 showing that the property of the Methodists in that year was about $80,000,000. The President replied that he was acting from a broad principle, wishing to do equal justice to all religious persuasions, and that the exemption of Church property was putting an unfair burden on other property. He cited as an instance the enormous wealth of the Trinity Church Corporation of New York City.' The fact is, that the Corporation of Trinity Church is taxed, under the laws of this State, precisely in accordance with the suggestions in your Message to Congress. Its property consists of church edifices, cemeteries, school-houses, an infirmary, a rectory, and several hundred lots of ground, which, with the exception of a few used for parochial purposes, are leased partly for short and partly for long periods. On the short leases the Corporation pays the taxes; on the long leases the taxes are paid by the lessees. I paid in September last, as Comptroller of the Corporation, on the former, $46,943 91; and we estimate the amount paid on the latter at $60,000, making over $100,000 paid to the city this year for taxes, besides a considerable sum for assessments. We pay taxes on every foot of ground used for secular purposes. We pay on our rectory, in which the Rector resides, on the office in which the business of the Corporation is transacted, although it is within the boundaries of St. Paul's Cemetery. In fact, nothing is exempt except the church edifices, the cemeteries, four school-houses, in which free schools are kept, and an infirmary, in which the sick receive gratuitous treatment. I know you will be glad to have this information. I have always been of opinion that the several States should tax all secular property belonging to Churches within their respective limits. Cemeteries are exempt by universal consent. I think church edifices should be, as I believe they always have been in Christian communities. To tax them would seem like making the Creator and Sovereign Ruler of the universe pay tribute to us for allowing a part of his footstool to be used for the worship which is his due." Morgan Dix, ed., *Memoirs of John Adams Dix* (New York, 1883), II, 203–4.

3. On Nov. 27 and Dec. 3, 5, Fish had recorded in his diary. "The President calls at the Department of State while Sen Ferry was talking about some consular appointments; after Ferry left the President asked if I had yet prepared that part of the message relating to Spain. I told him I had not, that I had attempted but was not satisfied with the draft and moreover the circumstances and the recommendations to be made might be materially varied by the terms of the note Mr Cushing had received from the Spanish Government and is now on its way accross the Ocean. . . . I thought the message should argue against

recognition of either belligerency or independence, should point to and suggest intervention as a possible necessity without recommending it at present; should state that propo-
sitions had been made to Cushing which had not yet been received which might dispose of
many of our causes of complaint and that Spain was at present making efforts for reform
in Cuba; that when the proposals have been received and considered he would make a further communication to Congress recommending such action by the United States as might
then be deemed advisable   He repeated each point as I had stated it and requested me to
prepare the message accordingly excepting that he would prefer no allusion to what Spain
was doing in Cuba, because they were in the habit of making such demonstrations each
year about the time Congress was to assemble and he had little faith in them." "The President had altered and emasculated what I had submitted to him on the subject of Spain &
Cuba . . . I then called attention to the part about Cuba and objected most strenuously to
it urging that it presented no argument against either Independence or Belligerency to
which the attention of the public and of the sympathizers with Cuba had alone been directed   That it presented the question of intervention without any argument in its suggestion which was of grave import being practically a suggestion of a possibility of War
That the people of the United States and the Nations of the World would regard such bald
presentation as insufficient and unworthy of the grave consequences to which it pointed.
That with his approval I had sent an instruction to Cushing on the subject, which had been
read in Madrid and in London and which committed us to a certain line of policy which
should be sustained and enforced by his Message. That the passages which he had read
would make Mr Cushing and myself unsustained and render all our effort abortive. Bristow & Pierrepont sustained my views, generally expressing the opinion that the subject
should be treated more argumentatively. Jewell wished the same thing and Chandler that
the message should go as far as the instruction to Cushing which he and Jewell thought
presented the matter in a strong and defensable light" "Called upon the President and read
to him the telegram of last night from Cushing, of a friendly interview with the Minister
of State. Expressed my anxiety that he should adopt the draft of the message with relation
to Cuba which I had submitted to him. He told me he had concluded to do so with the exception of two paragraphs; but would submit the whole argument as prepared against recognition of Independence or Belligerency and of the ultimate necessity of either mediation
or intervention, but would omit the passages relating to the increased Military efforts of
Spain against Cuba and the concluding passage which I regret very much" DLC-Hamilton Fish. See message to House of Representatives, Jan. 21, 1876.

On Nov. 20, Thomas Murphy, New York City, had written to USG. "I take the liberty
of intro[d]ucing to you Mr. J. M. Mestre who [d]esires an interview with you in re[g]ard
to the claim established by his [w]ife against the government of Spain. Mr. Mestre is a
gentleman of high culture and refinement, much esteemed and respected by his country[m]en, and his statements can be thoroughly relied upon" LS, DNA, RG 59, Miscellaneous Letters. On Jan. 17, 1876, USG endorsed this letter. "Refered to the Sec. of State."
AES, *ibid*. On the same day, USG had received a memorandum. "Mrs Paulina Alfonso de
Mestre is an American citizen by naturalization and lives in New-York since February 1869. At the death of her father in Cuba, the Spanish authorities commenced proceedings against her for alleged disloyalty, and seized as a precautionary measure the portion
of the estate which had to descend on her. Mrs Mestre succeeded in proving her innocence
before the Court martial convened at Havana to try her case. The Court acquitted her, and
ordered her property to be released and restored to her. The decision of the Court was approved of by Captain General Pieltain, September 26th 1873. The Board of managers of
confiscated and embargoed property were directed to comply with the order for the release
of Mrs Mestre's property on the 2nd of January 1874. No attention has been paid to such

orders, and the estate remains still under the control of the Spanish officials. His Excellency the President is respectfully requested to cause the matter to be referred to the American Consul at Havana, as has been done in other cases already settled like this." Copy, DLC-Jose Ignacio Rodriguez. The memorandum is endorsed. "The President said 'he will undoubtedly refer the matter to the American Consul at Havana.' On the 19th I saw Mr. Fish.—He objected my going first to the President. He tried to find fault in the word *Pieltain*. He said: Well, I will refer the matter to the American Consul.—He asked what could be expected from the intervention of the American Consul." E, *ibid.*

On Nov. 30, 1875, William Willock, Croton Landing, N. Y., had written to USG. "We are informed that a plantation near the Guantanamo Bay owned ~~by~~ and lived upon by a Mr Brooks whose Father was an Englishman born in England is guarded by English marines from incursions by the Cubans   Mr Brooks we are told has three plantations and two have been raided on by the Cubans the third being protected by English marines   Our attention is directed to Cuba because we own property there but have found it impossible to get justice under Spanish rule" ALS, DNA, RG 59, Miscellaneous Letters.

On Dec. 8, E. S. Drew, New Orleans, wrote to USG. "I am more than pleased with the spirit of your eloquent Message, and feel more assured that you have met, and yet can, in your administration of public affairs, meet the wishes of the American people—Cuban and Mexican policy almost universally endorsed in the South—Louisiana especially. Let us have a *little foreign unpleasantness*, and untold honors will wreathe your brow. With sincere wishes in your behalf, . . ." ALS, USG 3.

On Dec. 13, George W. Sayler, Kaolin, Pa., wrote to USG. "Excuse the plain style of my address. Thou art aware that Friends endeavor to avoid the use of flattering titles; though from my appreciation of thy excellent administration I might in truth apply the word *excellent*. As soon as I received a copy of thy Message to Congress which I did very soon by an extra of our county paper ('Village Record') and also by 'The North American,' I read it over carefully with much approval. It was in my mind before the meeting of Congress to venture a suggestion to thee; but, a hesitation as to intruding my views on thy attention, and that I might not in anywise interrupt thy labors in the preparation of thy Message to Congress, prevented my writing. Now from thy concluding words upon the Cuban troubles, an opening seems to be presented for the expression of what I have had in mind a long time. There is a peaceable way in which the Goverment of the United States may (I think) interpose a motive for Spain to act upon, which would probably end the trouble which I think, grows out of the existence of Slavery in the island. And as it is well known that the United States has suffered intensely from that 'Sum of all villanies' (as Wesley called it) No nation could reasonably object to this nation taking such a step. That is, to enact a law, making discriminating duties on articles imported from islands and countries where a large part of the labor is performed by Slaves. If the tariff of duties should be fixed at double rates on the productions of Slave labor, it seems to me it would powerfully operate in favor of emancipation in Cuba and PortoRico, and hasten the work begun in that direction in Brazil. If those governments which still cling to Slavery, should obstinately adhere to it, the effect of their delay would stimulate the production of Sugar in our own country, and coffee wherever else it can profitably be grown. Dear Friend President   Whatever thou mayst think of my plan please let me know by a line, that thou hast received this. That thou mayst be satisfied that the writer is not a mere enthusiast, I would refer thee to our Representative Washington Townsend or to Charles O'Neal Rep. from Philadelphia, who knew me when I resided there. I may mention my life long labors in the interest of free labor—my maintenance of a Store in Philadelphia devoted to the Sale of the products of Free labor exclusively for twenty years; importing my sugar, molasses &

rice, & manufacturing my own cotton goods; obtaining the cotton from the small planters who did not employ Slave labor in W. Tenn. N. Mi. & Ala, & E. Arkansas; from which labor I was released by one good result of the war: My customers were in all the then free States & Several of the Slave States. Excuse this reference to myself. I cherish the opinion that the free labor testimony had some effect in creating that public opinion that put an end to Slavery in this country." ALS, DNA, RG 59, Miscellaneous Letters.

On Jan. 8, 1876, Ambrosio José Gonzales, New York City, wrote to USG. "I had the honor to address you at the time of the 'Virginius' controversy. On the eve of important action on Cuban affairs, as foreshadowed in your Message, I beg to repeat, in substance, what I then said, as far as I can remember. I was born in Cuba and educated in New York city, graduated in law in Havana and was sent by the Cubans to this country in 1848 on a Secret mission to Genl. Worth; was a member of the first Cuban Junta in 1849; was then sentenced to death by the Spanish Government and have been since that year a citizen of the United States. I raised, in New Orleans, the first Cuban expedition and went, in 1850, as chief of Staff to Genl Narciso Lopez, to Cardenas where I shed the first Cuban blood in the cause. I was recommended by nearly all the delegations in both Houses of Congress from the Southern States to Presidents Pierce and Buchanan for high diplomatic positions in Spanish America. Previous to the 'Ostend Conference,' Mr Soulé, our appointed Minister to Spain, brought me from Washington to New York and introduced me to Genl Dix, then *U. S.* Treasurer, with a view to my going as Secretary of Legation to France had Genl Dix received the appointment of Minister thereto. I 1856 I married a daughter of the Hon: William Elliott, of Beaufort, the head of the Elliott family in South Carolina and a cousin of the late Episcopal bishop of Georgia. The civil war found me a citizen and resident of South Carolina and I became the only chief of Artillery of the Dept of S. C. Geo. & Fla until the evacuation thereof when I acted as chief of Artillery to Genl Joseph E. Johnston until the surrender at Greensboro', N. C. Although my sympathies have always been with the Cubans, I have taken no part in Cuban movements since the time of Lopez expecting to act in the future as a citizen of the United States. When you were in Charleston, after the War, on a tour of inspection, I was one of a deputation of merchants and planters who called on you to request the removal of colored troops and was introduced to you by Genl. Sickles then in command of the Department. Ruined by the war, I have been to Cuba four times since its close, the last one with my wife and children. Mr Henry C. Hall, who knows me well, then U. S. consul at Matanzas and since Consul General at Havana, attended my wife's funeral. I have been in New York for the last five years supporting myself as Professor of Modern Languages and have recently been appointed by the Board of Education to teach the English language, to a very large class of Cuban exiles, in the Public Schools. I referred you in my former letter to the Hon: Caleb Cushing, then practising law in Washington. I will add that I have the life-long friendship of the Cuban leaders in New York. Having been one of the pioneers in the Cuban movement, and having, in consequence suffered a score and a half years of vicissitudes, it is very natural that I should desire to be at what I hope may prove the last scene in its history. I have, for many years, been well known to many of the prominent men in all parts of the country, and hope that I may indulge in the belief that I may be considered an instrument at hand for the Government of the United States." ALS, *ibid.*, Letters of Application and Recommendation. No appointment followed.

On Jan. 31, James Thomson, Blackville, S. C., wrote to USG. "I with other gentlemen of this section regarding the unsettled state of our country and the probability of a war with Spane are desirous of organizing a light battery of Artillery so as to be in a position to offer our services to our country in time of need—But being unable to procure the necessary guns and equipments—We would most respectfully apply for assistance to your Excellency and would beg if it be possible that you lend us four twelve-pounds guns with proper equipments provided there are any such which might be so disposed of by the war department   Hoping that your Excellency will condecend to give this your consideration . . ." ALS, *ibid.*, RG 156, Letters Received.

4. See *PUSG*, 20, 25–27.

5. See telegram to George M. Robeson, June 15, 1875; *HRC*, 44-1-343; *CR*, 44–1, 296–98, 4309–15, 4521–33, 4629–46, 4744–47, 4753–55.

6. On June 2, 1875, USG had written to Fish. "I would suggest that the Proclamation extending the time of the Alabama claims commission had better be made out and signed by me to-day before my departure for Long Branch." LS, DLC-Hamilton Fish. On the same day, USG signed a proclamation extending the court of commissioners for six months after July 22. DS, DNA, RG 130, Presidential Proclamations. *SED*, 44-2-21, 137–38. See *Foreign Relations, 1875*, I, xxxi–xxxv.

7. On Jan. 27, 1876, G. von Chanoin, managing director, Direct United States Cable Co., London, wrote to USG concerning damage to the co.'s two cables. ". . . The fractured ends which have been brought home from the places of the two first interruptions, show beyond a doubt that the cable was broken by main force, such as a ship's anchor being intentionally or unintentionally dragged across the line of the cable. . . . My directors have already offered a reward of £500 sterling to any person able to give information as to the name of the steamer, sailing-ship, fishing-smack, or other vessel concerned in any of the previous breakages, which reward is increased to £1,000 in case malice should be proved. My directors, therefore, pray that your Government will, for the protection of the exceedingly valuable property of the company, and for the protection of the interests of the telegraphing communities on both sides of the Atlantic, issue a notice warning the owners and captains of ships not to anchor near the course of the cable, and offering a reward on behalf of your Government in order to find out the vessels which have been concerned in the ruptures of this company's cables for the past. My directors beg to suggest the advisability of posting up, by order of your Government, such notice, accompanied by charts showing the course of our cables, (of which I have the honor to forward herewith four,) in the custom-houses or other suitable places in all the fishing-ports under the jurisdiction of your Government." *Foreign Relations, 1876*, pp. 174–75. On Feb. 21, Fish wrote to Robert C. Schenck, U.S. minister, London, that the U.S. had no jurisdiction over damage done to lines in international waters. *Ibid.*, pp. 175–76. On March 1, von Chanoin wrote to USG that "the third fracture the ends of which have been picked up during the last two days shews that the Cable has been cut with an axe or hatchet." LS, DNA, RG 59, Miscellaneous Letters. A report on the damaged cable is *ibid.*

8. On Dec. 11, 1875, Daniel Kerr, Grundy Center, Iowa, had written to USG. "The reading of your Message relating to the question of Expatriation, Suggests to me that your attention may have been called to cases similar to that of my own. It seems to me there should be some Treaty provision in reference to such Cases   In 1841 my father emigrated to the United States With his family consisting of my my mother my sister and myself. My Grandfather Died in Scotland in 1839 leaving $5000 00 or a little over one thousand pounds in the hands of Trustees the interest to be used by my father during life and the residue to be divided among his children or their survivors after his death. The money has only drawn from two to four per cent for the last thirty years   As we are all citizens of the United States and as I am married and have six American children, It seems (I served three years in the 117th Illinois regiment) It seems to me, my father and his posterity

should have the benefit of those funds and of the better rate of Interest in this country. . . ." ALS, *ibid.*

On Jan. 18, 1876, Frederic A. Bossard, Brittnau, Switzerland, wrote to USG. "Excuse the liberty I give myself to addresse a few lines to you. In the year 1854 I received my first papers in Cincinnati said declaration of intention to become a citizen of the U. Staates of America. . . . At my arrival in Switzerland I was forced against my oath into Swiss citizenship, the governement wanted to force me to military service however I was discharged from actif service on account of my eyes, but I was bound to pay military taxes. I have done no military service to any nation. I have sent to the President of Switzerland the original document of above mentioned oath and reclaimed   his Secrty told me to apply to the Hon. H Rublee, he however refuses to *attend* to his *duty* and to do any step. I now call on the Governement to which I sworn fidelity *for ever* and which is legaly bound to protect its citizens and the legal oath in which I was forced to call on God Allmighty to be my witness and expect orders directly from the Hon. U. S. Grant to this Governement by which Switzerland is forced called upon to acknowledge said oath. and that consequently Switzerland hads no right to treat me as a citizen of theyr owne. . . ." ALS, *ibid.* In March and April, Bossard wrote to USG on the same subject. ALS, *ibid.* On Sept. 9, 1875, Bossard had written to USG describing his invention of an improved art. shell. ALS, *ibid.*, RG 156, Letters Received.

On June 27, 1876, Francis Thomson, Koenigsberg, Germany, wrote to USG that as a naturalized U.S. citizen he had gone to study brewing in his native Germany, which now challenged his citizenship. ". . . I beg leave, to note, that I have fougt during the whole war in the years 1861–1867, and also during the ~~Spanish~~ war against the Indians at Compagnie L of the 1th regiment of cavalry under the comand of captain Passinger and that I also have been wounded. Therefore I beg obediently, to send me, if you please, as soon as possible the necessary legitimation . . . under my former name, Eugen v Lochstädt, what name I have carried formerly in Germany" ALS, *ibid.*, RG 59, Miscellaneous Letters.

9. On Oct. 26, 1875, Fish had recorded in his diary. "The President stated to the Cabinet that he would desire their suggestions for the Message to be sent to him by November 15th . . . The Secretary of the Treasury suggested an enquiry as to how it would be advisable for the President to discus the question of currency and hard money in the message   No definite conclusion was reached but a general concurrence that decided ground should be taken and holding that the faith of the nation was pledged by the act of the last Congress of specie payment in 1879 & that Congress was bound to enact the proper legislation for that end. Bristow asked if it would not be well to make some recommendation as to the means. Nothing definite was decided upon the subject but the President expressed himself favorable to a recommendation of the repeal of the Legal Tender Act as to future contracts. Bristow reminded him that he had recommmended that last year and he answered that he would repeat it again this year; he also thought that a conversion of the Legal Tenders into bonds bearing 3 65/100% at long dates would be desirable. Robeson objected that this would raise the cry of contraction   I suggested that instead of bonds the issue of interest bearing notes which would not diminish the nominal but which would when the interest had accumulated to a sufficient amount gradually retire the issue as investments and thus practically approximate the the value of the greenback and Gold Bristow thought that the Banks might hord them, which I thought would have no injurious effect, but would rather facilitate the process of resumption." DLC-Hamilton Fish.

10. On Nov. 24, Wednesday, Fish wrote to USG. "I beg you will excuse the non transmission to you at an earlier moment of the papers from Messrs Blow & Partridge in

reference to the question of the remission of duties on Coffee. I directed them to be sent on Monday and regret to find they have been overlooked" Copy, *ibid.*

11. On Jan. 19, Lettus B. Titus, Tryonville, Pa., wrote to USG. "I take the liberty to adress you the chief ruler of our Nation, in regard to an invention which my Father (*James Titus*) invented and filed in the patent ofice in the year (1842 if I mistake not) in the year 1844 he went to the capital to patent it, but there was many things to hinder him from doing so. a few days before he arived there the Secretary of war had been killed by the bursting of a piece of artilery. togather with limited meanes, prevented his going on and perfecting his design. his invention was to ignite powder under water. there was no invention in the patent ofice at that time that would explode Powder under water disconected withe land—. . ." ALS, DNA, RG 48, Miscellaneous Div., Letters Received. On March 12, 1844, James Titus had diagrammed and described his proposed torpedo. ". . . The grate Object of this invention is to preserve and protect Merchant Vessels from their Enemy and to keep off all Enemy from Our Coasts and to tareupp the Ice in harbours done by Sinking this Well Charged with Powder an[d] Sat to go off when We think the Enemy Wi[ll] be at the place This inventon I Caul my Diveing Peacemaker" ADS, *ibid.*

12. On Sept. 23, 1875, White Eagle and many others, Ponca Agency, Dakota Territory, petitioned USG. "We, the undersigned chiefs, head men, and members of the Ponca tribe of Indians, in council assembled, respectfully represent to our Great Father at Washington, by our names hereto attached, our strong desire to be removed from our present reservation in Dakota Territory to the Indian Territory, and there to have assigned to us a good and sufficient reservation in which to live in peace and prosperity. It is our desire to learn the arts of civilization, and to enjoy all the facilities that can be extended to us in this purpose, that we may become self supporting, as the Great Father wishes. To this end, we respectfuly request him to remove us, the said Ponca tribe of Indians, to a new reservation in the said Indian Territory, and that a delegation of our chiefs may be sent to select such a reservation, in compliance with this request." *SRC*, 46-2-670, 405–6. On Feb. 24, 1880, Arthur J. Carrier, Ponca agent (Jan., 1875–April 1, 1876), Washington, D. C., testified before a select committee investigating removals to Indian Territory and recalled a discussion with USG on July 30, 1875. ". . . I talked with him for an hour and a half or two hours, at his cottage at Long Branch. In that conversation I went over with these facts that I have stated here. He stated that he would aid in every possible way to secure the removal of these Indians. He told me just how I should proceed. He instructed me that, in making my report, when I got back to the agency—in making out my report to the Commissioner of Indian Affairs, if the Poncas wanted to go, and were willing to sign a paper signifying their desire to go, that I should draw up such a paper, and have them sign it, and send it to the department with my report; and that, when I sent it to the department, I should send a copy to him. I suggested that it might be—such a paper being among a mass of other official papers—it might be overlooked and inadvertently referred to the department. He said, 'You can see that some friend gets it to my notice personally.' And that I did. But I never heard a word from the President about it, nor did I ever, to my recollection, hear a single word from the department in regard to it. . . ." *Ibid.*, p. 146. On Dec. 17, 1875, Alfred J. Abbott, carpenter and superintendent, Ponca Agency, wrote to USG commending Carrier and conveying the desire of Ponca chiefs to move from their reservation because of harrassment from the Sioux. *Ibid.*, pp. 378–79. See *ibid.*, pp. vi–vii, 404–5, 410–13; *HED*, 44-1-1, part 1, I, 750–52. The subsequent removal of Poncas to Indian Territory and Standing Bear's return north with some followers in 1879 caused widespread controversy. See M. LeB. Goddard, "The Story of the Poncas," *International Review*, IX (Oct., 1880), 388–404; Kay Graber, ed., *The Ponca Chiefs: An Account of the Trial of Standing Bear*

[by] *Thomas Henry Tibbles* (Lincoln, Neb., 1972); Francis Paul Prucha, *American Indian Policy in Crisis: Christian Reformers and the Indian, 1865–1900* (Norman, 1976), pp. 113–19; Ari Hoogenboom, *Rutherford B. Hayes: Warrior and President* (Lawrence, Kan., 1995), pp. 449–54; Valerie Sherer Mathes, *Helen Hunt Jackson and Her Indian Reform Legacy* (Austin, 1990), pp. 23–30, 35–36.

13. On Dec. 30, 1875, Moses Jones, Blue Mound, Kan., wrote to USG. "after Reading your Mesage We felt Obligated to you for your Great Recomendations to the Congress yet it Seems that Which would iterest us Poor Homesteaders has failed to Reach your Notice   Brobly you have Saposed we have been Relieved last winter a year ago By a bill being Passed to give the railroad Companys lands in Lieu as they were stricted to the Limetts of the roads & there is no vacant land in the Ft Scott & Gulf road So we are yet Waiting Believing that if it was Brought to your Notice you yet wold Recomend Some way for Our Relief as Our homesteads have been Canceled in favor of the Ft Scott & Gulf   if we Do not get relief this winter of all that we have Done upon Our homes fall in to the hands of the Misouri river Ft Scott Gulf railroad Company   know One knows the hardships of a frontier life as well as them has tried it   will you help us" ALS, DNA, RG 60, Letters from the President. See *PUSG*, 23, 352–54; *U.S. Statutes at Large*, XVIII, part 3, pp. 482–83.

To Edwards Pierrepont

Dec. 13th /75

DEAR JUDGE:

Gov. Reynolds' dispatch to you was received this evening while the room was full of visitors, and then read, but not answered until the company had all left—at 11 pm. Without re-reading I made my endorsement. On thinking of the matter—if my memory serves me correctly—Gov. Reynolds speaks of his readiness to defend—&c. It is as one of the prosecutor[s] I spoke of his employme[nt.] If any dispatch has been sent inconsistent with this view I hope it will be corrected.

Yours Truly

U. S. GRANT

HON. EDWARDS PIERREPONT ATTY. GEN.

ALS, DLC-USG, VIII. In Dec., 1875, Thomas C. Reynolds, St. Louis, telegraphed to USG. "... my only solicitude now is to see my old friend the President triumph over the vile conspiracy against him ... my proper position is that of counsel, if he chooses to select me, for the defence of Gen'l. Babcock ..." Charles Hamilton Auction No. 48, Dec., 1964, no. 197. USG endorsed this telegram. "I should like to have Gov. Reynolds accept. It is for the Atty. Gen. to say whether he should come to Washington ..." *Ibid.* Born in 1821 in S. C., Reynolds settled in St. Louis in 1850 and served as U.S. attorney (1853–57). Elected Mo.

lt. governor in 1860, Reynolds supported secession, served as *de facto* governor, and moved to Mexico after the war. In 1868, Reynolds returned to Mo.; he was elected to the legislature in 1874.

On Dec. 14, 1875, Attorney Gen. Edwards Pierrepont wrote to USG. "Be quite sure that no word in the telegram to Gov. R. needs to be changed; it was a mere request to act as special counsel to aid the Dist. Attorney & the others in the *prosecution* of the whisky frauds. You will see by reading the reply, (more friendly than discreet) that there was no misunderstanding. Will see you in course of the morning" ALS, CtY.

On Dec. 10, a correspondent had reported from Washington, D. C. "The President, in order that he may divest himself of any seeming partiality in the removal of General Henderson, has requested the appointment of Samuel T. Glover, the well-known Democrat and lawyer, to assist Colonel Dyer in prosecuting General Babcock." *St. Louis Globe-Democrat*, Dec. 11, 1875. Also on Dec. 10, Pierrepont telegraphed to David P. Dyer, U.S. attorney, St. Louis. "The President and all the Cabinet are desirous that you secure the services of Hon. Samuel Glover in the place of General Henderson." *HMD*, 44-1-186, 6. Probably on the same day, USG drafted a letter to [*Samuel T. Glover*], apparently for Pierrepont's use. "The President expresses the desire, and I join him in it, that you accept the position of Asst. Counsil in the Rev. fraud cases now pending in Mo. It was the original desire of the former that you should be retained and if any error was committed in not so informing you it was from mistake of mine arising from my non acquaintance with the bar of St. Louis." ADf, DLC-John Russell Young. See *PUSG*, 24, 17. Glover declined, "stating that his business engagements would not permit him to accept, even if his inclinations prompted him to do so." *St. Louis Globe-Democrat*, Dec. 12, 1875. On Dec. 11, 9:50 A.M., Dyer telegraphed to Pierrepont. "I have communicated the wish of the President and Cabinet as contained in your dispatch to me of yesterday to Hon Samuel T. Glover, who declines the appointment, and he has written you to that effect,   Under the authority given me in your other dispatch I will during the day employ other counsel and communicate the fact to you." Copy (press, telegram sent), DNA, RG 118, Letters Sent, U.S. Attorneys, Eastern District, Mo. On Dec. 13, Pierrepont wrote to USG. "I send the telegram of Dyer & Glover—I have sent Dyer nothing since the Cabinet telegram—he construes that as authority to select, as Glover declined—before the Country we stand right now:—If we reject Broadhead, there is danger that it will re-act against Gen. Babcock and deprive him of any fair trial:—it will surely do that if they think the action here is to shield him. The action of the Military Court, the fact that Henderson has been discharged, Glover declined, and Broadhead *accepted* at Dyer's solicitation, complicates the matter, and as the telegram was sent from the Cabinet, if Broadhead is rejected without Cabinet-consultation, I fear it will do mischief. Will call during the morning" ALS, CtY. James O. Brodhead replaced John B. Henderson as special U.S. counsel. See Endorsement, Dec. 3, 1875.

On Dec. 11, George E. Seymour, St. Louis, had written to USG. "Permit me to suggest the name of Edmund T. Allen Esq, a man of eminent ability and sterling integrity, for the position of U. S. District Attorney at this point, in case you shall submit another name than that of D. P Dyer, for the action of the Senate. Mr. Allen has never sought office, nor does have the remotest idea that any one has even thought of suggesting his name. My warmest regards to Col Fred, and Ulysses Jr, whom I knew as excellent boys twelve years ago, when they were at Mr. Edward Wyman's School." ALS, DNA, RG 60, Records Relating to Appointments. See *PUSG*, 9, 130–31. Also on [*Dec.*] 11, H. B. Johnson, Jefferson City, Mo., telegraphed to USG. "I would accept Dyer's place. Have written the attorney Genl" Telegram received, DLC-USG, IB.

On Dec. 12, Elias W. Fox, Kirkwood, Mo., telegraphed to USG. "Frank J Bowman law partner of Britton A Hill is one of the very best me to be associated as special counsel for the prosecution of the Whiskey fraud cases. He is a democrat but not a politician. Will prosecute as a lawyer with great tact & ability & will not abuse the trust   St Louis County & the State of missouri have often employed him as leading counsel in most important cases" Telegram received (at 12:37 A.M.), DNA, RG 60, Records Relating to Appointments.

To Robert C. Schenck

Dec. 15th /75

Dear General:

Let me introduce to you an old friend of mine, Dr. Kittoe, of Galena, Ill. and his daughter, who visit Europe for a time. The Dr. served as surgeon during the rebellion, and was mMedical Director on my staff during the latter portion of my service in the West. He is a gentleman Galena people esteem very highly and I am sure you will be pleased with him also.

Yours Truly
U. S. Grant

Gen. R. C. Schenck, Minister &c.
London, England.

ALS (facsimile), eBay, Sept. 30, 1999.

On March 16, 1868, Edward D. Kittoe, Galena, wrote to Bvt. Maj. Gen. James H. Wilson. ". . . General Grant came to Galena in 1861 and engaged in the leather business in the House of J. R. Grant & Co   I saw but little of him although I attended his family, he always appeared to attend to his own affairs and to them only, he was very little known here except by a few persons. I learned to know and to love him after I went into the service, and a more thoroughly good man by nature or one with more heart and less selfishness never lived, he has his faults, but they are the faults of a good and generous nature. I knew his brothers both of them well, Simpson the older one who died of consumption was a good deal such a man as the General, an honest upright and str[aig]htforward business man, one who had an excellent mind, and abundance of good common sense, the most useful of all endowments—What little I have ever seen of the father leads me to think that the sons owe most of their good qualities to the maternal side of the house. . . ." ALS, Wy-Ar. See Charles A. Dana and J. H. Wilson, *The Life of Ulysses S. Grant,* . . . (Springfield, Mass., 1868), especially pp. 39–40.

On April 26 and May 15, 1869, Secretary of the Navy Adolph E. Borie wrote to USG. "I have the honor to inform you that Dr. E. D. Kittoe, of Galena, Ill., accepts the appointment as Member of the Board of Visitors to the Naval Academy." "I have the honor to inform you that Dr. E. D. Kittoe, of Galena, Ill., expresses to the Department his regrets at being unable to attend the examination at the Naval Academy as a member of the Board of Visitors. Hon. Wm. H. Wadsworth, of Ky., selected by you as a member of the Board of Visitors, has not informed the Department of his acceptance or declination." Copies, DNA, RG 45, Letters Sent to the President.

To Annie Campbell Babcock

———

Dec. 17th /75

MY DEAR MRS. BABCOCK,

I know how much you must be distressed at the publications of the day reflecting upon the integrity of your husband, and write therefore to ask you to be of good cheer and wait for his full vindication. I have the fullest confidence in his integrity, and of his innocence of the charges now made against him. After the intimate and confidential relations that have existed between him and myself for near fourteen years—during the whole of which time he has been one of my most confidential Aides & private Sec.—I do not believe it possible that I can be deceived. It is scarcely possible that he could, if so disposed, be guilty of the crime now charged against him without at least having created a suspicion in my mind. I have had no such suspicion heretofore nor have I now.

His services to the government, in every capacity where he has been employed, have been so valuable, and rendered with such a view to its good that it precludes the theory of his conspiring against it now.

My confidence in Gen. Babcock is the same now it was when we were together in the field contending against the known enemies of the government.

With great confidence in the full vindication of ~~the~~ him.

I remain, very Truly

U. S. GRANT

ALS, Galena Historical Society, Galena, Ill.

To Hamilton Fish

———

Dec. 28th /75

DEAR GOVERNOR:

Until reading the enclosed article I had no idea of the relations existing between us. It must be new to you also.

Yours Truly

U. S. GRANT

HON. HAMILTON FISH SEC. OF STATE.

ALS, DLC-Hamilton Fish. On Dec. 29, 1875, Secretary of State Hamilton Fish recorded in his diary. ". . . On my arrival today from New York I found the annexed article enclosed to me by the President in a letter which ran thus. . . . Calling this morning I told him I had not seen the article from the Cincinnati paper but added that my well known reliance upon newspaper statements would have alarmed me had I not received his note at the same time as I read the article, further that although it was new to me still I knew that the paper was better informed of all of his personal feelings than himself." *Ibid.* On Dec. 24, a correspondent had telegraphed from Washington, D. C. "Gentlemen who are well informed with regard to the relations between the President and Secretary Fish, assert that the President has had in his hand since the Virginius affair sworn documentary evidence to establish the fact that Mr. Fish has ever since 1869 inspired numerous newspaper articles on our affairs with foreign Nations, which, while they have been unsparing in criticism and abuse of the President, have also been filled with praise of the Secretary. These articles are said to have been written for the most part by Sidney Webster, Mr. Fish's son-in-law, who is the attorney of the Spanish Government, and to have been printed in one of the most prominent Democratic newspapers in the country. It is also alleged that other evidence of Mr. Fish's duplicity have been accumulating in the President's hands, and that he is merely awaiting the proper time to punish the offender. This is one of the chief reasons why the early resignation of the Secretary is confidently anticipated; and another one is that the Secretary is believed to be the chief obstacle at present to the President's purpose to bring about a war with Spain on behalf of Cuba." *Cincinnati Commercial*, Dec. 25, 1875.

On Jan. 10, 1876, Lehman Israels, New York City, wrote to USG. "I take the liberty of addressing you briefly touching an affidavit which I had occasion to make nearly two years ago on the relations between Secretary Fish, his son-in-law Webster and the World newspaper of this city. As I notice by the public prints that You Excellency's attention has been called to this matter, I beg to state respectfully and directly to you that said affidavit was brought about to sustain the accuracy of the statements made a short time previously in this city by the Rev. Dr. Hepworth with regard to the fact that the son-in law of the present Secretary of State was the highly paid legal agent and attorney of the Spanish Government and Legation in the United States. For this statement the Rev. Dr. was at the time grossly assailed by the World newspaper, whose virtual Editor on all Spanish-American Affairs is Mr. Sidney Webster, the son-in-law as aforesaid of the Secretary. In the which connection I beg to call your attention to the fact announced per telegram from Europe that by some mysterious process the Spanish Government was able to learn the contents of the circular said to have been addressed by the State Department to the several American Ambassadors at the principal courts of Europe concerning Cuba   Now that the matter appears to have been brought to your attention, I beg to assure you that I am ready to Substantiate the contents of said affidavit.—My record as a journalist of 18 years standing is well known in NewYork. It was only interrupted during the war when I served as 2nd Lieut. in the 55th N. Y. Vols and was wounded at Fair Oaks, as can be ascertained by the archives of the War Department, having been mentioned for honorable conduct at said battle in Brigade Orders." ALS, USG 3. On Jan. 30, 1874, Israels had given a deposition in New York City. "That from the year 1865 till 1873 he has been City and Foreign Editor of the World, on several Occasions acting as managing Editor during the absence of the manager. That since President Grant's accession there arose the Cuban Question, the Catacazy affair, the Santo Domingo Annexation plan and the Washington treaty all of which were editorially commented upon, often ably and showing a great deal of research with ready quotations from State paper precedents and knowledge of international law not possessed by either Manton Marble or any of the Editors regularly attached to the paper; that most of these articles contained excessive, licentious abuse of the President of the United States; but never a word or suggestion even of censure of Secretary Fish. That the majority of the articles on the Cuban Question and on the negotiations with Great Britain, this deponent further Saith, were written by Sidney Webster, Son-in-law of the said Secretary Fish. . . . That the object of making this affidavit and the revelations it contains is simply to disabuse the minds of the presses and people who may believe that there are no intrigues in the State Department against the well known views of the President; to Show to Cuban Sympathizers and others that Secretary Fish, who must be well aware that his Son-in-law writes the pro Spanish articles in the NewYork World has favored that journal on more than one occasion in preference to others, known to be politically friendly to the President; and further, in the interest and behoof of upright journalism to expose the bareface persistent prostitution of its columns by the World newspaper for a period of years, to the uses of parties, to whom its proprietor and Editor knew to be the regularly employed and paid attorneys for the very ends to secure or advance which, the whole weight and influence of the journal was thus given under circumstances too extraordinary, not to suggest corrupt inducements.—" ADS, Babcock Papers, ICN.

To John M. Brodhead

Dec. 31st 1875.

Dear Sir:

In accepting your resignation of the office of Second Comptroller of the Treasury "to take effect on the qualification of your successor" instead of this date as you tender it, permit me to express regret at parting with an official who has rendered such long, faithful and valuable service to the government as has fallen to your lot. But few men have held responsible positions under the government for so many consecutive years as you have. None have enjoyed more

fully the confidence of the public, and I wish now to bear testimony
as to my appreciation of those services.

Hoping you may find peace and comfort in retirement denied to
the ever vigilant official, I subscribe myself,

With great respect

your obt. svt.

U. S. GRANT

DR. J M. BRODHEAD SECOND COMPTROLLER OF THE TREASURY

Copy, DLC-USG, II, 3. On Dec. 30, 1875, John M. Brodhead wrote to USG. "In accordance
with the declaration I made at the last interview I had with you—viz: that if my resignation would at any time relieve you of embarrassment—I have the honor to resign my position of Second Comptroller of the Treasury, from & after the 31st instant" ALS, DNA,
RG 56, Applications. On the same day, USG endorsed this letter. "Accept to take place on
the qualification of a successor." AES, *ibid.* Born in Canaan, N. H., Brodhead graduated
from Dartmouth Medical School (1825), served as second comptroller, U.S. Treasury
(1853–57), and later held local offices in Washington, D. C. On Dec. 14, 1863, President
Abraham Lincoln renominated Brodhead as second comptroller. In Nov., 1875, Secretary
of the Treasury Benjamin H. Bristow appointed a committee to investigate claims for supplies allegedly seized by federal forces in La. and Tenn. On Dec. 30, a newspaper reported.
"The committee find both claims fictitious and fraudulent, and that they were passed
through the offices of the Third Auditor and Second Controller without such examination
as the law requires; . . . The Secretary submitted the report to the President this morning, and on his return to the department showed it to Messrs. Brodhead, Rutherford, and
Curtis, who promptly agreed to tender their resignations." *Washington Evening Star*, Dec.
30, 1875.

On Dec. 31, Allan Rutherford wrote to USG resigning as third auditor, U.S. Treasury. ALS, DNA, RG 56, Appointment Div., Letters Received. Rutherford later wrote to
USG. "PERSONAL:—*Memo for the President* . . . I beg leave to submit herewith a statement
of facts in relation to my resignation as 3d Auditor of the Treasury. In the Month of Sep't
1875, I was sent to England by Secretary Bristow on business connected with the Syndi-
cate, and returned home during the Month of Decr. On my return I learned that a Committee had been appointed by Mr Bristow to examine into the method of conducting business in the Offices of the 3d Auditor and 2d Comptroller of the Treasury, and that this
Committee had been in session several weeks and had about concluded their work. At the
head of this Commission was Mr Pratt, the Commissioner of Internal Revenue, a person
with whom I was not on friendly terms. On hearing of this Commission and understanding that they had been investigating the alleged fraudelnt Cases of Sugg Fort and Julius
Witowski, I asked to be called before them, supposing that the Commission was honestly
seeking information on which to protect the public interests, and having no idea that I was
myself on trial. . . . I refer but briefly to these two cases, alth'o they were selected from the
hundred of thousands settled by the Office during my administration of Six years to Show
that the Office had been managed carlessly by me, in this, that I did not *personally* examine
all the papers in *all* the Cases upon which I acted: To any one familiar with the duties of
the head of a large Bureau such as that of the 3d Auditor, this proposition is simply ridiculous. . . . I felt satisfied at the time, and subsequent events have only strengthened that conviction, that I was made a victim to Mr Bristows Presidential Aspirations, as it was well

known that he was not my choice or the choice of my friends for the nomination. The Committee which made the report before referred to was composed of but two Heads of Bureau. Mr Platt, Comr of Internal Revenue and Mr D Mahon the 1st Auditor. Mr Robinson the Ass't Solicitor had long been known as an aspirant for a place as Head of a Bureau in the Treasury Dep't, and I now believe, thought he could accomplish his object by making such a position vacant. The other two members of the Commission were Clerks, not familiar with the laws or the routine of business as transacted in the Offices of the Auditor & Comptroller. And as an evidence that the alleged Carelessness was but a very thin excuse for a report, the substance of which had no doubt been decided on even before the Commission was formed; I would refer to the fact, that the manner of transacting business in the 3d Auditors Office now, is substantially the same as it was under my administration. During a period of fifteen years of faithfull and honorable service, nine years of which was in the Army, in the Regular and Volunteer service I am conscious of no act that would bring disgrace or discredit upon myself or my friends: and I now seek a vindication from the unjust imputation of carelessness which was thrown upon me to aid the mad ambition of Mr Bristow." ALS (undated), *ibid*. On Sept. 4, 1876, William H. Crook, act. presidential secretary, endorsed this letter. "The President directs me to say that he is satisfied that Gen Rutherford has been harshly & unjustly treated, that he believes him to be honest, capable & faithful, and suggest his appointment, to the position now held by Mr. Mahon" AES, *ibid*. No appointment followed. See letter to Edwards Pierrepont, Nov. 13, 1875; *HED*, 44-1-2, LI–LV, 363–79; *New York Times*, Sept. 23, 1876.

On Dec. 31, 1875, Edmund B. Curtis had written to USG. "In compliance with your request I herewith tender my resignation of the Office of Deputy Second Comptroller of the Treasury. And in doing so I beg leave to say that had the statements in the endorsement which was prepared by another, and signed by me in the regular course of business, been correct my signature thereto would have been justified. As my means are very limited, and as I have been in this Office long enough to become somewhat familiar with its duties, I respectfully ask that the place about to be vacated by Mr Wilson, who examined the account and made the endorsement which I signed, may be given to me." ALS, DNA, RG 56, Applications. On July 10, 1876, Curtis wrote to Secretary of the Treasury Lot M. Morrill. "I respectfully ask to be re-appointed to a fourth-class clerkship in the Office of the Second Comptroller of the Treasury." Copy, *ibid*. Brodhead endorsed this letter. ". . . I *know* that the President directed his reinstatement in some position, & his capability, experience and exemplary character entitle him to consideration, and would make him valuable to the public service." Copy, *ibid*. Related papers are *ibid*. No reinstatement followed.

On Dec. 31, 1875, a correspondent had reported from Washington, D. C. "Gov. C. C. Carpenter, of Iowa, has been appointed Second Controller to succeed Dr. Brodhead. Gov. Carpenter is the present Governor of Iowa, but his term of office will expire next week. . . ." *New York Times*, Jan. 1, 1876. See Mildred Throne, *Cyrus Clay Carpenter and Iowa Politics, 1854–1898* (Iowa City, 1974), pp. 196–99.

On Jan. 6, 187[6], U.S. Representative Horace B. Strait of Minn. telegraphed to USG. "I feel wholly justified in saying that Gov Austin will accept the third Auditors   He has been away from Telegraph lines in Minnesota for the last seven days" Telegram received (misdated), DLC-USG, IB; DNA, RG 107, Telegrams Collected (Bound). On Dec. 8, 1875, U.S. Senator William Windom of Minn. and three others petitioned USG to appoint Horace Austin, former Minn. governor, to a territorial judgeship. DS, *ibid*., RG 60, Records Relating to Appointments. On Jan. 6, 1876, USG nominated Austin as third auditor.

On June 8, 1875, Bristow had written to USG. "In view of the reorganization of this Department to take place under the law which goes into effect on the 1st of July next, it has become important that the matter of the Sixth Auditor shall be definitely fixed. I learn from Governor Jewell that it is your purpose to appoint Mr. McGrew, the present chief clerk, to that place, and will thank you to advise me whether I am correctly informed in this respect. I have no doubt Mr. McGrew would make a good officer, and, so far as I am concerned, have no objection to his appointment—indeed no other person has been named to me in connection with the office, except Col. A. H Markland, who is suggested to me by Governor Morton and two or three others. I ought to say that I would have no objection to his appointment either, but only desire to know your wishes in the premises." LS (press), DLC-Benjamin H. Bristow. On June 10, Orville E. Babcock, Long Branch, wrote to Bristow. "In reply to your letter of the 8th the President directs me to inform you that he thinks it best to appoint Mr. Mc Grew the present Chief Clerk, and that you may consider the matter so settled, in reorganizing your Department on the 1st of July." Copy, DLC-USG, II, 2. On June 13, U.S. Senator Algernon S. Paddock of Neb., New York City, telegraphed to Babcock. "I beg of President to appoint Taffe Sixth auditor or secretary colorado and I think now I should have alonzo gG Paddock marshall Utah   please answer" Telegram received, *ibid.*, IB. On June 14, Bristow telegraphed to Babcock. "I have directed Mr McGrews commission to be issued in accordance with your note" Telegram received, *ibid.* On June 23, a correspondent reported from Washington, D. C., on Jacob M. McGrew's appointment as Sixth Auditor in place of Charles C. Sheats. ". . . Sheats was for some years Congressman from Alabama, and was made Auditor upon the adjournment of the last Congress. He soon proved utterly incapable of filling the office, however, and was found to be mixed up with the Hinds-Spencer postal ring. McGrew is from Ohio, and his appointment is regarded generally with satisfaction. There are a few who charge that he has been connected with the Post-Office rings, but the charge has never been clearly established." *Chicago Tribune*, June 24, 1875. On Jan. 19, 1876, U.S. Senator John Sherman of Ohio telegraphed to USG. "Did Mr Sheets Sixth Auditor, resign, or was he removed," Telegrams received, DLC-USG, IB; DNA, RG 107, Telegrams Collected (Bound). On the same day, Levi P. Luckey telegraphed to Sherman. "Mr Sheets resigned" ALS (telegram sent), *ibid.*

On June 29, 1875, Bristow had written to USG. "By the act of the last session of Congress to reorganize the Treasury Department, it is provided that the duties heretofore performed by the Chief Clerks of Bureaus should be hereafter performed by deputies to be appointed for that purpose. This involves the necessity of appointing deputies for each of the Comptrollers and Auditors, the Commissioner of Customs and Register. The Attorney General holds that these officers must be appointed by you, by and with the advice and consent of the Senate, and that you have the power to make temporary appointments during the recess of the Senate. I have no doubt this opinion is right and have caused to be transmitted to you commissions for ten deputies. They are all good men, as I believe, and the only one about whom I have any doubt is Hemphill Jones for Deputy First Comptroller. I understand he is a Democrat in politics, but he has long held the position of Chief Clerk, is a very good officer, and is strongly recommended by Tayler, First Comptroller. Tayler has also recommended two of his Democratic clerks to be promoted to be heads of division. I have declined to follow his recommendation in this respect, and have appointed Republicans. I give you this explanation for the reason that I do not desire to have you sign Jones' commission without being informed of the facts." LS (press), DLC-Benjamin H. Bristow.

Calendar

1875, JAN. 3.   U.S. Senator Phineas W. Hitchcock of Neb., New York City, to
USG. "Just returned from West and learned appointment Irish third Auditors
It is excellent one, will do credit administration,   On behalf Nebraska strong-
est republican state I wish to thank you"—Telegram received (at 9:46 A.M.),
DLC-USG, IB. See *New York Times,* Jan. 28, 1883.

On April 12, 1869, U.S. Senator John M. Thayer of Neb. had written to USG.
"My colleagues, Tipton & Taffe united with me in asking for the appointment
of Col. *O. H. Irish* for the of *Nebraska* for the *Portugese Mission* or any other 2d
class Mission. . . ."—ALS, DNA, RG 59, Letters of Application and Recommendation. Related papers are *ibid.* On Dec. 6, USG nominated Orsamus H.
Irish as consul, Dresden.

1875, JAN. 5.   Orville E. Babcock to Knowlton & Co., New York City. "I send
you enclosed the President's check for $255 25 gold in accordance with the re-
quest of Mr. Henry. C. Hall U. S. Consul General at Havana. Will you please to
acknowledge the receipt and oblige."—Copy, DLC-USG, II, 2.

On Nov. 3, 1869, Danford Knowlton, Havana, had written to USG. "In view
of the retirement of E. L. Plumb Esq, as Consul General of the United States in
this Island, I take the liberty of recommending for the same position Henry C.
Hall Esq, who is well known to the Department, having had some seven years
of Consular service in this Island. From an extensive acquaintance with merchants here, and in the United States, I assert with confidence, that Mr Hall is
not only acceptable to all, but that he is eminently qualified for the duties required in the present unsettled condition of political affairs here: and while attending with scrupulous care to the interests of American citizens having business in this Island, will not render himself obnoxious to the government with
which he is brought in contact"—ALS, DNA, RG 59, Letters of Application and
Recommendation. On Dec. 11, Miner Knowlton, USMA 1829 and art. instructor at USMA (1837–44), Burlington, N. J., wrote to USG. "My brother sends
me a letter from the island of Cuba with a recomendation for Henry C. Hall Esq.
as the successor of the Consul General, of the U. States in Cuba. At my brother's
request I forward his recommendation to you. And as his letter to me is calculated to give you desirable information I take the liberty to send it in company.
My brother has been many years engaged in business between N. York & Cuba,
spending a part of every year in Cuba. His business, as commission merchant,
has made him extensively acquainted with the whole island, its inhabitants,
its officials, and especially its merchants, American and Spanish. He is of undoubted reliability, great experiance, and takes no part in party politics."—
ALS, *ibid.* The enclosure is a letter of Dec. 3 from D. Knowlton, Havana, to his
brother. ". . . We are fearful that some mere politician will be sent who dont
know his business, or even the Spanish language. Mr Hall speaks the language
like a native, . . . I hope Congress will keep quiet about Cuba—years of preparation are wanted before we can talk of annexation, with profit to us, or to the
people of the Island—The Cuban policy of destroying property to cut off
the government resources, is a very bad one; for once beggars, they are not the
people to build up prosperity—That has been done by Spaniards, aided by negro muscle, for which the climate is so favorable—Cubans, reared in luxury,

and unaccustomed to labor, with free negroes, would make slow progress—. . ." —ALS, *ibid.* On Aug. 23, 1873, Edward L. Plumb, Havana, wrote to Secretary of State Hamilton Fish. *"Personal.* . . . I am irresistibly led to address you to suggest whether it may not be practicable to extend to Mr Hall the full appointment of Consul General at this port, . . . I do not know that such a step may at present be practicable, but it may be at no distant period, and I beg to be permitted in view of my past connection with this office, to lay before you in this manner this expression of views which I have previously, just after my retirement from this port, had the honor verbally to submit both to the President and to the Department, . . ."—ALS, *ibid.* Related papers are *ibid.* On Dec. 2, 1873, USG nominated Henry C. Hall as consul gen., Havana.

1875, JAN. 5.   Orville E. Babcock to F. H. Shallus, Baltimore. "Enclosed please find the President's check for $216.78 in payment of expenses on one case of cigars from Cuba which came to hand safely. Please acknowledge receipt of check . . ."—Copy, DLC-USG, II, 2.

1875, JAN. 6.   USG endorsement. "Respectfully refered to the Sec. of War. Let special attention be directed to this application."—ALS, DNA, RG 94, Correspondence, USMA. Written on a letter of Dec. 28, 1874, from Commodore John Guest, Beltsville, Md., to USG. "I had the honor to apply for an appointment to West Point for my son John Guest Jr by letter dated 22nd Novr 1874, with the endorsements of Commodore Ammen & Admiral Porter. I now have the honor to renew the application for an appointment for Him to enter in 1876 at which time he will be nineteen years of age. I shall esteem it a great favor if it pleases the President to appoint my son, who is a well trained youth of unexceptionable habits"—ALS, *ibid.* Guest's letter to USG, dated Nov. 22, 1873, is *ibid.*
     On June 13, 1876, Guest again wrote to USG. "I have the honor to solicit an appointment for my son John Guest Jr as Second Lieutenant in the Army."— ALS, *ibid.,* ACP, 3521 1876. On June 15, USG endorsed this letter. "Refered to the Sec. of War. When apts. are made to the Army I wish special attention called to this application."—AES, *ibid.* On Aug. 11, USG nominated John Guest, Jr., as 2nd lt., 8th Cav.

1875, JAN. 6.   Levi P. Luckey to William S. Sneden, Long Branch. "The President requests me to acknowledge the receipt of your favor enclosing annual pass over the New Jersey Southern Railroad & Branches, and express his thanks for the continued courtesy."—Copy, DLC-USG, II, 2. On the same day, Luckey acknowledged a pass from the Baltimore and Ohio Railroad.—Copy, *ibid.* On Jan. 9, Luckey wrote to D. M. Zimmerman, Camden & Atlantic Railroad, Camden, N. J., acknowledging a pass for USG and Julia Dent Grant for 1875.— Copy, *ibid.* On May 15, 1876, Ulysses S. Grant, Jr., wrote to Zimmerman acknowledging passes for 1876.—Copy, *ibid.,* II, 3.

1875, JAN. 8.   Chester A. Arthur, collector of customs, George H. Sharpe, surveyor, Thomas Murphy, and five others, New York City, to USG. "We respectfully ask the appointment of Mr. William Dowd of this city as one of the Board of Visitors to the Military Academy at West Point for the year 1875."—LS, DNA, RG 94, USMA, Board of Visitors. On Jan. 25, Charles H. Fowler, president, Northwestern University, wrote to USG. "Allow me to call your attention to Prof. Julius F. Kellogg, Prof. of Math. in the Northwestern University, as a person *every way qualified* to perform the duties of an Examiner at the Military Academy at West Point."—ALS, *ibid.* On Feb. 2, Ambrose E. Burnside, Chicago, wrote to USG. "I promised one of my constituents, Mr H. H. Fay of Newport that I would recommend him to you as a proper person for appointment on the Board of Visitors to West Point this year. . . ."—ALS, *ibid.* On Feb. 23, U.S. Representatives James M. Pendleton and Benjamin T. Eames of R. I. wrote to USG recommending Henry H. Fay, prominent preparatory educator.—LS, *ibid.* USG appointed William Dowd (see *New York Times,* Oct. 8, 1899), Julius F. Kellogg, Fay, Vice Admiral Stephen C. Rowan, Jacob Ammen, Nathaniel B. Baker, and Daniel C. Gilman to the board of visitors, USMA, for June, 1875. See *HED,* 44-1-1, part 2, I, 351–64.

On Dec. 12, 1874, Edward W. Serrell, Fort Montgomery, N. Y., had written to USG. "If it is entirely agreeable to you, not otherwise, I should like to be on the Board of Visitors to West Point: . . ."—ALS, DNA, RG 94, USMA, Board of Visitors. On Jan. 6, 1875, Orville E. Babcock wrote to U.S. Senator Reuben E. Fenton of N. Y., following conversation with USG and Secretary of War William W. Belknap, "that without the records of the War Department they can not decide whether the State of New York, is entitled under the laws relating to the matter, to an appointment this year. . . ."—Copy, DLC-USG, II, 2. On Dec. 21, 1874, U.S. Senator Frederick T. Frelinghuysen of N. J. had written to USG. "Mr. Nathaniel Niles—formerly a Member of The Legislature of New Jersey—and a Lawyer of intelligence, and good education, wishes to be appointed one of the Board of Visitors to West Point—and I take pleasure in presenting him as entirely worthy of the position. There is another Jerseyman—Genl James F. Rusling—of Trenton, who has a wish for the position. He is a gentleman of character and education; and did good service in the War. You may remember him, in the West. I present these two names—not that I expect two to be appointed from New Jersey—but because so requested. Whether any one is appointed from New Jersey, of course, I submit to your better Judgment."—LS, DNA, RG 94, USMA, Board of Visitors. On Jan. 16, U.S. Representative Robert S. Hale of N. Y. wrote to USG. "I beg to submit for your consideration as a member of the Board of Visitors to the Military Academy at WestPoint for the coming year, the name of Genl John Hammond of Crown Point, Essex County, NewYork. . . ."—ALS, *ibid.* On Jan. 27, U.S. Representative Eppa Hunton of Va. wrote to USG. "I have the Honor to ask the appointment of Dr James F. Harrison one of the visitors of West Point Military Academy—He is Chairman of the Faculty of University of Va and well qualified to fill this position   He has an application on file"—ALS, *ibid.* On Feb. 8, U.S. Representative Stephen A. Hurlbut of Ill. wrote to USG. "I have the honor of requesting you to appoint the Rev. J. S Burroughs Chancellor of Chicago University on the Board of Visitors either to West Point or the Naval Academy. It is I think due to this Institution that its head should be considered. He is also a leading Minister in the Baptist denomination"—ALS, *ibid.* On Feb. 15, Sewall L. Fremont (USMA 1841), Wilming-

ton, N. C., wrote to USG. "Allow me to request of you the favour of an appointment on the Board of Visitors to West Point for the next annual Examination
of Cadets—As we have known each other there and elswhere so many years I
will not ask a member of congress or any one else to present this letter. I trust
there will be a pleasant re-union of the graduates on the 17th of June and that
I may meet you there with many others—I think perhaps North Carolina may
have some claim to a member of the Board of Visitors and if so and you think
me a Suitable person to represent her in the Board I shall be please to receive
the appointment."—ALS, *ibid.* On Feb. 19, Col. William F. Barry, Fort Monroe,
Va., wrote to USG. "If it can be done with propriety, I respectfully ask to be
named by you as a Member of the Board of Visitors to the U. S. Mil: Acad: at
West Point for this year."—ALS, *ibid.* On March 19, Thomas L. Alexander
(USMA 1830), Louisville, wrote to USG. "I would be pleased to receive the
appt. of a member of the 'Board of Visitors' from Ky. to our 'Alma Mater' whom
I left just forty five years ago. If you *can* grant this, it will be a favor most highly
appreciated, and not soon forgotten; but if it at all interferes with other
arrangements, just think no more of it"—ALS, *ibid.* Letters to USG recommending Isaac N. Arnold, Samuel M. Gaines, Thomas A. Parker, and Robert G.
Bickle, other unsuccessful applicants, are *ibid.*

1875, JAN. 12.   To Congress. "In accordance with the requirements of the Joint
Resolution Approved March 25 1874 authorizing an inquiry into, and report
upon the causes of epidemic cholera, I have the honor to transmit herewith reports upon the subject from the Secretaries of the Treasury and War Departments"—Copy, DNA, RG 130, Messages to Congress. *HED*, 43-2-95.

1875, JAN. 12, Tuesday.   William H. Rightmire and Jacob W. Starr, Camden,
N. J., to USG. "At a meeting of the Young mens republican club held Tuesday night at Camden, Hon, James M. Scovel was unanimously recommended
to you for appointment as Collector for the Port of Camden vice Judge Gray
[*de*]ceased   we sustain your ad"—Telegram received (on Jan. 13), DLC-USG,
IB. On Jan. 14, Rightmire and Starr wrote to USG on the same subject.—LS,
DNA, RG 56, Collector of Customs Applications. On Jan. 12, James M. Scovel,
Camden, had telegraphed to USG. "We want peace in the south but we want the
democracy to do equity before they ask it."—Telegram received, DLC-USG,
IB. William P. Robeson, Secretary of the Navy George M. Robeson's brother,
succeeded Philip I. Gray as asst. collector of customs, Camden. See *PUSG*, 19,
410; *ibid.*, 21, 239; *New York Times*, Sept. 17, 1881, Dec. 3, 1904.

1875, JAN. 14.   Henry Sherman, Washington, D. C., to USG. "In submitting
the accompanying petition and statement, I desire simply to say, I have had
some printed to facilitate your examination of them, and for the convenience of
further copies should any others than the one now submitted to you be called
for or required. You will perceive, however, that both are subscribed with my
autograph signature."—*HMD*, 44-1-170, part 5, p. 311. Sherman, a lawyer and
former Treasury Dept. official, represented Fayette Hungerford in a claim
against the Navy Dept. for property seized in Memphis in 1862. On April 3,

1875, Hungerford, Monroe County, N. Y., petitioned USG concerning his claim.—DS, DNA, RG 45, Subject File, Div. PN. On Oct. 25, Sherman wrote to USG. "It is now full nine months since you directed the Secretary of the Navy to re-open the Hungerford claim and hear me, as his duly-authorized attorney of record, on the points upon which he rejected it in December last, and yet no result has been reached. . . ."—*HMD*, 44-1-170, part 5, p. 314. On March 9, 1876, Sherman testified before the Committee on Naval Affairs, House of Representatives, investigating alleged corruption by Secretary of the Navy George M. Robeson, that he had met several times with USG to discuss the claim, and that Robeson had refused to hear the case. See *ibid.*, pp. 312–30; *HRC*, 53-3-1968.

1875, JAN. 18.   USG endorsement. "Refered to the Sec. of War. Let special attention be called to this application when appointments come to be made."— AES, DNA, RG 94, Correspondence, USMA. Written on a letter of the same date from Maj. Henry L. Abbot, Washington, D. C., to USG. "I would respectfully renew my application of last year, for the appointment of my son, Frederic Vaughan Abbot, as a cadet at West Point. . . . Respecting my own record, I was refused permission at the beginning of the War to accept the command of a volunteer regiment; on the ground that 'my services as an engineer could not be spared.' Thus, although constantly in the field, and once wounded, I had from the rules of the Service, to suffer for two years the hardship of remaining a subaltern, while many of my associates in the regular Army were enjoying high rank and its emoluments. Finally, permission to enter the volunteer Service having been granted, I had the honor of serving immediately under your own orders, as Commander of the Siege Artillery in front of Richmond and Petersburg; where it was always my endeavor to merit your approbation. . . ."—ALS, *ibid.* Related papers are *ibid.* On March 11, Orville E. Babcock wrote to Secretary of War William W. Belknap. "The President will be pleased to have you make the following change in appointments of Cadets to the Military Academy:—Place young Abbot on the list to enter next June, and young Roberts on the list to enter one year from next June. This is in accordance with the wishes of the parents of both of the boys."—LS, *ibid.* Frederic V. Abbot graduated USMA in 1879, first in his class.

1875, JAN. 18.   To J. Hall & Son, Liverpool. "I have the honor to acknowledge the receipt by the Inman Steamer, of the Southdown sheep which you were kind enough to send me. It arrived in splendid condition and was one of the finest specimens I have seen. It was enjoyed very much by my family and myself, and I beg to tender to you my sincere thanks and appreciation of your kindness."— Copy, DLC-USG, II, 2.

1875, JAN. 18.   John P. Grant, York, Maine, to USG. "You see that By the enclosed, my Claim is rejected. I volunteered in 1862, served nearly 3 years was in 43 Engagements, of 1st Maine Cav, Co K, Army, of the Potomac. Chargeing on the weldon Rail Road my Horse fell on me crushing my Ribs on right side. . . . there is a number of men Here that get a Pension that are no way disabled and have no Family's to surport, while I Have wife 6 children Father and grand mother to suport . . ."—ALS, DNA, RG 48, Miscellaneous Div., Letters Received. Grant received six dollars monthly for chronic rheumatism as of March 15, 1876.

1875, JAN. 18.   Pierce M. B. Travis, Bible Grove, Mo., to USG. "I understand that you have the power to appoint ten young men every year to the Military Academy of West Point, without regard to locality. I write you soliciting an appointment to West Point,   I have long had a strong desire to get a military education and lead a military life; to spend his life in the service of his country I conceive to be the noblest to which a young American can aspire. I am a young man; just twenty years of age, of good health and well developed bodily, my education is such, that I am able to teach in the public schools; as I have been teaching for some time past. I can give references and recomendations if need be, in regard to my character, education and ability. By hard efforts I have obtained what education I have, poverty has surrounded me since my child-hood. I have ever been ambitious to rise and be something in the world.   if I can get a military education, I am willing to spend the remainder of my life in the Army of the United States; leading a soldier's life as many of my relatives and ancestors have done before me,   my father was a Soldier in the Mexican War, he belonged to the Palmetto Regiment of South Carolina under Colonel Butler; he also served during the Rebellion. During the war between Texas and Mexico in 1835 and '6, one of my uncles, William B Travis was commander of Fort Alamo, and died with the garrison, when the fort fell March 6th 1836. I have no powerful friends in Washington City to plead my case for me, but I appeal to you who have been a soldier, and won laurels on the field of battle, to place me in the long wished for position from which I may rise to honor in the service of my country,   if you will do so, you will place me under lasting obligations to you." —ALS, DNA, RG 94, Unsuccessful Cadet Applications. Travis graduated USMA in 1880.

1875, JAN. 21.   George F. Robinson, Washington, D. C., to USG. "I have the honor to ask to be appointed a Paymaster. in the U. S. Army, when the present law shall be so modified as to allow the same to be done."—ALS, DNA, RG 94, ACP, 5979 1872. On Feb. 19, 1877, Robinson wrote to U.S. Representative Latimer W. Ballou of R. I. "Two years ago I made application to the President to be appointed Paymaster in the army, and filed therewith recommendations &c, copies of which I enclose. . . ."—ALS, *ibid.* On Feb. 20, Ballou endorsed this letter to USG. "I know not how I can present Mr. Robinson's request with more clearness and force than by enclosing his letter to me received last evening, which request I hope it may be in your power to grant. Mr. Robinson is earnestly recommended to the position of Paymaster,—not only for his competency but for his gallantry and service during the war, and especially for his personal courage in saving the life of Secretary Seward on the night of the attempted assassination by Payne, . . ."—AES, *ibid.* On June 19, 1879, President Rutherford B. Hayes nominated Robinson as maj., paymaster. See *U.S. Statutes at Large,* XVI, 704.

1875, JAN. 22, Friday.   Orville E. Babcock to Secretary of War William W. Belknap. "The President goes to Philadelphia tomorrow leaving on a special train at 1 P. M. B & P. RR to return Sunday night, and will be pleased to have you accompany him."—Copy, DLC-USG, II, 2. USG planned to attend a party at the home of George W. Childs. See *Philadelphia Public Ledger,* Jan. 23, 1875.

1875, JAN. 22.   N. C. Representative Appleton Oaksmith to USG. "A Restricted state Convention is desired by a majority of both parties to make needed amendments to Constitution of North, Carolina   Democratic opponents of Convention here assert upon telegrams received from Democratic Members of Congress that the President of the United, States will interfere   I respectfully ask authority to Contradict this assertion provided the action of Proposed Convention is strictly in accordance with Constitutions of United, States & North, Carolina."—Telegram received (at 1:45 P.M.), DLC-USG, IB. See *PUSG,* 19, 538–40.

1875, JAN. 24.   Lewis Wallace, Crawfordsville, Ind., to USG. "The bearer of this, Mr. Thomas W. Durham, in anticipation of the establishment of a territorial government for the Indian Nation, and the organization of a judicial district therein, will apply for appointment as U. S. Marshal of the same, and requests from me a letter to you; which I give with pleasure. He is a young man of excellent character, good education, considerable business experience; at one time he studied law; for several years he was a resident on the frontier between Arkansas and the Indian Territory, and was besides a lieutenant in my old regiment, (the 11th Ind. Infy) in which he served from the beginning to the end of the war. In fact, he counts his residence at this time in Arkansas, though his family is amongst oldest in this county. He is republican in politics. In brief, in the range of my acquaintance I hardly know a person in every way ~~better~~ so qualified for the appointment he seeks."—ALS, InHi. No such law passed.

1875, JAN. 26.   William Davis, Charleston, West Va., to USG. "The writer of this communication requests your influence to secure an appointment at some of the Departments as Usher or messenger. Perhaps I am the 1st one of color of this State who has made application for an appointment of this kind. I have unflinchingly supported the administration and the Republican party ever since citizenship was conferred upon me   Awaiting A favorable reply . . . P. S As to character & Qualification References T. B Swann G W Atkinson P. M. & others"—ALS, DNA, RG 56, Applications. In March, 1877, George W. Atkinson and four others, Charleston, wrote to President Rutherford B. Hayes recommending Davis. ". . . He has held the position of Principal of the colored schools of this City for several years, . . ."—LS, *ibid.* No appointment followed. See Louis R. Harlan, ed., *Booker T. Washington Papers* (Urbana, Ill., 1972–89), II, 17–18, 69.

1875, JAN. 27.   Lt. Gen. Philip H. Sheridan, New Orleans, to USG. "It gives me great pleasure through the medium of this note to introduce Mr: Effingham Lawrence, a dear friend for whom I have a warm attachment—Any kind con-

sideration extended to him—would be but a recognition of a substantial and
and praise worthy citizen of this state."—Copies (2), DLC-Philip H. Sheridan;
ADfS (undated), *ibid.* Effingham Lawrence, La. sugar planter, contested the
election of U.S. Representative J. Hale Sypher of La. and secured the seat for the
Democrats on March 3, the final day of the session.

1875, JAN. 27.   U.S. Representative William Lawrence of Ohio to USG. "The
Attorney general yesterday recommended the pardon of Kills at Indianapolis
prison whose term is nearly   I respectfully ask you to issue the pardon if you
can deem proper   I believe it is advisable"—Telegram received, DNA, RG 107,
Telegrams Collected (Bound). On Jan. 28, USG pardoned John M. Kills, convicted for submitting fraudulent claims and sentenced to four years in prison on
June 8, 1871.—Copy, *ibid.*, RG 59, General Records.

1875, JAN. 29.   Ransom Balcom, N. Y. Supreme Court, Binghamton, to USG.
"A friendly letter . . . I beg leave to say to you that thousands of true Republicans
voted against the reelection of Govenor Dix last November. I so voted—He
went to Newyork City & slurred you by declaring against electing you President a third time. I do not find a Republican, whether he voted for Dix or
against him last fall, who does not heartily approve of your course & Sheridans
acts in the Louisiana affairs—. . . There are thousands of quiet Democrats as
well as the masses of the Republicans who are not politicians or office seekers—
that believe in you as the wisest and best patriot in the Union—you have saved
the Union and will preserve law and order in the Southern States—The masses
of the good loyal people pay no attention to what Wm M. Everts, (whom you
did not appoint Chief Justice) *or* William Walter Phelps, M, C, from NewJersey,
(who owns stock in the NewYork Tribune & was justly defeated last fall by the
votes of colored people) *or* Ellis Roberts (in whom the people have little
confidence) *or* Wm E, Dodge (who paid a penalty for violating our Revenue
Laws) *or* William Cullen Bryant, (who is a *Free trade* Democrat & desires to
break up the Republican Party & supported you in 1872 *only* because he *hated*
Greeley more than he did you,) *or* any other Republican traitor, *or* coward *or*
disappointed *or* defeated office seeker *says or proclaims!* The mean, cowardly editors, who pretend to publish neutral news papers—& lie respecting the condition of affairs in the Southern states, do not represent the real patriotic sentiments of the masses of the people—. . . We shall have another war for the
destruction of the Union unless the Northern Democrats shall cease to encourage & approve of the Southern Rebels in their riots & murders in the Southern
States,   We shall all feel safe as long as you are President—for the people will
sustain you—I believe they will forget temperance crusades & all extreme
moral measures until the Southern Rebels shall be subdued and the Union is
clearly, firmly & fully established—"—ALS, USG 3. See *New York Times*, April
18, 1872.

1875, JAN. 29.   U.S. Representative Horace H. Harrison of Tenn. to USG.
"This will be handed you by Mrs Snyder of Nashville Tennessee whom you will
no doubt remember when you see her. Just before I resigned the office of U. S.

District Atty for the Middle District of Tennessee, Mrs Snyder's young brother, then about 18 years of age, was indicted by the Grand Jury in the U. S. District Court for abstracting letters from the private box of the Methodist Publishing House in the Post office at Nashville. He had been a clerk in the Methodist Publishing House. I drew the Indictmt, believing as I did, that the offense was covered by the U. S. Statute, the box being in the post office; but there may be some ground for doubting whether the statute fully covers the case. After he was indicted the defendant failed, as I have learned from inability to be present at the Court, to appear and a forfeiture was taken against him. The case, it seems, has never been tried. Mrs Snyder brings letters from Mrs Polk and Exchancellor East, and a letter from Rev Dr Redford of the Methodist Publishing House showing that the Publishing House has no desire whatever to prosecute the young man. In view of all the circumstances, which Mrs Snyder will state to you, I respectfully commend her application to your kind consideration and favourable action"—ALS, DNA, RG 60, Letters Received, Tenn. On Jan. 23, Mrs. James K. Polk, Nashville, had written to USG. "It would be esteemed a favavor, and an act of great kindness, Mr. President, if you would grant the petition accompanying this letter. The mother Mrs. Hill is an old friend of mine; an aged and highly respectable widow lady of this city. and the grand daughter of Genl James Robertson, the old pioneer of Tennessee. Mrs. Hill's unfortunate son, is a mere boy only 18 years of age. I ask your consideration in his behalf, for the distressed and grieved Mother."—ALS, *ibid.* On the same day, Albion H. Redford, Nashville, wrote to USG. "More than two years ago, a young man, by the name of W. T. Hill, then in my employ, was arrested by the United States authorities for extracting letters from my box in the Post Office in this city. He was brought before Hon C. F. Trigg, Judge of the United States Court—and held to bail for his appearance at a subsequent term of the Court. He has not appeared, and is now a wanderer—His mother is a widow with but little means, and the young man, still young may be saved. The object of this letter is to petition your Excellency to pardon him. . . ."—ALS, *ibid.* The other enclosure and related papers are *ibid.* No pardon followed.

1875, JAN. 30. USG veto. "I have the honor to return herewith H. R. No 4462 entitled 'An Act for the relief of Alexander Burtch, from which I withhold my approval for the reasons given in the accompanying letter of the Secretary of War."—Copy, DNA, RG 130, Messages to Congress. *HED,* 43-2-142; *SMD,* 49-2-53, 390. On Jan. 28, Secretary of War William W. Belknap had written to USG that Alexander Burtch, 1st Ind. Art., "deserted, at Fort Gaines, Alabama, September 25th, 1865, and was a deserter, at large, at date of muster out of his company, January 10th, 1866."—*Ibid.*; copy, DNA, RG 107, Letters Sent, Military Affairs. See *HRC,* 43-1-88.

1875, JAN. 30. Martin Ryerson, Newton, N. J., to USG. "I confidently expected to have resumed, long ere this, my duties as a Judge of the Court of Commissioners of Alabama Claims, but the state of my health has prevented, and there is no prospect that I would be able to resume them much before the 1st of April. Under these circumstances, duty to myself, as well as to the public, requires that I resign the Office, which I hereby do, my resignation to take effect on Wednesday, the 3d of February, proximo. I take this occasion to again express my thanks to you, personally, for your kindness & confidence, manifested in conferring upon me the appointment."—ALS, DNA, RG 59, Miscellaneous Letters. On Feb. 24, USG nominated Harvey Jewell, older brother of Postmaster Gen. Marshall Jewell, to replace Ryerson, who died on June 11. See Hamilton Fish diary, Feb. 1, 5, 19, 23, 1875, DLC-Hamilton Fish; *New York Times,* June 15, 1875.

[*1875, Jan.*].   Governor Silas Garber of Neb. *et al.* to USG. "Knowing that the name of Ex-Governor Robt W. Furnas of this State is favorably mentioned in connection with the office of United States Commissioner of Agriculture, we the undersigned Nebraska State officers cheerfully and cordially recommend his appointment to that position"—DS (10 signatures, undated), Nebraska Historical Society, Lincoln, Neb. Another undated copy of this petition with fifty additional signatures is *ibid.* No appointment followed. On Jan. 12, 1875, Garber had succeeded Robert W. Furnas.

1875, FEB. 1.   Mary Elliott, Lansing, Mich., to USG. "I adress you as Generel grant that was your office at that time   dont you recollect of and old lady comig to Caro the first year of the war i think it was sept or october it was before you went south to take memphis bringing nuwes of a Chain Cables being placed at fort pillow to catch the yankes boats on and i told you their was some 50 12 ponders placed on the hill side ~~in~~ when the boats got fast on the Cable theirs was to destry them   dont you remeber of giveng me a free ticket to go to St Luis and said uncle sam had got ~~news~~ nuws enough to give [you] a free ticket and you gave me a lett[e]r to Generel halleck and told me to tell him what you told me . . ."—ALS, DNA, RG 56, Applications. Elliott sought unspecified compensation for her services. In a letter of the same date to Secretary of the Treasury Benjamin H. Bristow, Elliott included a note to USG. "did you ever receive a bottel of mapel molases i sent you the time you was beseigeing Vickburg   i sent you by Dr forer i bileive was his nam   i have no Clames against you for that only want to know wethere you received it"—AN, *ibid.* See *PUSG,* 3, 278.

1875, FEB. 2.   Levi P. Luckey to Lt. Col. Henry F. Clarke, asst. commissary gen., Chicago. "The President desires me to write and say to you that at the time when he saw you early in the Winter and stated to you that he had no intention of making a change in the head of the Commissary Dept., he had no expectation that an occasion would arise unexpectedly to make such a change necessary. He finds now that on account of the request of the Commissary General himself a change is made necessary, which will be made in the customary way of choosing heads of departments without reference to seniority."—Copy, DLC-USG, II, 2.

On April 1, Lt. Gen. Philip H. Sheridan wrote to USG. "The recent illness of Gen. Shiraz has created much anxiety in my mind about who should be Commissary General in case of his death or retirement. It is well-known that Beckwith has been making great exertions for the place, and while we all consider him competent we do not think him a good officer because he does not confine himself to his professional duties, and resorts to means to accomplish his ends which we do not consider professional. His appointment would be very distasteful to the Army, and his constant interference with legislation will in all probability make his presence in Washington tiresome to the Executive and to Congress. I therefore beg of you, Gen. Grant, to give us some one that will not be objectionable, and whose ability and good sense will make a pleasant reminder of your consideration to the Army in this respect."—Copy (unsigned), DLC-Philip H. Sheridan. Brig. Gen. Alexander E. Shiras, commissary gen., died April 14.

On April 27, Luckey wrote to Secretary of War William W. Belknap. "The President directs me to say that he desires that you should cause to be made out the appointment of Robert Macfeely, Major and C. S. to be Commissary General; and when the promotions in that corps are made he desires the vacancy in rank of Captain to be filled by the transfer of Lieut. Fredk F. Whitehead."—LS, DNA, RG 94, ACP, 1906 1875. On April 28, Belknap wrote to U.S. Senator John A. Logan of Ill., Chicago. "Yours of April 25th was received yesterday. On the day previous (Tuesday, 27th), at Cabinet meeting, the President spoke to me concerning the section of the 'Revised Statutes', which prohibited the appointment of the acting head of a Bureau to continue for a longer period than ten days, and informed me that, on account of that Statute, he must make an appointment of a Commissary General, on that day, & then had addressed to me a communication directing that Col. Macfeely be appointed. Until that law was discovered, I am satisfied that he had no intention of making any change in the Bureau, until the meeting of Congress in December. I have frequently presented to him Gen'l. Beckwith's name, and thought that he would finally be appointed. I believe that the President, since the appointment, mentioned to Mrs. Logan, the reasons which induced him to make the selection. As soon as I learned from him that the appointment would be made on that day, I brought to his attention Capt. Whitehead's name & reminded him of your application, should there be a vacancy among the Captaincies. He, at once, directed me to appoint Whitehead to the position of Captain & Commissary of Subsistence, which has been done—"—ALS, DLC-John A. Logan. On Feb. 20, Logan had written to USG. "You will do me a very great kindness by giving the enclosed case your personal & favorable consideration as Maj Whitehead is certainly very worthy of this recognition of his services."—ALS, DNA, RG 94, ACP, 2005 1875. Related papers include an undated petition from John F. Long *et al.* to USG. "The undersigned citizens of the State of Missouri would respectfully present to your Excellency the name of Brevt Majr Frederick F. Whitehead U. S. A. (1st Lieut. 18th U. S. Inf) for transfer and promotion from the line, to the Staff Pay Department. . . ."—DS (17 signatures), *ibid.* On Dec. 6, USG nominated Maj. Robert Macfeely to replace Shiras, and 1st Lt. Frederick F. Whitehead as capt., commissary of subsistence, both to date from April 14. See *Calendar*, Feb. 10, 1874.

On April 15, 1875, Ezra Millard, president, Omaha National Bank, and three others wrote to U.S. Senators Phineas W. Hitchcock and Algernon S. Paddock of Neb., recommending 1st Lt. John F. Trout for a vacancy in the commissary dept.—LS, DNA, RG 94, ACP, T168 CB 1870. On April 22, USG endorsed this letter. "Refered to the Sec. of War, application transfered for Qr. Mr. Dept."— AES, *ibid.* Related papers are *ibid.*

On April 20, U.S. Senator Hannibal Hamlin of Maine, Bangor, had written to USG. "Allow me to call your attention to the application of Lieut Henry B. Osgood of the 3d Reg of Art. for the place of Commissary of Subsistance—He is well recommended by officer who know him well, and by Several of the delegation from Maine, in Congress. . . ."—ALS, *ibid.*, 1748 1875. On Nov. 23, Hamlin telegraphed to USG on the same subject.—Telegram received, *ibid.* Related papers are *ibid.* Letters recommending Capt. Michael J. Fitzgerald for a vacancy in the commissary dept. are *ibid.*, F96 CB 1863.

1875, FEB. 2.   Anna L. Clapp, Lee Center, Ill., to USG. "Permit me to engage your attention a few moments while I prefer a request. In order to do so, allow me to introduce myself as Mrs Anna L. Clapp of St. Louis, who all through the War was, the Pres. of the Ladies Union Aid Soc. of that city, and the coadjutor of the Western San. Com. in its noble work for the Soldiers. With the breaking out of the rebellion, I enlisted in the service of my country, and never ceased my labors, as long as there was a sick soldier to be cared for—My son in law Frank H. Fletcher was appointed a Paymaster in the Volunteer service—He served till the end of the War, was then mustered out, with a Brevet for faithful and efficient services, his accounts being perfectly correct, and he in all points irreproachable. He now desires a reappointment as Paymaster in the regular army. He has made an application to the Sec. of War, and I have intruded upon you, to beg that you will grant his application—Trusting that you will pardon the intrusion and bestow the favor, . . ."—ALS, DNA, RG 94, Applications for Positions in War Dept. A related letter is *ibid.* On Nov. 8, Dec. 14, March 18, 1876, and Feb. 5, 1877, Clapp wrote to USG on the same subject.—ALS, *ibid.* No appointment followed.

1875, FEB. 2.   Pa. Representative Henry Huhn *et al.* to USG. "The undersigned members of the General Assembly of Pennsylvania most cordially recommend Charles E. Slade Esq for re-appointment in the regular Army of the United States, and urge your Excellency to give his claims a favorable consideration."—DS (30 signatures), DNA, RG 94, ACP, S265 CB 1868. USG wrote a note. "Chas. E. Slade formerly of the 15th Inf.y desires to get back. See record of this officer and if good apt."—AN (undated), *ibid.* On March 23, Secretary of War William W. Belknap endorsed these papers. "The President directs that after the assignment to Regiments of the present 1st Class at the M. A. Mr. Slade be appointed a Lieutenant (2d) of Inf'y. if a vacancy exists—"—AE (initialed), *ibid.* On April 10, Belknap wrote to Charles E. Slade, Washington, D. C. "Since the verbal notification to you that you would be appointed a Second Lieutenant in the Army, the Department has received two sets of charges and specifications against you, when you were formerly in service. These papers have been submitted to the President, who instructs me to say that the notification that you would be appointed, is rescinded."—LS (press), *ibid.*

1875, FEB. 4.   John Bell Hepburn, Port-au-Prince, to USG. "PRIVATE . . . Pray pardon me for thus again obtruding on your valuable time, but your Excellency will permit me to suggest that it would be a want of gratitude if a man, like my humble self, whom God has endowed with a proper appreciation of men and things, should be wanting in manhood and good-breeding not to break through the formalities of etiquette which your high Office commands and communicate to yourself what a grateful heart feels and a sensible mind thinks for all that you have done for the colored Race. In your message, now two years ago, you showed to Congress that notwithstanding the fifteenth amendment to the Constitution of the United States, its benefits to the colored people were merely theoretical and not practicable to them so far as Liberty and Equality are concerned; and in your succeeding message you plead for those native born americans who have left their native land and residing in foreign countries and who, by the State Department, if not by law, have lost the protection of the United States Government. Again in your Excellency's last message you renewed the question and asked Congress to act on the subject. For all this, President, please accept my hearty thanks and may God Almighty, in His Allwise Providence, inspire the Senate and House of Representatives to bring this matter to a close during this present session. President, I thank you also for the compliment you have paid to my race, by sending the Honorable E. D. Bassett to represent the United States of America in Hayti. I must, in this circumstance, humbly request of your Excellency to excuse the remark when I am forced to say that that Gentleman is totally unfit to fill the Office he occupies, as the Representative of the People of the United States of America—whether white or black—in their policy, their interest and their dignity, and I repeat, President, what perhaps no other individual has as yet said to your Excellency that the interests of the United States of America would be better served in Hayti by a *White* Representative rather than a *Black* one. In conclusion I must further crave your Excellency's excuse for this lengthy epistle and may God Almighty in His Supreme Wisdom hold you and your dear family in His Holy Keeping . . ."—ALS, DNA, RG 59, Miscellaneous Letters. See *PUSG*, 21, 299–301.

1875, Feb. 8.   Mary McCook Baldwin, Poughkeepsie, N. Y., to USG. "Tell me about Alex   I am so anxious   time short"—Telegram received (at 12:46 A.M.), DLC-USG, IB. USG endorsed this telegram. "No probability of any change being made at West Point at this season."—AE (initialed, undated), *ibid.* No appointment followed for 2nd Lt. Alexander McCook Guard, USMA 1871.

1875, Feb. 9.   USG endorsement. "Refered to the Sec. of the Treas. I see no objection to the apt. here recommended."—AES, DNA, RG 56, Collector of Customs Applications. Written on a petition to USG of the same day from U.S. Senators Zachariah Chandler and Thomas W. Ferry of Mich. and all nine members of the Mich. congressional delegation, recommending Digby V. Bell as collector of customs, Detroit.—DS, *ibid.* On Feb. 12, USG nominated Bell.

1875, Feb. 10.   Attorney Gen. George H. Williams to USG. "I have the honor to acknowledge the receipt of House Resolution No. 650 transmitted to me this day for examination; and to say that no objections appear to me to its approval. It is herewith returned."—LS, OFH. On Feb. 11, USG signed this bill to reimburse John Brennan for janitorial work on federal buildings in Indianapolis. See *HRC,* 43-1-152.

1875, FEB. 10.   Orville E. Babcock to Bluford Wilson, solicitor of the treasury.
"I send you back Genl. Lawlers letter. I read it to the President who remarked
that he did not see why Genl. Lawler had no right to ask a favor, for if a good
soldier had, Genl. L. had. He said he did not know however of any place he could
offer him and repeated the kind remarks of him as a soldier."—LS, ICarbS.
A Feb. 13 letter from Wilson to Michael K. Lawler is *ibid.* No appointment
followed.

1875, FEB. 11.   William J. Purman, Tallahassee, to USG. "Jones democrat
elected united states senator by fusion of Democrats and Independents and
in combination with the governor"—Telegram received (at 6:00 P.M.), DLC-
USG, IB.
    On Feb. 24 and 25, John Tyler, Jr., Tallahassee, wrote to USG. "In Washing-
ton you best know what Mr Conover is now after, since being defeated here in
all things, and at all points, but his Democratic Competitor here, His Excellency, the Florida Ass, M L Stearns, is still playing out Democratic Cards in his
Judicial & other appointments, after having yealded up to the Democracy the
Speakership of the Assembly, the President Pro: tem: of the Senate, the United
States Senator, and the public printing, . . ." "I neglected to say in my letter of
yesterday that, since the decision of the Senatorial contest here, resulting in the
failure of both Conover & Stearns to secure their real ends—the object of
Conover being to get a Democrat elected who would favour him as Governor in
1876, and the object of Stearns being to be elected to the Senate himself, and,
therefore, playing his Cards into the hands of the Democracy for speakership of
the Assembly and president pro tem of the Senate, which failing ultimately as
to his own election thus resulted in his choice of Jones to defeat Conovers movement for Bloxham that would have been the next card of the latter—now both
are aspirants for the Gubernatorial office in 1876, and the old Democratic game
of both is to be more vigorously conducted than ever. Heretofore the struggle
between Reed & Osborn for the Succession to the Senate tore the Republican
Party to pieces. . . ."—ALS, Tyler Papers, College of William and Mary,
Williamsburg, Va. See Jerrell H. Shofner, *Nor Is It Over Yet: Florida in the Era of
Reconstruction 1863–1877* (Gainesville, 1974), pp. 295–97.
    Between Sept., 1875, and Jan., 1876, Tyler wrote ten letters to USG con-
cerning Republican factions in Fla., Tyler's feud with U.S. Senator Simon B.
Conover and Governor Marcellus L. Stearns, and Tyler's editorials in the *Fer-
nandina Observer*, some of which he enclosed.—ALS, Tyler Papers, College of
William and Mary, Williamsburg, Va. On May 17, 1876, Tyler, Jacksonville,
wrote to USG. "POLITICAL. . . . The enclosed letter received yesterday from the
Hon Josiah T Walls gives me the opportunity of saying, concerning the political situation here, that, in despite of the loss by fire of my paper, and the strenuous efforts of all the Factionists in the Republican lead, together with those of
the Democratic Leaders, to prevent the reestablishment of the Press before the
31st May Nominating Convention, *I shall still hold, I believe, through Walls, the balance of power in that Convention, with the ability to defeat the aspirants of the Factions
and thereby to prevent the scheme of the Democracy taking effect in favour of some Fac-
tionist as the Republican Nominee leading to Democratic success through Republican*

apathy in the contest. I am very poor, tis true, and greatly need your official help, yet I am still strugling energetically to save the Republican Party in the State, . . ."—ALS, *ibid.* On May 18, Tyler wrote to USG. "In answer to the letter of your Secretary of the 26th April I *specified*, as requested by him in your name, the office that would be acceptable to me as the Post Office here now vacant. Should Senator Conovers influence be brought to bear against me for the place, and the responsibility of the appointment be thrown by you upon him, then I pray you to consider the propriety of my appointment as Consul to Rio-Janeiro in South America in the place of a man by the name of Hines now holding it at the instance of Mr Spencer of Alabama. . . ."—ALS, DNA, RG 59, Letters of Application and Recommendation. See *PUSG*, 22, 426. In early June, Fla. Republicans renominated Stearns as governor; a smaller, breakaway convention nominated Conover. In mid-June, at Cincinnati, the Republican national convention seated a Conover-led delegation instead of the regular Fla. delegates. See Shofner, *Nor Is It Over Yet*, pp. 301–3. On June 6, USG nominated Tyler as postmaster, Jacksonville; on June 8, the Senate confirmed Tyler. On June 14, Tyler wrote to USG denigrating Stearns and Conover. ". . . The Delegates to the Madison Convention were all literally bought and held in the Pantaloons pockets of either the one, or the other, and in all that occurred there it was the ~~it was the~~ foulest and most corrupt and corrupting business I have ever yet beheld. The Purse of Stearns was drained, and it is no exaggeration to say that Conover was completely bankrupted. . . . *In the present posture of the Party will be found the realization of all that I have said to you in my communications from time to time during the past three years.* Yet, judging from all that I hear, these two men will, most likely, while at Cincinnatti, buy and sell each other, the one to the other, and then endeavour to prevail on you to hold my Commission as Postmaster here in abeyance, ~~until~~ so that ~~I may be compelled~~ they may compel me, as they suppose, into their joint arrangements still to secure to themselves and their Carpet-bag Brethren *exclusively*, as usual, every other place of honor, profit and emolument in the state, although constituting only six per cent of the Party in the state, as against ninety-four per cent of Southern Republicans. . . ."— ADfS (marked "Duplicate"), Tyler Papers, College of William and Mary, Williamsburg, Va. On June 20, on the motion of U.S. Senator Hannibal Hamlin of Maine, the Senate voted to reconsider Tyler's appointment. On June 27, Tyler wrote to USG. ". . . By recurring to my letter of the 14th June the President will also see how correctly I foresaw and read the game being played against me as Postmaster. The fact is just this. If these Gentlemen are determined that I shall not live then in self-defence I must and *surely* will destroy them."—ALS, *ibid.* On June 29, Dennis Eagan and eight others, Republican state committee, Jacksonville, wrote to USG supporting Tyler's appointment.—Copy, *ibid.* On the same day, the Senate rejected Tyler. On July 6, Tyler, Washington, D. C., wrote to USG blaming Conover for the reversal. ". . . It is equally due to the living, and to the memory of the dead, that the matter shall not be permitted to rest here. I have seen Mr Hamblin and appointed to meet him in the Morning upon the subject. Believe me, Mr President, I sincerely appreciate the friendship you have manifested towards me, . . ."—Copy (on U.S. Senate stationery), *ibid.* On July 7, Tyler wrote to USG. "I have seen Senator Hamblin this morning and he says that, in relation to my nomination as Postmaster at Jacksonville, Florida, and its final rejection by the Senate, 'if any mistake has been made the Corrective power is entirely with yourself and the Postmaster General, and that the burthen of the responsibility of making the correction should not be thrown upon the Committee of the Senate, and that such a course is unusual.' As to this I do not pretend to be informed beyond what he states; But I beg your Excellency to permit me to say that, if the Communication from Jacksonville endorsing my Nomination received by you on yesterday is not sufficient to be the basis of further action in my behalf for the office, then I pray you to send in as Postmaster of Jacksonville, either the Name of the Hon: Thomas W. Osborn, or that of John J Holland, both of whom are true Republicans and certainly fit to hold the office, although I have no special relations with either. . . ."—Copy, *ibid.* Possibly concerning Tyler, USG wrote on the same day. "Send for Senator Hamlin a request that he call here to-morrow morning before going to the Senate Chamber."—AN, OHi. On July 13, USG nominated Manuel Govin, one of the Conover delegates at Cincinnati, as postmaster, Jacksonville. On July 18, Tuesday, Tyler, Clifton, Md., wrote to USG. "On Friday last, being in Washington, I learned from Governor Stearns the final action taken by your Excellency in relation to the Post-Office at Jacksonville, in consequence of your having been informed by Senator Hamlin, as he said, that the Committee of the Senate on Post-offices and Post-Roads, in the interest of Senator Conover, had refused to change its unfavourable attitude towards me. . . ."—ALS, Tyler Papers, College of William and Mary, Williamsburg, Va. Tyler met USG on Aug. 12, and wrote to him the same day.—ALS, *ibid.* On Sept. 1, Tyler, Washington, D. C., wrote to USG, Long Branch. "You will see from the enclosed copy of the Chronicle how I have defined my position with the public at this time. It was only this week that I was informed by the Attorney General that a Commission as District Attorney had been forwarded to my address at Key-West, hence my apparent delay in responding to it. Not wishing to be longer idle in the important canvass for the Presidency now engaging all minds in the country, I shall proceed, without delay, to my post of duty, which, however, is most hazardous to do at this yellow fever season at that point. As I have frankly told you of my wants and wishes, you will please to consider my application for the Judgeship lately made vacant by the death of Judge Frazer as still before you. Having full confidence in your disposition to serve me in a manner that would be most acceptable, as well as in your power to do so, I rely in faith upon your recollection and friendship in relation to that appointment."—Copy, *ibid.* On Feb. 27, 1877, USG again nominated Tyler as postmaster, Jacksonville; the Senate adjourned before acting. As of Sept. 30, Tyler served as customs inspector, Richmond.

1875, FEB. 12.   USG veto of a bill granting a pension to "Lewis Hinely," because of a spelling discrepancy.—Copy, DNA, RG 130, Messages to Congress. *HED*, 43-2-168; *SMD*, 49-2-53, 390–91. On March 3, USG signed a bill pensioning Louis Heinley.

1875, FEB. 12.   USG order setting aside land in Idaho Territory "for the exclusive use of the mixed tribes of Shoshone, Bannock and Sheepeater Indians, to be known as the 'Lemhi Valley' Indian reservation. Said tract of Country is estimated to contain about one hundred square miles, and is in lieu of the tract provided for in the 3rd Article of an unratified treaty made and concluded at Virginia City, Montana Territory on the 24th of September, 1868."—DS, DNA, RG 75, Orders. *HED*, 45-2-1, part 5, I, 637, 45-3-1, part 5, I, 747, 47-2-1, part 5, II, 329, 49-2-1, part 5, I, 544–45; *SED*, 48-2-95, 295; *SD*, 57-1-452, 839. Subsequent orders are printed in the sources listed above.

On April 23, USG ordered Camp Verde reservation in Arizona Territory restored to the public domain.—DS, DNA, RG 75, Orders.

On Oct. 20, USG ordered land near Fort Stanton in New Mexico Territory set aside for the Mescalero Apaches. On Dec. 20, 1876, Gen. William T. Sherman wrote to Lt. Gen. Philip H. Sheridan, Chicago, concerning a band of Mescalero Apaches seeking to return to the agency at Fort Stanton. ". . . the President would much prefer that these Mescalero Apaches should be conducted and subsisted, to the Reservation at Fort Sill—I explained to him the inveterate hostility between the apaches and Kiowas, when he modified his instructions to them. If those Indians cannot be persuaded to go to Fort Sill, then to give them the food necessary to enable them to reach Fort Stanton, there to be turned over to the resident Indian Agent their ponies to be taken and sold for their account and the proceeds invested in Beef or Sheep for their maintenance, the military to escort them into their reservation, and to protect them whilst there. . . ."—Copy, *ibid.*, RG 107, Letters Sent, Military Affairs.

1875, FEB. 12. U.S. Representative J. Ambler Smith of Va. to USG. "The Bill removing the political disabilities of Harry Hetze Genl. in the confederate Army and an Officer in Mexico, passed the House some time since He is alive and well in Richmond, I send this as I understand you have been informed that he was dead."—Telegram received, DLC-USG, IB; DNA, RG 107, Telegrams Collected (Bound). On the same day, USG signed a bill removing the political disabilities of Henry Heth, USMA 1847.

On May 14 (Friday) and May 17, Heth, Richmond, telegraphed to USG. "Can I see you a few minutes this Evening at nine 9 oclock" "Republican Committee will leave tonight can they see you tomorrow in relation to the matter I spoke to you about on Saturday"—Telegrams received, DLC-USG, IB.

On Dec. 31, Heth wrote to USG. "This will be handed you by our mutual friend Mr A. B. Hagner of Annapolis Md We (Mr H. and myself) are very anxious to get our nephew Heth Harrison a Lieutenants appointment in the Army. if you can consistently grant our request, we will be under many obligations to you, and I think the Service will gain a first rate Soldier. With the compliments of the Season . . ."—ALS, DNA, RG 94, Applications for Positions in War Dept. Related letters are *ibid*. No appointment followed.

1875, FEB. 13. USG note. "Will the Sec. of the Treas. please see Miss Bootes whose father recently died after forty years of service in the department leaving a dependent family."—ANS, DNA, RG 56, Applications. On the same day, Alexander R. Shepherd, Washington, D. C., wrote to USG. "I beg to introduce Mr Anthony Hyde an old & estimable citizen of Washington who wishes to ask your help for the young lady who accompanies him   She is the daughter of a person who served 40 years in the Treasury Dept & died leaving a helpless destitute family   There can be no case more deserving"—ALS, *ibid.* Related papers are *ibid.* Sophia S. Bootes clerked in the Treasurer's office.

1875, FEB. 16.   Nathan W. Duck, Shelby City, Ky., to USG. "I am a native of Kentucky, and reside in Shelby City, Boyle Co Ky. I served (3) three years in the Federal Army, and was honorably discharged—Have voted the Republican ticket since the war; Hence I have rendered myself odious to all KuKlux and enemies of the Goverment. On the night of the 26th November 1874, A man by the name of Joseph S. Wright entered my house and attempted to force himself into my wifes bed room, when I ejected him by force. He returned on the next morning armed with an Army Pistol & shot me in the neck inflicting a dangerous wound from which I may never recover. I will here state that Wright some two or three years since was charged with the crime of KuKluxing in this County and to avoid arrest & punishment he fled the state of Ky & went to Mo—where he killed a man. Finding that the Rebels had regained the state of Kentucky he returned to his home in Ky with *blood stained hands* to renew his former occupation, being well satisfied that no Ex Rebel could be punished in this state for murder or other crimes. . . . I will state without fear of successful contradiction, for two years last past there has been more outrages committed in Ky than any other state in the Union. *La. Miss, or Arkansas not excepted.* As a law abideing American Citizen, I respectfully ask and demand of united states protection,   Trusting that I will receive a speedy reply . . ."—ALS, DNA, RG 60, Letters Received, Ky. Also in Feb., John Ogden and John Henderson, Cave Spring Station, Ky., wrote to USG. "this moning I am very mutch destrest a bout my Coulerd frinds   we ere ofley prest here in logen county Kentucky and morless all over the land they do suffer.   the matter is now of the county here at Russellvill   the first yeare of mancerpation they hav made us pay $550 Dollars and did not own eny propety nothing but what was on thire baks and nothing to Eat an the white dimmorcrats they ever ritch an had onley five Dollars to pay   they hav cattel and land an we pore pepoel hav nothing   they hav they Big Scools an free at that   we trid to hav scool and they burint it down ~~moth~~ mothan that they Elected a Shirff in the year of 1870 Who name wars george gillom a drunkerd negleterfull   maney of us pad tax an he give no reset for it and he drunk run thrugh and destroyed untell Logen County is a bout Sixteen thousand Dollars bhind   they taxs us to make it good of us   our taxs is 400 Dollars an half   they poles taxs 200 dollers half   I am a pore minster of the gospel & hav three little Childrens an no propety   Iv nothing   I am tax 400 an half dollars   I am advertised for Sale even my bead Clothan   the hole cuntrey is in just such a fix   they sell us out and we ere fread to chepe and murders us   we can not get gustus in nouthing   what ere we to do   we will but starve ere Stile: it is truth genral Grant   I ~~fot~~ fort under the Stars and stripes under you for my libete   I hav non   you hav the power there to help us here I do wosh to no of you is it lawfull us to be treted eny such away   oh if I wars abel to come I could tell you all a bout the way we ere pursercuted . . . thrug the powers of the most high God you hav domenon over the land in this great pow-

ers he give to you is to Exercise Rightness for the lord sake   tell me what am
I to do . . ."—LS (docketed Feb. 17), *ibid.* In [*Sept.*], L. C. Rill, Massack, Ky.,
wrote to USG. "My house was torn down the other night (I forget the date)
Six men were prowling through the neighbourhood last night, dressed as Ku-
klucks, inquiring for my name   I am a loyal son of the government, and anti
slavery; and have been from the very start. I have suffered severⅼely for my
senti[m]ents. I want protection. I do not know to whom to apply. South western Kentucky was the hot bed of secession during the war   My patrimony is so
arranged I cannot leave it. My family are females or miners. When they tore the
house down, they left this note   'Mr *Henry Tilsworth if this house is occupied by
you, you will have to abide by the cosequences* signed, C C C.' Heny Tilsworth is a
black man building on my land. I intend for him to—and I want him to have
protection   He do not know who they are   We live ten miles south west of Pa-
ducah   I am a minister of the Gospel, and peacible. . . . P. S. The state laws here
are administerd by secesh"—ALS (docketed Sept. 7), *ibid.*

On Sept. 29, Ned Trigg and fifteen others, Cave City, Ky., petitioned USG.
"We the undersigned colored people of Barren county State of Kentucky, In a
Meeting held by us for the purpose of consulting you in regards to the Tax paid
by the colored people of this section. We feel that we have been overloaded with
Taxation & have been defrauded by those who are in power here in this section
of the state. Sir at this present time the colored people are compelled to pay
$3.00 per head poll Tax & the whites who are more able are only paying $2.00
per head poll tax and we also pay 52¢ per hundred property tax & the whites
only 40¢ per hundred dollars worth. We are unwilling to do this & we do not
believe that you will approve of the above Measure taken by our office holders
to collect the Tax of the colored people.   believing you to be a friend of ours we
thought proper to write to you as our Gov. McCreary is a Democratic Governor, & w̶ you would answer us a give us all information needed,   Pleas do this
& we will not further disturb your Honor, . . . We the above named persons pati-
tion for all in this County."—D, *ibid.*, Letters from the President.

1875, FEB. 17.   USG proclamation convening a special session of the Senate on
March 5.—DS, DNA, RG 130, Presidential Proclamations. The Senate devoted
most of the session to USG's La. policy and passed a resolution of support before adjourning on March 24.

1875, FEB. 17.   Postmaster Gen. Marshall Jewell to USG. "Judge Hughes and
Mr Platt inform me that you desire to withdraw the nomination of Gibbons for
Post master at Winchester and substitute therefor the name of Mr Miller. Is
this s̶o̶ your desire? If so. I will bring you the papers tomorrow."—Telegram re-
ceived, DLC-USG, IB. On the same day, Levi P. Luckey telegraphed to Jewell.
"The President says he will make the change and see if that will bring quiet."—
ALS (telegram sent), DNA, RG 107, Telegrams Collected (Bound). On Feb. 8,
USG had nominated C. M. Gibbens as postmaster, Winchester, Va. On Feb. 20,
Saturday, Gibbens, Winchester, telegraphed to USG. "I am telegraphed that
you propose withdrawing my nomination upon objection that I was a confeder-
ate deserter   the objection and its deductions are untrue.   will you not give

me an opportunity to defend myself. Can I see you before Tuesday. Please answer."—Telegram received, DLC-USG, IB. On Feb. 23, USG nominated William Miller in place of Gibbens.

1875, FEB. 18.   Attorney Gen. George H. Williams to USG. "I have the honor
to return herewith House Bill No. 4546, and to inform you that in my opinion
there are no objections to its receiving your approval."—LS, OFH. On the same
day, USG signed this bill, to correct errors in the Revised Statutes.

1875, FEB. 19.   To Congress. "Under the requirements of section 6 of the 'Act
for the government of the District of Columbia and for other purposes.' approved June 20th 1874 I have the honor to submit herewith the report of the
Board of Audit, upon the amount equitably chargeable to the Street rail-road
companies pursuant to the charters of said companies or the acts of Congress
relating thereto, together with the reasons therefor."—Copy, DNA, RG 130,
Messages to Congress. *HED,* 43-2-170.

1875, FEB. 20.   James W. Denver, Washington, D. C., to USG. "The National
Convention of the Veterans of the Mexican War will be held in this city (at
Willards Hotel,) commencing on Monday next—February 22d—and will continue in session two or three days. I have been directed to request you to send
an order to the various departments of the government giving to such of the
clerks and employees as belong to the association in this city, leaves of absence
to attend the meetings of the convention, for, say three days without stopping
their pay during that time. By doing this you will much oblige them . . ."—Copy,
DNA, RG 60, Letters Received, D. C.

1875, FEB. 20.   B. McGuinness, Drogheda, Ireland, to USG alleging that he
was illegally confined in a Philadelphia insane asylum before being deported.
". . . Without proper protection, I would fear to travel the streets of Philadelphia, as the police there seem empowered to arrest anyone they think fit, fling
him into prison, *without judge or jury,* where he must remain as long as the 'authorities may deem fit, without any redress. If this is in accordance with the
spirit of liberty and the justice measured out in a free Republic, I dont want to
experience anymore than I have of it, yet it is my resolve to have indemnity for
the outrages inflicted on me COST WHAT IT WILL."—ALS, DNA, RG 59, Miscellaneous Letters.

1875, FEB. 21.   To U.S. Senator John Sherman of Ohio. "May I ask the favor of
a call from you on your way to the Capitol to-morrow morning?"—ALS, de-
Coppet Collection, NjP.

1875, FEB. 21.   William W. Smith, Washington, Pa., to "Dear General," presumably USG. "I beg leave to introduce the bearer Mr. J. T. Edgar at present residing in Omaha   Mr. Edgar was for several years a resident of this county, and
we can all most cordially recommend him to you, as an accomplished gentleman
and an honest & reliable man. It will give me great pleasure if you can forward

his wishes."—ALS, DNA, RG 59, Letters of Application and Recommendation. On Feb. 24, Admiral David D. Porter wrote to USG. "I had the pleasure of knowing Mr John T. Edgar in 1861. just after the late war of the Rebellion broke out, when I commanded the Frigate 'Powhatan'. Mr Edgar was then Consul at St. Thomas and afforded me many facilities and removed obstacles to my getting supplies and aided me materially in proceeding in chase of the rebel steamer 'Sumter' and driving her from those waters and ending her career. . . ."—LS, *ibid.* Related papers are *ibid.* On March 9, USG nominated John T. Edgar as consul, Beirut, in place of George S. Fisher.

On March 8, 1873, Amos T. Akerman, Cartersville, Ga., had written to USG. "Mr. George S. Fisher of Augusta, Ga. informs me that you have expressed a wish to know my views concerning his fitness for the mission to Japan. So far as a brief acquaintance enables me to judge, he is well qualified for the place. He came to Georgia a few years ago on account of health, and engaged in agriculture. Last year he took part in politics, and was put upon the Republican Electoral Ticket. In that position he was efficient and did all that could reasonably be expected. He seems to be a man of intelligence and culture, and is very much respected by those in Georgia who know him. I learn that he has had consular service in Japan, and this has no doubt tended to qualify him for the mission."— ALS, *ibid.* On Oct. 14, Fisher, Washington, D. C., wrote to USG seeking a consular appointment, and recommending Akerman as associate justice, U.S. Supreme Court.—ALS, *ibid.* On Jan. 14, 1874, U.S. Representative Alexander H. Stephens of Ga. wrote to USG. "I understand that Major Harry Wayne does not desire the consulship to Japan—If this be so I wish hereby to recall to your mind what I said in behalf of Hon. George S. Fisher of Georgia for that place— Judge Fisher is originally from Illinois but was appointed by Mr. Lincoln to Japan in 1860—Since the war he has been living in Ga"—ALS, *ibid.* Related papers are *ibid.* See Lincoln, *Works,* Supplement (Westport, Conn., 1974), p. 116. On March 3, USG nominated Fisher as consul, Beirut.

On April 26, 1875, Fisher, Beirut, wrote to USG at length refuting corruption charges. ". . . I have most respectfully to say this if I am removed, under all the circumstances of this case, it were better a thousand times I had staid right where I was in the Ku Klux, White Leaguers fires of Georgia, if there be such things, than as Minister Boker says have jumped into 'the flaming fires of Syria.' My sacrifices to get here took all the means I could raise and now I am to be left here without a Dollar after paying all my expenses and slight indebtedness, and how I am to be able to return to my native country I really know not. . . ."— Copy, DNA, RG 59, Miscellaneous Letters. On Nov. 29, Stephens, Crawfordville, Ga., wrote to Secretary of State Hamilton Fish. "This will be handed to you by Mr. George M. Fisher son of Hon. George S. Fisher late Consul to Beyrout—How ~~its~~ Stands the Matter of his removal I do not know: but he is now in Syria in great destitution and without means to return—The Son is I think an upright young man qualified for a clerk Ship in your department and I commend him to you Specially for such position, as he is qualified for if you can bestow it. upon him—It will enable him while rendering valuable services to the Government to Save something to enable his parents—both father & mother—are now in Syria—. . ."—ALS, *ibid.,* Letters of Application and Recommendation. As of Sept. 30, 1877, George M. Fisher served as Treasury Dept. clerk.

On Sept. 6, 1876, George S. Fisher, Washington, D. C., wrote to USG. "*personal* . . . You are doubtless well aware that I have studiously and of course purposely abstained [f]rom appealing through the Press for Justice at the hands of the Secretary of the Department of State—of exposing the indefensible and shameless corruption of my removal [f]rom Office—of the persistent inconsistency and injustice of it connected with my appointment under Civil service rules—and of the personal knowledge of Secretary Fish in connection with Wm E. Dodge of New York and A. S. Dennis of New Jersey, both very rich men, who have sons, 'poor missionaries' in Syria supported by the charitable large hearted loving christian American people who believe in foreign Missions. Now, Secretary Fish *knows* I have been outrageously treated—yes *he knows this from testimony* that cannot be impeached by any power on Earth—and he has personally promised m[e] justice—but that is the last of it. I do not hea[r] it. I do not receive it. I have before appeale[d] to you but either you, do not see my letters, or if y[ou] do, refer them to the Secretary, and, at least, I g[et] no answer to them. I confess I cannot unde[r]stand this, knowing you as I suppose I do persona[lly] and through your faithful friend Genl. Babcoc[k] as well as others equally devoted not necessary t[o] name. . . . I can get no hearing from Secretary Fish. He is in this whole matter under the personal particular influen[ce] of Messrs Dodge and Dennis *to* SAVE *the missionaries o*[*f*] *Syria*, whom he and *they know* have only libeled [me] and were the cause of my removal from office— and [in] that, he only does himself manifest injustice. I have only demanded right—nothing more, and no ma[n] with the common instincts of manhood could do less; a[nd] yet, repeatedly without avail. I shall make no furth[er] appeal to him. . . . I am anxious to go to Georgia to assist Col. Bryant my friend, upon the stump, to send him to the next Congress, to save his dDistrict, and possibly Markham in the 5th, Pierce in the 3d and Whiteley in the 2d provided he wishes any help from me, and I wish this matter disposed of before I go down there."—ALS, *ibid.*, Miscellaneous Letters.

1875, FEB. 22. Thaddeus S. Stewart, Mount Pleasant, Iowa, to USG. "I have concluded to drop you a few lines to inform you of the gross injustice now being used towards me in the Pension Office of the United States. I proved my claim up after you had been written to and had got it increased to $24 per month but the Pension sent out a Detective who come to see me and who had been using intoxicating liquors to such an extent as to render his breath really sickening who had got some birds of his feather to give him evidence that was nothing more nor less than malicious falsehoods . . ."—ALS, DNA, RG 48, Miscellaneous Div., Letters Received. Pensioned for neuralgia and ophthalmia after serving in the 137th Ill., Stewart had been dropped from the rolls on evidence that his condition predated his service. See *SRC*, 44-1-18, 50-1-893.

1875, FEB. 23. Martha Hall, York, N. Y., to USG. "I am A poor widdow living in york and have lived here for 40 years   My husband has been dead about 10 years   I raised A family but they have nearly all passed away   My only Son;

My only support; served in the last war. Wm S. Hall Co K 8th Cavalry N. Y. Volunteers he died at Andersonville Prison. I have tried for the last three and ahalf years to get A pension but without any succes . . ."—ALS, DNA, RG 48, Miscellaneous Div., Letters Received. Hall received eight dollars monthly beginning in June, 1876.

1875, FEB. 26.   Charles S. Hamilton, Milwaukee, to USG. "Please delay action on any petition affecting me until arrival of Senator Cameron"—Telegram received (at 10:00 P.M.), DLC-USG, IB. Hamilton continued as marshal, Eastern District, Wis.

1875, MARCH 1.   Speaker of the House James G. Blaine to USG. "Paymaster's bill has just passed"—Telegram received, DNA, RG 107, Telegrams Collected (Bound). On March 2, USG signed a bill to establish the number of army paymasters at fifty.—*U.S. Statutes at Large*, XVIII, part 3, pp. 338, 524–25. See *PUSG*, 24, 268, 280–81; *CR*, 43–1, 1799–1800, 3485–90, 43–2, 1985.

On March 5, Secretary of War William W. Belknap telegraphed to Postmaster Gen. Marshall Jewell. "The President selected personally from a long list of application the names of those whom he proposes to appoint Paymasters. He has the list in his possession & from what he said today I do not think he feels disposed to make any change in it"—ALS (telegram sent), DNA, RG 107, Telegrams Collected (Bound). On March 6, Belknap telegraphed to Charles P. Williams, New York City. "Several hundred names before the President for Paymaster. Merrills is among them. Like all the rest he has about one chance in one hundred fifty."—ALS (telegram sent), *ibid.* On the same day, Jewell telegraphed to Orville E. Babcock. "I want to see the President at one oclock with mrs Allyn wife of Capt Arthur W. Allyn applicant for Position of Paymaster unless he is engaged. If he is, please telegraph me."—Telegram received, *ibid.* Also on March 6, Jewell telegraphed to Belknap. "Mrs ~~Allyn~~ Arthur W. Allyn is here and I am going to take her to the President between this and one o'clock   She says she understood from you two years ago that you would advocate the case of Cap't Allyn and she has therefore largely relied upon your influence to bring it about. Is the affair settled beyond a doubt, and is it settled that Cap't Allyn is not on the list?"—Telegram received, *ibid.* On the same day, Belknap telegraphed to Jewell. "I have seen the President. The list is signed and Capt. Allyn's name is not on it. I presented the list to the President and called his attention to Allyn's name, with others. The President will not change the list now."—ALS (telegram sent), *ibid.* Papers related to USG's nominations for paymaster are *ibid.*, RG 94, ACP, 1203 1875. On March 8, USG nominated as maj., paymasters, Frank M. Coxe, Alfred E. Bates (USMA 1865), John P. Willard, William M. Maynadier, C. Irving Wilson, John E. Blaine, William H. Eckels, Cassius K. Breneman, James R. Roche, and Reginald H. Towler.

On Feb. 5, Breneman, Washington, D. C., had written to USG. "The undersigned a resident of the City of San Antonio, Texas, respectfully asks to be appointed a Paymaster in the Regular Army."—ALS, *ibid.*, ACP, 1438 1875. On Feb. 26, U.S. Representative John Hancock of Tex. wrote to USG. "I am but slightly acquainted with Mr. Breneman, but from statements of his neighbours, and acquaintances, feel warranted in recommending him to you as a man of good moral and social standing."—ALS, *ibid.* Related papers are *ibid.* On March 17, the Senate tabled Breneman's nomination. On March 14, 1876, Breneman wrote to USG. "In as much as I find it impossible to wait longer for an interview it occurs to me I can as well state in writing the reasons why I desired to have an interview with you. I am the man whom you nominated last Spring for the position of Paymaster in the Army. My nomination was not rejected by the Senate and I desired to state to you that I am satisfied all opposition to me has been over come and that the Senators who opposed my confirmation at that will actively support it should my name be again sent to the Senate. Senator Cameron says there will be no trouble at all about my confirmation now and that I would have been confirmed before if he had not opposed me. Senator Wright guarantees my confirmation. . . ."—ALS (on White House stationery), *ibid.*, Applications for Positions in War Dept. No appointment followed.

On Feb. 8, 1875, U.S. Senator Simon Cameron of Pa. had written to USG. "*Private* . . . You may remember that I spoke to you about the anxiety I had for the appointment of Wm H Eclees as Paymaster in the US Army, under the bill which will probably pass soon. When the war broke out Mr Ecles with the best young gentlemen of Harrisburg joined the army as privates. When his term of service was over he again enlisted. But my brother-in-law, Major Brua, took him for his clerk, and he has after fourteen years service been left out of employment by the order retiring ~~of~~ Major Brua. Inquiry at the Paymaster Generals will show that Major Bruas accounts are among the best in the Army, and they are largely the work of Mr Ecles. His acceptance of the place of clerk under Major Brua was from personal devotion. The place was never on a level with his talents. I hope you will oblige me by making this appointment, and I shall be very much gratified."—LS, *ibid.*, ACP, 1336 1875.

On Feb. 24, U.S. Senator John H. Mitchell of Ore. wrote to USG. "I respectfully and earnestly recommend R. H. Towler—M. D. late asst Surgeon in the U. S. Army for appointment as Paymaster in the Army;—Doctor Towler's Army Record—is of itself a strong recommendation in his favor—while his high character for integrity—his courteous and gentlemanly bearing as a man—are all that could be desired to fit him for the position named;—His appointment would be one worthily bestowed—and I would esteem it a personal favor to myself—"—ALS, *ibid.*, 1331 1875. Related papers are *ibid.*

On March 1 and 2, Speaker Blaine had written to USG. "I respectfully request the appointment of my brother John E. Blaine as Pay Master in the Army—I will vouch for him as a man in all respects competent & trustworthy—He has been in the Military service and has an excellent record in civil life" "*Personal* . . . The residence of my brother, whom I have recommended for Pay Master is Montana Territory—. . ."—ALS, *ibid.*, 1879 1875. On March 15, George F. Johnston "who was in the rebellion from Connecticut," Pittsburgh, wrote to USG. "I think you have been imposed upon in appointing Jno E Blaine Paymaster U. S. A. He was *not* in the service during the rebellion, but was away up in N Hampshire (clerk in the U. S Court) out of harms way, An uncompromising democrat, appointed June 16. 68 by Mr Johnston as Military Store Keeper Q. M department and got out of that position some how Feby 1870. I

suppose now he is a good republican. He has not no claims either on the repub-
lican party or the military service. Appointed from Penna by Mr Johnston from
Penna in 1868, now he looms up from Montana   Would it not be well enough
to withdraw his name and sent in one who fought for his country"—ALS, *ibid.*
On Feb. 3, 1871, USG had nominated John Blaine as surveyor gen., Montana
Territory.

On March 1, 1875, Col. James A. Hardie, inspector gen., Philadelphia, telegraphed to Col. Rufus Ingalls, asst. q. m. "Our friend James R Roche disbursing
Clerk War Department is Candidate for Captain pay Department   will you do
me a favor & yourself by going promptly to the President and asking him to appoint Roche   no time should be lost"—Telegram received (at 7:30 P.M.), DLC-
USG, IB. In an endorsement dated Feb. 27, Ingalls wrote to Babcock. "You
know Roche and his friends. Please lay this before the President. Roche wants
to be PayMaster."—AES, *ibid.*

On March 3, Col. Benjamin Alvord, paymaster gen., and U.S. Senator
Zachariah Chandler of Mich., wrote to USG. "We desire to recommend to your
favorable consideration the appointment of *Albert S. Towar* of Detroit Michigan—We have the testimony of Genl Alvord (to whom he was clerk for three
years before coming here) as to his admirable qualities—He is thirty years old,
of fine physique & high character & industrious habits & we shall be gratified
at his appointment"—LS, DNA, RG 94, ACP, 1380 1875. Related papers are
ibid. On March 9, USG nominated Albert S. Towar as maj., paymaster.

On March 15, U.S. Representative Jacob M. Thornburgh of Tenn., Knoxville, telegraphed to Babcock. "Tonights dispatches indicate that the Senate may
not confirm all the Pay Masters. If this is so and the President determines to
make any other appointment please say to him that I shall look with Confidence
for the appointment of Lieut Thornburgh"—Telegram received (on March 16),
DLC-USG, IB. On Dec. 6, USG nominated 1st Lt. Thomas T. Thornburgh
(USMA 1867) as maj., paymaster.

On Feb. 26, Lucy M. Porter, postmaster, Louisville, had written to USG. "I
beg leave to introduce to you my particular friend Mr. Charles B. Chapman of
this city. If not inconvenient to you he would be glad to have the honor of an interview with you. Mr. Chapman intends applying for the position of pay-master in the army should the bill increasing the number of pay-masters become a
law. He has recommendations from many of the prominent Republicans of the
state: and knowing him as I do I can safely say that in my own judgment a more
trustworthy or more competent person for the place could hardly be found.
Mr. Chapman served as a clerk in the pay masters Department several years
during the war of the rebellion   Respectfully commending him to your kind
consideration . . ."—ALS, DNA, RG 94, ACP, C450 CB 1868. Related papers,
including a letter of Dec. 15, 1873, from James Speed to USG, are *ibid.* On
March 1, 1875, U.S. Representative Isaac C. Parker of Mo. telegraphed to USG.
"Paymaster's Bill has passed. I desire to place the application Cap't Wm D
O'Toole of Mo. for one of these places."—Telegrams received (on March 2, at
10:25 A.M.), DLC-USG, IB. On the same day, U.S. Senator George E. Spencer of
Ala. wrote to Belknap. "SPECIAL . . . After constant and unremitting labor, we
have succeeded in securing the passage of the Senate Bill through the House,

providing for filling the vacancies in the Pay Corps to fifty. I now beg leave to claim the fulfillment of your promise to aid me in securing the appointment of one Paymaster, a promise which the President has also acquiesced in. I wish this position for my immediate personal friend, Hon. J. J. Noah, of Alabama, . . ."—ALS, DNA, RG 94, Applications for Positions in War Dept. On March 2, Ulysses G. White (USMA 1871), Washington, D. C., wrote to USG. "Having learned from the Pay Master General that under the provisions of Senate Bill No 320 there are at present nine vacancies to be filled in his department I respectfully ask that you take my name into consideration when making the appointments."—ALS, *ibid.*, ACP, 1954 1873. On March 3, U.S. Representative James Platt, Jr., of Va. telegraphed to USG. "Mr Thomas Mr Howell & myself together with all Virginia Republicans I have seen earnestly desire the appointment of E J Underwood as Asst Paymaster in the Army and trust he may be among those selected"—Telegram received, *ibid.*, RG 107, Telegrams Collected (Bound). On March 4, U.S. Senators Powell Clayton and Stephen W. Dorsey of Ark., and four others, wrote to USG. "We respectfully but urgently request that Edward Wheeler be appointed to the position of Paymaster in the U. S. Army. He was a good soldier during the war of the rebellion, is a very competent business man, and is in every way worthy and well qualified—"—LS, *ibid.*, RG 94, Applications for Positions in War Dept. On March 10, Mrs. William J. Martin, Philadelphia, wrote to USG. "What my feelings were, when I became aware of the fact, that the Paymasters were actually appointed, and my husband was not one of the fortunate ones, I have not the power to express—. . . I remembered the interview you granted me, that it had given me great hope—Your kindly manner and Sympathetic look, I never *shall* forget, as I had always imagined you stern in the extreme,   Turning all these things over in my mind, I determined to write to you. Mr. Borie proposed to me that I would write, on the occasion when the bill had passed, fixing the number of Paymasters, he said just a few lines, merely to remind you of us, I feeling that a letter would require more time, resolved to telegraph and did so, knowing how many there were on the spot ready to apply—. . ."—ALS, *ibid.* The telegram, dated March 1, and related papers are *ibid.* On March 16, Chief Justice Morrison R. Waite wrote to USG recommending Dudley W. Rhodes for paymaster. "I called this morning to hand you the enclosed papers, but you were engaged and I did not see you— Mr. Rhodes was the Secretary of the late Constitutional Convention in Ohio, and I there came to know him very well. He is one of the most careful and trustworthy men I ever knew. . . ."—ALS (press), DLC-Morrison R. Waite. On April 3, 1876, Waite again wrote to USG concerning Rhodes.—ALS (press), *ibid.* On April 20, James M. Comly, *Ohio State Journal*, wrote to USG. "*Personal* . . . There is such a pressure for office, and so large a share of the drudgery of the Executive comes from the examination of the claims of contestants, that I have carefully refrained from adding anything to the literature of the Executive office. Pardon me, therefore, for complying with an urgent request of many influential friends on behalf of Dudley W. Rhodes, of Ohio, who applies for an appointment as Paymaster in the army. . . ."—ALS, DNA, RG 94, ACP, 2693 1875. Related papers are *ibid.*; *ibid.*, 2506 1875. On April 2, 1875, Robert T. Lincoln, Chicago, had written to USG. "I understand that at the request of Senator Logan, the Secretary of War has placed upon the list of names to be submitted to you for appointment as Paymaster in the Army, that of Col. John P. Baker, now of Springfield Ills. Col Baker was by my father personally appointed a Cavalry Officer in the Regular Army at the beginning of the rebellion and he remained in the Army until his resignation in 1868 at which time he was Captain in the First U. S. Cavalry. I understand that he was an excellent officer but as to that reference would of course be had to his official history in the office of the Adjutant General. Col Baker is my cousin by marriage and I believe him to be a most excellent and trustworthy man. He has lately met with a severe loss by fire and I am very anxious to help him in any way I can, and I most earnestly hope that his application will meet with your favorable consideration—"—ALS, *ibid.*, Applications for Positions in War Dept. On April 14, John P. Baker, Springfield, Ill., wrote to Babcock. "Your kind reply of the 10th inst to my letter of the 26th ult came to hand yesterday   I am sorry that I was so late in making my application, but trust if there is any show I may be the fortunate one. . . ."—ALS, *ibid.* On April 29, Manning F. Force, Cincinnati, telegraphed to USG. "Cannot Gen T C H Smith who was on Gen Popes staff in the war be appointed PayMaster in the army.   there is not a better or nobler man in the United States.   his appointment would do honor to the service"—Telegram received, DLC-USG, IB. On May 10, Frederick Watts, Jr., Washington, D. C., wrote to USG. "I have occupied the place of Chief Clerk in the Department of Agriculture for the past two years, and during that time must have made an impression of my fitness for business. Desirous of obtaining a more permanent situation I beg leave to submit an application to you for the appointment of Paymaster in the U S Army. I have many friends who will be pleased to recommend me to you, and I can give any security which shall be required. I shall feel under great obligations to you if you will confer the appointment upon me."—ALS, DNA, RG 94, Applications for Positions in War Dept. Letters to USG from Cameron and U.S. Senator Oliver P. Morton of Ind., and others, recommending Watts, son of the commissioner of agriculture, are *ibid.* On July 23, Henry Porter, Philadelphia, wrote to USG. "I respectfully ask to be appointed Pay Master in the U. S. Army. As long as my brother Horace was connected with you I refrained from asking you for any appointment, and even now feel a great delicacy in doing so. Horace has said that if there should be a vacancy in the Army, or elsewhere, he would, now, aid me. He has been a good brother to me. Genl Cameron, who has been very kind, said if I could only point out something in the way of an appointment, he would do his share. I learn that Mr. Martin was an applicant but was found too old. The Porters never get old. I can satisfy your Excellency fully as to integrity, sobriety, energy, vigor, bond education &c. Some of your personal friends will recommend me and have often volunteered. I have been Hon. John A. Hiestand's Special Deputy Naval Officer since May, 1st 1871, having been re-appointed May, 1st 1875. He will recommend me in the strongest terms. I know Hon. Secy. Bristow, and the Comr of Customs will endorse me officially."—ALS, *ibid.* No appointment followed for these and other paymaster aspirants.

1875, MARCH 1.   U.S. Representative Clinton D. MacDougall of N. Y. to USG. "Allow me to suggest that in disposing of the case of L. M Drury, the pension Agent at Canandaigua, he might be made a paymaster in the Army? That having passed the House this morning—he is fitted for such a position   Col. Mead is a wounded soldier shot through the legs at Gettysburg, competent and worthy   I trust you may see some to appoint him & at the same time oblige Senator Conkling by a provision for Drury"—Telegram received, DLC-USG, IB. On March 5, MacDougall telegraphed to USG and Secretary of the Interior Columbus Delano. "If deemed desirable I will agree to leave the Pension Office Canandaigua,   Col Mead could leave Auburn every morning to attend the duties or remove to Canandaigua,   as Mr Drury was imported from Washn to take the place originally certainly the people there can not find any fault if the same be done for Mead. With this modification I trust there may be no trouble about the appointment"—Telegram received, DNA, RG 107, Telegrams Collected (Bound). On the same day, MacDougall telegraphed to Orville E. Babcock requesting his assistance in this matter.—Telegram received, *ibid.* On March 8, USG nominated Sidney Mead as pension agent, Canandaigua, N. Y.; on March 13, USG withdrew Mead and nominated Leander M. Drury.

1875, MARCH 1.   U.S. Representative Isaac W. Scudder of N. J. to USG. "I have had a personal acquaintance with Mr John D. Buckalew of Middlesex County New Jersey, for Several years past. He is a man of upright character, good capacity and educated to business. He asks the appointment of Marshall at Yokahama Japan. I have been informed relative to the duties of that position, and I am satisfied that Mr Buckalew can perform them in a proper manner. I therefore beg leave to reccommend his appointment"—ALS, DNA, RG 59, Letters of Application and Recommendation. Related papers are *ibid.* On March 12, USG nominated John D. Buckalew as consul, Stettin.

1875, MARCH 2.   Secretary of State Hamilton Fish to Secretary of the Navy George M. Robeson transmitting USG's order to station a warship at Acapulco in response to a mob attack on a Protestant church that killed a U.S. citizen.—LS, DNA, RG 45, Letters Received from the President. See *Foreign Relations, 1875,* II, 855–73, 881–84, 888.

1875, MARCH 3.   U.S. Senator Timothy O. Howe of Wis. and three others to USG. "The undersigned members of the Wisconsin delegation in the 43d Congress, respectfully recommend to your favorable consideration, Hon Gerry W Hazelton for the position of Commissioner of Claims under the Act of March 3d 1871, in case a vacancy should occur."—LS, DNA, RG 60, Applications and Recommendations. No appointment followed to the Southern Claims Commission.

On March 8, U.S. Representative Jeremiah M. Rusk and U.S. Senator Angus Cameron of Wis. wrote to USG recommending Conrad Moser, Jr., for a territorial judgeship. ". . . He is a german, and his appointment is urged by the germans throughout the State of Wisconsin."—LS, *ibid.*, Records Relating to Appointments. On July 2, Attorney Gen. Edwards Pierrepont wrote to USG, Long Branch. "I enclose copy of letter this day received   I have no information upon the subject, but recommendations are on file. I await your direction."—LS, *ibid.* On July 3, Orville E. Babcock, Long Branch, wrote to Pierrepont. "The President directs me to say in reply to your letter enclosing one from Mr Moser, that his recollection is that the appt was to be made from Wisconsin—as the removal contemplated was from that State—but that he was under the impression that Hazleton was to be appointed—but that he is probably mistaken in this."—ALS, *ibid.* On Sept. 20, Rusk, Viroqua, Wis., wrote to USG. *"Personal* . . . At the close of the last session of Congress, Senator Cameron and myself recommended the appointment of the Hon. Conrad Moser, of Eau Claire, Wis., to a Judgeship in Dakota Territory, in place of one of the present incumbents. I believe we understood that the change would be made by the 1st of July. Having heard nothing from the Attorney General, although I have written him on the subject, I have concluded to address you, and would urge that the appointment be made. . . ."—ALS, *ibid.* No appointment followed.

1875, MARCH 3.   T. S. Scoville, real estate dealer, Elmira, N. Y., to USG. "I take pen to give a few hints, though you may already know more than I can state. I have Studied Southern Characters forty years well, and I am prepared to dissect them. I also Study the Prophets, and Revelations, and am prepared to prophecy a little too,   'Slaveholders' now, 'White Leaguers' are determined to ruin every man who goes into the south by law or force,   The great mistake of Republicans was in being generous & trying to win the devil by Kindness,   they will Soon find they have thawed out a frozen Serpent,   Once again the Rebs in Congress, they plot to rule, they intend next Session to Controll Congress,   when they do Your Honour, and the Vice President will be shortlived. You will not be the first President they have cleared from their track   three have so departed by their hands, 'a word to the wise' &c   Then Congress will be called on to replace the loss. A Southern man will take your place, the Ropes will be then drawn tight, and an Emperor declared, political parties will be instantly in arms all over the land, the Blacks & Repubs South against white Leaguers,   The North will run into ~~as~~ Civil Strife betwee[n] Democrats and Republicans,   as the party here is Made of Catholics they will go for protestant Churches, and burn them, in turn Protestants will fire their Churches & schools and burn them, Cities and towns will be scorched, And the great battles will be over church property, and it will result in a religious War. White Leaguers will have Congress the Presidential Chair, State Governments. And all the petty offices in cities and Towns, and we Protestants ~~will~~ will have the out side of the ring and become rebels to the government,   the Leaguers will try again to Enslave the blacks North & South, and God will blow their ship to atoms and sink them in water so deep they will never again rise to the surface. Our hope now is, Your life may continue, the Repub Party may take stringent Measurs instantly, if Martial Law could instantly be declard in half the old Slave States,   If the Blacks South could be enlisted in the US Army, and taught to fight, *now, before it is too late,* they would save the South, if not taught to fight many of them will be slain. A rod of Iron is what they need. I wish You and Butler could be permitted to handle them at will. You have handled them, and I hope will continue to do so. I want you to live to whip them again.   if they can strike you down they will do it, if not they will strike as soon as you leave the office. Imperial Government alone will satisfy them,   And that Keg of Powder will blow them up."—ALS, USG 3.

1875, MARCH 5.   William H. Taylor, "of Brooklyn N. Y. formerly a member of the firm of Mess S. B. Chittenden & Co," St. Marys, Ga., to USG. "It is my desire to say a word in favor of Mr Joseph Shepard Collector of this Port, under the following circumstances. I am spending the Winter here with my family and having known Mr Shepard for a number of years he has been to consult with me for the reason that he has today recd a letter from the Member of the House from this the 1st Dist of Geo in which said member advises Mr S to resign only saying in explanation of his action that 'a fight will made over his case. I wish to state that I have known Mr Shepard for a number of years and can say of my own knowledge that there is not a more *loyal* Republican in this or any other State, and none more worthy to represent the government. . . ."—ALS, DNA, RG 56, Collector of Customs Applications. On Jan. 24, 1872, USG had nominated Joseph Shepard as collector of customs, St. Marys, Ga.

On Feb. 15, 1876, USG renominated Shepard; the Senate took no action. On Jan. 5, 1877, USG nominated William S. Mayfield in place of Shepard. On [*Feb. 3*], USG wrote. "Suggested by Mr. Platt that Jos. Shepard Surveyor Collector of Customs at St. Mary's, Ga. in place of _____ Mayfield, not confi[rm]ed"—AN (undated), Wayde Chrismer, Bel Air, Md. On the same day, USG withdrew Mayfield and renominated Shepard, who was confirmed on Feb. 6.

1875, March 6.   U.S. Senator Samuel B. Maxey and U.S. Representative John Hancock of Tex. to USG. "If it is not your purpose to present again the name of, Judge L. D. Evans, to be marshal of the Eastern Federal judicial district of Texas, we have the honor to present, for your favorable consideration, for that position, the name, of, George H. Giddings, who, from his long residence in that state, and extensive business connections with the people, would, we beleive, be generally acceptable to all parties."—LS, DNA, RG 60, Records Relating to Appointments. No appointment followed. See *PUSG*, 23, 171–72.

George H. Giddings, C.S.A. vol., wrote memoirs that included a discussion with USG and James Longstreet in Washington, D. C., concerning a possible British invasion of Tex.—Typescript, DLC-George H. Giddings.

1875, March 8.   USG endorsement. "Refered to the Sec. of War. Approved."— AES, DNA, RG 94, ACP, 3269 1873. Written on a letter of March 1 from Lt. Col. Quincy A. Gillmore, New York City, to USG. "I have the honor to request that my son, Quincy O'M. Gillmore, a graduate of the Military Academy, may be appointed in the Army, as a second Lieutenant of Cavalry. In a regiment not serving in the Department of Texas. His resignation took place last fall under such peculiar circumstances, that his friends regard his re-appointment as entirely fit and proper."—ALS, *ibid.* On March 16, USG nominated Quincy O. Gillmore as 2nd lt., 8th Cav.

1875, March 8.   Arthur Rich, Baltimore, to USG. "Permit me to say that I think you have been greatly misled in relation to Maryland matters—I beg to call your attention to the fact—that Andrew Johnson's Naval officer for 4 years Wm S. Reese is now running the Custom House and the Republican party with Booth as an *ineligible figure head* now with Andrew Johnson in the Senate and Andrew Johnson likely to be the Democratic Candidate for the Presidency—

The *true Republicans* feel discouraged and much disgusted thereat—I will also state that Dr Luther Cox an Amateur Physician from the Easten Shore a through Rebel Democrat holds the position of *Medical referee* in the Pension Bureau—If their is not to be through changes in Maryland as well as elsewhere— The Republican party will have a difficult task to elect the next President—you having been twice honored Mr Presidt by the great union Republican party— I do hope that *you* will not permit Democrats to hold more offices than Republicans and more particularly friends of the Administration"—ALS, DNA, RG 56, Letters Received from the President. On Nov. 14, 1876, Rich again wrote to USG. "Although rather late—Allow me to express my *thanks—many thanks* for the utterance of your dispatch from the Centennial grounds—it is worthy of the Centennial period and so expressive of the times,   It also presents a *Mirror* in which Saml. J. Tilden—Jno. Lee Carroll and the Sham Democracy can see themselves reflected in political naked deformity, from Head to foot, and from one end of the Country to the other—I am sure had it not been for the shotgun policy of the south—and the fraudulent vote at the North whereby Hayes was elected out of New york N. Carolina—Connecticut & Missipi His vote would have been more than 225 in the Electoral College—. . ."—ALS, USG 3.

1875, MARCH 8.   Wilson G. Richardson, Central University, Richmond, Ky., to USG. "I was in Maysville last summer[.] I of course went to see my old school-friend Judge William Henry Wadsworth, whom you and I there must have regarded as among the 'big boys.'—Bill Conway, Elijah Phister, Austin Richardson (my eldest brother);—my next brother, Warfield and Charlie Shultz represented the intermediate grade; whilst your distinguish self (Dr) John Phister, your cousin Noah (my classmate), and mself were among the smaller boys. Wadsworth talked of you in a way that keeps friendship aglow. Ever since our talk over our school days, I have resolved to draw an autograph note from you as a keepsake for 'auld lang syne.' My daughter's lecturer in history has asked her to furnish her at some time with the names of your cabinet. Some time when you are right well, congress adjourned, and not specially busy, if such a moment ever comes, please copy them off, or write me a note. My father removed from Maysville to Tuscaloosa in 1837. I graduated at the University of Alabama in 1844—(my two brothers in 1843—both living in Alabama yet)—I was Prof. there—visited Europe 1850–53—Prof. in Univ. of Mississippi, & am here Prof. of Greek. Maysville is a dear old place to me. Pardon the liberty I have taken . . ."—ALS, USG 3. On the same day, Richardson again wrote to USG. "In my letter just mailed I omitted to write my given name in full. My sister-in-law Mrs. Evans is poor motherless children. She often speaks in high terms of you and your army from her Oxford, Mississippi standpoint. The drill of the federal troops was certainly splendid. They got better all the time whilst I believe we got worse, if any thing. You perceive, General, I was a rebel, but like a true soldier gave it all up as soon as the news reached me from Appomatox & Greensboro' reached me."—ALS, *ibid.*

1875, MARCH 9.   Owen King, Clinton, La., to USG. "Griffith who opposes me on the second district for collector, is a man of no principle"—Telegram received, DLC-USG, IB. On July 29, 1876, USG nominated Oscar Holt as collector of Internal Revenue, 2nd District, La., in place of Oscar A. Rice.

On Feb. 9 (Wednesday) and May 3, 1876, King, Jackson, La., wrote to USG. "You may think it strange in me writing again, I do it from a feeling of gratitude which is due to the name It is Strange that Blaine & Mortin have not better sense than to try and run for the Presidency The Democratic Party want either of them to run, but, t'would be like Greeleys. Do the remember what a time Abraham Lincoln had to get in. the Democrats will not bring out two candidates this time. I think their policy will be to bring out a military man and the only man who can [b]eat them is President Grant. The Republican Party had better take warning in time. one bad man now and they are gone. There are a good many traitors in the camp who will sell out at any price, and I have reason to believe that Gov Kellogg is one of them. I believe Senator West is another. I believe Kellogg is a scoundrel and traitor to you—he has brought down the odium of the papers on your head—let them take pattern by your humble servant—There is in N. O. a merchant Mr Thos King a brother of mine some 35 years in business seven years since we spoke because I would not denounce the name of Grant! he tried to buy me with his money, but failed My enemies here and in N. O. tried to defeat me in every way but they have not been able to buy me yet. They have broke me up in business, but a kind Providence has taken care of myself and family. I told you last Fall that unless your name was at the mast head of the Republican Party, that the South would go Democratic next Novr there is none other name that they fear but yours, Ex Gov Wickliffe told me last saturday that Blaine nor Mor[ton] would not get the vote that Greely did, and that the only hope of the Party was President Grant." "I feel very much flattered—inasmuch as—Mr Law has failed to get his position here as P. M. of Jackson La. and I have endeavored to show to those who are opposed to you that these bad appointments have not come through you, but through bribed congressmen: and as to the candidates for the Nomination—I think that ~~that~~ the Democrats have settled on Hancock as their strongest man, to oppose you, whom I have ~~not~~ no doubt will get the nomination from the Republican Party—as they must know, without the name of U. S Grant at their mast Head that Republicanism is dead—and as for Hancock—it is strange that he should ever want to behold that dismal spot in Washington where once hung the body of Mrs Surratt. And as to those officials who are endeavring to expose frauds—I should not be troubled about such matters—your past history as a warrior—will endear your old comrades in arms—the closer—and your history as a Statesman and Executive—will cause you to come out in flying colors —and you name will stand out in bold relief at the head of hundreds of your ranks—very soon as the Nominee of the Republican Party for the third Term— as President of these U. S."—ALS, USG 3.

1875, March 9. Ben: Perley Poore, clerk of printing records, U.S. Senate, to USG. "The Boston Journal telgraphs me that the news from New Hampshire is very encouraging. in five out of six of the numerous towns heard from the Republicans have gained and in the others, they held their own Cheney may be elected Governor by the people."—Telegram received, DNA, RG 107, Telegrams Collected (Bound).

1875, MARCH 10.   USG endorsement. "Refered to the Sec. of War. May be considered in case of vacancy in Sept. not already provided for."—AES, DNA, RG 94, Correspondence, USMA. Written on a letter of March 9 from U.S. Representative Charles Hays of Ala. to USG. "Permit me very respectfully to ask the appointment of John O. Mallet as Cadet at large to the Military Academy at West Point. Mr Mallet is a son of the Professor of Chemistry at the University of Virginia, and is a young gentleman of fine attainments and a brilliant mind. He belongs to one of the best families in the Southern States, and I am sure he would, if appointed, reflect credit upon himself and honor upon the country."— L, *ibid.* Related papers are *ibid.* John W. Mallet had worked to improve ordnance and ammunition for the C.S. Army; his son, John O., did not attend USMA.

1875, MARCH 12.   A. E. Camp, jailer, Jefferson County, Ky., Louisville, to USG. "I write you in behalf of David Prewitt a colored boy who has been in my custody four years charged with murder in Powell Co Ky—The facts are these. Party of Ku Klux visited house of David's father ordering entire family to leave County.   on Second visit of the party to enforce the Order David fired through the door, killing one of the men. Case has been in U S Court, but Hon Bland Ballard has not as yet tried the case. If the boy is transfered to Powell Co for trial there is Scarcely a doubt but that he will be mobed. Gov Leslie declines to pardon the boy before trial—His punishment already is more than adequate to the crime imputed to him. If your Excellency would advise with Gov Leslie I have no doubt the boy would be released from his long confinement. He is a good & deserving boy & ought to be at liberty."—ALS, DNA, RG 60, Letters Received, Ky. On April 5, Gabriel C. Wharton, U.S. attorney, Louisville, wrote to Attorney Gen. George H. Williams recommending clemency.—ALS, *ibid.* No pardon followed.

1875, MARCH 13.   Eli A. Collins, "your *old time* friend," Shelby, Iowa, to USG. "I here with enclose an application for the position of Indian commissioner My Son Gilbert who has just returned from Washington & the East informs me you are willing to give me the appointment as soon as a vacancy occures   If the Suggestion is not an improper one I would prefer assignment to Territory West of the Miss. River   I am going to New York & Washington the last of this month.   & If the appointment is given will indevour to fill it to the satisfaction of yourself & those with whom I am thrown in contact   With best wishes for the future Success of yourself & your Administration . . ."—ALS, DNA, RG 48, Appointment Div., Letters Received. The enclosure is *ibid.* No appointment followed. See *PUSG,* 23, 332.

1875, MARCH 16.   USG endorsement. "See Sec of War in relation to transfering Mrs. Gnl. Plummer to Qr. Mr. Dept."—AN, DNA, RG 107, Appointment Papers. Filed with papers concerning Frances H. Plummer, widow of Brig. Gen. Joseph B. Plummer, a copyist in the Pension Office. On April 22, Plummer, Washington, D. C., wrote to "Dear General," probably USG. "I am so sorry I cannot see you to day. Have you spoken to the secretary of War about giving me the clerkship in the Quarter Masters Dept?—which will soon be vacated by Miss Knowlton—who is to be married in June. I wish also to ask you to give my daughter a clerkship in one of the Departments—she has not been in Office for over six years, and was always considered a competent clerk. Hoping you will pardon the liberty I take, as we are so much in *need* of employment, and have no political influence to aid us in getting it,"—ALS, *ibid.* On April 24, Henry T. Crosby, chief clerk, War Dept., endorsed this letter. "To be called up when the first vacancy occurs after Miss Davis & Miss Jones are provided for."—ES, *ibid.* See *PUSG*, 22, 284–86. Jennie B. Jones and Annie G. Davis received positions in the q. m. gen.'s office.

On May 2, Betty M. Heath, Washington, D. C., wrote to USG. "I respectfully ask for your influence in obtaining a clerkship in the quarter master's department for my unmarried Sister—Miss Susan Mason—who has not one dollar—having been deprived, by the ravages of the war of her independence. She is thoroughly competent to fill the position writes an admirable hand and is a most conscientious woman—We are daughters of Hon. John Y. Mason—died in Paris as minister to France. 1859. If you will be so kind as to recommend her to the Secretary of War, you will confer another favor upon a Virginia woman, for which, both she and I will be so grateful!"—ALS, DNA, RG 107, Appointment Papers. A letter of April 6 from Heath to Secretary of State Hamilton Fish recommending Susan Mason for a clerkship in the State Dept. is *ibid.*, RG 59, Letters of Application and Recommendation.

On May 27 and June 1, Mrs. Lewis M. Smith, Washington, D. C., wrote to USG. "Having heard so much of your kindness of heart and being in *great* trouble as to how to earn my daily bread I have come to you to ask you to help me; bear with me until I have stated my case and I feel sure your kind heart will prompt you to do something for me. My husband a clerk for some years in the Q. M. G's. Office and a faithful and efficient one as his office record will show left the office on Saturday Jan 23rd apparently in perfect health was taken sick that night at half past twelve oclock and lived but three hours, leaving me with seven children. An application was at once made for a position for me as copyist in that office, the application was approved by the Q. M. G. and sent to the Sect'y of War for his approval. I went to see the the Sect'y a few days after that and he said he had marked my case *special*, he also treated me very kindly. It is now over four months since my husbands death & I have still nothing to do. I am utterly disheartened. I need not tell you that these things require influence. Now Mr President one word or line from you will give us food. A young lady in the Q. M. General's office will resign the last of this month to be married next week. Will you not ask the Sect'y to give me the first vacancy that occurs? Has not the Saviour said 'Inasmuch as ye have done it unto the least of one of these ye have done it Unto Me'. I ask you now for the sake of these fatherless children as well as my own that you will grant my request." "Pardon me for importuning you again, but I feel so desperate I do not know what to do. When I received your message that I should go and see the Secretary of War, and that you had spoken to him, I felt inspired with new life. ~~but~~ I went to the War Dept yesterday, and was told by a young gentleman that it would be no use to send my card in that the Sect'y was preparing to leave for West Point and ~~and~~ would not see any one. What to do then I did not know, and now after spending a sleepless night (which is nothing unusual for me, but why trouble you with this because I know you feel for those in distress) I come again to ask you if you will not give me a line to the Secretary? May God bless you for what you have already done in my behalf."—ALS, *ibid.*, RG 107, Appointment Papers. On May 27, John Foley, New York City, had written to USG. "I Will thank you for a note to Sec'y of War, in favor of *Laura Callan.* She is a most respectable young Woman, 25 y of age a native of the District and thoroughly qualified for a Clerkship, having passed a perfect examination before the Civ[il] S Board, Smart Well educated, with the ability and disposition to earn two dollars for every one doll the Government may pay her,   As the plaintiff in the famous *Foley injunction Suit* agt the Tammany Ring resulting as you have admitted in So much Public good, I think I am fairly entitled to Some little Consideration and therefore ask your Excellency to Send me the *needful* Letter for my friend and I will take it as a Special favor . . ."—ALS, *ibid.* On May 28, Laura Callan wrote to USG. "Having made repeated visits to the Executive Mansion, without gaining admission to your presence, I must resort to this medium to solicit of you a favor. I am a daughter of the late John F. Callan, for many years Secretary of the Military Committee of the Senate and compiler of the U. S. Military and Naval Laws. By his death, his widow and four daughters, were left wholly unprovided for, and since that time, I have been trying for an office. The Vice President, Genl A. G. Myer and other prominent persons have given me letters, and added to this, a year ago I passed a successful examination, for a position in the Quarter Master General's Office, and all this assistance has been in vain. I am so much discouraged, but, feel sure that a note from you to the Secy of War, will be the only aid that can secure me a place, and it is to ask this, that I write. If you will only grant this request, you will be doing an act of Charity, for we are actually in want, and an office is the only relief that I can have, there is no other employment, I could follow, or I would most cheerfully do it."—ALS, *ibid.* On May 31, Secretary of War William W. Belknap wrote to Smith. ". . . The vacancy referred to has been applied for by a great many persons, and the President some months ago named a person to fill it   I have placed your name upon the list for future consideration, but cannot say when there will be a prospect of your appointment."—LS (press), *ibid.* A similar letter of the same day from Belknap to Callan is *ibid.*, Letters Sent, Military Affairs.

On Aug. 19, Maria C. Page, Washington, D. C., wrote to USG seeking reappointment as copyist, Q. M. Dept. "Tho' I am a Stranger to Genl Grant, he is not one to me—I will not apologize, for addressing you, for, to whom else, (save our Heavenly Father) can the widow & orphan, appeal for justice—All my friends, and relatives, who could have aided me, have passed away—They procured me an appointment in the Qr. Mr. Genls Office, when it was first organized,   'Abraham Lincoln' was my personal friend, & Col. E. D. Baker U. S. S. was my protector, & Guardian, which I can prove by his letters in my possession—. . . My Son lives in Mo. is, your friend, & a voter—He is not able to help me, as he has a family—I have adopted a little Orphan girl, whose father, was a soldier and am educating her, myself—by self-denial, and economy, I have saved from my Salary, of $75. per Month, to *partly* pay for a *home*—On the 1st of July, for no fault of mine, I was 'discharged' to give a place to Miss Jones— Tho' in the same Office, there were two Sisters and many Ladies, who had sis-

ters in other Dept's, and some, with comfortable homes, and no children—I
never had a relative in Office, and was the only lady in Qr. Mr. Genls Office appointed from Kansas—I dont know, what will become of me, and my little one,
unless, I am reinstated, as my lungs are too weak now, for me to teach again—
I have not been out evenings, for years, that I might save all my Strength, to be
promp in my duties—If I cannot meet the payment of my notes, I shall lose my
home. . . ."—ALS, *ibid.*, Appointment Papers.

On Aug. 25, Mary C. Ringgold, Washington, D. C., wrote to USG. "PRI-
VATE . . . I have several times called to see you but been disappointed, and hence
I now appeal to you by letter. I appeal to you for your assistance and aid in my
behalf as the Chief Magistrate of the Country—I appeal to your aid as the Genl
of the Union Army of which my deceased husband was a faithful servant, and a
most devoted and loyal defender. I appeal to your aid, as *one* whose kind heart,
and generous nature has never refused to aid poor womankind; or denied your
help to the orphan or the widow of the true soldier. I beg *from you,* a position in
the Quarter master Genls Office, to which have generally been assigned the
widows of Army Officers; I have enclosed a note, I did not then receive the appointment; it had been already made and my eldest boy got a small Compensation *soon after* from the Govt Printer, which enabled me by *great* economy to
provide for the family—This promising boy *is now in a consumptive state*; rapidly
declining—unable to provide for his *actual necessities,* or lend any aid to my support. I *need* a *friend,* believing that as the widow of a faithful Officer, you will assist me   I beg from you as the President of my Country a position which will
give me the means of providing for my sick son; and my own necessities. Be assured gratitude will not be wanting. That God may extend to you prosperity
and many blessings . . ."—ALS, *ibid.* Related papers are *ibid.*; *ibid.*, RG 108, Letters Received. Ringgold, widow of Lt. Col. George H. Ringgold, deputy paymaster gen., worked as a copyist, Q. M. Dept., as of Sept. 30, 1877.

In an undated letter, Ellen E. McCoy, Washington, D. C., wrote to USG. "I
address this appeal to you as the former 'General' of the Army, knowing well
your old time kindness to all under you in authority—& to whom an appeal
from a companion in arms never came in vain. My Husband Col. James McCoy
is dead—died as I truly believe from desease contracted during the war, thro'
which he served faithfully & entirely—he has left his family unprovided for; &
to take care of myself & three of my five children I solicit from you a place in
any of the departments where they employ women that you may be kind enough
to appoint me to. I only ask this Mr President untill my two oldest sons both of
whom have just entered into business (one being 18 & the other 21 years of age)
are able to share with me the burden of taking care of the family—Hoping that
this may meet your approval & that you may speedily grant my request . . ."—
ALS (docketed Aug. 23, 1875), *ibid.*, RG 107, Appointment Papers. On May 29,
Col. James C. McCoy, aide to Gen. William T. Sherman, had died, leaving
official financial accounts with irregularities. See Col. Orlando M. Poe to Sherman, June 24, 28, and 29, 1875, DLC-William T. Sherman.

1875, MARCH 17.   USG pardon for Benjamin Williams, "convicted of larceny,
and, also, of assault and battery," because George P. Fisher, U.S. attorney,

Washington, D. C., believed the offences "small affairs" and nearly eight months served in prison sufficient punishment.—Copy, DNA, RG 59, General Records. On Aug. 1, 1874, "Benjamin Williams, colored," had been convicted for stealing shoes worth five dollars from a storekeeper and having "pelted him with paving stones" while being pursued.—*Washington Evening Star*, Aug. 1, 1874.

1875, MARCH 17.   U.S. Senator Richard J. Oglesby of Ill. to Orville E. Babcock. "Intended to call on the President this morning but could not—Will be pleased if the President can nominate Lieut J. M. Marshall now acting A. Q. M. at West Point Academy one of the Assistant Quartermasters to be sent in—He is a first rate young man with large experience and I think he has the approval of the Secy of War for his promotion   Will you read this to the President . . ."—Telegram received, DNA, RG 107, Telegrams Collected (Bound). On Dec. 6, USG nominated 1st Lt. James M. Marshall (USMA 1865) as capt., asst. q. m.

1875, MARCH 18.   William H. Smallwood, Topeka, Kan., to USG. "I take the liberty to make a personal appeal to you. I am too poor to come to Washington and beg an office; though in so doing I presume I could procure the co-operation and unqualified endorsement of every member of the Kansas delegation. I was four years in the army, have served in both branches of the Legislature, and have been four years Secretary of State. . . . The newspaper business (the business of my life time) is largely overdone in Kansas at this time. Now, although I am poor, I am still patriotic, and am willing to serve my Country in peace as in war. Can I have a consulship? I refer you to our delegation in Congress—especially to Senator Harvey & Judge Lowe."—ALS, DNA, RG 59, Letters of Application and Recommendation. On Feb. 25, 1876, USG nominated Smallwood, former capt., 79th U.S. Colored, as land office register, Vancouver, Washington Territory.

1875, MARCH 19.   Patrick O. Hawes, "Contingent M. C. from Nebraska," Washington, D. C., to USG. "Senator Hitchcock informs me that the name of Henry Atkinson is mentioned for the office of Comr of Pensions. I desire to say his appointment would give eminent satisfaction to the Republican Party of Nebraska"—ALS, DNA, RG 48, Appointment Div., Letters Received. On the same day, U.S. Senator Algernon S. Paddock of Neb. telegraphed to USG. "I desire to say to the Secy of Interior that Atkinson having been in Military service and having good legal and administrative abilities I withdraw Ashby in his favor" —Telegram received, *ibid.*, RG 107, Telegrams Collected (Bound). Also on March 19, John P. C. Shanks, Washington, D. C., telegraphed to USG. "Can I be appointed Commissioner of pensions?"—Telegrams received, DLC-USG, IB. On the same day, Orville E. Babcock telegraphed to Shanks. "A nomination for Commissioner was sent in to the Senate this afternoon—The President is not in his office."—ALS (telegram sent), DNA, RG 107, Telegrams Collected (Bound). On March 17, USG had nominated David P. Lowe as commissioner of pensions and former commissioner James H. Baker as surveyor gen., Minn.; on March 19, USG nominated Henry M. Atkinson as commissioner of pensions after nominating Lowe as chief justice, Utah Territory.

On Jan. 29, 1876, Atkinson wrote to USG resigning his office.—ALS, *ibid.*, RG 48, Appointment Div., Letters Received. On Jan. 31, USG nominated Charles R. Gill as commissioner of pensions. On March 8, Gill wrote to USG resigning his office. ". . . The cause for this step is, that I find the duties after this brief trial, that the duties of the office are so arduous, and the responsibilities so great, that a conscientious & faithful discharge of them, requires a stronger constitution and better health than I possess; . . ."—ALS, *ibid.* On March 20, David L. Gitt, pension clerk, Washington, D. C., wrote to USG. "I beg leave to make this informal application for the office of Commissioner of Pensions, which I am informed is to be made vacant by Mr Gill's resignation on the first proximo. I have been connected with the office for five years as Chief of Division and I am thoroughly familiar with the routine and details of the office. This, I admit, is my only claim to your consideration in this matter. . . . Without expressing any opinion as to former occupants of the position, I must be pardoned for adding, that it would not be a bad idea for a Commissioner to commence his career with some knowledge of Pension Business. Should you see fit to favor me, I pledge my honest and constant endeavors to bring the office up to the mark and to keep it there. . . . Since writing this application notice of Mr Gills resignation has been published. I would suggest that Mr J W Babson be advanced to the Commissioners position and that this application be considered for the Deputy Commissionership"—ALS, *ibid.* On March 22, USG nominated John A. Bentley as commissioner of pensions.

On Dec. 9, 1875, U.S. Representative John D. White of Ky. had written to USG. "Allow me to urge the appointment of Maj. A. T. Wood of Mt. Sterling Ky., to the position of Deputy Commissioner of Pensions, vice Mr. Lockey. Maj A. T. Wood you may remember was the Republican candidate for Cong. from the 9th Dist. Ky. in 1872. But it is not for this reason alone that I request his appointment. He is a good worker a true man to the Republican cause. In conclusion I will say that there is but one representative (subordinate) from my district in any of the departments. By judicious management we should hold the 9th Cong. Dist. Ky. I think this appointment very important; and if you can-not recommend his appointment to this position, I hope you will recommend him shortly to one equally as good."—ALS, *ibid.* No appointment followed.

1875, March 20.   Col. Henry W. Benham, Boston, to USG. "In the fear that I might not otherwise be able to make this statement to yourself only, and, as briefly as possible, I offer you this letter to give the reasons for the request I now make,—which I trust may be such, that you may be willing to decide at this interview even, if such request can be at once granted—which is that I shall not be made an exception to the other engineer officers over 62, in being immediately made, when the time comes, subject to the retiring law—or at least during your authority. And I came direct to you, as the only official who knows my faithfulness to duty, or on whose justice I can rely in this case . . . And I would state, that in addition to my desire, and full competence for continued duty, I indispensably need the means for the simply comfortable support of my family, for the privation of income (with the allowances) is *nearly one half* on retiring; and I have very little else besides and that uncertain. . . ."—LS, DNA, RG 94, ACP, B447 CB 1864. Benham, born April 8, 1813, remained on active duty until 1882.

1875, MARCH 20. George D. Damon, Clarksburg, West Va., to USG. "I was confined in the asylum at washington and the Officers of that institution not discharging me as soon as I thought they should I ran away   General I am entitled to a discharge and my money which amounts to about five hundred dollars   I wish you to take the matter in your hands, personally, and see that I get my money and discharge   I was sent there from the 3rd Cav. Band"—ALS, DNA, RG 94, Letters Received, 3876 1874. On April 10, Damon, Elizaville, Ky., wrote to USG on the same subject.—ALS, *ibid.* On April 24, AG Edward D. Townsend endorsed papers concerning Damon. "The man is evidently wandering about & it is impracticable to send any party to follow & arrest him. He will probably bring up somewhere where he can be taken care of until he is returned to the Asylum."—AE (initialed), *ibid.* On Aug. 10, Damon, Elizaville, wrote to Col. Joseph J. Reynolds claiming that he had been "drugged & kidnapped and put in the Insane Asylum . . . there has been a rascally game played on me which you are hardly cognizant of. My papers should have been taken to Washington City with me unless the hounds ~~ment~~ meant to rob me of the money due me. . . ."—ALS, *ibid.* Related endorsements are *ibid.*

1875, MARCH 23. USG endorsement. "Refered to the Sec. of the Treas. I approve of the change of Collector in the 4th Ga Dist. from information gathered outside the recommendation of Mr. McWhorter."—AES, DNA, RG 56, Collector of Internal Revenue Applications. Written on a letter of March 22 from J. G. W. Mills, Washington, D. C., to USG. "I most respectfully submit the name of Hon William H. McWhorter, of Georgia, for appointment as Collector of Internal Revenue for the 4th District of that State, feeling fully assured that his appointment will give the greatest satisfaction to the friends of the administration. Mr McWhorter is a good and true Republican, controlling a very large circle of influential friends who, would at once, be brought into an active service in the reorganization of the Party."—ALS, *ibid.* On Oct. 2, 1874, USG had written concerning this office. "The proposed change of Collector of Int. Rev, for the 4th district of Ga need not be made for the present, and if the Sec. of the Treas. is satisfied with the explanation of Mr. Holtzclaw the Col. the change need not be made at all."—ANS, *ibid.* On March 9, 1875, Henry C. Rogers, 1st deputy commissioner of Internal Revenue, wrote to Jesse A. Holtzclaw, collector of Internal Revenue, Atlanta. "I received yours of the 1st inst. a day or two since, and immediately made enquiry and found that certain letters—among them, one long communication from your present Deputy—was on file in this Office making complaints and asking for your removal. I was introduced yesterday to Mills and Jackson by late Representative Freeman. I communicated freely with Mr. Freeman and Mr. Gavett who is here, and they represented your case to the Commissioner and I am satisfied forestalled any movement that is on foot against you. I also had Mr. Gavett place another strong letter on file in your behalf. I understand also that Mr Freeman called upon the President yesterday in your behalf . . ."—Copy, *ibid.* On May 1, William H. McWhorter, Atlanta, wrote to Secretary of the Treasury Benjamin H. Bristow. "About the 15th March, I was in Washington City   I then applyed for the Collectorship Internal Revenue 4th Ga District in view of the fact that there was a probability that Collector Holtzcla[w] would be removed.—My application was approved by

the President and refered to your *Honor* as I was infor[med]   a few days after
my application Collector Holtzclaw goes on to Washing[ton] via Raleigh, and
Supervisor Perry prefers Charges against me, which said charges, I incidentally
learne[d] of, and answered before I left Washington City and filed my answe[r]
with Commr Douglass. Supervisor Perry in the same Connexion with *his*
charges recommended that Collector Holtzclaw be not removed   The charges
prefered against me are frivolous and absurd and in the main false   I have
learned that supervisor Perry will not consent to Collector Holtzclaws removal
and that, He in Connection with others will be able to prevent His removal
supposing that the facts in the case had not come to your knowledge I thought
proper to write you direct[ly]   I was Endorsed by Ex Gov Parsons and other
leading men of Alabama also Mr Stephens and other Representativ[e] men from
Ga and am satisfyed that the Republicans here desire my appointment"—ALS,
ibid. On May 26, USG suspended Holtzclaw. On Dec. 8, USG nominated John
L. Conley as collector of Internal Revenue, 4th District, Ga.; on Nov. 20, USG
had suspended interim appointee Jack Brown. On April 4, 1877, John T. Brown,
Atlanta, wrote to Secretary of the Treasury John Sherman indicating that
Holtzclaw had been removed for appointing and sustaining a "drunken brother-
in-law" of Rogers as special deputy collector.—ALS, *ibid.*

On March 6, 1881, Jack Brown, Washington, D. C., wrote to USG. "In May
1875 you appointed me Colr of Internal Revenue for the Atlanta Dist in Ga—
in Novr of the same year I. obtained ten day's leave from Comr Pratt to visit
Washington—While en route I was *dismissed for drunkenness,* and knew nothing
about it until I had been in W— for two or three days—I was so indignant
about my unjust, peremptory and uncalled for dismissal that I refused to call on
you (with Genl Logan) for the purpose of protesting against such treatment—
but concluded at once to look after a settlement with the Govt—two months
latter this settlement of accounts was made to my satisfaction, then I called to
see you at yr office, and to my astonishment you knew nothing *of* my *disgrace—*
Upon investigation the whole thing was traced to Pratt and Bristow over
whose heads, and against whose protestations you had appointed me—My old
friendship for you was immediately rerevived, and to this day has remained 'in
tact'   I have made no effort to obtain any position since yr retirement—To the
point—I am not a *drunkard*—do not *drink*—and will *never drink*—I want one
of two places—either Marshal of Ga—or solicitor of the Treasury. It is in your
power to get me one or the other—You, I, and other Grant men elected Genl
Garfield—*This is conceded—make me Marshal of Ga or Sol of the Treasury*"—ALS,
USG 3.

1875, MARCH 23.   Orville E. Babcock to U.S. Senator Roscoe Conkling of N. Y.
"I am in receipt of your telegram. I have seen the President and he authorizes
me to say to you that he sees no trouble in the way of making the change suggested, but he does not wish to send any more nominations to the Senate. He
has informed a number of people that he does not intend to send any thing more
to the Senate this session and he hopes not to do so. Should he decide to send
any thing more I shall call his attention to this matter."—Copy, DLC-USG,
II, 2. On the same day, Conkling had telegraphed to Babcock. "Recommenda-

tions from McBass [*Bass*] and others for Buell are in hands of Commissioner of Internal Revenue."—Telegram received, DNA, RG 107, Telegrams Collected (Bound). On March 24, USG nominated Frederick Buell as collector of Internal Revenue, 30th District, N. Y., to replace George R. Kibbe.

1875, MARCH 25. USG note. "Will the Postmaster Gen.l please see Mrs Bleickar whos husband was in the Navy and died in service during the war. Mrs B. is desirous of a position to enable her to support her self and orphan daughters."—ANS, DNA, RG 56, Appointments. On March 29, Admiral David D. Porter wrote to Secretary of the Treasury Benjamin H. Bristow. ". . . Myself and other friends of Mrs J. V. B. Bleecker whose husband served under my command during the rebellion and died of disease contracted in the service, are extremely anxious to get this lady who is really destitute with a large family to support a situation under government . . ."—LS, *ibid.* Appointed Aug. 16, Sarah R. Bleecker clerked in the Treasury Dept.

1875, MARCH 29. Edward P. Smith, commissioner of Indian Affairs, to Orville E. Babcock. "A delegation of Wisconsin Winnebagoes wants to see the President for a few minutes—They have no official business which they wish to present but would be gratified with an informal interview of three minutes any time today just to shake hands   Will it be convenient?"—Telegram received, DLC-USG, IB. On the same day, Levi P. Luckey telegraphed to Smith. "President will receive Winnebagoes this after-noon at two o'clock."—ALS (telegram sent), DNA, RG 107, Telegrams Collected (Bound).

1875, MARCH 30. A. J. Hopkins, Topeka, Kan., to USG. "Our Governor T A Osborn, is in Your City for the purpose of trying to Secure the Removel of Superintendent Enoch Hoag—Honest People of the State of Kansas believe Mr Hoag to be an *honest competent* Person for the position he is filling—Your Excellency is aware that the Indian Agency business in this Section of Country has been Shamefully handled and abused prior to Mr Hoags Admisrstration and I *verily* believe that I represent the Sentiments of the honest People of the State of Kansas when I Say that they would *heartly* regret to hear of Mr Hoags revmovel—We regard Hoag as Strictly honest, and ~~and~~ if he was removed we might get a Rascal in his place—I am not a Quaker, nor a Granger, but a farmer and beliveing you are as willing to hear what a farmer may have to Say on this Subject as a Politician . . .—"—ALS, DNA, RG 48, Appointment Div., Letters Received. A related clipping is *ibid.* On Dec. 17, USG nominated William Nicholson as superintendent, Indian Affairs, Central Superintendency, replacing Enoch Hoag.

1875, APRIL 1. Mrs. James K. Polk, Nashville, to USG. "Be pleased to allow me to unite with other friends in recommending, to your notice & favorable consideration, the application of Mr. James N. Southworth, of this City, who wishes to be appointed, Cadet, at West Point Military Academy. He is a worthy young man, and is highly recommended."—ALS, DNA, RG 94, Correspondence, USMA. A related letter is *ibid.* James N. Southworth did not attend USMA.

1875, April 2. L. Desnoyers, Philadelphia, to USG seeking U.S. aid to build a prototype thirteen-foot boat. ". . . This being done, I engage myself to furnish you the exhibition at sea of this little vessel, travelling at the incredible speed of from 124 to 155 miles per hour; (the exhibition successful, it will belong to me), the preference over all offers which I would accept and the offer of the lease of my invention. This invention would appear so incredible (nothing opposes it in nature, the free whale makes 80 leagues) that of two things one (must be the case?): either I am a lunatic who at the cost of $10000 which he has spent on his work, the future of his wife and children, still loses his time in pursuit of a chimerical idea, or my invention exists. (I hold the theoretical proof of it at your disposal.). . ."—ALS (in French), DNA, RG 45, Letters Received from the President; translation, *ibid.*

1875, April 6. To Secretary of the Treasury Benjamin H. Bristow, addressed "Confidential." "Will the Sec. of the Treas. please let me have the letters which I returned yesterday before Cabinet meeting. I do not know that the letter addressed to the Sec. of the Treas. is necessary."—ANS, DLC-Benjamin H. Bristow.

1875, April 7. USG endorsement. "The recommendation of the Secretary of War is approved, and the Secretary of the Interior will cause the proper notation to be made in the General Land Office"—Copy, DNA, RG 107, Letters Sent, Military Affairs. Written on a letter of April 5 from Secretary of War William W. Belknap to USG, recommending that the boundaries of a military reservation near Carlin, Nev., be modified to exclude land covered by a prior claim.—Copy, *ibid.* Also in 1875, USG ordered land set aside for military reservations at Fort Ripley, Minn., Fort Whipple and Camp Lowell, Arizona Territory, Fort Abraham Lincoln, Dakota Territory, and the San Juan Islands, Washington Territory, and for the national cemetery at Fort Smith, Ark.—Copies, *ibid.*, RG 94, Military Reservation Div.

1875, April 7. Sarah E. Kirk, Washington, D. C., to USG. "I most earnestly regret the necessity that compels me to bring my case before you again. I presented a letter of introduction to you a short time since from Judge Tremain, and endorsed by Senator Ramsay, Gen'l Garfield, and Senator Jones, these gentlemen, and others have tried to get me a position at the Post Office Department, and they advised that I should present my case to you as they regarded my failure as an act of injustice You refered my case to the Secretary of War, but I have no place yet. I have tried to succeed through personal merit, and political influence. I am told that a great many ladies get places here with but very little influence, . . ."—ALS, DNA, RG 107, Appointment Papers. As of Sept. 30, 1877, Kirk worked as a Justice Dept. copyist.

1875, April 8. To Detective Richard O'Connor authorizing the extradition from Canada to New York County, N. Y., of Jacob and Davis Ripstein, charged with forgery.—Copy, DNA, RG 59, General Records. On April 2, Governor Samuel J. Tilden of N. Y. had written to USG requesting this extradition.—DS, *ibid.*, Extradition Case Files. See *New York Times*, April 18, 1875.

1875, APRIL 8.   James R. Robbins, Seattle, to USG. "All business upon puget Sound is suffering from Mail Irregularities and frequent failures   Can we have no RELIEVE   answer"—Telegram received (at 11:40 P.M.), DLC-USG, IB. On Jan. 15, USG had nominated William H. Pumphrey as postmaster, Seattle; Pumphrey took office on April 9.

1875, APRIL 9.   To James M. Leary authorizing the extradition from France to N. Y. of Charles Claremont, charged with forgery and embezzlement.—Copy, DNA, RG 59, General Records. The request for this extradition, dated April 6, is *ibid.*, Miscellaneous Letters.

1875, APRIL 9.   USG note. "Can the Appointment Clerk of the Treas. give Mrs. Sarah Boudin employment? I believe her to be a very worthy Colored woman who has worked for my family in former years. She has several dependent upon her."—ANS, DNA, RG 56, Applications. On Aug. 21, 1866, USG had written to Secretary of the Treasury Hugh McCulloch. "Permit me to recommend to you for employment about the Treasury Building Mrs. Sarah Boudin, widow of a Colored soldier who died in the service of the Country. Mrs. Boudin has one child and herself to support by her labor."—ALS, *ibid.* Related papers are *ibid.* Sarah E. Boudin was appointed Dec. 1, 1870, as laborer, Treasury Dept.

1875, APRIL 9.   Alexander Falconer, Springfield, Ill., to USG. "Will you favor me with an answer to my letter by telegraph first."—Telegram received, DLC-USG, IB. See *HED*, 49-2-137; *SRC*, 49-1-1575.

1875, APRIL 10.   USG endorsement. "It seems to me the order releiving Lt. Marcotte is rather summary taking in view the recommendations of the court and what I learn of the unfit condition of this officer—the result of honorable wounds—for field duty."—AES, DNA, RG 94, Letters Received, 5356 1874. Written on court-martial papers dated April 2 concerning 1st Lt. Henry Marcotte, 17th Inf., assigned as asst. q. m., Newport Barracks, Ky., convicted of illegally employing an enlisted man as carpenter.

1875, APRIL 10.   Postmaster Gen. Marshall Jewell to USG. "Bard will be in to see you very soon,   I am more & more satisfied that the appointment of Conley will be sustained by a large majority of the republicans of Atlanta and am quite certain the people generally approve your action in the matter,   I have letters & dispatches from reliable sources this morning indicating that Mr Bard is mistaken in saying the people of Atlanta regret the change."—Telegram received, DLC-USG, IB. On Dec. 9, USG nominated Benjamin Conley, former Ga. governor, as postmaster, Atlanta, replacing Samuel Bard.

1875, APRIL 12.   Leopold Karpeles, Washington, D. C., to USG. "The undersigned respectfully request your Excellence for a strong indorsement to the

Secratary of War ore of any other Department for any possition if only fore $60 or $75 pr Month. As I am a father of 3 Children and my Wife sick, and entirely out of means for there support. I have had the strongest reccommadations—as a hart working Republican, and also as a Soldier I received a Medal of Honor, I have also receive a Wound inat the Battle of North Ana Rever, and for the only reason that I have no Members of Congress to push forward my appointmet I have not been able to receive one   Hoping to receive such a indorsement from you to anable me to gat a appointment. . . ."—ALS, DNA, RG 107, Appointment Papers. On Dec. 19, 1872, Karpeles had written to USG seeking appointment to the 1873 Vienna Exposition.—ALS, *ibid.*, RG 59, Letters of Application and Recommendation. Beginning in Nov., 1875, Karpeles clerked in the Treasury Dept. See Robert Shosteck, "Leopold Karpeles: Civil War Hero," *American Jewish Historical Quarterly*, LII, 3 (March, 1963), 220–33.

1875, APRIL 14.   To Commander George C. Remey. "During the temporary absence of Commodore John C. Howell, Chief of the Bureau of Yards and Docks, from the Seat of Government, you are appointed to act as chief of that Bureau."—DS, DLC-Remey Family Papers.

1875, APRIL 15.   Col. Benjamin H. Grierson, 10th Cav., Jacksonville, Ill., to USG. "Please order my transfer to fifth Cavly when Col Emory is retired,"— Telegram received (on April 16), DNA, RG 94, ACP, G553 CB 1865. On July 8, 1876, USG nominated Wesley Merritt as col., 5th Cav.

1875, APRIL 20.   Tunis G. Campbell, New York City, to USG. "I Respectfully call your Attention to certain outrages Perpetrated, and being Perpetrated upon me under Color of law; in the State of Georgia, on account of My Political Principals,   Pleased find inclosed here with, a Printed Statement of my case now being Carried up to the Supreme court of the State of Georgia, on a Bill of Exceptions, said Bill acting as a Supercedious,   I was Released on Bonds from confinement in the jail of Fulton County in the City of Atlanta, and on my way home, I was again Arrested and Put in jail in the City of Savannah Chatham County, upon another indictment Which they had against me, upon a Charge trumped up so as to heap Cost upon Cost, And Prevent me from geting Bond, And also keep me from geting Counsel. as I Will not be able to Pay fees and costs,   I came North three Weeks ago for the Purpose of Coming to Washington to See your Exelencey, but my confinement in damp and cold cells, and Exsposesure other wise in this Severe Weather has caused my feet to Swell and Pain me to that degree, that I have not been able to get to Washington, And now I am compeled to Return Home, not having time, as I am under Bond to appear at the April term of the Mcintosh County Superior court to be held Next week I Called upon Col Farrow the United States Attorney General of the State of Georgia, When I was in Atlanta, but he said Nothing could be done for any Republican in Georgia, and all We had to do was to Submit, for the Laws could not be enforced.   and as I have been Personally in formed by your Exelency that the Laws of the United States Should be inforced, I do hereby Respectfully Request that your Exelency will So instruct through the department of justice, as to you may seem best, That when I Shall make Affidavit as Required by Law, that such Steps shall be taken as will insure justice to me against these Malicious Persicutions goten up for the Purpose of driving My Family and My self from the State of Georgia   all of Which I Respectfully Submit"—ALS, DNA, RG 60, Letters Received, N. Y. Campbell, former Ga. senator and McIntosh County justice of the peace, enclosed a clipping protesting his conviction for false imprisonment.—*Ibid.* In [*May*], "Citizens of McIntosh County" petitioned USG "to protect us from the illtreatment of the demercratic party for the demorcrat ~~have~~ are trying to kill us all out: ~~See 1, See~~ 1 They have take our right from us By apointed Boad of Commissioners of democrat Contrary to Will of the majority of people of ~~the 271 District~~ McIntosh and Contrary to the Laws and they are trying to kill all of the Republican party out Because the majority is Republican in ~~the 271 District~~ MCIntosh county By having cruil Demercrats officers and they Shooting Collord people up and Send them to the State prisson By Numbe[r]s and taking away they property from them that they Leagaly Bought and paid for and Runing them out of the county: and on the 29 inst of April 1875 A Suprior Court Was take place in Darien ga Mctouch County of ~~Said 271 District~~ and Said Judge have an inimosity against the collord people   he was trying to ran Mr T G Campbell Sr to the State prissons Because he is a Leader of the Republican and the Republican Went to the court house to See him off and the Judge [Command about 50 fifty demercrats mens] to fire in to the Republican and they done So and that comence a great Reiot With the demercrats and the Republicans and they Shot ~~down Womens and~~ mens Republicans down (and taking Wemen Bound them in jail and going to Send them to the State prissons for they Said they Will either Send every Republicans to the State prison or kill them out of this district . . . and Sworn they Will either Send old T G Campbell ~~to~~ out of Georgia or to State prisson or kill him . . ."—DS (docketed June 1), *ibid.*, Letters Received, Ga. On May 26, C. B. Clark, Buffalo, wrote to USG. "I would respectfully call your attention to the enclosed account of outrages that have lately come under my notice while returning from Florida—I was in Washington about the 15th, but sudden illness prevented me from bringing this case fully before the proper authorities. I left the matter in the hands of Judge R L B Clarke who published my statement substantially in The 'Chronicle' Since my return I have prepared the enclosed statement which was published in the 'Buffalo Commercial Advertiser'   Mr Campbell appealed to me to call upon you as he felt assured that you would have his case investigated   He wished me to say that he visited Washington in 1868 as one of the Georgia delegation and had a a personal interview with you—He can now only appeal to you through the medium of some friends who have had access to him in his prison in Savannah. I, as one among several citizens who are cognisant of these persecutions, implore you to have the cause of Mr Campbell and fellow prisoners looked into —I can if necessary furnish you the names of at least six persons who were witnesses to the attempted drowning of the three colored men mentioned   These outrages while meant by their Legal persecutors to destroy their political power, yet strike down the personal liberty of law abiding american Citizens—We trust and believe President Grant, that this honest appeal made to you will not be in vain,"—ALS, *ibid.*, Letters Received, N. Y. On June 24, Clark wrote to USG on the same subject.—ALS, *ibid.*, Letters Received, Ga. On Sept. 2, Campbell, Chatham County jail, Savannah, wrote to USG. ". . . in 1871 & 1872 they got an act Passed and under said act governor James M. Smith appointed a Board of Commissioners, to take charge of McIntosh County & Prevent colored men from holding office in McIntosh county, ~~with~~ with power to act as a ~~Boa~~ Board of Alderman & Mayor for the city of Darien, with a right of appointing there sucessors in office, thereby repealing the charter of the city Virtuely and de-nieing the citizens ~~of~~ there right to Elect the Mayor & Alderman by Ballot, they also have a right by Vertue of office to take the Bonds of the county officers, and they have defeated 3 Elections held in the County of McIntosh this year, & have also, after My haveing 290 Majority compeled me to contest for my seat by not appointing Managers, & then when as required by Law Managers were appointed got the ordinary one of these *tools* to appoint a man who swore he was a freeholder, and afterwards upon the takeing of testimoney Said he did not know whether he was or not;—but to Make sure of the seat they arrangd a Plot; to kill me, & while I was on to see your Exelency this spring in April your were on to the celebration of the Bunkerhill, & Lexington centenial, & being very un-well from cold caught during my confinement in chains, at the convict camp, & in Prison I could not walk, & was also under a *Bond* to appear at the McIntosh superior court, on April 27th 1875. therefor I came back without waiting to have an interview with you. . . . all through the county they have Spys, colored & White, Watching the Meetings of ~~the~~ the colord People, & Pretending to Pick up letters, & hear things said by the People & then Warrants are Issued for there arrest, & these Witnesses have there testimoney arranged by the clerk of the Superior court, & that is the way all through the South where there is a ma-jority of colored Voters, & in this State there are now over (200) Leaders of the colored People now in the chain gang, or States Prison, and many thousands have left the State & gone to Arkansas, . . . I aske your Exelency, can not some-thing be done for me, & for the colored, & White Republicans of the *South,* in many countys of this State the People to day do not know that they are free & any White man can have them Whiped just when he Pleases, for they dare not say they are free, . . . these chain gangs are for the Purpose of Breaking the Leaders of the colored People: & god only knows how many have been mur-dered in cold Blood in there houses & in the Swamps of this State. President grant I appeal to you in the Name of My god, & the Loyal People of this State, to consider this matter, & if you want Proof Bring from the States Prisons those now Suffering in chains & let the records of the judicial tribunals show upon what Testimoney they were sent, and let Witnesses who were Starved & beaten untill they were compeled to tell what was wanted as testimony against Loyal men. ~~and~~ I know if there is not something done for us, thousands will have to leave & Seek homes some where else, or make up there minds as I have to die at our Posts, trusting in god for our reward hereafter May god Bless you & yours . . . P Sript In 1873, they arrested the gaurd that watched my house, & put them under a Bond, & of course they could not watch, & they told me there was no danger of my house being burnt. But last April the house & my wife & sons store with groceries adjoining too it were burnt to the ground"—ALS, *ibid.* On

Nov. 13, Campbell again wrote to USG, asking that his case be transferred to a
U.S. court.—ALS, *ibid.*, Letters from the President. On Nov. 6, Harriet Campbell, Atlanta, had written to USG. "I Call upon you in the name of high heavens
to assist me in Some Way to Save My husbands Life—he is laying in Savannah
jail Sick   the Court Sits in Darrien this month & I Dont know how Soon he
may be Draged their in irons to lay in a Cold jail to finish out his days.   the
Bond that they ask above the homestead Cant be got   the best Lawyers in the
South Says his Charges is persicution & they will Clear him for a few hundred
Dollars, but I have not got the money.   tell me in gods name if you Cant give
him any protection.   the jailer in Darien has Shot a prisoner in jail for asking
for Some thing to eat. When Collord men are put in jail he throughs bucets
of Water over them & tells them that is the remainder of the Sivil Rights Bill.
this I have Stood & heard   the Collord people Dare Assisted Mr Campbell
nor Say a word in his favor. or they are taken up & put in prison false Charges
trumped up agin thim & put in prison for 10—or 15—years   in the name of
high heavens is there no protection for us on the earth.   for this is a true Statement of things here in Mcintosh Co.   good lord good lord people is flying in
evry Direction Evry Day to Save their lives. We are destitute   do please & Send
me Some money to assist my husband in his law Suits.   it would be a great act
of Charity   I know no other friend to Send. Do Send to my assistance in this
trying hour, & god will bless you. My heart is bleeding in Sorrow & Greef. I beg
of you to assist me in Some Way. . . . Poscript.   My Son had to escape for his
life & I am Secritly hid. & you See there is no one to aid My husband   do Send
to my assistance for you are the president of the united States. I know you never
Can miss what you give me & by So doing it will Save my husbands life. I
Dont want to leave Georgia untill I See what becomes of My husband.   please
write me an answer & Direct it to benjeman Conly atlanta post office."—ALS,
ibid. On Jan. 10 and Feb. 27, 1876, Harriet Campbell telegraphed and wrote to
USG. "Judge Erskine has decided that Mr Campbell must be turned over to the
Keeper of the penitentiary   is there no help for him," "I am oblidge to Write to
beg you to Please have a Spetial order Sent to mr pharrow to take the papers
out of the State Court, for the papers in that Case are not & Will not be got
from the Clerk of the State Court Without a Special order from the Department of Justice at Washington."—Telegram received and ALS, *ibid.* See Russell
Duncan, *Freedom's Shore: Tunis Campbell and the Georgia Freedmen* (Athens, Ga.,
1986), pp. 99–109.

1875, APRIL 23.   James M. Edgar, Huntsville, Ala., to USG. "I herewith enclose you a clipping from a Democratic paper of this City (Bourbon to the core)
eulogistic of your recent appointment of a Ku Klux Grand Cyclops of the K. K.
Klan in preference to an old soldier of the Union Army (Z E. Thomas) even if
he has the Stigma attached to him of being a Northern man from Iowa. This appointment is repugnant to every man (democrat or republican!) in North Alabama, and it is not only requested by the few Soldiers resident here; who have
acted under you from Donelson, to Appomattox, for you to reconsider and revoke this appointment and reappoint the present incumbent, . . ."—ALS, DNA,

RG 60, Letters from the President. The enclosure is *ibid.* Edgar had served in
the 11th Mo. Cav. On March 16, USG had nominated Robert P. Baker as marshal, Northern District, Ala., replacing Zachariah E. Thomas.

1875, APRIL 27.   USG speech welcoming Mr. de Pestel, who replaced Bern-
hard de Westenberg as Dutch minister.—*Philadelphia Public Ledger*, April 28,
1875.

1875, APRIL 27.   James F. Casey, New Orleans, to USG. "I transmit herewith,
letters from several gentlemen, personal friends of mine, urging the appointment of Lieut. L. E. Campbell, 22d U. S. Infantry, to the position of Captain and
Commissary of Subsistence. You will probably remember that this is the appointment I spoke to you about while I was in Washington, and I trust you will
oblige me by making the appointment."—LS, DNA, RG 94, ACP, 3611 1876.
Related papers are *ibid.* On March 11, 1876, Ulysses S. Grant, Jr., wrote to 1st
Lt. Lafayette E. Campbell, Detroit. "The President desires me to say that the
brook trout which you so kindly forwarded to him by express were received in
excellent condition and were very fine. He begs you to accept many thanks."—
LS, Gallery of History, Las Vegas, Nev. On May 31, USG nominated Campbell
as capt., asst. q. m.
     On Sept. 7, James T. Clarke, bandmaster, 22nd Inf., Detroit, wrote to Camp-
bell concerning an appointment to USMA.—ALS, IHi. On [*Sept. 18*], USG endorsed this letter. "Answer Capt. Campbell that is now to late for any more apts
~~from~~ during my term of office"—AE (undated), *ibid.*

1875, APRIL 29.   Attorney Gen. George H. Williams to USG. "I have considered the papers referred by you to me relative to the claim of the United States
against E. Delafield Smith, Esq. for a succession tax upon the transfer of a house
in New York to him by his wife. It appears that he purchased the house with his
own money, and that the conveyance was made to Mrs. Smith. Subsequently it
was thought advisable to have the legal title to the property vested in Mr.
Smith. . . . I am inclined to think from my examination of the case that the Government has a technical right of recovery against Mr. Smith for a succession
tax; but in view of the fact that the transaction was in 1867, and that Mr. Smith
acted under the advice of the Commissioner of Internal Revenue, I am satisfied
that it would be unequitable and unjust to enforce the payment of this tax
against Mr. Smith. . . ."—Copy, DNA, RG 60, Letters Sent to Executive Officers. See *PUSG*, 23, 316–18.

[*1875, April*].   Juan Nicolas Tapia *et al.* to USG. "We, your petitioners, Natives of the Pueblos of the Territory of New Mexico, present ourselves before
your Excellency, by means of this suplicatory petition, which will be handed
to you by our representatives, who have been selected to represent the Pueblos
of San Juan, Taos, San Yldefonso, Santa Clara, Picuris, Nambe, Pujuaque,
Tesuque, San Felipe and Sandia. These 'Pueblos' most Excellent Sir, humbly
present themselves before your Excellency, who is the father, after God, of the

poor natives of this Territory, and beg to represent to you, as our father, that the King of Spain gave us possession of our lands and confirmed them by grants, which were approved by the mexican government, which gov't turned us over to the US. government, in accordance with the treaty of Guadalupe Hidalgo and Washington, with all rights and privileges to our lands, pastures and woods: We also beg to represent to your Excellency, that there are some persons who wish to impede us from pasturing our animals,—cattle and horses—and not only this, but they even wish to deprive us of the privilege of cutting wood for our use, which privilege we have always had in common,   nobody was ever before deprived of these privileges, but we are now being deprived from pasturing our animals and from cutting wood, and the people even wish to take our lands. Therefore, Most Excellent Sir, in view of the fact that we are manaced and oppressed, &c. to whom can we present our complaints for a remedy, if not to your Excellency, our father and our protector. Your Excellency, after God, can only pity us, and grant us the justice that we implore. We beg your Excellency to issue an order—a peremtory order—that no citizen shall enter within the limits of our lands, and that we may not be deprived of the public pastures and woods, but that we may be allowed to use them as formerly. By doing this you will grant us grace, mercy and justice."—D (in Spanish, undated), DNA, RG 75, Letters Received, New Mexico Superintendency; translation, *ibid.* On April 26, Benjamin M. Thomas, agent, Pueblo Agency, Santa Fé, wrote to Edward P. Smith, commissioner of Indian Affairs. "I have the honor to introduce to you the bearers of this paper, a delegation of Pueblo Indians from the Pueblo of San Juan, New Mexico. They go to Washington on their own expense, to see the President, Hon Commissioner of Indian Affairs, Hon Secretary of the Interior, and to others,   They make the trip with a view to combining business and pleasure. Their business I leave them to state. I respectfully recommend them for your kind consideration."—LS, *ibid.* See *HED,* 44-1-1, part 5, I, 584–86, 834–35; *PUSG,* 20, 342–44; *ibid.,* 23, 472–73.

1875, MAY 1.   USG note. "I will be willing to give the bearer, Mr. Brewster, one of the best consulates now vacant. I have known Mr. B's family for many years, quite favorably."—Copy, Society of the Cincinnati, Washington, D. C. On Aug. 2, 1885, William F. Brewster, Detroit, wrote to Hamilton Fish, New York City, asking to have the note returned.—ALS, DLC-Hamilton Fish.

1875, MAY 2.   Micah J. Jenkins, Summerville, S. C., to USG. "The writer had the misfortune to lose his Father Genl. Jenkins, and his Grand father Genl. Jamison during the last war. The Mother was left with four little children of whom I am the eldest (now nearly eighteen). She has struggled bravely to educate us, and I am permitted to enclose testimonials from the Faculty of the Charleston College in the Junior Class of which I am at present. I have taken a first position in the class hitherto, and beg leave to refer your Excellency to Mr. B. C. Pressley, Lawyer, and to Mr. Hastie, Broker, and Mr. Geo. W. Williams, Merchant, or any one else in the city of Charleston who may have heard of me as to capacity, and character. I have sprung from a military family, and all my aspirations tend that way. You are aware how difficult it is for a white youth of good social standing to get and appointment to West Point from the district representatives of So. Ca. I have in vain struggled for a competitive Examination, which was all I desired. Under these circumstances, knowing my full ability to meet every requirement, and being desirous of aiding my family, I would respectfully beg your excellency to entertertain this my letter of application for an appointment 'at large' to West Point, or should all these be taken for one to the Naval Academy at Annapolis. Very Respt, and hoping I may receive a favorable response, . . ."—ALS, DNA, RG 94, Correspondence, USMA. Jenkins graduated USMA in 1879.

1875, MAY 2. John S. Mosby, Warrenton, Va., to USG. "I enclose a slip cut from an Alexa. paper simply for the purpose of giving you information concerning a matter which may have escaped your notice. I learn from other sources that an attempt is about to be made to procure the dismissal of a few persons from office who happen to be my friends & who were appointed through my agency. I do not write this letter to intercede in their behalf but to submit the question to your sense of justice. If their removal will add anything to the popularity of the Administration in this State I will certainly raise no objection to it. I have *three* appointees in Genl. Spinner's Dept. & three mail-clerks, whom, I learn, there will be an attempt to remove for no other reason than that I recommended their appointment. Some of them voted for you—the others were too young to vote at the Presidential election. One is a great-nephew of Genl. Washington & bears his name & is only 19. You know well the grounds on which I supported you for President—to these I have consistently adherred during a trial to which few men have been subjected. But no matter what may be your action in this matter I shall earnestly desire the properity & success of your administration. . . . I wd call in person to see you but my appearance at the White House wd occasion a great deal of newspaper criticism which I know wd be as annoying to you as to myself."—ALS, DLC-Benjamin H. Bristow.

1875, MAY 3. Orville E. Babcock to Gen. William T. Sherman, St. Louis. "I submitted your favor of the 28th ultimo to the President who says he remembers the hospital you refer to well. He says also that the matter of renting out the Chicago Marine Hospital had been brought to him before the receipt of your letter by the Secretary of the Treasury, and that he had decided not to lease any other of the Hospitals, and the Secretary has so informed other applicants. Please remember me to Mrs. Sherman and your family."—Copy, DLC-USG, II, 2. On April 28, Sherman had written to Babcock. "I enclose you two papers that you may find it difficult to understand—Sister Angela Gillespie, a nun, a relation of Mrs Sherman and Speaker Blaine—and whom I knew well as a School girl, thoroughly educated and as persevering as the veriest Yankee, wants to secure the Hospital at Chicago, which she says is to be leased out, by the Secretary of the Treasury—She wants me to ask the President to endorse her paper—I have written her the President ought not to endorse her paper—and at the utmost should only manifest a personal interest in her behalf, and in that of the Sisters of Charity generally—This Nun Angela—had charge of the Hospitals at Cairo and Memphis in 1863, and Genl Grant himself saw how neat & thorough they were kept, by these Sisters. and if he will simply say to Genl Bristow that all other conditions being right, he would favor the application of the Sisters of Charity who managed that large hospital at Mound City, he would do a personal kindness to this very Sister Angela, who was the very person in charge—She is as industrious as an ant—and as persevering as a Washington Claim Agent—Please answer her direct—as she is at Baltimore."—ALS, Duke University, Durham, N. C. See Anna Shannon McAllister, *Flame in the Wilderness: Life and Letters of Mother Angela Gillespie, C. S. C. 1824–1887* (Paterson, N. J., 1944), pp. 170–71.

1875, MAY 3.   Governor James L. Kemper of Va. to USG. "I respectfully ask that a Board of National Officers be authorized and directed to act in conjunction with the State Harbor Commissioners of Norfolk and Portsmouth, Virginia, in the manner and for the purposes explained in the enclosed copies of communications from the Superintendent of the U. S. Coast Survey and the President of the Harbor Commissioners."—LS, RG 77, Letters Received. Related papers are *ibid.*

1875, MAY 10.   USG endorsement. "Refered to the Sec. of War."—AES, DNA, RG 94, ACP, 1872 1875. Written on a letter of the same day from Montgomery Blair, Washington, D. C., to USG. "The Revd Geo W Simpson of Baltimore of the Methodist Church will present with this testimonials of the highest order both from the Clergy of his denomination & from the citizens of Baltimore in favor of his appointment as a chaplain in the army. His endorsers are well known to me & were among my former warm political friends when I was acting with the Republican party, & are still among my best personal friends & I know that you would be doing right to act on their recommendation. It would be very acceptable to me both on their account as well on account of Mr Simpson who impresses me very much, if you would make this appointment"—ALS, *ibid.* On Nov. 4, George W. Simpson, Baltimore, wrote to USG renewing his application. ". . . So far as I am able to judge, every one by the name of Simpson who has held and who may now hold a position at the hands of the government has proved himself to be a faithful and efficient servant. . . ."—ALS, *ibid.* A related letter is *ibid.* On Jan. 10, 1876, USG nominated Simpson as chaplain.

1875, MAY 10.   To President Ponciano Leiva of Honduras congratulating him on election to office.—*New York Times*, May 13, 1875.

1875, MAY 10.   Secretary of the Treasury Benjamin H. Bristow to USG. "On examination I find that Mr. Anthony stands well as Collector of Internal Revenue, but, inasmuch as all the sureties on his official bond insist on his resignation in order to relieve them from further liability of which they cannot be otherwise relieved, and as the entire delegation in Congress from Kansas unite in asking that Mr. Anthony be removed and the Honorable A. M. Blair appointed, I respectfully recommend that Mr. Anthony be requested to resign. To prevent inconvenience which might result from a sudden change in the office while he is now engaged in the collection of special taxes I suggest that his resignation should take effect the first of June, or not later than the end of the present fiscal year. I return herewith the papers transmitted me this morning."—Copy, DNA,

RG 56, Letters Sent to the President. On June 17, Bristow again wrote to USG. "Referring to the request made some weeks ago by your direction for the resignation of Mr. George T. Anthony, Collector of Internal Revenue for Kansas, I think it proper to advise you that papers have been forwarded here signed by the two Republican representatives elect to the 44th Congress from that State, by the Governor and other State officials, and by prominent bankers and business men throughout the State, earnestly remonstrating against Mr. Anthony's removal. On the other hand, the two Senators claim that the removal was promised, and, by telegraph, insist on it. On inquiry at the Commissioner's office I find that Mr. Anthony stands as well as any ~~man~~ Collector in the United States for efficiency and integrity. In view of these facts I am inclined to the opinion that it would be well to withdraw the request for his resignation and permit him to remain. Col. Phillips, Member of Congress from Kansas, desires to present Mr. Anthony's case to you in person, and at his request I have handed him the papers filed in behalf of Mr. Anthony. I await your pleasure in the matter."— LS (press), DLC-Benjamin H. Bristow. On Dec. 13, 1876, USG nominated Alexander M. Blair to replace George T. Anthony as collector of Internal Revenue, Kan.

1875, MAY 10. Judge William McKennan, 3rd U.S. Circuit, Pittsburgh, to USG. "I hope you will not consider it intrusive or indelicate in me to ask a favor in behalf of an old and valued friend—Mr. W. T. Minor is in the Dept. of Justice, where he has held a position since the close of the War. He did himself great credit in the Army, and was wounded. . . . His father, at whose instance I write this letter, informs me, that it is understood a change in the Chief Clerkship in the Atty. Genls. office will probably be made, and ~~that~~ is apprehensive that this with other consequent changes, may involve the displacement of his son. . . ."—ALS, DNA, RG 60, Letters Received, Pa. In [*June, 1876*], Lawrence L. Minor wrote to USG. ". . . I have learned an unpleastness has occured betwen the Chf Clerk and my son Minor. I have not learned the cause of it; but am left to conjecture   My son has the frailty of taking an occasional spree and when in one is indiscreete and may have given offence. . . . I feel more anxious about from the fact that I know his position has operated as a check and restraint on his unfortunate periodical weakness—. . ."—ALS (docketed June 27, 1876), *ibid.*, Letters from the President.

1875, MAY 11. J. Young Scammon, Chicago, to USG. "*Private and personal.* . . . You doubtless know from rumor that misfortune after misfortune has visited me in consequence of my determination to establish and maintain an administration republican paper in this great center of the north west. I do not conceal from myself that I should have had a heavy burden to carry, as events have turned, under any circumstances, but I should have probably been able to bear the same had I not invested so large a sum in in replacing the power of the republican press in Chicago, which [the] treachery and perfidy of the managers of the Chicago Tribune attempted to destroy. Alone and unaided I established and maintained until it was the grandest poliical success of modern newspaper enterprises, the Inter Ocean newspaper; but in so doing I brought down upon me all that malignity and treachery could exert to destroy my character and credit in the hope of thereby silencing the only powerful administration newspaper in Chicago. It is not silenced and today has more readers than any other polical newspaper west of the Alleghennies, but its power is with the people rather than with the business men who have advertising patronage in the City. Hence it has given me no pecuniary return, but has constantly taxed me. I know that I am not saying too much when I assert that no other individual has done so much for your administration in this region as I have done, and no other person has pecuniarily suffered so much in consequence. I have never asked the President for an office for myself, but I am impelled to do so now. I had intended to apply for the Judgeship on the Court of Claims about to be vacated by Judge Peck, but I am told it has been promised to Mr. Paine. I therefore do not ask it; but I do ask that my services and ability and my situation shall be recognized and that you will give me an appointment at home or abroad—such an one as I am entitled to by my acknowledged services to the Country and to the republican party, and to you personally, as its head, in our great contests. With great respect, and ever faithful devotion to our principles, and you personally as their representative, . . ."—ALS, USG 3. No appointment followed.

On Jan. 18, 1876, Scammon, Washington, D. C., wrote at length to USG alleging that recent indictments against Scammon's Chicago bank amounted to blackmail in order to collect a private debt. ". . . These indictments have caused great astonishment and indignation in Chicago where my character, as you well know, was above reproach and among my friends here. In one of my first interviews with Mr. Wilson, the Solicitor of the Treasury, I suggested to him that he had been needlessly intermeddling in a matter where it was not pretended that any wrong had been done to the Government, even if the complaints were true, while they were not. . . ."—LS, DNA, RG 60, Letters Received, Ind. On Jan. 19, Levi P. Luckey endorsed this letter. "Respectfully referred to the Attorney General with the suggestion that the subject of this communication receive the earliest practicable attention and that any and all injustice that has been done Mr. Scammon be corrected as far as possible and without delay. The position Mr. Scammon has occupied in Chicago for many years as a man of integrity, benevolence and generosity entitle him to this attention. No man that knows him, whether personally friendly or not, will believe for one moment that the proceedings which have been had in Chicago imputing dishonesty to Mr. Scammon can have any good foundation."—ES, *ibid.* On Feb. 23, Scammon wrote to USG. ". . . I understand this matter has been examined in the Department of Justice by the Solicitor General, and by him declared to be an indecent proceeding, and that he advised the immediate dismissal of all the proceedings touching the same. The Attorney General fully concurred in these views, and wrote to the District Attorney in Chicago, to dismiss the proceedings at once, if the facts were as represented; and if not to report any additional facts to him. I am informed by the Attorney General that the District Attorney reported to him that there were no further facts. Still the proceedings have not been discontinued, . . . I have thus been detained here more than a month waiting to have this injustice corrected. The papers in the Attorney General's Office, and the opinion of the Solicitor General condemn these proceedings as a blackmailing

operation, and the Attorney General has given his full and entire concurrence
to that opinion. In this state of the case, I respectfully yet urgently appeal to you
once more to set in motion the wheels of the Department of Justice, . . ."—ALS,
ibid. Scammon also addressed a lengthy report on his case to USG, incorporating copies of related correspondence. ". . . Finally: I am and my friends ~~proceed~~
are forced to the conclusion, that the quarrel of the Secretary of the Treasury &
his Solicitor of the Treasury, with the Inter Ocean newspaper, the leading Republican morning paper, which I established in Chicago; and which has been
shown among other things, by his causing the removal of one of its editorial
writers from an office in the Chicago Custom House, without any cause connected with the discharge of his duties, may explain the zeal shown by the Department *in furthering these unheard of blackmailing and Star Chamber proceedings.*
I demand justice, and that such necessary steps shall be taken as to render in
the future impossible the repetition of such acts, as in the past of the Employees of the Government. . . . N. B. Papers in the Office of the Attorney General,
and the records and correspondence in the Treasury Department, and especially in the Office of the Comptroller of the currency prove the statements contained in the above communication."—DS (docketed March 1, 1876), *ibid.,*
RG 206, Miscellaneous Letters Received.

1875, MAY 13. Isham G. Benton, Paris, Tex., to USG claiming $700 due his
late father Willis Benton for removing Indians from Ala. in 1836.—ALS, DNA,
RG 75, Letters Received, Miscellaneous. On July 7 and on June 16, 1876, Benton wrote to USG on the same subject.—ALS, *ibid.; ibid.,* Letters Received,
Creek Agency. No action followed.

1875, MAY 15. USG note. "Will the Sec. of the Treas. please see Miss Carr?"
—ANS, DNA, RG 56, Applications. On May 7, Henry H. Wells, Washington,
D. C., had written to USG. "Miss H. Carr, whose petition accompanies this, is
a most deserving young lady with whom my family became acquainted in Richmond in 1868. She is in most distressed circumstances and greatly desires some
employment. I think you may rely upon all her statements as absolutely true. I
write this at her request."—LS, *ibid.* Related papers are *ibid.*

1875, MAY 15. Horace W. King, Dallas, to USG. "I have just came back from
a trip over Tenn Georgia Ala, and Miss. My object was to See my old associates
in Lees Army that we might have an organization of more cohesive power than
we did in the last canvass (when you was Elected,). in the next Six months we
will have matters so perfected, that we will control the Electoral vote of the
South, and we have decided to give it to the Rebublican Candidate, If we think
he will control matters and give us and the country generally the protection you
have. if you Should allow your name to be run, we will willingly Support you,
for the reasons that you have done your duty, lived up to the Treaty you made
with us, administering the Government in a way, Especially the Finances,
which is remarkable, nothing like it Since the days of Richielu, and if you had
not have interfeared in the La. Affairs, all of this magnificent State, La, Miss and
Ala, would at this moment be like a midnight revel in 'Hades,' . . ."—ALS, DNA,
RG 60, Letters Received, Tex. An enclosure is *ibid.*

1875, MAY 17.   U.S. Senator John H. Mitchell of Ore. to USG. "I understand E. S. Kearney is soon to resign his position as U. S. Marshall of Washington Territory—in such event—I *earnestly* recommend the appointment of Capt Chas Hopkins—of Walla Walla Washington Territory—Capt Hopkins was formerly in the Army,—is a man of *unquestionable integrity,*—in fact a *model man* in all relations of life—he is thoroughly competent   he is married to the daughter of the late Senator Baker of Oregon—has in the past few years—been a great sufferer by fire—and also by sickness in his family—I hope he may be appointed"—ALS, DNA, RG 60, Records Relating to Appointments. Similar letters to USG from George H. Williams and Cornelius Cole are *ibid.* On Dec. 15, USG nominated Charles Hopkins as marshal, Washington Territory, in place of Edward S. Kearney.

1875, MAY 19.   Robert S. Lacey, Washington, D. C., to USG. "I have the honor to state that thousands of citizens of Virginia and District of Columbia have petitioned the Forty Third Congress for a free bridge over the Potomac at Georgetown. In view of this it was not deemed essential to extend the petition for detail of engineer, presented your Secretary to day, beyond the names of the property holders contained therein. It is, perhaps, pertinent to add as an argument in favor of a bridge as desired, that its erection would permit transfer of road from the east bank of the Potomac to the west, and far greater developement of water facilities for manufacturing purposes at Georgetown"—ALS, DNA, RG 77, Rivers and Harbors Div., Letters Received. The accompanying petition, signed by Alexander R. Shepherd and more than forty others, complained "that the present bridge erected upon the piers of the Aqueduct exact an onerous and exhorbitant toll from all using it, and operates as a bar to improvement of a large portion of Alexandria and Fairfax Counties, Va., and to the exclusion of visitors from Arlington and the National Cemeteries; . . ."—DS, *ibid.* See *SED,* 44-1-39; *SRC,* 46-2-383; *HED,* 47-1-156.

1875, MAY 20.   James D. Cameron, Harrisburg, to USG. "Can I see you between three & four o'clock tomorrow afternoon,   Answer,"—Telegram received, DLC-USG, IB.

1875, MAY 21.   "A. White," Corinth, Miss., to USG. "Would you be pleased to call the attention of those haveing Jurisdiction in Such cases to the case of J. E. Gillenwaters formerly of Corinth Miss. for the Murder of Dr. Dunn who was an officer of the Government and was murdered while Sleeping in his room at a late hour of the night. The Said Gillenwaters made his Escape from Justice, and his friends assert that it was favored by Some officials. Gillenwaters also had a Black man Kukluxed at Corinth and tried to prove an Alibi. It is evident that he is a very bad man and for him to run at liberty does not Speak well for our Courts. Have the matter investigated at Corinth and Oxford Miss."—L (incomplete, name from docket), DNA, RG 60, Letters Received, Miss.

[*1875, May 22*].   USG endorsement. "Thirty-one years ago. I was so frightened however that I do not remember whether it was warm or snowing."—AES (undated, signed "Ulys."), USG 3. Written on an undated letter from Julia Dent

Grant. "How many years ago to day is that we were engaged? Just such a day as this too was it not?"—ALS, *ibid*. Julia Grant later noted. "I find this among some old letters. I suppose I just then remembered that it was the *anniversary* of our engagement   22nd May 1844"—AE, *ibid*.

1875, MAY 24.   Orville E. Babcock to Secretary of the Navy George M. Robeson. "The President directs me to say that the several departments of the Government will be closed on Saturday the 29th inst., in order to enable the employees to participate in the decoration of the graves of the soldiers who fell during the rebellion."—LS, DNA, RG 45, Letters Received from the President. Babcock wrote similar letters to other cabinet officers.

1875, MAY 26.   USG endorsement. "Refered to the Sec. of the Treas. who has the card on which my memorandum was made."—AES, DNA, RG 56, Applications. Written on a letter of the same day from Virginia Dunnavant to USG. "At the close of my interview with you Thursday 20th I left my fate in your hands, and fearing you may leave the city before it is decided, I cannot resist the impulse to address you on the subject that is of such great importance to me, according to the rules of decorum I have made no movement since I saw yourself,   will you grant me farther indulgence and see me for a short time—President! on you my hopes depend,   let them not be crushed—"—ALS, *ibid*. USG had written an undated note concerning Dunnavant. "Has an aged mother to support. Were Union people from Va. Place obtained through Genl. Canby who became acquainted with them while in Command in Richmond after the close of the War. Desires restoration as only means of support of two otherwise helpless ladies."—AN, *ibid*. On Sept. 14, 1876, Dunnavant wrote to USG. "In the discharge—of the clerks from the Treasury Dept—on the 1st of September I was among the number, and haveing been called to the notice of the Secretary of the Treasury one year ago last May, I feel much surprised at not being retained, as I *filled my position* in a *satisfactory manner* and the *chief* of the *Division* asserts that there is naught against me. On my referring to the card of your Excellency which you gave to Secretary Bristow and which is on file in the Sec-s office the reply was it is only a 'reference not a request.' Secretary Morrill being absent I cannot reach his notice. . . ."—ALS, *ibid*. Related papers are *ibid*.

1875, MAY 26.   Orville E. Babcock to Frederick A. Schmidt, president, Shakespeare Club. "Your favor of this date—with enclosure for the President—is received. I am requested to say that the President and Mrs. Grant accept with pleasure your polite invitation for the 28th inst. I beg to tender many thanks to the members of your Club for their kind invitation, and my regrets that sickness in my family will not permit me to accept."—LS, Cincinnati Historical Society, Cincinnati, Ohio. Schmidt clerked in the Treasury Dept. The Shakespeare Club performed John B. Buckstone's "Married Life" at the National Theatre. See *Washington National Republican*, May 28, 29, 1875.

1875, MAY 28.   Philip Bell, Philadelphia, to USG offering $300,000 for aid in settling his claim against Haiti "for eight hundred thousand spanish dollars or

the value of it in gold or gold and silver."—ALS, DNA, RG 59, Miscellaneous
Letters. Similar letters from 1871, 1872, and 1876 fail to reveal the nature of
this claim.—*Ibid.*

1875, MAY 28.   Mishahquahnahum, seven other "Chiefs and head men," and
nineteen "private men holding no office," Mount Pleasant, Mich., to USG. "We,
the undersigned, Chippewas of Saginaw, Swan Creek and Black River, respectfully represent to our Great Father at Washington, as follows: I. Rev. George I.
Betts of Lansing Mich, is the Indian Agent, but his relations with us are unfriendly for reasons hereinafter given. He refuses to look after our interests or
to listen to our grievances and seems wholly indifferent to our welfare. In the
Spring of 1874 we requested him, instead of giving us seeds to sow, to give us
their value in money as we could buy seeds to better advantage, but he became
angry, and refused to listen to us. II. The members of our tribe have long since
selected and received patents for all the land, to which they are entitle[d,] but
recently nearly if not quite all of the remaining lands of our Reservation have
been absorbed by new selections, made under the advice of bad white men and
with the knowledge of the Agent, and a list of such new selections is now in the
hands of the Secretary of the Interior upon which patents are expected to issue.
Such selections are generally made by poor ignorant widows who are improperly prevailed upon by the Interpreter and the white man to apply for the
lands. . . . IV. We charge the Interpreter with being wholly unfit and unworthy
of the position he fills and respectfully represent that he is intemperate, a fre-
quenter of bad houses, an oppressor of our poor and fully in league with bad
white men in the cruel work of stripping us of our lands. An additional evidence
of his unfitness is the manner of his obtaining the position. Knowing that he
could not obtain the recommendation of the chiefs he forged their names to his
application. V. Finally we call your attention to the alarming increase of drunkenness among our young men—Your laws prohibiting the sale of liquor to our
people are not enforced, and liquor is dealt out freely. When drunk our people
fall easy prey to the land pirates who are fattening upon ill gotten gains. Homestead after homestead is passing away beyond reach of our people, and their former owners reduced to a condition of beggary. We are helpless unless actively
aided and constantly protected by the Agent. When he turns against us as he
has done we are indeed helpless. We therefore turn to our Great Father for that
relief we so much need—and we will ever pray"—DS (by mark), DNA, RG 75,
Letters Received, Mackinac Agency. On Aug. 2, Lyman Bennett *et al.*, Isabella,
Mich., wrote to USG. "We, the undersigned, Chippewas of Saginaw, Swan
Creek and Black River respectfully represent to you as follows: It appears that
a former petition from us to you, respecting our rights and interests in the Indian Reservation in Isabella County, Michigan, reached you in good time and
that you cause it to be referred to our Agent Geo. I. Betts. He in turn referred
it to I. E. Arnold and John M. Collins, both of whom were complained of in said
first petition. As soon as the latter received it they at once called a meeting of
our people, and asked them if they had forwarded such a complaint to you. We
answered in the affirmative—and upon assuring themselves that our petition
had placed them in danger, they at once commenced to intimmidate us and
threaten us with harm unless we withdrew our first petition—Some of the

weak ones among our people and some addicted to the use of fire water have
yielded, but we your petitioners reaffirm the statements made to you in our former paper and again respectfully and earnestly ask you to take active and
efficient measures in our behalf—Said Arnold and Collins manipulated the new
selections and if not prevented by your strong arm they will reap a rich harvest
of spoil, to our injury and damage—. . . In conclusion we have to say that we are
trying to live a christian life and are getting our living by cultivating the soil
and this is our sole dependence—We combine together as one man in shaking
hands with our Great Father   Hoping he may have compassion upon his children is their prayer to the Great Spirit"—DS (68 signatures, by mark), *ibid.* On
April 17, 1876, USG nominated George W. Lee as agent, Mackinac Agency, to
replace George I. Betts.

On Oct. 15, 1875, Nancy Miner, L'Anse, Mich., had written to USG. "I have
the honor to state that [o]n the 19th of July last there was issued to me a Patent under the provisions of the treaty with the Chippewas of Lake Superior and
Mississipi of Sept. 30, 1854. and in said Patent there is a clause restricting me
in the power of alienating in any way said land 'without the consent of the President of the United States.' The land is discribed a follows viz the North half of
the North west quarter of Sec. fifteen in Township fifty North of Range thirty
three West, in the State of Michigan containing Eighty acres. Now therefore
your petitioner respectfully requests that you will grant her permission or the
power to dispose of said land and for the following reasons. 1st I am an aged female and widow entirely unable to clear or cultivate the land and have no children to assist me in doing so. 2nd To hold the land will be but a bill of expence
to me for taxes. 3rd My home is and has been for a number of years some forty
miles away from the Reservation, with no likelihoods or desire to remove from
it and lastly the only possible benifit the land could ever be to me would be to
sell it for what I could get for it and use the proceeds for my comfort and support which would be a great relief to me. I respectfully request you therefore to
either change my Patent and give me one in fee simple or in some other way em-
power me to sell my land—"—ALS, *ibid.* On Feb. 19, 1877, Mary Smith, Detroit, wrote to [USG]. "I beg your atention a few moments   will you please tell
me if it is possible for me to have value of this land that I have in Money as I have
Six children all girls who could not be able to clear the land and I want to make
a home for my children here in the city where I can give them a chance of being educated, . . ."—ALS, *ibid.*

1875, May 29.   Albert K. Owen, Washington, D. C., to USG. "I have the honor
to report that, in accordance with your instructions, I conferred, on the 26th.
inst., with Brig. Gen. A. A. Humphreys. The General said that if the President
desired that the territory lying between the 29th. and 31st. parallels and between Austin and the Rio Grande should be examined and reported that it could
readily be done—the extra expense being nothing to speak of. On the 27th.
inst. Brig. Gen. A. A. Humphreys consulted with the Secretary of War. On the
28th. inst. Secretary Belknap told me that he had not any money, but if Gen.
Humphreys could arrange the survey without expecting money from him that
he would not object. President Grant! the Northern, Central and Southern

routes to be examined have a distance of some 1,500 miles. Time required 3 months. Two engineers and myself and an escort of six men would complete examination and report with an extra expense to the Government of but $1,000. If President Grant will Commission me to make the examination and report, and allow an escort of two men, I will execute the required work with $500. In Mexico I examined and reported 5,000 miles of Mountain and Coast lines, for Gens. Rosecrans and Palmer, the last 2,000 miles at an expense of but $800. The section in question should not only be recorded at the Engineer Bureau for highway purposes; but for Military movements on the Mexican border the information gained would be valuable."—ALS, DNA, RG 77, Letters Received. On June 25, Secretary of War William W. Belknap wrote to Owen. "Your letter of the 29th ultimo, to the President in relation to the survey of the Austin and Topolovampa Railroad route was referred to the Chief of Engineers, who reports thereon as follows:—'The survey proposed by Mr. Owen is a part of a railroad route from Austin to the harbor of Topolovampo on the west coast of Mexico, proposed by him, and which he advocated before the Senate and House Committees at the last session, with a view of obtaining an appropriation of $20.000, for a War Department survey. The bill failed to receive the action of Congress and there are no funds applicable to the purpose at the disposal of this Department. It may be further remarked in reference to the cost of the survey between Austin and the Rio Grande, which is about one half of the distance from Austin to Topolovampo, contemplated by the bill before Congress, that the estimated cost of the survey of the entire route, $20,000, was thought by a Board of Engineers, to whom the question was referred, to be inadequate to the purpose.' It would seem to me judicious, under these circumstances, to await the action of the next Congress."—LS, *ibid.* A related letter is *ibid.* See *CR,* 44–1, 2730–32, 3704–6.

On Oct. 12, 1889, Jesse Root Grant, Jr., El Paso, wrote to Owen about a Mexican railroad project.—Copy, CSmH. See letter to Matías Romero, Aug. 10, 1880; Sanford A. Mosk, "A Railroad to Utopia," *Southwestern Social Science Quarterly,* XX, 3 (Dec., 1939), 243–59; Thomas A. Robertson, *A Southwestern Utopia* (Los Angeles, 1964).

1875, MAY 29.   William J. Pollock, Washington, D. C., to USG seeking "a suspension of the proceedings against him now pending in the District Court of the United States for the Southern District of the State of New York, for conspiracy to defraud the Revenue, . . . Your petitioner, alarmed, left the jurisdiction of the Court and has not been arrested. He has returned without means, and deeply desirous to enter into some business on a comparitively small capital which he can command by reason of an inheritance of which his wife has just become the recipient,   He has determined, if without the dishonor and ruin of a public prosecution it can be done, to enter upon the business of the manufacture of Chemicals, abandoning permantly that of importing, . . ."—LS, DNA, RG 60, Letters Received, N. Y. On May 18, Chester A. Arthur and Thomas Murphy, New York City, had each written to USG introducing Charles S. Spencer.—LS, *ibid.* Related papers are *ibid.* On Jan. 5, 1876, Attorney Gen. Edwards Pierrepont wrote to USG. "The enclosed paper is intended to be referred to the Solicitor General and not to the Attorney General. the Attorney General having been formerly counsel for Mr Pollock."—LS, *ibid.*, Letters from the President. Related papers include a written statement by Pollock describing Spencer's legal efforts on his behalf and unexpected "exorbitant demands" for money.—D (undated), *ibid.* USG endorsed these papers. "Refer to Solicitor Gen."—AE (undated), *ibid.* On Jan. 24, Solicitor Gen. Samuel F. Phillips wrote to USG summarizing Pollock's allegations. ". . . Even if, according to Mr. Pollock's theory, there has been a combination between the U. S. Attorney and Mr. Spencer, to serve the interests of the latter by a prostitution of a high office, it were better that the further prosecution of the case should be *compelled* (even), to the end that the affair may be *established* and *made public*—in which case the proper consequences to all concerned will be sure to follow. At present I submit that there is no ground for interfering. . . ."—LS, *ibid.*; copy, *ibid.*, Opinions.

Following the 1868 election, USG had received petitions recommending Spencer, "*President of the Union Republican Presidential Campaign Club of the City of New York,*" as U.S. attorney, Southern District, N. Y.—DS (undated), USG 3 and NHi. No appointment followed.

1875, MAY 31. William H. Miller, Jefferson City, Mo., to USG. "As all my former appeals to you for assistance have not yet met with any response whatever, I should feel discouraged thereby from attempting any further in that line, but my present condition of utter destitution causes me, like the drowning man catching at straws, to lay hold on one more hope that your heart may yet be moved to render me some assistance. You have seen me and talked with me, and 'though it was only for a few moments, yet that was sufficient time to enable a man of your intelligence and penetration to know my condition, physically and mentally. When I wrote you of difficulties of my position on account of the great prejudice of color in this State, you, probably could not credit it. It is worse now then it was then. The Democrats and the Grasshoppers have overrun the state, and between them both, the State is going to the Devil. Business of every sort languishes; people are starving, or to appease their hunger and clothe their nakedness, they are stealing, and thus augmenting the crowd now in the State Penitentiary! I am still Notary Public, but I have no salary, and no business, and no money; nor have I any friends who are able to help me. You can help me, if you will. Of I want money, or employment by which I may earn money. I am so reduced, every way, that I cannot furnish, nor obtain, the means of leaving this place;—otherwise, I would throw up my Commission and go to some other state, and there renew my efforts to make an honest living. Can you not give me some position,—a clerkship—Postmasters position in some state as South Carolina or Mississippi? You may recollect that I stated in my former communications that I was born in Mississippi. Or can you not give me some small post in some foreign country similar to that held by Messrs. Bassett & Turner? Well; perhaps you may think that I am very bold in making such requests of you; but sir, I am suffering, and hence this is no time to give way to any ideas or scruples of a mawkish modesty. As to my physical qualifications, you have seen them. As to my mental qualifications, I have before stated that I am a regular graduate. But in consequence of never having held a position commensurate with my acquirements, since I left College, I am somewhat rusty now; nevertheless, like a blade of true steel, a little rubbing up will soon make me as bright as ever. Relying on your honor as a Gentleman, I respectfully entreat an early reply."—ALS, DNA, RG 59, Letters of Application and Recommendation. Miller served as notary public, Cole County. On Sept. 7 and on July 17, 1876, Miller wrote to USG. ". . . Should the democracy succeed in securing the executive branch of the government, next general election, as they are aiming to do, it is very improbable that any Colored man would ever receive a governmental appointment; if, even, they did not decapitate all those whom they might find holding such positions, on their accession to power. But, I hope better things of the Country and the Republican Party. At any rate, I shall not give up the Old Republican Ship as long as there's a plank left of her." ". . . A Colored man of good natural and acquired abilities, can hope for, and aspire to, nothing beyond an ordinary existence in this State. The State seems to be hopelessly Democratic. The Republicans have little or no energy or 'get up' in them. Indeed, they are a lukewarm, poke easy set—wholly lacking in the requisite enthusiasm for the political principles which they profess to hold; while, on the contrary, the Democrats are as lively as crickets, and equally as noisy. . . ."—ALS, *ibid.* Related letters are *ibid.* No appointment followed.

On Sept. 28, Miller wrote to USG. "Yesterday evening John H. Chambers, of Fulton, Callaway County, Missouri, discharged Solder formerly private in Co., F, 60th U. S. C. T., called at my office, and desired me to lay his case before you as follows, viz; While at the Battle of Big Creek, Arkansas, on or about 4th July 1863, while in the line of duty, fighting the enemy, he was wounded by a musket ball, which struck him in the right hand, near the wrist, cutting the cords, and injuring said hand in such a manner as to cause it to close and become comparatively useless. . . . And now, he respectfully prays that you, the General of the Army & President of the United States, will look into this matter and see why he is, as he thinks, so unjustly denied an Invalid Pension. . . . Don't be alarmed, Sir; I am not asking for anything for myself."—ALS, *ibid.*, RG 48, Miscellaneous Div., Letters Received. On Aug. 30 and on Feb. 14, 1877, Miller wrote to USG on behalf of veterans seeking pension increases.—ALS, *ibid.*

1875, MAY.   "A. Rebel." to USG. "Prepare for your assassination be fore the 31st   Let no one see this or Instant Death."—L, USG 3.

[*1875*], JUNE 4.   To Levi P. Luckey, from Long Branch. "PLEASE SEND TO MRS. ZEBRIGHTS FIVE HUNDRED AND FIVE ELEVEOTH ST. AND GET KATY DENNIS TRUNK AND SEND IT HERE BY EXPRESS."—Telegram received, DLC-USG, IB. USG, family members, and Orville E. Babcock had taken a train to Long Branch on June 3.—*Washington Evening Star,* June 3, 1875.

1875, JUNE 4.   Governor John L. Beveridge of Ill. to USG. "I wish to add my testimonial to the worth and honesty of Major James R. Hayden of Washington Territory, and recommend him for the appointment of U. S. Marshal of that Territory, or any other office."—ALS, DNA, RG 60, Records Relating to Appointments. Related papers are *ibid.* On Sept. 6, Brig. Gen. Oliver O. Howard, Portland, Ore., wrote to USG. "I write you privately, at the request of a friend of yours, with the hope of calling special attention, to Major James R. Hayden. He and many of his friends wish, very much, to get him the position of a Paymaster in the Army. You are doubtless familiar with his excellent record during the War, and of his persistant friendship to yourself since the war. I think he is an able and upright man and therefore join with others in commending him to your favorable consideration. That you might call him fully to mind I have had the accompanying transcript of his record prepared in the form of memoranda."—LS, *ibid.*, RG 94, Applications for Positions in War Dept. The enclosure is *ibid.* On Jan. 10, 1870, USG had nominated James R. Hayden as assessor of Internal Revenue, Washington Territory; on May 18, 1876, USG nominated Hayden as collector of Internal Revenue, Washington Territory.

1875, JUNE 4.   U.S. Representative Jeremiah Haralson of Ala., Selma, to USG protesting the removal of Robert A. Moseley as postmaster, Talladega. ". . . He is the Proprietor of the only two Republican papers now published in this State, and he is a true and ardent Republican, and a strong supporter of the present administration. I can but believe that he has been removed from the position of Postmaster by the misrepresentations of some parties who are envious and jealous of him without a sufficient cause. Without these papers the Republicans of this State will not have any medium through which they can speak, and I think it the duty of the great National Republican party to encourage such measures as will have a tendency to keep the organization of the Party up, and without the assistance of some Federal appointment through which they can maintain these journals, it will be very difficult here in the South, and especially in Alabama, for the party to keep up their papers. . . ."—LS, DNA, RG 56, Appraisers of Customs Applications. On Dec. 9, USG again nominated Moseley as postmaster after Joseph H. Parsons had declined the office.

1875, JUNE 5.   To Secretary of the Interior Columbus Delano. "Offer Axtell Governorship New Mexico and appoint Emery in his place if he accepts. Emery may be appointed to New Mexico otherwise."—Calvin Horn, *New Mexico's Troubled Years: The Story of the Early Territorial Governors* (Albuquerque, 1963), p. 175. On the same day, Delano had telegraphed to USG. "Geddings Gov of New Mexico is dead   who do you desire as his successor   Mr Ewing will start this evening & see you"—Telegram received, DLC-USG, IB. Also on June 5, Chief Justice Morrison R. Waite wrote to USG. "Gen. Charles Ewing is, as I understand, a candidate for appointment to the office of Gov. of New-Mexico, now vacant by reason of the death of the late incumbent. My long acquaintance with and great respect for his father, naturally interests me in his f[a]mily, and I shall feel personally much gratified, if you find it consistent with your own views of the public good to give him the position—"—ALS (press), DLC-Morrison R. Waite. On June 8, Delano telegraphed to USG, Long Branch. "Send by mail today appointment of axtell for New Mexico and Emery for Utah"—Telegram received, DLC-USG, IB. On Dec. 9, USG nominated Samuel B. Axtell as governor of New Mexico Territory to replace Marsh Giddings, who had died on June 3. For George W. Emery, see *PUSG*, 23, 218–19.

1875, JUNE 6.   U.S. Senator William M. Stewart of Nev., San Francisco, to USG. "My son in law, Lieutenant R. C. Hooker, has what I regard a good opportunity to go into business in San Francisco—He has applied for a year's leave of absence—You will confer a great favor on him and me if you will order the Navy Dept to grant his request."—ALS, DNA, RG 45, ZB, Richard C. Hooker. On June 9, Stewart telegraphed to USG, Long Branch, on the same subject.—Telegram received, *ibid.* A clerk endorsed these papers. "a leave of absence for six months may be granted at the expiration of which another six months leave will be granted if the Officer desires to resign at the end of that time."—E (undated), *ibid.* Lt. Richard C. Hooker resigned as of June 30, 1876.

1875, JUNE 10.   William J. Murtagh, *Washington National Republican,* to USG. *"Personal* . . . I am very much interested in the case of the Rev Dr Atkinson, a most worthy gentleman and christian. I have endeavored to have him appointed chaplain, but he was found to be over age. You will bear me witness that it is not my habit to add to the pressure which you undergo for office, and I do so reluctantly on this occasion. I would be greatly gratified if he could have a Consulship anywhere in Europe at a salary of abt $3000. I would make application to the Secretary of state if he were friendly to me, and this is my excuse for writing you."—ALS, DLC-USG, IB.

1875, JUNE 11.   To Secretary of the Treasury Benjamin H. Bristow, from Long Branch. "This will introduce to the Sec. of the Treas. Mr. Carson, formerly of South Carolina, grand-son of the late Mr. Pettigrew, so well known for his loyalty to the Govt, as well as for his high social standing. Mr. Carson will state his business and I will only add that if he can be accommodated I will be pleased."—L (signature clipped), DNA, RG 56, Applications. On June 8, William Carson, New York City, had written to Bristow. ". . . I am a grandson of the late James L Petigru of South Carolina and am one of the few young Carolinians who remained loyal during the Rebellion—I lost all my property during the struggle and was accounted a good enough patriot to be drafted into the National forces in New York and reported for duty—I am out of work now and should be glad to have a Whiskey Guagership out West or some place in the Treasury at Washington—. . ."—ALS, *ibid.* Related papers are *ibid.* On March 10, U.S. Representative Stephen A. Hurlbut of Ill. had written to USG. "Mr William Carson seeks an appointment as Lieut. in the Army. He is the grandson of James L Petigru of Charleston. My personal obligations to Mr Petigru with whom I studied Law are very great, but I know that the Country owes him far more than they can pay. I was sent to Charleston by Prest Lincoln ten days before Fort Sumpter was fired upon—& found Mr Petigru the only outspoken Union man in that City and so he continued to the day of his death. I need say nothing of his eminent ability and great public service. His daughter Mrs Carson mother of the applicant, inherited & exercised the feelings of her father & Mr Wm Carson stood ready in New York under the draft in 1864—to bear arms for the Country. All the other members of Mr Petigru's family his son & younger daughter Mrs King have died—& this applicant is the eldest representative of the family. I think he has the material for a good soldier and good officer and I desire to give to his application all the influence personal and official which I possess"—ALS, *ibid.*, RG 94, Applications for Positions in War Dept. On Dec. 11, 1876, John C. Hamilton, New York City, wrote to USG on the same subject.—ALS, *ibid.* As of Sept. 30, 1877, William Carson worked as an Internal Revenue clerk in Washington, D. C. See William H. Pease and Jane H. Pease, *James Louis Petigru: Southern Conservative, Southern Dissenter* (Athens, Ga., 1995), pp. 127–29, 160–61; Jane H. Pease and William H. Pease, *A Family of Women: The Carolina Petigrus in Peace and War* (Chapel Hill, 1999), pp. 166, 176–77, 270–72.

1875, June 11.   William P. Jones, Nashville, to USG. "My son—Quintard L Jones solicits of yr Excellency an appointment to West-Point   He is diligent industrious sober & moral—In its peril, I was an unfaltering friend to the Goverm't have been yr personal friend & supporter, as well as State Senator Reprsenting this—the Nashville district. I may further say of my son, he is 20 yrs of age & pretty well advanced in his studies   Though I have written you from time to time—saying 'well done' etc. I have at no time solicited a reply. I however, beg of you a response to this"—ALS, DNA, RG 94, Correspondence, USMA. On June 12, William F. Prosser, Nashville, wrote to USG. "Dr W. P. Jones, late State Senator from this county, for some time Superintendent of the Insane Asylum of this State, and always a firm, consistent and uncompromising friend of the U. S. Government is, I am informed, applying for an appointment to West Point for one of his sons. . . ."—ALS, *ibid.* Related papers are *ibid.* Quintard L. Jones did not attend USMA; his father, a physician dedicated to the mentally ill, especially advocated facilities for blacks.

1875, June 12.   John R. Barret, Louisville, to USG. "I have a young friend here, born & raised in this city, who has been well off, but by his great generosity, & some bad luck in business, has about lost all his estate. He was in the Confederate Army during the War, but he is a great friend & admirer of yours. I should feel under great obligations, if you would give him an office of Some Kind. He has travelled over Europe several times, is well educated, speaks almost all the languages, & is a high toned elegant gentleman. He would be a splendid representative abroad, would make a splendid Consul. His name is William Johnston. He was capt. in the Confederate Army. I am acting upon my own motion in asking a position for Capt Johnston."—ALS, DNA, RG 59, Letters of Application and Recommendation. No appointment followed.

1875, June 12.   William W. Duffield to USG. "Your petitioner William. W. Duffield of Inkster, Wayne county Michigan respectfully represents: that he served in the Army of the United States as a line and staff officer of Volunteers during the War with Mexico, and also as a field and general officer of Volunteers during the War of the Rebellion from May 1861 until disabled from further service by two severe gunshot wounds received at the battle of Murfreesboro Tennessee. Wherefore your petitioner prays your Excellency to select his only son William. W. Duffield Jr to fill any vacancy in the appointments at large of cadets at West Point which is now or may hereafter be placed at your Excellency's disposal . . ."—ALS, DNA, RG 94, Correspondence, USMA. Undated favorable endorsements include one from U.S. Representative Alpheus S. Williams of Mich. "This candidate for a Cadetship is of a family distinguished for generations for its patriots & scholars   His Grandfather (Rev.d Dr Geo Duffield) was well known to the President—. . ."—AES, *ibid.* William W. Duffield, Jr., did not attend USMA; his grandfather, George, who died in 1868, had been a Presbyterian minister and temperance advocate in Detroit.

1875, June 14.   Charles E. Mayer, chairman, Republican State Executive Committee, Mobile, to USG. "One Richards is seeking collectorship of Internal Revenue at Mobile   The best interests of government & party require retention of present incumbent"—Telegram received (at 10:17 P.M.), DNA, RG 56, Letters Received from the President. On Jan. 5, 1876, Charles W. Buckley, probate judge, Montgomery, wrote to USG. "I have the honor to hand you herewith a petition signed by a few leading Republicans of Alabama in favor of Ex. Gov William H. Smith for collector of the Port of Mobile. The request is based on information that there is shortly to be a change in that office. Ex. Gov Smith is recommended in furtherance of a recent movement in the State for harmony and a thorough organization of our party for the coming Presidential campaign. This movement has been generally supported and attended with gratifying results. In all these efforts, Gov Smith has been called upon to take a prominent part, and his name is suggested to you as the representative of the best elements and aims of the best and controlling Republicans of Alabama."—ALS, *ibid.*, Collector of Customs Applications. The enclosure is *ibid.* On Dec. 1, 1873, USG had nominated Louis H. Mayer as collector of Internal Revenue, 1st District, Ala. Mayer continued in office. See Sarah Woolfolk Wiggins, *The Scalawag in Alabama Politics, 1865–1881* (University, Ala., 1977), pp. 89, 109–13, 121–23.

On June 17, 1875, John W. Youman, Mobile, wrote to USG. ". . . I would have held my peace, and tried, to stand insult, injury and political calumny, but the pressure is so great that I am at last compelled to give way, and ask at your hands some relief or at least an alleviation of our present condition,   Politically, I was appointed by the Treasury by influence of Genl Canby, now dead, as Hull Inspector of steam vessels at Mobile Alabama, and am now turned out and my place occupied by one of Mobile's rankest and most bitter democrat Mr Geo. Blakeslee, . . . Mr William Rogers Supervising Inspector appointed Mr Blakeslee and knew at the time of making the appointment knew that he was opposed to the administration and knew of his cursing you and the entire cabinet calling them a damn set of thieves. I heard on one occasion when Mr Blakeslee was reading the Report of the investigation of Vice President Colfax, before the Credit Mobilier committee, I heard him repeat this language of you and the Cabinet and all this in the presence of at least one dozen persons. This man Blakeslee was nominated by Mr Rogers and the Hon Richard Busteed the then district Judge appointed him. Mr Rogers alone is responsible for his appointment, because when Judge Busteed signed the nomination or appointment he was in a beastly state of intoxication, and was not able to tell what he was doing and did not even know Blakeslee from any other man. If a man is to be judged by his acts and the company he keeps I think I could be safe in saying that Mr Rogers is a democrat. . . . The native Republicans control all the parties interests, do all the work at the Polls, and do the drudgery generally only to be told that they can not hold office under this administration. If there is any

thing or a place to give out, some one North of Mason and Dixons line is
brought here to fill it,   Is this Just, where we have plenty to fill any position
they can offer? No sir my word for it, the present parties in power under the administration, can not do anything to help the party and do not even know the
names of the streets of the city. Now sir Mr. R. H. Goodloe is our present Collector, and has a son also in his department—he is from away up in North Alabama and during his appointment to this place for the whole time since he has
been in office, I do not think he has been in his office two weeks, . . . In my experience I find after ten years in the Republican party that the whole native element or scalawags as they are called, are the most re-reliable, they are the one's
who are feared at the polls and are of necessity the most despised and can not be
wined and dined. The Carpet Bagger is more pliant and for a few dollars can be
gotten to forget his duty at times, but not so with the scalawags, he is uncompromising, staunch and true, and has some little interest in his own town to
check him in any acts of fraud that he might undertake. . . . There is not a Republican in office outside of the Custom House, there is not even a Policeman, and
the Democrats are sworn never to employ a Republican, why not adopt the same
rule with them? If the democrats are going to fight it out on this line, it is the
more reason that the government should at once purge our offices at this place
of all democrats, and all white washed Republicans, and supply their places with
Scalawags, the democracy can not tamper with them, and you will never again
have what is called a split in the party; select Mobile men, and we will carry Mobile, not only in the coming election, but at all times, . . . I organised the Loyal
League, presided over the first negro convention to select candidates to the first
Republican Legislature that ever met in Alabama, I voted for the negro constitution for the State of Alabama, that made us our free schools, and for all this I
am stiled the arch scalawag of the state. I never shouldered a gun during the
war, I never served the rebellion a day, I never drew a dollar from the confederacy for services or in any other shape—I did not pilot the first gun boat into
Mobile as is charged to me by the democrats, I wish I had been afforded the opportunity and pleasure of doing so—I was rendering service at another point
and I was rewarded by General Canby's influence in getting me appointed as
Inspector of Hulls for the 1st District of Alabama at Mobile. I remained in said
office about two years when one H. C. Baldwin the steam boat King of Mobile
became displeased with me because I would not look over the fraud on the certificate hereto attached and enclosed. The figure five erased and the figure six
forged, this and similar acts led to indictments against me by Mr Southworth
the District Attorney. Mr Southworth sent for me, two weeks before the grand
jury met and told me if I did not withdraw an order that I had served on the
Steamer Reindeer for some repairs that I would be indicted, this I did not do,
consequently the indictments followed, and I was indicted. At that time the U. S.
Courts was nefariously used by Southworth to intimidate & further his ends by
threatening indictments to carry his points,   when a Republican was to be gotten out of the way, all that was necessary was to get Southworth to indict and
O. H. Cotton the Deputy Marshal to pack Juries to convict and it was done in-
stanter. The Marshal's office is another rotten hole,   I am not prepared to connect him with any fraud, but his deputy Mr O. H. Cotton has been guilty of acts

which is a curse to the country, . . . I ask that a special agent may inquire into all my statements, and am ready to prove any and all that I have herein stated, though if an agent comes here, spies in Washington always communicate with these men, and they are always ready to wine and dine the agent sent, and he is generally sent back with his eyes closed, unable to find anything out, If you can send a man that can not be bought and we can get at him, I think that matters will come to light equalling the Whiskey ring. . . ."—ALS, DNA, RG 56, Letters Received from the President. The enclosure is *ibid.* On Jan. 29, following recommendations from George M. Duskin, U.S. attorney, Southern District, Ala., and former U.S. Attorney John P. Southworth, USG had pardoned Youman from a $500 penalty for "being pecuniarily interested in a steam vessel, while holding the office of Inspector of Steam Vessels," upon condition that he pay "costs of the prosecution."—Copy, *ibid.*, RG 59, General Records. On Aug. 10, 1876, Youman, New Orleans, wrote to USG. "Notwithstanding your pardon & the remission of the fine of $500 00 & because I did not have the money to pay the cost of court, I was put in jail by that reconstructed rebel Duskin now at present Dist Atty at Mobile Ala, he remarked to Judge Bruce, that he would like to send me to the penitentiary, it is more then he has ever done, for those Ku Klux rebels that was brought before him for murdering union men in open day, he is a Rebel convinced against his will & is of the same opinion still, he knew as well as everybody that the charge against me was false & malicious, although he prosecuted me as if every cent of money in the treasury depended upon my conviction, that Kind of Republicans made by reconstructing rebels has been the cause of the defeat of the party in the south . . . President I beg you to give me a letter of recommendation to Marshal Packard or Collector Casey enabling me to make a living for my family—I must make a living out of the party, for I have made a breach between myself & the rebels, that can never be healed, I cannot ask them for anything without making concessions & I would rather starve then do it. . . ."—ALS, *ibid.*, RG 60, Letters from the President.

1875, JUNE 15. F. Kauffmann, Stuttgart, Germany, to USG. "For the first time in my life I regret that I have not a well known name, and that I must address you as a plain private citizen.—As a man, however, I have a right to speak in the name of humanity, and, in that name, to demand great things. I conjure you: Put an end to the horrors in Cuba! Give freedom to the slaves and the the doubly enslaved masters of the slaves! Give the Indian paradise, now desolated by demons, back to mankind! A good work needs no thanks, but, without seeking it, you can earn the deepest gratitude, and be placed by posterity by the side of Abraham Lincoln."—ALS (in German), DNA, RG 59, Miscellaneous Letters; translation, *ibid.*

1875, JUNE 17. 2nd Lt. Harrison G. Otis, 4th Cav., "Cantonment on Sweet Water," Tex., to USG. "I have the honor to address you a few lines, combining business with pleasure, if I do not encroach too heavily on your many past kindnesses towards me. To begin the matter before me, I wish to ask you if you will order me to report to the Artillery school at Fortress Monroe, at the beginning of the next session, may, 1876. I am very desirous of graduating there, and I ap-

ply to you as the only source through which that end may be attained. . . . It has
been quite a long time since I have heard from Buck; but moving about as much
as has been my lot of late, has played sad havoc with my mails. Shall write to
him by this opportunity. Please give my kindest regards to Mrs. Grant, who I
hope is in excellent health."—ALS, DNA, RG 94, ACP, 2965 1874. On March 7,
1876, AG Edward D. Townsend wrote to Otis, Fort Elliott, Tex. "The President directs that you report in person on or about the 1st of May next to the
Commanding Officer Artillery School, Fort Monroe, Virginia for duty at the
School."—Copy, *ibid.* On Aug. 1, Otis, Fort Monroe, Va., wrote to USG. "I have
the honor to request that in the event of United States signal service being organized into a Corps I may be transferred to it"—ALS, *ibid.*

On Dec. 29, Otis, Fort Fetterman, Wyoming Territory, telegraphed to "Mr
U S Grant," presumably Ulysses S. Grant, Jr. "Expedition returned today
Letters received will I be ordered to Monroe or is an application to adjutant
General necessary being temporarily relieved from duty there wish to get
back as soon as possible"—Telegram received (on Jan. 3, 1877), *ibid.* Probably
on Jan. 3 or 4, 1877, Grant, Jr., wrote to Townsend. *"Confidential . . .* The President says that he would like to have Lieut Otis recalled now, since the expedition is over and he would not like to see the young man suffer by his too great
willingness to be where there was duty."—ALS, *ibid.* See *PUSG,* 20, 261, 329.

1875, JUNE 18.   Sister M. Mercy, Convent of Mercy, West Troy, N. Y., to USG.
"Having heard of your charity and generosity to those in need, I take the liberty of soliciting your aid in behalf of our little community here. Though we are
of a different creed, I trust you will not deem it an intrusion on my part. I am
very much in need of funds at present I was obliged to make some improvements owing to the dampness of the grounds around our Convent, for the comfort of our poor children. For any donation you may kindly send you will have
the prayers and gratitude of our Sisters & children."—ALS, OFH.

[*1875*], JUNE 19.   To Secretary of War William W. Belknap from Long Branch.
"IF THE ASSIGNMENT OF GEL. BARNARD TO DUTY WITH HIS
BREVET RANK IS TO INTERFERE WITH HIS SUBORDINATION TO
THE ORDERS OF THE CHIEF OF HIS CORPS THE ORDER SHOULD
BE REVOKED. SEE GEN. HUMPHRIES IN THIS."—Telegram received,
DNA, RG 94, ACP, 1745 1874. On the same day, Belknap had telegraphed to
Orville E. Babcock, Long Branch. "was the president aware when the order of assignment of Genl Barnard to duty in accordance with his Brevet rank was made
that such assignment would cause him to rank Genl Humphreys I was not but
issued the order without inquiry this assignment cannot legally be limited to
his duty on the light house board it would seem that Genl Barnard propose under this assignment to claim authority to reside in washington & also to claim
that he is not subordinate to the chief of engineers. under The circumstances
it seems to me that the order should be revoked please present this subject to
the Prest the information above referred to comes from letter written by Genl
Barnard to the adjutant general"—Telegram received, DLC-USG, IB.

1875, JUNE 19. Secretary of War William W. Belknap to USG. "I have the honor to transmit copy of correspondence in regard to the flight of Hualpai Indians from the Colorado Reservation and their return to their former home in the mountains; and of the endorsement of General Schofield requesting that the matter be brought to your notice."—LS (press), DNA, RG 94, Letters Received, 4727 1874. On May 24, Maj. Gen. John M. Schofield, San Francisco, had endorsed related papers. "The Hualpai Indians have been our firm friends for many years, and our active allies whenever their services have been required against the hostile Apaches. In return for their fidelity they have been treated with great injustice and cruelty. They were forced to leave their homes in the Mountains and go upon a reservation in the Colorado desert, where they have suffered from the extreme heat, to which they were unaccustomed, from disease, and from hunger. This was done, in spite of the protest of the Military commanders who were familiar with the wants of these Indians and were anxious to repay by kind treatment the faithful services they had rendered. The Indians were bitterly opposed to this change, and it was only the great influence which Genl. Crook and Captain Byrne had acquired over them that enabled the removal to be made without war. The Indian Agent having seen fit to relinquish the aid of this powerful influence the effect was at once manifest in the return of the Hualpais to their former homes. I am decidedly opposed to the use of any coercive measures to force them back upon the Colorado reservation. The injustice and bad faith shown by the government toward the Hualpais and the Indians which Genl Crook had collected upon the Verde reservation are calculated to undo as far as possible the good work which Genl. Crook and his troops had accomplished with so much wisdom and gallantry. It is useless to attempt to disguise the fact that such treatment of the Indians is in violation of the just and humane policy prescribed by the President and a disgrace to any civilized country. I respectfully suggest that this subject be laid before the President, as being worthy of his personal consideration, involving the question of peace or war, the preservation or sacrifice of many lives, and the saving or expenditure of millions of money. It is simply one of many illustrations of a self-evident principle, viz; that the management of Indian affairs, by temporary, poorly paid, irresponsible Agents, must mean, in general, extravagance, dishonesty, folly injustice, inhumanity and war."—ES, *ibid.* On Sept. 25, John A. Tonner, agent, Colorado River Indian Reserve, Arizona Territory, reported to Edward P. Smith, commissioner of Indian Affairs. ". . . Upon the approach of the planting season I removed the Hualpai Indians from the control of the military to a point near the agency, intending to teach them planting, and oblige them to labor for their rations; but they went off the reservation to their old range, saying they would not work or return to the reservation; after a consultation with the commanding general of the department, we decided to let them remain during good behavior. They have, thus far, kept their promise, and given no trouble. . . ."— *HED*, 44-1-1, part 5, I, 712.

1875, JUNE 22. Pedro P. Rioseco, New York City, to USG. "I have taken the liberty to address you, knowing how great is your benevolence. Sir, I am a Mexican. My family have sent me to this country that I may pursue my studies at the Military Academy at West Point, and thus follow the career of my father, General Rioseco, who fell a victim to the French bullets. Now, in order to be admitted at West Point, I require some recommendations, and although I have some already, such as that of Mr. Mariscal, Mexican Minister in this Republic, I nevertheless take the liberty of asking you, directly, to give me yours, on no other grounds than those of my poverty and my condition as an orphan, not doubting that you will grant me this small favor."—ALS (in Spanish), DNA, RG 94, Unsuccessful Cadet Applications; translations, *ibid.*; *ibid.*, RG 59, Miscellaneous Letters.

1875, JUNE 25. Secretary of the Treasury Benjamin H. Bristow to USG. "I have the honor to hand you herewith a communication from the Commissioner of Internal Revenue making certain statements affecting Internal Revenue Collector Rose of the Cleveland District. Mr. Pratt expresses the opinion that there should be a new Collector appointed for that District, in which I fully concur. I would be pleased to receive your direction in the matter, and, inasmuch as neither Mr. Pratt nor I have anyone to suggest for the office, would thank you to name the successor if you concur in the opinion that Mr. Rose should be removed."—LS (press), DLC-Benjamin H. Bristow. On Dec. 8, USG nominated Charles B. Pettengill as collector of Internal Revenue, 18th District, Ohio, to replace Peter Rose, suspended on July 10.

1875, JUNE 25. Secretary of the Interior Columbus Delano to USG. "S B Dutcher Pension Agent in N Y tenders his resignation requesting immediate appointment his successor on account of business arrangements   If you will name the successor I will forward papers immedy"—Telegram received, DLC-USG, IB. Jacob M. Patterson, Jr., replaced Silas B. Dutcher as pension agent, New York City. See *New York Times,* Aug. 15, 1875, June 1, 1899.

[*1875*], JUNE 26. To Orville E. Babcock from Long Branch. "THE SEC. OF WAR MAY APPOINT W. H. RAPLEY TO WEST POINT FROM THE DISTRICT OF COLUMBIA."—Telegram received, DNA, RG 94, Correspondence, USMA. On April 8, Judge Arthur MacArthur, D. C. Supreme Court, had written to USG recommending William H. Rapley on the strength of his education and family's past military services.—LS, *ibid.* On June 26, USG endorsed this letter. "Refered to the Sec. of War. Application approved."—AES, *ibid.* Related papers are *ibid.* Rapley entered USMA but did not graduate.

[*1875, June*]. Governor Cushman K. Davis of Minn. *et al.* to USG. "The Undersigned citizens of the State of Minnesota would respectfully bring to your notice Professor Alexander Loemans, Artist, a citizen of this State and a resident of the city of Minneapolis and most heartily recommend him as a fit and proper person to receive the appointment of United States Consul at any post where a thorough knowledge of the French language is requisite. Prof Loemans has been a citizen of the United States for more than thirty years, and is a gentleman of the strictest integrity, speaks and writes the French language with fluency and is the fullest meaning of the word a gentleman: His appointment as Consul would give great pleasure to your petitioners"—DS (55 signatures, undated), DNA, RG 59, Letters of Application and Recommendation. Related papers are *ibid.* No appointment followed. See Peggy and Harold Samuels, *The Illustrated Biographical Encyclopedia of Artists of the American West* (Garden City, N. Y., 1976), p. 292.

1875, July 2. Levi P. Luckey to William R. Holloway, postmaster, Indianapolis. "The application of Senator Morton for leave for Lieut. Reynolds has been recd. from Long Branch and the President has approved it for one year. Gen. Babcock says, in a note to me, that the President telegraphed to Washington upon receipt of a telegram and is under the impression that sick leave was granted early in June."—Copy, DLC-USG, II, 2. 1st Lt. William F. Reynolds, USMA 1867, began a year's leave as of July 24.

1875, July 13. Secretary of the Treasury Benjamin H. Bristow to USG. "I have the honor to inform you that the resignation of William Ames as Collector of Internal Revenue for the district of Rhode Island has been accepted, to take effect upon the appointment and qualification of a successor. Senator Anthony, Honorable L. M. Ballou and B. F. Eames unite in recommending William E. Pierce for the position. Mr. Pierce formerly served in the Internal Revenue service, and is highly recommended by the honorable gentlemen above mentioned. Senator Burnside presents the name of Col. Elisha H. Rhodes, and states that he is an active working Republican, an honest and intelligent citizen, and was a most gallant and meritorious soldier during the war. I have no doubt that they both are suitable candidates for appointment, but after a personal conference with Senator Burnside I am inclined to favor Col. Rhodes and would be pleased to have your instructions in the matter."—Copy, DNA, RG 56, Letters Sent. Elisha H. Rhodes replaced William Ames as collector of Internal Revenue, R. I. See Robert Hunt Rhodes, ed., *All For The Union: The Civil War Diary and Letters of Elisha Hunt Rhodes* (New York, 1991).

1875, July 14. Secretary of the Treasury Benjamin H. Bristow to USG. "The Commissioner of Internal Revenue and Supervisor A. P. Tutton, having recommended the consolidation of the 1st and 2nd collection districts of Pennsylvania, which recommendation I deem for the best interests of the service. I have the honor to transmit herewith for your approval, should you concur, the necessary order carrying into effect the proposed consolidation."—Copy, DNA, RG 56, Letters Sent. On July 16, Orville E. Babcock, Long Branch, wrote to Bristow. "In the consolidation in Pa. the President thinks Elliott should be retained"—Copy, DLC-USG, II, 2.

1875, July 14. Secretary of the Treasury Benjamin H. Bristow to USG. "The Commissioner of Internal Revenue has addressed a communication to me recommending the removal of Mr. Flanigan, Collector of Internal Revenue for the First District of Michigan (Detroit), for incompetency and inattention to his duties. The Commissioner transmits with his letter, memoranda from the heads of divisions of his Bureau, all concurring in the statement that Mr. Flanigan has been neglectful of his duties, and that he has failed to give attention to directions from the office, and to make reports when required by the Commissioner of Internal Revenue under the law. It is also alleged that his reports, when made, are incorrect and incomplete, and that the business of his office is not well conducted. For these reasons the Commissioner requests the removal of Mr. Flanigan and the appointment of a competent successor. The reasons given by the Commissioner seem to require a change in that District. Should you concur in this opinion, I will thank you to suggest the name of a successor, or if none occurs to you, to advise me with whom I shall confer on the subject."—LS (press), DLC-Benjamin H. Bristow. On July 28, USG suspended Mark Flanigan as collector of Internal Revenue, 1st District, Mich.; Luther S. Trowbridge replaced Flanigan. See *PUSG*, 20, 357.

1875, July 15. Attorney Gen. Edwards Pierrepont to USG. "Herewith I enclose copy letter this day received. Shall I prepare the papers for the President to carry out the wishes of the Senator? If so shall there be a suspension or a request to resign? The record of Mr Lammon the present Marshal so far as my office reveals is good; no complaint appears and no fault in his accounts."— Copy, DNA, RG 60, Letters Sent to Executive Officers. On July 19, Orville E. Babcock, Long Branch, wrote to Pierrepont. "The President directs me to say in reply to your letter of the 15th; that he has no objection to your requesting the resignation of the present Marshal, and appointing the gentleman named by the two Senators from the State of Nevada—"—ALS, *ibid.*, Records Relating to Appointments. On July 2, U.S. Senators John P. Jones and William Sharon of Nev., San Francisco, had written to USG. "We have the honor to unite in the request that R. S. Clapp, Esq, be appointed United States Marshal for the State of Nevada, in place of Mr George I. Lammon, the present incumbent. Mr Clapp's residence is at Pioche, Nevada."—LS, *ibid.* On Nov. 17, R. S. Clapp, Carson City, wrote to USG resigning as marshal, Nev.—ALS, *ibid.*, Letters Received, Nev. On Jan. 31, 1876, USG nominated Augustus Ash as marshal, Nev.

On Aug. 5, 1875, Robert H. Lindsay, U.S. attorney, Nev., Virginia City, had written to USG resigning his office.—ALS, *ibid.* On Aug. 11, Jones and Sharon wrote to USG recommending Charles S. Varian to replace Lindsay.—LS, *ibid.*, Records Relating to Appointments. On Dec. 15, USG nominated Varian as U.S. attorney, Nev.

1875, July 15. Manuelito and eleven others, Fort Wingate, New Mexico Territory, to USG. "We the undersigned Principal Chiefs of and representing the Navajo Nation, in council assembled at Ft Wingate New Mex this 15th day of July 1875 do respectfully, for the preservation of peace in our nation, repeat our petition to the Great Father in Washington made the 28th day of May 1875. First   For the removal of Agent W. F. M Arny   Because a man in whom the Navajo Nation has no faith cannot promote the welfare of our people   Because Agent W. F. M. Arny does not fail to create the opportunity to enrich himself at the expense of the people he should protect. Because he is trifling, vacilating and unreliable in all matters connected with his Agency and the people composing the Navajo Nation. Because of the parade, pomp and circumstance of all his actions and sorroundings. His high sounding and meaningless words; the

application of the property of our people to the support of his personal popularity and ridiculous dignity, his waste of public property and missaplication
of public funds, designed to be expended for our use. Because we beleive he is
false to his trusts as a public servant, and false to the people whose interests he
should serve   Because he has never talked candidly to our people, nor have we
ever discovered that he has ever uttered the truth in our councils. Second   And
because we desire to have an Agent in whom we all may have confidence; who
will give to us that which our Great Father has provided and directed; one who
will distribute with the least ostentation our annuities and our rations; who will
not waste the nations money, in travelling over the country on personal business, but will expend it for bread and meat to feed the poor and needy of our
people—to sum up the whole matter, we pray our Great Father to send us an
Agent who will talk less and do more, give use less show and more justice.
Third   We beleive Thomas Keams to possess all we ask for; He has lived many
years among our people, he knows us, he spea[ks] our language, we can make
known our wants to him, without the danger of false interpretations of wicked
and selfish interpreters. Our people are law abiding and peaceable, and so we intend to continue; and we think that in the matter of selection of an Agent who
should distribute to us the benefactions of our Great Father, our interests, as we
understand them should be respected   Praying immediate attention to this our
oft repeated application for releif we are faithfully our Great fathers freinds and
servants."—DS (by mark), DNA, RG 94, Letters Received, 4354 1875. Related
papers are *ibid.*; *ibid.*, RG 75, Letters Received, New Mexico Superintendency.
On July 22, William F. M. Arny, Washington, D. C., wrote to Secretary of the
Interior Columbus Delano resigning as agent for the Navajos. ". . . I will do all
in my power as an humble Citizen to make the wise policy of the President a
success, and show that Indians can be civilized Christianized and made Self sustaining."—ALS, *ibid.*, RG 48, Appointment Papers, New Mexico Territory. On
Oct. 1, 1876, Alexander G. Irvine, agent, Navajo Agency, Fort Defiance, Arizona Territory, reported to John Q. Smith, commissioner of Indian Affairs.
"Upon my taking charge of this agency last December, I found everything in
confusion, . . . I must say for the Navajoes, notwithstanding the difficulty with
their former agent, Wm. F. M. Arny, that they have conducted themselves in a
quiet and orderly manner. They would receive whatever was given to them in
the way of supplies, and they are the only Indians that I have any knowledge of
who will say 'Thank you' in return. The progress made during the past year has
been all that could have been expected. . . ."—*HED*, 44-2-1, part 5, I, 513. See
William Haas Moore, *Chiefs, Agents & Soldiers: Conflict on the Navajo Frontier,
1868–1882* (Albuquerque, 1994), pp. 137–65.

On Sept. 1, 1870, Arny, "Now special agent for Indian service in NewMexico," Cimarron Agency, had written to USG. "When I saw you in Washington
you kindly said you would at the proper time aid my efforts in the establishment
of schools &c for the Pueblo Indians of NewMexico. The change of the Super-
intendnt and agents in New Mexico by the relieving of the Military officers
from Indian duty, induces me to believe that you can now place me in the position where I can do much towards the improvement of the Indians of the nineteen Pueblos (villages) of New Mexico. I therefore most respectfully ask the ap-

pointment of *'Indian agent for the Pueblo Indians of NewMexico'* My appointment to this position will enable me to carry out my educational plan for these
Indians, of which you was kind enough to express your approval when I last saw
you."—ALS, DNA, RG 48, Appointment Papers, New Mexico Territory. Related papers are *ibid.* On Jan. 18, 1871, USG nominated Arny as agent, Pueblo
Agency; on Dec. 2, 1873, USG nominated Arny as agent, Navajo Agency.

1875, July 15. Francis G. Servis, Canfield, Ohio, to USG. "Oweing to my
financial Embarrassment I am Compeled to tender this my resignation as associate Justice of the Supreme Court of Montana Territory:"—ALS, DNA, RG 60,
Letters Received, Montana Territory. On July 28, Attorney Gen. Edwards
Pierrepont wrote to USG concerning this resignation and recommendations
for Henry N. Blake.—Copy, *ibid.*, Letters Sent to Executive Officers. On the
same day, Orville E. Babcock, Long Branch, wrote to Pierrepont. "The President directs me to acknowledge the receipt of your favor of the 27th, and to enclose you a telegram that he has received on the subject, and to say that so far
as he knows, the appmt recommended by Gov. Potts and Secty Belknap will be
agreeable to him—but if you have information to the contrary you may forward
it to him here."—Copy, DLC-USG, II, 3. On Dec. 15, USG nominated Blake as
associate justice, Montana Territory.

1875, July 16. USG endorsement. "Respectfully refere[d] to the Sec. of the
Treas. I hope it may prove consistent with the interests of the public service to
continue Mr. Furguson in his *old position* in the Treasurers office. . . . Asks continuance until Oct. when he can go back into the ministry"—AES, DNA, RG
56, Applications. Written on an undated letter from William M. Ferguson, a
Methodist minister, to USG requesting *"immediate* interposition" for his restoration as clerk.—ALS, *ibid.* John P. Newman endorsed this letter. "I know Mr
Ferguson so thoroughly & so well, that I give him my most cordial endorsement. He is so competent as a clerk, so earnest as a Republican, so useful in
society, that I was surprised when I heard of his dismissal & I hope the President will restore him to his position."—AES, *ibid.* Ferguson also wrote an undated memorandum to USG outlining his Civil War services.—ADS, *ibid.* As of
Sept. 30, 1877, Ferguson clerked in the Treasury Dept.
    On April 15, 1869, Ferguson had written to USG. "I respectfully ask to be
appointed 'Commercial Agent,' or Consul for St Domingo. My residence is District of Columbia—"—ALS, *ibid.*, RG 59, Letters of Application and Recommendation. Related papers are *ibid.* No appointment followed.

1875, July 19. USG endorsement. "Referred to the Attorney General.
Mr. Burwell was a loyal citizen of Vicksburg at the breaking out of the Rebellion. I have always regarded him as a trusty man and believe he has ranked as a
good lawyer."—Bruce Gimelson, Autographs, *The First Hundred* (Fort Washington, Pa., Jan., 1966), no. 27. Written on a letter of July 16 from Armistead
Burwell, Washington, D. C., to USG requesting help finding a position and securing a court judgment.—*Ibid.* See *PUSG,* 9, 419–21; *ibid.,* 19, 432.

1875, July 19.   Secretary of the Interior Columbus Delano to USG. "I have the honor to invite your attention to the accompanying copy of a letter, dated the 8th instant, from the Governor of Montana Territory, reporting the necessity for military protection for the people of the Territory—and for the Crow Indian Agency—from the Sioux who are making predatory incursions into the Yellowstone and Gallatin Valleys, and who have recently captured all the stock at the new Crow Agency, killed the herder and captured a mule team engaged in the transportation of supplies to the new Agency. The subject is respectfully submitted for such suggestions as by you may be deemed appropriate, for adoption by this Department. . . . Since writing the above a further communication from the Governor has been received; and isa copy is herewith enclosed together with the newspaper slip therein referred to."—LS, DNA, RG 94, Letters Received, 3517 1875. The enclosures are letters of July 8 and 9 from Governor Benjamin F. Potts of Montana Territory to Delano. ". . . No Agent can live at the New Agency unless a military Post is established near it. . . . I appeal to the Department to afford the Crow Agent and the people of Gallatin & Yellowstone Valleys protection, from the raids of the worst Band of Indians on the American Continent. As this Band has steadily refused to treat with the Government, I hope that they soon may be whipped into submission. . . ." "I enclose Agent Clapp's report of the Sioux attack on the new Crow Agency. I am very apprehensive that the Agent and all of his employes have been butchered,   the military has sent no assistance, because the major part of the force is in the neighborhood of Fort Benton where there has been no hostilities for five years. How long is this policy to last?. . ."—Copies, *ibid.* Related papers and the clipping with Dexter E. Clapp's report are *ibid.* See *HED,* 44-1-1, part 5, I, 803–5; Keith Algier, *The Crow and the Eagle: A Tribal History from Lewis and Clark to Custer* (Caldwell, Idaho, 1993), pp. 328–30.

On Oct. 20, USG ordered land along the Yellowstone River in Montana Territory added to the Crow reservation, "provided that the same shall not interfere with the rights of any *bona-fide* settlers who may have located on the tract of country herein described."—D, DNA, RG 75, Orders. *HED,* 45-2-1, part 5, I, 639, 45-3-1, part 5, I, 753, 49-2-1, part 5, I, 556; *SED,* 48-2-95, 460–61; *SD,* 57-1-452, 857. In [*Dec.*], George W. Monroe and more than sixty others petitioned USG. "Your petitioners residents of the county of Gallatin Montana Territory learning that an effort is being made to detach a portion of our county and set it aside as a portion of the Crow Reservation would respectfully represent First, that there is and can be no necessity for this change as the Crow reservation is at present large enough for all purposes   That the country proposed to be detached is a portion of an organized county in this Territory and is fast settling up with a thrifty and enterprising people and the segregation of it would work a great injury to the people of this Territory and the County of Gallatin. That through it is the only natural direct Eastern communication and is on the line of the proposed Northern Pacific railroad   Second. That the country is not sought for by the Indian & is of no advantage to the Indians as by reason of its settlement there is no game for the Indians to subsist on and is a country which they do not inhabit. That the people of this Territory look with great hope to the full settlement of all this country lying to the East of us and connecting us in a direct line with the Eastern markets   That this development will more surely settle the vexed Indian question and protect us from Indian depredations."—DS (docketed Dec. 16, 1875), DNA, RG 75, Letters Received, Montana Superintendency. Another version of this petition is *ibid*. Potts and U.S. Delegate Martin Maginnis of Montana Territory favorably endorsed the petition.—AES (undated), *ibid*. On March 8, 1876, USG revoked the previous order and returned the land to the public domain.—DS, *ibid.*, Orders. Printed in the sources listed above. See Algier, *The Crow and the Eagle*, pp. 288–89.

1875, JULY 20.   Secretary of the Navy George M. Robeson to USG. "In view of the hospitality of the breaking out of Yellow fever at New Orleans during the present Summer or approaching Autumn, I have the honor to inquire if in that event, it would never the less be desirable for our vessels of war to remain there for the protection of public interests."—Copy, DNA, RG 45, Letters Sent to the President. On July 24, Levi P. Luckey wrote to Robeson. "The President directs me to acknowledge the receipt of your letter of the 20th inst., relative to the retention of our vessels at New Orleans and say that he approves your suggestion that they remain there."—LS, *ibid.*, Letters Received from the President.

1875, JULY 20.   James Longstreet, Washington, D. C., to USG, Long Branch. "Since my arrival, here, I have heard that there will probably be a vacancy of 'Commissioner' of this District; soon. I beg your favorable consideration of my application for this place; in the event of a vacancy, or any other position that you may be pleased to assign me. I feel that I have no personal claim and am only encouraged to prefer this petition by your great magnanimity."—ALS, DLC-USG, IB. On the same day, Longstreet wrote to Orville E. Babcock, Long Branch. "I have your valued favor of the 19th instant, and thank you kindly for your good offices in the matter of the records. Since writing you on the 14th instant I have heard that there will probably be a vacancy of 'Commissioner' of this District in a month or so; by the resignation of Mr Dennison, and it has occurred to me to write to the President and ask, in the event of a vacancy, for the place. Please find inclose, my application and I beg of you the favor to lay it before the President. Gen Bristow Gen Ingalls and Gen Alvord have kindly proffered their assistance in this, or other proper vacancy that may occur When I mentioned to Gen Bristow that the vacancy would probably occur he advised me to go to Long Branch and see the President, Gen Ingalls advised me to the same course; but he thinks the resignation extremely doubtful: which leaves me without a defined plan of opperations. I have concluded therefore to write to the President and yourself, and to leave to Gen Ingalls—who has kindly promised to do so—to advise me of a vacancy, that I may hope secure"—ALS, *ibid*. No appointment followed. Longstreet wished to examine "the rebel archives in possession of the Government in order to refute certain charges made against him by Georgia newspapers that it was his mismanagement which lost to the rebels the battle of Gettysburg."—*Washington National Republican*, July 16, 1875.

1875, JULY 20.   Governor Samuel J. Tilden of N. Y. to USG. "I have the honor
to transmit herewith a copy of a concurrent resolution of the Senate and Assembly of this state, and, in accordance therewith, to apply for the appointment
of officers in the service of the United States to examine and revise the exterior
and bulkhead lines of the Harbor of New York on the Staten Island side and report such revised lines to the legislature."—LS, DNA, RG 94, Letters Received,
4150 1875. The enclosure and related papers are *ibid.* See *PUSG*, 23, 372–73.

1875, JULY 22.   Secretary of the Treasury Benjamin H. Bristow to USG. "Dr.
Linderman, Director of the Mint, writes me from Carson, Nevada, that Mr.
William H. Doane, coiner of the Mint at that place, has fallen into bad habits,
and that the interests of the service require his immediate dismissal. In accordance with the recommendation of the Director, I have the honor to hand you
herewith, with request for your signature, an order suspending Mr. Doane, and
have requested the Secretary of State to issue a commission to Mr. Levi Dague,
who is recommended by the Director of the Mint."—Copy, DNA, RG 56, Letters Sent to the President.

1875, JULY 23.   Secretary of the Interior Columbus Delano to USG. "A. C.
Hawley who was nominated and confirmed as Receiver at Cheyenne Wyoming
failed to procure his bond & has declined. Senator Hitchcock backed by the
Governor, Attorney General, Marshal and State Treasurer for Nebraska
strongly recommend Major William Caffrey for a Territorial appointment. I
think Corey, the present Receiver should be removed. I submit Caffrey's application for your consideration."—LS (marked "Not sent"), DNA, RG 48, Appointment Papers, Wyoming Territory. USG appointed William Caffrey as
land office receiver, Cheyenne, in place of Alfred C. Hawley. On Dec. 13, USG
nominated Ithamar C. Whipple to replace Caffrey, who had resigned.

1875, JULY 27.   USG endorsement. "The resignation of A. S. M. Morgan, Mil.
Storekeeper, if accepted, may be withdrawn. If not acted upon no action need be
taken."—AES, DNA, RG 94, ACP, M1632 CB 1866. Written on a letter of July
21 from Moses W. Field, Detroit, to USG. "I beg to introduce Col. Morgan,
Military Storekeeper, now on duty at Allegheney Arsenal. Two or three months
ago, the Colonel on being ordered to Rock Island, fearing that the change of climate would be dangerous to life, sent forward his resignation. He is in delicate
health, which is the result of being shot through the body during the war. After receiving the wound the Colonel laid on his face in bed for 13 long months.
His record and Character are good, and I beg of you on *personal grounds* to allow the Colonel to withdraw his resignation."—LS, *ibid.* Related papers are *ibid.*
On June 22, Secretary of War William W. Belknap had written to U.S. Senator
Simon Cameron of Pa., Harrisburg, explaining why he had rejected the request
of Capt. Algernon S. M. Morgan, former col., 63rd Pa., for reinstatement.—
LS (press), *ibid.*, RG 156, Letters Received. On June 25, Cameron wrote to Bel-
knap requesting "mercy" for Morgan.—ALS, *ibid.* Related papers are *ibid.* On
Sept. 14, Belknap wrote to U.S. Representative James G. Blaine of Maine, Au-

gusta. "Since my return I find that in my absence the President has revoked the order accepting the resignation of Colonel Morgan. This action, of course, is perfectly satisfactory to myself, and as no further steps are necessary in the matter, I herewith return to you Mrs Morgan's letter, which you enclosed to me."—Copy, *ibid.*, RG 107, Letters Sent, Military Affairs.

1875, July 27.   Secretary of the Navy George M. Robeson to USG. "I have the honor to state in reply to your request of the 16th instant, that the recommendation of Mr. C. E. Heath for Cadet Midshipman, made by Senator J. P. Jones, is on file in the Department, but the same does not appear to have been transmitted through, nor has it any endorsement from the President."—Copy, DNA, RG 45, Letters Sent to the President. C. E. Heath did not attend the U.S. Naval Academy.

1875, July 27.   F. M. Fulkerson, Saline County, Mo., to USG. "I hope you will pardon me when you here my complaint   I am now in my 66th year   through Dint of hard Labor has made A Little Living for my family of 7 sons & 3 daughters   5 of my sons one son in Law & A youth I partly raised and My negro man making 8 persons from my house went in to the servise of the government against the Rebels untill ~~that~~ the war Ended and was all honorbly dischard at the the close of the war but one whoo died while in servise   I cauled the only union meeting that was held in our county in 1861   I was appointed County Court Judge & served for six years   in the faul of 64 I was Elected A member of the constitutional convention to frame A new constitution for the state . . . My youngest son that was in the army Thomas Benton Fulkerson has been Indited for Murder in the first degree said to be done some ten or twelve years since the kiling was certainly done by some one or more persons & I was strongly opposed to all such acts And dont pretend to Justify the act But do protest to stiring this thing up and not saying one word About the Mayny brutal Murders done on the personsons of union soldies during the war & since the war & also on Many private upright cittizens for no cause only their Adhering to the government   now they the rebels is in full power from constabl to governor   there is but one Attorney that has ever has made Any pretensions to Loyalty as I know of   now wee have to give the rebel Lawyiers Large fees whoo per haps has Aided in getting up inditements Against My son and another person whoo has been Absent fom the state for more than two years whoo they intend to try to use Against My son   he has been put under arrest and is Looked for hourly here   I fear they will get him to yield to do there dirty work for them   wee find by sad Experience that A rebel of 61 is A rebel of 75   still wee had strong hops that our government would protect us not only in the war but ever after wards   will not president Lincoln Amnesty proclamation meet this case fully if so please have it forwarded to me with full instructions how to Avail ourselvs of its Bennifits . . . my son the Acused is A sober peacable cittizen with A wife & two children A stay at home farmer interrupting no person   the men kiled were rebels and was said to feed Bush whackers   some conjectured that that they may of Been kiled by negroes as they had Been recently whiped by the parties kiled   I know not whoo done the killing But I do solomly protes Against this one sided matter when wee were in power wee made no Efforts to have them indited which wee could of found plenty of evidence the war was over & wee thought that by gones be by gones . . . I write this under great secrecy for fear of great Excite in the country and & perhaps my own personal safety be pleasd to have this matter attended to as Early as possible wee are in great suspense concerning it as the trial will come up in the Latter part of september next I am Exceeding sorry to caus you any trouble whatever But I hope you will pardon me under all the circumstances if it was possible for us to have A fare trial with imparl judges Juror & witnesses I think wee would have but Little to fear as it is there is no positive telling you will Look over Bad writing spelling & so on"—ALS, DNA, RG 60, Letters from the President. In Nov. and Dec., Levi Hagan and Thomas B. Fulkerson were tried and acquitted in Marshall, Mo., for the murder of two men in Feb., 1864. See *History of Saline County, Missouri, . . .* (St. Louis, 1881), pp. 385, 509–10.

1875, JULY 29. USG endorsement. "Returned to the Sec. of the Int. his action approved."—*The Collector*, No. 767 (1958), m259. Written on a letter of July 9 from Secretary of the Interior Columbus Delano to USG concerning the actions of G. W. Woolley, involved in the 'Rio de Santa Clara' Calif. land claim, who "admitted in a personal interview of his own seeking to one of my clerks, that he was acting as attorney for the settlers, and would receive a handsome fee in case he succeeded in getting the United States to intervene in their behalf. Thus disclosing the motive that animated him to such persistence, he at the same time stripped himself of all claim to disinterestedness."—*Ibid.* Congress rejected calls for resurvey of the contested land. See *SRC*, 44-1-413; *HRC*, 44-2-217; James F. Stuart, *Argument on the Survey of the Rancho "Rio de Santa Clara," Situated in the County of Santa Barbara, State of California* (Washington, 1872); G. W. Woolley, *An Exposition of Facts Connected with the Survey and Patent of the "Rio de Santa Clara" Land Grant, addressed to Congress . . .* (Washington, 1876).

1875, JULY 30. Orville E. Babcock, Long Branch, to James H. Marr, act. 1st asst. postmaster gen. ". . . The arrangements for the President's mail, and the Cottagers along the beach are now fine, and are highly appreciated."—Copy, DLC-USG, II, 3.

1875, JULY 31. Levi P. Luckey to Francis D. Clark, New York City. "The President directs me to acknowledge the receipt of your letter of the 22d inst. and convey to you his thanks for the badge of the Association of early Californians. He wishes me to express to you his willingness, and desire, to be enrolled among your number."—Copy, DLC-USG, II, 3. See *New York Times*, March 11, 1879.

1875, JULY 31. Parish B. Johnson, land office register, Walla Walla, *et al.*, to USG urging "construction of a Wagon Road from at or near a point on the present Stage road over the Blue Mountains, known as Meachams Station to Walla Walla" because "its construction will not do any material damage to the Reservation while it will greatly benefit the people of Eastern Oregon and Washington Territory."—DS (31 signatures), DNA, RG 75, Letters Received, Oregon Superintendency. About this time, Lot Livermore *et al.* petitioned USG for permission to reroute another road on the same Umatilla reservation, despite objections from officials controlling a trading station and hotel along the existing road.—DS (38 signatures, undated), *ibid.* Brig. Gen. Oliver O. Howard endorsed this petition. "I think the proposed road would be no detriment to the Reservation & will benefit the travelling public."—AES (undated), *ibid.* On Aug. 5, Narcisse A. Cornoyer, agent, Umatilla Agency, wrote to Edward P. Smith, commissioner of Indian Affairs, that "this road would be very injurious to the interests of the Indians and they strongly object to its being done as it would run through the best portion of the range used by them to sustain their Stock during the winter months."—ALS, *ibid.* Cornoyer claimed no interest in the competing road even though he had signed the July 31 petition. See *HED,* 44-1-1, part 5, I, 855–56.

1875, AUG. 4. USG pardon for G. W. Swanton, convicted in May of "maltreating seamen on the high-seas" and sentenced to four months, "on account of the danger to which an unacclimated person is exposed by being imprisoned in New Orleans during the summer months."—Copy, DNA, RG 59, General Records.

1875, AUG. 4. J. D. Langworthy, Dubuque, to USG. "I write you for the purpose of enquiring whether a certain proclamation issued by you and signed by Hamilton Fish as Secy of State, bearing date Jany 17th 1873, is Still in force and considered binding or not? If it is so considered I hope that you will read the enclosed certificate, and please inform me, by what right D E Lyon now holds the office of Collr of Customs, and City Attorney at $1800 00 a year—And in case you should consider that he has no right to so hold them—Will you be so good as to notify him, that his resignation will be accepted, and allow another as good a republican, as he is to hold the office—As to my qualifications for the office, enquire from Wm B Allison, or any other of my numerous friends which will doubtless be as satisfactory as you could wish—. . ."—ALS, DNA, RG 56, Letters Received from the President. An enclosure is *ibid.* On Oct. 17 and Dec. 20, Langworthy wrote to USG on the same subject.—ALS, *ibid.* Nominated as surveyor of customs, Dubuque, on Dec. 22, 1870, and again on March 8, 1875, Delos E. Lyon retained the position. See *PUSG,* 24, 315–18.

1875, AUG. 5. Lemuel Perry *et al.,* Gallipolis, Ohio, to USG. "Your petitioners respectfully ask that Oberlin M. Carter, of Gallia County, Ohio, be appointed a cadet at large to the West Point Military Academy, to report for examination on the 27th inst., and in case there be no vacancy this year, that he be appointed next year."—DS (4 signatures), DNA, RG 94, Correspondence, USMA. Related papers include favorable endorsements from Rutherford B. Hayes, U.S. Senator John Sherman of Ohio, and Secretary of the Interior Columbus Delano.—*Ibid.* Admitted to USMA in 1876, Oberlin M. Carter graduated in 1880, first in his class. See *HRC,* 76-1-1045; *New York Times,* July 20, 1944.

1875, AUG. 9.   Green B. Anderson, Chattanooga, to USG. "I this Eavening take My Penn in Hand to Let you Know that I am A Calored Man 24 years of Age & Mr President ask you Beleveing you Will tell Me all A Bout what I want to No   I Want to Know what is our duty ~~was~~   We are trying to ognize A Campany what We Call A Homes Guard   Some of our Boys think We Can Be Called out of our own State   I Say Not So   I Wish you Will Bee So kind as to Let Me Know Soon As Pasible   Well are Willing to Came Like Salgers When We are Call any Where in the State of Tennessee   But Mr grant the Boys thinks We will Be Call in A year or tow to the frount to fight   I am the Second Sargent of Said Campany   My Captain Dont Know I Writing to you   I take A Bound My Self So I Will Close By Saying Write Me all the perticlars of Home Gaurds . . . Please Direct to My Address in Care Houston & Co Chattanooga   P. S. Mr President We also Have tow White Campanys Here   We ask them But the Woud Not give us any Satifacsion A Bout it   you Will Pleas Do So   Please Excause My Hand Write   I Have Not Had any Schooling But 4 Month"— ALS, DNA, RG 94, Letters Received, 4267 1875.

1875, AUG. 9.   John Gooseberry, Lockport, N. Y., to USG. "I inclose petition of several of the citizens of this place asking your Excellency to grant to myself & wife transportation to Govt land in Louisiana—I am poor & desirous of reaching there for the purpose named in said petition—I trust that your Excellency will give this matter your early attention"—ALS, DNA, RG 48, Miscellaneous Div., Letters Received. On Aug. 5, W. H. Baker *et al.*, Lockport, had written to USG. "The petition of the undersigned residents of the city of Lockport N. Y. respectfully showeth that John Gooseberry a private in the late war & a member of the 54th Regt. Mass. Volunteers who did good service for the Govt of the United States in said war is now a resident of said city & bears the scars he received with honor in the service aforesaid—he is poor & needy is willing to work & lend his assitance in building up the desert places in the South & is anxious to commence operations at once   We therefore pray your Exellency to give him & his beloved spouse a pass from this place to the Government lands in Louisiana where he proposes to devote the remaining years of his life to making the desert bloom like the rose—if your Excellency will grant this our petition we will see that he has funds sufficient to maintain him & his wife till he acquires title to a homestead under the laws of the U. S. And for which action by your Excellency we will ever pray"—DS (10 signatures), *ibid.*

1875, AUG. 10.   USG commutation of death sentence for Oscar Snow, convicted of murder in Ark., to life at hard labor, as recommended by Judge Isaac C. Parker, Western District, Ark.—Copy, DNA, RG 59, General Records.

1875, AUG. 10.   James Walsh, Bristol, "Va & Tenn," to USG. "I wish to apprise you of the fact that disguised, lawless bands are now organized in this town who go round of nights breaking up the furniture, knocking down the doors, and otherwise mistreating we Colored Citizens who are bold enough to declare ourselves in favor of the Administration—The town Officers are encourgeing them to acts of lawlessness and I hope you will for the sake of us who are your friends, and friends to the party will send a Company of troops to this point to break up the Mob—I would have sent to the Com'd't at Richmond but was afraid he would not reply at once to my wishes—Your friends and supporters are being imposed upon, and I appeal to you for protection—As the election draws nigh things will get worse—Hoping that you will not disregard this . . ."—ALS, DNA, RG 60, Letters Received, Va.

1875, Aug. 13.   To Mr. [*Thomas*] Murphy, from Long Branch, urging Murphy to invest $100,000 in rapid transit stock. "Private & confidential. . . . it would afford me much pleasure to see you have one thousand shares—if it is the success I believe it will be—than to have it myself and you left out . . ."—Charles Hamilton Auction No. 84, Jan. 23, 1975, no. 182.

1875, Aug. 17.   George R. Maxwell, U.S. marshal, Salt Lake City, to USG. "I am informed that the son of Robert T Burton, has been appointed as Cadet at West Point,   his Father was in command at the time of the Morrissite Massacre, and since the indictments, brought in 1872, has never been in Utah, until within the last 30 days,   If this son of a Murderer shall be appointed it will show to the world, that there is no limit to the endorsement of crime in Utah,"—LS, DNA, RG 94, Correspondence, USMA. No Burton attended USMA during this period. See C. LeRoy Anderson, *For Christ Will Come Tomorrow: The Saga Of The Morrisites* (Logan, Utah, 1981), pp. 153–56.

1875, Aug. 20.   James J. Swilley, Cold Springs, Tex., to USG. "Mingo, the chief of the 'Cushada' tribe of indians, comes to me complaining that the hogs, cattle &c of his tribe are often killed & maimed, and that he can not protect them— The tribe numbers only forty three and reside on a small tract of land purchased by Mingo, situate in this County—They are poor and needy, are honest and have ever been friendly towards the white people—They wish some protection, and, if possible, some assistance from the general government—They have no white agent to represent and protect them—Not knowing the proper department to whom to write this I have written to you—"—ALS, DNA, RG 75, Letters Received, Miscellaneous. Swilley served as justice of the peace, San Jacinto County. See *PUSG*, 24, 491–93.

1875, Aug. 21.   USG endorsement. "Refered to the Sec. of War. This application may be filed for the class of /77 and special attention called when apts. are made."—AES, DNA, RG 94, Correspondence, USMA. Written on a letter of Aug. 20 from Francis Darr, New York City, to George Deshon soliciting his "friendly aid" to obtain a USMA appointment for his son Francis J. A. Darr.— ALS, *ibid*. Deshon endorsed this letter to USG. "It would gratify me very much if General Darr's application meets a favorable response as he is one of my best and most esteemed friends"—AES (undated), *ibid*. On Oct. 20, Col. James B. Fry, New York City, wrote to Col. Rufus Ingalls. "A few weeks ago I wrote you concerning the cadet's appointment for Frank Darr, son of Genl. Darr, which the President told Father Deshon & Darr that he would give. Darr is very anxious to know that the thing is not overlooked & is in proper way to be certain. Wont you do Deshon, Darr & me the favor to see how it stands."—ALS, *ibid.* On Oct. 22, USG endorsed this letter. "Refered to the Sec. of War. Special attention"—AES, *ibid.* On May 8, 1876, Deshon, New York City, wrote to USG on the same subject.—ALS, *ibid.* On a card printed "Francis Darr" USG wrote: "Jr. may be placed on the list of supernumerary at West Point for /76"—AE (initialed, undated), *ibid.* Darr graduated USMA in 1880.

1875, AUG. 21. USG endorsement. "Refered to the Sec. of War for examination, and if practicable to remove all disabilities in the case of Lt. Col. Foulk. I understand Col. F. does not desire position but relief from disgrace which he thinks has been unjustly brought upon him"—AES, DNA, RG 94, ACP, F38 CB 1870. Written on papers concerning former 1st Lt. William B. Foulk, including a telegram of [*Aug.*] 17 from Governor John F. Hartranft of Pa. to USG, Long Branch. "Permit me again to invite your attention to the application of Capt. Foulke for Reinstatement in the army. His services during the war and the Earnestness of his friends impel me to join in asking his restoration & I sincerly hope that you will find it in your power & in accordance with your judgement to grant his request"—Telegram received (dated on docket), *ibid.* On Sept. 1, Judge Advocate Gen. Joseph Holt endorsed these papers. ". . . This Bureau has made five unfavorable reports upon various applications for his reinstatement. In the last report, under date of July 9, 1874, it was remarked as follows:—'The offences of this officer—striking his superior a severe blow with an unsheathed saber in the presence of enlisted men; making a false official report; and instigating a malicious prosecution—were regarded as satisfactorily proved; and the unfavorable impression thus conveyed of his unfitness to remain an officer of the army was increased by the indication in the testimony of an attempt on his part to suborn witnesses in his behalf.'. . ."—ES, *ibid.* On April 3, 1874, Secretary of War William W. Belknap had written to U.S. Senator John Scott of Pa. "The President has referred to me your letter of the 27th ultimo and accompanying papers—application of Wm L. Foulk, late Captain 10th U. S. Cavalry, for re-instatement—. . . In view of the action already taken, and of the fact that Mr. Foulk now offers nothing new in his case, I am compelled to decline taking any favorable action on his application."—Copy, *ibid.*, RG 107, Letters Sent, Military Affairs. On July 20, Belknap wrote to U.S. Representative James S. Negley of Pa. on the same subject.—Copy, *ibid.* See *HRC*, 44-1-826; *SRC*, 45-2-117; *U.S. Statutes at Large*, XX, 499.

1875, AUG. 21. To AG Edward D. Townsend, from Long Branch. "You may pardon Joseph Trigg a deserter from the Eighteenth (18th) Infty now Confined at Governor's Island N. Y."—Telegram received, DNA, RG 107, Telegrams Collected (Bound). On Aug. 25, Townsend issued orders restoring to duty without trial Joseph Trigg, private, 18th Inf. band; on Sept. 15, Trigg was ordered discharged.—Printed, *ibid.*, RG 192, Orders Received.

1875, AUG. 25, Wednesday. To "Dear Judge," from Long Branch. "It was entirely your luck. It poured here all day on friday last so that I could not get out of the house."—ALS, Gallery of History, Las Vegas, Nev.

1875, AUG. 25. Zebina Eastman, Maywood, Ill., to USG. "I send you enclosed copy of the biography of Benjamin Lundy, the most complete as a sketch that has been made. I infer from the interest you expressed in the life of the man, that, in relief from the cares of state, you would be pleased to spend a little time in reviewing his life. I returned to my home about a week ago, an absence of nearly ten weeks, two weeks of which I spent pleasntly at Fayetteville Vermont. I saw Mr. Smith, the Collecter of Customs, on Saturday, who received me most cordially"—ALS, OFH. See *The Biographical Encyclopædia of Illinois of the Nineteenth Century* (Philadelphia, 1875), pp. 510–11.

1875, AUG. 27. USG endorsement. "Refered to the Sec. of War. The Leave of Absence of Lt. Smead, 3d U. S. Cavalry may be extended for six months from the 1st of Jan.y, 1876."—AES, DNA, RG 94, ACP, 5014 1874. Written on a letter of Aug. 26 from Sarah M. Smead, Carlisle, Pa., to USG. "My Son, Bache Smead Lt in the 3d Cavalry obtained leave of absence last Winter and is now in Europe As his furlough will expire on the 1st of January, he must cross the ocean in the month of Dec. that inclement season of the year, and as the time approaches for his return, I am growing anxious to have his furlough extended to three or six months if possible—There does not now remain sufficient time to obtain the extension by the regular process and I therefore apply directly to you as the one person who might grant this favor without [delay.] His Physician considers it would be very imprudent for him to come home and rejoin his Company in mid-winter, now stationed at Fort Laramie—I am myself the Widow of an Officer, Capt. R. C. Smead of the 4th Artillery, who died during his passage home from the Mexican War—and my Eldest Son Capt. J. R. Smead of the 2d Art. was killed at the 2d Battle of BullRun and this Son Bache is the only one I have left, therefore I feel that I may presume to ask this favor of you Hoping to hear from you favorably . . ."—ALS, *ibid.*

1875, AUG. 31. Samuel H. Winsor, land office register, Cheyenne, to USG. "I beg leave most respectfully to state that I have been advised of the appointment of Mr. L. Edwin Dudley, as my successor. In order to place myself in the proper light before the world and the many friends who recommended me for the position, and in simple justice to myself, I would earnestly ask that if there are any charges or complaints against me I may have an opportunity to vindicate myself. Or, if there are no complaints against me, then, that the name of my successor be with drawn."—ALS, DNA, RG 48, Appointment Papers, Wyoming Territory. On Sept. 3, William A. Carter, Fort Bridger, Wyoming Territory, favorably endorsed this letter.—AES, *ibid.* William S. Harney also favorably endorsed this letter.—AES (undated), *ibid.* On July 19, Levi P. Luckey had written to Secretary of the Interior Columbus Delano. "The President directs me to say in reply to your letter of the 10th instant, that you may appoint Mr. Dudley

Register of the Land Office at Cheyenne Wyoming Territory."—LS, *ibid.* L. Edwin Dudley, appointed in place of Winsor, failed to qualify. On Dec. 13, USG nominated George R. Thomas in place of Dudley.

1875, SEPT. 1.   Secretary of the Treasury Benjamin H. Bristow to USG concerning gold medals for ten men from Westerly, R. I., to recognize their gallantry in saving 32 persons after the wreck of the steamer *Metis* on Aug. 31, 1872.—Copy, DNA, RG 56, Letters Sent to the President. See *CG*, 42–3, 1401; *U.S. Statutes at Large*, XVIII, part 3, p. 205; *New York Times*, Aug. 31, Sept. 1, 5, 7, 25, 1872.

1875, SEPT. 1.   Governor John F. Hartranft of Pa. to USG. "An old College mate of mine a Clergyman of the Episcopal Church and a gentleman of Education and ability Rev. J. C. Laverty will make application for an appointment as chaplain in the United States Army and I respectfully commend him to your favor. Mr. Laverty's claims to the position and his merits will be properly and earnestly presented to your Excellency by his other friends, and I join with them in the expression of the belief that no more competent or estimable gentleman could be selected for a chaplaincy. Trusting that the application of Mr. Laverty may meet with your favor, . . ."—LS, DNA, RG 94, ACP, 1596 1876. On March 1, 1876, USG approved James C. Laverty's appointment as chaplain.—AES, *ibid.* On March 3, USG nominated Laverty as chaplain, 24th Inf.

1875, SEPT. 4.   S. A. Andrews, Sparta, Ga., to USG seeking authorization and arms for a military co. ". . . We has on role 45 nam out Sid of officers mySelf Captain   Please give us Some answer as Soon as Posible   We have bin Weaighing Evry Since July and now hop to hear you Soon"—ALS, DNA, RG 94, Letters Received, 7456 1875.

1875, SEPT. 7.   A. P. Merrill, vice president, American Academy of Dental Surgery, New York City, to USG. "Please excuse me in behalf of the Academy for trespassing upon your enjoyment at the Sea side. But the question is now being discussed in reference to some legal provission being made by the Government for the appointment of Dental Surgeons on the Staff of instructors at West Point & the School of Anapolis and if found practicable to the departments of the Army and all come under the head of the Surgeon Genl at the War Department . . ."—ALS, DNA, RG 94, Correspondence, USMA. On Sept. 20, Secretary of War William W. Belknap wrote to Merrill. ". . . So far as the Military Academy at West Point is concerned, I do not see how, without interfering with other pursuits of great importance to the education of an officer, an appointment of Dental Surgeon could be made, as suggested in your letter. There are now already at West Point, under the supervision of the Surgeon of the Post, sufficient dental facilities to meet the requirements of the Officers and their families, of the Corps of Cadets and the soldiers who are stationed there; and in my opinion a change at this time would be the cause of much embarrassment. . . ."—LS (press), *ibid.*

1875, SEPT. 9.   Smith Green, Waterproof, La., to USG. "as regards to Color
some of the White people regards us as no more than dogs   I went on the
Steamer Ouachita Belle to day with some white boys and they went in the Cabin
and got some Ice water and I went in too and got some and as I were drinking
I saw Capt Campbell approaching and I put the cup down and he caugh me by
the hand and slapped me thre or four times and led me down to the steps and
kicked me down the steps and did not do nothing to the white boys, and now I
think there are better laws in the state for us if we are Negroes   I am a boy only
15 years old and I thought I would write to you"—ALS, DNA, RG 60, Letters
from the President.

1875, SEPT. 14.   L. Cass Carpenter, collector of Internal Revenue, Columbia,
S. C., to USG. "On the morning of the 8th inst. Hon Joseph Crews, representative in the legislature of this state from the county of Laurens was deliberately
assassinated while en-route from his home to this city. He was riding in a buggy
with a young man, about 6 oclock in the morning, and while crossing a small
creek about 3 miles from Laurens court house was fired upon by persons in ambush, who discharged two shots from a shot gun, both of which took effect ion
the person of Mr Crews and his friend. Mr Crews received five Buck shot in his
back, one of which pierced his spine, paralyzing his lower extremities, one entered his lungs, and the others lodged underneath his shoulder blades. His companion received one shot in his shoulder. Mr Crews died from his wounds at
midnight the 13th. There is but little doubt here, that Mr Crews was assassinated for political purposes. He was the leading republican ~~republican~~ in Laurens County, and was regarded by his political opponents as being the only man
in the way of democratic ascendancy. The county is strongly republican, providing the votes can be got out, but without some one to organize and give the
colored men confidence, there is no chance to carry the county for the republicans. Mr Crews was a resident of that county, and had been long before the war.
He identified himself with the republican party, and for that reason was obnoxious to those who 'accept the situation,' from a democratic standpoint. This is
the way our democratic politicians 'shake hands across the bloody chasm,' and
this is the way they propose to inaugurate that 'era of good feeling,' so glibly
talked about by our Centennial orators. I have not a doubt that this murder was
deliberately planned, and as deliberately executed. If the democratic leaders
can secure the 'taking off' of a few leading republicans, they have but little to
fear from the result of the next elections. Mr Crews was one of my 'Special
Deputies,' but so far as I have been able to learn, his murder had nothing to do
with his official position in the Revenue Service."—ALS, DNA, RG 60, Letters
from the President. On March 15, USG had nominated Carpenter, a newspaper
editor, as collector of Internal Revenue, 3rd District, S. C. See *PUSG*, 21, 264–
65; *ibid.*, 23, 72.

1875, SEPT. 18.   USG endorsement. "Refered to the Sec. of State. I have no objection to this apt. being made if the vacancy exists or if a removal is advisable."—AES, DNA, RG 59, Miscellaneous Letters. Written on a letter of Sept.
16 from Solomon Sternberger, New York City, to USG. "I beg herewith to hand

you my application for United States Consul at Cardenas (Cuba). I am a citizen of the U. S., resident of the State of Pennsylvania, born in Germany, 52 years of age, have been a resident of the United States for 38 years and am by occupation a merchant."—LS, *ibid.* A related letter is *ibid.* On Oct. 12, M. & S. Sternberger, bankers, New York City, wrote to USG recommending "our brother Mr Solomon Sternberger" as consul, Minatitlan, after learning there were no vacancies in Cuba.—L, *ibid.*, Letters of Application and Recommendation. On Dec. 9, USG nominated Solomon Sternberger as consul, Minatitlan. On Dec. 24, M. & S. Sternberger again wrote to USG complaining about their brother's low income at Minatitlan.—L, *ibid.*, Miscellaneous Letters. On July 29, 1876, Sternberger resigned his consulship.—LS, *ibid.*, Consular Despatches, Minatitlan.

1875, SEPT. 18.   Jay Cooke *et al.*, Philadelphia, to USG. "The undersigned respectfully request the appointment of Louis Henry Scott as Consul to reside at the city of Chihuahua State of Chihuahua Mexico,   Mr Scott is of the mercantile firm of Day Brothers & Co of Peoria Illinois and is about removing to Chihuahua with his family, and we recommend him as a gentleman of high character and one who will in our opinion energetically and discreetly represent the interests of American Citizens in that portion of Mexico   Some of the undersigned have recently invested a large amount of Capital in mercantile and mining enterprises at Chihuahua and our trade being wholly with the United States we find it an absolute necessity that a consulate should be established for our protection and comfort & the proper developement of the increasing business between the two sections   We respectfully ask for your kind consideration of this request"—DS (7 signatures), DNA, RG 59, Letters of Application and Recommendation. Related papers are *ibid.* On March 3, U.S. Representative James W. McDill of Iowa had written to Secretary of State Hamilton Fish. "I desire to recommend Rev Joseph *Knotts* of this District, formerly of West Virginia to the appointment of consul at Chihuahua Mexico   He is in ill health and goes to Mexico for its benefit. As this place is vacant I venture to recommend him for it he desiring it more for protection than for any profit therefrom"—ALS, *ibid.* Related papers are *ibid.* On Dec. 9, USG nominated Joseph Knotts as consul, Chihuahua; on Aug. 5, 1876, USG nominated Louis H. Scott to replace Knotts.

1875, SEPT. 18.   G. Miligan to USG. "i now take My pen in hand to Deliver A Messeage unto you to Let you know that we the paopel of Shelby Co Calera Ala are uneducated in Genel and we had A Gentleman here A teachen A writen School and the White men did Beet them and Drove them from us But we do not know what they did it for But we know that we herd him Say that he would not teach the chool   we know that is what they did beet hem a bout and we wold like to get aid from you a bout this case and would have written to the governer but we know that it is would not do no good becasus we have not the money to enter in Law with for the man that we are inploied with dos not pay us money not onely him it is so all over this countery) and we ask you for to aid us) and in the regard of school here and now mr president plese here hour con-

session and send us somthin to in corage us in hour minds)   So I Will Close..."
—ALS, DNA, RG 60, Letters Received, Ala.

1875, Sept. 22.   USG endorsement. "Refered to the Atty. Gen. for such action
as he may choose to take. Any nomination sent to me at St. Louis, to fill Mr. S'
vacancy I will approve."—AES, DNA, RG 60, Letters from the President.
Written on a letter of Sept. 21 from Walter H. Smith to USG. "I hereby tender
my resignation of the office of Assistant Attorney General, to take effect on the
first day of October next. I embrace this occasion to thank you for the honor
conferred on me and to express the hope that you may continue to be prospered,
both as an individual and as the Head of the Nation."—ALS, *ibid.* On May 24,
USG had written to John Goforth accepting his resignation as asst. attorney
gen.—Copy, DLC-USG, II, 2. On Dec. 15, USG nominated Augustine S. Gaylord and Thomas Simons to replace Smith and Goforth. On the same day, USG
nominated Edwin B. Smith as asst. attorney gen. to replace Clement H. Hill.
    On Oct. 25, 1876, USG authorized Edwin Smith to serve as act. attorney
gen. during the temporary absence from Washington, D. C., of Attorney Gen.
Alphonso Taft and Solicitor Gen. Samuel F. Phillips.—DS, DNA, RG 60, Letters from the President.

1875, Sept. 22.   W. J. A. Smith, Los Angeles, to USG. "The undersigned would
respectfully represent to your excellency that there are now in this city two
chiefs of tribe of Indians mentioned in the enclosed slip cut from the Los Angeles Express of Sept 18 /75.   despairing of obtaining redress in San Diego,
they have come here to see if they can find an agent who has been living among
them but is now absent, and to get some advice if possible as to what they ought
to do. They have been preyed upon by sharpers here who have heard their tale
of distress, charged them 10 or 20 dollars for listening & then sent them to
other villians to be treated again in the same manner. They are almost crazed
with the anxiety in respect to their family & property and the apparent hope-
lessness of any effort to obtain redress. They are now actually turned out of
their homes & know not where to go. They fought well for the U. S. in the war
with Mexico & doubtless will die bravely fighting, if driven to it, for what they
feel is their right in the sight of God and man. Hoping that in your wisdom and
kindness, some means of averting such a desperate resort on their part, may be
found . . . Signed for myself and many citizens present."—ALS, DNA, RG 48,
Letters Received, California Superintendency. A Calif. court had ordered nearly
300 Temecula Indians ejected from land in San Diego County.—Clipping, *ibid.*
On June 30, D. A. Dryden, special Indian agent, Hollister, Calif., had written to
Edward P. Smith, commissioner of Indian Affairs, concerning the Temecula and
other Mission tribes in southern Calif. ". . . The valleys of San Pasqual and Pala,
in San Diego County, which were once set apart for a reservation would afford
good homes for a large part of the people, *and ought to be restored to them.* The
abolishment of this reservation four years ago was secured by interested parties, through a shameful perversion and falsification of the real facts of the case
at that time, and the Indians yet remaining in these valleys are being shame-

fully imposed upon by the settlers; but these lands would not be sufficient. But the chief difficulty in the way of a general reservation is that the Indians themselves are universally opposed to such a disposition. . . . I venture to recommend, as soon as these surveys are completed, certain townships, including the principal Indian settlements, be selected and set apart for exclusive Indian occupation; . . ."—*HED,* 44-1-1, part 5, I, 725–26. On Feb. 17, 1871, after settlers had protested, USG revoked an earlier order and restored reservation land to the public domain. See *PUSG,* 19, 526. On Dec. 27, 1875, and May 15, 1876, USG ordered more than one hundred sections of land in San Diego and San Bernardino counties set apart as reservations for the Mission Indians.—DS, DNA, RG 75, Orders. *HED,* 45-2-1, part 5, I, 634, 45-3-1, part 5, I, 734–35, 47-2-1, part 5, II, 313, 49-2-1, part 5, I, 524; *SED,* 48-2-95, 227–28; *SD,* 57-1-452, 820–21.

1875, SEPT. 23.   John C. Howell, act. secretary of the navy, to USG. "I have the honor to intrust herewith the Record of the proceedings of a Naval General Court Martial in the case of Lieutenant Cornelius R. Meeker of the Navy who is found guilty of the charges of 'Drunkenness' and 'Scandalous conduct tending to the destruction of good morals,' and sentenced to be dismissed from the Naval Service of the United States. I respectfully recommend that the sentence be approved."—Copy, DNA, RG 45, Letters Sent to the President. See *New York Times,* Oct. 5, 1875.

1875, SEPT. 24.   E. Green, Methodist minister, Pennington, N. J., to USG concerning "nearly $7000.00" worth of defaulted St. Clair County, Mo., bonds. "Will you allow an humble citizen of this great republic, of which you have the honour to be the Chief Magistrate, to call your attention to a most grievous wrong which myself, together with many others, am now suffering. You are doubtless aware that some of the western states, and more especially that of Missouri, have within the past few years, enacted laws holding out inducements to counties and towns to loan their credit to aid in the construction of R. Roads. and other public improvements; by means of which hundreds of thousands of Bonds have been put in the markets. and have been largely purchased by innocent, unsuspecting creditors mostly I presume residing here in the east, and among whom your humble correspondent happens to be one. . . . We of course sued, and after long and patient waiting for the court processes. and being subjected to the most grievous embarrassments, ~~we~~ obtained judgment against the Co. in the U. S. District court sitting at Jefferson City, having beaten them in all the Courts below. A mandamus was issued several months ago, but was defeated by a dishonerable artifice now becoming common in ~~the West.~~ some parts of the West. viz that of *resignation by the County Judges.* Another peremptory writ was issued by the last Court, but as I learn there are no judges upon whom to serve it. in office. it must also fail to bring the money. . . ."—ALS, DNA, RG 60, Letters from the President. See *The History of Henry and St. Clair Counties, Missouri* . . . (1883; reprinted, Clinton, Mo., 1968), pp. 903–24.

1875, SEPT. 24. William H. Polk, postmaster, Paris, Ky., to USG. "Special Agent Beard, of the P. O. Dept, yesterday called on me to investigate my Money Order business. The balance due the Dept I paid him & *squared* the acc't. I acknowledge that I have been somewhat remiss in rendering my returns, though often it was on account of inability from sickness & other causes. My lack of promptitude seems to have been the cause of the Dep't sending an Agent to look into the matter. My bondsmen, who are men of means and standing, I requested to examine my books, After so doing they wrote a letter to the Hon Post Master Gen'l (to which I refer you) asking that I be *retained*, and that I gave satisfaction & they would continue on my bond, At the request of Spec Agent Beard, I wrote out my resignation, by his direction directing it to Mr McDonald, of the M. O. office. As *you* commission me, I dont see what it amounts to, unless directed to *you*. Therefore, at the suggestion of friends & my bondsmen, I have recalled it and await your action. If there is no other way, I would like to be allowed to resign, provided you request me. But if you can overlook some little *past* delinquencies, and accept my assurances that I will give no further cause for trouble in the future, you will place me under renewed obligation to you for all you have done for me in the way of appointing me & sustaining me against those who sought to *oust* me, You have no conception how much I *regret* ever having given any *cause* for trouble. I have, since I joined your old Regt at Springfield, when 17, been in the Army & routine of P- O- Business, & understand no other, I have a family of 5 to take care of, It is hardly necessary for me also to say that I have given more money towards the success of your & other republicans races, than all the republicans in this county. In fact, they have always *bled* me for campaign purposes. On several occasions I have had knives & pistols drawn on me at the polls because I would not give an inch from the democratic rascalities. But of these things you can take no account, unless you wish to consider them in my favor. One thing I will pledge you, 'on the honor of one soldier to another,' nothing shall hereafter cause you to regret any *favor* you may show me in this matter, I will strive to do all I can to please my superiors and perform my work to their satisfaction. As to the reliability of my father-in-law & bondsman—Jesse Talbott, I refer you to his kinsman Benjamin Holladay, of your city. I want to work in the traces, as long as you are President, anyhow, and hope you will favor me with an early reply. There are enemies of mine who heard of the Spec Agents visit & of course will be trying now to get my place, They are the fellows who got mad at me, Gen Croxton & others on account of the difficulty regarding Col Kelly, when Collector at Lex Ky, A woman, I suppose, will be trying for the place, She is in *good* circumstances. Hoping you will consider the matter & reply. . . ."—ALS, DLC-John M. Harlan. On Oct. 1, Postmaster Gen. Marshall Jewell wrote to John M. Harlan, Louisville, seeking information concerning Polk.—TLS, *ibid.* On Dec. 9, USG nominated Elliott Kelly to replace Polk.

On Nov. 3, 1872, and March 5, 1875, Polk had written to USG. "I congratulate you on your triumphant election and complete and thorough vindication by the people, We hope we have also carried Ky for you, This County—Bourbon—which heretofore has given over 300 Dem maj, we carred for you by 108 maj—the first time it ever went Rep, With best wishes for your future success & health . . ." "I see by the papers that a bill has passed to increase the Pay-masters force of the Army, by the appointment of eight additional Paymasters. Having always had a predilection for the Army, and as the position of Pay-master is a *permanent* one, I hereby respectfully make application for one of the appointments, if they are to be made from *civil* life. Having served over three years in your old Regt—the 21st Ill—I have had much experience, as you know, as a soldier. My business avocations since the War have been such as to familiarize me with money and give me facility in handling the same."—ALS, USG 3 and DNA, RG 94, Applications for Positions in War Dept. No appoint-ment followed.

1875, SEPT. 26. Thomas T. Ricketts, Hamden, Ohio, to USG. "I wish to Lay A matter befor you which I hope it will be duley noticed by you   the Matter which I Shall alude too is Respecting Wm H. Newman A Clerk in the Solicitors office of the treasury Department   he was ~~y~~ my Captain in the 39th Ohio Reg-iment when i Reinlisted as A vetran   on our way home I give him my money for Safe keeping & to give it back to me when we Should get to the City of Cincinnati   when we got their he give me the Slip & i never Seen him untill i Rejoined my Regiment At Nashvill tennisee but he had Spent it All & he Still owes me it . . . he is one of those men that Come from Washington City to ohio to vote the Democratic ticketts   that is the kind of A union man he is   Here is his notes for the Ammount"—ALS, DNA, RG 206, Miscellaneous Letters Re-ceived. William H. Newman, clerk, solicitor of the treasury's office, responded to the allegations. ". . . In the fall of 1863 while our Regiment was stationed at Prospect, Tenn. Ricketts, came to me with about $800.00 which he had won from the boys of the Reg't at a game called 'chuck-a-luck' and asked me to take care of it for him as he was afraid if he kept it himself he might lose it again. I took the money and left it with the sutler, until the Reg't. went North on vet-eran leave about the 1st of January 18~~76~~64. Riketts then asked me to keep his money while he was at home as he was afraid if he took it with him his mother would get it. . . ."—ADS (undated), *ibid.* Related papers are *ibid.*; *ibid.*, RG 56, Letters From the President.

1875, SEPT. 29. Thomas Pratter, Chattanooga, to USG asking about the le-gality of interracial marriage under civil rights legislation.—ALS, DNA, RG 60, Letters Received, Tenn. See *PUSG*, 21, 495–97.

1875, OCT. 2. James Bradford, Eastman, Ga., to USG. "My object in writing to you is to inform you of how I have been grossly wronged cheated out of my wrights & to see if possible if there is any redress   In the year 1812, I was bound to one Nathan M. Grafton of Hartford Co, Maryland after which he re-moved to Baltimore & there I was learned the trade of Boot & Shoe-maker   In the year 1838 the Legislator of the State of Maryland passed & act that all free persons of color that commited any criminal depredation should be ~~transported~~ tried before the court & if found guilty should be transported for sutch a length of time according to the crime committed. In 1839 I was accused & arrested of being in company with another negro & of the knocking down & robing a little slave negro of the sum of seven ($7 00) dollars & was put in jail   The 18th of Feb, 1839 I was brought before the court & got no hearing; It was then advertised in the Baltimore Sun that I should have my trial in three days; that knight I was slipped out & heavily ironed   next morning found myself at Cat's Tavern Alexandria; From thence I was removed to Wilkinson Co, Georgia: soon after I arrived there I was sold to one Wm Calley; soon afterwards removed to Baker County, soon afterwards was sold to Elija Fann; soon afterwards I made it known through Elija Fann that I was a free man of color; I then wrote back to Samuel Bradford of Hartford Co, Maryland for a coppy of the record which he sent & I received: Mr Fann in 1841 entered a lawsuit against Mr Cally in Bainbridge Decatur Co,   He succeeded with the case far enoughf to get judgement & a fiew weeks before he would have got the execution he died; then the Callys had me sold & rebought me again; there I remained until 1857: I then went to Americus Ga, & made my case known to to another lawyer: He carried the case far enough for Gov, Brow to advertise me & that I should be supported as an orphan child & the Gov, of Maryland also demanded me when up steps the Calleys & pays this lawyer five hundred ($500.00) dollars to nulify the whole thing which they did   My object in writing to you is to appeal to your sympathies for help; I am now 68 years old almost blind & badly ruptured,   I have no meanes of support but my labor & being so afflicted I am able to do but little of that This appeal is my last resort & if I fail to enlist your sympathies in my behalf I dont know what will become of me; but knowing that you have a generous nature & feeling that you will lend a year to my helplessness & sufferings . . ."— ALS, DNA, RG 60, Letters from the President.

1875, OCT. 3.   Louis Philastre, Paris, to USG. ". . . My father, Eugène Philastre has leaved us in France (I am a French) a long while ago without help or any resources. After having robbed my mother of whatever she possessed, he sett off and come to New Orleans, with the title of painter of the Opera in that city. Perhaps he is now in another country, but I am sure he is yet in United States. Accordingly, I beseech you, honoured President, to oblige him to pay my mother the income he was condemned to pay by the French Justice, . . ."—ALS, DNA, RG 59, Miscellaneous Letters.

1875, OCT. 6.   USG pardon for J. Knox Lyons, "convicted of introducing spirituous liquors into the Indian country," after eleven months of a one-year sentence.—Copy, DNA, RG 59, General Records.

1875, OCT. 7.   Capt. VerPlanck Van Antwerp, Upper Marlboro, Md., to USG. "Advanced in years—verging upon my 'three score years and ten'—stricken down in health, and with but little of life left to me, I respectfully ask a favor at your hands. I have an only son, Robert Yates Van Antwerp, who expresses to me a wish to receive a commission in the Army, and I am desirous that he may procure it. . . . To you, Sir, I am personally known—better, perhaps, through my late and much esteemed friend, the venerable Mr. Frederick Dent, than any other channel. Mr. Dent, (many years my senior,) and I co-operated zealously, more than thirty years ago, in electing, for the last term—from 1845 'till

1851—of his 'Thirty years in the Senate,' Missouri's Great Statesman, THOMAS H. BENTON, a man whom every true friend of his was justly proud of being classed as such, by him—. . . When, however, the war of the rebellion was forced upon us, I, like so many other Democrats, tendered my serices to help save the Union. I was in Iowa—which I had helped to found as a State—and asked from its Governor a Regiment, for such service. More of a partisan than a patriot, he refused it to me! I was the oldest military man in Iowa, had been her first Adjutant General, more than twenty years before, and, prior to that, educated at West Point. Nobody, therefore, questioned, for a moment, my capacity for the position asked for by me, and I felt, keenly, the refusal of it as an insult! The partizan Governor, however,—unlike him of the adjoining State of Illinois—allowed his narrow partizan views to control his action, in my case. I thereupon applied, through Iowa's U. S. Senators, (men of higher motives,) to the President—one as great as he was truly patriotic—who gave me a Staff commission, . . . And now, conscious that, by the act of God, I must very soon 'step down and out,' thus vacating my commission, it would be exceedingly gratifying to me to know, or feel, that my wishes, as well as those of my son, could be gratified, by his receiving one in the Army. . . ."—ALS, DNA, RG 94, Applications for Positions in War Dept. Van Antwerp wrote to USG again in Oct.— ALS, *ibid.* Related papers are *ibid.* No appointment followed. Van Antwerp died Dec. 2.

On Dec. 4, 1866, USG had favorably endorsed a letter of Nov. 14 from Van Antwerp, Washington, D. C., to President Andrew Johnson requesting an army appointment.—ES, *ibid.*, ACP, 914 1873. On Aug. 29, 1867, Van Antwerp, military storekeeper, San Antonio, wrote to USG, secretary of war *ad interim*, seeking transfer to Fort Leavenworth, Kan. ". . . The late wife of Senator Williams, as I believe you know, was *my daughter*,—who died in Oregon, four years ago. Their *only* child, a little girl now six years old—*the child of my deceased daughter*—is now with my wife, *in Iowa.* I am of course anxious—*how* anxious you will readily conceive—to have them both, the child and her grandmother, with me during the few years of life that may be left to me—which I feel are to be *but few.* I CAN NOT DO so HERE—at this remote point, *so difficult to be reached*; for Judge Williams is, most naturally, unwilling to have the child so far removed that he could not visit it occasionally—as it would be impossible for him to do at *San Antonio*; but as he might, and would do, at Fort Leavenworth, or some point nearer than that to Washington—where he will be *most of the time*, for some years at least to come. . . ."—ALS, *ibid.*, RG 92, Consolidated Correspondence, Van Antwerp. On Nov. 15, U.S. Senator George H. Williams of Ore. wrote to USG on the same subject.—ALS, *ibid.*

1875, OCT. 7. U.S. Senator John P. Jones of Nev., San Francisco, to USG. "I have the honor to invite your attention to the fact that a very widespread dissatisfaction exists with regard to Judge Dunn of Arizona, and a general desire that he should be replaced, in the important office he holds, by some person who would dischage its duties with commendable ability. In case a change should be made I venture to request your kind consideration in behalf of Judge W. F. Anderson of White Pine, Nevada who has been long known to me as a man of unquestioned ability and sterling integrity. I am certain his appointment would be as popular with the good people of the territory as it would be conducive to the best interests of the public."—ALS, DNA, RG 60, Records Relating to Appointments. U.S. Senator William Sharon of Nev. favorably endorsed this letter.—AES (undated), *ibid.* On Dec. 7, 1873, U.S. Senator William M. Stewart of Nev. had written to USG recommending Edmund F. Dunne as chief justice, Arizona Territory.—ALS, *ibid.* On March 6, 1874, USG nominated Dunne. On Oct. 8, 1875, Stewart, San Francisco, wrote to USG. "I Enclose a letter recently received from E F Dunne Chief Justice of Arizona—Judge Dunne is undoubtedly an honest man—I have known him for many years and urged his appointment—The request for an investigation which he makes is a reasonable one and if his removal is to be bassed upon charges of corruption he ought to be heard—But I fear he has been a partisan in too many matters & has made himself so unpopular as to impair his usefulness. His opposition to the free Common schools of the Teritory as reported to me on good authority has made him enemies, and I suppose you will find it your duty to make a change—But while I cannot advise his retension in office I d[e]sire to bear testimony to his high character & honesty of purpose. In the Event of a change I wish to join Sentors Jones & Sharon in recomending Wm F Anderson of Nevada for the place. Mr Anderson is a lawyer of experience & standing and a man who enjoys a spotless reputation—In short he is a fit man for the place and his familiarity with mining law will enable him to be of great usefulness in a mining territory—No better man can be found any where who would take the office—I feel warranted in urging the appointment of Mr Anderson because I know the importance of the position & the difficulty of securing the right man for such a place"—ALS, *ibid.* Related papers are *ibid.* On Nov. 29, a correspondent reported from Washington, D. C. "It is said, upon apparently good authority, that President Grant has determined to remove E. F. Dunne, Chief Justice of the Supreme Court of Arizona Territory, on account of the position which he has assumed in public speeches on the school fund question. He is an ardent Catholic, and has indicated his desire that his coreligionists shall have a share of the common school fun[d] set apart for their special control. This places him in open opposition to the President's Iowa speech on the school question."—*New York Times,* Nov. 30, 1875. See Speech, [*Sept. 29, 1875*]. On Dec. 21, William Markoe, on behalf of Minn. Catholics, St. Paul, published resolutions protesting Dunne's removal. ". . . *Resolved,* That we condemn the policy, from whatever source emanating, that would stifle the discussion of minority grievances by an appeal to religious antagonisms, as vicious in principle and disastrous in effects. *Resolved,* That we are opposed to a centralization of educational powers in the national government, and re-assert as correct in principle the retaining within the people of all liberty of action, not incompatible with the general safety and happiness. . . ."— Clipping, DNA, RG 60, Letters from the President.

On Oct. 22, U.S. Senator Algernon S. Paddock of Neb. and U.S. Delegate Hiram S. Stevens of Arizona Territory had written to USG. "We have the honor to recommend the appointment of Nathan K. Griggs of Nebraska as Chief Justice of the Territory of Arizona vice Dunne against whom serious charges are preferred. Mr Griggs is an able lawyer, at present President of the State Senate of Nebraska. He was recently a candidate for Circuit Judge in his state but not successful although very strongly supported."—LS, *ibid.*, Records Relating to Appointments. On July 22, 1876, USG nominated Nathan K. Griggs as consul, Chemnitz.

On Nov. 10, 1875, Elisha M. Pease, Austin, had written to USG. "Understanding that Hon Colbert Caldwell of El Paso in this state is an applicant for the Office of Chief Justice of Arizona Territory, I beg leave to say that I believe him to be well qualified in every way for the position. He was a Union Man during the late Rebellion and was much persecuted for it. When Gov Hamilton returned to Texas as Provisional Governor at the close of the War he appointed Judge Caldwell as one of the Judges of our District Court, the duties of which he discharged with much credit to himself and to the satisfaction of the people of his District   Afterwards when Genl Sheridan became Commander of the 5th Military District, including Louisiana and Texas he appointed Judge Caldwell one of the Judges of our Supreme Court, which office he continued to hold until he was displaced by the organization of a Constitutional Government under the Reconstruction laws. At present he holds the office of Collector of Customs of the District of El Paso. . . ."—ALS, *ibid.* Related papers are *ibid.*

On Nov. 2, Charles A. Tuttle, Calif. Supreme Court reporter, Oakland, had written to USG. "For fifteen years last past I have been intimately acquainted with C G W French of Sacramento and have been associated with him in the conduct of Several very important cases, in which we have been Attorneys both in the District Courts and Supreme Court and have had therefore had a good opportunity to become conversant with his knowledge of the law, and his character as a man,—As a lawyer I know of no one in this State more thoroughly versed in all that pertains to the Statute and common law, and as a man he is what a lawyer Should be above reproach—He would adorn the bench and administer justice without favoritism"—ALS, *ibid.* Related papers are *ibid.* On Dec. 13, USG nominated Charles G. W. French as chief justice, Arizona Territory.

1875, OCT. 11.   James B. Thompson, agent, Ute Indians, Denver, to USG. "Referring to an interview between your excellency and Ouray, Chief of the Ute Indians, held in this city October 9, 1875, at which I had the honor to be present in an official capacity, and complying with your direction given at that time, I respectfully represent the following as the causes which led me to solicit that meeting. First. It is a notorious fact that, notwithstanding the solemn promise made to the Utes in the 'Brunot Treaty' of 1873 (ratified by Congress in April 1874), to the effect that they should receive from the government $25,000 per annum for having ceded to the United States a certain portion of their reservation (more fully described in said treaty), *not one dollar has yet been appropriated* for the purpose referred to. Secondly. It is claimed by Ouray, and by all his subchiefs with whom I have talked, that they have been deceived in regard to the amount and kind of land proposed to be ceded by the 'Brunot Treaty,' and he specially calls attention to the proviso contained in article 1 of said treaty. This proviso absolutely excludes from the cession all the region known as the 'Uncompahgre Valley' and sets it apart as a portion of the Ute Reservation, although it is known now, and was known at the time the treaty was made, that the direct northern boundary line of said cession, as laid down in the treaty, passes through the middle of said valley. This Uncompahgre Valley, or park, and the valleys of the streams flowing into the San Juan River, in the extreme southern portion of the reservation, comprises all the farming land available for this people within the limits of their present reservation; therefore it is easy to comprehend their solicitude that these regions should be excepted from the provisions of the treaty. It now appears from indubitable evidence that, in contravention of the articles of said agreement, white settlers have located both in the reserved portion of the Uncompahgre Valley and on the tributaries of the San Juan, heretofore referred to, and although these settlers have been driven out by the agent this summer, Ouray believes that as soon as it is understood that the northern line has been run by the government surveyors, these squatters will return and claim the protection of the government. It may be well to state here that gold has been discovered on the head waters of the Uncompahgre this summer. Thirdly. About the middle of August, this year, a party of surveyors belonging to the United States Geographical and Geological Survey, known as 'Hayden's Survey,' were attacked in the Sierra la Salle, or Salt Mountain, Southeastern Utah, by a small band of Indians, and lost (according to their report) four mules, all their instruments, pack-saddles, blankets, and provisions. It was represented by the leaders of the surveying party that the Indians who made the attack were Utes and that they were in the habit of visiting at the Ute Agency, where they obtained arms and ammunition; some of the surveyors going so far as to say that they had met certain members of the attacking party at the agency the year previous. The impression that they were *Utes* seems not only to have been carefully conveyed through the press to the people at large, but, through some means unknown to me, to have obtained with the Commissioner of Indian Affairs. (See copy of press telegram herewith.) This telegram makes Ouray, as chief of the Utes, responsible for the acts of a renegade band of Indians, none of whom belong to any of the tribes of which he is the head, and but one of whom, he assures me, has been at either of the Ute agencies for years; although the tribes to which they belong have always been at peace, and on friendly terms, with the Utes. The *one* Indian, to whom Ouray refers, is named 'Nubes Azul' or 'Blue Clouds,' and he was at the Los Pinos Agency *one day* early in 1874, from whence he was ordered by Ouray to take his departure as soon as his presence became known to him (Ouray). The surveying party was not at the agency until more than a month later. (See Agent Bond's annual report for 1874, page 92.) Fourthly. Referring to the fourth article of the 'Brunot Treaty,' Ouray respectfully asks that the agreement therein made may be fulfilled as soon as possible; and that your excellency may be pleased to make such recommendation as will secure an early appropriation for that purpose. The appropriation of last Congress for that object and for the removal of the Los Pinos Agency was only $10,000, all, or nearly all, of which will be required to effect said removal and to erect suitable buildings at the new location in Uncompahgre Valley; leaving little or nothing available for the establishment of the proposed agency for the Muache, Weeminuchee, and Capote bands. I think the argument which Ouray uses in this connection is a strong one, viz, that the Indians desire to go to farming and stock-raising, and that the Uncompahgre Valley will not accommodate them all; in fact, that said valley will only be adequate to the support of the Tabequache band; whereas the three tribes named will find abundance of good farming and grazing land on the tributaries of the San Juan which flow through the southern border of the reservation. A number of Indian families have been for years—and are now—farming in the valleys of the Dolores, the Mancos, and the Animas; and it is certain that many others will speedily follow their example, provided they can be secured in their title to the land and have an agent among them who will guard against encroachments on the part of the whites. Ouray desires that his agent be directed to employ, permanently, some competent person as interpreter in his place. He resigned the position last January; but up to this time the agent has declined to accept his resignation. He says he cannot faithfully discharge the duties of the office owing to the fact that he does not speak English and the agent does not understand Spanish. Ouray finally asked me to call your excellency's attention to the injustice done to his people through the enforcement of the order requiring all Indians to remain upon their reservations. The winter hunting-grounds of the Utes are almost entirely off the reservation; especially is this true as regards the region frequented by the buffalo, by the chase of which animal the majority of the warriors support themselves and their families. In support of argument that the Utes should be excepted from the provisions of that order because they are perfectly peaceable, and so nearly support themselves by the chase, I would respectfully state that the appropriation for subsistence of the Utes from year to year is $25,000, and that this amount, applied upon the basis of the Army ration, would support the 5,000 Utes exactly sixteen and two-third days. In consideration of the foregoing representations, which I believe to be correct and just, I would be pleased to have an opportunity of communicating to Ouray your excellency's early and favorable reply."—*SED*, 46-2-29, 18–19. Thompson enclosed an Associated Press dispatch dated Sept. 22. "Commissioner of Indian Affairs Smith sent the following dispatch to Agent Miles to-day in reply to a dispatch received Monday: Tell Ouray that the Brunot treaty very carefully defines the boundary of the cession, and the surveyors are following that line exactly and must not be disturbed; also that *the President* regards the attack upon Hayden's party *by the Utes* as a violation of the treaty, and expects *Mr. Ouray* to secure the capture and punishment of the bad Indians, and to recover the valuable surveying instruments which have been lost."—*Ibid.*, p. 20 (italics added by Thompson). See *PUSG*, 24, 239–44. On Nov. 22, USG signed an order extending the northern boundary of the Ute reservation.—DS, DNA, RG 75, Orders. *HED*, 45-2-1, part 5, I, 636, 45-3-1, part 5, I, 739, 47-2-1, part 5, II, 319, 49-2-1, part 5, I, 533; *SD*, 57-1-452, 834. On Dec. 15, Thompson wrote to USG. "Respectfully referring to my report of October 11th 1875, furnished, and f[o]rwarded, at your request, I would suggest that early action be taken, by the proper department, as regards the rights of the Ute Indians in this Territory, under the celebrated 'Brunot Treaty.' I would especially call Your Excellency's attention to the encroachments of white settlers upon the 'Uncompagre Valley'—"—ALS, DNA, RG 75, Letters Received, Colorado Superintendency. *SED*, 46-2-29, 23–24.

On March 25, 1876, Governor John L. Routt of Colorado Territory wrote to USG. "Article 14 of the Ute Treaty of Nov. 6, 1868, contains the stipulation 'that whensoever, in the opinion of the President of the United States, the public interest may require it, that all roads, highways, and railroads, authorized by law, shall have the right of way through the reservations herein designated.' I, therefore, respectfully request in behalf of the settlers of the Uncompahgre country, that, if you can consistently do so, you will accord permission to the 'Uncompahgre Valley Wagon road Company,' organized under the laws of this Territory, to have the right of way across the southeastern portion of the Ute reservation. This is rendered necessary by the topography of the country as the mines of that section are practically inaccessible during one-half of the year, unless the route above mentioned should be opened. Hon. T. M. Patterson, our Territorial delegate, is now endeavoring to secure the establishment of a post-route over this same line, and if travel be unrestricted it will be of immense advantage to settlement of that portion of the Territory, and the development of its vast resources."—LS, DNA, RG 75, Letters Received, Colorado Superintendency. On March 27, Mayor William J. Barker of Denver wrote to USG. "A portion of the mines in the San Juan country are surrounded on the East South & West by the Snowey Range and on the North by the Indian Reservation. If permission could be obtained to build a Road across the extreme Southern portion of the Reservation for a few miles those mines would be accessable the entire year, otherwise only for a short time in the Summer. The Cheif Ouray is willing and desirous that the Road be constructed. I am going to move to those mines this spring and if you could grant the permission to open the Road I will esteem it a personal favor"—ALS, *ibid.* A related paper is *ibid.* On April 21, Carl Wulsten, Cañon City, Colorado Territory, wrote to USG. "From all signs the Ute nation is very much dissatisfied with proceedings going on in and about La Plata County and other of the counties within the borders of the San Juan Country, of Southwestern Colorado. They complain, that the treaty with them and the U. S. Government is not kept faithfully and seem deterimed to drive out the whites when grass is growing. I in my mind, have no doubt, that the Utes are right and have every cause for complaint. Now Sir, there ought to be a thorough investigation of this case made, and *honest* men send out to settle this differences, who will act promptly and without treachery. to the Indians. The Utes are our friends and we ought to keep faith with them. I am a personal friend to several of their chiefs and warriors, and I know, that they have just cause for complaint. I know also that they are in dead earnest and determined to maintain themselves. I Sir, implore you to send out the right men and settle the difficulty, and, save us a bloody trouble, for it is brewing."—ALS, *ibid.* On Aug. 17, USG signed an order restoring part of Uncompahgre Park to the reservation.—DS, *ibid.*, Orders. Printed in the sources listed above. See *U.S. Statutes at Large,* XVIII, part 3, p. 37; *SED,* 46-2-29, 24–33; *HED,* 44-1-1, part 5, I, 735–36, 44-2-1, part 5, I, 422–23.

On Jan. 24, Thompson had written to USG. "I have the honor to apply for the appointment (in case of a vacancy) of U. S. Indian Agent at Los Pinos Agency in this Territory—I respectfully call Your Excellency's attention to the accompanying testimonials—"—ALS, DNA, RG 48, Appointment Papers,

Colorado Territory. On the same day, Routt favorably endorsed this letter.—ES, *ibid.* Related papers are *ibid.* On March 18, Thompson, Washington, D. C., wrote to USG. "Referring to an application, for appointment as U. S. Indian Agent at Los Pinos Colorado, made by me about February 1st, I have the honor to call your Excellency's attention to the enclosed letter of 'Ouray,' head chief of the Utes, and to ask that you will cause it to be filed with the application above mentioned—"—ALS, *ibid.* On Feb. 27, Ouray, Los Pinos Agency, had written to USG. "as chief of the Ute Indians and in behalf of that Portion of them who make their home at this agency I respecffully ask that an agent be appointed for them who will guard ther intrests and in whom they have confidence based upon actual acquantaince In case you are disposed to change the Present management of the agency which has not been Satisfactory to us I ask you to appoint in Place of the Present agent Mr J. B. Thompson late Specal agent at Denver Mr Thompson is the choice of my self and of all the head men of the different bands who acknowledge me as chief; and my People know and respect him"—LS, *ibid.* See Thomas F. Dawson, "Major Thompson, Chief Ouray and the Utes," *Colorado Magazine,* VII, 3 (May, 1930), 113–22. On May 1, 1874, USG had nominated Henry F. Bond as agent, Los Pinos Agency; on Dec. 6, 1876, USG nominated Willard D. Wheeler to replace Bond.

1875, OCT. 15. To Albert E. Knapp, Poultney, Vt. "I take much pleasure in acknowledging the receipt of the very handsome family bible which you were kind enough to send to me through Senator Edmunds, and beg you to accept my sincere thanks. I regret that this acknowledgment has been delayed on account of my absence from Washington."—Copy, DLC-USG, II, 3.

1875, OCT. 15. To Frederick Vokes. "I beg to acknowledge your kindness in presenting me with the little work of yours and ask your acceptance of my sincere thanks for it."—Copy, DLC-USG, II, 3. Possibly Frederick M. Vokes, who with his sisters had formed a popular touring theater company. See *New York Times,* June 6, 1888.

1875, OCT. 15. Arthur Shepherd *et al.,* D. C. Art. Corps, to USG. "For the purpose of assisting those, who have suffered so heavily through the late Texas floods, a Grand Promenade Concert and Ball will be given by Companies "A" and "B." of the D. C. A. C. (incorporated as a Volunteer Corps May 25, 1874, according to Act of Congress) on Tuesday evening, October 26 1875, at Masonic Temple,—*all* profits of which will be forwarded to Texas. Knowing Mr. President, your readiness to assist every good object, We the undersigned Committee, most respectfully beg your Excellency to order the U. S. Marine band to play on that occasion. Hoping that our application will meet with your kind consideration, . . ."—DS (more than 20 signatures), DNA, RG 45, Letters Received from the President. Secretary of the Navy George M. Robeson favorably endorsed the docket.—AES, *ibid.*

On Feb. 15, 1877, Shepherd wrote to USG. "I have the honor to respectfully apply for the appointment as Surveyor General of the territory of Arizona, for which place the name of Mr Culver. C. Sniffen was withdrawn from before the

Senate. . . ."—ALS, *ibid.*, RG 48, Appointment Papers, Arizona Territory. No appointment followed. See Alan Lessoff, *The Nation and Its City: Politics, "Corruption," and Progress in Washington, D. C., 1861–1902* (Baltimore, 1994), p. 112.

1875, OCT. 18, Monday.   Postmaster Gen. Marshall Jewell to John W. Garrett, Baltimore. "The president says he will accept your invitation to visit your house & has named saturday of this week as the d[ay]   any communication in regard to it you may make to me as I have permission to make all arrangements"— Telegram received, DLC-Garrett Family. On Oct. 22, Jewell again telegraphed to Garrett. "Arrangements all complete   The President will be at the Station at ten oclock with probably three members of the Cabinet and three or four other gentlemen"—Telegram received, *ibid.* On Oct. 23, USG took a special train to visit Garrett's "country seat, 'Montebello,' in Baltimore county, . . . The Presidential party embraced President Grant, Postmaster General Jewell, General Belknap, Secretary of War; General Babcock, the President's private secretary; Marshal Sharpe, of Washington; Judge Jewell brother of the Postmaster General; Collector Casey, of New Orleans, and Mr. Orvil Grant, brother of the President. . . . After the visitors had been shown everything of interest at Montebello they were driven through Clifton, the estate of the late Johns Hopkins and the site of the Johns Hopkins University, which he so richly endowed. The President and the other gentlemen were much interested in listening to the details of the bequest, . . ."—*Baltimore American and Commercial Advertiser*, Oct. 25, 1875.

1875, OCT. 18.   Camm Patteson, Howardsville, Va., to USG. "The fortunes of war have left but two adult survivors among the male members of my immediate family—myself and a young brother who was an infant during the late Struggle and of course took no part in it—He is burning with military ardor and wishes you to give to him the appointment as a Cadet at West Point—I well know that I have no claim upon you greater than any other citizen.—probably not as much as my northern fellowcitizens from the fact that I was an officer in the Confederate Army (Captain Co' D 56th 'Reg' Va. Volunteers) and an advocate of the constitutionality of Secession. . . ."—ALS, DNA, RG 94, Unsuccessful Cadet Applications.

1875, OCT. 20.   USG endorsement. "Will the Sec. of War please see Miss Greenwell, and, if he can consistently grant her request."—AES, DNA, RG 107, Appointment Papers. Written on a letter of Oct. 19 from Mary Greenwell, Washington, D. C., to USG. "As the great-great neice of George Washington, I feel confident that it is only necessary for me to appeal to your kind and generous sympathies, and to say I am *in want*, to insure from you the grant of my request. I am but sixteen years of age and the obtainance from the Secretary of War of copying from the War Record Fund, to be done at home will enable me to greatly assist my mother and to pursue my studies. I write, for fear a personal interview would so embarass me that I could not make myself properly understood, altho' I should much like to see the one who now fills the honored position once occupied by my illustrious ancestor, and whom I know possesses the same liberality and charity of heart."—ALS, *ibid.* A related note is *ibid.* On March 29, Greenwell had written to USG. "No doubt you will be some-what surprised to find on reading this letter that it is from the hand of the great, great neice of General George Washington 'the Father of our Country' My Grandfather was John Augustin Washington the last heir to and owner of Mount Vernon and feeling that you fill the position with the same heart and sympathy as did our countrys 'Father,' I am sure you cannot refuse the request of one of his kindred. I am a girl of but sixteen years, poor and desirous of finishing my education, and having no other resources, ask you to give me a letter to Adjutant General Townsend, having me appointed among the number of those employed in copying war records, an appropriation for that purpose having been made at the last session of Congress As the work is to be done by ladies at their homes it would give me a means of support and at the sametime enable me to pursue my studies, *Do*, Mr President, approve my request, . . ."—Copy, *ibid.*, RG 94, Letters Received, 1757 1875. On April 5, AG Edward D. Townsend wrote to Greenwell that "the appropriation for preparing the Records of the War for publication will be expended mainly in printing, all the copying needed for some time having been already done. There are as many persons already engaged on this work as can be employed to advantage"—Copy, *ibid.*, Letters Sent. In 1877, Greenwell served as temporary clerk in the Treasury Dept.

On Oct. 29, 1875, Secretary of War William W. Belknap had written to Marcie Elliotte, Washington, D. C. "Your letter of the 27th instant, has been received, enclosed in one from the President, with an endorsement by him referring your communication to the Secretary of War. There is no vacancy at present in the War Department; there are many applicants, and no immediate prospect of the appointment of any of them. . . ."—Copy, *ibid.*, RG 107, Letters Sent, Military Affairs.

1875, OCT. 20. USG endorsement. "War Dept. Please let special attention be invited to this application when apts. to West Point are made for /77."—AES, DNA, RG 94, Correspondence, USMA. Written on a letter of the same day from Maria B. Judah, Washington, D. C. "I respectfully apply for a cadet-ship at West Point for my son Theodore D. Judah, who will be seventeen years of age, next January—"—ALS, *ibid.* On June 25, Col. Benjamin Alvord, paymaster gen., had written to USG. "*Personal* . . . I enclose herewith a note from Mrs Genl H. M. Judah to you, as also her note to me on subject of her son being appd to West Point. You know fully her claims & it is not necessary for me to add any thing— By the way—my application has been made as you suggested to Secy of War for appointment of my own son to West Point to enter in June 1877—He will be 17 in May of that year,—& a very promising boy. Mrs. Judah asks me to call on you—Regret I cannot give myself that pleasure"—ALS, *ibid.* The enclosures are *ibid.* Admitted to USMA in 1877, Theodore D. Judah, son of USG's classmate Henry M. Judah, did not graduate.

On Jan. 29, 1876, Alvord wrote to USG requesting a cadetship for his son.— ALS, *ibid.* On the same day, USG endorsed this letter. "Refered to the Sec. of War. Let special attention be called to this application."—AES, *ibid.* Benjamin Alvord, Jr., graduated USMA in 1882.

1875, OCT. 20. USG note. "I ordered that Capt. T. should not be sent to Alaska and spoke to the Sec. of War of my recommendation of last spring that he should be appointed Lt. Gov. of the Soldiers Home."—Americana Mail Auction, Dec. 28, 1978, no. 283. On July 17, Mary Throckmorton, Washington, D. C., had written to [USG]. "I see by the Papers that the position of Sub-Governor at the Soldiers Home has been made vacant. My son has been eleven years with his Company, and is entitled to a detail. So dear Gen'l can you not order him there. You know not the happiness it will bring to our little family to be once more united, & I feel such faith in the regard you have for me that I know you will give it if you can."—ALS, DNA, RG 94, ACP, 5307 1875. Related papers are *ibid.*

On Feb. 4, 1875, U.S. Senator Oliver P. Morton of Ind. had written to USG. "In case of promotion on the staff of the Army, I beg leave to recommend Capt. Chas B Throckmorton, for promotion to Assistant Adjutant General, and commend him to your favorable consideration."—ALS, *ibid.*, Applications for Positions in War Dept. No promotion followed.

1875, OCT. 21.   Thomas M. Linley, formerly Co. E, 1st Ala. Cav., Wedowee, Ala., to USG. "When the war broke out, I was opposed to Secession, & from oppression, I left my family & went north & joined the U. S. Army,   I was poor, & gave my only horse, bridle & Saddle to the government,   at its close I had nothing, & continued bad crop years has kept me so,   I am now in dept, but if I can get my horse claim, that has been pending for 5 yrs—*this fall*, I can pay out & save my family from ruin, . . ."—ALS, DNA, RG 217, Third Auditor, Letters Received. A related letter is *ibid.*

1875, OCT. 22.   James Brown, San Francisco, to USG. "I regret to have to complain of the U. S. Consul at Acapulco, Mr John A. Sutter. A man named Henry Morris, left here a number of years since owing me $250, and went to Acapulco. After having been there some time, I wrote to him and wished to make arrangements for the payment of the debt with interest. He arranged with the Consul to pay $50 every 60 days until the debt was cancelled. . . ."—LS, DNA, RG 59, Miscellaneous Letters. Brown accused John A. Sutter, Jr., of keeping part of the money collected. On Aug. 24, Sutter had written to Brown's lawyer denying the charge.—ALS, *ibid.* On Jan. 20, 1876, William Hunter, 2nd asst. secretary of state, notified Brown that an investigation had cleared Sutter.—LS, *ibid.* On May 23, Brown wrote to USG disputing the ruling.—LS, *ibid.* See *PUSG*, 19, 414–15.

1875, OCT. 27.   Orville E. Babcock to George H. Sharpe, surveyor of customs, New York City. "The President directs me to say that if you can give Genl. Parker (E. S.) a position without injury to the service he would be pleased to have it done."—Copy, DLC-USG, II, 3. See William H. Armstrong, *Warrior in Two Camps: Ely S. Parker, Union General and Seneca Chief* (Syracuse, 1978), p. 165.

[*1875*], OCT. 28, Thursday.   Joaquin Miller, Washington, D. C., to USG. "I am to talk on literature and the literery outlook of America as compared with that of England, the treatment of Artists and litery men &c, at Lincoln Hall Sat. evening. I will take it as a very great personal favor if you can be present, as this is

my begining.”—ALS, Barrett Collection, ViU. See *Washington Evening Star*, Oct. 30, 1875.

1875, OCT. 28.   Mary Howard Schoolcraft, Washington, D. C., to USG. “My late husband, went out in 1816, as an explorer of the *then* unknown West, that was principally inhabited by bears, wolves, and blood thirsty savages. . . . In 1832 he discovered the Sources of the Mississippi River, & named it Itaska. He wrote thirty one works in prose and poetry all descriptive of his beloved country’s history. His whole life was spent in the service of the Government until finally a stroke of paralysis imprisoned him in his Library sixteen years   Even then, as his brain was not affected I became his amanuensis, and constant nurse, so that he wrote those six Great Quarto Volumes, of Indian history, for the Government, and then died in 1864 without leaving a dollar for his family—his only son, being then in the Federal Army, and he too died in hospital shortly afterwards, from wounds received at the battle of Gettysburg. If my said husband, were alive now he would be eighty four years old. I have travelled much and studied deeply the Races of Mankind, But a more splendid specimen of exalted perfected manhood, than Henry. R. Schoolcraft God never made. I say this defying contradiction though I know politicians believe, that ‘a living dog, is better than a dead lion’   Since my august husbands death, I have given up all society and try to serve my country, by seeking out the children of wicked parents to save them from the gallows   I have adopted into my family, several of these born miserables, and now they are highly educated, useful men, & women, & ~~now~~ they are on the high road to success. You are the only President of the United States, that I have never seen, during the last thirty, or forty years. I am deeply concerned about the education of the South, where I have great influence; and two years ago, wrote to you, to ask an interview on *that* subject. But receiving no answer, I knew it was impossible that you could have received my communication. The object of this letter, is to appeal to your gratitude, as a Western man, who knows what my husband did for that portion of the country, in its childhood, to aid his widow, in the following particulars. I was swindled out of my home, two years ago   Since then a friend, in New York has paid my board here. I have lately become possessed of Gen. O. O. Howard’s beautiful villa, on 7th Street—the house stables, et cetera cost $29000 to build them. The lot some 60000 square feet is valued by the neighbours at 50 cents a foot—The property in ‘*good times*’ ought to sell for $60.000, I am told—There is an incumbrance of $11000 on it and one years tax. The location is so very high that a perfect panorama of this whole city can be seen from it, with all the romantic forest surroundings for 20 miles. The air is so mountainous in its purity, that there is no necessity to go to Watering Places, in summer, for coolness, or health. In the hands of a rich owner, of taste, & interest this villa, from its commanding height, could be made the pride of the nations capital. and as you are the only millionaire President the United States ever did have, I should be rejoiced to see you enhance the value of property here, by such a splendid improvement of the Street—or by your presenting it to the Freedmans College. I am in so much need that I will sell it, exclusive of the mortgage for $20.000. cash. May the God of the Republic, founded by George Washington guide you

through our national dissentsions, . . ."—ADfS, DLC-Henry R. Schoolcraft. On
the same day, Schoolcraft drafted a nearly identical letter to USG and Julia Dent
Grant.—ADfS, *ibid.* A partial draft, dated Oct. 29, is *ibid.* On Oct. 14–17, 1872,
Schoolcraft had drafted numerous versions of a letter to Julia Grant complaining about black rule in her native S. C.—ADf, *ibid.* See Richard G. Bremer, *Indian Agent and Wilderness Scholar: The Life of Henry Rowe Schoolcraft* (Mount
Pleasant, Mich., 1987), pp. 284–90, 341–46.

1875, OCT. 29.   USG speech welcoming Nicholas Shishkin as the new Russian
minister.—*New York Herald*, Oct. 30, 1875.

1875, OCT.   Harry H. Andrew, Boston, to USG. "I take the liberty of you in order to apply to you as a candidate for West Point next June. I thought I might
apply to you as you knew my father who was governor of Massachusetts during the rebellion. Please excuse me if I have made a mistake in applying to
you."—ALS, DNA, RG 94, Correspondence, USMA. On Nov. 30, Eliza H. Andrew, Boston, wrote to USG on the same subject.—ALS, *ibid.* Andrew did not
attend USMA.

[*1875, Oct.*].   A. Gondet, Paris, to USG. "I take the liberty of writing to you
for the purpose, of inquiring what has become of one of my relatives named
Julien Bonnet. This relative, who was born in France, was drafted for the army
in 1813, and sailed for America while he was still a soldier. If he is still living, he must be in the United States, where he married a lady of quality who had
the face of a pig; her nearest relatives even declare that she was a princess. The
newspapers must have spoken of this event. My family, who can neither read
nor write, have preserved none of the letters addressed to them by him after his
marriage; for this reason I am no longer in possession of his address. It is at
least a dozen years since any tidings concerning him have been received. It is a
matter of great importance for me to learn what has become of him, or, if he is
dead, to learn the whereabouts of his widow."—ALS (in French, stamped Nov.
5, 1875), DNA, RG 59, Miscellaneous Letters; translation, *ibid.*

1875, Nov. 1.   Alexander Ramsey, St. Paul, to USG. "Geo. D. Bowman Esquire
of Penna. and formerly for many years a resident of Minnesota where he was &
is esteemed to be a gentleman of great integrity and business capacity desires
an appointment as Register of a land office and I take great pleasure in joining
his other frie[n]ds in cheerfully commeding him for such position"—ALS,
DNA, RG 48, Appointment Papers, New Mexico Territory. Related papers are
ibid. On Jan. 5, 1876, USG nominated George D. Bowman as land office register, La Mesilla.

1875, Nov. 1.   William S. Winder, Baltimore, to USG. "Some months since I
made application to the Hon Secretary of War asking asking permission to examine the 'Confederate Archives' now in his custody, for the purpose of getting
material to be used in defence of the memory of my Father Gen John H Winder
who has been so cruelly slandered. My application was denied and the Secre-

tary informed me by letter and verbally that he could not grant my request. I then asked if he had any objection to my making an appeal direct to your Excellency he informed me that he had no objection to my doing so. I now most respectfully ask that your Excellency will grant me permission to Examine the papers and documents captured at the close of the war—known as the 'Confederate Archives' for the purpose indicated above and none other, which I trust may be deemed a sufficient excuse for this letter."—Copy, DLC-Jubal A. Early. Winder endorsed this letter. "The answer to the above has been mislaid, it was answered very promptly, and signed for the President by Gen Babcock and said that the President endorsed the decission of the Sec of War in denying my request, but added it 'might be otherwise if you would designate any particular pages.'"—AE (undated), *ibid.* On Dec. 11, Winder wrote to Belknap requesting ". . . a copy of Gen Winders reply to Col Chandlers report, which reply included statements of the Chief Quarter Master Chief Commissary Chief Surgeon and the Commander of the Prison at Andersonville. Gen Winders reply with these statements were forwarded to Richmond I think in August 1864. I also desire copies of all letters and tellegrams from Gen Winder relating to the prisoners; Soon after reaching Andersonville in *June 1864,* the prison was then crowded and Gen Winder wrote to the Adjt Gen or Sec of War, and sent that letter by an officer to Richmond. I would like a copy of that letter. At various times he telegraphed and wrote concerning the Exchange of the sick, all of these letters and telegrams must have been among the papers captured, and I respectfully ask copies of them—. . ."—Copy, *ibid.* Related papers are *ibid.* See *PUSG,* 17, 598–99; Arch Fredric Blakey, *General John H. Winder C. S. A.* (Gainesville, Fla., 1990), pp. 203–7.

1875, Nov. 3. George W. Childs, Anthony J. Drexel, and Adolph E. Borie, Philadelphia, to USG. "We have learned, very much to our regret, that Col McMichael U. S. District Attorney of Philadelphia intends to resign that office, and feeling a strong interest in having a proper successor appointed we respectfully invite your attention to Col. McMichaels present assistant John K. Valentine Esq . . ."—LS, DNA, RG 60, Records Relating to Appointments. Related letters are *ibid.* On Dec. 15, USG nominated John K. Valentine as U.S. attorney, Eastern District, Pa., replacing William McMichael.

1875, Nov. 4. USG endorsement. "Referred to the Secy of War with recommendation that Col: O'Rourke be appointed in charge of one of the Nat. Cemeteries if Vacancy exists."—Copy, DNA, RG 94, ACP, 4154 1876. Written in response to a letter of Nov. 1 from Patrick J. O'Rourke, Nashville, to AG Edward D. Townsend. "I have the honor to make application for the position of superintendant of one of the National Cemeteries, and base my claims upon my Military record—I served as Capt Co E 1st Regt Penna Reserves for three years, . . . I was wounded at Charles City cross roads in the Seven days battle before Richmond—As to my Civil life I take pleasure in submitting testimonials from Citizens & Soldiers of high character. . . ."—ALS, *ibid.* Related papers are *ibid.* As of Sept. 30, 1877, O'Rourke served as cemetery superintendent, Fort McPherson, Neb.

1875, Nov. 5.   William W. Hanes, Covington, Ky., to USG. "I most respectfully ask your serious attention to following   Genl S. V. Benet Chief of Ordnance Deplores the condition of his Department owing to the lack of rifled Guns of large caliber when he has any amount of Smoothe Bore large and Small which I Say can be made more effective and De Structive than Rifled guns of Same caliber By having Percussion Projectiles fired from Smoothe Bore guns . . ."—ALS, DNA, RG 156, Letters Received. Hanes sought $100,000 in return for $75,000 worth of his shells, patented in 1862. On May 21, 1872, Secretary of War William W. Belknap had written to Jesse Root Grant, Covington. "I have the honor to reply to your reference of the letter of W. W. Hanes, Esq., who desires to introduce his improved projectile and to obtain a contract for furnishing Ordc Stores, that the Department will take pleasure in testing or examining them if Mr. Hanes will furnish samples or drawings of the same; but that having large quantities of shot and shell on hand, the Department has no present intention, as he presumes, of giving out contracts for such."—Copy, *ibid.*, RG 107, Letters Sent, Military Affairs. See *HRC*, 45-3-175.

1875, Nov. 12.   USG note. "Sec. Hitchcock is very anxious for this apt. as a personal favor to him."—AN, DNA, RG 94, Applications for Positions in War Dept. On the same day, Secretary of War William W. Belknap wrote on the reverse of this note. "The P. informed me that he knew nothing about this beyond H's request & had no wish to express"—AN, *ibid.* On Oct. 23, Wilbur B. Hugus, Omaha, had written to Belknap. "I have the honor to apply for the appointment of Post trader at Fort Fetterman, Wyoming Territory, which, I understand, is now vacant. . . ."—ALS, *ibid.* Brig. Gen. George Crook favorably endorsed this letter.—AES, *ibid.* No appointment followed.

1875, Nov. 17.   USG endorsement. "Refered to the Sec. of War. Please call special attention to this application when appointments to the Military Academy are made."—AES, DNA, RG 94, Correspondence, USMA. Written on an undated letter from Eunice Tripler to USG. "Will you give my Son Ned an appointment to West-Point among those for the *last* year of your Second term?— The enclosed letter has comforted me by its promises, in many an hour of trouble. I send it to you as a reminder—It has done duty before, you may perhaps remember the occasion, it is now on its last mission, I hope and pray it may be a successful one. I think Ned will do you credit. I have great faith in him. He is a namesake of Genl Townsend (Edward Townsend) whom I have asked to be the bearer of this note & who will I think be glad to convey your answer to me if it be favorable—"—ALS, *ibid.* Edward T. Tripler did not attend USMA. See Eunice Tripler, *Some Notes of Her Personal Recollections* (New York, 1910), pp. 103–4, 152–56.

1875, Nov. 18.   To Joseph W. Sawyer, Boston. "I have your very cordial invitation to participate with the members of the Old 19th Massachusetts Volunteers in their celebration of the anniversary of the crossing of the Rhappahannock river in 1862—You are very kind to think of me in connection with the celebration of that event and I thank you, but the public business will not admit of my absence from the Capital at the time set in your invitation and I am therefore obliged to deny myself the pleasure of being with you."—LS, Robert L. Markovits, Middletown, N. Y.

1875, Nov. 18.   Alton R. Easton, pension agent, St. Louis, to USG. "The facts as set forth in the enclosed are substantiated by letters and other papers, accompanying the letter from Lieut Charles Morton to me, and dated Sept 25. 1875. He is a Son-in-Law of Genl L. C. Easton of the Qr Mr Dept—I believe him to be a worthy young officer, and your favorable action towards his promotion, will confer an additional obligation on me."—ALS, DNA, RG 94, ACP, 285 1876. On Sept. 25, 2nd Lt. Charles Morton, USMA 1869, Sidney Barracks, Neb., had written to Easton seeking promotion.—ALS, *ibid.* On Dec. 4, 1876, USG nominated Morton as 1st lt., 3rd Cav.

On Jan. 10, 1877, Mary E. Sibley (Easton's sister), St. Charles, Mo., wrote to USG urging a staff appointment for Morton.—ALS, *ibid.* No appointment followed.

1875, Nov. 19.   USG note. "Steven J. Mulhall applies for Lieutenancy. Entered the service during the War, at 12 years of age, Residence Buffalo N. Y.   Papers now in the War Dept.   Now in War Dept. as Clerk."—AN, DNA, RG 94, ACP, 5064 1875. On July 13, Stephen J. Mulhall, Washington, D. C., had written to USG. ". . . I am the son of an old Soldier, & entered the 4th U. S. Arty. as a musn. at the breaking out of the War, at the early age of eleven (11) years & served my time out. . . ."—ALS, *ibid.*, 5142 1875. Related papers are *ibid.* On Dec. 19, Secretary of War William W. Belknap wrote to AG Edward D. Townsend. "The President directs that Mr. Mitchell & Mr. Mulhall have another examination by February 1. 1876—"—AL (initialed), *ibid.*, 5344 1875. See *PUSG,* 24, 410.

On Nov. 19, David D. Mitchell, Jr., Washington, D. C., had written to USG. "I have the honor to apply to you for the appointment of Second Lieutenant in the regular Army. I am a native of Missouri, Age 27 and the Eldest son of the late Col David D. Mitchell, who participated in the Mexican War and whose record is on file in the War Department. I graduated at the Kentucky Military Institute and beleive that I am well qualified for the above position. Trusting that my application may be favorably received, . . ."—ALS, DNA, RG 94, ACP, 5256 1875. Related papers are *ibid.* On Feb. 23, 1876, USG nominated Mitchell, Jr., as 2nd lt., 15th Inf.

1875, Nov. 20.   H. S. Williams, Wetumpka, Ala., to USG. "I write you to inform you of the condition of the colored people of Elmore Co. and to ask your advise. The colored people are very ignorant and poor and I fear they will ever remain so from the fact they are cheated out of their just earning and defeated of their rights by those who have the power and brain to do it, to such an extent that some of them are forced to do that which is not consistent with their will or character to sustain themselves and families and the ones that cause them to do thus by the way of figuring their just earnings from them are the first to take them up an thrust them into Prison without a fair trial in Court. and rejoice at the fall of the poor ones   They make their brags that they will enslave us by putting us in Prison and then take us out and work us on their farms like they have many now that have been convicted to prison and they have got them out on their farms under the whip and lash   They are taking the ignorant people without on false accusation and without legal warrants and thrusting them into prison. and in Tallapoosa. they are taking the colored people up for carrying fire arms and going to their houses and taking arms and they are agreat many things going on here against both the laws of this state and of the United States   There must a surden change or we must suffer from unjust treatment   what must ~~me~~ we do. Please write me as soon as you get this   I speake these words having good will toward all men and malice toward none   I call your attention to these things because I see the ill-treatment and suffering of my people and believe it to be my duty to inform you of the eviles now going on   As I have been a slave and my chance for education have been poor please excuse my deficiency in scholar-ship."—ALS, DNA, RG 60, Letters from the President.

1875, Nov. 23.   Marcus C. M. Hammond, USMA 1836, Beech Island, S. C., to USG. "I have a Son who has recently Set his mind upon the *Army*, if there is any possibility of procuring a commission. He is in his 21st year & competent in all the attainments & qualities of the grade which he could Seek. When at the right age, I applied to a Congressional Representative for a Situation at West Point— there was then no vacancy, & he has grown, too old for so Slow a process at his time of life—and he has been recently preparing on the programe for a commission—I had hopes that backed by political influence if the personal had no weight, that I could Secure the kindness of your attention.—I am not personally acquainted with you, but we have certainly known each other—you must have heard of me in the Regiment, when you first joined it—I must have left a reputation for geniality & Sociability which must have existed longer than 4 months, between my departure & your arrival—mutual friends like Alvord have linked—our memories together these many years, & the tie of Hoskins & others, bound in the bloody Shroud of battle, Should render all their intimate associates more friendly than others. While the Sentiments Suggested by Such deeds have been deadened by frequent, repetition, by your active Career in the war, their first blush would be most indellibly retained, *Hence* there is a prospect of being kindly remembered by Genl, Grant.—Besides we claim the Same Alma Mater. My Son is named *James H. Hammond*. & as far as politics are concerned, his mood is as blank as this paper. He is not like the citizens of Athens, in the time of Solon—Compelled to be a partizan,   He is now prepared to be chained to the car of his chieftain, & Should you confer this favor on him, he would, no doubt belong to you for life. General Alvord, will inform you that I was Stricken with Paralysis a year ago, & in consequence, I am now confined to bed—"—L, DNA, RG 94, Applications for Positions in War Dept. On Dec. 17, Col. Benjamin Alvord, paymaster gen., wrote to USG recommending James H. Hammond as 2nd lt.—LS, *ibid.* No appointment followed. See Carol Bleser, ed., *The Hammonds of Redcliffe* (New York, 1981), pp. 12–14.

1875, Nov. 23.   Harvey Lindsly *et al.*, American Colonization Society, Washington, D. C., to USG. "By official dispatches just received, the painful intelli-

gence is announced that an engagement took place at Cape Palmas on the 10th
of October, between the troops of the Liberian Government and the Natives of
that region, in which the former were repulsed, leaving their cannon and ammunition in the hands of the enemy. The relation of the Government of the
United States to the Republic of Liberia is '*sui generis.*' It is not like that of Great
Britain to one of its colonies, exposed to extreme peril, not to say annihilation,
yet were Liberia a colony of America, more could not have been done for its
founding and fostering, than has been bestowed upon it from this country.
We[re] either of the great Powers of Europe placed in like relations to Liberia,
no scruples as to propriety would prevent their immediate interposition. With
this view of the State of the case, as a Committee of that organization to which,
under God, Liberia owes its existence, we respectfully and earnestly solicit the
attention of the President and his Cabinet to the very critical condition of that
young Republic, with limited means of self-defence against the hostile attacks
of populous and savage tribes in their immediate vicinity, with scarcity of provisions actually existing, and *famine* immediately threatening; an[d] we respectfully ask that a Government steamer be sent to Liberia with the least possible delay. We believe that such action is right and just in itself, and urgently
demanded by every consideration of humanity and sympathy with this
people:—the most of whom were born in America, and who are struggling to
build up a Christian Nation in Africa, and that it will be universally approved,
not only in the United States but throughout the civilized world. The presence
of such a vessel as requested will inspire with fresh courage the Liberians, and
in equal degree restrain from further hostilities their savage enemies."—LS
(4 signatures), DNA, RG 59, Miscellaneous Letters. On Nov. 30, Bishop Edmund S. Janes and five others, New York City, wrote to USG. "The undersigned
managers of the Missionary Society of the M. E. Church respectfully represent
to you our great interest in the Republic of Liberia and join our solicitations to
those already received by you that a government vessel be immediately sent to
the seat of war in the south part of that Republic. For more than forty years we
have been engaged in mission work on that part of the African coast, expending per annum, sums varying from $8000 to $35000. We have erected school-
houses churches and parsonages, and have a conferenc[e] of ministers there, and
a goodly number of church members. All our interests are imperille[d] by these
warlike demonstrations, and we invoke the power of the United States government for their protection   All the other aspects of the case have, no doubt, already been represented as fully as need be. Humanity, Civilization, and Christianity deman[d] the interference of our government."—LS, *ibid.,* RG 45,
Letters Received from the President. On Oct. 29, Secretary of State Hamilton
Fish had recorded in his diary. "The Secretary of the Navy exhibited a chart of
the coast of Liberia, and referred to the insurrection now pending in that country. He read the heads of instructions proposed to be given to one or more of
our vessels of War, to proceed thither, practically giving authority to them to
intervene and in his language 'to shell the woods where the insurgents might
be supposed to be; and declare the intent of the United States to extend its protection to the Republic of Liberia, which had been established and maintained
by this government.' The President remarked that he thought that the instruc-

tions were right; and should be sent   I thought they ~~were~~ went further possibly than was intended; and asked Mr Robeson whether the government of the United States had in any way contributed to the founding of the government of Liberia, or had at any time expressed itself as especially interested in its existence: adding that I knew that individuals had been thus interested, but asked for information with regard to the government   He said the Colonization Society had contributed; but allowed that he knew nothing of any action on the part of the government. The President asked me if I thought the proposed instructions committed the government to anything more than a declaration of friendship and sympathy. In reply I referred to an expression as used by Mr Robeson that the government promised to extend its protection to that of Liberia, in case of assaults of any of the neighbors, and to the allegation made, that those tribes were being instigated by the British Government and British influences   That if such protection was assured, and the fact of such influence were established, we might be called upon to extend our protection in case of hostility, even with Great Britain, sustaining the insurgent tribes. That I did not think it wise to promise protection which, under the Constitution, we might not be at liberty to give. The President assented, though playfully remarking 'Robeson will only have to drive the British ships away.' Mr Robeson said he would carefully prepare the instructions and submit them to me   I told him I thought that this was sufficiently delicate, to be decided in full Cabinet."—DLC-Hamilton Fish. On March 1, 1876, warring parties signed a peace treaty witnessed by Capt. Alexander A. Semmes, U.S.S. *Alaska.*—Copy, DNA, RG 59, Miscellaneous Letters. On Feb. 29, King Weah and other chiefs, Cape Palmas, had written to USG. "We the undersigned humbly beg to make the following petition, through Captain Semmes to the United States Government, to establish public schools in the different sections of our Tribe, through the Foreign Committee of the Protestant Episcopal Mission of New York, by furnishing the said Foreign Committe with the means of purchasing the books & stationery etc. for the said schools and to pay the teachers therewith for a certain number of years, for we are perishing in heathenism for the lack of knowledge, and we stand in need of help of the United States in this disideratum"—Copy, *ibid.* See *Foreign Relations, 1875*, II, 832–36; Gary R. Kremer, *James Milton Turner and the Promise of America: The Public Life of a Post-Civil War Black Leader* (Columbia, Mo., 1991), pp. 78–86.

On March 8, 1875, U.S. Senators Thomas J. Robertson and John J. Patterson of S. C., and two others, had written to USG. "We the undersigned most respectfully represent that the great commercial relations between our Country, and the Republic of Liberia and its growing importance demands a renewal of efforts to develop its growth and augments its value to our Country. And believing that to have a representative from this government as minister whose energy and ability would encourage those relations between the two countries; allying them closer; by mutual commercial benefits derived, by a more perfect union of interests, We respectfully and earnestly request the appointment of Hon. Richard. H. Cain, of South. Carolina, as minister and consul general, to that Republic, Believing that his appointment will greatly enhance the interests of both countries."—DS, DNA, RG 59, Letters of Application and Recommendation. No appointment followed. Richard H. Cain, African Methodist Episcopal minister and newspaper editor, had just completed a term as congressman.

On Dec. 20, Charlton H. Tandy, St. Louis, wrote to USG. "The undersigned, your obedient Servant, respectfully represents that rumors prevail indicating that ere long the position of U. S. MINISTER PLENIPOTENTIARY to the REPUBLIC OF LIBERIA will become vacant by reason of the resignation of the present incumbent—the Hon J. Milton Turner. Conditioned upon this rumor proving to be a fact, I desire to express to you my wish to fill the vacant place, pledging in advance the strictest fidelity to duty and the fullest possible exercise of whatever of ability I possess. Besides having the honor of Your personal acquaintance, I have that of many others here who are known to you, and with their kind consent, I will refer to what they may say in my behalf."—L, *ibid.* John F. Long, Henry C. Wright, and others favorably endorsed this letter.—AES, *ibid.* On Aug. 3, 1876, Tandy wrote to USG on the same subject.—ALS, *ibid.* Tandy served as messenger, St. Louis Customhouse.

On July 10, C. O. H. Thomas, African Methodist Episcopal pastor, Smithfield, Ohio, wrote to USG. ". . . I am 32 years of age, and has a knowledge of the Portuguese as well as the Spanish language, as well as a ready facility of acquiring languages. . . . P. S. If the Liberian Mission should not be available, I am at your service for any other position of the Government, that you may (in your judgment) deem fit to impose upon me"—ALS, *ibid.*

On Aug. 10, W. Hines Furbush, sheriff, Lee County, Marianna, Ark., wrote to USG. "Allow me to informally ask a favor at your hands   I see by the papers that J Milton Turner is about to resign ~~his~~ as Minister to Liberia   For two reasons I ask for the appointment   1st Because I am tired of southern politics and if I continue I am sure a life policy would be the best thing I could procure   I have been Sheriff of Lee County for four years and on last saturday was unanimously nominated again   But I fear the result of two years ago when I had to shoot two men that cut my throat in the dark   2nd Because I am aquainted with the country having spent some time there (in /66 & /67 Returning to Arkansas in /68   I have written to our Senators about the matter and I am sure they will consider my claims   There is hardly any one that wants the place on account of the helth of the country   If you can without injury to any one nominate your humble servant (that is if our Senators should approve of it) you will have confered a great favor upon one that has faithfully Served you"—ALS, *ibid.* A related petition is *ibid.* J. Milton Turner continued as minister to Liberia.

1875, Nov. 23.   Thomas B. Swann, Charleston, West Va., to USG. "Major Slack, the present Marshall of W. V. informs me there is an effort on foot to remove him, & requests of me a note to your Excellency. It gives me pleasure to say Major Slack won a good reputation as a soldier, & has been a faithful, & efficient officer as Marshall of W. V. for the last eight years. It appears that in the item of summonsing his Jurors Major Slack has not given entire Satisfaction to republicans of extreme views, but he has had great difficulties to contend with. No one doubts he is an ardent republican. Major Slack is a man of fine sense, & as an officer he is competent & faithful."—ALS, DNA, RG 60, Records Relating to Appointments. On Jan. 8, 1876, George H. Henderson, Charleston, wrote to USG. "We the republicans of this State very much desire a change in the Office of U. S. Marshall,   the present Marshall uses his Office more for the benefit of the Democrats than for the Republicans—We would also submit for your consideration the name of G. W. Patton of this place a *veteran soldier*, an honest worthy republican for the appointment instead of the present incumbent Mr. Slack"—ALS, *ibid.* Related papers are *ibid.* On March 2, 1875, George W. Patton, Charleston, had written to USG. "I see by the papers that you want some of the younger business men, to apply for the position of Paymaster's in the army. I would therefore offer my name for your consideration. . . ."—ALS, *ibid.*, RG 94, Applications for Positions in War Dept. On May 15, 1876, USG nominated Hedgeman Slack to continue as marshal, West Va. On May 25, USG withdrew this nomination in favor of Patton.

On May 26, Swann wrote to USG. "We are deeply exercised here today at the news that you had withdrawn the name of H. Slack for Marshall of W. V. from the Senate; & Sent in the name of another Gentleman. Major Slack is a faithful public servant, & is just & honest & there can be no just reason for his removal."—ALS, *ibid.*, RG 60, Records Relating to Appointments. On the same day, USG wrote a note. "Withdraw nomination of ___ [Geo W.] Patton as Marshal [of US for Dist of] of West Va & renominate Slack"—AN (bracketed material not in USG's hand), Wayde Chrismer, Bel Air, Md. On May 28, John S. Carlile, Washington, D. C., wrote to USG. "I stopped off here this morning on my way to Balto and was surprised to learn that some one by the name of Patton had been recommended to you for Marshal of our District (the District of West Virginia) over the present incumbent Maj. H. Slack. Maj Slack is a West Virginian Patton is not. The Republicans of our state have felt heretofore the injustice that has been done them by the appointment of nonresidents credited to our state and I think I hazard nothing when I say that if the app.t had to be made by yr friends in West Virga Patton would not get ten votes. The reappointment of Maj. Slack is expected by the citizens of our state. He is a good officer, honest, faithful, and capable, and I am sure if you were properly advised you would reappoint him. We have carried our state for you over a democratic majority of thousands, and could do it again, because we all have confidence in you—more than we have in any party—"—ALS, DNA, RG 60, Records Relating to Appointments. Related papers are *ibid.* On May 29, USG again nominated Slack. On Jan. 5, 1877, USG nominated Patton to replace Slack.

1875, Nov. 29.   USG endorsement. "Refered to the Sec. of War. Let special attention be called to this application"—AES, DNA, RG 94, Correspondence, USMA. Written on a letter of the same day from Brig. Gen. George Crook to AG Edward D. Townsend. "I have the honor to apply for the appointment 'at Large' of George Crook jun. as cadet at West Point for 18677—"—ALS, *ibid.* George Crook, Jr., did not attend USMA.

1875, Nov. 29.   Albion W. Tourgee, Greensboro, N. C., to USG. "I have the honor to recommend to your Excellency's favorable notice Master William Andrews of Raleigh, North Carolina. Master Andrews is a bright sturdy lad of excellent parts and good parentage: the son of a widow and one whom the Republicans of North Carolina would be glad that your Excellency should honor with the appointment he desires."—ALS, DNA, RG 94, Correspondence,

USMA. Other papers recommending William R. Andrews for an appointment to USMA are *ibid.*; he did not attend.

1875, Nov. Benjamin H. Cheever, Jr., New York City, to USG. "I have the honor respectfully to solicit an appointment as Lieutenant in the Army I was born in the District of Columbia, received my early education in Rhode Island, and graduated at Eagleswood Military Academy. Have had two years frontier life in Hayden's Geological Survey. I am personally known to Senators Anthony, Burnside, and Logan, to whom I beg to refer as to my capacity for such position."—ALS, DNA, RG 94, Applications for Positions in War Dept. On Aug. 11, 1876, USG nominated Cheever as 2nd lt., 6th Cav.

1875, DEC. 1. Julia Ingeröe, Fort Howard, to USG. "Please excuse a poor womans petition But as it is a higher power that prompts me I can not help writing hoping for results Eight years ago God with his almighty hand began to work one my mind that I aught to try to get Christian Missionaries to labor among the Indians ~~from~~ who dwell between Omahaw and Salt Lake Citty It would be for America a great and woundefull blessing to bring the Indians on terms of friendship with the whites in ~~thi~~ese parts As It is Brigham Young politics to do all that he can to Enslave these poor Creatures by allowing his Bishops and highest men to take the females of those tribes for wives so as in case of need and hostility to make use of those tribes . . . I am an old Scandinavian woman and have come to this country with this purpose alone if anything in this way will be done I shal feel richly paid"—ALS, DNA, RG 75, Letters Received, Miscellaneous.

1875, DEC. 1. Francis Woodbridge, Allegheny Arsenal, Pittsburgh, to USG. "I have the honor to ask of The President a commission as Second Lieutenant in the Army of the United States. I am the only son of Captain Francis Woodbridge, 2nd Artillery, who graduated at the Military Academy in 1837: was twice brevetted for conspicuous gallantry during the Mexican War and died at Barrancas Barracks, Fla. (from the effects of a disease contracted in Mexico) October 20, 1855, leaving his family destitute of means. I was born at Detroit, Mich, January 25, 1853, and am now in the twenty-third year of my age."—ALS, DNA, RG 94, ACP, 5489 1875. On Dec. 4, AG Edward D. Townsend endorsed this letter. "The President directs that Mr. Woodbridge be appointed if he passes the examination as 2d Lieut."—AES, *ibid.* On July 29, Kate Woodbridge Michaelis, Allegheny Arsenal, had written to Julia Dent Grant concerning her brother and the acquaintance between the Grants and Woodbridges formed while both families lived in Detroit.—ALS, *ibid.* On Jan. 10, 1876, USG nominated Woodbridge as 2nd lt., 7th Inf.

1875, DEC. 2. USG endorsement. "Refered to the Sec. of War. Let special attention be called to this application when appointments to West Point are made."—AES, DNA, RG 94, Correspondence, USMA. Written on a letter of Nov. 1 from 1st Lt. William N. Sage, 11th Inf., Fort Richardson, Tex., to USG. "I have the honor to request that my son, William. H. Sage. may be appointed to the Military Acadamy at West Point, and to enclose herewith reccommendations for his appointment. He will be 17 years of age in April next, and I desire if possible, to have him appointed to the class which will enter in June 1877."—ALS, *ibid.* Related papers are *ibid.* William H. Sage graduated USMA in 1882.

1875, Dec. 3. USG speech acknowledging the promotion of J. H. de Hegermann-Lindencrone from chargé d'affaires to Danish minister.—*New York Times,* Dec. 5, 1875.

1875, Dec. 3. USG pardon. "Whereas, on the 19th day of July, A. D. 1875, in the Police Court of the District of Columbia, one Annie Kelly was convicted on two informations of larceny, and was sentenced to be imprisoned for one hundred and eighty days; And whereas, in view of her extreme youth, she being but thirteen years of age, the Judge before whom she was tried, and the United States District Attorney believe that she has been sufficiently punished. Now, therefore, be it known, that I, . . . hereby grant to the said Annie Kelly, a full and unconditional pardon. . . ."—Copy, DNA, RG 59, General Records.

1875, Dec. 4. Herman Tuerk, Lübeck, Germany, to USG. "Will please forgive the liberty I am taking in addressing you and depriving you of your valuable time, by laying the following petition before you. At the battle of Pearidge Ark. on the 8th of March 1862, being then a 2nd Lieut. of Comp. E 12th Mo. Vols., and 20 years of age, I lost both my eyes by an enemical gunshot. After having had an audience with our never to be forgotten and deeply lamented President Lincoln in Feb. 63, who then allowed me a personal pension of 25 doll. per month, which Congress has now raised to 50 per month, I left in 1864 for Europe, as living is so much cheaper here. Since my stay here I have been principally associating with German Officers here in Hamburg Berlin etc., and am also a member of the military club. I have always born the title of Lieutenant and now being more advanced in years, also married since Spring, it is not very agreeable, as Lieutenants here are all so much younger, than myself, to rank with them as such.—Therefore, your Excellency, I most urgently beg of you, as the Chief Commander of the Army and Navy of the United States, to present me with the title of 'Captain' of U. S. Vols., or U. S. Army, or U. S. Invalid Corps; by doing so, I should ever be indebted to you. . . ."—LS, DNA, RG 94, ACP, 120 1876. A related letter is *ibid.* See *CG,* 37–3, 1237–38; *U.S. Statutes at Large,* XII, 918.

1875, Dec. 6. To Detective James G. Tilley authorizing extradition of William J. Sharkey from Canada to N. Y.—Copy, DNA, RG 59, General Records. The person Tilley found in Montreal was not Sharkey.—*New York Times,* Dec. 21, 1875. In June, 1873, Sharkey had been convicted of murder in New York City; on Nov. 19, he escaped from the Tombs disguised as a woman with assistance from female accomplices and thereafter evaded recapture. See *ibid.,* June 22, Nov. 20, 1873, March 17, 1877; Thomas S. Duke, *Celebrated Criminal Cases of America* (San Francisco, 1910), pp. 611–12.

1875, DEC. 6.   Levi P. Luckey to Secretary of the Navy George M. Robeson. "The President directs me to say that he has no objection to the Marine Band playing at the Concert in aid of the Protestant Orphan Asylum on next Monday Evening—the 13th."—ALS, DNA, RG 45, Letters Received from the President.

1875, DEC. 6.   Larkin Smith, USMA 1835, Atlanta, to USG. "If I could have had it otherwise my first effort towards renewing old asociations, would not consist in asking a favor, but it so happens that on the rare occasions, when in recent years, I could visit Washington, you have been elsewhere, preventing the opportunity to make my respects to you. The favor I would ask is to place my son, Albert Triplett Smith, at West Point, as a Cadet at Large in June 1877. Since they disrupted the country in 1870, I have shunned politicians and therefore cannot expect support in this petition from them, the only field open to me is with officers of the old Army, and among them, I know of none more likely to make an effort in my behalf, than you would be, in inclination, to favor me. I therefore come directly to you trusting my hopes to that favor. It may not be amis to state that my son is the Grandson of the late Major General Jacob Brown."—ALS, DNA, RG 94, Correspondence, USMA. Smith had served as col. and asst. q. m. gen., C.S. Army. On Dec. 3, Smith had written to Secretary of War William W. Belknap on the same subject.—ALS, *ibid.* On Dec. 8, Belknap wrote to Smith. "Yours of December 3d has been received. I have placed the name of your son, Albert T. Smith, upon the list to be submitted to the President, when he makes his selections for appointment to West Point, for 1877. The list is very large and the applicants very pressing; but I shall see that this case receives full consideration from the President."—LS (press), *ibid.* On Feb. 3, 1876, U.S. Representative Alexander H. Stephens of Ga., Crawfordville, wrote to USG. "Allow me to commend to the special consideration of your Excellency Master Albert Triplett Smith who desires the appointment of Cadet in the Military Academy at West Point. . . ."—LS, *ibid.* Albert T. Smith did not attend USMA.

1875, DEC. 6.   Chief Justice Morrison R. Waite to USG. "At the request of an esteemed friend in Richmond, Mr. W. H. Haxall, I ask leave to introduce to you his sister in law Mrs. Jane R. Haxall. She wishes to have a nephew placed at the Naval Academy & will call upon you for that purpose. May I ask your attention to her application—"—ALS (press), DLC-Morrison R. Waite.

1875, DEC. 10.   Levi P. Luckey to U.S. Senator Roscoe Conkling of N. Y. "As you requested I handed the President Mr. Bailey's letter to you. He instructs me to say that he thinks it hardly probable that Major Enos will be retired. There are several officers before the Retiring Board but there are only three or four vacancies and it is unlikely that any officers of the Staff Corps will be retired as there are others that will have to go out."—Copy, DLC-USG, II, 3. Maj. Herbert M. Enos, USMA 1856, on sick leave as of July 12, 1870, was retired as of May 29, 1876.

1875, DEC. 10.   Miguel Tejera, Paris, to USG. "The love which I bear to my native land, America, has induced me to establish an illustrated journal in this capital, the title of which is 'El Mundo Americano.' My design, in so doing, is to make better known in the old world the history, geography, statistics, commerce, industry, manners, customs and literature of the new; and, inasmuch as I cannot for a moment doubt that this enterprise will meet with Your Excellency's approval, I have taken the liberty to send you the numbers of 'El Mundo Americano,' which have thus far appeared. Your Excellency will thereby be enabled to see the manner in which we have adhered to our programme. I congratulate myself in advance on the interest which Your Excellency will not disdain to take in this publication, and on the efficient aid which you will be pleased to lend to an enterprise which is calculated to subserve the interests of an entire continent. I avail myself of this occasion to offer Your Excellency my most sincere wishes for the prosperity of the nation over which you so worthily preside, . . ."—ALS (in French), DNA, RG 59, Miscellaneous Letters; translation, *ibid.*

1875, DEC. 11.   Samuel Colson, "A poor black man redy to bee turn out doors for rent," Washington, D. C., to USG. "i right these fue line to in form yo of my want   i Sarve 3 three years in the yo nitid State navy   i umbole ask yo pleas to Sume Work if yo onner pleas as i am stranger in this Cuntry   i have A Wife an to Childen nuting to eat no shoes on my feat my Children Crying for bread . . . i list in the navy in 1864 in i was in the war at forth fisher on Boord of the U S Steammer forth Jackson . . ."—ALS, DNA, RG 56, Applications.

1875, DEC. 13.   Postmaster Gen. Marshall Jewell to USG. "A gentleman will come to you today by the name of Begole from Flint Michigan where there is a controversy in regard to a Post Office. I shall be at your Office between twelve & one oclock. Permit me to advise that no decision be made in the case until I have explained some matters as to the position of Secretary Chandler & Senator Ferry—the latter gentleman will give Mr Begole a letter of introduction to you as he explained to me this morning because he was asked to do so & not because he approves of Mr Begole."—Telegram received, DNA, RG 107, Telegrams Collected (Bound). On Jan. 6, 1876, USG nominated Washington O'Donoughue as postmaster, Flint, Mich.

1875, DEC. 13.   F. F. Millen *et al.*, New York City, to USG urging the release of Edward O'Meagher Condon, an alleged Fenian, from prison in England. ". . . We respectfully submit to Your Excellency, on behalf of an honorable American citizen, that his is a case which requires the immediate attention of your administration. We claim that he has been unjustly condemned, and is now illegally detained in a foreign prison; and that upon a legal review of the evidence, or a new trial, it will appear that he has been made the victim of a vicious tyranny; has been suffering years of torture in violation of all principles of law and Justice; and that upon a demand being made by Your Excellency's administration for an investigation into his alleged guilt, and for copies of the testimony and charges on which his conviction has been based, which we consider is due to him, it will be found that the facts and circumstances herein stated, in this connection will be more than corroborated; and that the freedom for years of an honorable citizen of this Republic has been abridged, and himself unjustly persecuted. . . ."—DS (18 signatures), DNA, RG 59, Miscellaneous Letters. On Nov. 12, 1872, Thomas Murphy, New York City, had written to Secretary of State Hamilton Fish recommending Millen as consul, Aspinwall.—LS, *ibid.*, Letters of Application and Recommendation. No appointment followed. See *New York Tribune*, Nov. 24, 1875, April 13, 1889; *PUSG*, 21, 221–23.

1875, DEC. 13. Wendell Phillips, Boston, to USG. "Excuse a citizen for troubling you so far as to ask leave to introduce the bearer Mr E. A. Hutchins—He comes to Washington to call public attention to the Helyotype copies of Hogarths works made for the house of Osgood & Co of this city—Desirous of the President's countenance, he has asked me to name him to you in this way—" —ALS, USG 3. On March 28, 1876, James R. Osgood & Co., Boston, wrote to USG. "Would you be kind enough to inform us if a Mr. E. A Hutchins soliciting orders for an edition of 'Hogarths Works' left a letter of introduction to you from Wendell Phillips in your possession, and what the facts are about his taking your order for the work—We wish to carry out every thing he may have promised in relation to the delivery of the work honorably—"—L, *ibid.* On April 19, Culver C. Sniffen wrote to James R. Osgood & Co. "In reply to your very kind favor of the 14th instant the President directs me to say that he is in receipt of the copy of 'Hogarth' which you forwarded by Express. and that the binding is elegant and in every way satisfactory He begs that you will consider the delay of its delivery a matter of no consequence ~~but~~ and regrets that the bad faith of your Agent should have made ~~the work~~ his copy such a very expensive ~~issue~~ one to you—Thanking you for the Consideration you have shown."—ADf (initialed), *ibid.* See *The Works of William Hogarth, Reproduced by the Heliotype Process from the Original Engravings.* . . . (Boston, 1876).

[*1875, Dec. 13–14*]. Mrs. George L. Brent, "At Genl O. M Poes," Washington, D. C., to USG. "I fear that in my trouble and distress, I did not state to you clearly what I wished to obtain for my husband, and that from the letters left, you might suppose Mr Brent desired the place of Purser, in the Navy.—What I do wish ~~for~~ is to obtain employment for Mr Brent under the Goverment. If you could know the happiness it is in your power to give us I am certain you would help us. Understanding, as my husband does, French spanish & Portuguese would it be possible to obtain work as translator? By the love you feel for your children, whom God has blessed so abundantly, I pray you to enable me to give some of the comforts of life to my two little girls—Will not your Christmas be made happier, with the thought that we are asking Gods blessing on you & yours.—Relying upon your goodness, . . ."—ALS (undated), DNA, RG 59, Letters of Application and Recommendation. Related papers are *ibid.* On Dec. 14, 1875, USG handed Brent's letter to Secretary of State Hamilton Fish for an answer.—Hamilton Fish diary, DLC-Hamilton Fish. No appointment followed.

1875, DEC. 17.   USG endorsement. "Refered to the Sec. of War. Let special attention be called to this application when appointments come to be made."—AES, DNA, RG 94, Correspondence, USMA. Written on an undated letter from Lyman W. V. Kennon, Providence, to USG. "I respectfully ask for one of the appointments at large, as a cadet in the Military Academy at West Point. I was born September 2nd 1858, in the city of Providence R. I. where my residence now is. My father entered the Army on the 18th day of November 1862, and died in the service at Brashear City in the Red River Expedition, May 23rd 1863. He was a Quarter Master Sergeant in Co. D. 2nd Reg. R. I. Cavalry. I beg you to consider the accompanying recommendations from the representation of the State of Rhode Island."—ALS, *ibid.* The enclosure is *ibid.* Kennon graduated USMA in 1881.

1875, DEC. 18.   Thomas C. Fletcher, St. Louis, to USG. "I beg to submit herewith the endorsements and recommendations of Ira E Leonard of Boulder Colorado, for appointment as a Judge of the U. S. court of Colorado. Certainly no man in all the West can have better recommendations than those herewith enclosed. Judge Leonard has resided in Colorado for about two years, or nearly so, and it is everywhere conceded that his appointment would give satisfaction to the people of Colorado. If however it is not deemed best to appoint him for Colorado, he would accept a Judgeship for one of the other Territories. It is not often the case that men of his ability can be had to accept the Judgeship in a Territory."—ALS, RPB. No appointment followed.

1875, DEC. 20.   Dawson A. Walker, Dalton, Ga., to USG. "I desire to be appointed United States District Attorney for Georgia. I have been thirty years engaged in aiding in the administration of the law; six years of the time as Judge of the Superior Courts of this State, and two and a half as Judge of the Supreme Court. In addition to these facts I refer for my capacity and fitness for the position to Col. Akerman, Ex Gov. Conley, and to any other leading Republicans in this State. As to my political record I will say I was on the Grant electoral ticket as alternate electer for the State at large in 1868, attended the Philadelphia Convention as a delegate from the State at large in 1872; was the nominee for Governor in 1872, of the Republican party, and addressed the people in favor of Grant and Walker daily, after getting my appointments published, from the time of my nomination until the election. You know my connexction with the Civil Service Commission"—ALS, DNA, RG 60, Records Relating to Appointments.

On Jan. 1 and March 12, 1876, Samuel P. Warren, Republican Executive Committee, Fulton County, Ga., Atlanta, wrote to USG. "I am informed from reliable sources that Mr Candler the Democratic member of Congress from this District has for the last two weeks been hunting up FACTS upon which to base a resolution of the House asking for a Committee to visit Georgia and examine into the past management of the Offices of the 'U S District Attorney,' 'U S Marshall,' 'Supervisor of Internal Revenue' and 'Collector of Internal Revenue 4th District,' and that he has knowledge of large frauds, that will greatly damage the party here, besides making an outcry against your administration, therefor I write you to suggest if it would not be better to remove these Officers and appoint new men before this investigation is had, for I am satisfied it cannot result but disastrously to the Republican party here. You will please pardon me for writing you but the interest I take in the welfare of the party and the success and popularity of your administration prompts me to furnish these facts and I know that my humble suggestions can do no harm,"—ALS, *ibid.*, Letters from the President. "I have the honor to hand you herewith slips cut from the 'Daily Constitution' of March 12th 1876, on the one side you will find the paid advertisements of Benj Conley Post Master and John L Conley Collector of Int Rev 4th Dist of Ga, on the other a fair sample of the slang and filth thrown at you and your family, this by a newspaper receiving the patronage of two of the highest federal Officers in the State when the 'Atlanta Republican' *receives none.* I ask you most earnestly Mr President how long will such things be tolerated in Ga,"—ALS, *ibid.*, RG 56, Letters Received from the President. The enclosures are *ibid.* On March 27, 1869, Warren, Washington, D. C., had written to USG. "I have the honor, very respectfully, to solicit appointment to the position of Collector of Customs at Galveston Texas. During the recent Civil War I served the Government as Quartermaster of the 15th Kansas Cavalry, . . ."— ALS, *ibid.*, Collector of Customs Applications. Related papers are *ibid.* No appointment followed.

On Feb. 19, 1876, Henry C. Holcombe, Atlanta, wrote to USG. "I *most respectfully* write you this Special letter in behalf of many colored citizs of Ga, as well as many whites who feel the importance of a change in a U. S. District Attorney for Ga. There having been such backing down & catering to the favor of the outlawed class of whites, on the part of Col Farrow, the presant incumbent, that a large majority of voters are *sadly* discoraged under his operations. I have attended several republican meetins in the City (Atlanta) this Winter, being a member of an important committee, and the expression is *frequently* made by white, & more *unanimous* by *colored,* that Col G. W. De'Costa would be satisfactorily received here as U. S. District Attorney. Col Fitch of 1866—Col Pope who followed, nor Col Farrow has seemed to give that attention that the exigencies that exist seem to require & it is believed that Col G. W. De'Costa will be *prefferable.* The colored vote want him because they hear he is *capable* & *reliable,* & *that will arouse their energies in the opening campaign Please give him to us.*"—ALS, *ibid.*, RG 60, Letters from the President. On Feb. 22, Lewis Alexander *et al.*, Atlanta, wrote to USG. "we want our ~~manes~~ moses remove we dont consider him nothing but a demacratic pet we are in hopes Sir that you will give us a moses that will give us the power to go the Ballot Box in peace and can walk free to the ballot Box we hope sir these thing will prove faitfull by the nex November we hope by the nex President Election that he will send us a man that will exhibed the demacratic ring from keeping the raticals from voteing the raticals party is almost squished down Mr President the republicans long to hold thier heads up once mor Mr President we are longing to hear that Pharroe is thrown over bard if it kills him let him die I will close" —LS, DNA, RG 60, Letters from the President. Other communications from Ga. blacks condemning Henry P. Farrow, U.S. attorney, Ga., are *ibid.* On Feb. 28, Farrow, Atlanta, telegraphed to USG. "Please read letters from Judge Erskine

and Mr Akerman ~~and~~ written last week to Attorney General Pierrepont and
postpone appointment of Dist. Att'y for Georgia till I can reach Washington
and see you"—Telegram received (at 1:38 P.M.), *ibid.,* Letters Received, Ga. On
March 3, USG wrote. "Re-nominate Henry P. Farrow—whos term as Dist.
Atty. for ~~Northern Dist.~~ ~~of~~ Ga—whos term of office expires on the 5th of March
1876"—AN, OHi.

1875, DEC. 20.   U.S. Representative John D. White of Ky. to USG. "Your remarks to me in Horticultural Hall led me to expect a communication from the
Secretary of State concerning a consulate in Germany. As no letter came, I
thought it not improper to call upon the Secretary. He conversed freely and
concluded by saying that the President was mistaken about the matter, that
other states had better claims than Kentucky; since she already had more than
due proportion. I did not then know as I am, now, credibly informed that at least
two of those accredited to Kentucky are residents of other states and should be
charged to Ohio & New York respectively. He stated, however, that there would
be, possibly, another vacancy on the South—Mediterranean, which, for one not
conversant with the German nor French languages, would be more desirable
than the consulate to Germany. Hoping that you will carry out your intention
as indicated to me in Philadelphia, I take pleasure in recommending a scholar, a
brave soldier, a true Republican and a wise gentleman Dr. S. M. Ferguson of
Laneville Floyd co., Kentucky to be appointed to the position in Germany, . . ."
—ALS, DNA, RG 59, Letters of Application and Recommendation. No appointment followed. See Henry P. Scalf, *Stephen Meek Ferguson, Lieutenant-Colonel
of the 39th Kentucky Volunteer Regiment, U. S. A.: Physician-Soldier-Industrial Leader*
(Prestonburg, Ky., 1962).

On Dec. 14 (Tuesday) and 17, George W. Childs, *Philadelphia Public Ledger,*
wrote to George H. Stuart. "Your friends President Grant and his family are
coming on Friday to remain until Monday, and I would like you to come on Friday and take a quiet family dinner with them at my house. All our party were
deeply impressed on Sunday night, particularly Col. Scott." "I find the President
& Cabinet will arrive about 8. o'clock and we will have dinner immediately &
hope & expect you to be present. Come not later than 8. as Mrs. Childs will be
glad to see you. I hope we can persuade the President & his family, and members of Cabinet to hear Messrs Moody & Sankey on Sunday night. The Ledger
will have a leading editorial article tomorrow on the Meetings, and it will be
read by at least half million persons. I have also ordered [th]e advertisement to
be placed at the head of Religious Notices tomorrow."—ALS, DLC-George H.
Stuart. On Dec. 18, a correspondent reported from Philadelphia on the "enter-
tainment" for "members of the press, public officers, and other invited guests"
to promote the Centennial celebration, which included a banquet at Horticultural Hall. ". . . Here the President, Secretary Robeson, Secretary Chandler, Attorney General Pierrepont, Chief Justice Waite, and the Justices of the Supreme
Court met informally before sitting down to the table. The President was surrounded by a host of friends, prominent among whom was Bishop Simpson, of
the Methodist Church. The President said to him that he read his opinion respecting Bishop Haven's prayer for a third term, and a rambling conversation

ensued, in which the topics most prominently mentioned in the President's Message, his position on the diversion of the public school fund, and the Mormon question were referred to. . . . The President sat in the central seat at the main table, occupying a handsomely carved chair, made specially for the occasion by a Philadelphia manufacturer, and presented to the President as a souvenir of the Centennial. . . ."—*New York Times,* Dec. 19, 1875. See *ibid.,* Dec. 18, 1875; *Philadelphia Public Ledger,* Dec. 17–18, 1875. On Dec. 19, USG attended the evening revival meeting of Dwight L. Moody and Ira D. Sankey.—*Ibid.,* Dec. 20, 1875.

1875, Dec. 21. USG endorsement. "Refered to the Sec. of War. Let special attention be called to this application."—AES, DNA, RG 94, Correspondence, USMA. Written on a letter of Dec. 16 from Sophie Schimmelfennig, Washington, D. C., to USG. "I once more turn to you with a petition, as you so generously conferred a favor upon me several years previous; I sincerely trust, you will gratify my wish, if in your power. I now petition you in behalf of my only son, Hermann, A. Schimmelfennig, for whom I beg at your hands the favor of a Cadet-ship to the M. A. of West Point. Having lost his father in the defence of the country, I am not able to give him the education, said institution could afford. He will be sixteen years old next February, and is a very active and intelligent boy. He won the scholar-ship for the Columbian University this year, having passed the best examination of all the Grammar-scholars in the District. He also was honored with the medal for Grammar, and ~~he~~ is, like his deceased father, a soldier from head to foot. Mr. John Hill Martin, Attorney at law in Philadelphia, a schoolmate of your Excellency, while at West Point, and who is a friend of our family, wishes to be kindly remembered to you, and wants to say, that you would oblige him too, in granting my request. Hoping, that it may find ~~find~~ your approval, . . ."—ALS, *ibid.* Hermann A. Schimmelfennig did not attend USMA. See *PUSG,* 15, 596.

1875, Dec. 24. Robert Crowley, New York City, to USG. "I am desirous of obtaining an appointment to the Military Academy at West-Point for my Nephew John. E. Cook—the Son of my Brotherinlaw of that name who was Executed at Harpers Ferry for complicity with John Brown—my Friend Mr McDonald will give you the Boys history, and it being his Fathers wish that he should enter West-Point—I trust in the event of an appointment being in your gift, that you will view favorably my application—"—LS, DNA, RG 94, Correspondence, USMA. On Jan. 26, 1876, Speaker of the House Michael C. Kerr wrote to USG. "Permit me to commend to your most favorable attention the application of young John E. Cook, to be appointed a cadet at large to West Point. I have known the family for nearly twenty years. Since the execution of the boy's father in Virginia, he has been under the charge of his uncle, Mr. Crowley, in Brooklyn N. Y. I have the highest assurance that the boy is in all respects worthy and gives promise of future usefulness. He is poor, and such an appointment would be a special boon."—LS, *ibid.* John E. Cook did not attend USMA. See *New York Tribune,* Dec. 17, 1859; Oswald Garrison Villard, *John Brown, 1800–1859: A Biography Fifty Years After* (1910; reprinted, Gloucester, Mass., 1965), pp. 569–72, 680–81.

1875, DEC. 27.   USG pardon. "Whereas, on the 4th day of October, A. D. 1875, in the United States Circuit Court for the District of Massachusetts, one George Miller, and one William Smith, *alias* Ephraim Clark, were adjudged Pirates, and were sentenced to suffer death; And whereas, the commutation of their sentences to imprisonment for life has been recommended by Governor Dingley, Governor-elect Connor and ex-Governor Perham, of Maine, and by Senators Morrill and Hamlin, and Representatives Frye, Burleigh and Plaisted, of the same State; and, also, by Bishops Haven and Wiley, of the Methodist Episcopal Church, and some seventy other ministers of the Gospel, together with many other respectable citizens of Maine and Massachusetts; . . . I do hereby grant unto each of them, . . . a pardon,—*on condition* that he be imprisoned, at hard labor, in the State Prison, situated at Thomaston, in the State of Maine, for the term of his life. . . ."—Copy, DNA, RG 59, General Records. See *The Jefferson Borden Mutiny. Trial of George Miller, John Glew and William Smith for Murder on the High Seas*. . . . (Boston, 1876).

1875, DEC. 27.   Matthew Callaghan, New York City, to USG seeking payment and recognition for postal innovations. "I respectfully as a matter of public importance send you the enclosed stamp which cannot by any means be washed again or used   the stamp is taken from wood engraving or electrotype and Consequently the Application of acids rubing or erasive matter of any kind totally destroys it   this has been sought by the Post office for years as the loss to the Post office revenue from the washing of Post stamps and their use again have been enormous   I am also the person who suggested to Post master General Holt in 1859 the plan by which Dead letters have been reduced to an insignificant number . . ."—ALS, Boston Public Library, Boston, Mass. The enclosure, a stamp with USG's picture, is *ibid.*

1875, DEC. 28.   USG endorsement. "Refered to the Sec. of War. Let special attention be called to this application for /77."—AES, DNA, RG 94, Correspondence, USMA. Written on a letter of Sept. 27 from Edward W. Meredith to USG. "The undersigned respectfully requests the appointment to a cadetship in the U. S. Military Academy, if practicable and meeting with your approbation."—ALS, *ibid.* On the same day, Governor John F. Hartranft of Pa. and eight others petitioned USG to appoint Meredith. ". . . The father of this worthy lad is a Methodist Clergyman of excellent character, being a Member of the Philadelphia Annual Conference of Ministers, and was a *faithful chaplain during the war*. Mr Meredith was commissioned Chaplain of the 50th Regt P. Vol. by Gov. A. G. Curtin, April 2nd 1862. He *was present with his Regiment in the battles* of Second Bull Run, South Mountain, Antietam, and Fredericsburg. In these engagements he had charge of the field hospital of his Regiment, and rendered valuable service to the wounded and dying by skill in nursing and the consolations of prayer. . . ."—DS, *ibid.* Related papers are *ibid.* Meredith did not attend USMA.

1875, DEC. 28.   Levi P. Luckey to John B. Drake, Grand Pacific Hotel, Chicago. "The President directs me to acknowledge the receipt of your letter of the 23d and convey to you his thanks for your kindness. I enclose you his check for

$109 28 the amount of Mr. Brown's bill. The hams had not yet arrived this morning but as soon as they do, I have given orders to have them hung up"— Copy, DLC-USG, II, 3. For Drake, see *Encyclopædia of Biography of Illinois* (Chicago, 1894), II, 95–99.

On Sept. 24, [*1870*], Drake, Tremont House, had written to USG recommending Albert Erskine as appraiser of merchandise, Chicago, to replace Charles H. Ray, deceased. ". . . I will keep a eye to him that he does his duty faithfully and would Consider it a *personal favor*. He is a good Republican and has Seen Service in the Cause for his Country."—ALS (docketed Sept. 29, 1870), DNA, RG 56, Appraisers of Customs Applications. On April 25, U.S. Senator Hannibal Hamlin of Maine, U.S. Representative John A. Logan of Ill., and ten others, had petitioned USG to nominate Erskine as marshal, New Mexico Territory.—DS, *ibid.*, RG 60, Records Relating to Appointments. No appointment followed. See *Chicago Tribune*, Nov. 23, 1875.

1875, Dec. 28.   U.S. Senator Aaron A. Sargent of Calif. to USG. "I have the honor to recommend the appointment of Benjamin H. Brooks, of California, to a Marshalship in some Territory. Mr. Brooks has many influential friends in my State, who will be gratified with his appointment. He is represented to me to be exceedingly well qualified for such a position."—LS, NHi. U.S. Senator Algernon S. Paddock of Neb. favorably endorsed this letter.—ES, *ibid.* No appointment followed for Benjamin S. Brooks. See *SRC*, 44-2-689, 50–63, 901–28.

[*1875, Dec.*].   USG note. "Mrs. Crockett, whos papers are before the Treas. Dept. desires a place to support her children   ~~She is~~ The ~~family~~ children are grand nieces of Pres. Madison, and are related to Patric Henry Pres. Taylor, Pres. Harrison and Pres. Tyler. Address St. James Hotel."—AN, DNA, RG 56, Applications. Enclosed with a letter of recommendation from U.S. Senator John W. Johnston of Va., dated Dec. 18, 1875. "I have known Mrs S. G. Crockett for several years and state positively of my own personal knowledge, that she is a lady of high moral and social standing and is an accomplished and sensible woman"—ALS, *ibid.* On June 26, 1876, Roderick R. Butler, Washington, D. C., wrote to Secretary of the Treasury Lot M. Morrill recommending Susan G. Crockett for a better position in the Treasury Dept. than the one she held "through the especial favor and kindness of the President."—ALS, *ibid.* On April 11, 1877, John S. Mosby, Warrenton, Va., wrote to Secretary of the Treasury John Sherman. "The bearer—Mrs Crockett—a member of one of the oldest & most distinguished families of Va—was appointed by President Grant to a 75 clerkship in the Treasury—She has lately been reduced to $39—She has several children dependent upon her for support—I commend her case to your favorable consideration—"—ALS, *ibid.*

[*1869–1875*].   USG note. "Invite Senators Scott, Cameron & Anthony, and Mr. Schenck to dine with us socially to-morrow at 6.30"—AN, ICHi.

1875.   Louis Riel to USG on political discontent in western Canada.—Hartswell Bowsfield, "Louis Riel's Letter to President Grant, 1875," *Saskatchewan History*, XXI, 2 (Spring 1968), 67–75. On Oct. 3, 1870, Riel and others had petitioned USG for help in alleviating grievances against the English and Canadian governments.—George F. G. Stanley, "Riel's Petition to the President of the United States, 1870," *Canadian Historical Review*, XX, 4 (Dec., 1939), 421–28. See *PUSG*, 20, 381–82; *ibid.*, 23, 384–86; Harry James Brown and Frederick D. Williams, eds., *The Diary of James A. Garfield* (East Lansing, Mich., 1967–81), II, 387–88; John Perry Pritchett, "The Origin of the So-Called Fenian Raid on Manitoba in 1871," *Canadian Historical Review*, X, 1 (March, 1929), 23–42; Stanley, *Louis Riel* (Toronto, 1963), pp. 161–63, 169–73, 222–23.

Index

All letters written by USG of which the text was available for use in this volume are indexed under the names of the recipients. The dates of these letters are included in the index as an indication of the existence of text. Abbreviations used in the index are explained on pp. xvii–xxii. Individual regts. are indexed under the names of the states in which they originated.